MAINE

MAINE

The Pine Tree State
from Prehistory to the Present

Edited by

Richard W. Judd

Edwin A. Churchill

Joel W. Eastman

UNIVERSITY OF MAINE PRESS

Copyright © 1995 by the University of Maine Press
Published by the University of Maine Press
Orono, Maine 04469

First edition 1995
02 01 00 99 98 97 96 95   1 2 3 4

The paper used in this publication meets the minimum requirements of American
National Standard for Information Sciences—Permanence of Paper for Printed
Library Materials, ANSI z39.48-1984. ∞

Library of Congress Cataloging-in-Publication Data
Maine ˙ : the Pine Tree State from prehistory to the present / edited by
Richard W. Judd, Edwin A. Churchill, Joel W. Eastman. — 1st ed.
p.   cm.
Includes bibliographical references and index.
ISBN 0-89101-081-5. —ISBN 0-89101-082-3 (pbk.)
1. Maine—History.
F19.5.M355   1994   94-15106
974.1—dc20   CIP

Manufactured in the United States of America

For Howard Schonberger and Edward O. Schriver

FRIENDS & COLLEAGUES

Contents

🌲

Maps

Preface

This book originated at a conference on rural Maine history at Bethel, Maine, in 1985. A luncheon conversation involving several attendees touched on the point that Maine educators at all levels suffer from the lack of a good survey history of the state. Richard D'Abate, associate director of the Maine Humanities Council, suggested that his agency might help fund such a project, and Joel Eastman and I naively accepted the challenge. On sober reflection we found the prospect too formidable to undertake alone, so we sought the advice and ultimately the help of scholars around the state.

The project that evolved out of this discussion drew together the work of twenty-seven Maine scholars and was underwritten by two major grants from the Maine Humanities Council. It brought together the scholarly representatives, resources, and services of several institutions involved in the production of history in Maine: the University of Maine System, the Maine State Museum, Bates College, Bowdoin College, the Maine Historical Society, the Maine Historic Preservation Commission, and the Maine Humanities Council.

Production of this volume was a cooperative effort in every sense of the word. The editors would like to thank, first of all, each of the scholars who contributed chapters to this volume. Setting aside time from busy professional schedules to create synthetic pieces on topics in Maine history—in some cases where no history had ever been written before—required a remarkable act of faith in the early stages of this project. The unanimity with which these individuals responded to our appeal is a testament to their commitment to preserving the state's history. It goes without saying that this book results from their efforts, dedication, and good will.

We would also like to thank those who read and commented on chapters or on the text as a whole. Charles E. Clark read carefully and provided insight and perspective on two drafts of the book, and Robert York likewise offered his considerable expertise on a draft of the text. Laurel Thatcher Ulrich helped similarly with a reading of chapters. Especially important was the help provided by Sarah McMahon and Eileen Eagan, who contributed their expertise in Maine women's history to various chapters. David C. Smith also read the manuscript, providing valuable commentary. Richard D'Abate, who encouraged the project throughout its long development, also deserves our thanks. William D. Barry performed an exemplary service as art editor of the project, and Richard D. Kelly prepared a fine selection of maps. Elizabeth Johns, who coordinated the project's relations with the University of Maine Press and prepared these pages for publication, deserves our special thanks. And finally, we acknowledge the inspiring example of professional scholarship left by Ronald F. Banks, as well as the contributions of people like Elizabeth Ring, Francis M. O'Brien, and James B. Vickery, who dedicated themselves to Maine history as an avocation.

Richard W. Judd

MAINE

Introduction

This book has three goals. First, we hope to provide a comprehensive core volume covering the sweep of Maine history from prehistoric times to the present. The last such effort, Louis Clinton Hatch's *Maine: A History*, was published in 1919. This new volume, although long overdue, comes at a time when Maine is enjoying a renaissance in published history. Although gaps still exist, particularly in gender and ethnic studies and in twentieth-century Maine, the historical record is much fuller today than it was even twenty years ago. This volume brings together the work of twenty-seven scholars currently working in the field and draws their various perspectives into a new survey of Maine history.

Second, these essays are designed to convey an appreciation of the scholarly craft of writing about the past. The chapters present several different facets of historical research, reflecting the different styles, methodologies, interests, and perspectives of their authors. These interpretations are derived from the fields of archaeology, anthropology, ethnohistory, material culture studies, ethnic studies, and various historical subdisciplines, including social, political, cultural, economic, business, military, maritime, labor, and statistical history. Rather than homogenize these various approaches into a standard textbook presentation, we have made every effort, while preserving continuity in theme and chronology, to keep intact the perspectives of the individual authors. Thus, the book reflects the broad spectrum of approaches that currently make up research and writing about Maine's past.

Finally, this collaborative rewriting offers several new synthetic interpretations of Maine history. Although each author's work remains discrete, together they form a greater whole, combining in ways that yield new conclusions about, for instance, Maine's interaction with the outside world, the forms of social tension and stability that have shaped this history, Maine's blend of localism and cosmopolitanism, and the role of geography, environment, and natural resources in Maine's past. A tremendous amount of exciting history has surfaced since

1919, and we have done our best to reflect the richness of this new scholarship and to show how it has changed the meaning of Maine history.

These three goals—producing a narrative history, demonstrating the variety in Maine scholarship, and achieving new syntheses—are not easily reconciled. Thus, the editors have taken substantial liberties with the essays as they were submitted, altering emphases, inserting new material, and sometimes diffusing an author's point of view through adjacent chapters, when those insights seemed applicable in more than one context. Where it was not too cumbersome, we have indicated individual authorship, but the matter remains somewhat murky. We take responsibility for errors in the volume.

This volume seeks to give students a sense of the varied approaches that can be used in understanding Maine's past. Each scholar has a unique sense of curiosity about past events. Were this not so, our histories would be a featureless plain, an unprioritized listing of mere detail. Appreciating this diversity is an important part of understanding how scholars work and how they provide us with our image of the past.

Researchers differ, first of all, in their focus of interest. Social historians are interested in questions relating to work, leisure, entertainment, education, and the institutions that embody these pursuits. They try to understand how people coalesced into groups or classes, and how these various segments of society interacted with each other in the framework of momentous events such as the American Revolution. Economic historians trace the evolution of transportation, commerce, agriculture, and manufacturing, and the links between these developments. Political historians identify and describe the influence of political forces. Thus, scholars can view the same period in very different ways. This volume, for instance, contains three chapters on colonial Maine, each derived from a different discipline: ethnohistory, historic archaeology, and social history. Together they give a multidimensional image of the time based on the viewpoints of authors interested in different historical questions.

Scholars define themselves not only according to their topics, but also according to their choice of evidence and the methods by which they interpret that evidence. Archaeologists and ethnohistorians rely heavily on artifacts, usually for insight into periods when written accounts were nonexistent or rare. Cultural historians also rely on artifacts—paintings, clothing, furniture, for example—not so much because written sources are scarce, but because physical remains, or objects of "material culture," can uniquely illuminate the trends, patterns, and processes of the time. Interpreted in proper context, a piece of hollowware in a local museum, or a photograph of a Maine-built schooner on the ways, becomes a richly nuanced entry into the past. Economic historians also rely on artifacts—the products or tools of a changing manufacturing or trading sector.

Other scholars choose different evidence. Economic historians find censuses useful; political historians rely on autobiographies, correspondence, administrative records, and newspapers as primary expressions of political life. In this volume, three chapters on twentieth-century Maine demonstrate how statistics, blended with traditional forms of evidence like newspaper accounts, official reports, family papers, and autobiography, can be used creatively to draw a lively and detailed image of the past. Historians interested in nonelites—people like rural women, Franco-American or Irish mill workers, fishers or farmers, who left few first-hand accounts—must interpret traditional historical documents creatively, in ways sometimes reminiscent of the work of anthropologists and ethnohistorians. They also devise new techniques for analyzing aggregate data, such as those found in censuses and industrial reports. Obviously, the histories that are drawn from these various sources will differ markedly, but each is revealing in its own way.

Scholars differ, thirdly, in their interpretation of events. All historians seek to relate primary evidence to larger events or transformations in society, but ways of making these connections are infinitely varied. Moreover, history is never written in stone; differences of opinion among scholars studying the same topic generate the debates that keep scholarship ongoing, dynamic, and, indeed, argumentative. In this volume, for instance, readers will encounter not only descriptions of the past, but arguments about the mental outlook of French colonists, the role of diplomacy in the English-Indian wars, the importance of women in Maine's economy, and other topics.

Still, in the midst of this diversity, we find patterns. The mix of foci, methodologies, and interpretations, after all, simply provides different windows into a single past. Maine people worked, thought, worshiped, and expressed their culture in a manner that identifies them as Americans, as New Englanders, and as Mainers. Thus, certain overarching themes weave these various stories together into a distinctive history.

These chapters have indeed taken Maine history in new directions. Generalizing is hazardous because Maine is such a diverse state, and each subregion—southern Maine, the midcoast, the western mountains, the "Maine woods," Aroostook County, eastern Maine, and others—bears the mark of its own "Maine" history. Maine also encompasses a wide range of cultural, political, and economic differences. There are, however, threads that bind together this heritage. Pointing them out enriches our understanding of the state's history and at the same time offers an appreciation for the past we share with people across the nation.

Certain themes are inherent in any regional history. The most apparent of these is the link between local experience and "outside" processes or events. The larger structural changes in the nation—market trends, technological advances, wars, depressions, demographic flows—obviously impinge upon the everyday world of Maine people, and state history must be set in this broader context. But our interest lies in the characteristic manner in which people in a given locale—Maine—respond to these events. This is what gives a region its identity and its special place in national history. Keeping this interaction between regional history and national events in mind, we avoid the narrowed perspectives all too common in local or state history, and the equally disastrous assumption that local inhabitants are simply the passive subjects—or victims—of broader historical trends. Maine people have always demonstrated resourcefulness and ingenuity in dealing with events beyond local control.

Creative interaction with outside events and processes is a pervasive theme. In prehistoric Maine, we see this in the constant cultural upwelling caused by influxes of new peoples, new technologies, and new trade goods. The impact of outside events became more compelling with the arrival of Europeans in the seventeenth century, but again it is important to consider the perspective of local inhabitants. Theirs was a world undergoing wrenching changes, but Maine's Wabanaki were not simply the objects of "outside" forces; as historical actors, they chose from a variety of responses to external threats to their sovereignty. Diplomacy and war, dispersal and resistance, and ultimately consolidation of a French-Wabanaki alliance were the bleak choices Maine native peoples had before them in the face of outside pressures.

As Europeans settled, they, too, felt the pressure of outside events: Old World rivalries, ambitions, and politics set the bounds of Maine history, as each tiny colony struggled to secure its foothold on the new continent. First England, then Massachusetts, claimed control over Maine, but within these parameters Maine settlers worked out their own destiny, establishing a viable government, legal system, and economy in the face of shifting external authority and constant military threat. The interplay of outside control and local adaptation is most evident in the French outposts in Acadian Maine. Wracked by conflicts that had their sources in France, Boston, and the diplomatic courts of Europe, the fragile French outposts nevertheless were able to recreate, on their own terms, at least an echo of French aristocratic styles, practices, manners, and material life.

During the American Revolution, Maine people began the process of thrusting off outside domination, participating in this world-changing event once again in their own way. Shays's Rebellion, the War of 1812, the sectional crisis, and the great reforms of the early nineteenth century—these events precipitated changes in Maine's political history, but at the state level they had much different meaning than they did nationally.

Maine's culture and economy reflected this creative interaction between outside influences and local reactions. Situated advantageously on Atlantic sea

lanes, Maine developed a culture that blended cosmopolitanism and provincialism. Local insularity was tempered by maritime activity that connected
Maine with the rest of the world. Rural Mainers retained close family and community interdependencies alongside their broader commercial contacts. Even
Maine's industry, a mixture of small, locally financed shops and large factories
dominated by outside capital, reflected these polarities of localism and cosmopolitanism.

Perhaps the most sustained external force on Maine's history has been its
hinterland relation to Boston. Economic and cultural forces radiating from this
metropolis have been important factors in Maine's economic growth and stagnation and in the alternating periods of friction and cooperation. Pitched
battles between Maine settlers and agents of Boston land speculators colored
Maine's early history; metropolitan capital, on the other hand, built Maine's
textile cities and paper mills. Maine developed a "love-hate" relation with
Boston, as one scholar called it, a struggle against economic domination coupled with appeals to the metropolis for financing to develop untapped local
resources.

Although Civil War battlefields were far from Maine, this national crisis, too,
became a watershed in Maine history. Politically, the war years marked the beginning of a long Republican Party ascendancy; at the same time it shook the
foundations of Maine's economy. After the war other national trends and
processes threatened the state's traditional industries, particularly expanded
market competition and the rise of monopoly capitalism. Maine producers reacted to these outside pressures by shifting to new markets, adopting new
technologies, and developing new industries. Maine people responded to other
national events—the Great Depression, for example—in ways consonant with
their own past.

A second theme that runs through Maine history, again a strain in the history of any region or state, is the importance of geography. As a borderland
region, Maine was a battleground for several colonial wars. Situated on the edge
of the continent, the region was also vulnerable to naval assault by French and
Dutch privateers during the colonial period and by British warships during the
American Revolution and the War of 1812. Maine's long contiguous border with
Canada gave it a history of international conflict and cooperation few other
states could claim. The Aroostook War, an incident that almost plunged the
nation into a third conflict with Great Britain, demonstrated the longevity of
Maine's role as an internationally contested region. On the other hand, the
coming and going across the border, also part of this special relation between
Maine and the Canadian provinces, has given the state its characteristic demographic and ethnic mix.

Maine's economy was profoundly influenced by geography. In the first half of the nineteenth century, location and topography provided Maine with a splendid transportation system. Under this influence commercial networks spread through upland and coastal Maine, supplying raw materials from outside and carrying out finished products. As a result, small-scale manufacturing spread quickly into the remote corners of the state.

Location was a controlling factor in Maine's distinctively maritime culture. Authors Sarah Orne Jewett, George Wasson, and Louise Dickinson Rich transformed a coastal geography into the rich metaphors that the nation has come to associate with the state of Maine. Seascape painters like Winslow Homer, Fitz Hugh Lane, and Andrew Wyeth reinforced this popular image of Maine as a maritime culture.

Maine's maritime tradition illustrates a central fact about American history: the importance, in the first half of the nineteenth century, of the sea as a commercial artery and as a source of protein for a growing population. Close to North Atlantic fishing grounds and blessed with productive rivers and estuarian spawning grounds, Maine became the nation's premier fish exporter in the mid-nineteenth century. On the other hand, Maine's position at the end of a heavily trafficked coastwise shipping corridor, the most vital commercial route in America in the early nineteenth century, gave Maine tremendous advantages as a shipping and shipbuilding state.

In the second half of the century, transportation changes altered this favorable situation as railroads shifted American trade flows to an east-west axis. Situated north of the major rail lines linking the eastern seaboard and the interior, Maine became geographically insular. Maine's eastward-thrusting frontier proved to be a long-term disadvantage in a nation that had set its sights to the west. Isolated from the great streams of trade and immigration, and increasingly distant from the nation's westward-trending center of gravity, Maine shows that industrial development was not a given in the United States, as some historians seem to imply. In the age of railroads, upland Maine farm communities were disadvantaged, too. Partly as a result of this, market forces were relatively weak; Maine farms experienced less consolidation, less technological change, and less crop specialization than regions to the west.

A third constant that runs through these chapters, along with the influence of external forces and geography, is the balance between conflict and stability. Conflict is apparent in the series of wars in which Maine participated, but it is also a constant fact of Maine's domestic history. The question of who was to control Maine—whether the French, Indians, or English; the heirs of Ferdinando Gorges or the Massachusetts General Court; the Anglicans or the Puritans—seemed interminably in dispute, and resolutions were never very convincing. Disputes over trade, proprietorship, land titles, religion, and administration kept the colony in turmoil. Deprived of stable leadership and direction, Maine remained a backwater in the expanding colonial system until a few decades before the Revolution.

Class and sectional tensions emerged during the American Revolution, affecting Maine's response to the wartime crises. These same social tensions, a rift between coastal and inland Maine and between farmers and merchants, shaped the movement to separate Maine from Massachusetts. Conflict, not surprisingly, manifested itself in party politics, and, indeed, within the parties themselves during the antebellum period. The second half of the century was marked by a new form of conflict, between workers and capitalists. Apparent first in the fishing and quarry industries, class conflict led to the formation of numerous labor organizations in Maine in the 1880s. This, too, reflected national trends, but class conflict retained a characteristic Maine flavor, based on the state's ethnic mix, its industrial structure, and its rural heritage.

Perhaps the most pervasive theme in these chapters, and certainly the most powerful single factor in Maine history, is environment. This is abundantly illustrated by Maine's prehistory. Glaciers began receding from the area some 13,500 years ago, leaving in their wake a rapidly changing environment. Tundra evolved into forest, and woodland mammals moved into the area as other mammals died out. Lake levels receded, while the climate alternately warmed, cooled, then warmed again. This changing natural world had a tremendous impact on prehistoric cultures.

Environment determined the strategies for survival in colonial Maine: French habitants depended on fur-bearing animals for their export economy, British settlers on fish and forest resources. Unlike the soils that drew immigrants to southern New England, these natural resources scattered inhabitants widely across the area and complicated the problems of government and defense.

Environmental influences shaped Maine's industrial development. Raw or semifinished natural products like lumber, fish, farm produce, granite, and ice were among Maine's most important nineteenth-century industries. Work in these trades shared certain features: Maine men and women shaped, molded, lifted, caught, or transported bulky natural materials, and their work was vulnerable to the uncertainties of weather, the limitations of climate and season, and the prospects of resource depletion. Scarcity or abundance of resources also determined town locations and local economies. Waterfalls and shoreline configurations were locational factors of absolute importance for frontier upland or coastal towns, and, thus, these features explain demographic patterns in Maine. Town locations, occupational patterns, industrial rhythms—all were shaped by

the location of resources and by the natural conditions under which these resources could be dug, cut, mined, netted, or processed. An equally important
story in these chapters is the precariousness of Maine's resource-based economy
and the impact these industries had on all forms of opportunity in Maine.

Maine people frequently responded to these environmental forces by diversifying their survival strategies. Wabanaki survival depended on seasonal
adaptations to various sources of energy, protein, and materials located in the
landscape. Colonial frontier communities learned quickly to adapt to these
same seasonal rhythms, supplementing agriculture with foraging, timber
cutting, hunting, and fishing. Nineteenth-century farmers, like their colonial
forebears, practiced varied crop and livestock production and added a number
of nonfarm crafts and labor exchanges to their sources of income. In addition
to crops, Maine farm men and women produced a fascinating array of home-
manufactured products. Maine's farms—"miniature factories," one scholar calls
them—were a relatively unique adaptation to Maine's proverbial high-risk
farming. Spreading risk over several sources of income was one way of insuring
against adverse weather, crop failures, high transport costs, and variable markets. Even urban industrial workers, typically on the move from town to town
in the nineteenth century, used diversified occupational patterns to preserve
their independence, achieve some security in an uncertain world, and perhaps
gain a better life.

Much of Maine's history could be summarized by reference to its most important natural resource: the forest. Forest resources have been the mainstay of
the economy since colonial times, and the forests have succored other Maine
industries—shipbuilding, brick-firing, and lime-burning, for instance. Winter
woods work provided supplemental income for Maine farmers and a major
market for oats, hay, potatoes, beans, and other crops. Hunting, fishing, guiding,
and providing facilities for tourists in the forested uplands have been important
industries since the 1880s. Forests continue to shape the economy, while much
of Maine's image—captured in the writings of Sarah Orne Jewett, Henry David
Thoreau, Holman Day, Gladys Hasty Carroll, Kenneth Roberts, and Fannie
Hardy Eckstorm—drew inspiration from the Maine woods.

Finally, the importance of environment throughout Maine's history highlights another development: concern over conserving and protecting the
natural resources that are so important to Maine's economy and the welfare of
its people. In the late nineteenth century, Maine played a leading role in protecting fish, forest, wildlife, and water power resources, and in the next century
the state assumed a similar role in the national movement to regulate water
pollution.

There are other threads that run through this lengthy story. Maine, for instance, in addition to responding to national events, led the nation in a number of ways. Maine's state motto, *Dirigo* ("I lead"), has been realized in a number of ways. Maine's fishing activity fed and its textiles clothed the nation's people. Maine loggers contributed heavily to the technologies of cutting, hauling, and driving timber. Maine led the nation in the production of wooden ships—and supplied the expertise to sail them. Maine's nineteenth-century political leaders, among the most powerful in the nation, illustrate the importance of Maine in national politics, and Maine's contribution to nineteenth-century reform, especially temperance, brought national recognition. Maine history is rich in material that illustrates the variety of human interaction. The following chapters spell out the details of these and other themes.

Richard W. Judd

1

Prehistoric Indians of Maine

BRUCE J. BOURQUE

The study of prehistoric peoples—those whose culture predates the written record— is the domain of archaeology, a discipline with methods much different from those of history. While historians work mostly with written documentation, archaeologists interpret clues found in the material remains of vanished cultures. Such clues, although often fragmentary and enigmatic, can tell us much about the lives of prehistoric peoples. Moreover, these physical remains are intellectually "inert"; they reflect none of the biases that are sometimes written into historic documents, and thus they leave archaeologists free to draw conclusions of their own.

Despite their differences, historians and archaeologists both strive to define patterns or regularities in the cultures they study. Prehistoric societies, like historic ones, behaved in patterned ways. They reproduced their houses and tools time and again with little change; they left remains of their preferred foods in location after location in characteristic ratios. The manner in which they buried their dead reflects consistent beliefs about afterlife. It is largely through the study of such patterns, revealed in the physical record, that we can construct models of the cultures that produced them.

The succession of prehistoric peoples that moved in to occupy our region as the glaciers receded illustrates some important and pervasive themes in Maine's history. These themes prevail into the era of European settlement, despite the obvious difference in cultures, and indeed they help inform our understanding of Maine's place in the modern world. First, prehistoric peoples and the Europeans who followed them were profoundly influenced by the rhythms and contours of the complex New England environment. Prehistorically and historically, survival strategies, population distributions, and social organization responded to an environment that changed daily, seasonally, and in longer climatic swings. A variety of ecosystems—coastal, mountain, wetland, riverine—added another complex of influences. In the early post-glacial period, this relation between culture and environment seems particularly dramatic because the landscape was rebounding rapidly, or seems so when we measure time in millennia rather than in decades or centuries. But the environment was no less a dominant force in the era of European settlement. In both cases, Maine's peoples accommodated in dynamic and creative ways to their physical surroundings. This chapter illustrates the diverse ways in which Maine's prehistoric inhabitants responded to a changing post-glacial environment.

A second theme important for understanding both prehistoric and historic eras is an appreciation for the influx of new cultures and new technologies, the dynamic mix of peoples and ideas that generated change and accommodation throughout the region. Constant interaction with the outside world, so evident in the overlays of prehistoric cultures in Maine, continued as a basic driving force in regional history in the era of European settlement. Environment and exogenous influences, then, set the parameters for prehistoric culture and European settlement. When either of these two conditions changed, the inhabitants of the region adapted, and an older way of life disappeared.

Humans in the New World

Modern *Homo sapiens* has existed for at least forty thousand years in Europe, Asia, and Africa, but the date of human entry into the New World is much less clear. Certainly humans were in the Americas by about twelve thousand years ago, for finely crafted spear tips called fluted points and other tools in styles dating just after this time have been found in all states and Canadian provinces and as far south as Guatemala. Indeed, generally similar tools were deposited in caves at the southern tip of South America about ten thousand years ago.

The people who made these fluted points are called Paleoindians. They are regarded as the ancestors of most New World natives except for the more recently arrived Inuit (Eskimo), Aleuts, and, perhaps, Athabascan-speaking peoples of the western United States. The uniformity of their tools, whether found in northern Mexico, northern Maine, or even southern Argentina, suggests a very rapid dispersal. But from where did they disperse? If these were the first people to enter the New World, we might expect to find similar archaeological evidence in Siberia, which was connected to Alaska by land during the late Pleistocene (glacial) epoch, but to date no such evidence has come to light. Yet if Paleoindians are not the first Americans, there should be evidence of their ancestors in the New World, and again no convincing evidence has been discovered.

The question of their origins is complicated by a further issue: the fate of the species they preyed upon. As mobile hunters and gatherers in a post-glacial

1-1. Human beings have flourished in what is now the state of Maine for twelve thousand years or more. This exhibit in Augusta's Maine State Museum shows a meat cache built by Paleoindians some ten to eleven thousand years ago in what is now Oxford County. It is the earliest example of rock construction in Maine yet discovered. Collections of the Maine State Museum, Augusta.

environment, Paleoindians probably hunted caribou and musk ox, which now live only in northern regions. But they also had available to them several large species collectively referred to as Pleistocene megafauna, which included horses, camels, ground sloths, two types of elephant, two of giant bison, and even a giant beaver. These animals became extinct about the time Paleoindians arrived on the scene.

The disappearance of musk ox and caribou from the central and northern United States is understandable in terms of climatic change following the last ice age, but great debate surrounds the extinction of the Pleistocene megafauna. Some feel this mass extinction was the result of the first wave of humans entering the New World. According to this scenario, the abundance of these large animals fueled a Paleoindian population explosion that sent a wave of people rolling across the North American landscape, extinguishing their prey as they went. Others, noting that humans failed to extinguish elephants, camels, and horses in the Old World, argue that there is no compelling reason to expect they should have done so in the New World. Furthermore, the Pleistocene extinctions wiped out small species as well as large ones, including many birds and small mammals that were not likely to have been the focus of Paleoindian hunters. Those who dispute the "overhunting" hypothesis believe the extinctions to be the result of profound yet poorly understood ecological changes accompanying the disappearance of the ice sheets.

Paleoindians in Maine

Many of the arguments surrounding Paleoindian origins do not pertain to this region of the continent, which was still emerging from under glacial ice sheets when Paleoindians inhabited regions to the south and west. But sometime between eleven and ten thousand years ago, Paleoindians did enter the region. Their remains, though widely dispersed in Maine and adjacent areas of Canada, seem clustered in compact areas where fairly large numbers of people may have made seasonal visits. The total Paleoindian population of Maine was probably small by comparison to those of more southerly regions and may even have been seasonal.

The landscape Paleoindians encountered in Maine differed considerably from that of modern times. After the sea and glaciers retreated, sedges, willows, grasses, and a few dwarf trees began to spread. This combination of plants, called tundra, is similar in some ways to the modern Arctic ecosystem. Mammoths and perhaps other now-extinct species occupied these open and relatively barren landscapes but may have been locally extinct by the time Paleoindians arrived in Maine.

This landscape was changing rapidly. Unlike the modern tundra of northern Canada and Alaska, which is the product of a harsh climate, the New England tundra resulted mostly from the relatively slow spread of tree species into the newly exposed landscape. Pollen samples from southern Maine bogs and ponds show the widespread presence of poplar, spruce, and jack pine as early as 12,000 BP (before the present time, or about 10,000 years BC). At first these species grew only in sheltered areas, but in southwestern Maine true forests had developed, and by 11,000 BP tundra had vanished from all but northern Maine.

Inference suggests that the predominant big-game species in Maine during Paleoindian habitation was caribou. Archaeologists initially felt Paleoindians were big-game specialists who ignored other animal and vegetable foods, a notion that resonated well with the Pleistocene overkill hypothesis. But many now believe Paleoindians throughout North America relied on a variety of food sources. After all, humans do not generally restrict their diets if they have access to a variety of edible materials. Further, varied diets require less energy to procure, provide more complete nutrition, and are more reliable in the face of fluctuating resource availability.

Even the popular notion that nonagricultural peoples like the Paleoindians relied mainly upon meat has been discounted. This theory derived in part from analogies made with the modern-day meat-eating Inuit hunters. But Inuits live in a region where large mammals are virtually all there is to eat, while Maine's Paleoindians very likely had more than megafauna or caribou herds available to them. Unfortunately, the remains of smaller mammals and plants are even less likely to survive in Paleoindian sites than elephant and caribou bones, so we still know little with certainty about the Paleoindian diet.

Whatever the diet of the Paleoindians, the climate that emerged after the ice age had profound effects upon their culture. Over much of their range, including Maine, they seem to have dwindled or disappeared entirely. In other areas, particularly the Southeast, Paleoindians adapted to changing conditions by becoming more sedentary, developing new kinds of tools, and exploiting an increasing range of food resources. However, between 10,000 and 8,500 BP, these cumulative changes characterized a new kind of hunting and gathering culture that archaeologists refer to as Archaic.

The Archaic Period in Maine

The Archaic period in eastern North America is usually divided into the early (ca. 10,000–7,500 BP), middle (ca. 7,500–6,000 BP), and late (ca. 6,000–3,000 BP) subperiods. The sizes of Archaic Indian populations during these subperiods are difficult to estimate, since the cultures were at least somewhat migratory and the settlements short-lived, and many sites have been destroyed by natural forces, particularly along the seacoast where land subsidence and attendant coastal erosion have been ongoing for the past ten thousand years. Nevertheless, it is significant that evidence for human occupation is much more abundant for each succeeding subperiod of the Archaic.

In Maine, Early Archaic artifacts are scarce, even in comparison to what remains of the much older and probably more mobile Paleoindians, suggesting that the population immediately following the Paleoindian period was very small and may have dropped to zero. The few known Early Archaic sites are near watercourses or lakes in western and southern Maine, and some were occupied by later Archaic peoples. These sketchy data suggest that Early Archaic Indians relied upon fish as well as game.

By Middle Archaic times, Maine's Indian population had risen appreciably, and the artifact record is correspondingly better. Known sites range from far in the interior to the coastal islands. In general, however, they are more common in western Maine than to the eastward, and to date, few Middle Archaic artifacts have been reported from New Brunswick or Nova Scotia. The reasons for this distribution are not clear, but it is at least consistent with the notion that population was increasing from the southwest to the northeast.

Evidence suggests that Middle Archaic Indians were adapting to a more complex and varied landscape. White-tailed deer were probably the predominant game species for this period, as the projectile points that dominate their tool assemblages would imply. But sites of this period are often situated along streams at rapids, falls, river confluences, or lake inlets or outlets, where seasonal runs of shad, alewives, salmon, and eels were probably harvested. The importance of fishing is also suggested by their use of weights, or plummets, which probably accompanied fishing lines or nets.

Changes in the marine environment may have prompted other adaptations. Extensive erosion of early coastal sites makes it difficult to estimate the importance of coastal resources during Middle Archaic times. However, the Gulf of Maine, which began as a huge, fairly tideless bay of questionable productivity during Early Archaic times, was becoming more tidal and turbulent as crustal down-warping caused sea levels to rise through the seventh millennium BP. Increasing biological productivity probably did not go unnoticed by Middle Archaic populations. Indeed, Middle Archaic stone gouges, tools which are associated with dugout canoe construction, suggest both forest and sea resources were becoming richer. The notion that such a craft was used at sea is supported by the discovery of a few Middle Archaic artifacts from islands in Penobscot Bay.

Between 6,000 and 3,000 BP—the Late Archaic subperiod—northern hardwoods like beech, maple, ash, and elm became increasingly common, providing

1-2. Beautifully carved plummets or weights from the Late Archaic period (5,000–3,000 BP) are utilitarian objects crafted in the form of fish, ducks, seals, and other animals by highly skilled, imaginative individuals. Collections of the Maine State Museum, Augusta.

better habitat for deer and other food species. Perhaps in response to this change in food supply, late Archaic sites are richer and more widely distributed throughout the state. This clearly suggests higher populations. The archaeological record for the late Archaic is also more varied. Populations in different parts of the state sometimes exhibited very different forms of behavior, and from time to time, these late Archaic patterns shifted from one locality to another.

A third important change pertains to evidence for animal exploitation. Late Archaic coastal sites provide us with our earliest samples of food-bone refuse, an invaluable aid in reconstructing past diets. Most animal remains are found in refuse heaps called shell middens. They are composed mostly of mollusk shells, which render these middens slightly alkaline, thus protecting bones and other organic materials from the destructive effects of Maine's typically acid soil. Furthermore, shell refuse is bulky and accumulates rapidly in distinct layers or "strata," which incorporate artifacts and bone refuse from different periods of occupation. These stratified middens are a boon to Maine archaeologists, who must otherwise deal with generally thin, unstratified deposits close to the surface, where they are subject to disturbance. Over the last century, the wealth of data in the middens has led to considerable debate about the importance of cultural differences during Late Archaic Maine. However, during the past decade some consensus has emerged about who the Late Archaic peoples were, how they lived, and what external influences they brought with them. The Late Archaic is generally divided up into three somewhat distinct cultures.

Laurentian Tradition

Maine's Late Archaic Indians were apparently related to populations occupying the St. Lawrence Valley and adjacent drainages, people collectively referred to as the Laurentian tradition. Their historic origins are obscure, but linkages with earlier Middle Archaic cultures are apparent in their artifacts, particularly the flaked-stone hunting equipment and ground-stone woodworking tools. Laurentian sites are most prevalent in interior areas of the Penobscot and St. Croix river systems. We have little evidence of their food-getting activities or migrations, but again their sites lie on watercourses, many of them near likely fishing spots, and their small size suggests a relatively mobile lifestyle. Radiocarbon dates are also scarce, but those we have suggest that they may have arrived in Maine at about 6,000 BP. They disappeared as a recognizable group by about 5,000 BP.

Small Stemmed Point Tradition (SSPT)

The next group appeared by 5,000 BP. Unlike the Laurentian tradition, characterized by large flaked projectile points, the Small Stemmed Point Tradition is typified by small quartz projectile points and a variety of other quartz tools. These artifacts, like those of the Laurentian tradition, show links with Middle-Archaic cultures, harking back to earlier times. The SSPT sites, however, are found primarily in southwestern Maine, on or near the coast, and extend as far south as Long Island, New York. In some places this tradition dominates the whole Late Archaic period, but its appearance in Maine seems to represent a northern fringe population of the larger tradition.

We know more of SSPT subsistence patterns than those of any earlier group. Data come primarily from three sites: Seabrook, New Hampshire, where the bones of cod and swordfish were recovered in association with several plummets; the Turner Farm site on North Haven Island in Penobscot Bay, where a refuse pit produced clam, sea urchin, cod, swordfish, deer, and duck remains; and finally, the tidal falls on the Sheepscot River estuary, where cod and probable deer bones came from a stratum containing small quartz stemmed points. This evidence and the coastal location suggest the inhabitants consumed a mix of fish, birds, and game, focusing more upon marine resources than earlier peoples. Indeed, their ability to capture swordfish presages later deep-water maritime hunting along the central and eastern Maine coast.

The Moorehead Phase

What follows the SSPT is a cultural phenomenon that has attracted international attention for more than a century. In the late nineteenth century—a period of increasing interest in America's ancient past—amateur and professional archaeologists began focusing attention upon so-called Red Paint sites. These were characterized by pits filled with bright red ochre (powdered hematite) and unusual stone artifacts, some carefully ground and polished, others made of visually appealing stone. Soon they realized these were ancient cemeteries from which virtually all bone had decayed.

Perhaps the first to study such sites was Bangor Mayor Augustus Hamlin. In 1882, Orland farmer Foster Soper showed him several blood-red puddles in a plowed field on the banks of Alamoosook Lake. Near the puddles they found pecked, ground, and polished stone artifacts that differed from those found in the better-known shell midden sites along the coast. Since then, similar pits have been discovered and excavated by people with widely varying levels of competence. One superb early excavation was conducted near Soper's initial discovery by C. C. Willoughby of Harvard University's Peabody Museum. Willoughby later exhibited the artifacts and a model of his excavations at the World's Columbian Exhibition held in Chicago in 1892.

Far more aggressive and much less careful was Warren K. Moorehead, of the R. S. Peabody Foundation at Phillips Academy in Andover, Massachusetts, who opened several cemeteries between 1912 and 1920. Avid interest in these cemeteries has continued unabated to recent times, and it now appears that few if any undisturbed Red Paint cemeteries remain. Archaeologists have given the label Moorehead phase to the culture that produced these elaborate mortuary remains.

Some archaeologists compared these spectacular cemeteries to the relatively humble artifacts from middens left by more recent cultures and concluded that there were no links between the two. They speculated wildly about the origins and disappearance of the "Red Paint People." The perception that these Indians were not related to later cultures began to change after the 1930s, when Douglas Byers, Moorehead's successor at the Peabody Foundation, discovered red-paint burials beneath the Nevin shell midden at Blue Hill Falls. Shortly thereafter, John H. Rowe recovered artifacts like those from red-paint cemeteries at a shell midden in Sorrento.

More recently archaeologists have excavated villages at the Turner Farm site on the island of North Haven, the Eddington Bend site on the Penobscot River, the Goddard site in Brooklin, and the Candage site on Vinalhaven. This, along with other data, make it clear that the Red Paint People were indeed Indians, although they seem to have undergone some sort of cultural flowering that set them apart from their forebears.

The geographical distribution of the Moorehead phase is not easy to define, in part because archaeological sampling throughout Maine and New Brunswick is so uneven. Secular artifacts have been found from Casco Bay east to New Brunswick and Nova Scotia, and northward into central Maine, but cemetery discoveries are confined to the area between the Kennebec and St. John rivers. Some flaked-stone projectile points from these cemeteries come from sources as far distant as the Lake Champlain area and the north Labrador coast. Cemeteries resembling those in Maine have been found in Labrador and Newfoundland.

Analysis of bone refuse from the Turner Farm site suggests that deer were the most important protein source during the Moorehead-phase times. More recent analysis of carbon and nitrogen isotopes from individuals buried at the Nevin site, however, indicate that cod and swordfish were more important than deer. Both fish species were presumably caught in deep water from seaworthy dugout canoes. The Turner Farm site on North Haven, at least, seems to have been occupied nearly year round. Insight into the origins of the Moorehead phase may be evident in its similarities to the SSPT. They were both coastal people who relied upon cod and swordfish, and they both used very similar plummets, woodworking gouges, and stemmed projectile points. In one respect, however, the production of ground-slate lance tips, the Moorehead phase resembles the Laurentian tradition or later cultures of the Gulf of St. Lawrence.

Sometime around 3,800 BP, all known traces of the Moorehead phase vanish, for reasons we do not yet understand. Some local environmental change, perhaps involving the waters of the Gulf of Maine, may have been the cause. However, a similar rapid disappearance occurred among the culturally related Indians in Newfoundland and Labrador, suggesting more pervasive cultural or environmental influences.

Susquehanna Tradition

The void created by the disappearance of the Moorehead phase was filled by a new archaeological culture known as the Susquehanna tradition, arriving, probably from the south, as suddenly as the predecessor left. The archaeological remains of the Susquehanna tradition are so different from those of the Moorehead phase that a complete population replacement is likely. Susquehanna-tradition sites yield distinctive thin, broad projectile points and other blade tools. Other technological changes suggest that people of the Susquehanna tradition, although occupying many of the same coastal sites as the Moorehead phase, apparently did not venture far from shore to hunt and fish. Both bone refuse and human bone isotope data indicate that marine resources were less important in their protein diet, which came largely from white-tailed deer and to a lesser extent from moose, shallow-water fish, shellfish, and seals. More Susquehanna sites have been found in the interior than those of the Moorehead phase.

A distinct break with the past is also apparent in Susquehanna ceremonial behavior. Typically, their cemeteries contain burned human remains and mortuary offerings and less commonly burials in the flesh or burials of "bundles" of bones, perhaps exhumed from temporary graves or from raised scaffolds—practices known from many areas of North America during historic times. The remains are often richly furnished, though the number of artifacts dedicated to each individual is difficult to determine because they are found in common burial sites.

In southern New England and New York, the Susquehanna tradition persisted for several centuries, during which its tool forms underwent several stylistic changes. After about 3,500 BP, these southern groups developed the novel practice of carving cooking vessels from soapstone (steatite) and other soft rocks. In Maine, however, only one such stylistic shift is apparent among the artifacts, and only a handful of steatite vessel fragments have emerged from the extensive excavations at Susquehanna tradition sites. Indeed, virtually all distinctive elements of Susquehanna technology disappear from the archaeological record sometime before 3,500 BP.

The demise of the Susquehanna tradition in Maine is even more difficult to explain than that of the Moorehead phase. It was soon replaced by a very different artifact pattern, suggesting again a change in population. At present, we have little evidence of human activity in Maine during the centuries following the Susquehanna tradition decline. No appreciable archaeological data appear until about 3,000 BP, when thick, rather crudely flaked projectile points only vaguely resembling those of earlier times were deposited at several coastal and interior sites. These points have not been found in association with the Susquehanna tradition, and links between the two periods are anything but certain.

The Ceramic Period

Sometime before 2,500 BP, Maine Indians joined other northeastern Indians in a technological revolution of considerable importance: the making of ceramic pottery. This practice continued throughout the remainder of the prehistoric period, dying out rather quickly in Maine following the arrival of Europeans willing to trade kettles made of copper. The remains of these clay vessels are so ubiquitous at archaeological sites that the term "Ceramic period" is used in reference to the rest of Maine's prehistory.

Throughout the region, the earliest pottery style was characterized by coarse, one- to two-gallon cylindrical vessels with pointed bases bearing the impressions of cordage. The vessels are called Vinette 1 ware, after the New York site where they were first identified. Within a few centuries a new, more refined, thinner pottery with various kinds of simple linear stamped decorations replaced the earlier Vinette 1 throughout northern New England. Even later, the vessel walls became thicker and less well fired. Stamped decoration remained in vogue until about 1,000 BP, when cord impression became the dominant decorative mode. Toward the end of the prehistoric period, a thin, well-fired pottery once again appeared, sometimes with globular bodies rather than the traditional cone form.

It is from the early Ceramic period that we have our first clear evidence of prehistoric house forms. A site near Isle au Haut dating from this period revealed a floor of darkly stained beach gravel about five meters in diameter, surrounded by a ring of clamshells. The house site is but the earliest of several now identified in central and eastern Maine. Although the sites vary in detail, the homes probably resembled the conical wigwam found throughout the greater Northeast during the early historic period. Such structures had pole frames covered by sheets of birch bark or matting, left open at the top to allow smoke from a small interior fire hearth to escape. In western Maine and much of New England, wigwams often had domed roofs, while to the east and north, as far as Labrador, the conical, tipi-like form was more prevalent.

Although the wigwam was perhaps the most common house form in Maine during early historic times, larger forms made of similar materials also existed. Some could hold thirty people in council. In the large agricultural villages of late prehistory, even larger "long houses" often housed several families.

Since Ceramic-period groups occupied most coastal shell middens, we know a great deal about their diets. The data suggest some basic differences from earlier times. Most important was the renewed dependence on fish and marine mammals. Unlike the more specialized Moorehead-phase Indians, however, Ceramic-period populations added marine species as part of a general trend toward dietary diversity. This is the sort of change anthropologists expect to see when a growing population finds that its preferred protein sources are no longer sufficient to sustain it.

One particularly marked aspect of this trend is the heavy exploitation of gray and harbor seals, which are especially nutritious because of their high fat content. Both species were hunted when they hauled out for pupping and molting, the former species between January and March and the latter between April and August. Ceramic-period people also made extensive use of shallow-water fish like flounder and sturgeon, but relatively less use of deeper-water species like cod. Finally, the importance of moose rose relative to deer, probably reflecting vegetational changes resulting from a slight but persistent cooling trend.

During two brief intervals, Ceramic-period populations abandoned a tradition of provincialism to participate in regional trade with areas to the east and north. The first period of exchange dates from early in the Ceramic period and is evident in the appearance of certain ceremonial artifacts from the Midwest, often similar to those found in the famed Adena burial mounds of the Ohio Valley. The second period begins after 1,000 BP and involves small chert tools originating from as far away as Ramah Bay, Labrador.

The Goddard site on Blue Hill Bay yielded an outstanding collection of such "exotic" stone tools, mostly scrapers and projectile points, along with numerous tools made of "native" copper quarried at Cap d'Or, Nova Scotia. But most interesting of all are two objects from the far north: a ground chert cutting tool typical of the Eskimo-like Dorset culture of Labrador and Newfoundland; and a Norse penny, minted between AD 1065 and 1080. Some commentators see this

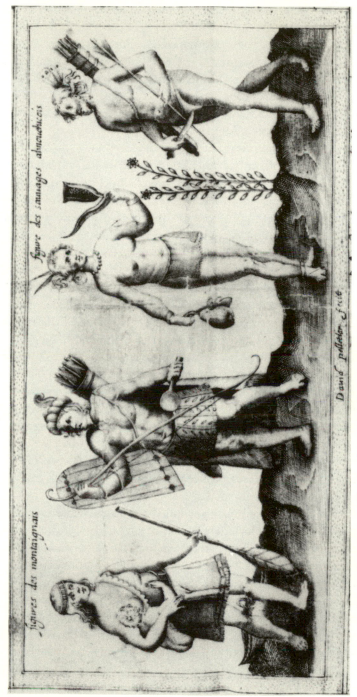

Figure des montaignais

Figure des sauuages almouchiquois

David pelletier fecit

1-3. From the map of New France in Champlain's *Voyages* (1612) comes this image of Montagnais tribesmen from the St. Lawrence (left) and two Indians (right) from Maine. The first European visual artist to visit the area described the inhabitants as "an agile people with well-formed bodies," armed with pikes, clubs, and bows, and living in homes constructed of tree branches and covered with bark. Courtesy of the John Carter Brown Library at Brown University.

coin as evidence of a Norse visit to Maine, but there is little support for this inference. All other Norse artifacts found on native American sites have been from Inuit contexts well north of the St. Lawrence. The number of other exotics of northern origin at the Goddard site suggests that this coin too originated with Inuit or Indian groups farther north and that it moved south through the native trade networks. It is probably best regarded as a highly noteworthy false clue, for there is no further evidence suggesting that the Norse explored or colonized as far south as the Gulf of Maine.

In discussing the late Ceramic period, it is tempting to draw upon the accounts of early European explorers for descriptions of native life "at contact." This approach has its pitfalls, however. By the time Samuel de Champlain, Henry Hudson, and John Smith arrived in the New World, waves of cultural change caused by earlier European contacts far to the north were washing over what is now Maine.

When Jacques Cartier sailed into the Gulf of St. Lawrence in 1534, Europeans had already been taking cod and whales there for many years. As a sideline, some traded metal goods and trinkets to Indians in return for furs and hides. After 1580, when felt hats became increasingly fashionable in Europe, the St. Lawrence fur trade intensified and focused upon the beaver, whose fur made the best felt. The effects of this trade were profound. By 1600, an entire population of Iroquoian-speaking people in the St. Lawrence Valley adjacent to northern Maine had vanished, probably because of warfare related to the growing European presence. Indians from Maine were among those trading furs to Europeans on the St. Lawrence by 1603, when Champlain met some of them there. These Maine Indians were also allied with Montagnais and Algonquin Indians in warfare against other Iroquois.

When Champlain arrived in Maine the following year, he found that Indians from Nova Scotia had for some time been sailing European vessels called shallops into the Gulf of Maine to trade European goods for beaver furs. And by the time John Smith arrived in 1614, many Indians had already been struck down by European diseases to which they had little immunity.

Nevertheless, the peoples described by these explorers clearly retained many aspects of their traditional cultures. Two of these represent important Ceramic-period innovations. The first, agriculture, arrived in New England relatively recently when compared to its adoption by other North American cultures. This was because the corn, beans, and squash that originated in Mexico thousands of years ago were adapted to arid, hot climates, and required considerable genetic modification before strains hardy enough to be grown in New England were developed. Furthermore, it is becoming apparent to anthropologists that peoples used to hunting and gathering do not always embrace agriculture as a

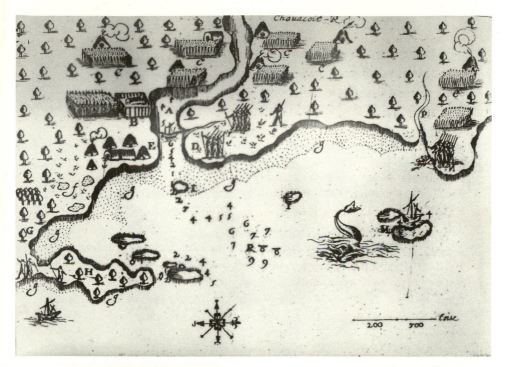

1-4. Samuel de Champlain (ca. 1567–1635) depicted this large Indian village at the mouth of the Saco River around 1605. Their fort was "a large cabin surrounded by palisades" and they grew crops including corn, beans, and squash in surrounding cleared land. Courtesy of the York Institute Museum, Saco, Maine.

more "advanced" lifestyle. Indeed, agricultural societies often work harder and achieve lower levels of nutrition than their hunting and gathering ancestors, and they adopt these strategies only because they can no longer support themselves with wild foods.

The spread of agriculture into the Northeast is poorly documented, because vegetable remains are rarely preserved in archaeological sites. Samuel de Champlain reported Indians growing corn, beans, and squash at Saco and on the Kennebec River in 1604, but to the eastward it appears that natives remained essentially hunters and gatherers. Possibly, the "Little Ice Age," a period from the thirteenth to the nineteenth centuries that brought significantly colder temperatures throughout the whole north Atlantic region, had forced agriculture out of the area. But it is just as possible the corn-growers were recent immigrants from Massachusetts.

A second important cultural development difficult to trace is the birch-bark canoe. So fascinated were European explorers with this supple craft that they took several specimens back to Europe, and by the middle of the seventeenth century Micmacs from Nova Scotia were making models for wholesale export to Europe. When Europeans first arrived, bark canoes were in use all across North America, particularly where birch bark was available. (Other kinds of bark were substituted in other areas.) Such a broad distribution implies that the basic development occurred long ago, unless it was as eagerly adopted by Indians as it was by the early French. Maine, however, was the southern limit of its predominance, for in Massachusetts wooden dugouts derived from archaic predecessors held sway. Therefore, it is possible that its adoption here was relatively recent.

A phenomenon which may mark the arrival of the bark canoe in Maine is the decline in abundance of large woodworking tools during the Ceramic period. Such tools are not absolutely required to make dugouts, but what interests archaeologists is the almost simultaneous appearance of other forms of smaller tools made of raw materials originating from the interior sections of Maine. It is tempting to see the fairly sudden onset of so much movement of material as the result of the bark canoe, which had great advantages over heavy dugouts on interior waterways.

European exploration and subsequent cultural, economic, military, and biological contact transformed the Indian way of life with breathtaking speed and generally disastrous results for native peoples. But we should not view prehistoric Maine cultures as static before the arrival of the white explorers. They, like the European-based cultures that came later, responded in dynamic ways to changes in physical surroundings and to the movement of peoples and goods in and out of the region.

Although we have much to learn about Maine's prehistoric peoples, we can extrapolate an important continuity from the complex overlay of their cultures. The choices they made about how they lived, got their food, fashioned their tools, celebrated the supernatural, and organized into social groups were made within the parameters set by landscape, fauna, climate, and other environmental opportunities and constraints. They made these choices consonant with human contacts outside the region through trade, technological exchange, population pressure, and war. Thus, their cultures evolved through dynamic interaction with both environmental and exogenous forces; when either changed, Maine's inhabitants adapted, moved, or, as a culture, disappeared. That Maine people responded dynamically and creatively to such forces is not exclusive to the prehistoric period, of course. Despite the differences in cultures across a vast gulf of time, these two powerful forces worked their influence on peoples of the historic age as well.

For Further Reading:

Maine was the focus of several early important archaeologists. One was Charles C. Willoughby, a careful excavator who described much of his work, including the excavation of several Red Paint sites, in *Antiquities of the New England Indians* (Cambridge, 1935) and *Indian Antiquities of the Kennebec Valley*, foreword and notes by Arthur E. Spiess (Augusta, 1980 [originated in 1892]). Working a bit later and with more flair and somewhat less care, Warren K. Moorehead continued the excavations of Red Paint sites and produced *A Report on the Archaeology of Maine* (Andover, 1922).

While work has continued since the efforts of these pioneers, it has been in the last two decades that major scientifically based studies have come to press. A recent overview of prehistoric Mainers is Bruce J. Bourque, *Prehistory of the Central Maine Coast* (New York, 1992). A number of carefully constructed thematic works have begun to fill in some holes and suggest new and creative ways to discover the makeup of these early societies. The maritime nature of many early cultures emerges in several works, including David Sanger, "Maritime Adaptations in the Gulf of Maine," *Archaeology of Eastern North America* 16 (1988), 81–100, and Arthur E. Spiess, Bruce J. Bourque, and Steven L. Cox, "Cultural Complexity in Maritime Cultures: Evidence from Penobscot Bay, Maine," in *Evolution of Maritime Cultures on the Northeast and Northwest Coasts of America* (Burnaby, B.C., 1983), pp. 91–108. Maritime influences also intrude in food sources in Bruce J. Bourque and Harold W. Kruger, "Dietary Reconstruction from Human Bone Isotopes for Five Coastal New England Populations," a paper presented at the Paleonutritional Conference, Southern Illinois University, March 1992, in press; and in exchange patterns in Bruce J. Bourque, "Evidence for Prehistoric Exchange on the Maritime Peninsula," in *Prehistoric Exchange Systems in North America*, ed. by John E. Erickson and Timothy Baugh (New York, 1994).

James B. Peterson and David Sanger provide a close look at Maine prehistoric pottery in "An Aboriginal Ceramic Sequence for Maine and the Maritime Province," in *Prehistoric Archaeology in the Maritimes: Past and Present Research*, ed. by Michael Deal (in press). Bourque scans one of the major time sequences in "Comments on the Late Archaic Populations of Central Maine: The View From the Turner Farm," *Arctic Anthropology* 12:2 (1975), 35–45.

The above works all evolved from field work and the attendant site records. Some of the more significant reports are listed below:

Bourque, Bruce, ed., *Diversity and Complexity in Prehistoric Maritime Societies: A Gulf of Maine Perspective* (New York: Plenum Press, in press).

Byers, Douglas S., *The Nevin Shellheap: Burials and Observations* (Andover, Mass., 1979).

Cox, Steven L., *Goddard: A Prehistoric Village Site on Blue Hill Bay, Maine* (in press).

Cox, Steven L., and Deborah B. Wilson, "4500 Years on the Lower Androscoggin: Archaeological Investigation of the Rosie Mugford Site." Maine Archaeological Society *Bulletin* 31:1 (1991), 15–40.

Dincauze, Dena F., *The Neville Site: 8000 Years at Amoskeag, Manchester, New Hampshire* (Cambridge, Mass., 1976).

Sanger, David, *The Carson Site and the Late Ceramic Period in Passamaquoddy Bay, New Brunswick* (Ottawa, 1987).

Sanger, David, *Cow Point: An Archaic Cemetery in New Brunswick* (Ottawa, 1973).

Sanger, David, Ronald B. Davis, Robert G. MacKay, and Harold W. Borns, "The Hirundo Archaeological Project—An Interdisciplinary Approach to Central Maine Prehistory," in *Amerinds and their Paleoenvironments in Northeastern North America*, New York Academy of Science *Annals* 288 (1977), 457–71.

Spiess, Arthur E., and Deborah B. Wilson, *Michaud: A Paleoindian Site in the New England–Maritime Region* (Augusta, 1987).

2

The European Discovery of Maine

EDWIN A. CHURCHILL

Maine was host to a number of dynamic cultures before the arrival of Europeans in the sixteenth century. Our review of these cultures illustrates the forces of change in the region: an environment rebounding after the glacial retreat and responding to climatic swings and the periodic arrival of new ideas, people, and goods from other areas. As we enter the historic period, with its comparatively rich sources of written documentation, our chronological focus narrows to the century and a quarter after Columbus made landfall in the New World, an intense period of change in population, culture, and land use along the coast of Maine. Despite the changed perspective, the themes are familiar ones.

Although the infusion of new ideas, peoples, and goods into the region is part of a much older story, during the sixteenth and seventeenth centuries the impact of these new exogenous forces became overwhelming and indeed devastating to existing Indian peoples. The balance between local stability and outside pressures for change shifted dramatically; in the courts and countinghouses of Europe, enthusiasm for New World colonization waxed and waned, and European contact with the coast of Maine pulsed accordingly. Thus the age of exploration served as prelude to a long period during which European events dominated colonial Maine. It is appropriate, therefore, that this episode in Maine's history begin with a discussion of events in Europe.

Between 1524 and 1618, Europeans made their first tentative ventures into the Gulf of Maine. They returned again and again to flesh out their understanding of the region; finally they planted a few scattered settlements along the coast. In dramatic fashion, these events reinforce the point that historic change in regional cultures often comes from the outside. The arrival of European explorers and settlers profoundly altered the human forces in the region.

European imperatives propelling the age of exploration formed the basis of the region's colonial economy. As a true picture of the continent emerged during the first decade of the seventeenth century, the possibilities of commercial exploitation crystallized in the minds of colonizers and their merchant-backers. Their objectives, for better or worse, decisively shaped Maine's colonial development. Thus Maine's environment—in this case, in the form of a European catalog of potential commodities—remains a central theme of the colonial period.

The period of European exploration also brought rival land claims, setting the stage for imperial wars that kept Maine and much of the North American frontier in turmoil throughout the colonial period. Other forms of conflict originated in this crucial period: clashes between Indians and Europeans and factionalism among the European colonizers themselves. These struggles—between French and English, Indians and Europeans, and among the settlers themselves—helped shape the history of colonial Maine.

European Background to the Age of Exploration

Numerous histories of Maine or its coastal communities indicate that around AD 1,000, Norse explorers sailed along the Maine coast and may have landed in the area. The evidence for these brave claims. however, is not terribly convincing. The ancient Norse sagas that describe New World exploration offer no precise geographic reference points, and time after time much-heralded "Norse" remains have proved to be no more than misread native or colonial objects, or even outright frauds. The eleventh-century Norse penny found at the Goddard site at Naskeag Point in Brooklin, Maine, was a different matter. Excavated in 1961 and reexamined in the late 1970s, the coin was found to be authentic. But as Bruce Bourque pointed out in chapter 1, the best explanation is that it was acquired by northern Indians and carried south to Maine along prehistoric trade routes. There is still no convincing evidence the Norse visited the Maine coast.

What can we say with certainty about the Norse travels? Their discovery and occupation of Greenland has been long known, and in 1960 Norwegian archaeologist Helge Ingstaad found an eleventh- or twelfth-century Norse occupation site at L'Anse aux Meadows in northern Newfoundland. Since then, other probable Norse artifacts have been retrieved from Labrador at similar latitudes. No artifactual evidence has been found that verifies voyages farther south, although it is conceivable that some of the early Norse voyagers traveled down as far as the St. Lawrence basin. We just don't know.

Ultimately, the extent of Norse explorations is of minimal historical consequence, since their discovery had little impact on European or American cultures. Medieval Europe at the time of the Norse discovery was simply too fragmented, too decentralized, and too conservative to take advantage of the exploits of the Vikings. Historically, it was not until the fifteenth century that western Europe was ready to expand outward, to probe beyond the limits of the known world. In contrast to the Norse landfall, the second discovery of the New World by Columbus was an epochal event, launching both Europe and America into a new age.

The age of exploration capped a period of vigorous political consolidation and modernization in Europe during which emerging nation states like Spain, Portugal, France, and England centralized political authority, reduced the power of the Church and the rural nobility, and developed bureaucracies capable of sustaining national programs. If the creation of powerful nation-states established the context for the age of exploration, the religious crusades of the late Middle Ages provided a motive. The great crusades of the eleventh through the thirteenth centuries, the expulsion of the Moors from the Iberian peninsula, and the long struggle with the Ottoman Turks in northern and central Europe in the fourteenth and fifteenth centuries gave intense religious import to the fifteenth-century exploration of the New World and the Far East.

A second motive, often inextricably entwined with the first, was the desire for commercial expansion and economic gain. Europeans had long known of the riches in the Far East, and their appetites were whetted by trading that developed out of the Crusades and by reports brought back by Marco Polo, Odoric of Pordenone, and others in the late thirteenth and early fourteenth centuries. The century following the last Crusades brought expanding commercial networks throughout Europe and into Asia. In the mid-fourteenth century, however, Islamic and other anti-Western empires arose in the Near and Far East and gradually consolidated their hold on the eastern Mediterranean. Although trade with the East continued, Islamic influence increased the already considerable risk to the Europeans of overland trade. The great overland caravan routes declined, forcing traders to sea-borne routes, where numerous Muslim intermediaries gouged them at ports along the way. Faced with rising prices, higher risks, and dwindling supplies of oriental goods, Europeans began searching for new routes to the East.

A third development necessary to the fifteenth-century explorations was a series of advances in ship design and navigation that made long, open-water voyaging possible. The vessels used by the explorers combined features of two earlier types of crafts, one from the North Atlantic and the other used by Mediterranean and southern European sailors. Neither by itself was satisfactory for transoceanic exploration. The North Atlantic vessel, a tubby, thick, high-sided craft designed for rough seas, featured a single mast with a large square sail. Although fairly stable in open seas, it was unsuitable for coastal navigation.

The Mediterranean craft was sleeker but less ocean-worthy. Its highly maneuverable lateen sail and fore-and-aft rigging were perfectly adapted to the Mediterranean coasting trade but performed poorly in the open sea. The explorers' vessels were ingenious composites of the two, borrowing the heavy structure, decking, and seaworthiness of the North Atlantic type and incorporating some of the sleekness of the southern style. Their rigging combined the best features of each type; typically, two of the three masts were square-rigged for open sea, and the third was lateen-rigged for maneuverability during coastal exploration.

Like ship design, the art of open-sea navigation improved during this time. In simplest terms, navigators solved the crucial problem of sailing in a straight line while out of sight of land. This was accomplished by devising a means of determining latitude which permitted sailors to keep to a direct east-west course. Borrowing from astronomers, navigators modified the quadrant and astrolabe for use on a rolling deck in the open ocean. Gradually these instruments were replaced by the cross-staff, essentially a calibrated shaft that was pointed due north (or south, if below the equator) with a sliding sight bar that was focused by sighting the upper end with a heavenly body and the lower with the horizon. It had the added attraction of being the simplest instrument to use on shipboard in the open sea. Despite their various shortcomings, these instruments guided mariners to landings far beyond the horizon of their home ports and back again.

First Contacts with the New Land, 1497–1527

Such was the situation when Columbus sailed west on his epic voyage of 1492. Europe was electrified by his discovery, and it was not long before other nations resolved to reach the East by sailing west. The first quarter of the sixteenth century brought several explorers to the Maine coast, each establishing an overlapping imperial claim to the region. Although these early voyages generated more disappointment than enthusiasm, each contributed to the small store of knowledge about the wealth of resources in the area.

By late 1495, John Cabot, "citizen of Venice," was in England urging Henry VII to grant letters-patent authorizing him to sail in search of a shorter route to the Indies. Cabot received his patent the following March and after a year's preparation departed from Bristol in May 1497 in the ship *Mathew*. He made landfall after a month and spent four weeks exploring a rugged and hostile-looking coastline. The crew of the *Mathew* observed great trees, evidence of human habitation, and—a matter of great importance to later visitors—remarkably productive cod-fishing banks.

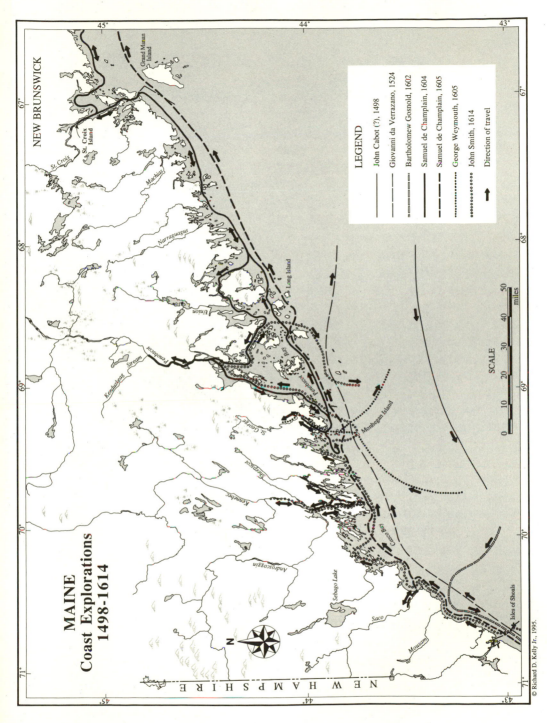

MAINE
Coast Explorations
1498-1614

LEGEND

————————	John Cabot (?), 1498
————————	Giovanni da Verrazano, 1524
–·–·–·–·–·–	Bartholomew Gosnold, 1602
————————	Samuel de Champlain, 1604
– – – – –	Samuel de Champlain, 1605
············	George Weymouth, 1605
∘∘∘∘∘∘∘∘∘	John Smith, 1614
↑	Direction of travel

SCALE

0 10 20 30 40 50
miles

NEW BRUNSWICK

NEW HAMPSHIRE

St. Croix
St. Croix Island
Machias
Narraguagus
Long Island
Union
Penobscot Bay
Kenduskeag Stream
Penobscot
St. George
Monhegan Island
Sheepscot
Kennebec
Androscoggin
Sebago Lake
Casco Bay
Saco
Mousam
Isles of Shoals
Grand Manan Island

N

GIOVANNI DI PIER ANDREA DI   BERNARDO DA VERRAZZANO
PATRIZIO FIOR. GRAN CAPIT.ᴺᴼ   COMANDANTE IN MARE PER
IL RÈ CRISTIANISSIMO   FRANCESCO PRIMO,
E DISCOPRITORE   DELLA NUOVA FRANCIA.

nato circa il MCDLXXXV.   morto nel MDXXV.

Dedicato al merito sing.ʳᵉ dell' Ill.ᵐᵒ e Rev.ᵐᵒ Sig.ʳᵉ Lodovico da Verrazzano
Patrizio, e Canonico Fiorentino Agnato del Med.ᵒ
Preso dal Quadro Originale in Tela esistente presso la sud.ᵃ Nobil Famiglia

G. Zocchi del.   F. Allegrini inci: 1767

2-1. Giovanni da Verrazano (ca. 1485–1528), a courtly, educated Italian navigator exploring for the king of France, made the first recorded European visit to the Maine coast in 1524. This image of 1767, based on an earlier portrait, was engraved by F. Allegrini after G. Zocchi. Courtesy of the Pierpont Morgan Library, New York. MA 766.

Historians are not certain where Cabot actually made landfall. Samuel Eliot Morison's authoritative history of the age of exploration favors the east coast of Newfoundland. James A. Williamson and David B. Quinn, eminent scholars who devoted substantial portions of their careers to the study of Cabot and his contemporaries, both feel he could have reached mainland America. Perhaps he and his crew were the first Europeans to set foot on the Maine coast.

The first clearly documented European visit to the Maine coast occurred in 1524. Italian explorer Giovanni da Verrazano sailed early that year for King Francis I of France seeking a passage to the Orient. He made landfall at or near Cape Fear, South Carolina, and then coasted northward along the Atlantic seaboard, providing the earliest known account of the area and its inhabitants. In early May he reached the Maine coast. Although pleased with the country, he found the Indians anything but cordial. Accustomed by Indians farther south to a warm reception, Verrazano paused to trade, perhaps at Bald Head at the tip of Cape Small. The Maine natives refused to allow the ship's crew to approach them. Ensconced on cliffs above the breakers and waving the small boat away from the land, they passed the items they saw fit to trade to Verrazano's crew using a rope, and accepted only a few items in return. "We found no courtesy in them," Verrazano complained, "and when we had nothing more to exchange . . . the men made all the signs of scorn and shame that any brute creature would make . . . such as showing their buttocks and laughing immoderately."

Some commentators have suggested the hostile reception stemmed from some previous unpleasant experience with other Europeans. But at this time few Europeans had reached Maine shores, and few would for over a half century. It is far more probable that these natives had heard of or witnessed hostile encounters between Indians and Europeans along the lower St. Lawrence River. Another possibility is that their behavior reflected precontact patterns that differed from other Indians that Verrazano had met and that had little to do with European influences. Unlike their proto-agricultural contemporaries to the south, this group of hunter-gatherers may have long exhibited caution and antagonism toward unfamiliar visitors.

Taking leave of the "land of the bad people," as he called it, Verrazano completed a leisurely investigation of the Maine coast and set a course for home, arriving in France on July 8, 1524. His accomplishments were most impressive. According to historian Bernard G. Hoffman, "he was the first to explore the gap between the Spanish ventures to the south and the English enterprises to the north; he was the first to establish the continental nature of the 'New Founde Land,' and he was the first commander to bring back anything resembling a detailed account of the natives of North America."

Learning of Verrazano's voyage on behalf of France, Charles v of Spain commissioned Portuguese sailor Esteban Gómez to find a western passage to the Orient. A year after Verrazano's voyage, Gómez carefully threaded his way down along the Maine coast looking for "el Cathays oryental." Thinking the Penobscot River might be the "Northern Strait," Gómez sailed upriver to the head of navigation near present-day Bangor. Disappointed, he was nevertheless impressed with the country, especially the timber, and continued his explorations along the entire Maine coast. Gómez subsequently captured several Indians at Newport, Rhode Island. Returning to Spain, he was severely reprimanded and forced to release those still alive. Beyond that, Spanish administrators found little of interest in his explorations and turned their attention to Central and South America.

Englishman John Rut, sailing for Henry vIII, was next along the coast in 1527. First probing northward in search of passage to the Orient, Rut returned to Cape Breton and sailed down along the American shores, "oftentimes putting [his] . . . men on land to search the state of those unknown regions." Rut sailed all the way to the West Indies before returning to England, but he found nothing really new, and his return coincided with mounting domestic problems in England. His efforts were of little import, and after Rut's voyage the Maine coast saw few European visitors for several decades.

At first glance, these early sixteenth-century voyages appear to be random and unrelated expeditions that passed by chance along the Maine coast. Each, however, was part of a broader pattern. The quarter century between the arrival of Cabot in 1497 and Rut in 1527 brought an explosion of new information about the Americas, as nation after nation sent expeditions westward. This was a period of high adventure and dizzying expansion of knowledge about the unknown western continent. But after Rut's voyage, the surge toward North America receded as quickly as it had developed. Failure to discover a Northwest Passage dampened enthusiasm for North America. Magellan's circumvention of the globe (1519–22) drove home the immense distance between Europe, America, and the Orient, and Portuguese explorers found easier passage to India by sailing eastward around Africa. Spain and Portugal were increasingly occupied in South and Central America, and neither England nor France, for the time being, retained much interest in the Gulf of Maine.

By the early seventeenth century, France was once again ready to move into Maine; but after Verrazano's voyage, French explorers had shifted their attention to the St. Lawrence region. French explorers returned to Maine, but the region would remain an outpost of the French North American empire that was centered to the north and east.

For the English, the sixteenth century had been a period of vigorous internal growth, centralization, and consolidation, during which monarchs brought the Church under state control and secured the hinterlands in Wales, Scotland, and Ireland. The country experienced impressive economic and maritime development, building an essential foundation for overseas empire. The defeat of the Spanish Armada in 1588 signaled England's readiness to take its place in the New World.

By the time England and France renewed their New World activities, the nature of exploration had changed greatly. One of the most obvious differences was the withdrawal of the crowns of both nations from direct participation. Far too often these New World expeditions had proved unprofitable, and monarchs chose to grant private individuals or organizations permission to carry out the various projects in return for a portion of the anticipated profits. More important was a growing emphasis on colonization. Earlier explorers, interested in the Orient, had merely searched for passages through or around the New World, while others hoped to establish trading bases with the North American natives. But no passages were found, and the Indians proved to be indifferent trading partners. It was obvious that a different approach was necessary; colonization would provide a settled population from which the home country could extract New World wealth.

Several examples existed that France and England found encouraging. The Spanish had developed a spectacularly successful colonial system, and the Portuguese were beginning to reap the rewards of Brazilian activity. English colonizing in northern Ireland had not only enriched the colonizers but was desirable for nationalistic reasons: it supplied England with cheap raw materials, provided markets for manufactured goods, offered convenient places to send idle populations, and helped bolster maritime and naval strength. Enthusiasts argued these precedents in both England and France during the late 1500s.

Explorers and Colonizers, 1579–1607

The second wave of Maine explorers thus arrived with radically different dreams and objectives. For the English, the new phase of exploration and colonial endeavor began when Sir Humphrey Gilbert sent Simon Ferdinando and John Walker to the Maine coast in 1579 and 1580 respectively. In search of a likely place to locate a New World colony, the explorers were drawn to the Penobscot region, for it was there they hoped to find Norumbega, a region and a city of fabled productivity, wealth, and splendor.

The myth of Norumbega blossomed during the mid-sixteenth century. The term first appeared as "Oranbega" on Girolamo da Verrazano's 1529 map of his brother's 1524 voyage. Three decades later, the region had acquired a reputation as a northern land of milk and honey, owing in large part to European publicists who obtained sketchy, second-hand information about the region and imaginatively embellished it. One of them, Pierre Crignon, stated that "the land overflows with every kind of fruit, there grow the wholesome orange and the almond, and many sorts of sweet-smelling trees." André Thevet, who had spoken with Jacques Cartier about his experiences in the St. Lawrence region, was slightly more accurate, but he too provided a glowing portrayal of Norumbega.

In the late 1550s, an English sailor named David Ingram grasped the opportunity to improve a good story. Ingram and two companions had been set ashore on the Gulf coast of Florida in October 1557. According to Ingram, they proceeded overland on Indian trails all the way to Maine. After a couple of years of wandering, Ingram turned up at the mouth of the St. John River and caught a French ship back to England. There he began recounting his adventures in the New World. Norumbega, he insisted, was the Cibola of the north. In "a town half a mile long" with "many streets far broader than any street in London," the men wore "hoopes" of gold and silver on their arms and legs. Their ornaments were "garnished with pearls, divers of them as big as one's thumb." Women were adorned in gold plates, and the houses were supported by pillars of gold, silver, and crystal. Ingram's adventures included finding gold nuggets as large as his fist in springs and brooks and being chased by creatures as big as a horse with tusks. Seldom had a single traveler done more to misinform one continent about the makeup of another.

If Ingram had done little to further truth about the New World, at least he sparked new interest. John Walker, who apparently landed near present day Camden on his 1580 voyage, climbed a nearby hill and described the surrounding land as "most excellent for soil, diversity of sweet wood and other trees." Walker visited an Indian lodge and stole some of four hundred hides that were stored there. Only once did he let his imagination get the better of him. Spying some mica sparkling in the rocks, he promptly decided he had located a silver deposit.

Humphrey Gilbert was sufficiently impressed by the accounts of Ferdinando and Walker to attempt a colony in the region in 1583. After sailing to Newfoundland, which he officially claimed for the Queen, he continued west, only to meet with disaster. The supply ship, the *Delight*, went aground off Nova Scotia and was beat to pieces, with the loss of all provisions for the projected colony and most of the crew. Gilbert was forced to turn back but never reached England; the *Squirrel*, a small pinnace in which he was sailing, foundered in heavy seas. Gilbert's half-brother, Sir Walter Raleigh, carried on the effort by commissioning yet another exploration, but reports from the voyage convinced him to shift his efforts farther south; soon thereafter he established the unsuccessful settlements at Roanoke, Virginia. This, along with the great war with Spain, once again shifted the focus of exploration and colonization away from Maine.

It was not until 1602 that English explorers returned to the North. That year Bartholomew Gosnold and Bartholomew Gilbert (the son of Sir Humphrey Gilbert) launched an expedition sponsored by the Earl of Southampton to establish a settlement in the northern portion of America. Sailing from Falmouth, England, in March 1602, they reached land on May 14, probably somewhere between Cape Porpoise and Cape Neddick. They proceeded around Cape Cod to Cuttyhunk Island, Massachusetts, where they erected a permanent storehouse and fort and loaded the vessel with sassafras, cedar, and furs obtained from the Indians. However, when Gosnold decided to return to England in late July, the twelve men who were to remain at the settlement refused to stay behind. The little colony was abandoned, and Gosnold, with his entire crew, returned to England. Despite these disappointments, Gosnold's reports and cargo renewed interest in colonizing the north Atlantic coast. In addition, his adventures resulted in the first known report of the excellent fishing along the New England coast, a matter that had important implications for the region's future.

By the next summer Raleigh had been imprisoned as a suspected foe of the newly crowned James I, but a number of merchants sent out Martin Pring with two vessels, the *Discoverer* and the *Speedwell.* Their ambitions were apparently scaled down somewhat by recent court events, for Pring was instructed merely to obtain sassafras and trade with the Indians; there was no mention of colonization. Pring struck the Maine coast somewhere near Gosnold's landing, ranged northeastward, then turned southwest into Massachusetts Bay. He probably landed at Plymouth or Provincetown and put up some sort of building with a palisade. Pring returned carrying a substantial cargo of sassafras and a glowing description of the soils, trees, fur-bearing animals, and fish awaiting European exploitation.

Though nothing very significant had come of Pring's 1603 voyage, the Earl of Southampton renewed his colonizing efforts the following year, interested this time in a New World home for discontented English Catholics (an idea that had been circulating since the 1580s). He enlisted the aid of his Catholic son-in-law, Sir Thomas Arundell, and by the spring of 1605, they had selected the experienced explorer George Waymouth to search out a location.

Waymouth's *Archangel* left London on March 5 and raised land in the vicinity of Nantucket Island on May 14. Since this was north of the proposed site, Waymouth turned back to sea and headed southward. The ship, however, was driven north for three days by strong winds, and on May 18 made landfall at Monhegan Island off the Maine coast. The next day Waymouth sailed to the

2-2. Turn-of-the-century reenactors recreate the landing of English explorer George Waymouth in 1605. Men dressed as Indians represent the native Americans kidnapped by Waymouth and presented to John Popham and Ferdinando Gorges. In the late nineteenth century Americans became fascinated by the colonial period and engaged in research, restorations, and reenactment. Courtesy of the Maine Historic Preservation Commission, Augusta.

Georges Islands and anchored in Pentecost (or St. George) Harbor. During an exploration of the nearby mainland, he used treachery to kidnap five Indians. On June 11, he sailed the *Archangel* up the St. George River to the site of the present ruins of Fort St. Georges. The river, he related, was among the most beautiful he had ever seen. Waymouth and a troop of men marched inland seeking a mountain they had spotted while at sea, but hot weather and cumbersome armor sapped their strength and they returned to the ship. The next day they sailed farther up the river in his shallop and on the way back erected a cross (probably near Thomaston). The *Archangel* then returned to Pentecost Harbor and on June 16 set out for England. On July 18, Waymouth reached

Dartmouth Haven with his cargo of sundry New World trade goods and the five captive Indians.

It is not clear exactly what took place when Waymouth returned. Arundell, the major backer, was off on another project and no longer interested. For some reason, Waymouth visited Sir John Popham, Lord Chief Justice of England, and Sir Ferdinando Gorges, commander of Plymouth Fort, giving to Popham two of the Indians he had captured and Gorges three. There is no evidence that either was especially interested in the New World, but both were related to other colonizers, and perhaps Waymouth was looking for support. If so, Waymouth's judgment was prescient: Popham and Gorges would become Maine's foremost English backers over the next few decades.

Their interest stirred by the captured Indians and Waymouth's reports, Popham and Gorges obtained a royal charter in 1606 incorporating two companies for the purpose of colonizing "in that part of America commonly called Virginia," a huge area covering most of the eastern seaboard north of Georgia. The London Company was to colonize the southern half of the region and the Plymouth Company the northern half. The two patents overlapped in the mid-Atlantic region, where either could establish colonies, as long as they were no closer than one hundred miles from each other.

The stage was set for an attempt at settlement. On December 20, 1606, the London Company sent three small ships to Jamestown in Virginia to begin the first successful English settlement in America. Not far behind, Popham and Gorges prepared for an expedition of their own. On May 31, 1607, the *Gift of God*, commanded by George Popham, nephew of the Lord Chief Justice, and the *Mary and John*, under Raleigh Gilbert, son of Sir Humphrey Gilbert, left Plymouth, England. The *Gift of God* was delayed by an encounter with two Flemish vessels, and the *Mary and John*, continuing on, made landfall along the Nova Scotia coast on July 30. The colonizers crossed the Bay of Fundy to the Penobscot region and arrived at the Georges Islands in early August. Two days later they sighted a sail, and to their joy the vessel proved to be the *Gift of God*.

Having brought along Skidwarres and Dahanada, two of Waymouth's captives, the expedition decided to visit the Pemaquid region where the Indians had been abducted. Understandably, they received a cool reception from the captives' kin. With no reason to expect a change in temperament and with summer slipping away, the settlers left Pemaquid and sailed to the mouth of the Kennebec River to establish a base for the winter. To their credit (or perhaps as an investment in future diplomacy), the English allowed Waymouth's captives to remain with their people. The *Gift of God* slid up into the Kennebec on the morning of August 13, and the *Mary and John*, after a harrowing bout with a storm at sea, arrived on the 15th. After locating a spot on the west shore near the

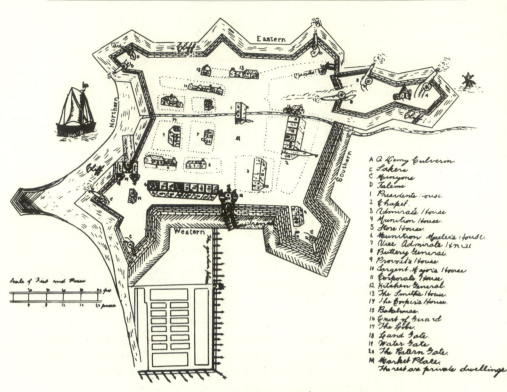

Plan of St. George's Fort, [Popham's] at mouth of Kennebec River.
By John Hunt. 1607. Oct. 8. — From Spanish Archives.

2-3. The first English attempt to settle Maine, then part of Northern Virginia, occurred
in 1607 near the mouth of the Kennebec River. Fort George, the first in a long line of
coastal defense works, is shown here in a sketch by John Hunt. Since the colony collapsed
the following year, such an impressive bastion could not have been completed. However,
a vessel, the *Virginia*, similar to the one in Hunt's sketch, was launched by the English.
Courtesy of the Maine Historic Preservation Commission, Augusta.

mouth of the river, they set to work building fortifications, a storehouse, and
quarters. The buildings were completed well before winter set in. Meantime,
Popham and Gilbert explored up the Kennebec, west to Cape Elizabeth, and
east beyond the Pemaquid peninsula.

As the warmth of summer gave way and winter enshrouded the little settlement, troubles set in. Although the men remained healthy through the winter,
they complained incessantly about the weather. In fact it was extremely cold,
for the northern hemisphere was suffering through the "Little Ice Age," which

lasted from 1300 to 1700 and plunged temperatures several degrees below the averages of today.

Furthermore, the community was torn by rivalries between President George Popham and Raleigh Gilbert. Feuding reached such a pitch that at one point each side attempted to induce the Indians to support its efforts. Spirits were not lifted when the storehouse burned in the late winter, leaving the settlement short of supplies. On top of that, the Indians remained suspicious and reluctant to trade.

For all its problems, the settlement might have survived had it not been for a series of untimely deaths. In England, Sir John Popham died shortly after the vessels departed for America, leaving financial and administrative màtters largely to Gorges, who was not nearly as well situated to support the venture. In February 1608, President George Popham died, and leadership fell to Raleigh Gilbert. Finally, Gilbert received news the following summer that his elder brother had died, leaving him heir to the family estate. Gilbert had no choice but to return to England to settle affairs. Since the colony was virtually leaderless, everybody clambered aboard the returning vessel, and in the fall of 1608 the once-promising settlement stood deserted amid the bright autumn foliage.

In England, the effect of the failure was catastrophic. Sometime later Gorges wrote that it had been a "wonderful discouragement to all the first undertakers, in so much as there was no more speech of settling any other plantation in those parts for a long time after." At another time he stated that "all our former hopes were frozen to death" for the country was considered "over cold, and in respect of that not habitable by our nation."

French Activity in the Gulf of Maine, 1604–13

During the first years of the seventeenth century, French explorers and colonizers returned to the territory of Maine, although, unlike the English, they focused on the northeast coastal regions. In November 1603, King Henry IV of France granted Pierre Du Gua De Monts a charter with trading and seignorial (ruling) rights in America roughly overlapping those the English king granted the Plymouth Company. A French nobleman, De Monts wanted a New World colony primarily as a personal estate; secondly, as a trading base with the Indians; and third, as a possible embarkation point in the search for a passage to the Orient. De Monts brought along explorer and geographer Samuel de Champlain to record and map the coast in the region. The expedition left France in two ships on April 7, 1604, and entered the Bay of Fundy in May. They skirted the shore, arriving at Passamaquoddy Bay in late June. Moving up the broad St. Croix River, which empties into the bay, they selected an island in the middle for their settlement (today known at St. Croix or Dochet Island). The site offered some advantages: a good anchorage, a fine growth of timber, a supply of clay for brick making, seemingly fertile soil, and security from attack. With the buildings and gardens established in September, Champlain and a small party headed west to explore along the Maine coast. Sailing close to shore, they passed between Mount Desert (which Champlain named) and the mainland and ascended the Penobscot as far as the Kenduskeag Stream at present-day Bangor. Although he was impressed with the area, Champlain found no Norumbega. He descended the river, sailed to the mouth of the Kennebec, and in October returned to St. Croix Island.

Winter came early and it proved to be severe. The desperate colonists quickly consumed most of the wood on the island, and cakes of ice churning in the tides kept them from crossing for more on the mainland. The men were reduced to eating frozen, uncooked food and shivering in their drafty dwellings. Frigid winds, unimpeded by the few remaining trees, stabbed across the island, intensifying the settler's misery. If this was not enough, the colonists found no natural source of water on the island and faced a constant shortage of drinking water. As the winter deepened, the harsh conditions took a fierce toll in scurvy. Over a third of the settlers died from the dreaded disease, and nearly as many suffered various degrees of permanent disability. The error of settling on an island was all too evident, and by spring De Monts set out to find a new location. He and Champlain spent the summer coasting southward, carefully surveying and recording what they saw. They ascended the Kennebec, perhaps as far as Augusta, but found the land along the shores of the river "very poor." They continued southward, observing the local Indians, their weapons, and their agricultural activities, eventually arriving in Massachusetts Bay after five weeks. With provisions low, they returned to St. Croix, not having encountered a place to the south that seemed promising for a new beginning. Thereupon they packed up their house frames and provisions and sailed for Port Royal (the present Annapolis Royal), Nova Scotia, where they reestablished their settlement.

Only a few years later the French again attempted a settlement in Maine, this time largely under the auspices of Jesuit priests. In the summer of 1610, Jean de Biencourt Poutrincourt et de Saint-Just sailed to Port Royal with a contingent of settlers and instructions to revitalize the habitation. Poutrincourt consciously avoided taking any Jesuits with him, concerned about the problems the zealous churchmen might cause. However, two members of the order, Fathers Pierre Biard and Enemond Massé, were not to be put off, and in early 1611 they arranged passage to the New World in a small vessel.

Relations between the Jesuits and the other settlers at Port Royal deteriorated through the winter, and shortly after, the Jesuits appealed to Antoinette de Pons, Marquise de Guercheville and lady of honor to the Queen of France, asking to be posted elsewhere. Concerned for the success of their mission among the natives, Madame de Guercheville fitted out a vessel and sent it to the colony in mid-summer 1613. After a few days, Biard, Massé, and the new arrivals sailed off, to the undoubted joy of all.

Although headed for the Kennebec, the Jesuits were enveloped in a fog and groped their way to Mount Desert Island, where they landed at the site of present-day Bar Harbor to rest and thank God for preserving them from the perils at sea. Shortly after landing, they were approached by a number of Indians, who pleaded that they remain in the area. Biard declined, being firmly resolved to settle on the Kennebec, but he agreed to visit their chief, Asticou, who, they informed him, was seriously ill and wished to be baptized before dying. This reference to baptism probably reflects efforts of earlier Jesuits in the region, most likely emanating from Port Royal. Whatever the case, the chief had nothing more serious than a cold, but the Jesuits found themselves at an ideal location for settling: the western shore of Somes Sound offered a protected harbor, cleared land, two springs, and excellent soil.

The colonizers elected to stay at Mount Desert but almost immediately became divided over plans for settlement: the Jesuits insisted on building fortifications, houses, and the like; the French commander, René Le Coq de La Saussaye, preferred to begin cultivating the rich soil. Whether or not La Saussaye's agricultural project seriously hampered the fortification of the small plantation is not entirely clear, but when the English captain Samuel Argall arrived at the mouth of the harbor shortly after, the French settlers were far from ready to defend themselves.

Argall, on a fishing voyage from the English colony at Virginia, had been told to keep alert for French settlements in the region. He learned of the colony from local Indians and was actually led to the site by an native who mistakenly presumed the French and English were friends. The English sailed into Somes Sound with "the banners of England flying and three trumpets and two drums making a horrible din," and after a few minutes of furious cannonade subdued the unprepared colonists. After sacking the settlement, Argall allowed about two-thirds of its inhabitants to make their way east along the coast, seeking passage from the French vessels plying the waters. He carried the Jesuits and other leaders to Virginia, then returned to destroy the settlement at Port Royal and the remains of the St. Croix Island colony. After this, the French abandoned all attempts at settlement in Maine for some time.

John Smith and the Promotion of New England

A year after Argall's foray, Maine was visited by one of the most colorful adventurers of the time: Captain John Smith. By the time he arrived in New England, John Smith's career as a colonizer was already well established. As a young man, he had performed heroic deeds in the religious wars against the Turks in eastern Europe, and later he kept the nascent Jamestown settlement from collapsing under the challenges imposed by the new land and its people. The trip to the northern shores of America was the beginning of still another phase in his remarkable career—historically, perhaps, the most important of all. When Smith returned from his North Atlantic adventures, he began a life-long promotion of the region he named New England, and it was largely his efforts that caused interest in the area to be revived in the late 1610s and 1620s.

Smith left for New England in April 1614. Sponsored by four London merchants, he was to hunt whales and look for gold and copper mines. After an uneventful voyage, Smith made landfall at Monhegan Island. Chasing the swift, powerful finback whales and searching for precious metals quickly proved frustrating, so Smith put most of his crew to fishing around Monhegan while he and eight others ranged along the mainland charting the coast and doing a little fur trading. Although the best season for both fishing and trading had already passed, Smith's thorough investigation resulted in a carefully drawn map of New England, with inlets, islands, harbors, soundings, sands, rocks, and other landmarks all meticulously recorded. Deeply impressed with the potential of the country, Smith sailed back to England fully determined to plant a new colony. Unfortunately, Thomas Hunt, whose vessel had accompanied the expedition, tarried after Smith sailed for England and captured twenty-four Indians, whom he sold as slaves. Outraged, Captain Smith reported that "this vile act kept him [Hunt] ever after from any more employment in these parts." Regrettably, this act would sour English-Indian relations for some time to come.

Upon his return Smith visited Sir Ferdinando Gorges, hoping for assistance in implementing his New World settlement plan. The old knight probably needed little convincing; with Gorges's backing, Smith left again in late spring 1615 with two ships, expecting to establish a small colony. He had gone but a hundred and twenty leagues when his ship "brake all her Masts, [and was] pumping each watch five or six thousand strokes," offering him no choice but to turn back. Smith reembarked on a smaller vessel, only to be captured by a French pirate shortly after leaving port. During the winter of 1615–16 he found himself sailing the Atlantic as the prisoner of a buccaneer.

Ironically, Smith probably did more to advance the settlement of New England by remaining at home than he would have in the New World. During his months of captivity, he occupied himself writing his *Description of New-England*, a thorough and convincingly laudatory discussion of his 1614 voyage and the territory he had explored and named New England. Published in 1616 along with a map of the region, its success was almost instantaneous. Smith filled his account with glowing stories of the riches to be recovered from the Gulf of Maine—the "strangest Fish pond I ever saw," as he called it. Fishermen began sailing to the region, and in less than a decade they had established small fishing stations from the Piscataqua to Damariscove Island. Justly, Smith has been called the father of New England.

Smith's voyage of 1614 once again galvanized Sir Ferdinando Gorges to action; the old knight sent repeated expeditions to the New England area, demonstrating that settlers could survive the cold season in the northern territories and that the Gulf of Maine could yield profitable cargoes of fish. In 1620, a group of English separatists known as the Pilgrims established the first New England settlement at Plymouth.

Smith's voyage and the subsequent publication of *Description of New-England* capped a long period during which Europeans yielded their old myths and unrealistic assumptions and came to understand the Gulf of Maine region in its own right. Transcribing explorers' reports into lists of profitable commodities, Old World merchants launched the first attempts at settlement based on a firmer understanding of what the land and sea had to offer. These halting early endeavors brought discouragements as colonizers encountered a harsh and unfamiliar environment and were sometimes subject to the uncertainties of European enthusiasm for New World intercourse. But this growing appreciation for the potential value of the Maine landscape was the basis for subsequent colonial development. A second important precedent for colonial Maine emerged during these years. The conflicts that prevailed throughout Maine's colonial history were already evident when Smith arrived in the Gulf of Maine: English explorers and colonizers had clashed periodically with Indians since the days of Verrazano, and the guns of imperial rivalry that first echoed off the steep cliffs of Somes Sound would not be stilled for another century and a half. By 1615 the shadow of European events had fallen across the coast of Maine.

For Further Reading:

Two of the best general works with material relative to Maine are Samuel Eliot Morison, *The European Discovery of America: The Northern Voyages, A.D. 500–1600* (New York and

London, 1971) and David B. Quinn, *North America from Earliest Discovery to the First Settlements: The Norse Voyages to 1612* (New York, 1977). While over a century old, Justin Winsor, *Narrative and Critical History of America*, vols. 3 and 4 (Boston and New York, 1884) still provides the best analysis of individual explorers accompanied with superb bibliographical information. From an Anglo perspective, Quinn, *England and the Discovery of America, 1487–1620* (New York, 1974) creates a plausible interpretation of early voyages westward, although he pushes his evidence hard to find earliest possible dates in the late fifteenth and early sixteenth centuries. Bernard G. Hoffman, *Cabot to Cartier: Sources for a Historical Ethnography of Northeastern North America, 1497–1550* (Toronto, 1961) is an underutilized but excellent work. Hoffman investigates early contact information, cartography, and explorers' reports in his analysis of the period, and he includes good coverage of such individuals as Giovanni da Verrazano and David Ingram.

J. H. Parry, *The Age of Reconnaissance* (New York, 1964) is still one of the best overviews of the European outward surge to the New World. Fernand Braudel offers a good update to Parry's views regarding the Mediterranean in *The Mediterranean and the Mediterranean World in the Age of Phillip II*, 2 vols. (London, 1972–73). Donald W. Meinig puts the story into a physically and culturally interactive framework in *The Shaping of America: The Geographic Perspective on 500 Years of History*, vol. 1: *The Atlantic America, 1492–1860* (New Haven, 1986). For those interested in the routes of the explorers, see Edwin A. Churchill and William F. Royal, "Early Explorations," in *The Maine Bicentennial Atlas: An Historical Survey*, ed. by Gerald E. Morris (Portland, 1976), pp. 1–2, plates 2 and 3.

The reader can look to *The Dictionary of American Biography*, 22 vols., New York (1928–58) and *The Dictionary of Canadian Biography, Vol. 1 (1000–1700)* (Toronto, 1966) for short discussions of specific individuals. Two of the era's greatest figures are discussed in Morris Bishop, *Champlain: The Life of Fortitude* (New York, 1948) and Philip L. Barbour, *The Three Worlds of Captain John Smith* (Boston, 1964).

There are numerous printed primary sources for the period of exploration. Maine's earliest documented visitor's story is published in *The Voyage of Giovanni da Verrazano, 1524–1528*, ed. by Lawrence C. Wroth (New Haven and London, 1970). Henry S. Burrage edited the records of later voyages in *Early English and French Voyages, Chiefly from Hakluyt, 1534–1608* (New York, 1932) as did Charles Levermore in his *Fore-Runners and Competitors of the Pilgrims and Puritans . . .* , 2 vols. (Brooklyn, N. Y., 1912).

French activities in the region are well documented in Harold Bigger, ed., *The Works of Samuel de Champlain*, 6 vols. (Toronto, 1922–36); Marc Lescarbot, *The History of New France*, 3 vols., trans. by W. L. Grant (Toronto, 1911); and Reuben S. Thwaites, ed., *The Jesuit Relations and Allied Documents*, vols. 3 and 4 (Cleveland, 1897). The efforts of two English adventurers are included in Edward Arber, ed., *Travels and Works of Captain John Smith . . . 1580–1631* (Edinburgh, 1910) and *Maine in the Age of Discovery: Christopher Levett's Voyage, 1623–1624 and a Guide to Sources* (Portland, 1988).

3

English Beachheads
in Seventeenth-Century Maine

EDWIN A. CHURCHILL

This chapter looks at the social, economic, and administrative history of the early settlement period in Maine, providing an encompassing view of the sources of stability and disruption in the emerging colony. The social institutions put into place in this period—government, courts, economy, the church, and the military—provided the foundations for colonial Maine. Their evolution, first under the fumbling but persistent overseas administration of Sir Ferdinando Gorges and later under the firmer guidance of Massachusetts Bay's General Court, show the impress of enduring forces in Maine history: a dynamic tension between outside pressures and local adaptations; the burden of severe climatic and environmental conditions; and the presence of conflict—in this case, a legal struggle over title to the formative Maine colony.

During the seventeenth century, English Maine grew from tiny beachheads established by fishermen and fur traders to stable colonial settlements, hosting durable governmental, religious, military, and economic institutions. Maine's early colonial period is characterized by a constant tension between the forces that disrupted society and those that fostered stability. Of these, external forces—an English proprietor's vision of a royal colony in New England, and later the economic, social, and military objectives of the looming Massachusetts Bay Colony—provided the primary impulse to create a government in Maine. Just as important, however, were local initiatives, which filled the gap between the English vision of this New World colony and the realities of living and working on the Maine coast. And finally, the physical world the settlers confronted—resources, climate, soils—limited what was possible in Maine. These three influences—external control, local initiative, and environment—explain the halting movement toward a stable society in Maine during the seventeenth century.

Ferdinando Gorges and Maine's Government, 1620–42

Before 1600, English experience with the Maine coast was confined to a few brief exploratory voyages. George Waymouth's diligent examination of the coast in 1605, for instance, turned up no evidence to indicate "that ever any Christian had ... [come] before," and Samuel de Champlain's voyage that same year drew him to similar conclusions. More important to the immediate use of the region, however, were reports from several early seventeenth-century explorers of the superb fishing and the potential for trade. It was these incentives that drew the earliest English, and to a lesser degree, French entrepreneurs, to the Maine coast. Attracted by the prospects for economic gain, scattered geographically by the demands of trade, and divided by their inherent competiveness, these speculators were not interested in permanent settlement. Nonetheless, the small fishing and trading posts that appeared in the 1620s initiated the slow process of reconciling the reality of New World colonization with the dreams proprietors had built upon scattered reports dating from the age of exploration.

After the collapse of the Popham colony in 1608, John Popham continued to sponsor annual fishing trips from England. The Jamestown colony, established in Virginia in 1607, was sending fishing vessels to the Gulf of Maine by 1610, and by the same time the French had begun small-scale fishing operations along Maine's eastern shores. In 1615, according to Captain John Smith, six English fishing ships arrived in New England, where they may have been joined by a few vessels from Virginia. The next year the number increased to eight, and by the 1620s forty to fifty vessels were fishing in New England waters.

As this activity increased, year-round fishing stations were established along the shores. One of the first was at Damariscove Island, financed by Sir Ferdinando Gorges and operated by thirteen men. Next came stations at Cape Newagen, Piscataqua, Monhegan, Pemaquid, and, by 1632, Richmond Island. These posts were not permanent settlements but rather working bases run essentially by men. A small number of women resided at a few of the stations, employed in domestic activities. These operations were viable only as long as English proprietors continued their provisioning and administration. They did, however, bring important economies to the fishing industry. In addition to offering a base of operations for year-round fishing activity, they lightened the complement of personnel and equipment on vessels carrying fish back to England. More important, they constituted the first continuous English presence on the Maine coast.

During these same years, prospects for fur trading brought another class of adventurers to the Maine coast. Local fur-trading stations were established at Pejepscot between 1625 and 1630, at Cushnoc (present-day Augusta) and

3-1. The most important furbearing animal in North America, the beaver, as drawn by John James Audubon (1785–1851) and published in volume 1 of his *Viviparous Quadrupeds of North America* (New York: V.G. Audubon, 1849).

Richmond Island in 1628, at Penobscot (present-day Castine) in 1630, and at Machias in 1631. These small posts, run by agents of English merchants or by the Plymouth Colony, competed aggressively for the lucrative trade in furs. Local merchant John Winter wrote in 1634 that "the traders do . . . under sell [one] another and over throw the trading with the Indians altogether." In the same year, John Hocking of Piscataqua and a Plymouth trader were killed in a fracus at Cushnoc, when Hocking tried to break the Plymouth Colony's hold on the Kennebec fur trade. Still, other than an ongoing dispute with French traders to the east, the business in furs gradually stabilized and, along with fishing, established a rationale for settlement on the northeastern coast.

As fishing and fur trading expanded, English merchants turned their thoughts toward establishing permanent colonies that would provide a stronger local base for extracting profits. Sir Ferdinando Gorges, the premier advocate of settlement in the region, hoped ultimately to develop New England as a royal colony governed by himself and others of his class. To accomplish this, in 1620 Gorges and over forty government officials and courtiers petitioned the Crown, asking for a proprietorial patent to the region. Funds to build the colony, they hoped, would come from a fishing monopoly along the New England coast.

Gorges and company received a patent for the Council for New England in 1621 and became sole owners of a domain reaching from the Chesapeake to the Penobscot and from sea to sea—that is, across the continent. (Of course, they had little concept of the actual size of the North American land mass.) They also received the coveted fishing monopoly, a feature which instantly created opposition from British West Country fishermen.

Gorges realized he had to move quickly to maintain the Council's authority in the New World. The Plymouth settlers were already securely established in the heart of the Council's claim. The Pilgrims had procured a patent from the Council, but Gorges feared that unless they saw evidence of Council authority, their cooperation would end. Even more serious were the increasing numbers of independent fishermen along the New England coast, decidedly unenthusiastic about obtaining licenses from the Council. To establish control over the region, in the summer of 1623 Gorges sent his son Robert across the Atlantic, along with Captain Francis West and an Anglican chaplain, William Morrell. As admiral of the coast, West was to enforce the fishing monopoly, routing out unlicensed fishermen; Morrell was to oversee religious affairs.

The effort failed miserably. Robert Gorges arrived at Wessagusetts, just below the Plymouth Colony, in September 1623 and immediately mishandled a confrontation with Thomas Weston, a contentious London merchant in the area. Unable to bring the Plymouth Colony under his control, Gorges sailed back to England. Captain West soon followed, having suffered rough treatment from the fishermen along the coast. The Reverend Morrell stayed only through the year. Events in England further doomed the mission: Parliament struck down Gorges's fishing monopoly in 1624, and a war between England and France and Spain preoccupied Sir Ferdinando for several years. Furthermore, the old knight was short of finances. Thus, official efforts to establish a colony languished for half a decade.

By the late 1620s, the war was ending and Gorges had restored his depleted purse by marrying a wealthy widow. Again free to pursue his interests in America, Gorges became involved in a fur-plantation scheme based at Piscataqua and called the Laconia Company. It soon proved to be an expensive failure.

In 1630, the colony of Massachusetts Bay was established and began to grow rapidly. Gorges soon realized that this new competitor seriously threatened his dream of a royal New England colony. With no money to challenge Massachusetts, Gorges and the Council began issuing land grants in northern New England, hoping to encourage settlement. Partly owing to the impetus of these grants, settlers began arriving in southern Maine in a steady stream, both directly from England and via Massachusetts. Joining Pemaquid, probably settled in the late 1620s, were new settlements established at York (1630), Cape Porpus (ca.

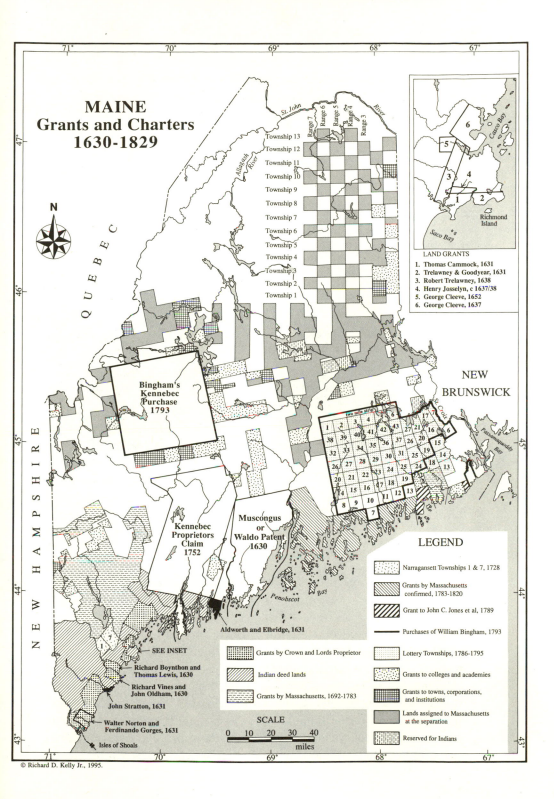

MAINE
Grants and Charters
1630-1829

QUEBEC

NEW
BRUNSWICK

NEW HAMPSHIRE

St. John River

Range 7
Range 6
Range 5
Range 4
Range 3

Township 13
Township 12
Township 11
Township 10
Township 9
Township 8
Township 7
Township 6
Township 5
Township 4
Township 3
Township 2
Township 1

Allagash River

Bingham's
Kennebec
Purchase
1793

Kennebec
Proprietors
Claim
1752

Muscongus
or
Waldo Patent
1630

two mile strip

St. Croix

Passamaquoddy Bay

Penobscot Bay

Aldworth and Elbridge, 1631

SEE INSET

Richard Boynthon and
Thomas Lewis, 1630

Richard Vines and
John Oldham, 1630

John Stratton, 1631

Walter Norton and
Ferdinando Gorges, 1631

Isles of Shoals

LAND GRANTS
1. Thomas Cammock, 1631
2. Trelawney & Goodyear, 1631
3. Robert Trelawney, 1638
4. Henry Josselyn, c 1637/38
5. George Cleeve, 1652
6. George Cleeve, 1637

Casco Bay
Saco Bay
Richmond Island

LEGEND

Narragansett Townships 1 & 7, 1728

Grants by Massachusetts
confirmed, 1783-1820

Grant to John C. Jones et al, 1789

Purchases of William Bingham, 1793

Grants by Crown and Lords Proprietor

Indian deed lands

Grants by Massachusetts, 1692-1783

Lottery Townships, 1786-1795

Grants to colleges and academies

Grants to towns, corporations,
and institutions

Lands assigned to Massachusetts
at the separation

Reserved for Indians

SCALE
0 10 20 30 40
miles

© Richard D. Kelly Jr., 1995.

3-2. The McIntyre garrison house in York was built around 1707 of horizontal courses of sawn logs sheathed with shingles, a building technique probably introduced by Scots settlers. The second-story overhang was a medieval feature also brought from the British Isles. Courtesy of the Maine Historic Preservation Commission, Augusta.

1630), Saco (1630), Kittery (ca. 1631), Scarborough (1632), Falmouth (1633), North Yarmouth (1636), and Wells (1642). Unlike the transient fishing stations, these new settlements were made up of people who viewed the Maine coast as a permanent home. They were settled not by single men but by families, generally young or middle-aged and often with young children. Straggling into the proprietorial claims, they were granted fifty- to one-hundred-acre tracts of land along the coast or river banks. Although more permanent than the fishing posts, these early farming settlements lacked the stability of the growing Massachusetts Bay towns. Unlike communities in Massachusetts, those in Maine were scattered—strung out in long, ribbon-like patterns, with no real center. They were also less homogeneous than the Puritan communities; Maine's settlers came from the West Country, London, interior England, and the Bay Colony—areas that were variously farming regions, fishing villages, cities, and small towns. The communities contained an assortment of Anglicans, Puritans, and Antinomians and a sprinkling of Quakers. They lacked the cohesive force of common origin and common religion. Despite their varied backgrounds, most settlers upon arrival turned to farming, which proved to be a more stable occupation than fishing or fur trading. Even Pemaquid, supposedly a fishing port, sent a load of twenty cattle to Salem for sale in 1640. Only after the communities established sufficient agricultural bases would they support more specialized artisan activities. In the meantime, ties to the soil anchored settler families to a particular locale, providing the social basis for permanent community settlement.

As the Maine coast settlements grew, so did the need for organized government. The first impulses in this direction originated in England. In the 1630s, Sir Ferdinando Gorges made the first of two major efforts to fulfill his vision of a royal colony in the New World. Increasingly aware of the rapidly growing Massachusetts Bay Colony's threat to his plans for a unified New England, Gorges dissolved the Council for New England in 1635, dividing its territory among various council members and taking for himself a grant, called the province of New Somerset, stretching from the Piscataqua to the Kennebec River.

After the dissolution of the council, Gorges moved rapidly to institute a government in his new province, appointing his nephew William Gorges as lieutenant governor. In late winter 1635, William sailed to the New World, and on March 21 he assembled a court at Saco, the first of several held over the next two years. The new government was generally well accepted, and it handled a series of minor disputes and transgressions, such as bad debts, drunkenness, and swearing.

William Gorges's governorship was short-lived. In the spring of 1637, the courts, acting on the king's initiative, revoked the Massachusetts Bay Colony charter; Sir Ferdinando recalled his nephew and discharged the commissioners, anticipating a proclamation from the king establishing a general New England government under his own command. Massachusetts, ever increasing in strength, successfully ignored the court's action, and the king, facing increasing problems at home, could do little but lend Gorges moral support. Plagued with bad debts from the bankrupt Laconia venture, the old knight had no funds to pay the fees for a royal charter. When he finally received the charter in late 1639, he sent another nephew, Thomas Gorges, to Maine as his deputy.

In fact, a number of settlements had begun forming local governments well before William or Thomas Gorges arrived in the New World. The inhabitants of Saco united in a "combination" by which they governed themselves, hired a minister, and granted tracts of land to individual settlers. Similarly, York began systematically apportioning its lands and formed plans for a new community meeting house. Between 1637, when William Gorges left New England, and early 1640, when Thomas Gorges arrived, individual communities maintained and elaborated these primitive governmental institutions.

Thomas Gorges, like his predecessor, faced opposition in bringing the colonists under Sir Ferdinando's authority. Local leaders were unwilling to relinquish power, and settlers generally worried that the proprietor intended to "draw them . . . into slavery." Through a careful mix of firmness and conciliation, Thomas Gorges prevailed. The settlers' fears were stilled by Gorges's insistence that they would be governed by "noe act but with their [own] consent." True to his word, Gorges called together representatives from four newly established counties and the incorporated city of Agamenticus (York) to develop a code of laws. These were sent to England for ratification and apparently became the standard by which Maine was administered. Maine government continued to bear the impress of Thomas Gorges's balance between local initiative and outside control.

Provision for direct participation—necessary because of the very tenuous legitimacy of Thomas Gorges's authority—and the local settlers' desire for stability and order were both addressed in the structure of the new government. The organization consisted of local and provincial bodies. Local governments were designed primarily to insure the communities' economic viability and to uphold accepted moral codes. At annual meetings, officials were chosen for the following year and major community decisions were made. As questions arose during the year, other meetings were held, while the selectmen, clerk, and minor local officials handled day-to-day administrative activities.

The settlements' overall enforcement agency was the provincial government, responsible for adjudicating disputes, enforcing agreed-upon social behavior, and otherwise insuring the smooth running of the society in general. The deputy governor and his counselors, appointed by Sir Ferdinando Gorges, administered the colony, participated in the various courts, and served as local magistrates. Grand and trial juries were chosen to decide the more serious cases before the provincial courts. Besides establishing a court system, Thomas Gorges also attempted to institute a provincial legislative body. In the summer of 1642, locally elected deputies from the four counties met with the deputy governor and counselors to impanel a grand jury and enact a set of laws for the province. By mid-summer 1643, however, Thomas Gorges was headed back to England, bringing that short phase of Maine's early government to an end.

Even though the effort failed, the public institutional structures so fundamental to the maintenance of an orderly society—town governments and the provincial court—proved surprisingly vital. Control over these civil institutions passed from Sir Ferdinando Gorges to Edward Rigby (a short-term proprietor of a portion of Maine), three times to Massachusetts, to the Dominion of New England, and to the Crown. Through these changes in leadership and through the chaos of intermittent political strife and warfare, they showed a remarkable resiliency and adaptability while retaining their basic functions and vigor.

Thomas Gorges's government did much to ensure the stability and permanence of the small communities along the coast. First, it assured inhabitants clear title to a piece of property. For seventeenth-century English people, land was the foundation of organized society, and in the New World it provided colonists with their basic necessities, their means of achieving wealth, and their sense of security. Not surprisingly, land transactions were systematically constructed, carefully prepared, and legally validated according to procedures borrowed largely from England.

Second, local governments regulated economic activity in the fragile colonies. Among other things, local governments controlled the number of trees cut in certain locations, restricted foraging by livestock, and stipulated methods used by local fish catchers. Timber resources were a matter of communitywide concern. Proprietors and inhabitants alike offered special grants to individuals proposing sawmills in their town. In return, local ordinances frequently stipulated that local people could procure lumber at special prices, that local people would be hired first, and that the town would be given special prices for boards.

Local government further ensured stability by maintaining standards of religion and morality. Nearly all the towns along the Maine coast experienced difficulties acquiring ministers. The small, isolated Maine plantations had to compete with Massachusetts and New Hampshire towns—and with each other—in their search for pastors. Because of this shortage, communities were frequently forced to settle for preachers who were at best less than stellar. One of the most notorious was the charismatic Reverend George Burdett, who, having been ousted from Dover, New Hampshire, arrived in York, Maine, where he combined the seduction of local women with his religious activities until he was driven out by Governor Gorges.

The provincial courts reinforced local efforts to secure economic and moral stability. Commissioners traveled from town to town holding court, and, in important cases, disputes were carried to the higher courts. Most disputes were resolved by arbitration or jury trial. Both of these legal tools were designed to provide systematic, prompt solutions and resolve issues to the best satisfaction of all concerned. Broad consensus was important in a frontier society where government legitimacy was tenuous and where divisiveness might endanger the whole system.

The court's effectiveness is exemplified in the experiences of one of Falmouth's irrepressible malcontents, James Cole. In 1636, Cole was fined five shillings and further costs for being "Drunck." Four years later, neighbor Arthur MacWorth declared Cole "an abusive and suspected person" and argued that the reprobate was "by reason of his former and still irregular living . . . injurious unto this complainant his family and goods." MacWorth asked the court to banish Cole from the province or "otherwise bridle his inordinate course of life by a due course of law." The exasperated court put Cole under a eighty-pound recognizance to be levied against his goods and chattels if he didn't straighten up. Apparently, he did!

Forces of Disruption: The Environment

Even as early Maine settlers strove to establish a way of life and to develop solid, peaceful communities, several disruptive forces shook the stability of their society. One of the most significant was the environment itself—the impediments of severe climate, thick, resisting forests, thin soils, and geographic isolation. Colonists had undoubtedly heard about the region's harsh winter weather, but Maine, after all, was at about the same latitude as England. Unaware of the arctic current running along the coast or the polar air masses that glided across the Canadian Shield into northern New England, the colonists discovered winters cold beyond all expectations. Not only were Maine winters colder than England's, they were significantly colder than those of present-day Maine, since this was the depth of the "Little Ice Age," a period from about 1300 to 1700 when the climate of the Northern Hemisphere was several degrees colder than it is today.

For Maine settlers, the winter season was an onerous presence. Repeatedly, Thomas Gorges noted the "tediousness" and deep snows of the winters. The clapboard frame houses kept the wind and snow off the occupants, but cracks and inefficient insulation let in liberal quantities of cold. Builders kept windows small and few in number. (Glass, in any case, was expensive.) Heavily draped beds gave the occupants a modicum of protection against the frigid temperatures. Fireplaces burned constantly but sent much of the heat directly up the chimney. Adding to the misery was a chronic shortage of clothing, for cloth was one of the most expensive necessities of the time, and most Maine people were not well off.

Every summer was dominated by preparations for the coming winter. Enormous quantities of wood had to be cut and hauled, clothing made or acquired, and food processed and stored. Most important, fields and gardens had to be tilled, planted, and harvested during a growing season substantially shorter than that enjoyed by Maine people today.

The primeval forest presented another barrier to settlers. Natural clearings for tillage and coastal and inland marshes for hay, portioned out to inhabitants, provided an initial opportunity to establish homesteads. Then came the back-breaking work of clearing new ground. Not only were settlers compelled to fell the great trees and clean off the underbrush, but they also felt obligated during the early years to grub out the stumps and haul off the seemingly endless supply of rocks.

Unfortunately, the new land offered other surprises. Unlike the rich, fertile earth of southern England, the soils along the Maine coast were both low in natural fertility and acidic. English grains, planted with little fertilization in the old country, grew best in a neutral or basic soil, and did not flourish in Maine. Indian corn did better, probably because settlers used fish as fertilizer. To this mix of discouragements, the Maine coastal environment offered up occasional droughts, wet spells, plant diseases, insect plagues, and early frosts. Getting in a crop could be a major accomplishment. Furthermore, the settlers had to contend with wolves. These predators were attracted by the settlers' stock of swine, goats, and calves, and they were fearless raiders. The settlers tried various methods of eradication, encouraged by governmental bounties, but from all evidence, the wolves were little hindered.

If this were not enough, Maine's settlers faced one more problem: geographic isolation. Maine was off the established English-American trade routes, and the settlements were too few in number to attract major mercantile business. Thus, even if they had products to exchange, colonists lacked suppliers. Merchants traded with them only at extremely high prices. Speaking of Boston merchants bringing supplies into the region, visitor John Josselyn remarked that "if they do not gain Cent per Cent, they cry out that they are losers."

Despite these hardships, by and large inhabitants generally scratched together sufficient food, clothing, and shelter to eke out a reasonably comfortable existence. Life was clearly above the subsistence level. Careful analysis of the extant inventories of mid-seventeenth-century Maine middle-class inhabitants indicate that even the average farm family had some amenities, such as stocks of linen, cotton, and wool cloth, pewter dishes, brass utensils, lanterns, and lamps. Similar patterns are suggested in archaeological findings at early Pemaquid and Arrowsic. Clearly, early Maine society offered some of the better things of life, and English settlers were learning to cope with the rugged Maine environment.

Internal Conflict and External Control, 1636–77

The fragile economic, political, and social structures of early Maine communities permitted little tolerance for discord and disruptions. A difficult season could quickly deplete limited surpluses, or an external military crisis could have the same effect, diverting the settlers from agricultural activities. As the colonists were soon to learn, political disputes could similarly disrupt leadership and diminish the cooperative effort so necessary as the new communities struggled for stability.

Political strife emanating from outside the small communities bedeviled Maine throughout the seventeenth century. The source of this turmoil was tension between two political and religious factions: Royalist Anglicans and their Puritan counterparts, both in England and in Massachusetts Bay, and each with its champions among community elites in Maine. Locally, the wrangling began with a seemingly minor dispute between proprietors George Cleeve of Falmouth and John Winter, agent for British merchant Edward Trelawny. Cleeve, whose claim to portions of Casco Bay was disputed by the aggressive Winter, sailed to England in late 1636 and convinced Sir Ferdinando Gorges that his representatives were not carrying out their duties in Maine. On Cleeve's advice, Gorges replaced Richard Vines as deputy governor with a commission headed by Cleeve. Back in Maine, Cleeve quickly obtained formal possession of his land. Meanwhile, Sir Ferdinando had second thoughts and returned the deputy governorship to Vines.

Cleeve surmised that his victory was in jeopardy and sailed back to England in 1642 with a new plan to save his property. With backing from Edward Digby, an English merchant, he managed to obtain a grant known as the "Plough Patent," which predated Trelawny's grant and covered a region stretching from the Kennebec to Cape Porpus. Carefully manipulating and in some cases falsifying the degree of backing for his project, Cleeve obtained parliamentary approval for his patent, thereafter known as the "Province of Lygonia." Having secured his authority by 1647, Cleeve began placating old foes by appointing some to high offices, holding frequent general assemblies, issuing new grants, and reconfirming old deeds. Cleeve's policies brought increasing stability to the region, a task made easier by the death of two powerful English opponents, Robert Trelawny in 1643 and Sir Ferdinando Gorges in 1647.

Cleeve and his former opponents soon faced a new, more powerful outside adversary, however. Massachusetts Bay had long coveted the territory to its northeast and was fearful of any controlling element tied to the Royal government, especially the heirs of Sir Ferdinando Gorges. The Bay colonists also had

3-3. The seal of the Massachusetts Bay Colony, which absorbed the Province of Maine in the 1650s. The seal has the native American improbably saying, "Come over and help us." Courtesy of the Archives Division, Office of the Secretary, Commonwealth of Massachusetts, Boston.

strong economic designs on the eastern area, where vast forests offered supplies of lumber and naval stores and huge tracts of land beckoned to ambitious speculators.

Those living in sections of territory still independent of Cleeves's Lygonia had little proprietorial support since Thomas Gorges's return to England. In 1649, the inhabitants of Kittery, York, and Wells formed an independent Province of Maine, governed by Edward Godfrey of York. By 1651, the province was attempting to obtain recognition from Parliament, something Massachusetts could not allow. Despite Godfrey's objections, Massachusetts moved resolutely, claiming, by a thoroughly contrived reading of its charter, that its northern boundary included all of Maine to northern Casco Bay. That said, the Bay leaders made good their claims, absorbing Kittery and York in November 1652 and annexing Wells, Saco, and Cape Porpus the following summer. Massachusetts gained some local support by providing liberal terms: inhabitants were assured that their land titles were secure; that local leaders would preside over administration; that freedom of worship would be allowed; and that Maine settlers would enjoy the same protection, favor, and justice other Massachusetts residents enjoyed.

Having annexed western Maine, Bay Colony officials halted, probably waiting to judge the response their actions brought. Returning from England in September 1653, Cleeve angrily reasserted his claim as deputy governor of Lygonia. Massachusetts hesitated, probably fearing adverse consequences from Parliament, and the verbal conflict continued over the next four years. By the late 1650s, however, conditions favored Massachusetts' plan to annex Lygonia. Cleeve's English backer, Edward Rigby, died, leaving only a young son to defend the Lygonia claim, and Parliament was too deeply immersed in problems at home to worry about the fate of a small colony in America. Furthermore, local resistance disintegrated as new settlers from the Bay Colony moved to Maine. Massachusetts moved into the last of Cleeve's domain in the spring of 1658. Again, generous terms minimized bitterness locally. In this case, two previous foes of Massachusetts, Henry Josselyn and Robert Jordan, were appointed as local commissioners, a decision Massachusetts leaders soon regretted.

For a time, the new administration worked well. However, in 1660, with the ascension of King Charles ii, Ferdinando Gorges, grandson of the old knight, began efforts to reclaim the region, and his petition to the newly formed Council for Foreign Plantations was favorably received. Not waiting for final confirmation, Gorges sent a commission to establish his government in Maine. In 1661, the commissioners met with their local counterparts in Wells and began planning a new provincial government. They also set out to collect a decade's worth of back quit-rents. Thoroughly agitated by these activities, Massachusetts sent commissioners to Maine to challenge the proceedings.

Massachusetts commissioners arrived on May 26, and the next few months saw heavy campaigning for the loyalty of Maine's inhabitants. The Bay Colony sent out warrants to individual towns ordering allegiance to its government. Gorges's supporters suppressed several of these and sent out similar documents of their own, some of which were similarly waylaid. By stripping a couple of Gorges's supporters of key administrative posts and throwing Robert Jordan in jail, the Bay leaders prevented the takeover attempt. On July 7, 1663, Massachusetts reopened its court in York with minimal opposition. When Gorges again tried to retake Maine in late 1664, the effort came to nothing.

As the Bay Colony leaders moved to reassert control to the east, they found themselves facing a more dangerous adversary to the south: a royal commission sent to America to settle affairs in New York, newly acquired from the Dutch. The commission was also to investigate complaints concerning the government in New England. Arriving in Boston in May 1665, the commissioners engaged in a stormy session with Massachusetts politicians, then sailed east, reaching Maine by late June. There they appointed eleven justices of the peace to carry on the affairs of Maine "until his Majesty will please to Appoint another government" and explicitly told Massachusetts to stay out. For the next two years, the area remained generally free of conflict, but each town harbored a substantial pro-Massachusetts faction just waiting for an opportunity to reestablish ties with the Bay government.

By the spring of 1668, many felt the time had come. The last royal commissioner in America, Colonel Richard Nichols, left for England, and on May 12, Massachusetts declared its right to Maine. A month later the Massachusetts commission arrived at York, "attended by 12 armed horse, their two marshals and several other gentlemen." After a number of minor confrontations, they were able to hold a fairly successful session. A relative peace settled over the region, and in 1677 the General Court secured clear title by purchasing the proprietary rights to Maine from Gorges's heirs. By this time, however, the shock of a native American uprising had descended over the territory, bringing a new and more terrible source of conflict to the Maine frontier.

While Gorges, Cleeves, Massachusetts, and the Royal Commissioners battled for control of the communities of southwestern Maine, a second group of English settlements was developing eastward near the mouth of the Kennebec River. Plymouth inhabitants explored the Kennebec in the fall of 1625 and established a trading post at Cushnoc in 1628. In 1630, the Pilgrims secured a patent for the surrounding lands on both sides of the river.

In 1653–54, agents for merchant Thomas Lake and later Thomas Clarke set up trading posts at Taconnet (Winslow) and Arrowsic Island (near the mouth of the Kennebec). The resulting Clarke and Lake Company gained title to much of the lower Kennebec. Numerous smaller fur-trading operations were developing in the area as well. At the same time, families were settling along the shores of the Androscoggin and Kennebec rivers, at Pemaquid, at Cape Newagen, and on the islands of Damariscove and Monhegan. In 1664, the Crown granted the Kennebec area to the Duke of York, who sent a Royal Commission to Maine in 1665. The commissioners met with local inhabitants, received oaths of allegiance, chose officers, and gave licenses to four entrepreneurs for the "re-tayling of wine or lyquors or strong drink." Despite this initiative, five years later the inhabitants of the "Eastern parts of New England" petitioned the Massachusetts General Court asking that they be brought under Bay government and protection. On July 27, 1674, the newly designated Devonshire County opened court—under Massachusetts jurisdiction. With this, Massachusetts brought all of Maine from Kittery to Pemaquid under its authority.

Colonial Maine Comes of Age

As the din of these jurisdictional conflicts died away and colonists turned to the task of survival, Maine settlers achieved a permanent hold on the land. Using local resources in various combinations, they managed a workable system of exports and subsistence activity. Pressured by local economic and demographic growth and by new administrative directives from Massachusetts, townspeople created a more stable social, religious, and political life.

By 1670, there were about 3,500 Anglo inhabitants in the region. Of these, approximately 900 were in the Kittery area and 400 to 500 resided in each of the other coastal communities, still largely arranged in shore-hugging, ribbon-like settlements. William Hubbard's description of Kittery as "a long scattering Plantation made up of several Hamlets" applied to communities throughout Maine.

The region's economic structure was organized on a gender-based, interdependent division of activities. Males played a dominant role in agriculture, fishing, lumbering, and a variety of crafts, whereas females directed and largely ran the domestic economy, including the management of the home, food, textiles and clothing, along with the rearing of young children. The occupational training of the young was largely carried on by the parent of the same sex. As might well be expected in a family-structured society, these lines of demarcation were often breeched, with members of the either sex performing work generally ascribed to their opposites when the need arose.

It was the men's activities of agriculture, fishing, and lumbering which were most often noted in contemporary descriptions of these early settlements. John Josselyn remarked that "all these towns have stores of salt and fresh marsh [hay] with arable land, and are well stokt with Cattle." Josselyn found Saco and Winter Harbor to be "well stored with Cattle, arable land and marshes" and Hubbard indicated that "upon the banks [of the Sheepscot] were many scattered Planters, . . . a thousand Head of Neat Cattel . . . besides . . . Fields and Barns full of Corn." Farther east lay Pemaquid, "well accommodated with Pasture Land about the Haven [harbor] for feeding Cattel and some Fields also for Tillage." Fishing was also much in evidence.

Even at this early date, however, some communities leaned towards a specific activity. Wells, Saco, Falmouth, and Sheepscot were centers of farming; Cape Porpus, Winter Harbor, Richmond Island, Damariscove, and Monhegan were more oriented to fishing. Islands and coastal areas with good drying spaces attracted fishers, while locations with arable lands, both along the coast and up the rivers, proved more attractive to farmers, especially if marshland for native grass and fertilizer was nearby.

The lumber trade also influenced the development of the Maine coast, as nearly every community had at least one sawmill and a number had several. According to Hubbard, "all or most of [the] ... Towns and Plantations are seated upon, and near some River greater or lesser, whose Streams are principally improved for the driving of Saw-mills: Those late Inventions, [are] so useful for the Destruction of Wood and Timber ... that there is scarce a River or Creek in those Parts that hath not some of those Engines erected upon them." The Berwick-Kittery area, on the well-timbered Piscataqua watershed, was particularly active. The first mill was built by Captain John Mason in 1634 on the Little Newchawannock River (Berwick). Although short-lived, it was followed by at least six other mills between 1648 and 1660. By the mid-1670s York supported at least ten mills; Wells and Saco had three each. Farther east, the Clarke and Lake sawmills in the Sagadahoc area readied a hundred thousand feet of boards for shipment in 1675. The Piscataqua region also provided numerous white pine masts and spars, many of which were being shipped directly to England.

Of the various trades in the region, lumbering was the most dependent on outside capital. In nearly all cases local millwrights and carpenters were financed from Boston and other nearby towns, and much of the lumber profit ended up in the pockets of the Boston financiers. Acting as merchants, these same Bostonians usually served the commercial needs of the small Maine towns. Here, too, their terms were generally disadvantageous for the Maine settlers, many of whom slipped deeply in debt to their suppliers. Even those who worked at the mills found their wages absorbed by debts to their employers.

As the towns matured economically, occupations diversified. Blacksmiths, carpenters, and millwrights were joined by coopers, wheelwrights, shoemakers, tailors, and other artisans related to an agrarian society. Essential to the economic and social stability was a vital domestic economy, an enterprise nearly invisible in colonial records and seldom mentioned in traditional economic studies. These domestic responsibilities fell almost exclusively to wives, daughters, servants, and extended female kin within the household.

Historian Laurel Ulrich notes that "a woman's environment was the family dwelling and the yard or yards surrounding it." This included the kitchen, cellars, pantries, brewhouses, milk houses, washhouses, and buteries, along with the garden, milkyard, henhouse, and perhaps the orchard. It also included the nearby woods and marshes, where women foraged for herbs, roots, and berries, and "the houses of neighbors and . . . the cartways of a village or town," where women traded work or bartered items they produced in the home or garden.

Women's economic contributions were fundamental to their families' well-being. They had to obtain foodstuffs—by growing, gathering, trading, or purchasing—and prepare them for the table, activities that could range from butchering a small pig to baking biscuits in a skillet over an open fire. Further, to extend the bounty of the harvest season into the winter and spring, they had to preserve a wide variety of foods, employing a diversity of techniques—salting, smoking, drying, pickling, root cellaring—that were handed down from generation to generation.

Women had to clothe their families and often their servants as well, and they were expected to be skilled at needlework. The yarns and cloth they used were home products or acquired through trade or purchase. Numerous other household tasks demanded attention, including laundry and mending, feeding the livestock, gathering kindling, and—most time consuming—raising children. Women, like the men, were adept petty traders, knowing what they needed, where to get it, its value, and what they might provide in exchange. At times, their offerings were home products or specific domestic labors. Other times, they would trade against their husband's credit. And each of their responsibilities they taught their daughters and servants.

There was yet one more major aspect to women's work in colonial Maine. At times, wives found themselves directly supporting their husbands' occupations. They might help their mate plant field crops, manufacture craft items, or handle business transactions in his absence. Ulrich observes, "almost any task was suitable for a woman as long as it furthered the good of her family and was acceptable to her husband."

The sexual division of labor was ingrained into the colonial society and economy, a fact underscored by the rapidity with which widowed persons, either male or female, replaced a lost mate. The structure was further solidified by inheritance patterns. Usually male heirs received the family real estate, which they used to continue the broader economic functions of the farm or business. Women usually received household goods, since these items were useful for establishing and maintaining the domestic unit. The importance of this dual system was well recognized by all, and without it early Maine never would have moved beyond the world of transient fishermen and fur traders.

As they responded to the growing complexity of their local economies and to the new initiatives from Massachusetts, Maine's towns found their administrative duties expanding. Certainly two of their most important governmental obligations were defense and transportation, and both proved to be major tasks for the small, scattered communities. The establishment of local militias probably began at some level soon after the first settlers arrived. However, the evolution of local and regional defense systems was much more evident after Massachusetts annexed Maine. This may partly reflect better records, but it also represents the Bay Colony's determination to bolster its eastern defenses.

As early as 1656, shortly after it took control of Maine, Massachusetts complained that several towns were not furnishing "sufficient armes, powder . . . as the law requires." A decade later, the king's justices recognized the problem and commanded local officers to order "their Souldgers armes . . . Well fixed and fitted with powder." Clearly this warning was insufficient, for in 1672 Kittery, York, Cape Porpus, Saco, Scarborough, and Falmouth were again admonished.

Most communities built one or more strategically located, fortified "garrison" houses. Of heavy construction, often the residences of the communities' leading figures, these structures provided a place to which nearby residents could flee in case of attack. Each town was also expected to maintain a militia unit. Local officers, usually a lieutenant and an ensign, were to see that citizens were appropriately supplied and periodically trained. Maine's militia forces in the 1660s consisted of over seven hundred men, a fairly formidable number, and it appears from extant inventories that ownership of firearms was fairly universal. Still, the value of inventoried guns ranged widely, and some were described as "ould"; one suspects that not all of these arms—or their bearers—were reliable. Furthermore, some militia officers were apparently less than distinguished. In 1663, Lieutenant Richard Hitchcock of Saco was criticized for "neglecting his office, by not commanding the souldgers to their due exercise . . . for the space of two years." Others were similarly reprimanded. Quite a few individuals petitioned for exemption from practices for reasons of age or occupation. Finally, the very scattered nature of the communities boded ill for any efforts to assemble the local forces quickly.

Creating a usable road system between and within the scattered Maine settlements proved another challenge. While necessary to tie the region together, the process of cutting roads through woods, across swamps, and over ravines and creeks must have seemed an unwelcome alternative to simply sailing along the coast and up the larger streams. In some stretches, especially between York and Wells, broad sand beaches provided a natural highway; those, unfortunately, were rare along the Maine coast.

By law, inhabitants were to build roads "sufficient for horse and man" between towns. Although this meant little more than a marked path through the dense woods, meeting even these minimal requirements proved nearly impossible. Every three or four years Kittery, York, Wells, and Newichawonnak (present-day Berwick) were admonished in court for not keeping up their roads. Hoping "for the more Convenient passage of strangers and others" beyond these southerly communities, in July 1673 the court ordered Wells, Saco, Scarborough, and Falmouth to "marke out the most Convenient Way from Wells . . . unto Falmouth . . . sufficient for horse and man." The next fall, a report was returned stating such a way was not feasible because "there are soe many bridges to bee made over the swampes and Rivers, [and] the ways being soe exceedingly bad." Unimpressed, the court repeated its demand the following summer. Equally uninspired, the local inhabitants ignored it. After all, by using the beaches at low tide, catching the various ferries, and putting up with some less than ideal paths, one could travel by land along the Maine coast.

Within the towns, crops, wood, and other items were moved about by carts, necessitating closer attention to local road and bridge building. In Saco, for instance, a bridge twelve feet wide, sufficient for horse and cart, was constructed. Usually town governments assigned local inhabitants to the tasks of building roads and making seasonal repairs. The towns also had to license taverns for travelers and see to the availability of ferry service over larger streams. At times, the towns had to deal harshly with their own inhabitants in order to keep roads open. Land travel in seventeenth-century Maine, whether local or regional, remained a considerable challenge.

Only with time were the small settlements able to build economic bases substantial enough to support a minister. Some, like Cape Porpus, never really did reach that point in the seventeenth century. Others found the task a formidable one, although the Bay Colony was ever diligent in seeing that efforts continued. In some cases, town residents attended services in neighboring towns. In others, ministers traveled between adjoining communities. Several towns were criticized for not providing places of worship or for letting meeting houses fall into disrepair. York's meeting house was cited for "great indesency and unsutableness" in 1679, "by reasons of Its being open to the weather and the Mischiefe of birds and swallows getting [into] it."

Maine's religious makeup at mid-century was anything but homogeneous, with Anglicans, Puritans, and Antinomians vying for ascendency. Puritan minister Thomas Jenner found Maine people "to be very superstitious, following man's invented formalities in devotion rather than the institutional worship of God"; in other words, those he encountered were good Anglicans. In 1643, the Reverend John Wheelwright arrived in Maine and established the community of Wells. The brother-in-law of Antinomian Anne Hutchinson, he moved to Maine to stay ahead of Bay Colony persecutors. Although he remained only briefly, he established a church at Wells and left behind several enthusiastic disciples.

Despite earlier promises of religious toleration, Massachusetts moved quickly and purposefully to eliminate its competitors, and by the 1670s, the Bay Colony had made significant progress in establishing Puritanism as the dominant religion in Maine. Anglican ministers were an immediate target. Not only were their religious tenets and practices unpalatable, but they represented a link with the royal government and Sir Ferdinando Gorges that could prove politically dangerous. Their first target was Reverend Richard Gibson. Moving about from Richmond's Island to Piscataqua, and then the Isles of Shoals, Gibson had made several anti-Massachusetts remarks along the way. In the early 1640s, the Bay leaders tossed him in jail and then forced him into exile in England. The Puritans' real adversary was Anglican minister Robert Jordan of Spurwink. Aggressive, politically powerful, and wholly unawed by the Bay Colony, Jordan built up a substantial following and flaunted Massachusetts directives. Jordan further roused Bay leaders by calling the revered Boston theologian John Cotton "a lyar [who] dyed with a ly in his mouth, and [went] . . . to hell with a packe of lyes." Jordan was censored, fined, and even jailed, but political connections and sheer tenacity enabled the Spurwink firebrand to continue his ministry right up to the Indian wars.

Generally speaking, an unorthodox minister was first warned to quit preaching. Shortly after, his town might be chastised for failing to support a qualified minister, and in most instances, the censured preachers eventually faded away. A few, like Jordan, gained sufficient local support to persist in spite of opposition from the community's Puritan leaders, but by the 1670s the Bay Colony had gained the upper hand throughout the region. Kittery's upper parish, along with York, Wells, and Falmouth, had settled Harvard graduate ministers, and the steady influx of Massachusetts settlers guaranteed that the trend would continue.

Maine's Quakers were the conspicuous exception. As early as the 1650s, Kittery harbored a substantial community of Quakers, some of whom were local political leaders. Despite periodic harassment and disenfranchisement, when Massachusetts retook Maine following the period of the Royal Commission, it found the whole Kittery government in the hands of Quakers. They were quickly dismissed and threatened with heavy fines if they assumed such roles again. Still, the group remained active, and in the 1660s signs of Quaker activity appeared in other southern Maine communities.

With substantial Anglican, Antinomian, and Quaker factions within the region, the Congregationalist Puritans were in no position to demand the level of orthodox conformity they maintained in Massachusetts. A current of tolerance, probably born as much from necessity as desire, permeated the religious structure of early Maine. A century and a half later, that same heritage of tolerance, coupled with the evangelical spirit of the early Antinomians and Quakers, would inspire Baptists, Methodists, and similar sects to seek full religious freedom and disestablishment of the state-supported Congregational church.

As early Maine towns stabilized in political, economic, and religious matters, they exhibited another characteristic of social maturation: institutionalized class differences. Class stratification reflected divergent levels of economic success, transmitted across generations by family or financial connections. In Falmouth, as in other Maine towns, class divisions were evident in landownership patterns as early as the 1660s and 1670s. Groups of substantial land holders were tied directly to Falmouth's early proprietors. The Jane Macworth–James Andrews clan, for instance, retained a large original grant on the northeast side of the Presumpscot River. Marrying into the clan, Francis Neale and George Felt contributed a two-thirds share in a giant Indian grant on the upper Presumpscot. The George Cleeve, Michael Mitton, and Robert Jordan clans similarly acquired large tracts. Poorer citizens seemed to show little such accumulation. Generally farmers and artisans, these middle-class residents lived out their lives on their original holdings. At the bottom of the social scale were a number of landless inhabitants. Some were young men in their twenties waiting for an inheritance, but most were involved in unremunerative occupations working as laborers or fishermen. They and their families rarely experienced much prosperity and often lived in truly destitute circumstances.

Wealthier inhabitants typically married within their own class, further consolidating social stratifications. The marriage of James Andrews and Dorcus Mitton, for instance, tied these two proprietorial clans together, enhancing the dominant stature of both. Some proprietorial matches spanned communities. Elizabeth Andrews of Falmouth married Thomas Purchase, a wealthy trader and political figure from the Androscoggin region. Conversely, the marriage patterns of small farmers and fisherfolk took place within their own occupational groupings, and, significantly, these marriages seldom augmented familty wealth and status. Usually the young man acquired a small plot of land, at times a small section from his father's farm or perhaps a modest plot from the town. The woman usually brought little more than her basic dowry. Such was the case of Benjamin Atwell and Thomas Cloyce, who married Alice and Susanna Lewis respectively. Even less promising economically was the union of Anne Lewis and James Ross of Boston. He brought no land to the marriage, and the couple was forced to live on property belonging to her family.

Like landownership patterns, the allocation of political offices reflected Maine's growing class stratification. George Cleeve and Francis Neale, deputies to the Massachusetts General Court, were both from the proprietorial group, as were community representatives for Lygonia, the king's commission, and York County. Selectmen's posts were overwhelmingly held by members of the same elite.

Local justice also reflected class biases, especially among the more common types of personal misbehavior, such as swearing, drinking, quarreling, assault, slander, and disturbing the peace. Those accused usually were fisherfolk or middling farmers—those of the "lesser sort" in terms of real property ownership, political achievement, and connections. Typical were the presentments of Thomas Greenslade and Thomas Standford for swearing and of George Lewis "for being In drink several Tymes." A bit more exciting was the presentment of Lawrence Davis "for rayleing at the Constable and for swearing and saiing the Constable was a lyar." Such transgressions brought fines ranging from six to ten shillings plus fees.

Two court cases clearly illustrate the biases of both sex and class inherent in the society. In 1675, the pregnant servant Mary Moore of Scarborough accused large land holder Robert Jordan of "committ[ing] folly and fornication with her." Persuaded of Jordan's guilt, the court ordered him to provide an allowance of two shillings a week for the child. However, Moore was also adjudged guilty of fornication and was either to pay five pounds in cash or its equivalent, or receive "15 lashes on the bare skine at the poast." The woman's father paid the fine, but it is clear that it was safer for one's "bare skine" to be well-to-do, or at least have ready access to money to pay for transgressions.

In a second case, George Rogers and Mary Batchelder of Kittery, after several warnings, were convicted of adultery. He was whipped and she was to have been after the birth of their child. However, she was also to have been branded with the letter "A," a painful stigma not inflicted on Rogers.

By every measure, from the establishment of militias to the stratification of the classes, colonial Maine was coming of age. In the 1670s, millwrights, artisans, and merchants arrived in the local communities, adding substance and diversity to the economy. Roads and bridges linked towns, facilitating local intercourse. Town governments matured, bringing stability to the frontier establishments, and the evolution of local elites signaled a society well beyond the rudimentary settlements of the 1640s. Unfortunately, these promising English communities were soon engulfed in savage warfare with Maine's native people, bringing ruin to both. Conflict, already evident in Maine from the age of exploration through the period of early settlement, would become the dominant theme in the late seventeenth and early eighteenth centuries.

For Further Reading:

The best general overview is Robert E. Moody, "The Maine Frontier" (Ph.D. dissertation, Yale University, 1933). Charles E. Clark, *The Eastern Frontier: The Settlement of Northern New England, 1610–1763* (New York, 1970) is more available and well worth reading, although the interpretation is somewhat dated. Two revisionary essays on early Maine are Edwin A. Churchill, "The Founding of Maine, 1600–1640: A Revisionist Interpretation," in Maine Historical Society *Quarterly* 18:1 (Summer 1978), 21–54, and Churchill, "World on the Edge: Life in Mid-Seventeenth Century Maine," a chapter in *The Land of Norumbega* (forthcoming, 1994).

Of several extant narratives and political-military works, three of the best are Henry S. Burrage, *The Beginning of Colonial Maine, 1602–1658* (Portland, 1914); John S. Reid, *Maine, Charles II and Massachusetts: Governmental Relations in Early Northern New England* (Portland, 1977); and Reid, *Acadia, Maine and New Scotland: Marginal Colonies in the Seventeenth Century* (Toronto, 1981).

A number of local studies go beyond simple narrative and provide substantial glimpses into lifeways in early Maine towns. Among the more useful are Charles E. Banks, *History of York, Maine*, 2 vols. (Boston 1931–35), esp. vol. 1, chaps. 2–23; Edwin A. Churchill, "Too Great the Challenge: The Birth and Death of Falmouth, Maine, 1624–1676" (Ph.D. dissertation, University of Maine, Orono, 1979); Emerson Woods Baker, II, "Trouble to the Eastward: The Failure of Anglo-Indian Relations in Early Maine" (Ph.D. dissertation, College of William and Mary, 1986); Baker, *The Clark and Lake Company: The Historical Archaeology of a Seventeenth Century Maine Settlement* (Augusta, 1985); William Avery Baker, *A Maritime History of Bath, Maine and the Kennebec River Region*, 2 vols. (Bath, 1973), vol. 1, chaps. 1–5; and Churchill, "Introduction: Colonial Pemaquid," in *Archaeological Excavations at Pemaquid, Maine* (Augusta, 1975), pp. ix–xix.

Although much scholarly work remains to be done with regard to specific topics, a number of specialized studies have explored various aspects of early Maine. Laurel T. Ulrich, *Good Wives: Images and Reality in the Lives of Women in Northern New England, 1650–1750* (New York and Toronto, 1980) illuminates the previously nearly invisible female world. Three studies examine the major male-oriented activities of fishing, lumbering, and agriculture. Edwin A. Churchill, "A Most Ordinary Lot of Men: The Fisherman at Richmond Island, Maine, in the Early Seventeenth Century," *The New England Quarterly* 57:2 (June 1984) finds a poor fit between the unexceptional characters of these men and the popular image of them as drunken, carousing rowdies. Richard M. Candee, "Merchant and Millwright," *Old-Time New England* 60:4 (July 1969–April 1970), 131–49, traces the development of the sawmill and lumber trade in early New Hampshire and southern Maine. Finally, a basic overview of seventeenth-century Maine agriculture is provided by Clarence Day, *A History of Maine Agriculture, 1604–1860* (Orono, 1954), in chapters 1 and 2.

Biographical material can be found in a number of sources. *The Dictionary of American Biography*, 22 vols. (New York, 1928–39) and *The Dictionary of Canadian Biography, Vol. I. (1000–1700)* (Toronto, 1966) have information on several of the region's more important inhabitants. Sybil Noyes, Charles T. Libby, and Walter G. Davis, *Genealogical Dictionary of Maine and New Hampshire* (Baltimore: Genealogical Publishing Company, 1972; first published in five parts, 1928–39) includes family histories and biographical data on hundreds of seventeenth-century inhabitants of Maine and New Hampshire. Supplementing these is the premier biography of *Gorges of Plymouth Fort* by Richard Preston (Toronto, 1953), which details the life of Maine's most important promoter and ties him to the story of the region.

Among the substantial body of primary materials, several are especially useful. James P. Baxter, ed., *Sir Ferdinando Gorges and His Province of Maine*, 3 vols. (Boston, 1890) contains most of the pertinent documents relating to Gorges's colonizing efforts. The correspondence of his nephew Thomas Gorges is transcribed in *The Letters of Thomas Gorges: Deputy Governor of the Province of Maine, 1640–1643*, ed. by Robert E. Moody (Portland, 1977). Charles T. Libby, Robert E. Moody, and Neal W. Allen record the activities of Thomas Gorges's and later courts in *Province and Court Records of Maine, 1636–1727*, 6 vols. (Portland, 1928–75). *The Trelawny Papers*, ed. by James P. Baxter, vol. 3 of the *Documentary History of the State of Maine* (Portland, 1884) provides the only extant records of a fishing station on the early American coast, the operation of Robert Trelawny located on Richmond Island, just south of Falmouth (present-day Portland). Samuel Maverick in "A Brief Description of New England and the Severall Townes Therein, Together With the Present Government Theseof," Massachusetts Historical Society *Proceedings*, 2d. ser., I (1884–85), pp. 231–33, briefly describes the settlements of the mid-seventeenth-century Maine coast. In his "An Account of the Voyages to New England," Massachusetts Historical Society *Collections*, 3rd ser., III (1833), John Josselyn writes vividly although not all that kindly of Maine's early inhabitants.

4

Acadian Settlement,
1607–1700

ALARIC FAULKNER & GRETCHEN FEARON FAULKNER

Archaeological evidence, as Bruce Bourque has demonstrated, opens a different window into the past. Combining documentary sources with physical artifacts yields an even richer collection of data, again with a perspective different from that of the historian. While Edwin Churchill's study of seventeenth-century English Maine focused on social and political events, this study of French settlement extrapolates, from artifacts and documents, information about colonizing strategies, daily life, and even the mentality of the colonizers.

Despite differences in approach, these authors identify themes similar to those that animated British colonial Maine. Most evident is the fact that Acadia was shaped by events and forces beyond its control—prevailing European cultural styles or maneuverings in the diplomatic courts of Europe, for instance. Still, local adaptation to these influences demonstrates again the creative agency of those who settled on the Maine coast. Second, we observe again the effects of conflict—internal struggles for control of the land, tension between the French and English, and encounters with Dutch naval expeditions. All this meant that the French colonies in Maine were, like the English settlements, vulnerable, fragile, and marginal to a larger locus of colonial activity—in this case, the French cities in the St. Lawrence region.

It is easy to convey the importance of Maine's English heritage in a book written for English speakers, some of whom can trace their ancestry back to the colonizers of the seventeenth century. In today's popular culture "down-east Maine" has become a sort of Yankee genesis, a fountainhead from which come all the virtues of New England wit, ingenuity, and frugality. That the early histories of Maine are often so patently British, however, is largely an accident. But for a few crucial shifts in political control, caused principally by decisions made in Europe, the history we commemorate would have been quite different.

Through much of the colonial period the role of French inhabitants, like that of native Americans, was fully as significant as the English accomplishments discussed to this point.

Indeed, it is fair to say that for most of the colonial period, eastern Maine was not part of New England at all, but rather a western extension of the French colony of Acadia, a fact recognized by the English as well as the French at the time. For example, in 1673 a French official described the capital of his colony as "at the head of all of Acadia near Boston." He was referring to the French post at Pentagoet, located at the mouth of the Penobscot River, midway along the coast of Maine. Few New Englanders would have considered this reference to Boston an exaggeration; the Acadian capital was barely more than a day's sail away.

As in English colonial Maine, Acadia was dominated by events beyond its control. In the great wars between the European powers in the seventeenth century, peripheral colonies, including Acadian Maine, were often used as bargaining chips. Political control switched back and forth between the English, the French, and even the Dutch during this period. But even though the area was periodically wrested from them by the English, the French remained the predominant European inhabitants of the northeastern half of Maine. English-speaking settlers did not actually begin to displace the French from the Penobscot basin until after 1759. Again like the English settlers to the southwest, the French colonists preserved some autonomy and local continuity in the face of larger controlling events. Daily life in Pentagoet, for instance, demonstrates creative adaptation to the harsh realities of the local environment, to geographic isolation, and to the larger world beyond control of the tiny French outposts.

Such similarities should not obscure fundamental differences between the French and English colonies, however. French merchant-backers had originally slated the coast of Maine for agricultural settlements like those developing in the English-occupied territory to the southwest. The ill-fated St. Croix Island colony established in 1604 and the more permanent habitation at Port Royal a year later were prototypes for such communities, and indeed French settlements in the St. Lawrence valley and the Acadian regions of present-day Nova Scotia were agricultural. But farming would not become became the principal attraction of Acadian Maine. For the French, central and eastern Maine remained a fishing, lumbering, and, most importantly, fur-trading frontier.

Religious motives, such as those that attracted the Pilgrims to Plymouth, were much less in evidence in Acadian Maine. There were several early attempts to establish Catholic missions—among them, Father Biard's brief attempt at Mount Desert Island in 1613 (see page 47). These missions had an important influence on the Wabanaki Indians and encouraged the regular contact between Indians and Europeans that was essential to subsequent colonial activity. But

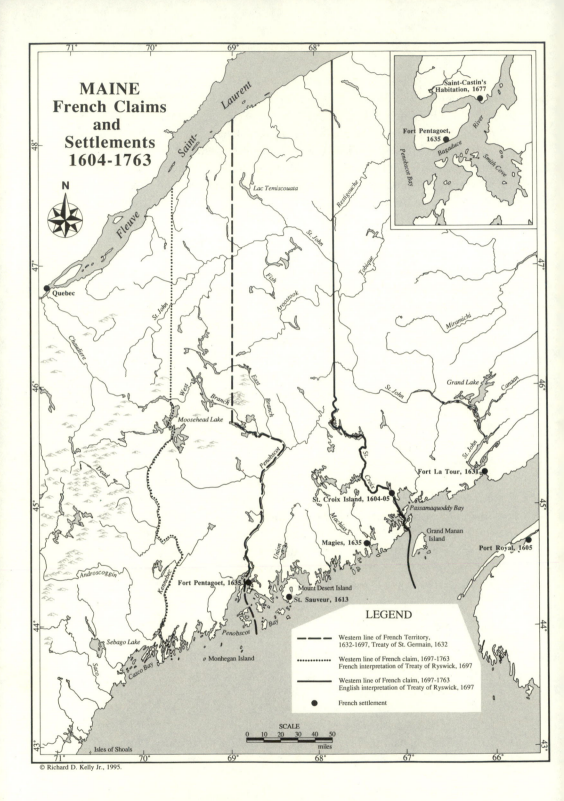

MAINE
French Claims
and
Settlements
1604-1763

N

Fleuve Saint-Laurent

Quebec

Chaudière

St. John

Lac Temiscouata

Restigouche

St. John

Fish

Tobique

Aroostook

Miramichi

West Branch

East Branch

Moosehead Lake

Penobscot

Dead

St. Croix

Grand Lake

Canaan

St. John

St. John

Fort La Tour, 1631

St. Croix Island, 1604-05

Passamaquoddy Bay

Machias

Magies, 1635

Grand Manan Island

Port Royal, 1605

Union

Androscoggin

Kennebec

Fort Pentagoet, 1635

Mount Desert Island

St. Sauveur, 1613

Sebago Lake

Penobscot Bay

Saco

Monhegan Island

Casco Bay

Isles of Shoals

Inset map (top right)
Saint-Castin's Habitation, 1677

Fort Pentagoet, 1635

Penobscot Bay

Bagaduce River

Smith Cove

LEGEND

— — — Western line of French Territory, 1632-1697, Treaty of St. Germain, 1632

········· Western line of French claim, 1697-1763 French interpretation of Treaty of Ryswick, 1697

—————— Western line of French claim, 1697-1763 English interpretation of Treaty of Ryswick, 1697

● French settlement

SCALE
0 10 20 30 40 50
miles

because of the seasonal movements of the Indians and their low population density, missions in the region were of comparatively brief duration and never gained large followings. Profits were the main impulse behind French settlement in Maine.

The French colony was different in other ways. Settlement patterns and colonial strategies, as we shall see, were markedly different, and unlike the merchants and nobility that controlled English settlement, French proprietors actually resettled in the New World, directing events from close at hand and building establishments that reflected their intention to remain in the area. Still, like the English, the French colonists bent to the powerful influence of outside factors and fell prey to incessant conflict, both internal and external. While the English settlements weathered these difficult obstacles and achieved some permanence by the end of the seventeenth century, the French outposts succumbed, although their influence among the Indians remained in evidence throughout the colonial period in Maine.

The French employed three major settlement strategies during their occupation of the region. The first, between 1635 and 1654, was initiated by civilian entrepreneurs like Charles d'Aulnay, who built Fort Pentagoet, the first European fortification in the region. During the second French occupation from 1670 to 1674, the area was placed under royal control and sponsorship, and Pentagoet, located at present-day Castine, became the seat of a military governorship. Under commanders Grandfontaine and Chambly, Fort Pentagoet became the capital of Acadia. After the fort was destroyed in 1674, a third and entirely new strategy was adopted by a former officer at Pentagoet, Jean Vincent de St.-Castin. Rather than install himself within the walls of a fortified European-style compound, St.-Castin placed his trading business at the center of an Indian village and married the daughter of its principal sachem. Even though the economic objectives of these three settlement strategies were similar, the differences were profound and, as will become apparent, each had a different effect on French relations with neighboring English and Indian inhabitants.

Control of the Penobscot

Although French traders ranged along the coast as far west as the St. George River, they focused their interest on the principal drainage of mid-coastal Maine, called Penobscot by the English and Pentagoet by the French. A less practical objective, nevertheless pursued in earnest through the 1670s, was the search for an alternate route to Quebec, a city virtually shut off from the outside world for the nearly six months each year when the St. Lawrence River was frozen.

The French influence in the Penobscot region apparently stretches back to a period for which there are few good records, either documentary or archaeological. Henry Hudson, in his 1609 exploration of Penobscot Bay, observed that the native peoples of the region were quite familiar with Europeans, particularly French traders. Not only was Hudson greeted by an Indian "who knew French words," but he encountered a number of "country people" sailing in French shallops and possessing European trade goods, who were either French traders or Indian intermediaries such as the Micmacs. Indeed, there is good evidence that French pioneer Claude de la Tour operated a trading post on the Penobscot as early as 1610–13. However, the earliest establishment confirmed by archaeological evidence is not French at all, but rather a trading house operated for the colonists of Plymouth, Massachusetts.

Like the French, the Pilgrims recognized the commercial potential of Maine, and to supplement their fledgling Plymouth colony they built trading posts on the Kennebec, Penobscot, and Machias rivers—the latter two in territory contested by the French. Of these, the Penobscot post is particularly important; it was built on the site of the later French fort. The Pilgrims hired Edward Ashley to manage the Penobscot post, then quickly fired the agent for selling or lending firearms to the Indians. But by refusing to trade muskets, powder, and shot, the Pilgrims made the post far less attractive to the Indians. More experienced traders recognized these as essential trade goods, since the Indians had become dependent upon such weapons for survival. After Ashley, the business muddled along until the post was taken over by the French.

French Civilian Entrepreneurs, 1635–54

Legal title to Acadia, including the Penobscot where the Pilgrim enterprise stood, passed to the French with the treaty of St.-Germain-en-Laye in 1632. Three years later, Charles d'Aulnay took possession of the Penobscot post. D'Aulnay's confrontation with the Pilgrims is a good example of the measured restraint often used at this time on the colonial frontiers. As Governor Bradford of Massachusetts tells the story (in *Of Plymouth Plantation*, p. 275), there was no fight, and indeed it was clear from d'Aulnay's manner that he intended to minimize provocation to the New Englanders:

> Partly by threatening and other wise, [he] made, Mr. Willet, their agent there, to approve of the sale of the goods there unto him, of which he set the price himself in effect, and made an inventory thereof, yet leaving out sundry things. But made no payment for them, but told them in convenient time he would do it if they came for it. For the house and fortification etc.

4-1. Charles de Menou d'Aulnay, Sieur de Charnisay (ca. 1604–50), took over the Plymouth Colony post at Penobscot (now Castine) and there constructed Fort Penta-goet as the southern line of French Acadia in 1635. He carried on a long feud with Charles Saint-Étienne de la Tour, who eventually took control of Acadia. Courtesy of the New Brunswick Museum/Le Musée du Nouveau-Brunswick, St. John, New Brunswick, Canada.

he would not allow nor account anything, saying that they which build on another man's ground do forfeit the same. So thus turning them out of all, with a great deal of compliment and many fine words, he let them have their shallop and some victuals to bring them home.

Small, isolated outposts like Penobscot were always vulnerable, and cooperation and appeasement were not mere expedients but essential aspects of survival. This was especially important to the French, who were greatly outnumbered by their neighbors to the south.

The Plymouth colonists, however, refused to abandon their trading post without a fight. In September 1635, Miles Standish led an expedition eastward to recapture the post. Standish found the French already well defended behind newly built earthworks. Following a brief and ineffective bombardment, the English expedition returned to Plymouth empty-handed. In his journal, Governor Bradford duly noted his fears: that the French would fortify themselves even more strongly. He worried they were "likely to become ill neighbors to the English."

The expulsion of the English and subsequent influx of new French colonists into Acadia marked the beginning of a period of exceptional turmoil. Soon after the French took the Penobscot, Lieutenant-General Isaac de Razilly, the principal colonizer of Acadia, died, leaving a number of rival entrepreneurs struggling for control of the colony. Among these French traders, competition gave way to warfare on the Acadian frontier. In this struggle the government of Massachusetts alternately sided with one faction or mediated between them, trying to prevent all-out war between New England and Acadia; the resulting diplomatic confusion brought down the Massachusetts government of John Winthrop and created animosities towards the Acadians that grew steadily over the following century.

The particulars of the ensuing conflict, a plot worthy of the most intricate soap opera or Dickens novel, are best recounted by historian M. A. MacDonald, in her *Fortune and La Tour*, and can only be summarized here. The principal contenders for western Acadia were Charles d'Aulnay, who solicited the backing of the French crown, and Charles de la Tour, who was more successful with the Massachusetts Bay Colony. D'Aulnay claimed the first victory when he destroyed La Tour's post on the St. John River, an assault that resulted in the death of La Tour's wife. La Tour's fortunes reversed, however, when d'Aulnay suddenly died in a canoeing accident in 1650, leaving his widow with a heavy burden of debts. In order to consolidate power, La Tour pressured Madame d'Aulnay into marrying him. La Tour became heir to his rival's debts but also managed to consolidate most of Acadia.

La Tour's victory left him in charge of Fort Pentagoet, built on the site of the Plymouth post shortly after the French takeover. The closest fortified French outpost to Boston, Pentagoet epitomized the differences between French settlement strategies and the nuclear communities of Massachusetts or the ribbon-like settlements of English Maine. It was a difference that Governor

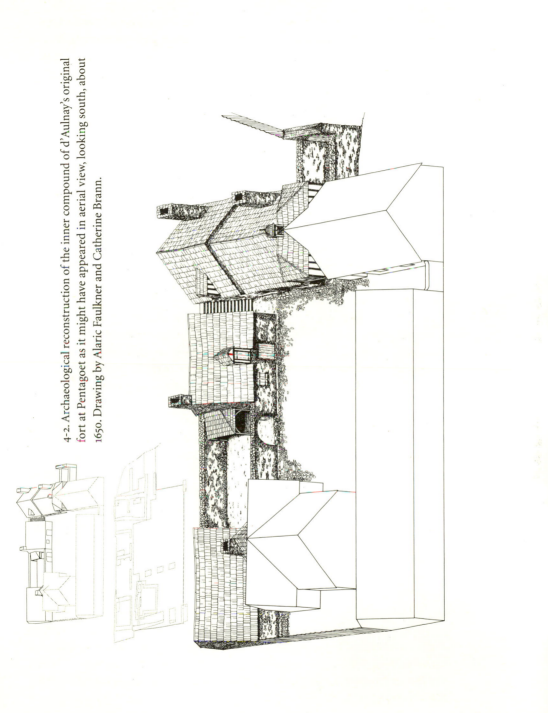

4-2. Archaeological reconstruction of the inner compound of d'Aulnay's original fort at Pentagoet as it might have appeared in aerial view, looking south, about 1650. Drawing by Alaric Faulkner and Catherine Brann.

Bradford understood all too well. The French, he complained, lie "closed up in their forts, well fortified, and live upon trade in good security," while the English "lye open and unfortified, living upon husbandrie."

Bradford was referring to the small, fortified seventeenth-century settlements established by entrepreneurs like d'Aulnay, La Tour, and others engaged in fishing, lumbering, or fur trading along Acadia's waterways. Of these, Fort Pentagoet is a particularly good example, as it is known both through documents and archaeological excavation. Built almost entirely of well-laid stone and protected by massive earthworks, it was a formidable construction with four bastions and a waterfront battery. Its inner compound of five major buildings measured no more than eighty feet square, but contained the minimal ingredients for the maintenance of a small garrison: a workshop and forge, a guard house, a magazine or warehouse for storing trade goods, officers' quarters, a barracks, and a small wooden chapel over the entrance. This diminutive but well-armed outpost allowed eighteen to twenty-five French soldier-employees to control trade throughout the Penobscot basin and along the coast from the St. George River to Mount Desert.

Pentagoet was a small, compact, and efficient establishment, harboring an enclave of Europeans in an architectural setting reminiscent of rural France. In one sense it had much in common with vernacular French farmsteads. But unlike its French counterparts, the fort was designed to exclude the outside world; mediation with visitors took place at its gates, not within its walls. Although primitive in comparison to French New World military architecture of the latter part of the century, this was the first stone fortification in the region and was more sophisticated in design than any of its New England contemporaries.

The permanence of Pentagoet's well-coursed slate masonry expresses a fundamental difference between the intentions of French entrepreneurs like d'Aulnay and many of his English counterparts. Most first-generation adventurers in Virginia, for example, intended to get rich quick on the fabled resources of the New World and then return home to England to enjoy their fortunes. Consequently, they often built relatively impermanent "earthfast" wooden structures whose framing was built of posts set directly into the ground. It was a construction technique chosen for convenience, and the resulting structures were destined to decay after only a few years. Similar post-in-ground architecture was chosen by the Plymouth traders at Cushnoc (Augusta). By contrast, the French, in choosing stone rather than wood as their construction material, expressed not merely a different building tradition but also their long-term commitment to occupation of the region. Their motives are not difficult to understand, considering the social background of the Acadian French leaders.

In searching for the motives that attracted French settlers to Acadia, it is tempting to draw parallels with the Pilgrim Separatists who fled the old country to practice their religion freely. Certainly French Protestants suffered political and religious persecution more than equal to England's Pilgrims, but there is little to document religious motives among Acadian migrants or even the presence of French Protestants among the settlers of Acadia. The principal lure of the region seems to have been economic opportunity rather than religious freedom.

During this first period of settlement, Acadia was controlled by a handful of adventurers. Men like de Razilly, d'Aulnay, de la Tour, and Nicolas Denys were mostly impecunious minor nobility who sought to augment their fortunes in a "respectable" commercial activity—an endeavor that would not compromise their social rank. Unlike English and Dutch leaders, many of whom were from urban merchant backgrounds, these Frenchmen came from rural settings that offered limited opportunities for financial improvement. They could not, for example, engage in most forms of manufacturing without forfeiting their birthrights. On the other hand, fur trading, lumbering, and managing fisheries were acceptable pursuits for these petty aristocrats. Consequently, they probably meant to stay permanently in the New World.

The leaders of these embryonic European colonies generally brought with them the symbols of their authority. Perhaps in the New World, even more than in Europe, it was important for French aristocrats to avoid "derogation," or acting beneath their station. The archaeological record from excavations at d'Aulnay's establishment in Maine and Charles de la Tour's fort at the mouth of the St. John River in New Brunswick shows the extreme measures that these French frontier nobles took to keep up appearances. Not only did they express their intentions in more permanent architecture, they also brought along many of the more portable amenities of life, suggestive of their efforts to dress and dine in a manner befitting their social status.

The elite of Acadia dressed in clothing which, although it may have been last year's fashion, was ornamented with gold braid and fastened with fancy hooks and buttons which were fully in keeping with their rank. They wore rapiers at their sides and spurs at their heels, dressing the part of true cavaliers and expressing their pretensions to knighthood. They put on this incongruous show even though there is little evidence that the swords saw regular use as weapons. In any case, there were no horses to ride in all of western Acadia, largely because there was no place to ride along the jagged coastline, and transportation by boat was far more practical. In fact, when Governor Winthrop of Massachusetts wanted to make amends to Charles d'Aulnay in 1646, after many years of siding with La Tour, he did so by presenting him not with a horse but rather with an expensive new sedan chair, whereby d'Aulnay was supposed to have been carried by his soldier-employees.

At the table these would-be aristocrats kept their food warm over gaily painted chafing dishes and served their guests brandy from miniature ceramic barrels, both made in the fashionable style of the renowned sixteenth-century French potter-artist Bernard Palissy. While they kept swine and sheep, they also ate a variety of wild foodstuffs, particularly fowl and fish. The birds were often prepared in deep pastry shells and served as casseroles or pies. On special occasions they feasted on bear, a meat praised as being "very delicate and white as that of veal." A common, albeit bizarre, presentation was stuffed bear's head, cut lengthwise and served in profile on a platter.

The pretensions of the leadership notwithstanding, frontier lifeways were hardly idyllic. The outposts of Acadia were at the end of a chronically unreliable line of supply. Shortages were also common in rural France during these years, and the situation in Acadia, although extreme, was probably very familiar to the colony's leaders. Judging from the refuse from Pentagoet's workshop/smithy, d'Aulnay came well prepared to cope with the shortages that characterized life on the Acadian frontier. This scrap tells an eloquent story of the means by which French colonists coped with isolation and a severe environment.

Many simple items were fabricated on site by the armorer from imported raw materials. Gunflints were made as required, as were cast-lead musket balls and shot. The forge supplied the various fittings and structural hardware needed by the fort—the strap hinges, nails, hooks, latch parts, and similar items. Tools were also manufactured or remanufactured as the situation demanded, particularly cutting implements such as saws, files, and axes. When an axe blade was broken, the eye was saved and welded to a new blade, and when an axe eye was damaged the blade was salvaged to be reused.

Most important was the maintenance of firearms, not just for protection, hunting, and sport, but especially for the conduct of the fur trade. To a large degree, it was the supply of powder and shot and the services of the gunsmith that brought Indians to Pentagoet. Pieces discarded in various stages of manufacture or repair indicate that gun mechanisms of diverse origins and forms were repaired, and parts for them were manufactured from scratch as needed.

Very little was discarded before the colony had extracted every last bit of usefulness. Scrap copper and brass sheets salvaged from worn-out kettles were reworked to make candle holders, hinges for small boxes, awls, and even rivets and patches for repairing other kettles. Kettle scrap was used in arms repair and as a brazing material. Like their Indian trading partners, the French employed sheet copper for ornamentation, making lace tips and "tinkling cones" to adorn the fringes of clothing. In fact, the artisans at Pentagoet were only carrying out in the extreme the recycling practices then common in Europe.

An English Interlude, 1654–70

A few years after d'Aulnay's death, Acadia fell into the hands of the English by a strange misfortune. The English and the Dutch were at war, and in the New World this pitted New England against New Netherland. Major Robert Sedgwick of Charlestown, in Massachusetts, was commissioned to lead an expedition from England against New Amsterdam (later to become New York). But by the time his expedition reached Boston, peace had been concluded between the two warring parties. Rather than return to England having accomplished nothing, Sedgwick "thought [it best] . . . to spend a lyttle time rangeing the coast against the French." Sedgwick's four ships arrived at La Tour's establishment on the St. John River on July 14, 1654. The fort, which was defended by seventy men and seventeen pieces of ordnance, surrendered within three days. The larger fort at Port Royal, with its garrison of 135 fighting men and twenty pieces of ordnance, fell just a week later. Pentagoet was the last to fall because, as Sedgwick noted, it was "a small Fort, yet very strong and a very well composed peece with eight peece of Ordnance one brass, three murtherers, about eighteen Barrels of powder, and eighteen men in garrison." With the fall of Pentagoet, the conquest of Acadia was complete. New Englanders rejoiced by proclaiming September 20, 1654, a day of thanksgiving.

The English allowed the agrarian families at Port Royal to stay, but they executed the superior of the Catholic Capuchin mission of friars and sent away the remaining Capuchins, soldiers, and sailors. They also sent back to France most of the individuals on the Penobscot and St. John and at St. Pierre Island, the chief Acadian fishery. For the next sixteen years England exercised political control over Acadia, now "Nova Scotia." Initially the area was patented to three men: Sir Thomas Temple, William Crowne, and the ever-resourceful Frenchman, Charles de la Tour. This tripartite division of Acadia dissolved, and eventually Sir Thomas Temple acquired exclusive rights to exploit Acadia. Unlike his French counterparts, Temple preferred to remain in Boston while his agents managed his assets for him. The fur trade continued, but under the direction of agent Thomas Breedon and various Boston merchants, who apparently cheated Temple unmercifully. While the merchants prospered, Temple lapsed further into debt. For most of Acadia, this was a period of neglect and mismanagement. Fort Pentagoet, or "Penobscot," was assigned various commanders, who lived in nearby Pemaquid, but there is no evidence, archaeological or documentary, to indicate that it supported a permanent garrison. By the end of the British occupation, according to the incoming French commander, Hector Andigné de Grandfontaine, there were but 389 French in all of Acadia.

Military Control, 1670–74

In the summer of 1667 the Treaty of Breda, concluded between Charles II of England and Louis XIV of France, restored Acadia to the French, and three years later Sir Thomas Temple's property was transferred. Acadia, briefly in the hands of private entrepreneurs, became a royal colony under a military governorship. The new governor and many officers and men were former members of France's first standing army unit, the Carignan-Salières regiment, raised in 1659 to fight the Turks and sent to New France in 1665 to subdue the Mohawks.

Hector Andigné de Grandfontaine, the new governor, was a noble like his predecessors, but his objectives were ostensibly military in nature and were dictated by his commission. Accordingly he placed his headquarters at Pentagoet, performed necessary repairs and minor renovations, and installed a permanent garrison. The new capital of Acadia, Pentagoet was strategically located for military purposes. Commanding Penobscot Bay, it protected the colony from encroachment by New Englanders and reestablished firm control of the Penobscot or "Pentagoet" River. The Penobscot, French military leaders thought, could provide a winter supply route for the St. Lawrence settlements. As a link, Pentagoet would facilitate control of all of the resources north and east of the river—not just fisheries, fur trade, and timber, but also the coal and other Acadian mineral resources New Englanders envied. Following his king's orders, Grandfontaine prepared a detailed if somewhat distorted chart of the route to Quebec via the Penobscot. As it turned out, the route proved to be neither easy nor direct.

Grandfontaine prepared for an expected wave of new immigration. But the return of Acadia to France had come a few years too late; the principal royal investments had been committed already to settlements farther north in New France. Similar attention to Acadia was not forthcoming, and the colony remained secondary in development to the settlements around the St. Lawrence. Consequently, Grandfontaine turned south, cultivating warm relations with merchants among France's traditional antagonists in Boston and Pemaquid, who supplemented the irregular supplies Grandfontaine received from France. There Grandfontaine also met with certain French merchants who dealt openly with these same New Englanders.

The artifacts recovered from this occupation at Fort Pentagoet help to characterize the daily lives of the soldiers, their resourcefulness, and their sources of supply. The population within the compound, with the brief exception of one

4-3. The 1983 University of Maine excavation of Fort Pentagoet, Castine, Maine, conducted by Gretchen and Alaric Faulkner. This view, looking east, shows the foundation of the fort's barracks/workshop, with the Maine Maritime Academy's training vessel, *State of Maine*, in the background. Photograph by Alaric Faulkner.

officer's wife, was entirely male. Although the workshop from this period has not been excavated, it is clear that recycling of scarce materials continued much as before. A pewter cap for a cartridge, such as musketeers wore suspended from their bandoliers, was recycled to make a thimble by cutting off the little eyes or loops by which it was suspended. Found stuffed with a woven button to form a sewing kit, it epitomizes the pragmatic all-male world of the frontier soldier. Similarly, when the bone grip of a knife handle was worn out, a soldier apparently replaced it with a new one carefully carved from a piece of Pentagoet's building slate.

A few pastimes are also represented. Gambling was an everyday part of the soldiers' lives, and they made the necessary checker-like gaming pieces by re-shaping some fragments of gaily painted majolica dishes scavenged from the trash dumps of the d'Aulnay period. During d'Aulnay's administration, smoking as a form of leisure had been confined to the fort's elite, who used ornate, long-stemmed pipes imported from Holland. By the 1670s, the practice had become universal. Fragments of short-stemmed work-a-day models, that were easily held in one's teeth and left the hands free for work, were recovered throughout the fort, particularly in work areas. While a few of the clay tobacco pipes seem to have come from New England, most of the pipes, pottery, glassware, and other common items reflect French sources of supply if not manufacture. Whatever dependence the garrison had on its New England neighbors was probably for perishable supplies, particularly foodstuffs.

The soldiers' diet still included large quantities of fowl and fish, but exhib-ited an increased dependence on domesticated mammals. The bones found in kitchen middens indicate that these new frontier Frenchmen had entirely aban-doned wild mammals in their diet, eating only beef, pork, and mutton, as was the trend throughout the more established French and English colonies. Al-though they kept their own livestock in a small shed west of the fort, they also apparently depended on barreled meats, which may have come from New Eng-land; even the French merchants who frequented the coasts of Acadia would procure such provisions from Boston rather than bring them from France. Still, famine struck the outpost during the winter of 1671–72, which may account for the presence of hawk and domestic cat bones and evidence of other "starvation foods" in the kitchen middens.

Despite his military appointment, Grandfontaine soon lapsed into the pat-tern of private entrepreneurship that characterized the previous period of French occupation. Like d'Aulnay before him, he became increasingly involved in the fur trade. It was for this reason and for his fraternization with the New Englanders that he was replaced at the end of his commission in 1673 by a new governor, Jacques de Chambly, a by-the-numbers officer with some experience as a military architect. Chambly planned to redesign defenses to forge stronger, more reliable economic ties with Quebec. His efforts, however, were cut short.

As was the situation two decades earlier, the demise of Pentagoet was the un-fortunate byproduct of a European power struggle, in this case involving a secret alliance between the French and English against the Dutch. War was offi-cially declared in 1672, and the following year the conflict spread to the colonies overseas. In 1674, Captain Jurrien Aernouts, commander of the Dutch corsair *Flying Horse* of Curaçao, received a commission to sail against the English who held New York, the former Dutch colony. Upon arrival in New York, he was informed that peace had been concluded between the English and the Dutch, but that no treaty had been made with the French. While refitting in New York, Aernouts became acquainted with John Rhoades, a coastal trader from Boston, who encouraged him to sail against the minimally defended French colony of Acadia.

On the first of August the *Flying Horse*, carrying a crew of fifty men and eight cannon and piloted by Rhoades, besieged "the Enemy's principal garrison" at Fort Pentagoet. During the brief skirmish which ensued, Chambly was severely wounded. Without their commander, the company of twenty-three poorly armed soldiers and settlers surrendered and agreed to swear allegiance to the Netherlands. Aernouts, realizing that he did not have "sofitient strenth to Leave to Garrison the place," took everything of value and proceeded to demolish the settlement. The buildings within the compound and some outside were burned, and then Pentagoet's guns were turned on its own stone walls. The tiny fort, which never housed more than about twenty-five men in garrison, was "levell'd wth ye ground."

Following the destruction of Pentagoet, Aernouts sacked the French posts to the northeast, at Machias, St. John, and, farther up the St. John River, at Jemseg, carrying away "the plundor and principle persons prisonors" to Boston. Once again Acadia had been ravaged by a naval force assembled too late to achieve its original mission and left with nothing better to do.

Aernouts's party claimed the Acadian coast from the St. John River to the Penobscot, renaming it New Holland. Upon hearing of the conquest, New Englanders again rejoiced. But for the next year, Acadia became a haven for a cadre of ten Dutch and English pirates—the participants in Aernouts's expedition. Claiming falsely that they were acting on the authority of the Prince of Orange, these buccaneers preyed on all shipping along the coast, taking prisoners and demanding ransom until they were captured by the English and brought to trial in Boston. Oblivious to the now desperate plight of the few remaining French habitants, the English at Pemaquid sailed to Pentagoet, scavenged the rubble for ironwork and planking, and abandoned the site.

The Beginning of the Indian Wars, 1675–78

Although the Dutch had no lasting influence in the area, their assault on western Acadia in 1674 had important consequences. The French had shown a measured commitment to the Indians as trading partners and allies, not simply as servants or adversaries. This was a critical relationship the English stubbornly refused to foster. More important, French gunsmiths had taken extreme measures to accommodate their clientele, remanufacturing gunlocks and even patching cracked gun barrels. The loss of Fort Pentagoet disrupted Indian supply sources, particularly in firearms, powder, and shot.

In 1675, King Philip's War broke out in southern New England. Its spread to Maine was in some sense the result of this disruption in arms trade to the eastern Indians. Thomas Gardiner, a prominent citizen of Pemaquid who had been in command of the Penobscot Fort during the period of British control, understood the situation clearly. In 1675, he wrote to Governor Leverett of Massachusetts:

> Sir I Conceive the Reason of your Troubles here may be occasioned not only by som southern Indianes which may come this way But by our owne Acctings . . . These Indians Amongst us live most by Hunting as your Honour well Knoweth [I do not see] how we Can Take Away their Armes whose livlyhood dependeth on it . . . And seeing these Indianes in these parts did never Appear dissatisfied Vntill their arms were Taken Away I doubt of any such Acctions whether they may be forced to go to the French for Releife or fight Against vs. [*Documentary History of the State of Maine*, vol. 6, p. 21]

Indeed, the Indians had little other recourse, since the English refused to provide the services the French had offered earlier. As one Indian leader, Diogenes Madoasquarbet, explained eloquently in a conciliatory letter to the "Governor of Boston":

> This is to let you understand how we have been abused. We love you but when we are drunk you will take away our coat and throw us outdoors. If the wolves kill any of your cattle, you take away our guns for it and arrows. . . . Because there was a war at Narragansett you came here when we were at peace and took away our guns and made prisoners of our chief sagamores, and that winter for want of our guns there was several starved. . . . Now we hear that you say that you will not leave us in peace as long as one Indian is left in the country. We are owners of this land and it is wide and full of Indians and we can drive you out, but it is our desire to be quiet. [*Documentary History of the State of Maine*, vol. 6, pp. 178–79]

Unfortunately these intolerable conditions persisted, with predictable results. In the summer of 1676 the Wabanaki systematically destroyed all but the southernmost English settlements in Maine. In essence, King Philip's War did not spread to Maine; a "Wabanaki War" was created in Maine independently, the result of the elimination of Pentagoet and the irrational English policy of disarming friendly Indians. This uprising was just the beginning of a series of wars between Wabanaki and English Maine lasting for over half a century.

St.-Castin's Habitation, ca. 1677–ca. 1700

While the Indians were driving back the English frontier in southern Maine, the French reoccupied the eastern sections, forging even stronger ties with the eastern Wabanaki, whom they called Etchemins. At Penobscot Bay, an entirely new method of settlement was adopted by Jean Vincent de St.-Castin, a former officer who served at the fort as a young man in 1670. St.-Castin reestablished French control over southwestern Acadia in about 1677. Abandoning the Pentagoet layout, a European design that separated French residents from the natives, he established his headquarters at the center of an Etchemin village about a mile and a half up the Bagaduce River from the ruins of the old fort. This new settlement consisted of two simple European structures: a dwelling and a storehouse of temporary construction. St.-Castin built no defensive works at all. Surrounding this nucleus, according to a general census of Acadia taken in 1687–88, was a group of thirty-two seasonally occupied wigwams housing 160 Etchemins.

Although St.-Castin received a commission to befriend the Indians in this fashion, most of the French considered his behavior to be scandalous and unbefitting his station in life as the heir to the title "Baron de St.-Castin." The fact that he lived among the Indians and followed their seasonal wanderings, living "without fixed habitation," was the very essence of the term *sauvage*, which the French generally applied to the Indians. As a result, St.-Castin earned the somewhat derogatory title "*capitaine des sauvages*." But he persisted in his support of the Indian cause; he married Pidiwamiska, daughter of the principal Etchemin sachem, Madockawando, and raised a family in this small village. And though he traded with the New Englanders at every opportunity, it is also apparent that in time of war he assisted the Indians against the English. When he returned to France in 1701, St.-Castin left the region in the hands of his sons, who were themselves to gain distinction in their support of the Indian and Acadian cause.

Acadia's rise and decline during the seventeenth century illustrates in even bolder relief the difficulties facing European communities on the Maine coast. Colonial settlers struggled to reconcile the social, commercial, military, and diplomatic demands imposed by their European background with the realities of survival in the New World. While the English settlers had completed a successful accommodation by the end of the century, the French were less fortunate. Still, it was not until the Treaty of Utrecht in 1713 that most of Acadia

BARON JEAN VINCENT de ST. CASTINE

4-4. Jean Vincent d'Abbadie, Baron de St.-Castin (1652–1707), who represented France at Pentagoet for thirty years after the destruction of Fort Pentagoet in an invented portrait signed "Will & Dow 1881." Collections of the Maine Historical Society, Portland.

was finally surrendered to the English. Even then, eastern Maine remained French and Indian territory until the expansion of Massachusetts settlement into the Penobscot Valley with the construction of Fort Pownal in 1759.

For Further Reading:

Archival sources useful for the study of Acadian Maine include the Public Archives of Canada; the Archives de la Marine, Paris, C7, dossier 169; the Fannie Hardy Eckstorm Papers, Special Collections Department, Fogler Library, University of Maine; and the Francis Parkman Papers, Archives of the Massachusetts Historical Society.

Key collected and bound documents for interpreting Acadian Maine include the following: the *Calendar of State Papers, Colonial Series*, vols. 1–25, available on microfiche; *Report of the Public Archivist of Canada* (1904); *Rapport de l'Archiviste de Québec* (1926–31); *Records of the Governor and Company of the Massachusetts Bay in New England* (Boston, 1853); *The Jesuit Relations and Allied Documents, 1610–1792*, edited by Reuben Gold Thwaites (Cleveland, 1896–1902), especially vols. 3 and 4; *The Trelawny Papers*, edited by James Phinney Baxter, *Documentary History of the State of Maine*, vol. 3 (Portland, 1884); and *The Winthrop Papers* (Boston: Massachusetts Historical Society, 1943).

Also important are three bound series of documents: *Documentary History of the State of Maine*, edited by James Phinney Baxter (Portland, 1869–1916); the *Collections* and the *Proceedings* of the Maine Historical Society (Portland, 1831–1906); and the *Collections of the Massachusetts Historical Society* (Boston, 1792–1871). See also *Memorials of the English and French Commissaries Concerning the Limits of Nova Scotia or Acadia*, vol. 1 (London, 1755); and *Nouvelle France: Documents Historiques* (Quebec, 1893).

Works by various colonial writers, officials, and observers that provide information on Acadian Maine include William Bradford, *Of Plymouth Plantation, 1620–1647* (New York, 1952); Mary Frances Farnham, "The Farnham Papers," *Documentary History of the State of Maine*, vol. 7 (Portland, 1901); Nicolas Denys, *The Description and Natural History of the Coasts of North America*, edited and translated by William F. Ganong (Toronto, 1908); Gargas, "General Census of Acadia by Gargas, 1687–1688," in *Acadiensia Nova*, edited by William Morse (London, 1935); Samuel de Champlain, *Voyages of Samuel de Champlain, 1604–1618*, edited by W. L. Grant (New York, 1907); John Winthrop, *Winthrop's Journal*, vol. 1, edited by James Kendall Hosmer (New York, 1908); *The Hutchinson Papers*, vol. 1 (Albany, 1865); John Josselyn, *An Account of Two Voyages to New England* (Boston, 1865); Thomas Gorges, *The Letters of Thomas Gorges, Deputy Governor of the Province of Maine, 1640–1643*, edited by Robert E. Moody (Portland, 1978); Samuel Purchas, *Purchas His Pilgrimmage or Relations of the World* (London, 1617); John Smith, *The Generall History of Virginia, New England, and the Summer Isles* (1624; facsimile of the first edition, Milan, n.d.); Louis-André Vigneras, "Letters of an Acadian Trader, 1674–1676," *New England Quarterly* 13 (1940), pp. 98–110; John Clarence Webster, *Relation of the Voyage to Port Royal in Acadia or New France by the Sieur Direville* (Toronto, 1933); and George Parker Winship, *Sailors' Narratives of Voyages Along the New England Coast, 1524–1624* (Boston, 1905).

Useful contemporary sources on this period include Alaric Faulkner and Gretchen F. Faulkner, *The French at Pentagoet, 1635–1674: An Archaeological Portrait of the Acadian Frontier* (Augusta: New Brunswick Museum and Maine Historic Preservation Commission, 1987); M. A. MacDonald, *Fortune and La Tour: The Civil War in Acadia* (Toronto: Methuen, *1983*); and John G. Reid, *Acadia, Maine, and New Scotland: Marginal Colonies in the Seventeenth Century* (Toronto: University of Toronto Press, 1981).

5

Turmoil on the Wabanaki Frontier,

1524–1678

HARALD E. L. PRINS

An ethnohistorian, Harald Prins interprets the documentary evidence of the seventeenth century to illuminate the world of the Wabanaki—the people who met the European "discoverers" when they arrived in the Gulf of Maine. This world was far different from that of the European colonists, and it was experiencing rapid change under the multiple blows of epidemic disease, intertribal combat, cultural decay, and steady European incursion. But here too it is important to view outside pressures (the arrival of Europeans) and local responses in dynamic interaction. Maine's Indians were not passive victims; they were historical actors in their own right. Certainly Europeans forced profound changes in the Indian way of life, but the Wabanaki peoples fashioned their own mix of resistance and accommodation to the European presence. Thus the themes of this chapter—European assault on a way of life, shifting Indian-white diplomacy, growing Anglo-Indian animosities, and the ultimate consolidation of a French-Wabanaki alliance—offer a somber variation on a familiar theme: creative adaptation to outside forces.

The history of Maine's Indians in the years following their first contacts with Europeans unfolds as a tragic story brimming with vice and violence, decay and despair. Virulent diseases, transmitted unknowingly by the Europeans, ultimately killed at least 75 percent of Maine's Indian inhabitants. Survivors in these ravaged lands hardly fared better; by stages they were uprooted by the never-ending inflow of colonists. The expanding fur trade profoundly altered their traditional relationship with the natural environment and brought periodic game depletions. Unpredictable fluctuations in European fur markets bewildered the tribal newcomers to international commerce. Competition between hunting bands for declining stocks of fur-bearing animals, along with growing friction between the colonizing nations, transformed the region into a volatile political arena and culminated in brutal warfare.

Piecing together a coherent picture of this tumultuous period in native American history is difficult. The history of Maine's tribespeople was preserved traditionally by word of mouth. Recounting the tribal myths, legends, and stories of events long past, elders in the community passed on their ancestral legacy. In the late nineteenth century, when white society intensified its repression of native cultural expressions, some of these oral traditions were put to pen by people such as Penobscot chief Joseph Nicolar, who wrote *The Life and Traditions of the Red Man*.

In addition to such indigenous sources of information, there were records produced by non-Indians. Information on the early historical period, for example, comes primarily from French and English documents. These, however, are often unreliable. European observers, confused by the effects of Indian migrations, new village formations, conquests, mass adoptions, and tribal name changes, wrote conflicting reports about the ethnic composition of local groups. All history, of course, is selective and to some degree biased by differences between the observer and the observed. But these inherent problems are accentuated where the record is either largely oral in nature or written across cultural barriers.

The native peoples of Maine, perhaps about twenty thousand strong before contact, are collectively considered Wabanaki— "the People of the Dawn." Organized in three major ethnic groups, commonly known as tribes, they spoke closely related Algonquian languages. Within each of these tribal communities people shared certain cultural traditions: a collective body of religious beliefs and practices; a sense of historical continuity; and a common ancestry or place of origin. In addition to the name used by the tribe's members themselves, they were also known by the way neighboring groups referred to them. Usually, such names alluded to distinctive characteristics, such as the type of land they inhabited or their mode of speech, distinctive dress, or particular habits.

The English typically named indigenous local groups after their geographic locations. Thus, English historic nomenclature records the "Eastern Indians" as the Saco, Androscoggin, Kennebec, Penobscot, Passamaquoddy, St. John, and Cape Sable (Nova Scotia) Indians, places where these people made permanent or seasonal occupation. French commentators, on the other hand, followed native practice, classifying native communities on the basis of ethnic or linguistic criteria. Thus they generally identified three major ethnic groups in the Gulf of Maine area. *Souriquois* (the ancestors of today's Micmac) possibly refers to the Souriqua River, which served as a travel route between the Bay of Fundy and Gulf of St. Lawrence. *Etchemin* (today's Maliseet and Passamaquoddy) may have derived from a Micmac or Maliseet word for human or man. *Armouch- iquois* (today's Abenaki) referred to a people then regarded as hostile by the

Micmac; it was probably derived from their word for dogs. Later, based on information obtained from their Micmac companions, the French adopted the names currently used by most ethnohistorians. *Micmac* probably meant "our kin-friends"; *Maliseet*, "those who speak badly"; and *Abenaki* derived from an Algonquian term, *[W]abanakiak*, which translates "people living in the land of dawn," that is, to the eastward. Historically, Abenaki residing in the Kennebec region were also known as Canibas (Kennebecs). In this chapter, the term *Wabanaki*, not to be confused with Abenaki, is a collective name used to refer to the Micmac, Maliseet, Passamaquoddy, Penobscot, Kennebec, and various Abenaki groups living as far west as Lake Champlain. All still speak Algonquian languages or dialect variants of this linguistic group and share many cultural features distinguishing them from other Indian groups.

Traditional Life

Native tradition holds that Maine Indians were created by Gluskap, an immortal super-being with magic power who also taught the Indians how to live good lives. Gluskap departed on the eve of the European invasion of America, which almost destroyed the Indians while it radically transformed their way of life. At the time of the first contact with Europeans, the Wabanaki living east of the Kennebec River pursued a way of life based on hunting, fishing, and gathering.

An early report by Jesuit missionary Pierre Biard noted:

> Their food is whatever they can get from the chase and from fishing; for they do not till the soil at all. . . . In the month of February and until the middle of March is the great hunt for beavers, otters, moose, bears (which are very good), and for the caribou. . . . In the middle of March, fish begin to spawn, and to come up from the sea into certain streams, often so abundantly that everything swarms with them. . . . From the month of May up to the middle of September, they are free from all anxiety about their food; for the cod are upon the coast, and all kinds of fish and shellfish. . . . In the middle of September [they] withdraw from the sea, beyond the reach of the tide, to the little rivers, where the eels spawn, of which they lay in a supply; they are good and fat. In October and November comes the second hunt for [moose] and beavers; and then in December . . . comes a fish [tom cod], which spawn under the ice. Also then the turtles bear little ones, etc.

Those living west of the Kennebec, on the other hand, also grew crops, and because these western Wabanaki used the land more intensively, their population

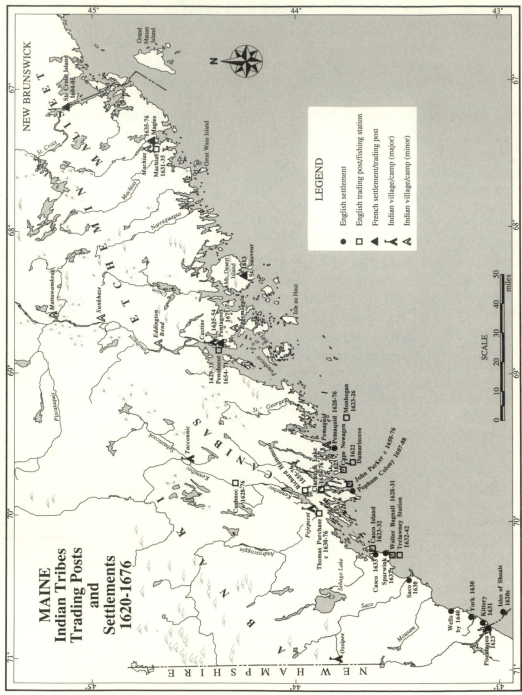

MAINE
Indian Tribes
Trading Posts
and
Settlements
1620-1676

NEW BRUNSWICK

NEW HAMPSHIRE

LEGEND

English settlement

English trading post/fishing station

French settlement/trading post

Indian village/camp (major)

Indian village/camp (minor)

SCALE

0   10   20   30   40   50
miles

St. Croix Island 1604-05

Maples 1635-76

Machias 1631-35

Great Wass Island

Grand Manan Island

Narraguagus

St. Sauveur 1613

Mt. Desert Island

Isle au Haut

Castine

Pentagoet 1635-54

Penobscot 1629-35
1654-

Eddington Bend

Mattawamkeag

Sunkhaze

Piscataquis

Pemaquid 1628-76

Monhegan 1623-26

Cape Newagen 1622

Damariscove

John Parker c 1650-76

Popham Colony 1697-08

Clarke's Lake 1654-76

Richard Hammond 1653-76

Cushnoc 1628-76

Pejepscot

Thomas Purchase c 1630-76

Casco Island 1623-32

Walter Bagnall 1628-31

Trelawney Station 1631-42

Casco 1633

Spurwink 1632

Saco 1630

Wells by 1640

York 1630

Kittery 1631

Piscataqua 1623

Isles of Shoals 1620s

Sebago Lake

Saco

Mousam

Ossipee

Androscoggin

Kennebec

Sebasticook

Tacconnic

St. George

Penobscot

Union

St. Croix

Machias

Togamoggin

© Richard D. Kelly Jr. 1995.

density was higher. The widely dispersed summer villages, usually located on the banks of the Kennebec, Androscoggin, Saco, and other rivers, differed in size, ranging from as low as 150 to as many as 1,500 inhabitants. Eastern Maine villages could be impressive as well. Missionary Biard, who accompanied a French trading voyage to the Penobscot in 1611, recorded eighty canoes, eighteen lodges, and about three hundred inhabitants at Kadesquit ("eel-weir place"), an important head village located near present-day Bangor. The expedition also visited a Sheepscot River village, probably Nebamocago. Describing a meeting with its chief, Biard wrote:

> When we arrived, Monsieur de Biencourt [the son of the French commander at Port Royal, Nova Scotia] armed himself, and thus arrayed proceeded to pay a visit to Meteourmite. He found him in the royal apparel of savage majesty, alone in a cabin that was well matted above and below, and about forty powerful young men stationed around it like a body guard, each one with his shield, his bow and arrows upon the ground in front of him. . . . They led [the French] to the largest lodge of all; it contained fully eighty people.

Generally, there was a clear sexual division of labor in these communities; while men engaged in hunting, trapping, diplomatic and military excursions, and clearing and burning the woods, the women in western Wabanaki villages planted, weeded, and harvested corn, squash, beans, and tobacco. Generally, Wabanaki clothing, also made by the women, came from the skins of game animals. For tanning, women used a mixture of animal brains, fish oil, and other ingredients, and they smoked the hides to make them more water-resistant. Usually these garments were decorated with paint, porcupine quills, and moose hair. Arranged in colorful designs, the applied motifs were often symbolic representations of ideas significant in Wabanaki culture—personal guardian spirits, status emblems, family totems, and other tribal insignia. Essentially, men and women wore the same type of dress, along with moccasins of seal or moose hide, leggings, and a soft leather loincloth attached to a belt at the waist. A fur robe of beaver, otter, deer, or moose was worn "like a mantle, and hanging downe to their knees, made fast together upon the shoulder with leather."

Certain men, renowned as warriors and hunters or endowed with oratory skills, qualified as leaders in the Wabanaki communities. Called *sagamores*, they were usually heads of large families and represented those who voluntarily associated themselves with such extended kin-groups. Great sagamores were known to possess special spirit power, or medicine, which enabled them to accomplish extraordinary feats. Occasionally, when a politically astute leader

5-1. A Micmac hunter in the seventeenth century depicted by Jacques Grasset de St.-Sauveur, later engraved on copper by J. Laroque. The hunter is tattooed and wears a wampum headdress. The engraving was published in *Tableaux des principaux peuples de l'Europe, de l'Asie, de l'Afrique, de l'Amrique et les dcouvertes des Capitaines Cook, La Prouse, etc.* (Paris et Bordeaux, chez l'auteur, 1796–1798). Courtesy of the National Archives of Canada (C-021112).

exercised influence over his allies, he could be recognized as a paramount chief of a confederation. A French Jesuit missionary familiar with the eastern Wabanaki penned this description of a meeting of such leaders in a 1616 report. Although the passage reflects a somewhat naive cultural bias, it indicates the basic intent and structure of these meetings:

> It is principally in Summer that they pay visits and hold their State Councils; I mean that several Sagamores come together and consult among themselves about peace and war, treaties of friendship and treaties for the common good. It is only these Sagamores who have a voice in the discussion and who make the speeches, unless there be some old and renowned *Autmoins* [shamans or medicine men] . . . , for they respect them very much and give them a hearing the same as to the Sagamores. . . . Now in these assemblies, if there is some news of importance, as their neighbors wish to make war upon them, or that they have killed someone, or that they must renew the alliance, etc., then messengers fly from all parts to make up the more general assembly. . . . In these assemblies so general, they resolve upon peace, truce, war, or nothing at all, as often happens in the councils where there are several chiefs, without order and subordination, whence they frequently depart more confused and disunited than when they came.

European-Indian Encounter

Initially, the Indians of the Gulf of Maine absorbed the European presence—particularly that of the French explorers—into their traditional patterns of trade, diplomacy, and war. Even before 1600, in fact, while the Europeans' exploring and fishing activities were mostly confined to the Gulf of St. Lawrence, certain Micmac and other coastal chieftains became intermediaries in the fur trade, carrying European goods into the Gulf of Maine. Wabanaki tribespeople, ranging north into the Gulf of St. Lawrence, may have encountered European mariners as early as 1504. Certainly by the 1530s Wabanaki were in regular contact with Europeans in the St. Lawrence region, exchanging furs and hides for commodities such as sharp steel swords, knives, copper kettles, iron arrowheads, cloth, and biscuits.

The first recorded contact between Maine Indians and European mariners in the Gulf of Maine took place in Casco Bay in 1524. Spying Giovanni da Verrazano's small landing boat making toward shore, local natives yelled and gestured from a steep rock that the crew were not to come on land. Apparently, they distrusted the newcomers, perhaps having heard unfavorable tales about the "boat people" from their Micmac neighbors.

One year later, Portuguese pilot Don Esteban Gómez, exploring the region for Spanish Emperor Charles V, sailed a fifty-ton caravel into the Gulf of Maine. Other voyagers followed. By the late 1500s a handful of Micmac entrepreneurs had acquired European shallops, small sailing vessels commonly used in fishing, and in these small boats they sailed enormous distances in pursuit of trade. When English, Basque, and French mariners ventured into the Gulf of Maine on a more regular basis in the early 1600s, they encountered these Micmac fur traders plying the coastal waters in their sailing boats, bartering with the Abenaki and their southern neighbors for skins of moose, deer, bear, sable, otter, mink, and especially beaver, along with corn, squash, beans, and wampum (white and blue shell-beads). Captain Bartholomew Gosnold, for instance, happened upon a Micmac trader in 1602 on the coast of southern Maine. According to his report, "six Indians in a Basque shallop with mast and sail, an iron grapple, and a kettle of copper, came boldly aboard us, one of them apparelled with a waistcoat and breeches of black serge, made after our sea-fashion, hose and shoes on his feet. . . . [W]ith a piece of chalk [they] described the coast thereabouts." French colonizing efforts, which began with the St. Croix experiment in 1604, added a new factor to traditional Indian alliances and animosities. Samuel de Champlain, who ranged with a small band of explorers and local Wabanaki guides into the Penobscot in that year, met the "great Captain named Bessabez [Bashaba], headman of that river." This Penobscot River sagamore was recognized as a paramount chief of a confederation of twenty-two Wabanaki villages in the territory they identified as Mawooshen, which stretched from south of Saco Bay to Mount Desert Island. Champlain's tactical move to establish a trading alliance added a volatile new element to the region.

When the French colonists from St. Croix relocated across the Bay of Fundy at Port Royal, Nova Scotia, in the spring of 1605, they also made friends with the region's Micmac Indians. As coastal traders, these natives possessed a keen knowledge of Gulf of Maine geography. Two local Indians, a young Micmac named Panounias and his Abenaki wife from southern Maine, joined Champlain on another expedition to the Kennebec. As Champlain's party approached the Kennebec, they encountered a small party of native bird hunters, and in the local dialect, Panounias's wife explained that her French companions were interested in trading for beaver and other furs. Champlain offered to help the tribespeople solve some bitter disputes with their eastern neighbors, in particular the Micmac. Interested, the hunters escorted the French party to their sagamore Meteourmite, who accepted Champlain's offer of an alliance. Like other Waba-

naki sagamores, Meteourmite was well aware that good relations with these for-
eigners meant direct access to the trade goods from across the waters.

Over time, trade and diplomatic contacts such as those established by
Champlain heightened animosities between local Indian chieftains. Direct linkages to European merchants and fishermen left Maine's coastal sagamores
independent of eastern Wabanaki traders (the Micmac and Maliseet), powerful men who had functioned as brokers in the fur trade for several decades,
and relations between the two peoples that were already strained predictably
began to worsen. Although the conflict remains difficult to reconstruct, it appears that the western and eastern Wabanaki raided and took captives from
each other's villages. In the fall of 1606, two eastern sagamores—Chkoudun, a
Maliseet from the St. John River, and Messamaoet, a Micmac from the Nova
Scotia coast—sailed to the Saco River looking for a chance to reconcile with
their opponents. At Saco, according to French accounts, they met with two
western Wabanaki sagamores—Olmechin, the local leader, and his ally Marchin from the Androscoggin. In a formal speech, Messamoet reminded his
hosts that "they had often had friendly intercourse together" and offered them
precious European commodities as gifts, including some copper kettles, iron
axes, and knives.

Despite such overtures, hostilities continued. Later that very summer, a
Micmac raiding party under sagamore Iouaniscou clashed with a group of
western Wabanaki, killing several warriors and abducting some of their women,
whom they put to death at Mount Desert Island. The young Micmac trader Panounias was murdered in retaliation at Penobscot Bay, probably by Olmechin's
warriors from the Saco. To avenge his death, Membertou, a Micmac sagamore
from the Bay of Fundy, assembled a fighting force of eastern Wabanaki allies in
the summer of 1607. Along with spears, tomahawks, bows, and arrows, the warriors were armed with muskets; possibly for the first time in New England
history Indians were intent on using firearms against other Indians. The warriors sailed in shallops to the Saco, where they launched a surprise attack.
Among those killed in battle were Olmechin and Marchin.

Early European encounters also set a precedent for animosity between the
two cultures. When Englishman John Walker landed at Penobscot in 1580, for
instance, his crew found a lodge filled with three hundred moose hides, stored,
possibly, by local hunters for barter with Micmac traders. It is indicative of the
cavalier disrespect many Europeans felt towards Maine's Indians that Walker
and his men thought nothing of looting the place and carrying these stolen
hides back to England.

A quarter century later, in 1605, five Wabanaki warriors belonging to
Bashaba's confederacy were kidnaped from Pemaquid by an English crew com-

manded by George Waymouth, who shipped them back to England. The captives, Dahanada, Skidwarres, Assacomet, Maneddo, and Amoret, fell into the hands of gentlemen-entrepreneurs Sir John Popham, then Lord Chief Justice, and Sir Ferdinando Gorges, at the time military commander of English Fort Plymouth. Two were taken to Popham in London, while the others were kept by Gorges, who had them "set me down what great rivers ran up into the land, what men of note were seated on them, what power they were of, how allied, what enemies they had, and the like." In 1606, Assacomet and Maneddo served as guides on an English voyage to the Maine coast, but the vessel was captured by Spaniards south of Florida. Assacomet, apparently confused to see whites fighting whites, screamed at the enemy: "King James his ship, King James his ship!" Severely wounded and captured, he was jailed with Maneddo in the Spanish port of Seville. Later, Gorges secured their release and arranged for their return to England. Meanwhile, Dahanada returned home aboard another English vessel, serving as guide on a separate reconnaissance voyage that same year. Accompanying Captain George Popham and the Sagadahoc colonists the following year, Skidwarres also returned. Assacomet, however, did not return until 1614, sailing aboard one of Gorges's vessels.

Being warned by local Wabanaki that the French planned to attack the place, Popham's colonists built a fort at the mouth of the Kennebec. Not surprisingly, the region's tribespeople were cautious in their dealings with these new neighbors, many of whom were convicted felons fresh from English prisons. The Wabanaki claimed that their god, Tanto, had "commanded them not to dwell neere, or come among the English." Still, according to Wabanaki oral tradition, some guileless tribal members were enticed into the English fort under the pretense of trade. "Causing them to take the drag ropes of a loaded cannon, [the English] fired off the piece when the Indians were in line, and blew them to atoms [Hubbard's *History of the Indian War*, 1680]." The would-be colonists abandoned the place in 1608, but English harassment continued from other quarters. In 1609, for instance, Henry Hudson, the English commander of the Dutch vessel *De Halve Maen*, anchored near a Penobscot River village, stole an Indian shallop loaded with fine pelts, launched a mortar attack on the peaceful village, and, when the Indians took flight, looted the deserted homes. Leaving the Penobscot behind, the Dutch vessel sailed for the Hudson River, named after *De Halve Maen*'s savage captain.

By this time, several French and English vessels were employed in fishing and fur-trade activities along the entire Wabanaki coast. The impact of the fur trade on native life was obvious to an early French observer of the native scene: "In Summer," he wrote, "they often wear our capes, and in Winter our bed-blankets, which they improve with trimming and wear double. They are also quite willing to make use of our hats, shoes, caps, woolens and shirts, and of our linen to clean their infants, for we trade them all these commodities for their furs."

Generally, the Wabanaki easily absorbed European trade goods into their existing patterns of culture and commerce, but growing competition between English and French traders complicated their encounters with the recent arrivals. Concerned about the English presence in the Gulf of Maine, a party of about twenty French colonists returned to Port Royal in 1610, after it had been abandoned by De Monts and Champlain in 1607. In the interim, the vacant habitation had been guarded by Chief Membertou and his Micmac kin. Father Pierre Biard, who arrived in Port Royal in 1611, mailed detailed reports to his superiors in Paris, describing the various Wabanaki nations, their way of life, the natural conditions of their lands, and, of course, the commercial opportunities for fur trading and fishing. Intent on missionary work rather than trading, Biard and fellow Jesuit Enemond Massé founded a settlement they named St. Sauveur on Mount Desert Island. Although both St. Sauveur and Port Royal were destroyed by an English raiding party from Virginia in 1613, French fur traders and fishers continued to sail the Gulf of Maine.

During these years of persistent feuding, the Micmacs and their allies, who controlled coastal Maine east of Penobscot, were armed by their French and Basque trading partners. The English lost a valuable opportunity to ally themselves in similar fashion with the western Wabanaki when John Smith arrived on the Maine coast in 1614. Smith found a willing guide and broker in sagamore Dahanada, one of the western Wabanaki chieftains who seven years earlier had guided Popham's expedition to the Kennebec. The English explorer promised Dahanada and his friends that the English would defend them "with a better power than the French did them," but having achieved his exploring and trading objectives within a few weeks, Smith simply returned to England. Part of Smith's crew stayed on Monhegan Island preparing a cargo of dried fish. While there, as Smith later found out, they abused their erstwhile allies, capturing twenty-seven and trying to sell them into slavery in Spain.

Plagues upon the Land

In 1615, a year after Smith's explorations, disaster struck the Wabanaki. Micmacs and their fellow eastern Wabanaki, sailing in shallops or paddling in war canoes, staged lightning raids against Bashaba and his allies on the central Maine coast. The Micmacs, an English document records, "surprised the Bashaba, and slew him and all his people near about him, carrying away his women and such other matters as they thought of value." With the death of Mawooshen's paramount sagamore, the confederacy of western and central Wabanaki villages collapsed, "and after his death the publique businesse running to confusion for want of an head, the rest of his great Sagamores fell at variance among themselves, spoiled and destroyed each other's people and provision, and famine took hould of many [Gorges 1658]."

Even this disaster was eclipsed, however, by a subsequent scourge that nearly brought an apocalyptic end to the Wabanaki world. Unbeknownst to all, the European vessels had transported alien pathogens, against which indigenous immune systems had not yet developed antibodies. Falling victim to highly contagious diseases, probably including hepatitis, the Wabanaki experienced a terrible pandemic. Already reduced in numbers by other calamities, more than 75 percent of the Wabanaki perished between 1616 and 1619. Many coastal villages were entirely wiped out. One English observer wrote that Indians "died on heapes as they lay in their houses and the living that were able to shift for themselves would runne away, & let them dy. . . . And the bones, and skulls upon the severall places of their habitations, made such a spectacle that as I travailed in that Forrest, . . . it seemed to mee a new Golgotha [Morton 1637]."

This "Great Dying" virtually depopulated the coastal area from Penobscot to Cape Cod. An English chronicler observed "that in a manner the greater part of that land was left desert, without any to disturb or oppose our free and peaceable possession thereof [Gorges 1658]." A year later, in 1620, English King James granted a large tract of Wabanaki lands, from the Kennebec to the Merrimack (later reduced to the Piscataqua River), to Sir Ferdinando Gorges, who thereupon claimed the title of Lord Proprietor of Maine. In the following decades, recurrent epidemics—smallpox, cholera, measles, plague, whooping cough—prevented the surviving Wabanaki from effectively resisting further European intrusion on their lands. English colonists, who viewed the catastrophe as God's good providence, founded new towns on abandoned Indian village sites, often located conveniently, and they grew crops or hay in the barren cornfields.

In the post-epidemic years, local Wabanaki leaders regrouped scattered families and used their power to exact tribute in furs, wampum, or other native commodities from less powerful neighbors. Having learned broken English, other Wabanaki traded with the growing numbers of English fishermen along the coast west of the Penobscot. While most eastern Wabanaki remained allied with the French in Acadia, those west of the Penobscot survived as clients of their new English neighbors, who soon outnumbered natives in their traditional homeland. Commenting on the emerging political situation, an English observer noted that the Wabanakis were "verie few in number." Although they lived close to the English settlements, "theire want of people makes them not feared by us as not beinge able to doe much mischeife."

Nevertheless, the new English settlers, inhabiting widely scattered homesteads on the edge of the forest, were gravely concerned about the trade in firearms. The Indians, one observed, "can use them with great dexterity, excelling our English therein, and have been vaunting with them." Accordingly, the authorities prohibited not only selling but also repairing such weapons. In 1632, having condemned a colonist for selling guns and ammunition to the Indians, the Massachusetts court ordered him "severely whipped and branded with a hot iron on one of his cheeks" and suggested that such an offense should be "punished hereafter by death." On Maine's remote coast, however, where the fur trade was in full swing, such laws were difficult to enforce and did not stop the flow of firearms into the interior. In addition to dozens of fishing vessels on the Maine coast, a lively trade in these weapons was carried on by England's rivals, particularly the French and Basques.

There were other sources of growing English-Wabanaki tension. Indian peoples in the coastal area, which was increasingly occupied by English settlers, were encouraged to sell their land. Signing quitclaim deeds, called "Indian deeds," the Wabanaki made a mark on the paper documents, usually an animal sign or some other symbolic representation, which concluded the transaction. In return for signing away full or partial title, they received European trade goods. Kennebec River sagamore Mattawormet's son, Monquine, for instance, received a large barrel of bread, a second barrel of beans, two cloth coats, two gallons of wine, and one bottle of rum when he agreed to sell the Pilgrims an enormous tract of Kennebec lands running from Cushnoc Falls (Augusta) north to Skowhegan.

In order to understand what the Wabanaki had in mind when they agreed to these transactions, we need to consider their traditional world view. To begin with, they did not distinquish between the so-called natural world and the supernatural. As Penobscot chief Nicolar explained in his *Life and Traditions of the Red Man*, the Great Spirit, whom they called grandfather, made it known to them "that the world was all spiritual, that there was a living spirit in all things, and the spirit of all things has a power over all." This spirit power, called *manitou*, was everywhere—in the sun, moon, stars, clouds, mountains, rivers, "and even in the trees of the earth." This land, which they shared with the animals and plants, was therefore sacred. Given to them by the Great Spirit, it was a collective resource to be used by the members of the local communities. Holding this heritage in a sacred trust for their children's children, they saw themselves as guardians of their ancestral lands. In contrast, Europeans viewed their lands as personal property to be bought and sold on the market like any other commodity. The English settlers talked local tribal representatives into transactions in which they agreed to "sell" tracts of land in exchange for a certain price in the form of trade goods or some other compensation. The Wabanaki, on the other hand, typically interpreted the "sale" as a ritual in which they gave permission to an English trader or settler to use a piece of their land for some period of time in exchange for certain gifts. Not surprisingly, given the opposite interpretations of these "Indian deeds," the Indians and the English soon found themselves embroiled in a bitter, long-lasting, and ultimately bloody dispute about land rights issues in the region.

The "Beaver Wars"

A third and more potent source of tension was Europe's ongoing demand for furs and the Wabanaki's own growing dependency on European commodities. As fur-bearing animals, especially beaver, grew scarce in traditional Wabanaki hunting ranges, small groups of western Wabanaki ventured into the upper St. Lawrence River valley, trying to establish themselves as brokers in the long-distance fur trade. In 1637, in an effort to stop these intruders from Maine, French authorities in Canada ordered the Wabanaki wigwams searched and their muskets confiscated. The French governor summoned the leaders of the Wabanaki expedition to Quebec City and informed them that "he was displeased that these peddlers should come trafficking in the footsteps of the French." Regardless of such warnings, the expansion of trading links between the Wabanaki and their interior woodland neighbors continued.

This growing competition for trade resulted in a series of violent clashes between the tribes. Commonly referred to as "Beaver Wars," these intertribal conflicts involved virtually all native groups from Cape Breton Island south to the Chesapeake and as far inland as the Great Lakes area. Although the Beaver Wars continued periodically throughout much of the seventeenth century, their importance in the 1640s was linked to the growing alliance between the Wabanaki and other Algonquian-speaking tribes, such as the Montagnais and Algonquins, as well as the French in the St. Lawrence Valley.

In 1640, Algonquin and Montagnais envoys from the St. Lawrence Valley invited the Abenaki to join them in league against the Iroquois, who received firearms from Dutch merchants on the Hudson River. French Jesuits, particularly those headquartered at the mission village of Sillery, near Quebec City, helped cement the alliance. Two years later, a Montagnais convert from Sillery evangelized among the Abenaki, wintering in a Kennebec village. Most tribespeople, debauched by alcohol acquired from the English on the coast, paid little attention to the native preacher, but one of the local sagamores must have been intrigued, for he accompanied the Montagnais back to the French mission. There, a visiting Abenaki sagamore told him: "If thou wishest to bind our two

5-2. A small Maliseet camp on the banks of a river, as depicted in a painting by William Robert Herries (1818–45). Courtesy of the National Archives of Canada (C-11891).

tribes by a perfect friendship, it is necessary that we should all believe the same." The sagamore, after religious instruction by the French priests, was baptized and renamed Jean Baptiste. This conversion symbolically expressed the new political alliance between the Maine Abenaki and the French and the Canadian mission Indians, in particular the Algonquins and Montagnais.

That fall, in 1642, a war party of ten Mohawks—members of the Iroquois confederation whose territorial base was in eastern upstate New York—raided the territory of the western Wabanaki. All winter they spread terror in the area and returned from northern New England with twenty-two captives, six of whom were Abenaki warriors. The Mohawks adopted the women and children into their tribe, but tortured and burned to death the warriors at their stronghold, Ossernenon, west of the Hudson River. Mohawk and other Iroquois raiders returned repeatedly to the Wabanaki homelands, carrying off furs, captives, and other spoils of war. Greatly alarmed by this situation, a number of Kennebec Wabanaki journeyed to Sillery in 1643 and, following the example of Jean Baptiste (pronounced by them as "Sabattis"), were baptized before returning to their villages.

In 1646, several tribal people from Norridgewock, one of the principal Wabanaki villages in the upper Kennebec River valley, traveled to Sillery to renew the pact with their mission Indian allies in the St. Lawrence River valley. From Sillery, two Kennebec River sagamores visited nearby Quebec, where they negotiated to have a "black robe" (Jesuit) establish a Catholic mission among the Wabanaki in Maine. That autumn, Father Gabriel Dreuillettes arrived at Norridgewock and stayed to preach the gospel and care for the sick along the valley. Remaining less than a year, Dreuillettes left when French Capuchin priests at Fort Pentagoet, who considered the Jesuit an intruder in their mission territory, objected to his presence. Nevertheless, he and others returned to evangelize, and over the next several decades the majority of Wabanaki became Catholic converts. Given the ongoing rivalry between the European colonial powers in North America, this turn of events was a political windfall for the French, who showed no reluctance in exploiting their advantage.

As the fierce Beaver Wars continued, a longstanding conflict between the Algonquian-speaking peoples and the tribes of the Iroquois Confederacy to the south and west began to intensify. In the 1660s, several Algonquian-speaking nations between the Hudson and the Kennebec formed an alliance against the Iroquois. This Algonquian league, associated with the French and their Algonquin and Montagnais allies, included the Mahican, their Sokoki neighbors of the Connecticut, the Pennacook on the Merrimac, and the western Wabanaki along the Saco, Androscoggin, and Kennebec. Despite the strength of this alliance, Iroquois depredations in the upper St. Lawrence Valley forced many beleaguered tribespeople into exile among the Wabanaki or pushed them farther westward toward the Great Lakes.

In 1661, a delegation of thirty Mohawk appeared in Maine, demanding that the Wabanaki at the Kennebec River pay tribute in furs and wampum and submit as a client nation under the Iroquois. Insulted, the Wabanaki murdered the Mohawks, allowing only one, half-scalped and with his upper lip cut off, to return to his village some three hundred miles away. The following year the Mohawks retaliated. A party of 265 warriors ventured deep into Maine to attack a band of Indian trading families camping near the English fortified trading post at Penobscot. They took about eighty captives, stole a considerable amount of English trade goods, and killed cattle. In the summer of 1666, six hundred French elite troops, well-primed after a campaign against the Turks in eastern Europe, marched against the Iroquois. Joined by Canadian militia and about a hundred mission Indians, they looted and destroyed the Mohawk villages after scaring off the inhabitants.

The focus of these regional wars began to shift in the late 1660s. One of the first signs of this change took place in 1666, as large numbers of Indians roamed the Connecticut River valley rustling English livestock. One of the guilty parties was a band of Wabanaki warriors from the lower Kennebec under sagamore Rawandagon, a shaman and chieftain commonly known as Robin Hood to his English neighbors. The raids indicated growing animosity toward English intrusion into northern New England. Over the next few years tensions between whites and Indians in the region began to replace intertribal warfare.

This shift in the focus of warfare was accelerated by growing bonds between the English and the Iroquois. By this time, the Dutch had been forced to relinquish their claims in the Hudson River area to the English. As successors to the Dutch traders, the English gained the support of the Iroquois, in particular the Mohawks, who had vested interests in the Hudson River fur trade. As the Wabanaki soon discovered, this new Anglo-Iroquois alliance seriously affected their struggle for survival.

Threatened by the new alliance, the Algonquian nations suffered two more dramatic reverses in the late 1660s. The first was a smallpox epidemic that raged through the St. Lawrence River valley in 1669, killing almost all the Algonquins and Montagnais in the area. This was followed by a disastrous military campaign. During the summer of 1669, a powerful force of more than six hundred Wabanaki, Pennacook, Sokoki, and Mahican warriors assembled. Armed with guns, pistols, swords, spears, and bows and arrows, they traveled hundreds of miles through the woods and crossed the Hudson to attack Kanagaro, a well-supplied and heavily fortified Mohawk village. The siege broke up when the allied forces exhausted their provisions and ammunition and some of the fighters became ill. After retreating some twenty miles, the Wabanaki and their fellow Algonquians were ambushed by a strong force of Mohawks and suffered a terrible defeat. Many warriors, including Massachusetts chief Josiah Cheka-tabutt, the expedition's leader, lost their lives. Afraid of renewed hostilities, many surviving Mahicans and Sokokis took their belongings and migrated to lands beyond immediate Iroquois reach. Some moved closer to the French in the St. Lawrence River valley, while others took refuge among the Wabanaki.

King Philip's War

In 1671, the Wabanaki and Iroquois agreed to a treaty, ceasing hostilities against each other, at least for the time being. By this time, however, tensions between the English settlers and local Indian communities along the New England coast were reaching a kindling point. The Indians had grown bitter about English encroachments on their land, about the temptations posed by English rum traders, and especially about free-roaming English livestock, which destroyed their crops. The Indians responded peacefully at first. Among the Saco River Wabanaki, for example, a local sagamore named Squando claimed that God had appeared to him and ordered him to pray and to stop drinking strong liquors. For a while, fellow tribespeople heeded his message, which helped them to cope with the burden of living in a world dominated by abusive English settlers.

Elsewhere, however, native reactions were less peaceful. The Wampanoags, who lived near the Plymouth Colony, armed themselves in the spring of 1671 and killed several colonists. Several Wampanoags were tried in an English court, and some were put to death; one was decapitated "and his head sett upon a pole on the gallowes." The incident inspired rumors of an Indian uprising that spread throughout New England. Tensions rose and a series of clashes in the summer of 1675 marked the beginning of King Philip's War, named after Wampanoag chief Metacomet, called King Philip by his English neighbors. A few weeks later, armed fighters from other Indian villages attacked some of the scattered white settlements. Moving within a widespread intertribal network formed during previous conflicts, native emissaries probably traveled from village to village, spreading Metacomet's rallying cry. Such a stratagem is suggested by a Saco River tribesman who informed the nearby English that "some stranger Indians" from the west had visited him: "They have endeavored to persuade us all to raise the tomahawk against the white people. They have gone farther east, and will probably soon come back with many warriors."

At the opening of the war, New England's colonial militia was well organized. Massachusetts alone raised seventy-four companies and struck back with

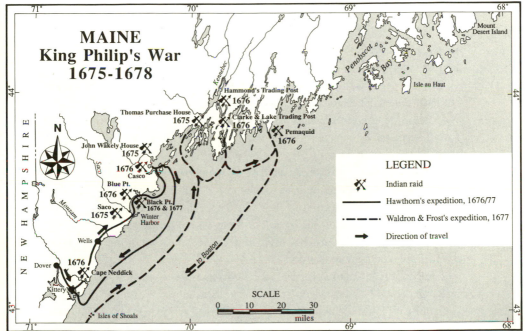

MAINE
King Philip's War
1675-1678

NEW HAMPSHIRE

Kennebec

Penobscot Bay

Mount
Desert Island

Isle au Haut

Hammond's Trading Post
1676

Thomas Purchase House
1675

Clarke & Lake Trading Post
1676

Pemaquid
1676

John Wakely House
1675

1676
Casco

Blue Pt.
1676

Saco
1675

Black Pt.
1676 & 1677

Winter
Harbor

Wells

Saco

Mousam

Dover

Kittery

1676
Cape Neddick

Isles of Shoals

to Boston

LEGEND

Indian raid

Hawthorn's expedition, 1676/77

Waldron & Frost's expedition, 1677

Direction of travel

SCALE

0   10   20   30
miles

© Richard D. Kelly Jr., 1995.

overwhelming force, killing thousands of Indian men, women, and children, looting their supplies, destroying their villages, and burning their cornfields. Those who surrendered or were captured were often executed or sold as slaves to plantations in the Caribbean.

Along the Kennebec, English traders, alarmed about the news from the rest of New England, removed ammunition and other commodities from their trading post at Taconnet (Winslow) and shipped the goods downriver to the larger station at Arrowsic Island. The English demanded that the local Wabanaki give up their weapons, including the firearms they used for hunting, and warned that noncompliance was punishable by death. Most refused, protesting that without guns they would starve. Many of the threatened Kennebec River Indians moved to the Penobscot River valley, where they began to negotiate with the Wabanaki bands farther east in order to resist any further English interference.

The already tense relations were further poisoned when English sailors at the Saco River deliberately overturned a canoe containing sagamore Squando's wife and child, thereby causing the infant's death. The inane reason proffered for this cruelty was curiosity to see whether "young Indians could swim naturally like animals." Predictably, Squando's sorrow turned into unrelenting hatred of the English. In the early fall of 1675, a party of embittered tribesmen ransacked an English trading post on the lower Androscoggin and skirmished with the English settlers at Casco Bay. Settlers in the Kennebec Valley, too few in number to feel safe and too remote from fellow colonists to solicit help, chose to abandon the Kennebec area. Until the following summer, things remained quiet on New England's eastern frontier.

South of the Piscataqua River, English forces, aided by their Iroquois auxiliaries, destroyed Chief Metacomet's hapless coalition in the summer of 1676. In the course of subsequent mopping-up raids, the English killed about three thousand tribespeople, including the ill-starred Wampanoag chieftain himself. Escaping from this carnage, a large number of natives sought refuge among the French in Canada, where they formed new tribal communities in the St. Lawrence River valley or joined the Jesuit mission at Sillery. Others escaped to the eastward, crossing the Piscataqua into Wabanaki territory. Not all made it to safer ground. At the Cocheco trading post (at Dover, New Hampshire), English troops captured about two hundred "strange Indians" who had taken refuge among the local Pennacook. These prisoners were sent to Boston, some to be hanged and the rest sold into slavery. Remaining centers of native resistance south of Maine were squelched in the late summer of 1676.

In Maine, however, Anglo-Indian hostilities resumed again later that summer, when a large war party of more than two hundred Wabanaki, commanded by noted warriors like Mogg Heigon, raided Falmouth, Black Point (Scarborough), Wells, and other English settlements. In addition, several fishing vessels and even a small warship were captured. Wabanaki forces were strengthened in 1677, when Penobscot sagamore Madockawando allowed his warriors to take up arms against the English. Several factors played a role in drawing these eastern Wabanaki into the conflict. Indian refugees from Massachusetts no doubt pressured Madockawando to take up arms, and the French may have done some coaxing as well. But the eastern Wabanaki also harbored grievances of their own. The English had included them under the arms embargo, despite the Penobscots' obvious neutrality, and destruction of the French trading post at Pentagoet deprived them of that source of firearms, ammunition, and other commodities. Also, they were furious about an incident at Machias, where some fifteen unsuspecting Wabanaki were lured onto the deck of a New Hampshire sailing vessel, then shipped off to be sold as slaves in the Azores. Perhaps the crowning insult was precipitated by an English expedition under Colonel Waldron of Cocheco, who beguiled a group of friendly Wabanaki with drink, then killed several, including Penobscot River sagamore Mattahando, plundered their camp, and took Madockawando's sister prisoner.

In May 1677, a few months after Mattahando's slaying, a composite band of Wabanaki fighters, joined by a medley of other tribesmen from southern New England, attacked an English fort at Black Point in Scarborough. On the third day of this fierce assault, Mogg was shot. In late July, the garrison was reinforced with forty young English recruits from Massachusetts and a company of thirty-six Indians from the Protestant mission village at Natick, near Boston. The next morning, Wabanaki fighters appeared not far from the fort. When the foolhardy English commander dashed out with his fresh troops, they were ambushed. Forty English soldiers and twelve Natick mission warriors were killed, along with a few Wanabaki fighters. The Wabanaki force subsequently left the garrison to range the coast, capturing no less than thirteen English fishing vessels complete with crews and cargoes.

A few weeks later, Governor Edmond Andros of New York sent reinforcements to Fort Charles at Pemaquid, then part of the Duke of York's jurisdiction (the province of New York, granted by English King Charles II to his brother, together with the area from the Kennebec to the Penobscot). In an effort to gain control over the Kennebec region, the fort's commander prohibited further English trading with the Wabanaki. Thus pressured, several Kennebec River chieftains offered to lay down their arms in return for an end to the trade embargo. Soon after, all of Maine's leading sagamores, including Moxus, Madockawando, and Squando, traveled to Pemaquid, handed over their English prisoners and returned captured vessels, and offered terms of peace.

Meeting again at Casco Bay in April 1678, both parties signed a formal treaty, bringing a much desired tranquility to the region's population.

From the perspective of Maine's native peoples, the early years of European settlement brought an unimaginable change in fortunes. Relations that began with mutually beneficial trade deteriorated over the first three quarters of the seventeenth century into bitter war, and combat would continue for nearly another century. Wabanaki history between 1600 and 1678 reveals the tragic paradox of European migration to the New World: the European quest for a better life in the Americas transformed native American existence into nightmarish reflection of their former existence. Although the Wabanaki peoples endured, somehow, the dramatic upheavals of the seventeenth century, their struggle for cultural survival had only just begun.

For Further Reading:

For general background, see Philip K. Bock, "Micmac"; Gordon M. Day, "Western Abenaki"; V. O. Erickson, "Maliseet-Passamaquoddy"; and Dean R. Snow, "Eastern Abenaki," in *The Northeast*, edited by Bruce G. Trigger, vol. 15 of *The Handbook of North American Indians* (Washington, DC, 1978). A native point of view can be found in a work by Penobscot historian Joseph Nicolar titled *The Life and Traditions of the Red Man* (Bangor, 1893). Primary sources include reports by explorers, such as the six volumes of Samuel de Champlain's *Works*, edited by Henry P. Biggar (Toronto, 1922–36). Detailed accounts by French missionaries were published in the seventy-three-volume series *The Jesuit Relations and Allied Documents, 1610–1792*, edited by Reuben Gold Thwaites (Cleveland, 1896–1902). English sources can be found in James P. Baxter's twenty-four-volume *Documentary History of the State of Maine*, containing the *Baxter Manuscripts*, published by the Maine Historical Society (Portland, 1889–1916). Much information can also be found in the Society's *Collections* and *Proceedings* (Portland, 1831–1906); in the *Collections of the Massachusetts Historical Society* (Boston, 1792–1871); in the six-volume *Records of the Governor and Company of the Massachusetts Bay in New England*, edited by Nathaniel B. Shurtleff (Boston, 1853–54); in the *Records of the Colony of New Plymouth in New England*, edited by David Pulsifer (Boston, 1859); in the *Calendar of State Papers, Colonial Series: America and the West Indies (1661–1668)*, edited by William N. Sainsbury (London: 1880); and in the 250 volumes of unpublished manuscripts relating to Massachusetts Affairs (1625–1791) in the Massachusetts Archives, State House, Boston. Information concerning Wabanaki political dealings with the Iroquois has been published in the fifteen-volume series, *Documents Relative to the Colonial History of the State of New York*, edited by Edmund B. O'Callaghan (Albany, 1849–51).

Secondary sources include works by early Jesuit historians such as Pierre F. X. de Charlevoix, who wrote a six-volume *History and General Description of New France* (New York, 1900) and early Massachusetts historians such as William Hubbard, who wrote a 1680 work titled *A General History of New England from the Discovery to 1680* (republished in 1815 by the Massachusetts Historical Society, Boston). More recent studies include Alvin H. Morrison's unpublished 1974 doctoral dissertation, "Dawnland Decisions: Seventeenth-Century Wabanaki Leaders and their Responses to the Differential Contact Stimuli in the Overlap Area of New France and New England" (Buffalo: State University of New York); P.-André Sévigny's *Les Abénaquis: Habitat et Migrations (17ᵉ et 18ᵉ siècles)* (Montreal, 1978); Kenneth M. Morrison's *The Embattled Northeast: The Elusive Ideal of Alliance in Abenaki-Euramerican Relations* (Berkeley, 1984); and Colin G. Calloway's *The Western Abenakis of Vermont, 1600–1800* (Norman, Okla., 1990), which discusses events and facts also pertinent to the Wabanaki groups of Maine. Finally, see also the following journals: *Proceedings of the Algonquianist Conference*, the *Maine Historical Society Quarterly*, *Man in the Northeast* (recently renamed *Northeast Anthropology*), *New England Quarterly*, and *Ethnohistory*, for relevant articles.

6

Diplomacy & War on the Maine Frontier, 1678–1759

DAVID L. GHERE

This chapter presents a diplomatic history of the French and Indian wars in Maine. It skirts the details of the mutual atrocities, recriminations, and massacres that punctuate the history of this tragic period to focus on a more fundamental issue: the sources of friction that perpetuated Indian-white conflict for more than eighty years. Local incidents triggered each of the wars, but larger forces lay behind them: imperial conflicts, cultural barriers, disregard of Indian sovereignty, abuse of the fur trade, incompatible styles of diplomacy, differing land-use strategies. Both the global and the local sources of antagonism are detailed below.

David L. Ghere, like Harald E. L. Prins, interprets this history largely from the Wabanaki perspective. This approach is important for two reasons. First, it shows that a simple "Indians vs. whites" perspective ignores important differences between and within the various groups of Wabanakis. These Indians disagreed among themselves and responded differently to each new series of outside events. Ghere identifies these loosely organized kinship groups by village or location rather than by the tribal labels used in English sources and most histories. Tribal names are only used after 1727 for the Kennebec and Penobscot when the terms more accurately reflect the diplomatic and political reality of those particular Wabanakis. It is important to be aware of these distinctions if we are to understand Maine's Indians as people rather than as generalizations.

Second, a Wabanaki perspective tempers our long-standing assumption that Europeans were destined from the start to control the area. As Prins has already pointed out, the Wabanaki people were active agents of history, even in the face of growing English military power. Negotiating between the shoals of English frontier expansion and French military ambitions, the Wabanaki left their own indelible mark on this period of conflict and European settlement. Again, from the Wabanaki perspective, history unfolds as a balance of local and outside forces.

The outbreak of King Philip's War in 1675 launched a seemingly interminable series of Indian-white conflicts in Maine and across the northeastern frontier. In these tragic times, Maine's Wabanaki, as ethnohistorian Kenneth Morrison recently pointed out, "shared with Europeans a driving need to maintain social order." Crowded by English expansion and drawn by circumstance into the Anglo-French imperial wars, Maine's Wabanaki nevertheless used various strategies—accommodation, diplomacy, reprisals, and war—to defend their sovereignty and their way of life. Although successful for a time, the Wabanaki people found their options disappearing after Dummer's War (1721–27). Weakened, scattered, and debilitated by destruction of their agricultural and foraging bases, Maine's Indians became increasingly less capable of resisting English frontier expansion. Like their English counterparts, the Wabanaki struggled to achieve autonomy and stability in the face of shifting and confusing external events. These efforts are a fundamental part of Maine history.

As the previous chapter demonstrated, diplomatic relations between the English and the Wabanaki people were fragile at best even before King Philip's War. As the English settlements moved eastward, coming in closer contact with the Wabanaki, relations between the two peoples deteriorated. The issues that arose were difficult to settle through normal diplomacy for several reasons. First, even under the best of circumstances, negotiations were strained by the structural and grammatical differences between Wabanaki and European languages. Official communications, such as treaties, conference dialogues, and written correspondence, suffered the distortions of translation. Translators were usually French missionaries or English and French militia officers who added their own interpretations, prejudices, and biases to the documents.

A second cultural difference added to the diplomatic confusion. The English considered written documents such as treaties and land deeds to be absolute legal proof of Anglo-Wabanaki rights and obligations. The Wabanaki, as an oral society, placed little importance on written documents, basing their diplomatic relations primarily on the reality of the existing frontier situation. At conferences, Indian complaints or objections usually drew adamant English demands for strict adherence to the written agreements and little regard for the circumstances that precipitated the problems. Faced with this intransigence, Wabanaki leaders would shift negotiations to other matters needing resolution, a strategy of setting aside especially difficult issues for later discussion that was consistent with the consensus politics of Wabanaki society. The English, however, perceived the shift as a concession to their point of view.

A third obstacle concerned the matter of sovereignty. Despite the reality of Indian military and political independence, neither the French nor the English believed that an "uncivilized" people could be sovereign; native Americans must either be French subjects or English subjects. Bent on forcing allegiance, the English through their treaties usually required Wabanaki submission to the English king; any subsequent failure to maintain this allegiance might be considered treason. Since the Wabanaki had no written language, these treaties were only recorded in English. In order to gain the Indians' acceptance of the treaties, English interpreters often mistranslated treaty provisions, informing the Wabanakis that they were merely exchanging salutes with the English governor and agreeing to peace with him. The Wabanaki would become aware of the discrepancies between the written text and the oral translation that had been given them when they took the documents to French officials or missionaries, whose translations were often influenced by their own biases.

A fourth difficulty was European in origin. Throughout the colonial period the boundary between Acadia and New England was in dispute, with the result that England and France each claimed the area between the Kennebec River and Passamaquoddy Bay. Both powers maintained that the Wabanaki in the region were their subjects and owed them allegiance. Anglo-French tensions or warfare in Europe would prompt colonial governors from both countries to demand the military support of "their" Indians and to threaten destruction or offer protection, depending upon the circumstances. Thus, a war between England and France almost invariably resulted in a new round of warfare on the Maine frontier.

English leaders pursued a variety of strategies to promote order on the Maine frontier. Many, however, were futile and some even counterproductive. During periods of mounting frontier tension, for instance, Massachusetts demanded (or simply took) hostages to guarantee the friendly behavior of the Wabanakis. Ironically, the Indians frequenting colonial settlements, where they could be captured, were generally those individuals already most friendly toward the English. Voluntary hostages surely came from the same group, since failure to offer themselves would tend to discredit their pro-British positions at council meetings. Thus, Massachusetts policy deprived the pro-English factions of some of their best leaders; at the same time, it had little impact on the pro-French factions.

On the other hand, the British gained some influence over the Wabanakis through trade. Private profit had been the motive for the first English trading posts, but in the late seventeenth century Massachusetts discovered the diplomatic importance of trade and began a colony-wide network of official trading posts. Interrupted by periodic warfare, the plan was finally implemented after Dummer's War, in 1727. It achieved limited success by enhancing English influence at the expense of the French, eliminating tensions on the frontier resulting from dishonest English traders, and promoting Wabanaki factions that favored peaceful coexistence. However, the termination of trade during wartime forced some Maine Indians to ally with the French to obtain basic necessities. English officials then had to decide whether to sell supplies to potential adversaries or to refuse to provision the Indians, thereby driving them into the arms of the French. Their decisions in this matter were not, as a rule, particularly astute.

French attempts to influence Wabanaki diplomacy were also unsuccessful. Many Massachusetts leaders (and early historians) believed that French missionaries wielded total control over the Indians and were the primary cause of Wabanaki hostility in Maine. However, in most cases, their diplomatic influence among the Maine Wabanaki was quite limited. The Penobscots, for instance, took the leading role in negotiating an end to Dummer's War, despite strenuous efforts by their priest, Father Etienne Lauverjat, to prolong the combat. During the 1730s and 1740s, no priests resided in the Maine Indian villages, and when permanent missionaries returned in the early 1750s, their influence was so limited that they forged Indian letters in an attempt to insert themselves between the English and the Wabanakis.

Colonial leaders from both countries sought to counter the perceived advantages of their opponent. During the 1720s and 1730s, Massachusetts instituted a policy of subsidizing pastors at their colonial trading posts in an effort to secure diplomatic influence over the local Indians. But since these ministers did not visit the Indian villages or learn their languages, it is not surprising that they had no perceptible effect on the Wabanaki religious orientation or diplomacy. French efforts to counter English trade influence were thwarted by the distance to the Maine villages and the unreliability of French supplies during periods of warfare. Despite several reorganizations of the French trade system and trade commissions paid to some Wabanaki leaders, Indians in Maine continued to trade at the Massachusetts posts.

Both England and France sought influence through diplomatic presents. They adopted various Indian customs of gift-giving, particularly the exchange of ceremonial presents at peace conferences or ambassadorial visits. The French usually provided gifts for a specific purpose, while the British held yearly conferences specifically to deliver annual presents and promote continued peace. Both countries granted commissions and awarded medals to Indian leaders, the French to reward past service and the English to recruit new allies.

Ironically, these gifts, medals, and commissions had little effect on Wabanaki diplomacy. Much to the chagrin of colonial leaders, some Wabanakis accepted commissions in both armies. French provisions dwindled during wartime, when they were most needed, and the English annual distributions proved totally ineffective in preventing attacks or securing allegiance. Anglo-Wabanaki diplomacy was shaped less by trade and gifts than by cultural differences, the irresolvable questions of sovereignty and European rivalry, and, most of all, by English incursions into lands that provided vital subsistence resources for the Indians. These issues created an enormous gulf between Indians and whites and helped to escalate the tensions caused by the eastward thrust of the English settlement frontier.

Early Wars, 1678–1720

The Treaty of Casco (1678), which concluded King Philip's War in Maine, was followed by a decade of uneasy peace. During these years settlers failed to pay the annual quitrents for their land that were promised to the Indians in the 1678 treaty. More important, they repeatedly placed large fishing nets across the Saco River, preventing fish from migrating upriver to the Wabanaki villages, and they allowed their livestock to roam freely, trampling Indian cornfields. Vigorous Wabanaki protests and occasional rumors of imminent Indian raids spread panic among the settlers and often resulted in angry verbal exchanges when Indians visited the settlements. These disputes became so heated that in 1684 the province called out the militia and improved fortifications along the coast.

Events leading up to the so-called King William's War (1689–99) demonstrate the pattern of racial tension and suspicion, indiscriminate mutual retaliation, and external events that precipitated the conflicts in this period. Open hostilities commenced in August 1688, when some Indians, after complaining repeatedly to no avail, killed four or five cows that had overrun their fields near the Saco River. Massachusetts retaliated by seizing twenty peaceful Wabanakis and imprisoning them in Boston. Indians then raided North Yarmouth and the settlements near the mouth of the Kennebec River, taking sufficient prisoners to negotiate an exchange. Edmond Andros, governor of the Dominion of New England, was furious with his subordinates in Massachusetts for needlessly escalating the conflict. Andros was on the verge of restoring peace with the Wabanakis when news arrived that his close friend and fellow Catholic, King James II, had been deposed by the English parliament. James's flight to France prompted fears of a Catholic conspiracy against England, and Massachusetts officials promptly arrested the highly unpopular Andros. Some colonials were convinced that Andros's conciliatory attitude toward the Indians was part of a plot with the French and Wabanakis to destroy the settlements in Maine. Andros was dispatched to England in chains, and negotiations with the Wabanakis ceased.

Growing hostility around Casco Bay and Merrymeeting Bay brought renewed Indian attacks in the summer of 1689, driving the English from the settlements east of Falmouth. After England and France went to war in Europe,

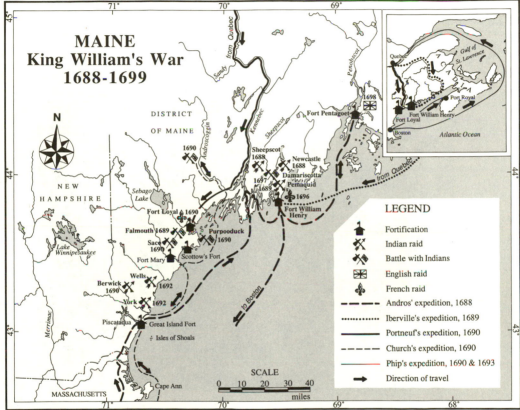

MAINE
King William's War
1688-1699

N

DISTRICT
OF MAINE

NEW
HAMPSHIRE

from Quebec

Sandy

Androscoggin

Kennebec

Sheepscot

Penobscot

Fort Pentagoet

1698

1690

Sheepscot
1688

Newcastle
1688

Damariscotta
Pemaquid

1697
1689

1696

Fort William
Henry

from Quebec

Sebago
Lake

Fort Loyal   1690

Falmouth 1689

Saco
1690

Fort Mary

Purpooduck
1690

Scottow's Fort

Lake
Winnipesaukee

Berwick
1690

Wells

York   1692

1692

Piscataqua

Great Island Fort

Isles of Shoals

to Boston

Merrimac

MASSACHUSETTS

Cape Ann

SCALE

| 0 | 10 | 20 | 30 | 40 |

miles

LEGEND

🏰 Fortification

⚔ Indian raid

⚔⚔ Battle with Indians

✠ English raid

⚜ French raid

– – – Andros' expedition, 1688

·········· Iberville's expedition, 1689

——— Portneuf's expedition, 1690

- - - Church's expedition, 1690

——— Phip's expedition, 1690 & 1693

➡ Direction of travel

Quebec

Gulf of
St. Lawrence

Port Royal

Fort William Henry
Fort Loyal

Boston

Atlantic Ocean

71°   70°   69°   68°

45°

44°

43°

6-1. Sir William Phips (1650/51–1694/95) was Maine's first rags-to-riches success. Born in what is now Woolwich, he became a ship's carpenter, master mariner, and successful treasure hunter. The first American knighted by the king of England, he served as the first royal governor of Massachusetts and led two invasions of Canada. Private collection.

France concluded an alliance with the Wabanaki in Maine, and several large French and Indian expeditions attacked the Maine frontier. Falmouth and Berwick were destroyed in 1690, and by the end of the year the English had abandoned the entire Maine frontier beyond Wells. The English countered by attacking French strongholds at Port Royal and Quebec in 1689. Expeditions led by Mainer Sir William Phips captured the former but failed to take the latter. In 1691, Phips was appointed the first royal governor of Massachusetts.

In the summer of 1692, Massachusetts launched an offensive against the Wabanaki. An expedition led by Benjamin Church built Fort William Henry at Pemaquid, then ranged the lengths of the Kennebec and Penobscot rivers destroying Indian villages and crops. During the previous four years, these Wabanaki had suffered severe food shortages because of the cancellation of the fur trade by Massachusetts and the disruption of their fishing, hunting, and gathering activities by English patrols. Now these problems were compounded by the disruption and destruction caused by Church's expedition and by the refusal of French officers to provide assistance or supplies. Discouraged by these conditions, a group of Wabanaki leaders sought to renew negotiations with the English.

Meeting with Madockawando and Egeremet, two Wabanaki sagamores, Governor Phips hastily drafted a peace treaty, assuming that all Wabanakis would be bound to this decision. The treaty, however, proved unpalatable to even the most ardent Wabanaki peace advocates. It demanded Wabanaki subservience to the British Crown, a confession that the Indians had caused the war, and an admission that the French had been the instigators. French officials meanwhile encouraged the war faction with presents, new promises of military support, and reminders of past English treachery. At the treaty conference, the Wabanakis learned that Madockawando had sold land around the St. Georges River to the English, causing a dramatic shift in sentiment away from the peace faction.

The Wabanakis renewed the war by attacking the area around Durham, New Hampshire, and killing scores of settlers. Hostilities continued sporadically during the next two years, but subsistence problems again prompted the Wabanaki to seek peace. In November 1694, four Wabanaki were killed under a flag of truce at Saco, and three others were taken prisoner a few weeks later in similar circumstances. When the Wabanaki released some of their captives during the following spring, the English refused to reciprocate. Then, in February 1696, several Indians were killed after they had been lured into Fort William Henry to negotiate a settlement. Five months later, a large force of Indians returned to the fort, forced its surrender, and killed the officers responsible for the atrocity. Frontier raids continued for the next two years, but Wabanaki suffering mounted as the militia destroyed their crops and the French failed to deliver supplies.

France and England concluded a peace in Europe in 1697. On the Maine frontier, King William's War continued for another two years, but on January 7, 1699, the major Wabanaki sagamores agreed to a treaty. Since the document

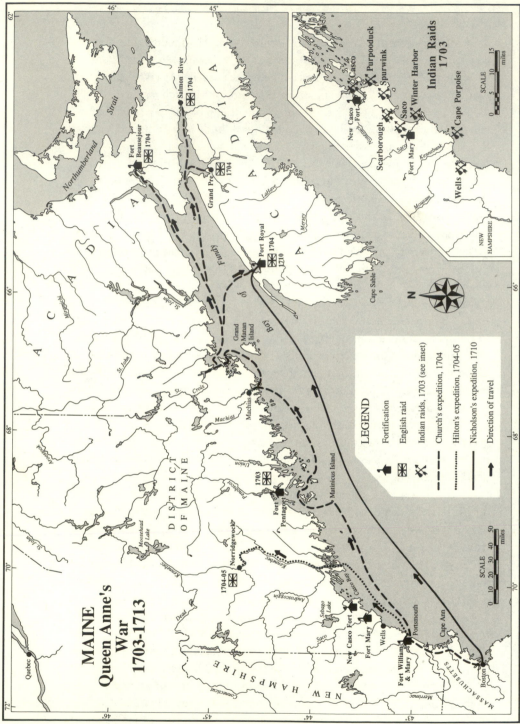

MAINE
Queen Anne's
War
1703-1713

© Richard D. Kelly Jr., 1995.

LEGEND

Fortification
English raid
Indian raids, 1703 (see inset)
Church's expedition, 1704
Hilton's expedition, 1704-05
Nicholson's expedition, 1710
Direction of travel

Indian Raids
1703

New Casco Fort · Casco · Purpooduck · Spurwink · Winter Harbor
Scarborough · Saco · Fort Mary · Cape Porpoise
Wells

NEW HAMPSHIRE

Salmon River 1704
Fort Beausejour 1704
Grand Pre 1704
Port Royal 1704 1710

ACADIA

Fundy
Bay of Fundy

Grand Manan Island
Machias 1703
Matinicus Island

DISTRICT OF MAINE

Quebec

Fort Pentagoet 1703
Norridgewock 1704-05
New Casco Fort
Fort Mary
Wells
Fort William & Mary
Portsmouth
Cape Ann
Boston

MASSACHUSETTS

SCALE
0 10 20 30 40 50 miles

SCALE
0 5 10 15 miles

simply restated Phips's terms, it failed to resolve the disputes that had led to war. Nevertheless, peace renewed the fur trade, allowed the Indians to replant their crops, and permitted the English to resettle around the Saco River and Casco Bay. Despite French efforts to promote distrust, Wabanaki leaders eagerly returned to the trading posts, seeking closer relations.

Nevertheless, English officials insisted that Indian diplomacy was controlled by French priests. When war erupted in Europe again in 1701—a contest known in the American colonies as Queen Anne's War—Massachusetts officials and Maine settlers assumed it was only a matter of time before the Indian raids resumed. Considering the assumptions about French influence and the mutual distrust generated by a decade of warfare, Massachusetts and Wabanaki leaders were surprisingly successful in their efforts to maintain peace. Isolated incidents during 1702 were resolved through negotiation, and the English continued to trade with the Wabanakis, who professed to be neutral. Even a series of Canadian Indian raids near the Kennebec River and a Massachusetts militia raid on Baron St.-Castin's home on Penobscot Bay failed to incite open warfare. Finally, in August 1703, an expedition of approximately five hundred French and Micmac Indians traveling from the St. Lawrence valley devastated the coastal towns and forts from Wells to Falmouth. Two months later, a similar force returned to attack York and Berwick. Although most local Wabanakis showed little interest in the war, Massachusetts leaders were unable to distinguish between the peace and war factions, and they declared war on all Maine Indians on August 18, 1703.

Fearing English attacks on their villages, many Wabanakis moved farther inland and dispersed into family bands. Others accepted French offers of sanctuary by migrating to the St. Lawrence River in 1704. These Indians provided limited military support when the French threatened to withhold supplies, but between 1704 and 1712, the Maine frontier was relatively quiet, aside from two large assaults on the coastal settlements in the summer of 1707. Canadian Indians dramatically increased their attacks on the Maine frontier in 1712, particularly at Wells, Kittery, York, and Berwick. Again, only a few Wabanakis participated in the raids; most of those who migrated to the St. Lawrence region resisted French efforts to recruit them.

In July 1713, directly after the cessation of hostilities in Europe, the Treaty of Portsmouth formally ended Queen Anne's War on the Maine frontier. Anglo-Wabanaki relations remained cool because the Massachusetts legislature proved unable to restrain the actions of individual settlers on the frontier and refused to comply with the trade provisions of the treaty. Nevertheless, settlers rebuilt the Saco River and Casco Bay towns between 1714 and 1716, and after construction of Fort George at Brunswick in 1715, families pushed east into the townships near the mouth of the Kennebec River.

Wabanaki leaders grew concerned over this expansion, since it violated their understanding of the Portsmouth treaty. They requested a conference in 1717, but the angry negotiations only served to increase tensions. Massachusetts Governor Shute repeatedly demanded Wabanaki submission to English sovereignty and recognition of English land claims, while Wabanaki negotiator Wiwurna outlined the Indian understanding of the treaty. In an attempt to inhibit further settlement in the three new towns, a band of Wabanakis killed some cattle and burned crops and buildings in 1720. Massachusetts seized four Wabanaki from the Kennebec region as hostages, demanding compensation for damages, and then refused to release the Indians when payment was delivered.

Dummer's War, 1721–27

During these years, Father Sebastien Rale, a French Jesuit missionary living in the Wabanaki village at Norridgewock, penned numerous letters to English officials, detailing these Indians' complaints and threatening war if their rights were not honored. These letters reinforced the English presumption that Rale was the sole cause of animosity along the Kennebec River. The English also assumed—again wrongly—that Wabanaki hostility in the Penobscot valley was caused by Joseph d'Abbadie, son of Baron St.-Castin and his Wabanaki wife, Pidiwamiska. This conviction inspired the militia to seize d'Abbadie in 1721. The Wabanakis retaliated, taking sixty-five captives, then releasing most of them to carry back an offer to negotiate peace and a prisoner exchange. Massachusetts eventually released d'Abbadie, but before this information reached the Indians, some disgruntled Wabanakis launched an attack on Brunswick. On July 25, Massachusetts declared war on the Wabanakis.

Governor Dummer's War (or Lovewell's, or Rale's war) was a disaster for all the Wabanakis in Maine. The French offered only limited aid, leaving Massachusetts free to focus its full attention on the Wabanakis. Aggressive militia patrolling in western Maine and repeated military expeditions up the Kennebec and Penobscot rivers forced the Wabanaki into more remote interior village sites or into dispersed family bands. The destruction of Wabanaki villages, the disruption of hunting, gathering, and fishing activities, and the constant threat of attack caused great hardship for the Indians. Reduced food supplies, combined with their mounting losses, eventually drove most of Maine's Wabanakis to migrate to the Jesuit missions at St. Francis and Beçancour, near the St. Lawrence River.

Two of the most widely known military incidents in colonial Maine history occurred during Dummer's War. In August 1724, on a day when many Wabanaki had returned to their village at Norridgewock to harvest corn, a militia

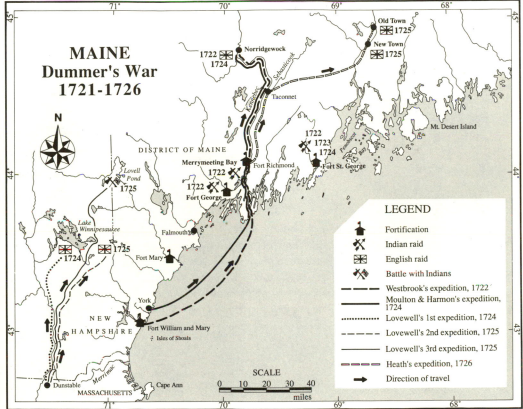

MAINE
Dummer's War
1721-1726

N

DISTRICT OF MAINE

Lovell Pond • 1725

Lake Winnipesaukee

Falmouth

NEW HAMPSHIRE

Fort Mary

York

Fort William and Mary

Isles of Shoals

Dunstable

Merrimac

MASSACHUSETTS

Cape Ann

Old Town ❂ 1725

New Town ❂ 1725

1722 ❂ Norridgewock
1724

Sebasticook

Taconnet

Kennebec

Mt. Desert Island

1722 ⚔
1723
1724 ⚔ Fort St. George

Merrymeeting Bay
1722 ⚔
Fort Richmond

1722 ⚔ 🏰
Fort George

Penobscot Bay

1724 ❂ ❂ 1725

SCALE
0   10   20   30   40
miles

LEGEND

🏰   Fortification

⚔   Indian raid

❂   English raid

⚔   Battle with Indians

— ▪ — ▪ —   Westbrook's expedition, 1722

———————   Moulton & Harmon's expedition, 1724

·················   Lovewell's 1st expedition, 1724

– – – – –   Lovewell's 2nd expedition, 1725

———————   Lovewell's 3rd expedition, 1725

▬ ▬ ▬   Heath's expedition, 1726

➤   Direction of travel

© Richard D. Kelly Jr., 1995.

6-2. The strongbox, chapel bell, and theological handbook which belonged to Father Sebastien Rale (1657–1724), the French Jesuit priest who ministered to the Kennebec Indians at Norridgewock. The strongbox, with a secret drawer in the base, was taken from Rale's house in Norridgewock by Colonel Thomas Westbrook in a raid on the village in 1722. The book was taken after a second attack on August 23, 1724, in which Rale was killed. The bell was hidden by Indians and discovered in 1808. Collections of the Maine Historical Society, Portland.

expedition attacked the village, killing Father Rale and over two dozen Indians. Had the expedition arrived a few days earlier or later, the village would have been abandoned. Massachusetts hailed Rale's death as a sign that the French grip on Wabanaki allegiances had been broken, but in fact the massacre accomplished little along these lines. Rale indeed had considerable influence among some of the Indians at Norridgewock, but he consistently refused to serve French interests in military matters, and in any case, the Wabanaki usually conducted their diplomacy independently of Jesuit admonitions.

The following year, in April, a group of thirty-four scalp hunters led by John Lovewell encountered a large Wabanaki force led by Paugus in the upper Saco River valley. A desperate struggle lasting until nightfall cost the lives of Lovewell,

Paugus, nineteen English scalp hunters, and an equal number of Indians. Volunteer expeditions like this were prompted by the bounties on Indian scalps that Massachusetts established during every war. (The French offered bounties on both scalps and captives to promote raids on English settlements.) This incident was extraordinary, however, for the sustained nature of the battle and the heavy casualties on both sides.

Dummer's War was officially terminated in July 1727 by Dummer's Treaty, signed by representatives from the Wabanaki villages of Norridgewock and Penawabskik in Maine and St. Francis and Beçancour in Canada. The treaty confirmed English rights to all land previously purchased and called upon the Wabanaki to submit to English sovereignty and provide military support against any Indians who broke the peace in the future. However, the implications of the treaty were not clearly spelled out to the Wabanaki. A series of letters and Indian actions over the next several years suggest that English interpreters had again mistranslated the provisions during the negotiations. Wabanaki submission to English rule, for instance, was translated simply as a salute to the Massachusetts governor. Since the governor responded by saluting the Wabanaki leaders, the Indians assumed this indicated equal status and not subjugation. The obligation to provide warrior support was translated as a pledge to attempt to dissuade other Indians from attacking. Finally, Massachusetts repeatedly misled the Wabanakis concerning the extent of English land claims and ignored Wabanaki requests for a definitive boundary.

Dummer's War marked a general shift in Wabanaki population to the north and east as well as some alteration in social organization. Internal factionalism, vulnerability to attack, and encroaching English settlements prompted various responses from the Wabanaki. Many chose to remain at the refugee villages of St. Francis and Beçancour rather than return to their homeland. Most Wabanaki sites near the Maine coast were abandoned, as their inhabitants merged into villages farther upriver or to the east. Those Wabanaki residing in the Kennebec and Penobscot river valleys consolidated into separate tribes with their principal villages, Norridgewock and Penawabskik respectively, at upriver locations. In contrast, Wabanakis inhabiting the Saco, Presumpscot, and Androscoggin river valleys chose to live in small villages and family band camps from this point onward.

These developments dramatically altered the military and diplomatic situation on the Maine frontier. First, it meant that the locus of Wabanaki power shifted appreciably. During the fifty years preceding Dummer's War, the Indians along the Kennebec River had played the leading role in warfare and diplomacy; thereafter, the Penobscots assumed leadership, a position they would hold for the next fifty years. Second, the Wabanaki in western Maine ceased negotiating and fighting in concert, becoming relatively insignificant in frontier relations. Concurrently, the refugee villages at St. Francis and Beçancour emerged as Wabanaki diplomatic and military powers. The third and most important change was the precipitous decline in Wabanaki military power after Dummer's War. During the first three Anglo-Wabanaki wars, united Wabanaki military power had dominated the Maine frontier. After Dummer's War the Wabanakis, weakened and scattered by long conflict and deprivation, were usually able to mount only harassment attacks against isolated cabins. The few major assaults that did occur were launched from the St. Lawrence or St. John river valleys with French support.

Dummer's Treaty was followed by seventeen years of peace, during which English settlement expanded with the establishment of seven new towns. Most were in areas that the Indians recognized as English territory, but the St. Georges River area was an exception. Here, English officials eventually responded to Penobscot protests by relocating the offending settlers. Similar complaints by Wabanaki in southwestern Maine were ignored because of their military weakness. The new town of Gorham was so close to Wabanaki camps that children of the Indians and settlers often played together in the 1730s and early 1740s.

Most disputes during this period concerned Wabanaki subsistence needs or the destruction of settlers' livestock. Between 1727 and 1739, Wabanakis living along the Saco and Presumpscot rivers complained repeatedly that settlers' nets kept fish from ascending the rivers. Historians have interpreted sporadic depredations on settlers' livestock as outbreaks of Wabanaki hostility or efforts to scare settlers off the land, but the timing and some documentary evidence suggest that hunger prompted some of these killings. Such disputes were generally settled at annual conferences at which the tribes compensated the settlers with furs.

Final Conflicts, 1744–63

Frontier tensions increased after the outbreak of another Anglo-French war in Europe in March 1744. During the following months, settlers reported the destruction of property, crops, and livestock in the Kennebec River area and Wabanaki involvement in raids in Nova Scotia, but both the Kennebecs and Penobscots maintained their innocence. The two tribes rejected a Massachusetts demand that they provide military support against the Canadian Indians, but they willingly gave information about Indian activities in the area and sought to dissuade other Indians from attacking. In October 1744, a group of English scalp hunters killed one Penobscot and wounded several others. Massachusetts sent its condolences to the tribe, but at the same time reiterated its

A view of the Landing the New England Forces in ye Expedition against CAPE BRETON, 1745.

When ye on Cape of Cape de Verd, this town and Colony of LOUISBOURG on the important Territories bound belonging were secured to the British Conquerors. The large & Adams Commodore Warren, since made Knight of the Bath &c, obtained of ye White commanded ye British Squadron in this famous Expedition. The Hon Will.m Pepperell Esq. (since Knighted) served a Volunteer Commanded the New England Men who bravely offer'd their services and went as private Soldiers in this Expedition but very glorious & the prey.

6-3. John Brook's engraving called *A View of the Landing of the New England Forces in ye Expedition against Cape Breton, 1745,* depicts the military forces that took the great French bastian of Louisbourg. The troops were led by William Pepperell (1696–1759) of Kittery Point and Samuel Waldo of Boston and Falmouth. For this astonishing triumph of provincial arms, Pepperell was made America's first baronet. Courtesy of Colonial Williamsburg Foundation, Williamsburg, Virginia.

demand for warrior support. Diplomacy continued to deteriorate until July 1745, when Canadian Indians attacked Pemaquid and Fort St. Georges. Despite minimal Penobscot and Kennebec participation, these raids prompted Massachusetts to declare war on the Kennebec and Penobscot Wabanaki in August 1745, seventeen months after the start of the European war known in the colonies as King George's War (1744–48). Colonial forces again attacked French strongholds, this time the fortress of Louisbourg on Cape Breton Island. Sir William Pepperrell of Kittery led the militia, one-third of whom were from Maine, in a successful attack on the French base.

This fifth Anglo-Wabanaki war, again touched off by events in Europe, forced difficult choices on the Maine Wabanaki. Two family bands living along the upper Saco River chose to provide warriors for the British and were transported to the Boston area. The Wabanaki inhabiting the upper Presumpscot valley (including about twenty-five warriors) divided, with some migrating to the Canadian missions and others perhaps withdrawing upriver into the White Mountains. A majority of the Penobscots moved upriver to more secure locations, but about a third of the tribe migrated to the Quebec City area. Presumably, the Wabanaki on the Kennebec and Androscoggin rivers had similar factional divisions between emigrants and those who chose to remain in the homelands.

Wabanaki involvement in this war varied widely. Many of the migrants to Canada enlisted as auxiliaries in French campaigns in Acadia (1746–48) and around Lake Champlain (1747). They also accompanied Canadian Indians in a number of raids on the Maine frontier. Numerous random incidents involving the destruction of settlers' property or livestock were presumably the work of those Wabanakis who remained in their homelands. These Indians experienced acute food shortages during the war, and references to mutilated cattle and warriors carrying quarters of beef indicate that hunger may have motivated some incidents. Food shortages apparently drove the remaining Penobscots out of the river valley in 1747–48, one group joining the earlier migrants in Canada, and the rest moving east to the St. John valley.

The Treaty of Falmouth concluded the fifth Anglo-Wabanaki war in October 1749, a full year after King George's War had ended. This agreement, a simple restatement of Dummer's Treaty, was again mistranslated to gain Wabanaki acceptance, but the following two years brought renewed strife along the frontier. A party of Kennebec and St. Francis Indians returning from the peace conference were attacked near Wiscasset, and one of the Indians was killed. The murderers were arrested and held for trial, but after numerous delays they were either acquitted or released from custody. Exasperated by these developments, some Kennebecs and Penobscots joined about a hundred Canadian Wabanakis

6-4. Fort Halifax was built in 1754 at Winslow by the Commonwealth of Massachusetts on a site selected by Governor William Shirley. It was named in honor of the Earl of Halifax, then British Secretary of State. Only this blockhouse survives. Collections of the Maine Historical Society, Portland.

to attack Fort Richmond and the surrounding settlements on the Kennebec River in September 1750. The English avoided disaster because other Kennebecs, fulfilling their understanding of their treaty commitments, warned the fort two days before the attack. The Kennebec and Penobscot Wabanaki continued to warn settlers of impending Canadian Wabanaki raids through the following summer. The conciliatory factions of these two tribes mediated an end to the warfare in 1751, and in 1752 all the Wabanaki tribes reconfirmed Dummer's Treaty. Again, however, the treaty text was mistranslated, and the English commissioners ignored all discussion of lands and boundaries. The conference ended with the Kennebecs protesting Frankfort, a new settlement north of Fort Richmond, which violated the Wabanaki understanding of Dummer's Treaty. The following year, Massachusetts officials permitted a blockhouse to be built at Frankfort, despite repeated protests, and finally revealed English ownership of land fifty-five miles upriver from Fort Richmond.

Frontier tension escalated in the months following this revelation. Threats and accusations were exchanged whenever Kennebec or Canadian Wabanakis visited frontier settlements. Heated confrontations led to the murder of two Canadian Wabanakis in late 1753 and two more in March 1754. Kennebecs again divided, some migrating to the Canadian missions and others threatening the settlers with exaggerated claims of French support. In January 1754, Massachusetts received three separate reports that the French had built a fort at the head of the Kennebec River. Acting on the basis of these false reports and on inferences from French behavior elsewhere, Governor Shirley launched a military expedition to eliminate the French installation and construct an English fort at Taconic Falls, thirty-seven miles above Fort Richmond. In early July the force of eight hundred militia arrived at the site, near present-day Winslow, but failed to find any evidence of French activity. Nevertheless, by October Fort Halifax had been constructed and garrisoned.

These events drastically altered the Wabanakis' situation. The new fort posed a direct threat to the Kennebec village at Norridgewock, and it blocked the Penobscots' route to Canada along the Sebasticook River. Uneasy about the new English garrison standing between the Penobscot village and French sanctuary, some Penobscot families migrated to the Canadian missions, although most remained in Maine. The Kennebecs, on the other hand, found themselves in an untenable situation, which resulted in the gradual disintegration of the tribe. The more antagonistic family bands migrated separately to the Canadian missions, while those seeking to remain neutral joined the Penobscots. The remaining Norridgewock community dwindled to nothing.

Hostilities commenced on October 30, 1754, when a party of Kennebecs and Canadian Wabanakis launched an unsuccessful attack on Fort Halifax. Massachusetts, in turn, demanded Penobscot warrior support. The Penobscots, hoping for peace, responded with a series of letters outlining their understanding of their treaty commitments. Massachusetts officials tacitly conceded by dropping their demands and praising the tribe's adherence to the treaty. Canadian Wabanaki warriors resumed hostilities in April 1755, and a series of early June raids in the St. Georges area caused many settlers to suspect Penobscot participation. As a result, Governor Shirley renewed his demand for Penobscot warrior support.

Following a conference at Fort St. Georges in late June, local militia officers seized the Penobscot negotiators and pressed their demand for warrior support. Although the Penobscots agreed to English terms, this forced alliance was shattered five days later when a band of scalp hunters killed fourteen Penobscot leaders at nearby Owls Head. Massachusetts officials sought to remedy the situation by expressing condolences, a release of hostages, distribution of presents, and the temporary withdrawal of the demand for warrior support. Tempers cooled over the next two months, but diplomacy was again interrupted by a Canadian Wabanaki attack near St. Georges. The Penobscots, fearing reprisals, fled the area, and this was interpreted by Massachusetts officials as confirmation of the tribe's involvement. War was declared on November 1, 1755.

This sixth and final Anglo-Wabanaki war became part of a general frontier struggle known as the French and Indian War (1754–60). During this conflict the Penobscots divided into three factions: one group migrated to Canada to join French expeditions near Lake Champlain and on the Maine frontier; another moved to the relative safety of the St. John valley; and a third withdrew up the Penobscot River, periodically returning to attempt peace talks. Frontier raids were sporadic and relatively ineffective throughout most of the war and decreased sharply after 1757. The only major expedition against the Maine settlements occurred in August 1758, when 50 Canadian militia and over 250 Penobscots and Maliseets attacked Fort St. Georges. The fort had been forewarned, however, and after several days of an ineffective siege, the warriors broke into small bands and raided throughout the area over the following month. These were the last Indian attacks on the Maine frontier, and in February 1759 Penobscot representatives renewed their peace efforts.

In May 1759, Governor Thomas Pownall led a force of four hundred militia up the Penobscot River seeking to humble the Penobscots and lay English claim to the region east of Fort St. Georges. Before reaching the abandoned Penobscot village at Penawabskik, near modern Old Town, the expedition returned to the mouth of the Penobscot and built Fort Pownall at present-day Stockton Springs. Even though Pownall failed to encounter a single hostile Indian, he returned to Boston proclaiming a glorious victory and the acquisition of all Penobscot lands through the "right of conquest." The same year, English forces defeated the French at Quebec, finally ending the long rivalry for control of North America. Peaceful relations on the Maine frontier were reestablished at a conference at Fort Pownall in 1762, although no treaty was actually signed.

During the next few years the various Penobscot family bands reoccupied Penawabskik and reunited into a tribe. Some Kennebec family bands returned to the area near Norridgewock, but they never formed a tribal group. Other Wabanaki returned to their homes in western Maine, but continued to live in separate small villages or family band camps, as they had prior to the war. Peace brought an explosion of white settlement eastward along the coast and up the river valleys, a trend the Wabanaki were powerless to prevent or direct.

This series of six Anglo-Wabanaki wars demonstrates the steady English encroachment upon Indian lands and subsistence resources and the military suppression of Indian protest. But through all this, English and French failed

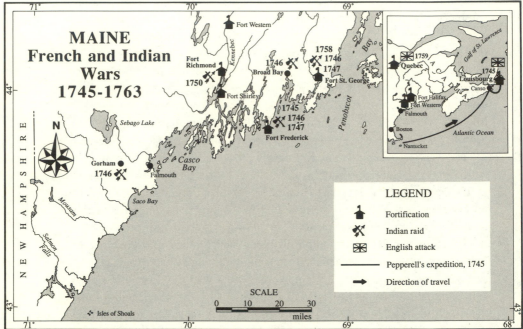

MAINE
French and Indian
Wars
1745-1763

NEW HAMPSHIRE

Fort Western

Fort
Richmond

1750

Fort Shirley

1746
Broad Bay

1758
1746
1747
Fort St. George

1745
1746
1747
Fort Frederick

Sebago Lake

N

Gorham
1746

Falmouth

Casco
Bay

Saco Bay

Kennebec

Penobscot Bay

Isles of Shoals

Gulf of St. Lawrence

1759
Quebec

1745
Louisbourg
Canso

Fort Halifax
Fort Western
Falmouth

Boston

Nantucket

Atlantic Ocean

LEGEND

Fortification

Indian raid

English attack

Pepperell's expedition, 1745

Direction of travel

SCALE

0   10   20   30

miles

© Richard D. Kelly Jr., 1995.

almost completely to dominate the Wabanakis in Maine. Caught between hostile forces on the St. Lawrence to the north and in Massachusetts and the Maine coast to the south, the Wabanaki chose their own path. Despite the influence of missionaries, the dispensing of gifts, the barrage of threats, the systematic mistranslation of treaty commitments, and the seizure of hostages, the Indians exhibited remarkable independence in their actions. Alone among these endeavors, trade policy offered the English some leverage, yet here again much of the impact was counterproductive.

English and French attempts to influence the Wabanakis were ineffective because they failed to respond to the Indians' most fundamental concerns: threats to their autonomy and encroachments on their land. Wabanaki diplomatic and military decisions were governed not by English or French maneuvering, but by these two overriding concerns. Colonial diplomacy also failed because it did not address the profound differences between European social and political perceptions and those of the Wabanaki. Colonial leaders saw the Indian villages as rigid tribal units, despite considerable evidence to the contrary. Indian leaders, they assumed, possessed the authority to sell Wabanaki lands and commit their people to diplomatic agreements. During periods of conflict, an incident involving one village or faction would usually result in declarations of war against all Wabanakis. Since colonial leaders were usually unable to identify and punish individual warriors, their only alternatives were to ignore the transgression or hold the entire group or village responsible. The first was unacceptable; the second was a prelude to war.

Early Maine historians shared this ethnocentric blindness, assuming that the Wabanaki were always organized as tribes and that a tribal village was an Indian's "official" residence. They perpetuated colonial misconceptions by failing to distinguish between villages, tribes, or factions and by using general terms, such as "eastern" Indians, to identify a small party of raiding warriors. Only recently have historians come to realize that the Indian wars, from the perspective of the Indians, involved historical choices at least as complex as those facing European-Americans.

One aspect of this older ethnocentric perspective was the disappearance from the history of the Wabanaki "tribes" in western Maine. When these Indians stopped appearing at major conferences and failed to reoccupy their old village sites after Dummer's War, historians assumed that they had permanently relocated to the Jesuit missions and had passed from Maine history proper. Actually, hundreds of Wabanaki, erroneously identified as wandering members of the Canadian St. Francis tribe, continued to inhabit western Maine in family band camps or small villages. Like the Penobscot and Passamaquoddy Indians in their villages in eastern Maine, these Wabanakis in the western part of the state continued to occupy a place in Maine history.

For Further Reading:

For a discussion of primary sources for the period of warfare between the Wabanaki and English, see chapter 5. In addition to the secondary sources cited in chapter 5, the interested reader might consult James Axtell, *The European and the Indian* (New York, 1981) and his *The Invasion Within* (New York, 1985) for a general view of Indian-white relations. Emerson W. Baker's Ph.D. dissertation, "Trouble to the Eastward: The Failure of Anglo-Indian Relations in Early Maine" (College of William and Mary, 1986), is essential to understanding this early period in Maine, as is Kenneth M. Morrison's *The Embattled Northeast* (Berkeley, California, 1984), and Colin Calloway's *The Abenaki* (New York, 1989). For a broader understanding of the wars in the context of colonial northern New England, see Charles E. Clark, *The Eastern Frontier* (New York, 1970); Douglas E. Leach, *The Northern Colonial Frontier, 1607–1763* (New York, 1966); Neal Salisbury, *Manitou and Providence* (New York, 1982); John G. Reid, *Acadia, Maine, and New Scotland: Marginal Colonies in the Seventeenth Century* (Toronto, 1981); or Alden Vaughn, *New England Frontier: Puritans and Indians, 1620–1675* (New York, 1979). The Maine Indian Program's *The Wabanakis of Maine and the Maritimes* (Bath, 1989) contains a wealth of teaching materials on the Wabanaki from the precontact period to the present. In addition, numerous articles in the *New England Quarterly* deal with Indian-white relations.

7

Maine in the American Revolution,
1763–1787

JAMES S. LEAMON

As we have seen, Maine's Wabanaki reacted to the events of the seventeenth and eighteenth centuries in diverse ways. Anglo society too was growing more diversified in late colonial Maine. Historian James Leamon is interested in how people formed themselves into occupational, social, and regional groups, and how these classes related to each other within the framework of momentous events such as the American Revolution. Indeed, in the formative period, Maine's increasingly complex society of merchants, clergy, commercial and frontier farmers, artisans, fishermen, and loggers progressively adopted differing outlooks on politics, religion, and society in general. Thus, Maine's inhabitants reacted to the movement for independence in different ways.

The themes that characterized colonial Maine history—internal conflict and imperial domination, local initiatives and outside forces, stability and disruption—culminate in this study of Maine during the American Revolution. But added to these themes is an overlay of social tension that could only surface once Maine had developed beyond the point of a subsistence frontier society.

Each of the American colonies participated in the events of the American Revolution, but each entered the fray under a distinct set of circumstances. Maine, like the other colonies, was subject to English rule, for instance, but the "District" was also tied to Massachusetts culturally, economically, and administratively. A colony of a colony, Maine was an undeveloped region carved up for exploitation by Massachusetts proprietors and merchants. Thus Maine's bid for independence was channeled in two directions: primarily against British imperial authority, but also against merchant control exerted from the coastal cities of Massachusetts and to a lesser extent from those of coastal southern Maine.

The war years in Maine were also characterized by local social tensions. Everywhere in the American colonies, the forces unleashed by revolution threatened the compact that bound social groups together. Common folk, who hoped to push the revolution to more radical conclusions, challenged elite leadership throughout the colonies. In Maine, these social tensions took on a geographical dimension; coastal towns like Falmouth (present-day Portland), dominated by relatively wealthy merchant elites, found themselves increasingly at odds with those on the frontier. Insular, impoverished, with little to lose from British reprisals, the backwoods and eastern coastal towns developed a different outlook on events leading up to the Revolution. Tension between these two sections and classes was an important part of Maine's Revolutionary War history.

A third set of circumstances distinguished Maine's experience in the Revolution. As a maritime territory situated on the boundary between the loyalist and rebel colonies, Maine was extremely vulnerable. British command of the Gulf of Maine, particularly after the occupation of Castine, left the eastern sections virtually at the mercy of this enemy power. Privateers and British warships cut off eastern Maine's all-important seaborne commerce with western towns, causing extreme suffering during the final years of the conflict. Caught in the swirl of larger events, responding with desperately inadequate resources to circumstances beyond their control, the eastern coastal towns present a culminating example of Maine bent to the hurricane force of outside events.

Social Groups in Late Colonial Maine

The conclusion of the Indian wars in 1763 brought swarms of settlers from older Massachusetts towns into York, Cumberland, and Lincoln counties, swelling Maine's population from 23,000 in 1765 to 47,000 by 1775. During the war-torn early 1700s, only 21 townships had been established in Maine, but between 1750 and 1775, no less than 120 more were settled. With France expelled from Canada and Spain from Florida at the end of the French and Indian War, American colonists could look forward to a future of peace, prosperity, and military might. Who then could have anticipated that in a dozen short years this vision would dissolve in rebellion, revolution, and then independence for the thirteen American colonies?

Maine during these years was a colony of a colony. Under the old Massachusetts charter of 1691, the Crown had legalized the Bay Colony's absorption of Maine, and over the course of the next half century politically prominent merchants used their influence to obtain large tracts of land from the provincial government. In 1714, for instance, several prominent Massachusetts men obtained the charter to the Pejepscot Patent, a tract of land granted by the old Council for New England back in 1632, in which they promoted the settlement of Brunswick, Topsham, North Yarmouth, and other towns along the lower

7-1. The permanent settlement of Machias began in 1763 when a group of settlers from Scarborough began to cut hay in the marshes. *A Sketch of Mechios Mills,* by Joseph F. W. Des Barres (published in 1777), is probably the earliest view of a Maine sawmill, the first of which had been built in York or South Berwick in 1634. Collections of the Maine Historical Society, Portland.

Androscoggin River. In 1730, Samuel Waldo was granted the Muscongus Patent, comprising what later became Knox and Waldo counties, while the heirs of the Clarke and Lake Company controlled the lower Kennebec.

The most prominent of these speculators were the Kennebeck Proprietors, who included among their shareholders leading Boston merchants such as Thomas Hancock, William and James Bowdoin, James Pitts, Dr. Silvester Gardiner, and a succession of royal governors of Massachusetts. In 1753, the proprietors assumed control of the old Plymouth Patent, a tract extending along the Kennebec from Merrymeeting Bay to Norridgewock and including territory fifteen miles on either side. The company claimed some three thousand square miles along the river, and proprietors James Bowdoin, Benjamin Hallowell, and Silvester Gardiner lent their names to towns founded under the auspices of the company.

At times even Maine towns gave birth to new settlements. In 1763, a group from Scarborough sailed down east and established a community at Machias. So vague was the jurisdiction over the region that the new settlers applied to both Nova Scotia and Massachusetts for title. By 1776, Machias numbered over 600 inhabitants and was the nucleus for several other minute settlements in the region, including Jonesborough, Gouldsborough, and a town named simply Number Four. To the south and west, settlements were more numerous and populous. In 1775, Georgetown, at the mouth of the Kennebec, had 1,700 inhabitants, while Pownalborough, farther up the river, had over 1,400. Falmouth was Maine's largest town, with 3,800 residents, but the center of Maine's population, as today, was defined by the well-established seventeenth-century towns of Kittery, York, Berwick, and Wells, each of which had between 2,500 and 3,300 inhabitants.

Each of these towns supported some combination of farming, fishing, and lumbering. Mainers exported vast quantities of building timber, shingles, clapboards, barrel staves, and firewood to Boston, New York, and Philadelphia. To England went naval timber, masts, and spars from the ports of Falmouth, Georgetown, and Wiscasset. Maine fishermen, with the French threat gone, were beginning to explore farther into the rich fishing grounds of the Gulf of Maine and the Newfoundland coast.

In Maine's newer eastern communities, the exhausting and time-consuming work of fishing and lumbering left little time for agriculture. These towns depended on imported food, which they paid for by exporting fish and lumber. Older communities in southwestern Maine enjoyed more diversified economies. While they too engaged in fishing and lumbering, they also supplied their own needs for grain and livestock and in some cases even exported some agricultural produce to Nova Scotia, Boston, and the Caribbean.

For each of these port towns or backwoods communities, Boston was the mart from which came money and credit for their underdeveloped economies. Here again Maine was a colony of a colony. Often, Boston merchants, individually or in their corporate capacity as land companies, financed the initial expense of transporting settlers to their new locations or underwrote the first saw- and grist-mills. Boston credit, provisions, and shipping kept the struggling communities alive and in touch with the outside world. From Boston, the Jones family—Ichabod, John Coffin, and Stephen—helped to found and maintain Machias, Jonesborough, and Jonesport. With Francis Shaw and Robert Gould, they established and supplied Gouldsborough as well. Nathan Phillips provided essential services to settlers on the Penobscot River, while Dr. Silvester Gardiner did the same on the Kennebeck Company lands. In southern Maine towns, resident merchants like Enoch Freeman in Falmouth,

Richard King in Scarborough, and Jonathan Sayward in York provided credit and shipping, but they in turn were tied by a delicate web of credit to merchants in Boston, who likewise turned to wholesale merchants in England for credit and goods.

Town development brought a bewildering diversity of occupations. In the more established commercial centers, merchants, doctors, lawyers, and the Congregational clergy formed the apex of a social pyramid. Their dwellings, clothes, education, style of life, and public responsibilities set them off from the rest of society. So too did the fact that this local elite frequently owned black slaves—a mark of status as much as a means of labor. Beneath the "better sort" extended a hierarchy of citizens of modest but independent means—smaller merchants, shopkeepers, artisans, fishermen, and farmers. Toward the bottom of the scale, usually without taxable property, were sailors and laborers associated with work on the docks, in shipyards, or on the farms. In the newer settlements, this social pyramid was truncated; merchants and professionals were scarce, while a large proportion of the population shared an equality of poverty and hardship.

Although contrasts in the distribution of property and social prestige could produce tensions among individuals and between towns and even geographical sections, the social fabric held together remarkably well in this frontier region. For one thing, inequalities were not static; many of Maine's poor could reasonably hope for improved status with time and maturity. Until the Revolution, at least, the promise of the future helped to mitigate the frustrations of the present.

Inequalities were accepted secondly because the colonial world was a deferential society, wherein the elite expected—and were expected—to lead. Both church and state upheld this traditional concept. Massachusetts law dictated that each incorporated town support an orthodox church and minister. In practice, this meant a Congregational Church whose university-trained preacher placed the events of ordinary life in the hierarchical perspective of Calvinist doctrine. By word and example, these preachers expounded the ideal Christian life which, in addition to love and charity, encompassed the values needed to restrain sinful people: sobriety, industry, thrift, honesty, and obedience. The church could count on the power of government to help protect a virtuous society against those who might disrupt it. The provincial court system extended from the Supreme Judicial Court, through intermediary civil and criminal courts, down to individual justices of the peace. All held royal commissions. Men of probity and property, chosen as judges and justices by the governor from the local elite, often enforced the very laws they themselves had helped to draft in a different capacity as representatives to the General Court.

7-2. African Americans have made up a small but vital element of Maine's population from colonial times. This painting is reputed to be a likeness of Phyllis, the mulatto servant who accompanied Elizabeth Wendell to Falmouth in 1766. Elizabeth married the Rev. Thomas Smith, who was a slave-holder. A number of freedmen and slaves served in the Revolution, but not until the Quock Walker case of 1783 was the hated institution abolished in Massachusetts. Photograph by David Bohl. Courtesy of the Society for the Preservation of New England Antiquities, Boston.

Each incorporated town in Massachusetts had the right and obligation to send a representative to the General Court, or legislative assembly. All towns cherished the principle, but as in Maine, many were poor, isolated, and so immersed in local concerns that they preferred to pay a small fine for failing to send a delegate. On the eve of the Revolution, perhaps 30 to 40 percent of eligible towns in Massachusetts failed to send delegates. In the assembly of 1770, Maine's total representation was but six from a total of twenty-seven eligible towns. The few Maine towns that did send representatives were generally coastal commercial communities, whose delegates aligned themselves with other coastal and commercial representatives, supporting legislation and taxation that favored commercial interests and discriminated against farmers throughout the province.

Those whose interests were ignored by the established institutions of government had only one recourse. Historians have recently pointed out that in the eighteenth century an urban mob, riot, or "crowd action" constituted a semi-legitimate means of social protest. Frequently, a community crisis arose for which there was no other remedy: the exportation of grain during time of local scarcity, a royal navy press gang, the existence of a house of ill-fame, or the establishment of a hospital, or "pest house," for victims of small pox which aroused local hostility. Whether in London, in Boston, or in Maine, citizens expressed public displeasure by harassing the individuals and destroying the property that symbolized their grievances. Even the elite occasionally joined in such crowd actions, although they were seldom comfortable about it. Crowds were useful if kept in control, but they were dangerously unpredictable; they remained "legitimate" only as long as they served the community interests—as defined by the elite.

Chafing under the British Yoke, 1763–75

Mobs were hardly a major concern in 1763 when the British triumphed over their traditional foes, the French, the Spanish, and their Indian allies. As British citizens, Americans too gloried in the empire's strength. A flourishing trade within a rich, expanding empire and a population doubling every twenty-five years reflected the dynamic quality of American society. To be sure, the British empire had a darker side. British merchants and officials envisioned the American provinces as perpetual consumers of British manufactures and producers of forest or agricultural products for England or for the sugar-producing islands in the Caribbean. It was a static concept that left little room for American economic or political growth. After the French and Indian War, a general depression added to the tensions inherent in this colonial system.

Settlers in Maine experienced their own particular frustrations with the British government. As a means of stabilizing the strategic supply of white pine masts cut in Maine and New Hampshire for the royal navy, the British Admiralty encouraged monopoly control over this lucrative trade by a few wealthy and politically connected colonial merchants. Felling and hauling or rafting these great pines took considerable planning, and these great merchants had the resources to conduct the masting operations on a large scale. As Maine's trade in masts and smaller wood products increased in the eighteenth century, it brought tensions between frontier settlers and the commission merchants who controlled the export trade in masts and the return trade in essential English manufactured items. These tensions extended to the British agents who enforced imperial regulations regarding the white pine timber. In general however, these were minor annoyances. For most Americans, including those in Maine, the British empire meant protection, prosperity, and liberty.

After 1765, the benefits of empire began to fade as Britain introduced new measures designed to tighten imperial regulation. The cost of defending and administering the newly won territory west of the Appalachians placed new burdens on the debt-ridden British government. Parliament quite naturally felt the Americans should pay at least a share of this cost. The result was the Stamp Act, which initiated an uproar in America over taxation and representation. Although Parliament repealed the obnoxious act, it passed the so-called Townshend Program, which resurrected the taxation problem and threatened the very existence of the provincial assemblies. By the time Parliament repealed most of the taxes associated with the Townshend Program in 1770, the damage had been done. Bostonians had clashed with British troops; blood had been shed, and Americans had been sensitized to expect the worst from a potentially despotic Parliament.

In 1773, Parliament removed most of the duties on East India Company tea imported to America. But since the tea still carried a small tax left from the old Townshend Program, radical leaders felt Americans were being tempted into drinking away their constitutional scruples against Parliamentary taxation. When ships carrying the tea reached Boston, a crowd thinly disguised as Indians threw the cargo into the harbor. Parliament's furious response, called the Coercive Acts, included closing Boston harbor and strengthening royal prerogatives on both the provincial and local levels. Massachusetts colonists retaliated by nullifying the royal provincial government and inaugurating their own Provincial Congress, county conventions, committees of correspondence and safety, and town meetings. The inevitable clash occurred on April 19, 1775, when British troops marched out from Boston to confiscate military supplies which the Provincial Congress was accumulating at Concord. The Revolutionary War had begun.

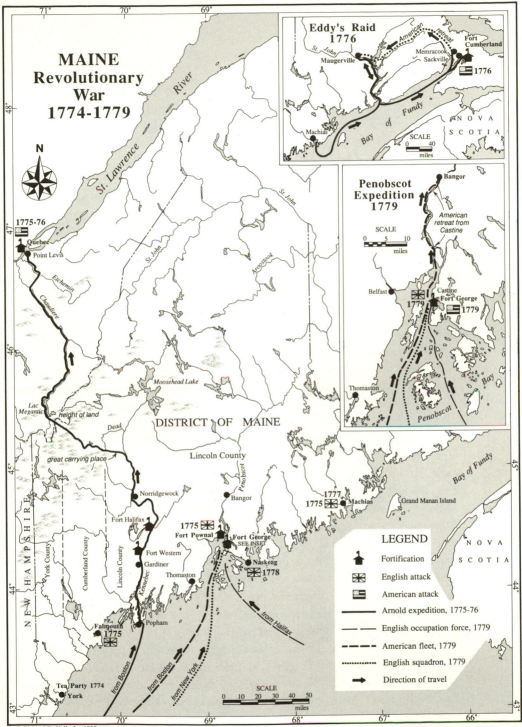

MAINE
Revolutionary
War
1774-1779

N

1775-76

Quebec
Point Levis

Chaudiere

Eichemin

St. Lawrence River

St. John

St. John

Aroostook

Lac
Megantic

height of land

Dead

Moosehead Lake

great carrying place

Norridgewock

Fort Halifax

DISTRICT OF MAINE

Lincoln County

Bangor

1777
1775 ⊞ Machias

Grand Manan Island

NEW HAMPSHIRE

York County

Cumberland County

Lincoln County

Fort Western
Gardiner

Kennebec

Penobscot

1775 ⊞ Fort Pownal

Fort George
SEE INSET

Naskeag
⊞ 1778

Thomaston

Falmouth
1775 ⊞

Popham

Tea Party 1774
York

from Boston

from Boston

from New York

from Halifax

Bay of Fundy

NOVA
SCOTIA

Eddy's Raid
1776

St. John

Maugerville

American retreat

Memracook
Sackville

Fort
Cumberland

1776

Machias

Bay of Fundy

NOVA
SCOTIA

SCALE
0   40
miles

Penobscot
Expedition
1779

Bangor

American retreat from Castine

SCALE
0   5   10
miles

Belfast

Castine
Fort George
1779 ⊞   ⊞ 1779

Thomaston

Penobscot

Bay

LEGEND

1	Fortification
⊞	English attack
⊞	American attack
——	Arnold expedition, 1775-76
– –	English occupation force, 1779
— —	American fleet, 1779
······	English squadron, 1779
→	Direction of travel

NOVA
SCOTIA

SCALE
0 10 20 30 40 50
miles

© Richard D. Kelly Jr., 1995.

Falmouth and Machias, 1775

Initially, the towns of Maine stood on the periphery of this tempest. As early as 1765–66, however, rioters in Falmouth publicly protested the Stamp Act, "rescued" a cargo of sugar from British customs officers, and prevented a British customs vessel from capturing several runaway seamen. The town also voted to support the nonimportation agreements, a series of colonial boycotts against British goods. The rising tempo of protest and reprisal stimulated the revolutionary ardor of Maine's inland towns as well. With less personal wealth or town property to protect, and insulated from reprisal from British ships, towns like Gorham, Brunswick, and Pownalborough responded enthusiastically to invitations from the Boston Committee of Correspondence to enforce the nonimportation agreements. Coastal towns, on the other hand, lay exposed to British sea power, and their merchants had grown wealthy as intermediaries in the lucrative exchange of British goods. When Falmouth leaders appeared reluctant to comply with the boycotts in 1773, an anonymous group known only as "Thomas Tarbucket, Peter Pitch, Abraham Wildfowl, Benjamin Brush, Oliver Scarecrow, and Henry Hand-Cart" ominously informed the ranks of genteel society that the boycott would indeed be enforced on everyone equally, be they "Great or Small, Rich or Poor."

By 1774, leadership in the resistance to Britain had passed from Falmouth's elite to the radicals in the frontier towns of Gorham and Brunswick. During 1774–75, militia from Gorham harassed loyalists in neighboring towns, while the Brunswick militia, led by Samuel Thompson, made periodic intrusions into Georgetown, Pownalborough, and even Falmouth itself. Seaport merchants grew increasingly apprehensive about the rising incidence of mob action aimed at those who violated the nonimportation agreements.

In the spring of 1775, tensions between local militia, Falmouth elites, and British officers came to a head in an incident involving a local merchant preparing a shipment of British goods. Although Thomas Coulson's actions violated the nonimportation agreements, Falmouth's leaders were reluctant to use force because of the presence of the *Cançeaux*, a British man-of-war, in the harbor. Exasperated by the timid response from the Falmouth merchants and townspeople, Samuel Thompson and the members of his militia took it upon themselves to end this stalemate by invading the town. On May 9, they seized the *Cançeaux*'s commanding officer, Lieutenant Henry Mowatt. Thompson's audacity achieved little. The boycott was quite forgotten in an uproar which forced him to release his captive. Mowatt sailed away, but neither he nor Falmouth forgot.

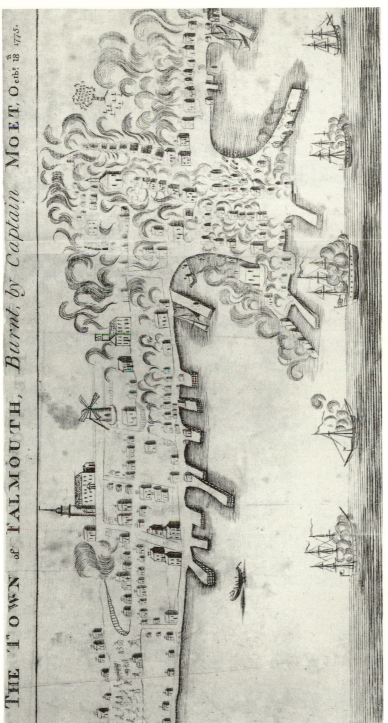

THE TOWN of FALMOUTH, Burnt, by Captain MOWET, Ocbr 18th 1775.

7-3. "I know not, how Sufficiently to detest [it]," wrote Gen. George Washington of the British bombardment and burning of Falmouth Neck (now Portland) on October 18, 1775. John Norman (1748–1817) created this image as an illustration in James Murray's *An Impartial History of the War in America* (Boston, 1782). Courtesy of the John Carter Brown Library at Brown University.

In June 1775, an even more unusual crisis occurred in the isolated town of Machias. Ichabod Jones, Machias's leading merchant, negotiated a profitable deal with the British occupying Boston, agreeing to supply them with wood from Machias provided he was allowed to ship goods out of Boston, which the British had blockaded, to sell at Machias. When Jones's two vessels arrived in company with the HMS *Margaretta* in Machias, local radicals led by Jeremiah O'Brien and Benjamin Foster repudiated his deal and moved to capture the officers of the *Margaretta*. The attempt went awry, and the British vessel drew offshore and threatened to bombard the little village. Instead of submitting, as at Falmouth, citizens of this frontier town rejected the authority of the Joneses, Ichabod and his nephew Steven, and threw their support behind the radical faction. Citizens equipped two sloops and set out after the *Margaretta*. They caught up with it on June 2, and in the ensuing conflict, the Americans mortally wounded the British commander. The British crew immediately surrendered, and the Machias rebels brought the *Margaretta* back in triumph. They easily captured two more British vessels investigating the fate of the first. The incident at Machias has been ranked as the first naval engagement of the American Revolution.

On October 16, Lieutenant Mowatt of the *Cançeaux* returned to Falmouth with a flotilla of gunships and orders to punish towns that were in open rebellion against the king. Falmouth and Machias were both on the list. Mowatt initially bypassed Falmouth on his way down east, but a change of wind brought him back to the unfortunate town. On October 18, the fleet, after warning townspeople to evacuate, brought home the cost of rebellion. By the end of the day, two-thirds of Falmouth lay in smoldering ruins, its merchant fleet resting at the bottom of Casco Bay. Such was the confusion and panic that Falmouth put up no resistance. Nor did Falmouth receive aid from the surrounding towns: the militia, convinced that the vacillating elites in the port town got what they deserved, were too busy looting the possessions and houses of those who had abandoned them. Burned by the British and plundered by the rebels, Falmouth bore witness to the fate of moderates in a revolutionary situation.

The burning of Falmouth drove home the vulnerability of the Maine coast to British sea power. Horrified by this example, Maine's coastal towns clamored for protection from a Provincial Congress already preoccupied by the task of containing the British army inside Boston. No troops were available to defend Maine. Given sufficient warning, local militias could offer effective defense, as in 1777, when a small British expedition under Commodore George Collier raided Machias, Boothbay, and Wiscasset. But usually citizen-soldiers were reluctant to leave homes and livelihoods and were slow to respond to an emergency, especially one distant from them. Maine could mount no effective defense against small enemy vessels that suddenly appeared to attack isolated towns or to seize sloops and schooners loaded with lumber, fish, or grain. For the vulnerable coastal communities, only their insignificance, in terms of military strategy, stood between them and the powerful British navy.

Although vulnerable, Maine was not passive; it served as the staging area for three separate attempts to invade British territory to the north and contributed many small armed vessels of its own which raided enemy shipping and towns. The first and most famous invasion was Benedict Arnold's ill-fated expedition against Quebec. Leading a thousand well-chosen volunteers from the army surrounding the British at Boston in the fall of 1775, Arnold's force advanced up the Kennebec River, then cut west and north across ponds and lakes, through swamps and over hills, finally reaching the Chaudière River, which brought them to the banks of the St. Lawrence. Six hundred and seventy-five men survived exhaustion, starvation, the terrors of a hurricane, and the temptation to desert. Reinforced by an expedition from the west, Arnold assaulted Fortress Quebec on December 31, 1775. It was a bloody disaster wherein a hundred men died and four hundred more were captured. Arnold himself was badly wounded. Overall, the event had little lasting impact on Maine.

More significant for Maine were two abortive expeditions launched from Machias by pro-American refugees from Nova Scotia. Convinced that Nova Scotia (which then included present-day New Brunswick) was filled with American sympathizers, Jonathan Eddy set out in October 1776, with seventy-two men in whaleboats and canoes to raise the standard of revolt. His little force laid siege to Fort Cumberland at the head of the Bay of Fundy, but the fort refused to submit. Nor did the local population rise up in rebellion. Instead, British reinforcements from Halifax surprised and scattered the intruders, who fled back to Machias as best they could. The second assault, also staged from Machias, was led by John Allan, another Nova Scotian convert to the American cause. In May 1777, Allan and an advance party of forty men in whaleboats and canoes sailed to the St. John River region, where they hoped to rally settlers and the Maliseet Indians to resist British occupation. Once again, the arrival of British troops put the Americans to flight. Only with the aid of the Indians were they able to reach Machias by an overland route.

Indeed, Indian support for the American cause was nothing short of astonishing. Led by their chief, Ambrose St. Aubin, a large number of Maliseets living along the St. John River accompanied the fleeing Americans to Machias, bringing with them their families and possessions. There they joined groups of Passamaquoddy Indians. The charismatic John Allan, appointed superintendent to the eastern Indians by the Continental Congress, cultivated their sympathies using a small allotment of supplies and gifts. The Franco-American treaty of

1778 strengthened pro-American sentiment among the eastern Indians, who retained feelings of friendship for the French. From the French warships which soon appeared in New England waters, John Allan was able to secure the services of French priests to minister to the spiritual needs of those Indians who still practiced French Catholicism.

Nonetheless, the Indians were understandably reluctant to take up arms in the American cause. Some actually fought the British, as when Collier attacked Machias in August 1777, or served as scouts watching the frontier to the north. But in general, the Indians preferred the role of friendly nonbelligerents. This enabled them to play off the Americans against the British to their own advantage—and to the advantage of the belligerents on both sides, who thereby were spared the horrors of frontier warfare, even as they tried to inflict it upon each other.

The Penobscot Expedition and Its Aftermath, 1779–83

In the summer of 1779, such issues of loyalty—Indian or white—received their ultimate test in the infamous Penobscot affair. In June, a British expedition from Halifax arrived in Penobscot Bay and disembarked 700 British regulars under Brigadier General Francis McLean. The troops began constructing Fort George in what is now the town of Castine on the Majabigwaduce (or Bagaduce) peninsula. The British had two goals in mind. First, they hoped to protect Nova Scotia from the Yankee privateers swarming out of New England ports to plunder the towns and shipping of the enemy to the east. These New Englanders—so reluctant to enlist as soldiers—served both the war and themselves as privateers, operating out of everything from open whaleboats to full rigged ships. Among the most famous were the O'Brien brothers from Machias and Agreen Crabtree from Frenchman's Bay, whose exploits were as colorful as his name. The second reason for the invasion concerned the British sympathizers who had fled the American revolution. The refugees themselves had suggested the idea of founding a new colony where dispossessed loyalists could begin anew. The British ministry approved to the point of sending troops to occupy the region adjacent to Nova Scotia. British officials drew up a frame of government for the province, called New Ireland, and selected governing officials.

Massachusetts acted quickly to prevent the loss of its easternmost counties. On July 19, an armada of forty vessels left Boston harbor. Half of them were transports, the rest warships, chiefly privateers, chartered and insured by the state. At Townshend (Boothbay), the fleet was to embark fifteen hundred soldiers recruited from the Maine militias and then proceed to Penobscot Bay to "Captivate kill or Destroy the whole force of the Enemy there both by Sea & Land."

On paper the American forces vastly outnumbered the beleaguered British in their half-built fort. But appearances were deceiving; the navy was chiefly a privateer force, unaccustomed to fleet maneuvers and fearful of being bottled up in the bay by a British fleet. The American troops were also five hundred men short, indicating the lack of enthusiasm with which citizen soldiers anticipated attacking British regulars in a fortified position. Nor was the leadership capable of inspiration. Commodore Dudley Saltonstall, commanding the fleet, disagreed with Brigadier General Solomon Lovell, the army commander, over tactics to be employed in attacking the British fort. After three weeks of maneuvering, cannonading, and internal bickering, the American commanders finally resolved their differences and on August 13 commenced a joint attack. But at that very moment, the Americans spotted the topsails of a strong British relief fleet sailing up the bay.

Amazingly, neither commander had anticipated such an eventuality. The American army quickly reboarded the transports, and the entire American fleet dashed precipitously for the Penobscot River. Those vessels that eluded the British continued upriver, only to be beached and burned by their own crews. Officers, troops, and crew members milled along the river banks without direction or discipline until singly or in groups they set off through the woods to their homes.

Secured by the British, New Ireland became a rallying point for loyalists from Maine and Massachusetts. Their arrival highlights another source of social tension in Maine and throughout the colonies. Perhaps 15 to 20 percent of adult white males were still loyal to the Crown, but their willingness to act on this loyalty depended on a variety of local circumstances, including the whereabouts of British troops. About three hundred families, former residents of Falmouth and Pownalborough, as well as local loyalists in the Penobscot region, joined the New Ireland colony. Reinforced by the occupying forces, loyalists acted out their British sympathies, plundering neighboring towns and kidnapping rebel leaders.

The failure of the Penobscot expedition, like the burning of Falmouth, underscored Maine's military vulnerability. Massachusetts, virtually bankrupted by the Penobscot defeat, could do little to protect Maine. The burden of defense fell upon Colonel John Allan, Brigadier General Peleg Wadsworth, and local militias. At Machias, Allan tried to assure the skeptical Indians that the situation was less desperate than it appeared and convince the local militia that it was worse, so they would help construct and garrison fortifications against an expected British attack. The Indians wavered but did not desert their basically neutralist position. Uncertain of Indian loyalties, the British dared not disturb eastern Maine, even though they controlled the Penobscot region. This was

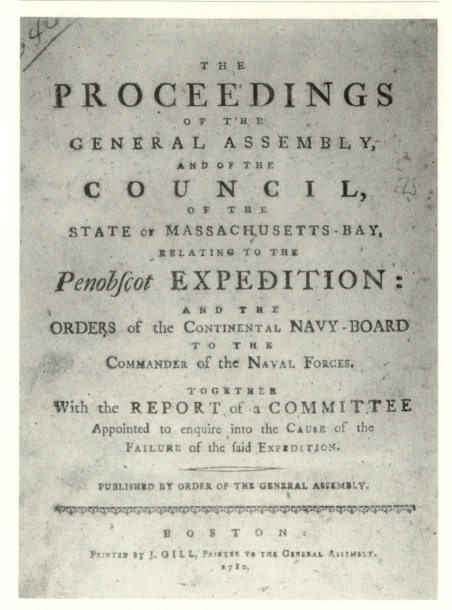

THE
PROCEEDINGS
OF THE
GENERAL ASSEMBLY,
AND OF THE
COUNCIL,
OF THE
STATE OF MASSACHUSETTS-BAY,
RELATING TO THE
Penobscot EXPEDITION:
AND THE
ORDERS of the CONTINENTAL NAVY-BOARD
TO THE
COMMANDER of the NAVAL FORCES.
TOGETHER
With the REPORT of a COMMITTEE
Appointed to enquire into the CAUSE of the
FAILURE of the said EXPEDITION.

PUBLISHED BY ORDER OF THE GENERAL ASSEMBLY.

BOSTON:
PRINTED BY J. GILL, PRINTER TO THE GENERAL ASSEMBLY.
1780,

7-4. The disastrous defeat of the Penobscot Expedition by the British in 1779 led to a
formal inquiry by the Massachusetts General Assembly and Governor's Council, the
results of which were published the next year. Courtesy of Rare Books and Manuscripts
Division, New York Public Library. Astor, Lenox and Tilden Foundations.

fortunate for the Americans, particularly during boundary negotiations following the war. The Machias militia, on the other hand, stoutly refused to perform hard labor to garrison the town. Nor were many willing to enlist for short-term duty at state pay. Indian neutrality was eastern Maine's chief defense.

Farther west, around Penobscot Bay, General Peleg Wadsworth fell back on state-paid, short-term enlistments to garrison little towns like Camden, Thomaston, and Boothbay. Try as he might, Wadsworth could not prevent British-backed loyalist raids and a disturbing tendency among coastal residents to resume their allegiance to the Crown when threatened by the British or when seeking trade with the enemy. So serious was the situation that on April 18, 1780, Wadsworth placed all of Lincoln County within ten miles of the sea under martial law. Military authorities arrested numerous loyalist suspects and even executed one, Jeremiah Baum, convicted of guiding a British raiding party. Nonetheless, raids continued and even intensified. John Jones, formerly of Pownalborough, led a British party to his former home town, where they kidnaped Colonel Charles Cushing, justice of the peace and brigadier general of the Lincoln County militia. General Wadsworth suffered the ultimate humiliation when he fell victim to a similar fate at Thomaston. Wadsworth's captivity at Fort George was shortlived, however. Once recovered from wounds incurred at Thomaston, he and another captive cut through the ceiling of their prison and escaped. Back in American territory, Wadsworth escaped once more—this time from the frustrations of his office. He resigned his commission and left Maine, not to return until after the war.

War, Patriotism, and the Economy, 1779–83

As the war dragged on, not only was there a growing disposition to trade with the British, but representatives for several of Maine's most vulnerable towns, such as Gouldsborough, Narraguagus, and Number Four, circulated a plan of neutrality for the region between Penobscot Bay and the St. Croix River. Their argument rested on the familiar premise that government was contractual and conditional ("Allegiance & Protection are Reciprocal"); if Massachusetts could not protect its towns, they would withdraw their allegiance and retreat into protective neutrality. Machias and most other eastern towns opposed the neutrality scheme and it collapsed, but not before revealing the growing disillusionment with a war that seemed to have no end and a provincial government that was not able to defend its territories.

Patriotism waned throughout Maine as drafts for military service with the Continental Army became more demanding. By early 1778, 18 percent of the adult males in a sampling of Cumberland County towns were in Continental service. Towns competed for scarce recruits to meet their quotas, paying ever higher bounties. By 1780, Scarborough voted a blank check to a town committee to hire recruits, while Arundel offered a hundred acres of land or three pounds per month in addition to military pay for those who would sign up for three years or the duration. In 1781, Pownalborough could find no recruits whatsoever; Vassalborough stopped trying. As patriotism declined, recruits willing to accept the bounties came from the poorest segments of society. The family members they left behind, already needy, often fell into desperate want. A Newcastle observer wrote that "the soldiers wifes in the eastern country suffer so much that should it be known in the army I should not wonder if all who have left families here should desert."

More than anything else price inflation and war taxation affected the lives of rich and poor. During the first few years of the war, state governments and the Continental Congress issued increasingly large sums of paper currency which, along with war-induced scarcities, drove prices to unprecedented heights. To debtors, inflationary currency provided an easy way to pay off obligations incurred when money was tight—and to challenge the patriotism of any creditor who refused to accept the cheap money. Beginning in 1777, Massachusetts withdrew old paper from circulation and replaced it with interest-bearing notes. For all practical purposes, by 1781 Massachusetts had adopted a hard money currency. The Continental Congress did the same in 1780, withdrawing its old currency at a ratio of forty to one and replacing it with new paper, backed by taxes and paying an annual rate of interest. The new financial situation favored creditors, who could demand payment in cash for debts incurred when money was plentiful and cheap. The new deflationary conditions especially favored commercial centers such as Maine's larger port towns, which, through privateering and wartime trade, had access to cash, in contrast to rural and interior regions where specie was scarce and prices for agricultural goods had dropped. Such inequities, serious enough during the war, would become a major grievance once the war ended.

Heavy taxation to pay for the war aggravated the situation. Not only was Maine's economy in ruins, but the Massachusetts policy of discriminating against landed property in favor of personal property placed a greater burden on agricultural regions than on commercial centers. Appeals for relief from taxes flowed in to the General Court from one end of Maine to the other, presenting the same doleful picture: trade dislocated, piles of unsold lumber rotting for lack of shipping, inadequate labor power, too little food, and insufficient money to pay taxes. A petition from Boothbay described the town as "nothing but the wreck of a Community in ruins." Added to the confusion was uncertainty over what taxes were due when, in what types of currency, and at what rate of depreciation. Depending on when they were levied, taxes were to be paid in old emission, new emission, hard money, in Continental currency, or on occasion in shoes, shirts, stockings, blankets, or beef. Some towns, overcome with the complexities and burdens of taxation, simply gave up and refused to tax.

Preoccupied by the burdens of war, Maine played little part in the creation of the new republican government that Massachusetts adopted in 1780. Although Maine delegates attended the state constitutional convention, they played only a minor role, and an average of only 14 percent of the electorate in seventeen Maine towns voted on the document. In general, opinion favored the new constitution, possibly as a more effective means of relief from the burdens and disruptions of war.

If so, such hopes were to be disappointed. Only an end to the fighting could bring relief, and peace came grudgingly to Maine. Throughout the United States in general, hostilities subsided after the surrender of Cornwallis at Yorktown in October 1781. In Maine, however, fighting and uncertainty continued. An attack by Canadian Indians on Sudbury Canada (Bethel) in the summer of 1781 spread fear along Maine's frontier, and as late as 1782, British privateers still raided periodically along the coast. Falmouth leaders worried that Machias, poorly defended as it was, might fall to the British, who continued to occupy Castine. They urged that part of the Continental Army be sent to protect eastern Maine. No help arrived, however. Britain and the United States signed a preliminary peace treaty in November 1782. The definitive treaty of September 3, 1783, renounced all British claims to Maine, but the troops at Fort George and their loyalist allies lingered until January 1784, without any official pressure from Massachusetts to depart. No American official was present when the last contingent of British and loyalists withdrew. Massachusetts did not even acknowledge the abandoned post it had once tried so hard to recapture until the spring of 1784, when an official arrived to make an inventory of what the British had left behind.

Even in peacetime Maine was not entirely free of its troublesome enemies. Most of the Bagaduce loyalists and many of the discharged British soldiers moved only as far as Passamaquoddy Bay, where they established the town of St. Andrews on the east side of what is now the St. Croix River. For the next fifteen years, the British and Americans quarreled bitterly over whether the settlement encroached on American territory, as John Allan insistently maintained. The dispute arose because the peace negotiators at Paris worked from an imperfect map of the area when designating the St. Croix as the boundary between Maine and British territory, soon to be named New Brunswick. After the war, neither side could agree on which of the several rivers flowing into

Passamaquoddy Bay was the St. Croix. If, as the Americans claimed, it was the easternmost river, the loyalists of St. Andrews would have to move yet again to remain under the Crown. If the St. Croix was the westernmost river, the loyalists were already in British territory. The two governments finally submitted their differences to a joint commission, which reported its decision in October 1798. In a masterpiece of political compromise, the commission acknowledged that the westernmost river—the Schoodic—was indeed the St. Croix, but mollified the Americans with the decision that the main course of the river flowed along its northerly branch rather than the one farther to the west. The Americans grudgingly accepted the decision, and the loyalists of St. Andrews could rest secure at last.

The Revolution was over, but basic differences over the nature of the Revolution divided the newly independent Americans everywhere. Was the goal of independence merely political separation from Britain, or did independence mean a democratic revolution transforming American society? Differences over this question led to deep and dangerous tensions in Maine's postwar society. A powerful conviction prevailed throughout Maine's backcountry that a man's right to possess land by occupancy and improvement was being denied by wealthy speculators who acquired legal title to thousands, even millions, of acres, merely to sell them again at a profit. The war with Britain might have ended, but to squatters the revolution was not yet over. A new class of American "Tories," in the form of speculators, merchants, and politicians, had arisen to deny people the fruits of their victory. Disguised as Indians, squatters fought back by assaulting surveyors and proprietary agents, even killing one.

Adding moral fervor to backcountry violence was a religious revival which swept through the interior of New England and even Nova Scotia during the Revolution. This "New Light Stir" filled a religious need that was both physical and spiritual. The District had grown so rapidly that as early as 1778 at least forty towns and plantations in Lincoln County alone lacked a regularly settled minister. In addition to a scarcity of clergy, traditional Calvanism failed to meet the emotional and spiritual needs of Maine's rapidly expanding population, especially in the turbulent backcountry, which was wracked by poverty, uncertainties over land titles, and the burdens of war. Inhabitants of Maine's frontier were attracted to the more enthusiastic sects—Shakers, Baptists, Universalists, and the even more radical but short-lived "Come-Outers" of Gorham and the "Merry Dancers" of Sanford, who expressed their religious excitement by dressing in odd costumes and by participating in wild dancing and even trances.

Despite the limited legal tolerance that Massachusetts allowed, traditional Calvinism remained the established religion of Massachusetts, supported by public taxation. To Maine's religious dissenters, many of whom were also back-country squatters, the only hope for full religious and economic liberty lay in separation from Massachusetts. Until then, physicial violence against their oppressors seemed to be the only immediate solution.

Backcountry violence, however, was a dead-end response to the powerful proprietors, who were backed by the state and the courts. As radical fontier leaders were silenced or imprisoned, their successors adopted more legitimate ways to express their demands. The experience of revolution had broadened political awareness through the lower ranks of society. Communities that before the Revolution had met only two or three times a year to elect town officers and conduct business, met much more frequently during the war to elect committees, draw up resolutions, raise taxes and troops, search out Tories, and evaluate constitutions. Maine towns still sent representatives to the legislature who were, as before, lawyers, merchants, and gentlemen farmers. The truly significant political change appears in the broadened political role assumed by the towns and a changing attitude toward political action. Traditionally, elected leaders had determined the good of the community, and virtuous citizens submitted to their decisions. In contrast to this corporate political outlook emerged a more democratic concept of political society as a series of competing groups from whose contests and compromises evolved the common good. In this changing political climate, Maine's dissenters gravitated to a new party of political opposition. By 1800 the Jeffersonian Republicans provided those who felt excluded from the opportunities of independence with a means of legitimate, organized political action which they had formerly lacked. In Maine this group included not only backcountry squatters and religious dissidents, but a new, vigorous merchant-lawyer elite, led by William King of Bath, for whom the old Federalist party had become too limited in ideology and in opportunity. This Jeffersonian Republican coalition achieved statehood for Maine in 1820, a development that opened the way for greater social reform in the new state.

For groups without political influence, the legacy of the Revolution was far more ambiguous. Loyalists who wished to return benefitted from the desperate need felt by newly independent states for leadership and entrepreneurial skills. As soon as the war ended, Massachusetts began to relax antiloyalist restrictions, and in 1785 it repealed all discriminatory legislation. Some of Maine's interior towns angrily passed resolutions barring returning loyalists from ever holding town office. In the coastal towns, however, loyalists received a warmer welcome, in hopes they might help stimulate the postwar economy. In Kittery and Falmouth, soon to be renamed Portland, several important merchants returned and successfully resumed their former roles as community leaders.

The Revolution did much to stimulate antislave sentiment throughout Massachusetts and the District of Maine. In 1783, the Supreme Judicial Court of Massachusetts declared that since the state constitution proclaimed all men were born free and equal, slavery in Massachusetts was unconstitutional. Slavery, of course, remained a national institution, and letters and even poems repeatedly appeared in the *Cumberland Gazette* denouncing slave-holding and those who participated in the slave trade. Perhaps the most dramatic antislave protest from Maine occurred in 1788 at the state convention to ratify the federal constitution. Several anti-Federalist delegates from Maine included its failure to abolish slavery among their reasons for opposing the new form of government. Samuel Thompson, delegate from Topsham, boldly condemned George Washington himself for continuing to hold in bondage those "who have as good a right to be free as he has."

Abolition of slavery did not imply economic and social equality for former slaves. Some simply remained as wage laborers for their former owners, who were now relieved of responsibility for their welfare. Others established their own communities on the outskirts of towns, where they maintained a precarious existence by doing odd jobs, raising vegetables, and accepting occasional charity from the town. A significant decline in the number of blacks among the postwar populations of York and Wells may suggest that some freed slaves made use of their liberty to move to Portland and other maritime communities in search of greater economic opportunity.

If independence provided Maine's African Americans with both ideological and legal leverage against bondage, the war's end deprived native Americans of whatever advantage they had enjoyed. The Penobscots, and especially the Passamaquoddys and Maliseets, could no longer use their strategic importance to play off the British and Americans. The fur trade had long ago disappeared, and so the Indians had no value to the Americans when the war ended. The Massachusetts government closed down its trading posts in Maine, and the Continental Congress relieved John Allan of his position as superintendent to the eastern Indians. In an effort to stimulate settlement down east, the state pressured the Penobscots into signing a treaty in 1796 whereby they surrendered 190,000 acres of land in exchange for annual supplies of guns, ammunition, clothing, food, and rum. Despite government aid, the Penobscots found it increasingly difficult to survive, except by selling off more land and timber rights, thereby further reducing their capacity for self-sufficiency. In 1818, they sold yet another large tract to the Commonwealth. and by the time Maine joined the union in 1820, the Penobscots were poverty-stricken wards of the government.

The Passamaquoddy and Maliseet Indians fared no better. Their lands stretched from eastern Maine into Nova Scotia, where the British government

7-5. Sarah Molasses (ca. 1812–80) by Jeremiah Pearson Hardy (1800–1887). Sarah was a Penobscot, the daughter of Molly Molasses, and she demonstrates in her attire the manner in which native Americans took European clothing and made it distinctively their own. Note the cross around Sarah's neck. Most Indians were converted to Catholicism by French Jesuit priests, like Father Sebastien Rale of Norridgewock. Oil on canvas, property of the Tarratine Club, Bangor, Maine. Photograph courtesy of the Maine Historical Society, Portland.

was hostile to Indians who had sympathized with the American cause. Through John Allan, the Passamaquoddies petitioned Massachusetts for a grant of land in Maine on which to settle, in exchange for surrendering their claims to other lands in the District. In response the state concluded an agreement in 1794 whereby they and Maliseets gave up whatever claims they had in Maine and received some 23,000 acres along the St. Croix River, at Pleasant Point and at Indian Township, as well as some islands in the river.

Although they acquired clearly defined lands within a nominally friendly environment, Maine's Indians in general appear as the losers in the Revolution. They suffered through the loss of their traditional lands and mobility, and through their humiliating new dependence on a government which regarded them as liabilities and as obstacles in the path of progress. The plight of the eastern Indians aroused no public protest, even though under the terms of the Federal Intercourse Act of 1790 the purchase of Indian land was illegal without the approval of the federal government. Two hundred years later, Maine's Indians finally obtained sufficient political and legal influence to secure a degree of compensation for the illegal loss of their land. In 1980 the Penobscot, Passamaquoddy, and Maliseet tribes received an award of $17 million in trust, and $54.5 million more to repurchase 300,000 acres of land. In 1992, Maine's Micmacs received federal recognition as a tribe and a $900,000 settlement in recognition of their land claim. Generous as the settlement may appear, it is at best compensatory, and Maine's native Americans still await the fulfillment of their Revolutionary legacy.

Women too contributed much to the Revolution, which in turn either ignored or exploited them afterward. Everywhere women were forced out of their traditional domestic roles to assume responsibilities normally filled by men. The well-worn image of Abigail Adams bravely managing her family and farm in Braintree, Massachusetts, while husband John conducted official business in France and Philadelphia, symbolizes what countless other women faced during the war. Recruits to the Continental army, generally from the lower ranks of society, left behind them wives struggling to support their families, frequently in the face of deepening poverty and even starvation. Everywhere, the war drew women out of their accustomed domestic roles and, regardless of their social station or political loyalties, forced them to assume new and unfamiliar activities as family defenders and providers.

At the end of the war, however, women generally resumed their familiar social functions. The genteel leaders and spokesmen of the Revolution had no intention of altering the traditional social structure, and women, even had they desired it, lacked the political leverage to do so. In the new American republic, women's roles were extolled, but their economic and legal privileges were curtailed, their recent revolutionary contributions largely ignored, and their political participation discouraged. The Revolution was no watershed for women, declares one modern historian: "As the new American nation moved toward independence from Great Britain, women remained in a state of submissive dependence."

The Revolution, however, did create an environment conducive to new ideas, if not action, regarding the role of women in the new republic. Some concepts, such as that of Republican Motherhood, while strengthening women's traditional domestic functions, acknowledged their political influence. Other ideas were more radical. The writings of English feminist Mary Wollstonecraft had a profound impact in America's post-revolutionary society. Clergymen and educators, apologists for traditional family values, expressed shock at her suggestions that women should be educated in the professions and enjoy full political and civil rights along with men. Yet, Wollstonecraft only articulated publicly what many Americans, men as well as women, were coming privately to believe. Correspondence between Maine's leading Federalist, George Thatcher of Biddeford, and his wife reveals that he could appreciate Mary Wollstonecraft, whose writings he and his wife had clearly discussed. Thatcher demonstrates the elusive change in attitudes and feelings regarding women, not necessarily created by the Revolution but nurtured in that atmosphere of change.

The legitimacy to seek change in the direction of greater freedom—this was the Revolution's most enduring legacy. Even in Maine, the eastern corner of Massachusetts, the Revolution fostered a new order based on freedom: freedom from the British empire, freedom to participate in the political process, to be free from bondage, free from the state church, and to have an equal opportunity to exploit the country's resources, especially its land, and eventually to be free from Massachusetts. It was also a legacy filled with controversy.

For Further Reading:

Two bibliographies will be of particular help in locating material on the American Revolution in Maine. Edwin A. Churchill compiled *Maine Communities and the War for Independence* (Portland, 1976). That same bicentennial year, Churchill and James S. Leamon published "Maine in the Revolution: A Reader's Guide," *Maine Historical Society Quarterly* 15 (Spring 1976).

Until now, there has been no general history of the American Revolution in Maine. The closest approximation was William Williamson's *History of the State of Maine*, 2 vols. (Hallowell, 1832)—written 160 years ago. Although not limited to the Revolution, Williamson's book devoted ten chapters to that era, and his work remained the source for virtually all subsequent accounts of Maine's revolutionary experience.

A modern history, synthesizing much primary source material and other resources that were unavailable to Williamson, is James S. Leamon's *Revolution Downeast: The War for American Independence in Maine* (forthcoming 1993, Amherst, Mass.). Building on these previous sources and studies, Leamon views the Revolution in Maine as an ambiguous and divisive experience that legitimized democratic change but also generated conflict over differing goals of the Revolution.

Many useful articles and documents relating to the Revolution in Maine can be found in the *Collections and Proceedings of the Maine Historical Society*, the *Maine Historical Society Newsletter*, and in the *Maine Historical Society Quarterly*.

SELECTED PUBLISHED PRIMARY SOURCES:

Bartlet, William S., *The Frontier Missionary: A Memoir of the Life of the Reverend Jacob Bailey* (Boston, 1853, 1979).

Baxter, James P., editor, *Documentary History of the State of Maine*, 24 vols. (Portland, 1869–1916).

Calef, John, editor, *The Siege of Penobscot* (1781, 1971).

Kidder, Frederic, editor, *Military Operations in Eastern Maine and Nova Scotia during the Revolution* (New York, 1867, 1971).

Roberts, Kenneth, editor, *March to Quebec* (New York, 1938).

Willis, William, editor, *Journals of the Rev. Thomas Smith and the Rev. Samuel Deane, Pastors of the First Church in Portland* (Portland, 1849).

ADDITIONAL SECONDARY SOURCES:

Ahlin, John, *Maine Rubicon* (Calais, 1966).

Gould, Edward K., *British and Tory Marauders on the Penobscot* (Rockland, 1932).

Hutchinson, Vernal, *When the Revolution Came* (Ellsworth, 1972).

Kershaw, Gordon E., *The Kennebeck Proprietors 1749–1775* (Somersworth, N.H., 1975).

Marini, Stephen A., *Radical Sects of Revolutionary New England* (Cambridge, Mass., 1982).

Seibert, Wilbur H., *The Exodus of the Loyalists from Penobscot to Passamaquoddy* (Columbus, Ohio, 1914).

Taylor, Alan, *Liberty Men and Great Proprietors* (Chapel Hill, N.C., 1990).

8

Separation & Statehood,

1783–1820

JAMES S. LEAMON,

RICHARD R. WESCOTT, & EDWARD O. SCHRIVER

The first section of this chapter was written primarily by historian James Leamon, who continues his discussion of the social groups and sectional conflicts he identified in the Revolutionary War era. Building on this social analysis, political historians Edward O. Schriver and Richard R. Wescott point out the political forces that frustrated the separationist movement through the next two decades. Thus we see earlier themes shaping Maine's own bid for independence.

As in the Revolutionary War, Maine first had to face external forces. Massachusetts administration was the most obvious of these, but the politics of the period responded to other exogenous events: Shays's Rebellion, the federal constitutional convention, the rise of the first American party system, the War of 1812, and the national debate over slavery in the western territories. Maine's separationist movement grew in the context of these momentous national events.

A second theme, the rift between coastal Maine and the interior, continued to be a feature of Maine politics after the Declaration of Independence. As will become clear in the following chapters, frontier Maine represented tremendous opportunity for a diverse mix of people. Among those who profited were land speculators, who were frequently coastal merchants, lawyers, or politicians. So did backwoods farmers, whose physical labor imparted value to the land if not outright ownership. The separationist movement was shaped by the ways rival groups responded to these opportunities. Maine's culture and its economy likewise responded to the expansion of opportunity in the early nineteenth century.

While the obvious task of the historian is to explain why Maine separated from Massachusetts in 1820, there is a more subtle, yet important question: why was the bid for independence so long delayed? For almost forty years following the Revolution, Maine remained a colony of Massachusetts. Vacillation and delay in the separationist movement stemmed from two primary causes. First, separationists—or at least factions within the movement—were distracted by national events such as Shays's Rebellion, the national debate over the federal Constitution, struggles between Federalists and Democratic Republicans, and the politics of sectionalism and slavery.

Closer to home, the movement was divided by conflicting visions of an independent Maine. Merchants and other prosperous leaders in the seacoast towns, aware of the enormous opportunity the frontier region represented, aspired to a state guided by their own conservative principles and economic interests. Backwoods farmers, chafing under an onerous tax and monetary policy and at odds with the great land speculators who controlled so much of the Maine backcountry, viewed separation differently. Coupling these two visions was a challenge; the uneasy alliance of elite and democratic forces in the separationist movement unraveled more than once as unfolding national events changed perspectives on Maine statehood. The delay becomes understandable in the context of national events and internal social developments in the post-Revolutionary War period.

Separation Politics in the Post–Revolutionary War Era
JAMES S. LEAMON

In 1783, the local elites who had guided the Revolutionary War in Maine had reason to be pleased. Despite the social and sectional tensions manifest during the Revolution, Maine's political and social fabric appeared to be secure. Yet revolution, independence, and republicanism weakened social restraints and inspired conflicting visions of Maine's future. Different segments of society held different views of what the revolution really meant and where it ought to lead. The years immediately after the Revolution brought two major challenges to the status quo—one from the coastal elites, the other from the impoverished settlers of the interior. These two groups united temporarily in Maine's first attempt at statehood, then broke apart in the debate over ratifying the federal Constitution.

After the war, thousands of settlers, principally from Massachusetts, moved into the District to take up land, most settling west of the Penobscot River and within fifty miles of the coast. In 1784, 56,000 people resided in Maine; six years later the number swelled to 96,540, and by 1800 the population topped 150,000. Some were merchants and artisans, but most were pioneer farm families from the more settled sections of New England. Speculators took steps to profit from this growth. Land companies such as the old Kennebec Proprietors and the Pejepscot Company reorganized and reasserted their claims to great stretches of Maine. In addition, former generals Peleg Wadsworth, Benjamin Lincoln, and

Henry Knox acquired thousands (and in Knox's case, hundreds of thousands) of acres in expectation of rising prices and lucrative profits.

Although an economic boon to speculators, the flood of settlers brought conflict over land claims along the northern frontier. New arrivals frequently settled on whatever tracts appealed to them, convinced that it had been the king's land won by common effort for the benefit of all, and not for a privileged few. Those who located on land claimed by absentee owners were subjected to threats of legal action and forcible removal; those who bought the land or accepted leases sometimes discovered that overlapping proprietorial claims left them open to challenges by other speculators. Tensions over land titles, combined with the problem of back taxes and a deflationary currency in a period of postwar depression, made the backcountry a very volatile region.

Other tensions developed in the years after the Revolution. Massachusetts pre-party politics was based upon the differing social and economic interests of commercial and agricultural groups. Commercial interests dominated national and state offices, controlled the upper house of the Massachusetts General Court, and exerted strong influence in the lower house. The farmers, in desperation, eventually resorted to extra constitutional conventions and violence to pressure the government to change its policies. The political rhetoric generated by both sides in speeches, pamphlets, newspapers, and handbills often portrayed these differences as a struggle between good and evil.

A chief source of conflict between coastal elites and backcountry farmers was the inequitable tax system. Maine's commercial interests—the merchants, ship owners, shipbuilders, artisans, and shopkeepers that made up about 12 percent of the District's population—supported a policy that taxed commercial and liquid property only lightly. Nearly a third of the taxes levied by Massachusetts between 1780 and 1786, for instance, were collected in poll taxes, assessed upon individual adult males regardless of their wealth. While local taxes were often paid in barter items, poll taxes and the state personal property and real estate taxes had to be paid in specie, paper money, or commercial paper, all of which were in short supply in subsistence farming towns.

Small farmers in Maine's recently settled smaller farming towns resented this inequity but felt powerless to change the situation. In 1784 Maine voters made up 15 percent of the Massachusetts constituency, yet the District had only 10 percent of the Senate seats, which were based on assessed property valuation. The House was apportioned by population, but usually only about 10 percent of Maine's towns could afford to send representatives to the General Court. Those that sat in session usually came from the wealthier coastal commercial towns. Backcountry subsistence farmers commonly regarded these commercially oriented politicians with suspicion and hostility—and with good reason.

Maine's commercial interests enjoyed close connections with their counterparts in Massachusetts, especially in Boston. These connections meant favorable economic legislation as well as a virtual monopoly on political and judicial positions in Maine. To be sure, some of Maine's merchants may have chafed under state mercantile policies restricting Maine's direct trade with Britain and Nova Scotia, but discontent was hardly sufficient to jeopardize the benefits of union.

The initiative for separation thus did not originate from debt-ridden farmers and harried squatters. Nor did it arise from Maine's self-satisfied commercial elite as a group. Rather it came from a small clique of merchants, wealthy farmers, and ministers who, in their own way, were speculators in Maine's growth. Convinced of Maine's potential and imbued with the revolutionary ideology of the period, they set out to create a state in which they themselves would play the leading roles. By doing so, these new elites challenged the older mercantile-judicial-political connections that bound the District to the Commonwealth. These older, established social leaders dominated the coastal communities and opposed separation as a threat to their vested interests, their civil and judicial commissions, and their status and influence.

The first public reference to separation appeared in the February 5, 1785, issue of the *Falmouth Gazette,* whose editor, Thomas Wait, devoted his paper to the cause. For the next thirty-five years, the argument justifying statehood for Maine changed little. Throughout the entire period, it remained largely political and economic in content, conservative and rational in tone. Supporters of statehood pointed out that Maine was geographically isolated from Massachusetts, and therefore had its own separate interests to pursue. Remote from the seat of government in Boston, Mainers could not take an active part in political and judicial matters there; statehood would mean more democratic government for Maine citizens. In addition, as a state, Maine would need a smaller, simpler form of government requiring less expense and lower taxes than in union with Massachusetts. Finally, the new state of Maine would acquire representation in the us House of Representatives and Senate, strengthening its own cause as well as that of the north against the south in the federal government.

Wait published a notice in the *Gazette* inviting all persons interested in separation to a meeting in Falmouth. Held in October 1785, the gathering was attended by thirty-three advocates of statehood. After some discussion, they elected a smaller committee to enumerate Maine's grievances against Massachusetts, estimate the costs of establishing a separate state, and draft an invitation to the people of Maine to meet in a convention in 1786.

At the subsequent September 1786 convention, delegates were split into roughly equal groups of radicals and moderates. Some called for immediate

8-1. On January 1, 1785, the first issue of the first newspaper to be printed in Maine, *The Falmouth Gazette*, advocated the separation of Maine from Massachusetts. The newspaper was published by Benjamin Titcomb, Jr., and Thomas B. Wait. Collections of the Maine Historical Society, Portland.

separation from Massachusetts; others for a more gradual approach, along with assurances that Maine did not intend to shirk responsibility for a fair share of the state's public debt. After much discussion, the convention approved a moderate list of grievances centered mostly on disadvantageous representation, taxation, and trade policies. The petition merely pointed out the difficulties of Maine's geographical situation respecting the rest of Massachusetts and humbly requested a separation. Rather than issue radical demands, the committee simply urged Maine towns to send representatives to the General Court to press for statehood in a legal, responsible manner. This done, the convention recessed until January 1787. The question of when to present the petition to the General Court was left to a committee headed by Revolutionary War radical Samuel Thompson, who had led the militia band that captured Henry Mowat of the *Cançeaux*. Thompson's presence symbolized a particular problem in the separation movement.

From the very start the promoters of separation were determined to keep the movement orderly and respectful. Newspaper articles supporting separation might appeal to historic rights of statehood, to natural law, and to the analogy between the colonies and Britain and Maine and Massachusetts, but the leaders of the movement had no desire to appear as revolutionaries. These community pillars were all the more conscious of their image in light of startling new events in Massachusetts. In the post–Revolutionary War years, the burden of debts and taxes weighed heavily upon inland Massachusetts farmers. The depression of 1785–86 heightened unrest, and in town and county conventions protesters complained about courts, taxes, the scarcity of money, and the costs of representation in a government situated in far-off Boston. Violence followed, as crowds closed courts and then resorted to armed rebellion under Daniel Shays, Luke Day, and Job Shattuck. In Maine, the news profoundly affected the movement to separate the District from Massachusetts.

The rebellion provided opponents of separation with the opportunity to compare Shaysites and Maine separatists, especially in their use of "illegal" conventions to achieve ends destructive to the Commonwealth of Massachusetts. Governor Bowdoin and the General Court condemned the movement as irresponsible. The charge was all the more embarrassing to separatist leaders as they realized their chief support did not come from the "respectable" segments of the population, but from the "dangerous" elements in the interior of Maine. Equally troubling was the realization that among the most energetic of separatists was none other than Samuel Thompson, whose turbulent rise to political prominence so alarmed leaders from the very beginning of the Revolution.

Actually, the restless towns of inland Maine were not Shaysites. Isolated, poor, struggling under heavy taxes, and contending with proprietary land agents and sheriffs, they nevertheless avoided radical demands for debt relief and the closing of courts; nor did they gather in armed bands to defy the state. Instead, at this point in time, they were seeking a nonviolent, politically legitimate solution to their problems: a truly republican government for Maine, free from the corrupting influence of powerful individuals and land companies and sympathetic to the needs of Maine settlers.

Despite their peaceful intentions, Maine's interior farmers and squatters appeared similar to Shaysites, and their support for separation tainted and even split the movement. As events in western Massachusetts became increasingly violent in the fall of 1786, Maine's representatives to the General Court supported the harsh measures advocated by Governor Bowdoin. By the time the Maine separationist convention reconvened in January 1787, General Benjamin Lincoln and a hastily recruited coastal militia were engaged in military action against western rebels. In Maine, many of the moderate separationists began to have second thoughts about pressuring the state for independence now, fearing that the radicalism might sweep northward into the District.

Not surprisingly, at the January convention the radical separationists lost ground, so much so that Thompson again refrained from submitting the September 1786 petition to the General Court. Discouraged by the lack of broad support, the advocates of separation recessed the convention until September 1787. Their assessment of the state of public opinion was based in part upon the fact that in a referendum on separation only about a third of the towns in the District had bothered to vote.

Indifference to statehood did not mean voters in Maine were happy about the state of political affairs. In the spring 1787 state elections, they and the voters in Massachusetts proper turned out in unprecedented numbers to defeat Governor Bowdoin and his conservative followers. Cued by this popular upsurge, the newly elected Governor John Hancock and the General Court followed a moderate course both in dealing with the Shaysites and in fiscal and financial matters. This, along with an improving economic climate, allayed discontent in frontier Massachusetts and undercut the separation movement in Maine. Thompson, newly elected to the Massachusetts Senate, finally forwarded the petition for separation to the General Court. He acknowledged that times were not propitious for pushing the issue, given the troubles in western Massachusetts. In this respect, he was correct: the General Court simply ignored the petition.

The coup de grace to the first separation movement came when the Constitutional Convention in Philadelphia presented the new federal constitution to the states for ratification in September 1787. The debate over ratification eclipsed state politics everywhere. In Maine, it utterly destroyed the brief, awkward alliance of Portland elites and interior separatists.

Maine's Federalists—those who supported the new national constitution—were more numerous in the commercial coastal centers among the mercantile-judicial-political establishment already hostile to separation. Frightened by Shays's Rebellion and the surge of popular participation in the 1787 state election, these socially conservative interests felt that a stronger national government could be a bulwark to their financial interests and their social prestige. On the other hand, a majority of Maine's secessionists were antifederalists, opponents of constitutional ratification. Secessionists, especially those in interior Maine where friction over taxes, debts, and land titles was most intense, feared that creating a stronger national government would only strengthen Massachusetts's grip over Maine and further concentrate power in the hands of a privileged few. The issue had changed, but the political alignments had not.

The 355 Massachusetts delegates who gathered in Boston to debate the Constitution in early January 1788 were closely divided between Federalists and Antifederalists. To the Federalist delegates ratification became a crusade against the evils of separation, national disunion, and Shaysism. As in Massachusetts proper, Maine's forty-six delegates were evenly divided. Those from more commercially oriented towns supported ratification, and those from small, frontier farming towns opposed it. The latter tended to confirm Federalists' images; Maine's Antifederalists were often self-educated and awkwardly self-conscious. Yet two of them, New Gloucester's William Widgery and Topsham's notorious Samuel Thompson, became leaders in the Antifederalist movement; their speeches remain classics in Antifederalism.

In the face of staunch Antifederalist opposition, the Federalists had to agree that the Massachusetts convention recommend a series of amendments to the Constitution. Only then were Federalists able to secure ratification by a narrow margin of 187 to 168. By four votes—25 to 21—the Maine delegation supported the majority. The amendments forced by Thompson and his Antifederalist allies set a precedent followed by many other state conventions, but Massachusetts ratified the Constitution. Despite the compromises, the mercantile-judicial-political establishment emerged victorious from the constitutional battles.

With consummate skill they also disposed of the separation threat. Only in January 1789 did the General Court consider the long-delayed petition from Maine for separation. Once more Widgery and Thompson rose to defend the measure, but it was a forlorn hope. Separatists were a splintered minority of Maine's population, divided over the implications of separation and tainted by Shaysism and by opposition to the new Constitution. Still, to avoid any appearance of insult to the advocates, the General Court voted to table the petition rather than kill it outright. The petition died a lingering but unobtrusive death. In March the last of the separatist conventions met in Portland, with but three members in attendance.

Renewal of the separation movement in the 1790s was largely the work of its earlier leaders, aided by some recent arrivals in the District. By and large this group believed that Maine's economic development—and their own prospects—were hindered by continued subordination to the Bay State. Among the general citizenry, on the other hand, there was no groundswell for separation, since the General Court had taken some measures to address frontier concerns about property titles.

The new separation movement began early in 1791, when some of Maine's delegates to the General Court attempted to take up the question. Although the initiative failed, separationists introduced a petition from their supporters in Portland asking for an official District-wide referendum on the question. In January 1792, following several days of debate, the General Court authorized a test vote for the following May. In the ensuing months secessionists worked hard to get a favorable vote, circulating tracts, publishing articles in newspapers, and making speeches. Daniel Davis, a Portland lawyer, wrote an influential tract titled *An Address to the Inhabitants of the District of Maine upon the Subject of Their Separation from the Present Government of Massachusetts*. He and others made the same basic arguments for separation as before, citing Maine's geographical isolation from Massachusetts and the discrimination the District suffered from its subordinate condition.

The May test vote was disappointing to the separationists. Only 4,598 people bothered to vote. Of those, 2,074 supported secession, while 2,524 rejected it. Predictably, the greatest support for separation came from inland farming towns, where friction between squatters and agents for land speculators stirred resentments against Massachusetts. The greatest opposition to separation came from southern coastal towns with substantial commercial connections to Boston. Despite the rather small turnout, the closeness of the vote encouraged separationists to persist; further unsuccessful test votes followed.

The General Court, meanwhile, had been moving to bind the District ever more closely to the Commonwealth by rectifying the grievances about which separatists complained. It established additional courts in Maine and divided Lincoln County into two additional county jurisdictions—Hancock and Washington. The Court undertook wholesale incorporation of communities within the new jurisdictions so the new counties could levy taxes and elect juries to support the legal system. The government promised to lay out roads running from the Kennebec River to Passamaquoddy Bay, and it approved in principle the incorporation of a college for the District. To alleviate discontent in the interior, the General Court suspended or abated taxes for over thirty percent of the towns in Maine, gave squatters occupying public lands prior to 1784 title to a hundred acres each, and urged private land companies to compromise differences with their tenants in return for tax exemptions on their lands.

Although this legislation addressed some of the complaints from the interior towns, its major thrust was not reform, but rather extension of the system of courts and town governments as a means of controlling Maine's frontier population. For those living on land claimed by private speculators, the 1790s brought an increasing number of civil and judicial officers to enforce the will of the land barons. Not incidentally, the Court also multiplied the number of civil and judicial officers who owed their commissions—and their allegiances—to the General Court of Massachusetts. The remedial legislation thus expanded the mercantile-judicial-political elite who would oppose future separation efforts.

For separationists, the vision of an independent Maine seemed more remote than ever. As Massachusetts officials and land speculators tightened their grip on Maine's back country, farmers and squatters drew together in armed bands and, imbued with a millennial-revolutionary ideology, resisted these new "Despots" and their agents. For them, the ideals of the American Revolution—life, liberty, and happiness—were yet to be realized. As long as statehood was denied and government lay in the hands of those who considered the Revolution over, these goals would remain unfulfilled.

Despite the consolidation of mercantile-judicial-political power in the 1790s, nothing could delay for long the forces of change at work in the new republic. The rise of a viable opposition political party, the Jeffersonian Democratic Republicans, gave dissident elements such as Maine's separatists and interior farmers a legitimate and peaceful means of expressing their concerns—and, by 1820, a successful one.

The Separation Movement in the Federal Period
RICHARD R. WESCOTT & EDWARD O. SCHRIVER

Regardless of what the secessionists thought, most Mainers remained indifferent to the prospect of statehood. Opposition to separation among the coastal towns stiffened in 1789, when the federal government passed legislation known as the "coasting law." Under this law, coastwise trading vessels had to enter and clear customs in every state they passed between their port of departure and their destination. Vessels were exempted, however, from clearing customs in states contiguous to the state where they were registered. Under this law, coasting vessels registered in the District of Maine gained a peculiar advantage: when sailing southward, they bypassed New Hampshire, Massachusetts, Rhode Island,

Connecticut, and New York—all contiguous with Massachusetts. If Maine were to separate, its vessels would reach a noncontiguous state after sailing only eighteen miles past the New Hampshire border.

Despite a frustrating lack of popular support, proponents of statehood continued to agitate. In 1793, secessionists again asked town and plantation selectmen to hold town meetings to choose delegates to another convention in Portland. Only fifteen sent delegates. Desperate to achieve some consensus, the convention delegates endorsed a scheme under which the two recalcitrant downeast counties—Hancock and Washington—would be left to Massachusetts, while York, Cumberland, and Lincoln counties would become a separate state. Under this plan, Maine would still enjoy an advantage under the coasting law by remaining contiguous to a part of Massachusetts. Despite the ingenious proposal, the separationists' next convention, called in 1794, was again meagerly attended. A vote on separation held in conjunction with the gubernatorial election in April 1795 was virtually ignored. Once again the movement faltered.

As the second round of separation politics ran its course to abject failure, a national political party system developed in response to controversies surrounding funding the national debt, assumption of state Revolutionary War debts, and creation of the Bank of the United States. For the most part the old Federalist leadership, still supporting a strong, centralized national government, became the backbone of the new Federalist party in the mid-1790s. Including such luminaries as George Washington, Alexander Hamilton, and John Adams, the Federalists were by and large wealthy lawyers, clergy, and merchants, and through the decade they maintained a powerful grip on the government. Conversely, their opponents—small farmers, artisans, middling merchants, and other nonelites—ended up in the Democratic Republican party. Thomas Jefferson, who helped found the party, was elected president in 1800, signaling the beginning of the end for Federalism.

Another referendum in 1797 attracted only five thousand votes, with a narrow margin in favor of statehood for Maine. Again, most voters had stayed away from the polls, and again the General Court ignored the results. But several developments at the turn of the century stimulated renewed interest in the subject of statehood. First, the population of Maine increased by 57 percent in the 1790s, as thousands of migrants moved northward from Massachusetts and New Hampshire. The population jumped another 51 percent between 1800 and 1810. Many if not most of the newcomers moved into the interior to take up land for farming. The immigrants, although far from wealthy as a rule, brought an infusion of capital into the District and generated a strong demand for goods and services that stimulated new business. Lumber production skyrocketed and Maine's shipbuilding and shipping expanded with equal vigor after the

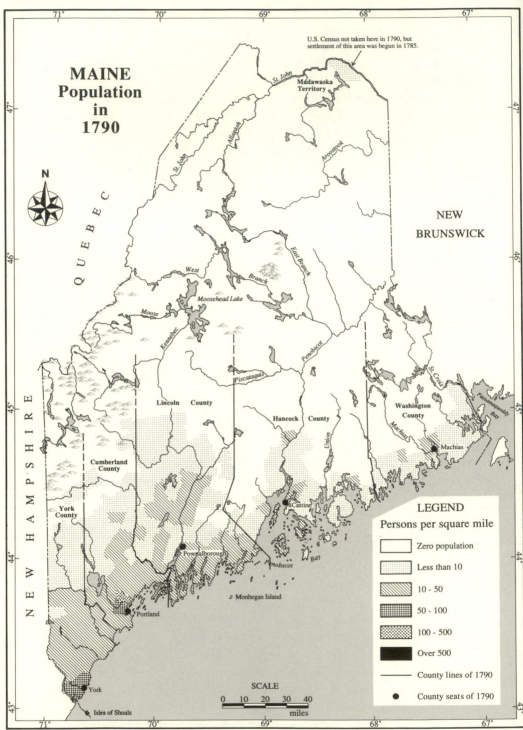

MAINE
Population
in
1790

U.S. Census not taken here in 1790, but settlement of this area was begun in 1785.

Madawaska Territory

QUEBEC

NEW BRUNSWICK

N

St. John

Allegash

Aroostook

West

Branch

East Branch

Moose

Moosehead Lake

Kennebec

Penobscot

Piscataquis

Lincoln County

Hancock County

Union

Washington County

Machias

NEW HAMPSHIRE

Cumberland County

York County

Powmalborough

Penobscot Bay

Castine

Monhegan Island

Portland

York

Isles of Shoals

St. Croix

Passamaquoddy Bay

Machias

LEGEND
Persons per square mile

☐	Zero population
░	Less than 10
╱	10 - 50
▦	50 - 100
▨	100 - 500
■	Over 500
——	County lines of 1790
●	County seats of 1790

SCALE

0 10 20 30 40
miles

© Richard D. Kelly Jr., 1995.

outbreak of war between France and Britain opened up commercial opportunities for neutral nations. Sentiment for statehood grew as Maine's population and economy expanded.

Second, partisan politics rekindled interest in Maine statehood. Maine's Democratic Republican party thrived on expansion in the frontier districts. Also, the party's rise was linked to the appearance of a few astute, well-connected political leaders. Richard Cutts of Saco, elected to Congress from 1801 through 1812, became a close associate of James Madison, who, with Jefferson, had founded the party. Kennebec County's Henry Dearborn, as a member of Congress between 1793 and 1797, had supported Jefferson and Madison during the party's early days. Dearborn became Jefferson's Secretary of War in 1801, and in 1809 he was appointed to the powerful patronage post of collector of the port of Boston. In Lincoln County, William King, a highly successful merchant-capitalist, left the Federalist party in 1803 and quickly became the District's preeminent Democratic Republican leader. By 1805, Democratic Republican voters were a solid majority in Maine.

Although Maine's Federalists had provided the early leadership of the separation movement, growing Democratic Republican power unnerved these moderates. Federalists remained strong in Massachusetts, but in a separate state of Maine they would be a minority. Realizing this, Federalists backed away from the statehood idea. As Democratic Republican fortunes waxed in the District, leadership of the separationist movement passed into the hands of William King and his associates.

Despite continuing indifference to statehood among the population at large, a third development—war with Great Britain—edged the District closer to separation and statehood. Britain and France, locked in war after the brief Peace of Amiens broke down in 1803, placed stringent regulations on neutral shipping, resulting in the seizure of many American ships by both nations. President Jefferson reacted to these depredations in 1807 by inducing Congress to enact an embargo barring all foreign trade by us vessels. The embargo had a disastrous impact upon American shipping interests, including those in Maine. The hard times cost Jefferson's Democratic Republican party some support in Maine, but it did not reverse the political balance of power before it was repealed in 1809.

Economic conditions improved only slightly after 1809, since trade with Britain and France was prohibited by the Non-Intercourse Act that replaced the embargo. As Britain continued to interfere with us neutral trading rights and encourage Indian hostilities along the western frontier, the two nations drifted into war. In Massachusetts, opposition to the War of 1812 revived the Federalist party and emboldened some to call for New England's secession from the

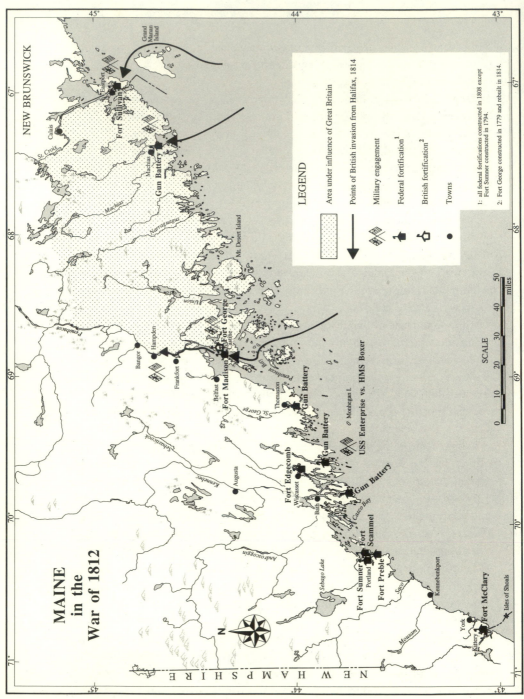

MAINE
in the
War of 1812

NEW BRUNSWICK

Grand Manan Island

Eastport
Fort Sullivan
Calais
St. Croix
Machias
Gun Battery
Machias
Narraguagus
Mt. Desert Island
Union
Penobscot

Bangor
Hampden
Frankfort
Fort George
Castine
Fort Madison
Belfast
Penobscot Bay
Gun Battery
Thomaston
St. George
Gun Battery
Monhegan I.
USS Enterprise vs. HMS Boxer

Schoodic
Augusta
Kennebec
Fort Edgecomb
Gun Battery
Wiscasset
Gun Battery
Bath
Casco Bay

Androscoggin
Sebago Lake
Fort Sumner
Fort Scammel
Portland
Fort Preble

Kennebunkport
Saco

York
Kittery
Fort McClary
Isles of Shoals
Mousam

NEW HAMPSHIRE

N

SCALE
0   10   20   30   40   50
miles

LEGEND

Area under influence of Great Britain

Points of British invasion from Halifax, 1814

Military engagement

Federal fortification[1]

British fortification[2]

Towns

1: all federal fortifications constructed in 1808 except
    Fort Sumner constructed in 1794.

2: Fort George constructed in 1779 and rebuilt in 1814.

45°   44°   43°

67°

68°

69°

70°

71°

United States. In Maine the war, like the embargo, cost the Democratic Republicans some support, but the party remained in control.

In mid-1814, British forces brought the war home to Maine by seizing control of the entire coast east of Penobscot Bay. British forces reestablished control over Castine, and, as they had during the American Revolution, administered the Penobscot region as a conquered territory. Shocked by this development, Governor Caleb Strong called a special session of the General Court, but the legislators proved unwilling to address the plight of Maine. Instead, they simply buttressed the defense of Massachusetts proper.

Since Massachusetts refused to resist British occupation in Maine, President Madison nationalized part of the Massachusetts militia and put it under the command of William King, a militia major-general. Preoccupied with more critical military situations elsewhere, the Federal government lacked the funds to launch an expedition against the British at Castine. When Madison turned to Governor Strong and Boston's predominantly Federalist bankers for financial support to defend Maine, they refused. King and other Democratic Republican leaders charged that Federalist leaders, including a few from Maine, were plotting with the British government to separate New England from the United States in a rank attempt to preserve the region as a bastion of Federalism.

Shocked and angered by the perfidy of the Federalists in control of the Massachusetts government, Maine's Democratic Republicans determined to organize another bid for statehood. Leadership in this third phase of the separation movement came from two who had been involved in the earlier campaigns: William King and John Chandler. They were joined by more recent converts, such as Albion K. Parris, William Pitt Preble, and John Holmes. The movement gained a valuable allay in the Democratic Republican *Eastern Argus,* an influential Portland newspaper.

Late in 1815, the "Junto," as the militant separationists were called, published a series of thirteen articles driving home the argument that statehood would bring more equitable taxation and lower government expenses. Given Maine's rapidly expanding population—now more than 250,000—the District undoubtedly could find leadership to conduct its own government affairs. Under pressure from the Junto, the General Court, still dominated by Federalists, agreed to another test vote on statehood for Maine.

Behind the Federalists' new sense of accommodation was a growing appreciation for two developments in Maine: first, the Democratic Republican party was obviously growing stronger; and second, Maine's population was growing faster than that of Massachusetts. Only by cutting away Maine could Massachusetts Federalists assure their continued control over Massachusetts proper. Federalists in Maine, on the other hand, realized that separation meant permanent minority status in the new state. Unlike their Federalist colleagues in Massachusetts proper, they vehemently opposed separation.

During the months preceding the May 1816 vote, all the old arguments for and against separation were rehashed in the press and public meetings. Interest seemed high, but the voting brought the same old story: substantial indifference to what the politicos saw as a burning issue. While the 1816 campaign turned out a larger percentage of voters than any previous referenda, it still amounted to slightly less than half the electorate. Coastal towns remained opposed to separation, in good part due to stipulations of the coasting law. Still, secessionists gained a three-to-two majority, with most of their votes coming from Democratic Republicans living in farming towns away from the coast.

The General Court agreed to allow Maine to vote again on separation and call a convention to oversee the returns. If a five-to-four majority preferred statehood, the convention delegates were to certify the election and call another meeting to draft a state constitution. As a condition of separation, Massachusetts was to retain title to fifty percent of the public lands in Maine, and the new state was to guarantee the sanctity of previous grants of land, franchises, and contracts. Passage of the bill reflected the Massachusetts Federalists' growing desire to be rid of the District, with its increasingly powerful Democratic-Republican organization. Harrison Gray Otis, chair of the joint committee and president of the Senate—and incidentally a business partner with William King in three townships of land—played the key role in pushing the bill through. Both Otis and King hoped that statehood would entice hordes of new settlers to take up their lands.

Back in Maine, proponents and opponents of statehood launched campaigns for the September election. When the voters had their say in September, 11,927 supported separation and 10,539 rejected it. The favorable votes were only 53 percent of the total—not the 55.5 percent margin needed to achieve separation. Stunned by the outcome, the Junto organized to control the upcoming convention, assuming that a show of support for separation could still sway the General Court. A majority of the delegates favored separation; the problem was circumventing the requirement for a five-to-four majority. At least some Junto leaders were willing to use chicanery to engineer the necessary count.

The convention met at the end of September at the Congregational Meeting House in Brunswick in an atmosphere made heavy by factional hostility and suspicion. Since the separationists had a straight majority of delegates, William King was elected president of the convention. In a crucial maneuver, King appointed thirteen delegates to a Committee to Examine the Returns; nine of them were committed separationists, including four members of the Junto.

8-2. William King, the first governor of Maine, in a portrait by one of the best-known American portrait painters of the era, Gilbert Stuart (1775–1828) of Boston. King was a leader of the separation movement and chaired both the Brunswick and Portland separation conventions. Collections of the Maine Historical Society, Portland.

William Pitt Preble was the Junto's most outspoken advocate of finding some way, fair or foul, to win separation. A former mathematics tutor at Harvard College, Preble devised a stratagem for manipulating the votes to gain the requisite majority for statehood. He declared boldly that the General Court had not intended a simple compilation of votes for and against separation. Rather, he argued, the convention was to tally the total vote in towns favoring separation, and weigh this against the total vote in towns with majorities against separation. By this sleight of hand, the five-to-four majority was achieved!

The carefully chosen Committee to Examine the Returns endorsed this obtuse construction and then assured the convention that, since a majority of voters in both May and September supported separation, the General Court would accept that result. Undaunted by their audacity, the separationists went on to recommend that King appoint a committee to draw up a constitution, and apply to Congress for admission to the Union, anticipating that the General Court would accede to these measures as a fait accompli.

These high-handed maneuvers brought forth a maelstrom of criticism in the Federalist press and even in some of the Democratic Republican papers. Opponents of separation heaped derision on the vote manipulations, and the General Court had no recourse but to order the Brunswick convention dissolved. The court refused to hear anything more about separation, and for the next three years the separation issue lay dormant.

In the years after the Brunswick Convention, King and the other separationist leaders developed a new, and ultimately successful strategy. It appeared that the chief stumbling block to separation was the coastal trading law. With this in mind, King went to Washington in 1818 to seek support from key members of Congress and the administration for a modification of the law. In early March 1819, Congress passed a new coasting law, lumping all the states from Massachusetts to Florida into one customs district. Except for the die-hard Federalists, opposition to statehood in Maine melted away.

Near the end of May 1819, the General Court met at the request of Maine's separationist leaders. By King's reckoning, at least three-quarters of the District's 127 members in the State House of Representatives favored separation. King weakened Federalist opposition in Maine by promising that one-third of all appointed offices under an independent government would be given to Federalists. Later, as governor, he reneged on this promise.

Maine towns deluged the General Court with requests for statehood; only 5 of the 130 petitions sent to the Court opposed separation. The committees appointed to receive the petitions acted expeditiously, and early in June a bill was introduced that outlined terms of separation similar to those set in 1816. The bill provided that voters in Maine would cast their ballots in July, and it specified that the majority for separation would have to exceed the negative votes by at least 1,500 votes. The bill easily passed the General Court. The public discussion in the District prior to the referendum broke no new ground; the old arguments, pro and con, were rehashed, sans the old coasting law issue. To ensure victory this time, the separationists organized county and town committees to distribute literature and get their supporters to the polls. This time they succeeded; the election resulted in a landslide victory—a 10,000-vote majority for statehood.

On October 11, 1819, 274 delegates, representing nearly all the 236 towns in the District, met at the Cumberland County Court House in Portland to set up a new state constitution. Present at the gathering were many who had worked hard for separation: John Holmes, Albion K. Parris, William Pitt Preble, William King, and John Chandler. The document would be submitted along with Maine's application for admission to the Union. The convention was overwhelmingly Democratic Republican, and nearly all the Junto leaders were present. None of the key Federalist leaders had been elected.

As could be expected, Junto leaders dominated the convention. William King was elected president of the convention and was expected as a consequence of this selection to be acting governor. As president, King controlled the sessions and named committee members. The all-important Committee on the Constitution, including Junto leaders John Holmes, Albion K. Parris, and John Chandler, drafted a document that was based broadly upon the Massachusetts constitution, with certain significant modifications that reflected conditions peculiar to Maine. Historian Ronald Banks, the leading authority on the emergence of Maine as a separate state, judged the 1820 document to be one of the most democratic state constitutions in the nation at that time.

Article I, a Declaration of Rights, enumerated the inalienable rights of Maine citizens. Its ten articles served as the basis for the political and legal life of the state. Maine citizens were guaranteed the exercise of free speech, freedom of the press, and freedom of religion. The latter freedom extended beyond the rights given Massachusetts citizens: under the Massachusetts constitution, the Congregational church was still the official state church. Other rights and freedoms were spelled out: the right of due process, the right to bear arms, the right of redress for injury and, among other things, a guarantee that no titles of nobility would be conferred by the state. These guarantees mirror those found in the Constitution of the United States. Article II gave suffrage to all males over twenty-one except paupers, persons under guardianship, untaxed Indians, and persons of recent immigration to the state, and spelled out the conditions for state elections. Article III provided for the division of governing power among the legislative, executive, and judicial branches, and Article IV

INDEPENDENCE ! !
July 26th, 1819.

CITIZENS OF MAINE,

Shall Maine be a free, sovereign and independent State, or shall you and your children remain forever the servants of a foreign power ? This is the true question that is to be settled by your votes on *Monday next.* The friends of liberty cannot hesitate in the choice between freedom and servitude.

What shall we lose by separation ? the privilege of being governed by Massachusetts. What shall we gain ? the right of governing ourselves.

☞ The last year we paid Massachusetts EIGHTY EIGHT THOUSAND DOLLARS for governing us. This is proved by the OFFICIAL CERTIFICATE signed by the SECRETARY OF STATE. It will cost us less, probably not more than ONE HALF this sum to govern ourselves. Almost the whole of this is now carried to Boston and expended there. Choose *freedom and independence* and one *half of this sum* will be saved to the people, and the *other half will be spent* at home.

☞ *Six Millions of acres* of Lands in Maine are now owned by *non-resident land holders ;* full *one third* of which is *owned in England.* These lands now pay but a *nominal tax.* Two THIRDS of the tax is taken off ; and who pays it ? ☞ It is paid by the FARMER AND MECHANIC *in addition* to his own proper share of taxes. ⬠ It is these non-resident land holders who are afraid of taxes. ☞ Their land is taxed at *two per cent,* yours at *six per cent.*

☞ They now pay a *Boston lawyer* ONE OR TWO THOUSAND DOLLARS A YEAR to manage this business with the legislature. *What is taken from their tax is added to yours.* Their taxes may be increased but yours will be diminished.

These land holders are now traversing Maine in every direction. They have their *agents in pay* in every quarter, and they are all *opposed to your independence.*

If you do not wish that you and your children should forever *pay the taxes of these nabobs of Massachusetts* and ENGLAND, turn out on the next Monday and give your voices for separation.

FELLOW CITIZENS,

The eyes of all America are upon you. Your enemies are active and vigilant, and already boast of their fancied success. We exhort you to turn out in your whole strength. Let not a vote be lost. Leave your private business for a day or half a day or an hour, and convince the world by an overwhelming majority that you deserve FREEDOM AND INDEPENDENCE.

July 21.

8-3. This broadside, printed on July 21, 1819, urged citizens to support separation from Massachusetts in a referendum to be held on July 26. An overwhelming majority did, clearing the way for statehood the next year. Courtesy of the Pejepscot Historical Society, Brunswick, Maine.

distributed seats in the legislature and outlined its duties and powers. In the House, representation was distributed by town, based on town population, with a maximum of seven seats for any town. Towns with less than 1,500 citizens were lumped together and the candidacy for representatives rotated among them from year to year. In the Senate, seats were distributed among the counties based upon population, rather than wealth as in the Massachusetts constitution.

Article v defined the qualifications for Governor according to age (thirty years) and residency (at least five years). Significantly, there were no property or religious qualifications, as was still true in Massachusetts. Article v also outlined the governor's powers and provided for an executive council, chosen by the legislature, to advise the governor in certain matters. As in Massachusetts, the secretary of state and treasurer were elected by the legislature. Article vi created the Supreme Judicial Court and inferior courts, and Article vii provided for a militia, the officers of which were to be elected by the men. The major generals were picked by the Senate and the House. The adjutant general and the quartermaster were chosen annually by joint ballot of the legislature.

Article viii titled "Literature," enunciated Maine's dedication to education. The people believed, it said, in a general diffusion of education. The legislature was enjoined to make certain that the towns provided, at their own expense, for the support and maintenance of the public schools. The state, for its part, was required to encourage and occasionally endow academies, colleges, and seminaries of learning. Additionally, Article viii gave the legislature authority to regulate any college to which the state provided funding in any form. The measure was particularly directed at Bowdoin College, a bastion of conservative Federalism and Congregationalism.

Article ix pulled other considerations together: oaths and subscriptions, tenure of office, impeachment, valuation, taxation, apportionment, and a variety of other matters not located in the other articles. Finally, the "Schedule" made provision for amendments, stating that "the constitution, with the amendments made thereto, in accordance with the provisions thereof, shall be the supreme law of the state."

The constitutional convention in Portland accepted the draft, and 236 of the 274 delegates were sufficiently satisfied to sign the document, suggesting that it would receive broad support from the electorate at large. The convention drafted an *Address to the People* explaining why it had introduced changes from the Massachusetts constitution and asking voters to ratify the document at the upcoming referendum in late 1819.

As expected, voters approved the Constitution by an overwhelming margin: only 9 of 241 towns returned majorities against the document. Two days later

8-4. An early version of the Maine state seal. The farmer and mariner represent two of Maine's major industries, while the pine tree in the center symbolizes a third. Resting in front of the tree is a moose, while above the pine is the North Star and the Latin motto *Dirigo,* "I lead." The seal is reproduced in John W. Barber, *History and Antiquities of New England, New York and New Jersey* (Worcester: Dorr, Howland, 1841).

petitions were filed in Congress asking for statehood for Maine. The District faced a deadline imposed by the Massachusetts Act of Separation. If Maine was not admitted to the Union by March 4, 1820, it would revert to its old status as a district.

Many separationists thought that once Maine's application for statehood reached the Congress, the rest of the process would be automatic, but this was not what happened. Congressional consideration of Maine statehood became entangled with consideration of statehood for the territory of Missouri and the attempts by some northern Congressmen to bar slavery there. Since December 1819, the Senate had been evenly balanced between free and slave states, and the Senate Judiciary Committee linked admission of Maine and Missouri with the intent of preserving this balance.

Republican Representative James Tallmadge of New York threw the hopes of the Maine delegates into momentary confusion by offering an amendment to the Missouri statehood bill that would prohibit the further introduction of slaves into Missouri and would free all children born of slaves already in Missouri when they reached the age of twenty-five. With the stipulation that Missouri would eventually become a free state, Maine's request was thrown in doubt, because the southern states would never allow parity in the United States Senate to be disturbed. Pro-southern Senator Jesse B. Thomas from Illinois offered an amendment to overcome the logjam. It provided that slavery would be forever forbidden in the area known as the Louisiana Purchase, north of the line 36°30', excepting in Missouri, which would enter the Union as a slave state. Based on this "Missouri Compromise," the Senate agreed to admit Maine to statehood on condition that Missouri enter as a slave state.

The Senate's Thomas amendment did poorly in the House of Representatives, however. Amazingly, despite their consuming interest in statehood, all seven Maine members of the Massachusetts House delegation voted against the compromise. When the House passed its own bill restricting slavery, the situation improved somewhat. A conference committee from the House and Senate, including John Holmes and James Parker from Maine, worked out a compromise package that was ultimately approved by the Congress in a series of votes. John Holmes, not wishing to leave anything to chance, sent his pro-compromise statement to Thomas Jefferson and a number of other prominent citizens. Jefferson's anguished letter about the dangers of slavery splitting the Union, along with the astute efforts of Henry Clay of Kentucky, won the day. Maine became the twenty-third state in the Union on March 15, 1820; Missouri entered as a slave state. With statehood, a new chapter in Maine's history was about to begin.

For Further Reading:

There are two principal works to read for an understanding of the political landscape of Maine from the end of the American Revolution (1783) to the Missouri Compromise (1820). Alan Taylor's *Liberty Men and Great Proprietors* (Chapel Hill, N.C., 1990) depicts the clash of economic interests between the settlers, many of them Revolutionary War veterans, who flooded into Maine in search of economic opportunities, and the wealthy owners of vast tracts of land such as the Kennebec Proprietors. The struggles between the two groups, Taylor makes clear, had political and religious overtones which exacerbated the level of conflict. Ronald F. Banks's *Maine Becomes a State* (Portland, 1970) lays out the rocky, twisting political road Mainers followed on the way to statehood. Banks pays particular attention to the shifting balance of power between the Federalist and Democratic Republican parties in Massachusetts and the District of Maine. The settlers Taylor describes formed the backbone of the Democratic Republican party, which became dominant in Maine and led the push for statehood.

A number of monographs provide a broader context for political developments in Maine during these years: William N. Chambers, *Political Parties in a New Nation* (New

York, 1963); Noble Cunningham, Jr., *The Jeffersonian Republicans in Power* (Chapel Hill, N.C., 1963; George Dangerfield, *The Era of Good Feelings* (New York, 1952), Paul Goodman, *The Democratic Republicans of Massachusetts* (Cambridge, Mass., 1964); and Glover Moore, *The Missouri Controversy, 1819–1821* (Lexington, Ky., 1953).

For a better sense of Maine in those days, a reader may turn to Moses Greenleaf, *A Statistical View of the District of Maine* (Boston, 1816) and his *A Survey of the State of Maine* (Portland, 1829). Contemporary insights on Maine include Luigi Castiglioni, *Viaggio: Travels in the United States of North America, 1785–87* (Syracuse, N.Y., 1983); Timothy Dwight, *Travels in New England and New York,* vol. 2 (Cambridge, Mass., 1969); and Edward Augustus Kendall, *Travels through the Northern Parts of the United States in the Years 1807 and 1808,* vol. 3 (Portland, 1809). Additional sources are given in Ronald F. Banks, comp., *Maine during the Federal and Jeffersonian Period: A Bibliographical Guide* (Portland, 1974).

9

Reform Movements & Party Reformation,

1820–1861

RICHARD R. WESCOTT & EDWARD O. SCHRIVER

In politics, culture, and economics, the first half of the nineteenth century was an era of new opportunities in Maine. While the structure of Maine government was dictated by the new Constitution, political parties evolved through a much less formal process: new coalitions formed around emerging national, state, or personal issues; old alignments were disrupted as leaders and constituents regrouped; and new political parties emerged from the chaos.

The reform impulse was a driving force behind party factionalism in this formative period. Gradually, the Whig-Democratic party system collapsed under the weight of two divisive issues: temperance and the abolition of slavery in the South. As political forces realigned, Maine's modern party system took shape.

Of course, this dynamic reform spirit was not confined to Maine; instead we see again the interaction between local impulses and national events. State politics reflected broader issues, but these were articulated in ways that embodied local concerns and local partisan maneuvering.

Similarly, a shifting balance between stability and disruption was a central dynamic in antebellum Maine. Changing party identifications—Democratic Republican, Federalist, Jacksonian Democrat, Whig—and the immense range of factions within each of these parties reflect the political instability of the times and the power of new ideas to rupture old organizations. Yet these chaotic decades prepared Maine for an era of remarkable partisan stability to come, during which Republican rule remained intact for nearly a hundred years.

Five years after statehood, newspaper journalist and humorist Seba Smith toured what he considered the settled portion of Maine. He began in the southwest, where most of Maine's three hundred thousand residents lived, and journeyed as far east as the Penobscot River towns—Bucksport, Bangor, and Old Town—and the small ports on Penobscot Bay. On his first stop, at Brunswick, he attended the Bowdoin College commencement, held in the fall because rain, snow, and mud made carriage travel over Maine's primitive roads at any other time of year almost impossible. Bowdoin College had been established in 1794 by Massachusetts authorities to bring enlightenment to Maine. Commencement in 1825 demonstrated the institution's rise as an eastern seat of learning: among the graduates were Henry Wadsworth Longfellow, Nathaniel Hawthorne, and several others who would gain fame in New England and beyond.

From Brunswick, Smith moved on to Thomaston, where he took occasion to visit the state prison, opened only one year earlier. He also made a pilgrimage to the grave site of General Henry Knox, whose visions of empire had begun to disintegrate well before the grand speculator died in 1806. Continuing north to Bangor, Smith noted the presence of the theological seminary and the frontier town's vast potential for growth based on lumber production and shipment. He traveled to Old Town, curious to observe the Penobscot nation firsthand. Like most white Protestants of the time, he saw the native people as shiftless, lazy, and tainted by Roman Catholicism. They would, he predicted, either adjust to the white way of life, abandon the region, or perish. (Such attitudes help explain the abysmal treatment Maine's Indians received at the hands of state officials over the next century.) Turning south, Smith stopped to admire manufacturing and educational facilities at Waterville and Gardiner. Everywhere he saw signs of a new state coming to life culturally and economically. Maine, according to Seba Smith, had tremendous potential.

Smith's impressions were typical in the new and acutely self-conscious state of Maine. Similar observations, based on the vast potential of the eastern frontier settlements, the newness of Maine's social institutions, and the promise of intellectual and spiritual life, permeated Maine politics. As the new state came of age, the years between 1820 and the Civil War brought shifting political allegiances, party consolidation and disintegration, reform, and conflict. The tremendous political energies vented during these years expressed the state's attempt to carve out a new niche in the Republic.

An upwelling of reform thinking churned Maine politics throughout this period, mixing with personal ambition to alter, time and again, the fragile coalitions that made up Maine's early political organizations. The triumphant Democratic Republicans, having led the people of Maine to independence and statehood, were divided between those who supported the democratic views of Thomas Jefferson and Andrew Jackson and others who believed in a more ambitious nationalistic approach, as outlined by Alexander Hamilton and the Federalists and championed by John Quincy Adams. By the 1850s, new issues— prohibition and abolition of slavery—agitated Maine politics, once again wracking the political structure and preparing the ground for the formation of the Republican party.

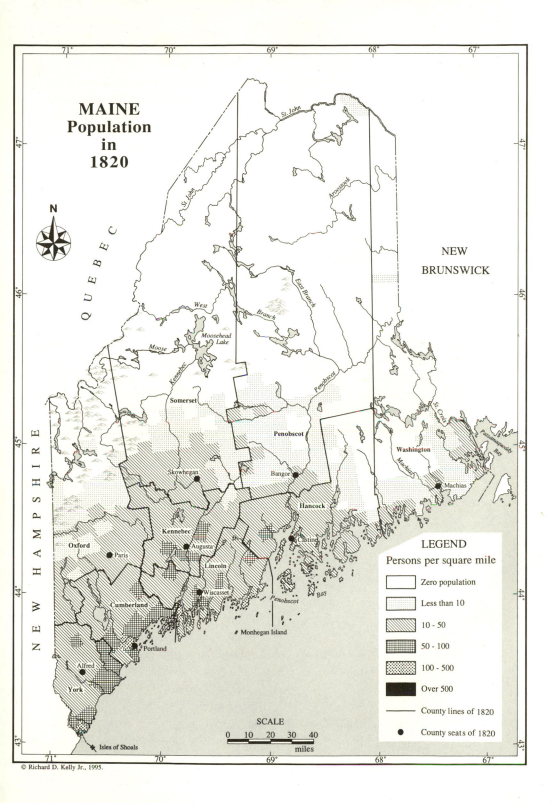

**MAINE
Population
in
1820**

QUEBEC

NEW

BRUNSWICK

NEW HAMPSHIRE

St. John

St. John

Aroostook

West

Branch

East Branch

Moose

Moosehead Lake

Kennebec

Penobscot

Somerset

Penobscot

St. Croix

Washington

Passamaquoddy Bay

Machias

Skowhegan

Bangor

Hancock

Machias

Kennebec

Oxford

Paris

Augusta

Castine

Lincoln

Penobscot

Wiscasset

Bay

Cumberland

Monhegan Island

Portland

Alfred

York

Isles of Shoals

LEGEND

Persons per square mile

☐	Zero population
▨	Less than 10
▨	10 - 50
▦	50 - 100
▦	100 - 500
■	Over 500
—	County lines of 1820
●	County seats of 1820

SCALE

0 10 20 30 40

miles

Such differences agitated Maine politics from its beginnings. In Maine's first state elections in April 1820, Democratic Republican leader William King, champion of Maine statehood, was elected governor in a landslide vote. This impressive consensus was not to last, however. In the spring of 1821 King resigned from office, in part because he failed to get legislative approval for two measures designed to foster economic development in Maine: purchase of the wild lands retained by Massachusetts under the Act of Separation; and property tax incentives designed to encourage manufacturing. King's desire to use state authority to promote economic growth, a policy reminiscent of the old Federalist program, failed to inspire his Democratic Republican colleagues in the legislature. Wedded to the original principles of Jeffersonian democracy, King's opponents looked with suspicion on policies that linked government to manufacturing or commercial interests. These Jeffersonians reasoned that state intervention necessarily favored members of the "privileged classes," and that an impartial, minimal government would eventually free the nation of parasitical wealth. King's resignation signaled a growing rift between these two factions of Democratic Republicans.

King was replaced by William D. Williamson, president of the senate, who in turn resigned and was replaced by Speaker of the House of Representatives Benjamin Ames. After this round of musical chairs, Albion K. Parris, one of the original Junto, emerged as the candidate of hardcore Democratic Republicans. Parris faced two rivals: one supported by a coalition of Democratic Republicans and Federalists, and the other an official candidate of the Federalist party. Both, like King, endorsed a Hamiltonian program of active state support for commerce and manufacturing. In the annual general election in 1821, the Jeffersonian vision triumphed: Parris was elected by a narrow majority, becoming Maine's first governor to remain in office for a full one-year term. Parris was reelected as governor each year through 1825, but this show of unity among Democratic Republicans masked deep schisms based on divergent trends in state and national politics.

The debate over government's role in economic development was indeed nationwide. President John Quincy Adams's support for internal improvements, the Bank of the United States, and tariff protection was unpopular with many Democratic Republicans, who lamented the party's drift from Jeffersonian principles. As Andrew Jackson began building his political following for the election of 1828, the forces opposed to Adams coalesced. When Jackson was elected, the old Democratic Republican party was irreversibly split into two new organizations: National Republicans and Democrats.

Although Jackson won the presidency in 1828, his Democratic followers in Maine fared poorly. Only the reelection of second-term Democratic Governor

9-1. This remarkable watercolor by Annah M. Bucknam, painted around 1821–25, is the only known painting of Maine's first State House (right corner), on Portland's Congress Street. Next door is the Cumberland County Courthouse and First Parish Church and across the street is Portland Academy. Portland remained the capital from 1820 to 1833, when the Bulfinch State House opened in Augusta. Courtesy of Berdan's Antiques, Hallowell, Maine.

Enoch Lincoln prevented the National Republicans from gaining full control of the government. Disarray within the new Democratic party became more evident during the following year when Governor Lincoln refused to accept renomination, and the party's legislative caucus, which usually made gubernatorial nominations, failed to agree on a candidate. The caucus called for a party convention, which after much debate came up with a compromise candidate in Samuel E. Smith, chief justice of the Court of Common Pleas.

The National Republicans nominated Jonathan G. Hunton, an undistinguished farmer and country lawyer from Readfield who had been a member of Governor Lincoln's council. Democrats responded to the selection of this political unknown with a vicious campaign; Hunton's forces responded in kind. Modern-day political rhetoric pales in comparison with that of the nineteenth century, but even by earlier standards this was a dirty campaign. Hunton won, but Smith and the Democrats returned to power in 1830 and retained control over state government and Maine's Washington delegation until nearly the end of the decade.

The popularity of the Democratic party in Maine during these years is not surprising. "Whigs," as the National Republicans came to be known for their opposition to "King Andrew" Jackson, emphasized tariff protection for American manufacturers, federal aid for construction of roads, canals, and other internal improvements, and a national bank—planks that favored manufacturing interests but offered little for a state economy based on agriculture, lumbering, and maritime commerce. Thus, during the early 1830s, Maine's Democratic party took on a distinctive Jacksonian cast. Governor Smith and his Democratic successors easily defeated their Whig opponents in a series of campaigns focused on Jacksonian policies.

The tide began to turn, however, in 1837. The Democratic party was again rocked by factionalism, this time growing out of dissatisfaction with President Martin Van Buren's administration. A sharp and prolonged depression further dampened enthusiasm for Democratic programs. Finally, Democrats nominated for governor Colonel Gorham L. Parks of Bangor, who had earlier defended a Penobscot County sheriff against a charge of adultery and was tainted by the scandal. Parks lost the election to Whig candidate Edward Kent by the slim margin of 479 votes.

Whigs renominated Governor Kent in 1838, but Democrats sought a new candidate in the place of the controversial Parks, and backed John Fairfield, a two-term member of the US House of Representatives. In an unusually large voter turnout, Fairfield won on a slight 3,000-vote majority. The margin was again reduced in 1840, after an extraordinarily dirty campaign between Governor Fairfield and ex-Governor Kent. The result was a virtual dead heat: Kent

emerged with a narrow margin of 45,574 votes to Fairfield's 45,507. The incon-
clusive results threw the election into the legislature, where Kent found enough
Whig support to prevail. Kent's narrow victory inspired an ironic piece of dog-
gerel famous in Maine's political history:

> Oh, have you heard how old Maine went?
> She went hell-bent for Governor Kent.

Ironically, success disrupted the Whigs' shaky unity, as bitter patronage contests pitted faction against faction. William Pitt Fessenden, a leading Whig,
complained in a letter to a political confidant, "I believe our friends to be office
mad." President Harrison's death a month after his inauguration worsened the
situation, as Vice-President John Tyler moved to strengthen his hand by re-
distributing federal posts. In Maine these divisions within the Whig party led
to Fairfield's election as governor over Kent in 1841, but patronage issues proved
equally as disruptive in the Democratic party. Fairfield reluctantly accepted a
draft from the divided 1842 convention and in the election again won over Kent.

The tensions caused by reform aspirations, national issues, and the quest for
spoils of office continued to disrupt Maine politics through the antebellum
years. Disarray in the Democratic party was evident in declining public interest in politics. The total gubernatorial vote dropped from 91,000 in 1840 to
63,000 in 1843. Old party issues lost their impact, and many voters stayed home,
revolted by the factional struggles for party control and patronage.

Among the most divisive issues during these years was President John Tyler's
determination to annex Texas, then engaged in a struggle with Mexico. John
Fairfield, now a US Senator, opposed annexation, believing it would lead to war
with Mexico. Nationally, the annexation question widened the rift in the Democratic party. The Whig party, on the other hand, fearing a sectional split
between the North and the South, refused to take a stand on the Texas question.
Meanwhile, in May 1844, the Democratic National Convention nominated
James K. Polk of Tennessee, a vehement advocate of annexation.

In Maine the annexation-minded Democrats supported Polk's nomination,
while the Fairfieldites supported Van Buren. In 1844, voters flocked to the polls,
drawn by the excitement of the presidential campaign, the annexation issue,
and a new style of campaigning characterized by vigorous newspaper editorials, local and out-of-state speakers, mass meetings, picnics, and rallies.
Democratic gubernatorial candidate Hugh J. Anderson, a Polk supporter, rolled
to a resounding victory. In the presidential contest Polk also won by a landslide
in Maine, prompting his supporters to call for the ouster of Democratic office-
holders who had received their appointments earlier under President Tyler.

Patronage, national issues such as annexation of Texas, and struggles for control of the fluid party organizations tore at the seams of the two young parties in the decades after statehood. In the 1850s, however, these party factions gradually coalesced around two new issues. During these years, the Maine Temperance Union and the Maine Antislavery Society abandoned attempts at reform through moral suasion and took up political cudgels. Increasingly, Democrats and Whigs opposed to slavery and liquor crossed party lines to support reform candidates, disrupting old factional and partisan alignments. Leaders of these two reform movements thus helped usher in a new party system in the years directly before the Civil War.

Institutional Reform, Peace, and Temperance

Although overshadowed by the temperance and antislavery campaigns, other reforms marked the state's effort to meet the needs of an expanding population. Seba Smith's visit to the Maine State Prison at Thomaston illustrated one of these measures. As county jails became increasingly inadequate to house the state's criminal population, the need for a state prison became apparent. The Thomaston facility opened in 1824 with a small staff of guards under Chief Warden Daniel Rose. At first both men and women were imprisoned at the facility; it was not uncommon to see a woman in the yard with a baby in her arms. The inmates carried on trades, such as shoe- and barrel-making and, outside the prison, quarrying. Ministers came in to teach illiterate inmates to read and write.

Prisoners were housed individually in small, one-person cells, which could only be entered by ladder from the roof. The purpose of this solitary confinement was to hasten the process of character reformation and prepare the prisoner to return to society. In the silence of the cells, the prisoners would contemplate their situation, discover the error of their ways, and rebuild their characters. This, at least, was the theory.

Ten years after the prison was completed, the state met another of its social needs by opening the Maine Insane Hospital. Before the establishment of this facility, the mentally disturbed were cared for privately—in many cases locked away in rooms at home or housed in county jails. In 1834, the state acquired land in Augusta and raised a building to house the patients. Treatment for the residents remained primitive, however; they were comforted if possible, restrained if necessary, and given different diets to see if this improved their mental state. Some were taken on outings to the coast as part of their cure. Until the Insane Hospital in Bangor was founded near the end of the nineteenth century, the Augusta facility was about the only public recourse for the mentally ill.

Maine also contributed to several nationwide campaigns to remold society. Over the centuries, reformers advocated peace as an alternative to a condition of seemingly perpetual war. After the American Revolution, for instance, the famous Philadelphia physician and reformer Benjamin Rush mounted a campaign to institute a Secretary of Peace to counterbalance the Secretary of War. Rush envisioned a world of peace ushered in by free schools teaching Christianity, citizens distributing free Bibles, and state and national governments inscribing Christian messages above the portals of public buildings. Other peace organizations followed, and in the 1820s, a small group of Maine citizens added its energies to this ancient hope.

Maine's Peace Society was essentially the labor of William Ladd. Born in Exeter, New Hampshire, in 1778, Ladd had a comfortable childhood and graduated from Harvard College in 1797. He made his fortune at sea and returned to devote himself to worthy causes. From his farm home in Minot, Ladd extended his influence throughout the state. In 1824, he began publishing a series of peace articles in the *Christian Mirror,* the Congregational church's weekly state paper. In *The Essays of Philanthropos,* which he published the following year, he listed the various causes of war: lust for applause, power, wealth, and revenge; the evils of ambition and avarice; the militia system; and, oddly enough, what he saw as women's weaknesses for men dressed in military uniforms and the public's penchant for military parades and other preparations for war.

In 1837, the American Peace Society and its branches, including those in Maine, were wracked by a series of acrimonious debates over such questions as a Christian individual's responsibility to defend loved ones threatened by violence, or the morality of a war to defend the nation at large. Plagued by limited public recognition and bedeviled by internal differences, Maine's peace movement dissipated rapidly when William Ladd died in 1841, and for all practical purposes, it disappeared when the Civil War began in April 1861. The dream, however, never completely died.

Liquor prohibition, one of Maine's two most influential reform movements, animated political debate well into the twentieth century. Popular concern over the evils of drinking emerged in the late 1820s, and in 1829 the state legislature passed a local option liquor law, thereby throwing the temperance issue into local politics. In 1837, a group of radical temperance advocates formed the Maine Temperance Union, which soon called for a complete prohibition of the sale of intoxicating liquors. The legislature responded with a law that effectively prohibited the sale of liquor for off-premises consumption. Enforcement, however, remained weak.

Young Neal Dow, destined to become America's preeminent temperance reformer, led the crusade to stiffen these restrictions on drinking. Dow was raised

9-2. Reform was in the air in the decades after statehood, and no cause was seized more passionately than that of temperance. After a campaign led by Neal Dow (1804–97), America's "father of Prohibition," the first antiliquor law was passed in 1851. Most towns of any size had a support society complete with paraphernalia. Charles Codman (ca. 1800–1842) painted this banner for Ellsworth's "Washington Total Abstinence Society." Collection of the Farnsworth Art Museum, Rockland, Maine.

in Portland in an atmosphere of strict morality and temperance. On his return from the Friends' Academy in New Bedford, Massachusetts, he began work in his father's tannery. In his free hours he roamed the streets of Portland intent on suppressing the evils of alcohol. In 1827, he joined the Portland Fire Department, as was the custom with well-placed young men in the nineteenth century, and two years later he demanded—and received—pledges of total abstinence from the members of his Deluge Engine Company.

Dow did not stop there. As a member of the American Temperance Society, he attacked the longstanding workingman's tradition of an afternoon grog (or rum) break, beginning in his father's tannery. In 1846, he took his campaign to the legislature and won a prohibitory law. Prohibitionists nevertheless remained discontented with the 1846 liquor law almost from the day it was enacted and continued to agitate for stricter provisions.

Elected mayor of Portland as a Whig in 1851, Dow used his power base there to rally prohibition forces across the state. In the same year Dow and his supporters won a legislative act prohibiting the sale of all liquor except for industrial or medical purposes. The "Maine Law"—prohibition—became a reality, and its influence spread well beyond the borders of the state. In Portland, Dow enforced the Maine Law to the point of being overbearing. His policies on search and seizure particularly irritated the public, including some of Portland's substantial citizens. As a result, he was defeated in the next election.

Dow received a second term as mayor in 1855, when he was returned to office by a mere forty-seven votes. During his second tenure as mayor, Dow became involved in one of the city's most unfortunate incidents. A shipment of alcohol was intercepted in Portland, and for safe keeping it was locked away in the city hall. This news spread quickly, and a crowd gathered containing a number of persons unhappy with the scarcity of drink in Portland. When the crowd became assertive, Mayor Dow used police, militia, and gunfire to protect the contraband liquor. The incident resulted in the death of one rioter and the wounding of several others; blame was attributed to Dow's fanaticism. Although Dow was cleared of blame, he never overcame the onus cast upon him.

Dow faced setbacks in the legislature as well. Even though he and his followers worked persistently to influence the selection of delegates to party conventions, leaders of both parties recognized the divisive potential of the prohibition issue and often distanced themselves by arguing that liquor consumption was a matter of individual conscience. Legislators, in turn, progressively weakened the Maine Law. The so-called New Maine Law, passed in 1858, trivialized penalties for selling liquor. Undeterred, Dow won a seat in the legislature and continued the fight there. Although frustrated in Maine, Dow carried his message afar; by early 1857, five New England states and Michigan had their own versions of Maine's pioneer temperance legislation. Dow also traveled to Great Britain to spread the temperance message. On the eve of the Civil War, the temperance crusade—and the chief crusader himself—still harbored a great store of energy to extend the battle into the second half of the century.

The Antislavery Movement

Undoubtedly the most vigorous and far-reaching reform crusade of the antebellum period was antislavery. Although slavery had been abolished in Massachusetts and the District of Maine in the 1780s, it was not until the 1830s that Mainers organized to fight the institution at the national level. Boston's renowned antislavery editor, William Lloyd Garrison, introduced abolition to Portland in 1833. Samuel Fessenden, an ex-Federalist Portland lawyer, and other like-minded people founded the Maine Antislavery Society in Augusta in 1834—about the same time the temperance movement started with the founding of total abstinence societies in many communities. Both crusades began by promoting their causes through moral suasion, denouncing intemperate drinking and slaveholding as immoral. Disenchantment with this approach eventually drove both movements to political action.

The Maine Antislavery Society sent traveling agents around the state to speak against slavery to anyone willing to listen, no matter how small the gathering. Opposition at these talks was often strong and sometimes threatening. Besides speaking tours, the Maine Society also petitioned Congress and the legislature. Annual meetings of the society passed and printed fiery resolutions, and Maine's antislavery newspaper, *Advocate of Freedom,* edited by Bowdoin College mathematics professor William Smyth, added its own rhetoric to the crusade.

Abolitionists tried unsuccessfully to obtain support from the Protestant churches in Maine. The major denominations—Methodists, Congregationalists, and Baptists—were reluctant to take a public stand on the issue. The Methodists argued that their task as Christians was to save individual souls, who would then free their slaves and sever their connection with the sinful practice. Baptists argued somewhat like the Methodists and pointed to their brethren in the South, whom they did not wish to offend. The Congregationalists insisted that each of its churches was independent; each would have to declare for itself.

To counter these refusals, the abolitionists organized their own Religious Anti-Slavery Conventions, which lasted from 1844 to 1852. Their message was persistent: because the Bible forbade fellowship with slaveholders, worshipers should withdraw from slaveholding churches. Letters were sent to churches in the South asking members to detach themselves from the sin of slavery. Slavery divided religious institutions across the nation; at the annual meetings, Christians who abhorred slavery passed resolutions against Christians who abided the practice.

By 1840, a minority faction of the Maine Antislavery Society had become convinced that slavery could not be reconciled by moral suasion. Interested in political action, several Maine abolitionists attended a meeting in Albany, New York, where they helped form the antislavery Liberty party. The delegates chose James G. Birney of Ohio as a presidential nominee. Despite continued opposition to political action by the Maine Antislavery Society, the Liberty party was officially organized in Maine in Winthrop on July 1, 1841. Traveling agents were again sent out to spread the message, this time with partisan overtones. The new party nominated Jeremiah Curtis of Calais for governor, and by 1842, it had

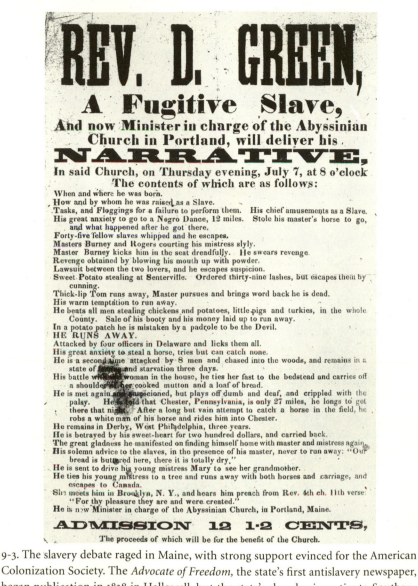

REV. D. GREEN,

A Fugitive Slave,

And now Minister in charge of the Abyssinian
Church in Portland, will deliver his

NARRATIVE,

In said Church, on Thursday evening, July 7, at 8 o'clock
The contents of which are as follows:

When and where he was born.
How and by whom he was raised as a Slave.
Tasks, and Floggings for a failure to perform them.   His chief amusements as a Slave.
His great anxiety to go to a Negro Dance, 12 miles.   Stole his master's horse to go,
     and what happened after he got there.
Forty-five fellow slaves whipped and he escapes.
Masters Burney and Rogers courting his mistress slyly.
Master Burney kicks him in the seat dreadfully.   He swears revenge.
Revenge obtained by blowing his mouth up with powder.
Lawsuit between the two lovers, and he escapes suspicion.
Sweet Potato stealing at Senterville.   Ordered thirty-nine lashes, but escapes them by
     cunning.
Thick-lip Tom runs away, Master pursues and brings word back he is dead.
His warm temptation to run away.
He beats all men stealing chickens and potatoes, little pigs and turkies, in the whole
     County.   Sale of his booty and his money laid up to run away.
In a potato patch he is mistaken by a padrole to be the Devil.
HE RUNS AWAY.
Attacked by four officers in Delaware and licks them all.
His great anxiety to steal a horse, tries but can catch none.
He is a second time attacked by 8 men and chased into the woods, and remains in a
     state of _____ and starvation three days.
His battle with a woman in the house, he ties her fast to the bedstead and carries off
     a shoulder of her cooked mutton and a loaf of bread.
He is met again and suspicioned, but plays off dumb and deaf, and crippled with the
     palsy.   He is told that Chester, Pennsylvania, is only 27 miles, he longs to get
     there that night.   After a long but vain attempt to catch a horse in the field, he
     robs a white man of his horse and rides him into Chester.
He remains in Derby, West Philadelphia, three years.
He is betrayed by his sweet-heart for two hundred dollars, and carried back.
The great gladness he manifested on finding himself home with master and mistress again.
His solemn advice to the slaves, in the presence of his master, never to run away: "Our
     bread is buttered here, there it is totally dry."
He is sent to drive his young mistress Mary to see her grandmother.
He ties his young mistress to a tree and runs away with both horses and carriage, and
     escapes to Canada.
She meets him in Brooklyn, N. Y., and hears him preach from Rev. 4th ch. 11th verse:
     "For thy pleasure they are and were created."
He is now Minister in charge of the Abyssinian Church, in Portland, Maine.

ADMISSION 12 1·2 CENTS,

The proceeds of which will be for the benefit of the Church.

9-3. The slavery debate raged in Maine, with strong support evinced for the American Colonization Society. The *Advocate of Freedom*, the state's first antislavery newspaper, began publication in 1838 in Hallowell, but the state's close business ties to Southern ports made support for abolition far from unanimous. This 1853 broadside summarizes the dramatic escape from slavery of a Rev. D. Green, who later served as pastor of Portland's Abyssinian Church (founded in 1828). Courtesy of the Portland Public Library, Portland, Maine.

completed a full slate of candidates in every county. Even more significantly, it
elected one member to each house of the legislature. Between 1845 and 1848,
Samuel Fessenden ran for governor on the Liberty party ticket, receiving, at his
best, 12,037 votes out of 82,277 in 1848.

Because women were generally barred from political activity, those in the
antislavery movement were compelled to work apart from the men. Some fused
their antislavery beliefs with their commitment to women's rights. "What can
women do in the great crusade?" asked Esther Gibbs in 1853. Her answer was
blunt: "Women can agitate the slavery question." The Maine Daughters of Freedom held a large meeting at East Livermore on July 3 and 4, 1854, and later the
women abolitionists went to Augusta to honor Governor Anson P. Morrill for
his strong antislavery convictions. At the February 1855 meeting at Augusta, they
presented the governor with a huge cake featuring antislavery sentiments in-
scribed in frosting.

In the 1840s, the prohibitionist and antislavery movements grew stronger,
and a few leaders were elected to the legislature. Under Neal Dow's astute
leadership the prohibitionists pushed hard for stronger liquor laws, and their
growing influence was indicated by the fact that by 1845 majorities in the executive council, senate, and house had signed the Maine Temperance Union pledge
forswearing the use of liquor. As temperance activists united with abolitionists,
both movements gained strength. Democrats, wrangling among themselves
over the fruits of repeated electoral victories, grew increasingly vulnerable to
divisions generated by prohibitionists and abolitionists. Nevertheless, the reformers were not yet able to disrupt the established political party system.
Further deterioration in the Whig and Democratic parties was necessary before
any fundamental political shift could take place.

Party Splits and Multiparty Politics, 1844–54

During the 1840s, the two major parties continued to react primarily to events
on the national scene. Even here, however, politics reflected fundamental re-
alignments based on sectional and slavery issues. Thus, national issues, too,
fanned the fires of political controversy down east.

The war with Mexico, long predicted by opponents of annexation, came in
May 1846. As us forces achieved victory after victory, Congress debated whether
slavery should be permitted in the conquered areas. The debate focused on the
Wilmot Proviso, a proposal to ban slavery from any territory acquired as a
result of the war. Maine's Democratic delegation to Congress was nearly unanimous in its support of the Wilmot Proviso, a position the Whig and Liberty
parties also endorsed in their press. In 1846, the dispirited Whig party nomi-

nated a relative unknown for governor and wrote a platform that mixed its standard positions on the bank and tariff with strident denunciations of the war and the southern slave power. Democrats, on the other hand, held out against mounting factional tensions, nominating John W. Dana for governor with a platform that endorsed the war with Mexico but studiously avoided the slavery extension issue.

The results of the election reflected the unsettled political times. Dana failed to win a majority, and the gubernatorial race was thrown into the legislature, where Dana won. The Democrats controlled the legislature, but the combined Whig and Liberty vote, representing opposition to the war and the extension of slavery, increased markedly, indicating a significant shift in voter sentiment. Some post-election commentators noted that a fusion of the Whig and Liberty parties might have given them control of the state government.

Sensing the growing resistance to slavery extension, most of Maine's Democratic members in the US House continued to vote for the Wilmot Proviso. Governor Dana endorsed antislavery sentiments, and following the unexpected death of Senator Fairfield late in 1847, the Democratic legislature chose Hannibal Hamlin, an outspoken supporter of the Wilmot Proviso, to replace him. Later in the session it handily endorsed resolutions denouncing slavery and slavery extension. Still, the Democrats ignored the slavery question in their 1847 campaign, hoping thereby to hold the party together. Whigs, on the other hand, attacked President Polk and condemned the war as an unconstitutional escapade to extend slavery. The Liberty party was equally outspoken in its condemnation of the war and slavery. The Democrats retained control over state government, but the issue continued to erode their margin over the other two parties.

That year a group of Ohio Free-Soil Whigs and New York Democrats called for a national convention to form a new political party opposed to the extension of slavery. Maine people responded in strong numbers, along with delegates from seventeen other states. At the August 9, 1848, Buffalo convention the delegates from Maine participated in the formation of the Free-Soil party, dedicated, as its platform stated, to "Free Soil, Free Speech, Free Labor, and Free Men." The party called for an end to government support of slavery, for conveyance of cheap federal lands to actual settlers (rather than to speculators), and for higher tariffs to pay off the national debt. In Maine, the Free-Soil party was dominated by former Liberty party leaders. However, it also drew in Whigs and Democrats who were committed opponents of slavery extension.

The 1848 campaign in Maine, for both the state and national elections, focused on the slavery extension question. Democrats emerged victorious again, but Governor Dana received only a plurality of the popular vote and had to be reelected by the legislature. The combined votes of the Whig candidate, Elijah

Hamlin, and of the Free-Soil candidate, Samuel Fessenden, exceeded by several thousand those cast for Dana; Free-Soilers now held the balance of political power in Maine. Over the next year there were signs of fusion between Whigs and Free-Soilers in several counties in Maine. Democrats, on the other hand, split into two factions in 1849: "Woolheads" were militantly opposed to slavery extension; "Wildcats" were more conciliatory toward the South; they supported opening up some of the territory taken from Mexico for slavery.

The rallying cry in 1849 was fusion, fusion, fusion. Whigs invited Free-Soilers into the Whig party; Democrats bid to win back Free-Soilers of Democratic origins; and Free-Soilers hoped to gain additional recruits from the other two parties. Despite the volatile impact of the slavery issue, the splintered Democrats managed a surprising sweep of offices, electing Woolhead John Hubbard as governor and retaining control of the legislature.

The question of extending slavery into the territories moved to the center of the national political stage in 1850, when Congress took up President Taylor's proposal for immediate statehood for California. Henry Clay proposed a compromise that included admission of California as a free state and organization of the rest of the territory acquired from Mexico without restriction on slavery. Maine's Democratic press generally backed the so-called Compromise of 1850, but Woolhead Democratic Senator Hannibal Hamlin voiced strong opposition, and his stand won praise from Whigs and Free-Soilers. Opposed by Maine's Wildcat Democrats and facing a reelection campaign in the Maine legislature, Hamlin sought allies outside the Democratic lines; he was elected, but only because leading Free-Soilers threw their support behind him.

Hamlin's senatorial election split the Democratic party, and neither side did much to pull it back together for the 1850 gubernatorial election. Governor Hubbard was renominated by the legislative caucus, but in the county and state district conventions chaos reigned. Antislavery Woolhead Democrats drafted platforms condemning the extension of slavery; Wildcats endorsed the Compromise of 1850. Whigs experienced similar divisions, while Free-Soilers squabbled over the issue of fusion with the antislavery Whigs. Amid this organizational confusion, Democrats easily won the election. A significant decline in the Free-Soil vote suggested that the major parties seemed to be stabilizing after years of factionalism. But just as antislavery reform was reaching an equilibrium in Maine, Neal Dow and his prohibitionist colleagues cut across party lines with a new issue, as they launched an all-out campaign to enact a statewide prohibitory law.

The collapse of the Whig-Democratic party system in Maine began in 1852, with a struggle between the Woolheads and Wildcats for control over liquor policy and patronage. Woolheads—opponents of slavery extension—also

9-4. Hannibal Hamlin (1809–91), a Hampden lawyer, served in the Maine legislature and in the US Congress and Senate. Hamlin, who opposed slavery, won national recognition when he switched from the Democratic to Republican party in 1856. Hamlin was selected as Abraham Lincoln's running mate in 1860, served as Vice-President from 1861 to 1865, and then returned to the Senate, where he remained until 1881. Collections of the Maine Historical Society, Portland.

adopted Neal Dow's reform crusade. Wildcats rejected both issues. When Governor Hubbard was renominated by the Democratic legislative caucus, Wildcats, angry with him for signing the prohibitionist 1851 Maine Law, bolted the meeting and held a convention of their own. Wildcats nominated Anson G. Chandler for governor and drafted a platform that endorsed the Compromise of 1850 but denounced the Maine Law. Both factions went on to nominate their own local candidates in most districts. Whigs, too, split over the Maine Law. Neal Dow and his Whig followers pledged to support Democratic incumbent John Hubbard, while so-called Liberal Whigs vowed to support Chandler, the Wildcat Democrat opposed to the Maine Law. The Free-Soil party, also in a state of disarray in 1852, nominated one of their long-time stalwarts, Ezekiel Holmes, but agreed that party members could vote as their consciences dictated.

In this unsettled political atmosphere, Governor Hubbard, a supporter of the Maine Law, received a large plurality of the votes but failed to get the constitutionally required majority. Apparently about half of his support came from Democratic voters, about a quarter from Free-Soilers and Whigs, and the remainder from Maine Law supporters. Efforts to suppress or accommodate free-soil and prohibition sentiment had failed; the breakdown of old party loyalties was obvious.

Principles, patronage, and personal ambitions: each was threaded into the new political fabric that began to take shape in Maine in 1852. The new legislature wrestled for over two weeks simply trying to fill the eight vacancies in the senate, where no candidate had received a majority. With Democrats unable to hold their party together, Whigs gained control of the senate, and when two Wildcat senators voted against their own party candidate, a Whig, William G. Crosby, was elected governor. Selection of a US Senator was equally difficult; no faction could muster enough votes to send up the name of a candidate, and thus Maine had only one senator in Washington until 1854.

In 1853, the factional struggle for control of the Democratic party was again fought largely in reference to the Maine Law. After intense factional bickering the party settled on Albert G. Pilsbury, who opposed the Maine Law but had not been outspoken on the issue. Having settled on a safe candidate, the convention adopted a safe platform based on old issues like tariffs, banks, and internal improvements. Woolheads called their own rump Democratic convention, endorsed the Maine Law, and nominated Anson P. Morrill for governor. Pilsbury received a plurality of the gubernatorial votes, but the Whig, Free-Soil, and Woolhead candidates—all of whom backed the Maine Law—outpolled him collectively by about eleven thousand votes. Again, the election was thrown to the legislature, where two Whigs were elected: the incumbent, Crosby, as governor, by a one-vote margin; and William Pitt Fessenden as

Senator. The results of the 1853 election raised the question: should prohibitionists and antislavery reformers unite into one party?

Fessenden's election took on greater significance when Senator Stephen A. Douglas of Illinois introduced a bill to repeal the Missouri Compromise that had brought Maine and Missouri into the union in 1820. The so-called Nebraska Bill reopened the question of slavery in the western territories and touched off a furor across the North. In Maine, it was denounced by most newspapers and in the legislature. Local gatherings held throughout the state culminated in a mass protest meeting called by a group of political leaders more or less evenly divided between prohibitionist Woolheads, now referred to as Morrill Democrats, and Whigs and Free-Soilers. The day following the meeting, the state temperance convention met and adopted a set of resolutions that urged all Maine citizens, whatever their party affiliations, to do battle for rigorous enforcement of the Maine Law. Most of those who participated in the prohibitionary convention had attended the Nebraska Bill protest. Opposition to slavery and support for prohibition were coalescing into a new, powerful political movement that threatened to burst apart old political boundaries.

In 1854, the Morrill Democrats, proclaiming the ideals of freedom and temperance, renominated Morrill and adopted a set of resolutions that condemned the Nebraska Bill. The other wing of the disintegrating Democratic party, now known as Liberals rather than Wildcats, held its own meeting and nominated Aroostook County's Shepard Cary. A "true Democrat," Cary condemned both abolitionism and prohibitionism. Finally, the "regular" Democratic state convention nominated a compromise candidate, Albion K. Parris, and called for all Democrats to return to the party fold. The Whigs, ignoring calls to fuse with the Morrill Democrats, continued on an independent course. However, their 1854 platform paralleled that of the Morrill forces, and they agreed to fuse with opponents of the Nebraska Bill in the congressional district nominations. Free-Soilers, satisfied with Morrill's stand on slavery and prohibition, nominated Morrill for governor by acclamation.

The potential for outright fusion of Morrill Democrats, Whigs, and Free-Soilers had not been fulfilled at the state level, but it did take place in some county and congressional district conventions. Most notably, in Franklin County the three factions adopted a platform condemning the Nebraska Bill and endorsing the Maine Law, and they agreed upon a division of the county offices among themselves. The Franklin County fusion organization was to be called the Republican party.

The political situation was further confused in 1854 by the formation of the "Know-Nothing" party. A national movement originating in the late 1840s, in Maine it sprang from a nativist reaction to the influx of Irish Catholic immigrants into the state's industrial and commercial cities. Viewing the newcomers as a threat to American Protestantism and democracy, the Know-Nothings wanted to exclude them from the political process. The new party threw its support to Anson P. Morrill.

The results of the fall elections amply demonstrated the strength of the fusionist movement. Morrill, drawing support from Democrats, Whigs, Free-Soilers, and Know-Nothings, only narrowly missed winning a majority. Much of his support came from the wealthier and more populous parts of the state, where manufacturing and maritime activities were more important than agriculture. Fusionists also won control of the legislature and, in the congressional elections, took four of the six seats. A political revolution was taking place.

The emerging fusionist party, called by some the Republican party, controlled the 1855 session of the legislature. With a symbolic burst of energy, it organized both houses in a matter of several hours and quickly elected Morrill governor, taking great care to see that Morrill supporters among former Democrats, Whigs, and Free-Soilers received equal shares of the spoils of victory. The fusionists rammed their program through the legislature. They adopted a set of resolves that condemned slavery and the repeal of the Missouri Compromise and passed legislation to strengthen enforcement of the Maine Law.

Along with abolition and prohibition, the fusionists dealt with a third concern: amending the state constitution to curb the governor's patronage power. Minor civil posts were made elective and the power to choose the state's land agent, adjutant general, and attorney general was switched from the governor to the legislature. Fourth, the fusionists moved to placate the Know-Nothing movement by stiffening naturalization and voting procedures. These measures also denied the Democrats some of their political support.

During 1855, the Republicans waged a strong campaign, holding mass rallies and bringing in nationally prominent speakers. Democrats urged the remnants of the Whig party to merge with them on an equal basis in opposition to the Maine Law, but the Whigs rejected the invitation. The superheated political atmosphere of 1855 brought a record number of voters to the polls. The Republicans increased their vote over 1854, but the Democrats did much better, winning control over both houses. It appears that the Republican defeat was the result of voter reaction to the violence of the Portland Court House riot of 1855, which the Democrats successfully portrayed as an example of prohibitionist fanaticism, and to the Republican party's association with Know-Nothingism. Although Republican gubernatorial candidate Anson P. Morrill gained a plurality of three thousand votes over the Democrat, Samuel Wells, Morrill did not receive a majority. When the legislature met in 1856, like-minded Democrats and Whigs cooperated to elect the Democrat, Samuel Wells, governor. Republicans

9-5. The arrival of Irish immigrants in large numbers swamped the job market and helped initiate the nativist "Know-Nothing" movement. On the night of July 6, 1854, a mob attacked and later burned Bath's Old South Meeting House, which was being used by Catholics. Depicted here by firefighter John Hilling (1826–94), the burning was one of several local outrages. Collections of the Maine State Museum, Augusta.

took heart from the fact that their party's permanence seemed assured, but a consensus developed that it would have to moderate its radical image by recruiting experienced leaders from the older parties.

Back in power, the Democrats and Whigs moved to overturn the principal actions of the Republicans in the previous legislature. First to go were the two laws that had been aimed at making it difficult for recent immigrants to become citizens and voters. Then, after extended bickering, they repealed the Maine Law and replaced it with a liquor license law.

In the 1856 campaign, Republicans perfected both their state and national party organizations, as slavery extension moved to the forefront of public attention during the conflict in "bloody Kansas." The party concentrated upon shedding the radical prohibitionist-abolitionist image that opponents tried to pin upon them. Before the state convention met, emerging leaders such as James G. Blaine and Israel Washburn argued that the party should nominate a candidate who had not been involved in earlier intra-party maneuvering and yet was a known opponent of the extension of slavery. Senator Hannibal Hamlin, they argued, was such a man. If he could be wooed away from the Democratic party, he could pull other Democrats over to the Republican side. Hamlin resisted the call until the 1856 Democratic national convention, where James Buchanan, a sympathizer with slavery extension, was nominated for the presidency. After delivering a Senate speech denouncing the Pierce administration, Hamlin quit the party.

Republicans greeted their new ally with hearty praise, and a few days after Hamlin's renunciation of the Democratic party nominated him for governor by acclamation. Their choice indicated that they were going to ride the slavery issue into state office, and the platform they adopted confirmed it. Devoting little attention to state affairs, it denounced the southern slavocracy and its puppet, Franklin Pierce. The Maine Law was studiously ignored.

The Republicans ran a high-powered campaign in Maine, insisting that their leaders were cautious people, as far removed from the fanaticism of rabid abolitionists and prohibitionists as they were from the disunionists of the Democratic party. With substantial funds raised from within and without Maine, they flooded the state with propaganda and canvassed from one end of the state to the other with stump speakers, mass meetings, clambakes, and chowder suppers. The Democrats emulated these tactics, but the effort was fruitless. In the state elections in September Hamlin won an outright majority over Wells, as thousands of voters deserted the Democrats and what little remained of the Whig party. Even more impressive, the Republicans pulled some 10,500 new voters into their camp. Their sweep extended to all congressional districts and both houses of the legislature, which they controlled by lopsided majorities. In November, as expected, Republican presidential candidate John C. Freemont also rolled to victory in Maine, even though he narrowly lost the national election.

The landslide Republican victory permanently altered Maine's political topography. Hamlin, elected governor, resigned when the Republican legislature elected him to the US Senate, and in 1857, Lot M. Morrill was nominated by an overwhelming vote in the Republican convention. Once again, Republicans triumphed over the divided Democratic party in the general elections. Morrill was easily returned to office the following year and continued in office to the eve of the Civil War. His platform pledged the party to "the encouragement of manufacturing industry, the settlement of our public lands, the development of our vast resources, and the improvement and perfection of our Common School system"—issues strikingly similar to those that had undermined Maine's first party system under Governor William King in 1820!

The Republican party emerged out of the turmoil caused by the issue of slavery and its wrenching impact on old party loyalties. Although antislavery remained a minority cause in Maine as the Civil War approached, the band of dedicated reformers had done much to alter Maine politics. As religious and moral stewards, Maine's abolitionists fought a good fight, finished their course, and kept the faith; they kept an unpopular issue before the people of Maine for nearly thirty years. Especially noteworthy was the fact that this was accomplished in a state which in 1840 had only 1,355 black citizens in a population of over half a million. Samuel Fessenden expressed their resolve best when he responded to William Lloyd Garrison's invitation to attend the antislavery society celebration in Philadelphia in 1863. Nearly blind and not far from death, Fessenden replied through his secretary that he could not attend, but that his heart was warmed by the realization that a dreadful enormity was soon to end. His last words to Garrison were, "Lord, now lettest thou thy servant depart in peace, for mine eyes have seen of thy salvation."

For Further Reading:

The key work to read for an overview of the development of temperance-prohibition and antislavery reform movements in Maine and their relationship to party politics is Richard R. Wescott's *New Men, New Issues* (Portland, 1986). Wescott discusses the intra-party factional fighting over patronage that was exacerbated on the one hand by the rise of a state prohibition movement led by Neal Dow of Portland, and on the other hand by the development of a national antislavery crusade led by William Lloyd Garrison, which had strong support in Maine. Ultimately, the new Republican party founded in the 1850s became the political sword of the antislavery and prohibitionist forces in Maine and the nation.

The national context for Maine politics is explored in Eric Foner, *Free Soil, Free Labor, Free Men* (New York, 1971); William E. Gienapp, *The Origins of the Republican Party, 1852–1856* (New York, 1986); George H. Mayer, *The Republican Party, 1854–1964* (New York, 1964); Roy F. Nichols, *The Disruption of American Democracy* (New York, 1948); and Glyndon G. Van Deusen, *The Jacksonian Era, 1824–1848* (New York, 1959).

At the state level, the role of religion in the antislavery crusade is depicted in Montague C. Clark, *American Slavery and Maine Congregationalists* (Bangor, 1940) and Austin Willey, *The History of the Antislavery Cause in State and Nation* (Portland, 1886).

Maine readers are fortunate to have a number of biographies available to them which portray key political figures of the era. The more important published works include Frank L. Byrne, *Prophet of Prohibition: Neal Dow and His Crusade* (Gloucester, 1961);

Philip G. Clifford, *Nathan Clifford, Democrat* (New York, 1922); Neal Dow, *The Reminiscences of Neal Dow* (Portland, 1898); Francis Fessenden, *The Life and Public Services of William Pitt Fessenden,* 2 vols. (New York, 1970); Gail Hamilton, *Biography of James G. Blaine* (Norwich, Conn., 1895); Charles E. Hamlin, *The Life and Times of Hannibal Hamlin* (Cambridge, Mass., 1899); Gaillard Hunt, *Israel, Elihu and Cadwallader Washburn* (New York, 1925); H. Draper Hunt, *Hannibal Hamlin* (Syracuse, N.Y., 1969); Charles A. Jellison, *Fessenden of Maine* (Syracuse, N.Y., 1962); William L. Lucey, *Edward Kavanaugh* (Francestown, N.H., 1947); David S. Muzzey, *James G. Blaine* (New York, 1934); and Edward Stanwood, *James Gillespie Blaine* (Boston, 1905).

Articles well worth consulting for a wider perspective on this topic include: David Demeritt, "Cuban Annexation, Slave Power, Paranoia, and the Collapse of the Democratic Party in Maine, 1850–1854," *Maine Historical Society Quarterly* 29 (Summer 1989); Rod Farmer, "Maine Abolitionists View the South: Images in Maine Antislavery Newspapers 1838–1855," *Maine Historical Society Quarterly* 25 (Summer 1985); Wayne M. O'Leary, "Who Were the Whigs and Democrats? The Economic Character of Second-Level Party Leadership in Tidewater Maine, 1843–1853," *Maine Historical Society Quarterly* 28 (Winter 1989); and Edward O. Schriver, "Antislavery: The Free Soil and Free Democratic Parties in Maine," *New England Quarterly* 42 (March 1964).

10

Family & Community Life in Maine, 1783–1861

JOYCE BUTLER

Local histories, memoirs, diaries, letters, journals, genealogies, and museum arti-facts provide the background for this cultural history of early Maine. Applying keen historical insight to these sources, Joyce Butler illuminates the patterns of work, leisure, entertainment, and education that emerged during the formative decades after the Revolution. Just as important, she describes the institutions and inter-actions that linked families and communities and formed the basis for future economic, social, and cultural development.

This chapter reconfirms points raised in the last chapter. First, culture, like poli-tics, reflects a rise in opportunity in Maine. As distribution points for a vast productive hinterland, Maine's coastal towns enjoyed a notable prosperity during these years. Frontier towns also offered a new beginning for farmers from southern New England, although their prospects were still limited by the harsh realities of wilderness living.

Second, we can see in cultural terms the growing divergence between coastal Maine and the interior settlements. In close contact with the rest of the Atlantic world, Maine's seaports prospered, matured, and developed an elite culture equal to that of their sister communities along the New England seaboard. Maine's inte-rior agricultural towns, on the other hand, matured much more slowly. This division, already reflected in the politics of the Revolution and statehood, remained an enduring part of Maine cultural and economic life.

Finally, we see once again the interplay of outside and local influences, or as Butler puts it, a mixture of "cosmopolitanism and provincialism." Culturally, this maritime region kept its windows open to the world, but the need for close-knit community cooperation lent a sense of inclusiveness and insularity to Maine life. These themes—economic opportunity, sectionalism, and a mix of local and out-side influences—characterized Maine in the early nineteenth century.

During the years of frontier expansion and town development in Maine, 1783 to 1861, fundamental social and cultural patterns took shape, preparing Maine's people for the important contributions they would make to America's industrial, commercial, and social life during the later nineteenth century. A remarkable influx of people during these years altered the frontier society enormously. New immigrants looked to Maine, with its vast tracts of undeveloped forestland and its access to commercial sea-lanes, as a place where they could better themselves economically. Along the southern coast, their success was reflected in a remarkably refined and cosmopolitan society. Farther east and inland, economic advances came more slowly, and the cultural attributes of a prosperous society were, in large part, far less evident.

Although Maine's fledgling seaports captured most of this expansion in population and trade, in 1783 even these flourishing coastal towns, some of them inhabited for over a hundred years, were still essentially frontier settlements. York, shire town or commercial center of York County since 1716, had itself dispersed men and women onto the eastern frontier and could claim the society, architecture, and culture of a well-established community, albeit on a modest scale. Wells and the Kennebunks were still small, struggling villages and Pepperelborough (Saco) a rough lumbering town. Bath, called "Twenty Cow Parish," was virtually unknown as a commercial port. On the Sheepscot River, Pownalborough (Wiscasset), the shire town for nearby Kennebec River towns, had yet to begin its ascent to prosperity.

Falmouth (Portland), Maine's most advanced seaport before the Revolution, was all but destroyed by the British. It reestablished commercial links with Boston and with the West Indies, shipping house frames, fish, country produce, and livestock. The community separated from the other Fore River towns in 1786 and became Portland. Ten years later it counted, among other structures, 409 houses, 86 mechanics' shops, 76 stores and shops, 3 rope factories, and 2 distilleries. Portland's vibrant economy attracted Maine's first newspaper, its first bank, and its first marine insurance company. Growth in the other southern port towns was only slightly less spectacular.

Settlement to the east and in the interior was also impressive. In the post-Revolutionary period, land speculators, merchants, artisans, and—in the greatest numbers—farmers flocked to the eastern and inland parts of the District of Maine. Veterans impoverished by the war and paid off in depreciated currency, along with families from the overcrowded, exhausted farmlands of eastern Massachusetts, needed cheap lands and abundant resources to begin anew. In 1797, missionary minister Paul Coffin declared Union, Maine, "a place for young men to make themselves."

Individuals of greater means also saw the district's frontier as a land of opportunity. General Peleg Wadsworth, originally of Plymouth, Massachusetts, commanded eastern Maine during the Revolution. In 1784, he brought his family to Falmouth and set himself up in trade. Three years later he paid less than a thousand dollars for 7,800 acres between the Saco and Great Ossipee rivers, holdings that would eventually encompass the town of Hiram.

In 1790, when the first federal census was taken, approximately half of the District of Maine's population lived west of the Androscoggin River. Over the next decade expansion beyond this frontier prompted the demarcation of new counties: Hancock in 1789, Kennebec in 1799, Oxford in 1805, and Somerset in 1809. Almost two hundred new towns were founded between the end of the Revolution and 1820. In most cases, the men and women who arrived in these new towns left behind them amenities carved out by an earlier pioneering society, and the hundred or more towns incorporated between 1820 and 1840 extended this pioneering sequence for another generation. Indeed, frontier development was a fact of life in rural upland Maine through the first half of the nineteenth century.

To reach these isolated settlements, pioneer families traveled on foot or on horseback, women and children riding "pillion" (on a cushion behind the saddle), following Indian paths or "spotted lines"—trails of blazed trees marked by settlers who had gone before and would soon be their neighbors. Timothy Chapman, who was seven when he moved with his parents from Methuen, Massachusetts, to Sudbury Canada (Bethel), never forgot their "long, lonely and tedious" journey.

Access to water to power gristmills and sawmills often determined the location of new inland settlements. But before the mills were erected and lumber had become available, settlers established rough camps and then put up log houses. The Chapmans built their twenty-foot-square log house of second-growth poplars from old Indian clearings. Ten family members crowded into the one-room house, which had loose boards laid down for a floor, rocks placed in one corner for a fireplace hearth, and a chimney made of crossed sticks plastered with clay. Usually the settlers completed more permanent one-story or story-and-a-half framed and clapboarded houses only after they had a barn. When the Chapmans were finally able to raise a two-story frame house, they called it their "mansion." For many families like the Chapmans, their first modest frame structure eventually formed the nucleus of a larger and more comfortable home.

Sustenance

The economy of Maine's inland farm communities revolved around subsistence production, a small export crop, a complex bartering trade between neighbors, and an assortment of small-scale crafts. Maine's early farmers usually plied a supplementary skill or occupation, since their homesteads were never fully self-sufficient. A farmer might also be a tanner, joiner, shipwright, blacksmith, or even a minister. Each, in fact, needed numerous skills: to be able to build and maintain chimneys; make farm tools, shoes, brooms, and baskets; repair looms and spinning wheels; and construct furniture. Farmers were also lumberers. During the boom years following the Revolution, harvesting timber brought a measure of prosperity to anyone willing and able to go into the woods to bring it out. Trees were an immediate crop. The forest provided not only material for home construction, but timber for shipbuilders and cargo for the vessels once they were seaborne. Maine settlers found ready markets for lumber, house frames, clapboards, shingles, and cordwood in Boston and the West Indies. In fact, Parsonsfield's historian saw lumbering as a distraction, drawing farmers from the plow. It was "a set back to improvements" in his town.

Trees supplied other products. Hemlock bark was raw material for tanners, who in turn produced leather for shoe and harness makers. Traders bought or gave credit for wood ashes from fireplaces, and frequently local manufacturers refined the ashes into pot or pearl ash, which was used in soap making or by ceramics factories in England. Since most farm products were bartered locally or used for subsistence, the cash such forest products returned was a scarce blessing.

A family's subsistence depended on the contributing labor of all family members—men, women, young and old. Women, who were responsible for meals and all aspects of running a household, also kept poultry whose eggs and feathers could be exchanged or sold to fill other family needs. They wove cloth, kept vegetable and herb gardens, and made butter and cheese for family use or sale. Some had special skills by which they could contribute to their family's support. Martha Ballard, a Hallowell midwife, was paid for her services with cash or goods. Eliza Wildes of Arundel, a weaver, made bonnets and capes for neighbors, and she kept in her home, for sale or exchange, a supply of "West India goods" brought by her shipmaster husband. Even children were involved in the family economy. Their chores—chopping wood, milking and pasturing the cows, churning butter, spinning flax—were a significant contribution to the welfare of the household.

Families bartered eggs, livestock, produce, logs, or disassembled house frames at the nearest port, earning credit for the purchase of coffee, molasses, rum, seeds, cotton, or English manufactured goods. Ann Bryant Smith of Portland ran a store with her husband. On January 22, 1807, in the diary in which she recorded the supplies of local produce that she bought for the store, she also noted, "Knitting on a stocking with yarn purchased of a country woman."

The barter system provided families the opportunity for significant use of their resources. A farmer might have the hides of his slaughtered cattle tanned in exchange for his or his hired man's services in the tanner's woods. An apprentice, learning a trade from a local farmer-artisan, might take a new pair of boots or shoes in partial payment for his services; likewise, a neighborhood or itinerant shoemaker could exchange his skills for a length of homespun cloth or room and board for a week. Labor, tools, livestock, and even fields were shared or rented in households aware of the market value of everything they "bot" or had to offer.

Barter continued as a crucial form of economic exchange even after a stable federal currency was available. This system, although far more personalized than cash exchange, was remarkably complex and involved assignments of comparable value for an amazing variety of items. On January 6, 1809, for instance, Joshua Whitman of Turner noted in his journal, "Bot 3 bowls of Reuben Thorp and agreed to give him a lb. of flax." On the same day he sold a local innkeeper "2 lb. flax. he paid me cash 2s." These are only two of the twenty different kinds of transactions by which Whitman conducted his business, including labor exchange, land sharing, lending, and borrowing. This neighborhood "mutuality," the sharing of resources through face-to-face transactions involving skill, tools, produce, and labor, challenge the traditional notion of the self-sufficient farm and testify to the strong economic bonds among pioneer neighbors, reinforced by ties of kinship, community, and shared faith.

Despite the increased number of new small towns in the interior, the focus of Maine's population growth and commercial activity remained in the older coastal towns, which benefited from the booming maritime trades and thrived on the exchange of frontier products brought down from the interior. Wiscasset, with three streets running north and south and eight or ten "majestic" houses, was the largest shipping center east of Portland. Augusta had emerged as the market town for Kennebec River settlements, and by 1803 Portland had experienced a spurt of growth unequaled by any other New England community to that time. In fact, the early years of the century would be the most prosperous in that seaport's history.

Society, Culture, and Education

In these older port towns, commercial prosperity reinforced a social hierarchy topped by bankers, lawyers, and merchants. The coastal elites were made up of the offspring of long-established families and the Harvard-educated clergy who were their intellectual mentors. These families prospered even as new arrivals—smaller merchants, artisans, mechanics, unskilled laborers, and mariners—transformed the village landscapes and economies. In the coastal towns, commercial connections to Boston and other world ports, along with rapid population growth, the rise of a local gentry, and growing economic wealth and diversity brought a flowering of social and cultural advantages.

In 1796, when Abigail May came from Boston to Portland to visit her aunt, she found Portland's houses with their elegant spread of rooms—lobby, parlor, drawing room, dining room, and breakfast room—"very handsome." The three-story homes built in Portland in 1800 and 1801 for the merchant-shipowners Hugh and Stephen McLellan are outstanding examples of the Federal-period houses built in ensuing years in Maine's coastal villages. With their delightful Palladian windows, delicate pilasters, urn-topped balustrades and fences, such mansions reflected not only coastal society's ability to have the best, but its awareness of what was fashionable.

Wallpapers and mirrors were made in Boston or Europe; glass, earthenware, engravings, and fabrics were of English manufacture; porcelain came from China; and silver was crafted by European or Boston artisans. Much of the furniture was of Philadelphia, Boston, or Portsmouth manufacture, although a share of the business went to Maine cabinetmakers like the Radfords of Portland, Saco's Ichabod Fairfield, William Hackett of Kennebunk, and the Berwick clock makers Paul and Abner Rogers. Those who could not afford Boston prices, or were too far inland to import bulky or delicate furnishings, patronized local cabinetmakers and hired itinerant artists like Moses Eaton to stencil their walls in lieu of wallpaper.

Prosperous families along the coast hired itinerant artists to produce silhouettes, miniatures, and portraits. The miniaturist John Roberts, silhouette cutter William King, and portraitist John Brewster, Jr., all toured coastal Maine at the turn of the nineteenth century. Brewster, who made his home with a brother in Buxton, began his career in Portland in 1796 and went on to paint many of Maine's prominent citizens.

In these towns the social life enjoyed by families of great or even modest wealth was extensive if somewhat provincial. Peleg Wadsworth's daughters attended balls at Portland's Assembly Room, gathered with others of their class at Broad's Tavern in Stroudwater, and attended parties in one another's homes.

It was Abigail May's opinion that her Portland companions lived in "elegant style" with "every species of enjoyment" available to them, even though it was she and a partner who introduced to them the "much admired" country dance "The Little Fifer." Another Boston lady, who spent some time in Wiscasset in 1809, found its inhabitants "genteel, remarking that she had been to more parties and teas in her short visit than in a whole year in Boston."

Besides dancing, Portland's wealthy young people enjoyed games like Blind Man's Bluff, Hunt the Whistle, and backgammon. Reading, letter writing, journal keeping, drawing, and painting were common pastimes. After receiving a common-school education locally, the offspring of Maine's professional and merchant families, like those of Stephen and Patience Longfellow of Gorham and Daniel and Sarah Cleaves of Biddeford, were sent to academies in southern New England. From there the young men went on to Harvard College or Yale to prepare for their life's work, and the young women returned home, where they employed their more narrowly contrived educations to embroider mourning pictures, paint Tiffany borders for their ball gowns, and to nickname their beaux after classical figures. (The Wadsworth sisters called their suitors "Narcissus" and "Despairing Pyramus.")

Yet just as more isolated, less cosmopolitan communites had their own social and cultural advantages, so too were townswomen obliged to work in the home, as did their more rural counterparts. Peleg Wadsworth was a representative to the United States Congress from 1792 to 1806. He was away from home each winter when Congress was "sitting," and his wife, Elizabeth, ran a household that included eight children. Daughters Eliza, Zilpah, and Lucia helped with household chores. In 1797, Zilpah wrote to a friend, "I have been hard at work all morn[in]g. We have no maid this long time, and I do not know when we shall be so fortunate as to get one."

Reestablished as Maine's premier port city in the 1780s, Portland led the coastal towns in social and cultural advantages. Maine's first newspaper, the *Falmouth Gazette*, began publication in Portland in 1785. Other refinements—a Boston theatrical group, a dancing academy with a French dancing master, musicals, and in 1805 a museum of wax works—testified to the growing diversity of cultural entertainments. Nevertheless, several "hinterland" towns preempted Portland in opening college-preparatory "grammar schools," or academies. Academies were chartered in Hallowell and Berwick in 1791, in East Machias and Fryeburg in 1792, and finally in Portland in 1794. By 1802, when Brunswick's Bowdoin College opened its doors, it was possible for a Maine youth to gain a complete education on home territory.

Individuals of privilege brought a measure of cultural refinement even to Maine's more remote towns. Thomaston had "Montpelier," the home of General Henry Knox and his family. There in 1796 the peripatetic Mr. Coffin

10-1. Fryeburg Academy, founded in 1792, is one of the scores of private educational institutions created to bring secondary education to Maine at the start of the nineteenth century. Daniel Webster (1782–1852) taught briefly at Fryeburg, which continues to provide secondary education to Fryeburg and surrounding communities. Courtesy of the Maine Historic Preservation Commission, Augusta.

dined with Mrs. Knox and her daughters and found the "little Misses talking French in a gay mood." Other guests were able to "talk European politicks and give the history of the family of the late King of France." After his two-month sojourn in backcountry towns, Coffin declared that Montpelier "exceeded all I had seen." In Hallowell, the wealthy Vaughan family, English born and educated, gave glittering parties at their estate and were liberal patrons of the arts. A family of remarkable musical ability, the Vaughans founded a reputation for Hallowell which was perpetuated by the Old South Church "chanting choir" and, beginning in 1800, regular publication of music books in the town.

10-2. Multigrade, one-room schoolhouses like this one in Old Town served Maine's smallest communities into the 1950s. This undated photo was probably taken in the early 1900s. Courtesy of the Maine Historic Preservation Commission, Augusta.

But if culture fed upon accessibility and prosperity in Maine's coastal towns, and upon the inspiration of a prominent family in a few other cases, inland towns generally showed their refinement in more modest ways. At the time when Fryeburg was establishing its academy, the children of Meduncook Plantation (Friendship) were attending classes in homes because there was no school building. In time, such simple beginnings evolved into school districts, each with its own modest schoolhouse. In 1798 Augusta had eight school districts; in 1825 Fryeburg had fourteen. Each district had a neighborhood school committee to administer its share of the local tax money earmarked for schools. As a state, Maine only began to provide financial support for education in 1828. This administrative fragmentation permitted an enormous range of educational conditions. One of Kennebunk's district schools, for instance, was a converted fish house. In most cases schooling involved simple curriculums, imperfectly taught by ill-prepared teachers. Moreover, it was not until 1875 that school attendance was compulsory for at least twelve weeks per year for nine-to-fifteen-year-olds. Mary Knight of Otisfield revealed the dilemma of many country students when she noted in her diary on December 12, 1836, that it was the first day of school and "don't know how often I can go."

Prospering communities eventually supplemented their free "common schools" with "grammar schools," which provided instruction above a elementary-school level and were attended by children whose parents owned shares. In 1800, Maine's 161 incorporated towns all had common schools, but only 7 had grammar schools. Other supplements to free common schools were private boarding schools for boys, usually run by ministers in their homes; dame schools for very young children and girls; and the academies, which drew their students, in part, from other towns. Most such educational advantages were enjoyed by males, but in 1816 a female academy with a woman preceptor opened in Augusta. In 1821, Portland opened Maine's first—and the nation's second—free high school.

Other educational institutions—libraries, debating societies, and public lectures—arrived in sporadic fashion along the Maine frontier. Usually they were preceded by less formal means of cultural exchange—story-telling as a form of oral history, or sharing printed materials whenever they became available. In 1787, Charles Vaughan organized the Kennebec Agricultural Society in Hallowell to promote agricultural knowledge. Wiscasset had a Social Library at the turn of the century, but Augusta did not gain one until 1817. The "Calais Club," whose paying members supported a library, was not formed until 1827. By 1825, debating societies, which provided a means of self-improvement as well as social intercourse, were general. By the 1830s, they were being called "lyceums," and their weekly meetings featured lectures by itinerant speakers as well as debates on moral, cultural, national, and international issues.

Despite Maine's somewhat provincial bearing, men and women in this generation made their mark intellectually, often exerting influence far beyond their home borders. The Abbott brothers, Jacob (born in Hallowell) and John (born in Brunswick), wrote the widely popular Rollo books as well as histories and biographies. Portland's Henry Wadsworth Longfellow influenced the world with his poetry. Hannibal Hamlin of Paris served as Abraham Lincoln's vice-president, and Kennebunk's Hugh McCulloch was his treasury secretary. Elizabeth Oakes Smith, born in Yarmouthville (North Yarmouth), was a nationally known author and lecturer; her husband, Seba Smith, was an equally prominent humorist and journalist. Each of these people was Maine-educated during the period when Maine was still a frontier. If credit for their achievement cannot be given to the schools, they were certainly influenced by daily life in Maine's small towns, with their home and community-taught values.

Cosmopolitanism and Provincialism

Outside influences were important as well. Maine's communities displayed a curious mix of cosmopolitanism and provincialism, a blend largely conditioned by the local transportation situation on one hand, and the pressing need for families and communities to band together—to turn inward—for cultural and economic survival. Like other American communities, Maine's seacoast towns expressed a prevailing interest in all things European. Indeed, this was reflected in the subject matter of novelist Sarah Wood of York, whose tales included *Julia and the Illuminated Baron* (1800) and *Ferdinand and Elmira: A Russian Story* (1804). The importance of ocean-borne commerce accounts for much of the cosmopolitan appearance of the seacoast towns. Maritime trades carried Maine men to distant ports, providing them, their families, and even their neighbors with a broad awareness of world events. Even those who were land-bound were familiar with the names and aspects of faraway ports. Most of Maine's coasting vessels ran south to American ports or the West Indies, but occasionally ships returned via Europe, and even wider horizons awaited Maine mariners shipping out of Salem, Boston, and New York to the Far East and the American Northwest.

Contact with people from far-off lands was second nature to Maine people. Inhabitants of Portland and Wiscasset, particularly, were exposed to foreign crews and passengers, and even smaller coastal communities occasionally welcomed foreign visitors. Maine people traveled abroad frequently as well. Packets and merchant vessels made the run between Maine ports and Boston regularly. On May 28, 1791, Eliza Wildes of Arundel (Kennebunkport) sailed to Boston on her husband's brig. She shopped, visited with friends, and after three days came home with Captain Benjamin Stone, who ran a coaster between Boston and Arundel, while her husband sailed on to Virginia. By 1816, the first steamer, the mode of transportation that would open up the Kennebec and Penobscot rivers to commerce and travel, was operating in Maine waters.

Farther inland, primitive travel conditions continued to plague travelers, causing these isolated communities to turn inward for cultural sustenance. Paul Coffin's 1796 complaint that the road between Phillip's Gore (Otisfield) and Bethel was "rocky, rooty, muddy and truly bad" describes most of the early roads that replaced the simple trails, and it also explains why travel in winter on hard-packed snow was easier and much preferred. Aside from pungs or sleighs, most inland travel in the early nineteenth century was by foot or horseback. In 1807, for example, fifteen-year-old Rufus Porter of Pleasant Mountain Gore (Denmark) was sent off to West Boxford, Massachusetts, to be an apprentice shoemaker with his brother. Deciding he would rather be in Portland making his fortune, young Rufus set out to make the 106-mile return trip—on foot!

Poor transportation was a source of persistent localism in the inland communities. Wagons were a rare sight in the early decades. A "rattler," an aptly-named, crude wagon whose body rested directly on its axles, was the first four-wheeled vehicle seen in Parsonsfield. It came into town on a Sunday and "more than half the men and boys staid out of [church] meeting to examine and discuss the 'flimsy notion.'" Brunswick counted only two or three carts, and wagons did not appear until 1816. Captain Peter Jordan, who owned one of the first, remembered that despite the poor construction and jolting ride, it was "considered a great luxury." Even these clumsy and primitive vehicles conveyed a certain prestige upon their owners, and their arrival marked a town's passage from frontier to civilization.

Communication with the outside world, by contrast to the bustling seaports, was difficult in the inland towns. Farmington received regular mail as early as 1793, but abominable roads delayed this service elsewhere: Dr. Moses Mason never forgot the moment in 1815 when he "heard the post-rider's horn and knew that the first regular mail was about to arrive at Bethel Hill." In 1793, the first stage passengers were carried from Portland to Hallowell, via Bath and Wiscasset, and by 1806, stages were running from Augusta to Boston. Mail delivery and stage service spurred the improvement of roads, but the widespread use of rivers and sea-lanes, coupled with the discouragements of broken terrain, thick forests, and innumerable swamps, rivers, and estuaries, curtailed this impulse generally. Considering this limited transportation, it was the immediate community that provided a framework for daily life, and even more isolated communities had their own "society," culture, and, in some cases, educational advantages sooner than more cosmopolitan communities.

Within the community, the family was the primary economic and social unit. Although the ideal was the nuclear family (father, mother, children), in reality households were often far more complex. Widowed, infirm, or indigent parents; widowed or single adult brothers and sisters; nieces and nephews who had lost one parent or were orphaned; stepsons and daughters resulting from second or third marriages; apprentices and hired hands who lived in—all were apt to be part of the "family," particularly as larger houses replaced the simple early dwellings. Following her 1795 marriage to the Kennebunk shipwright John Bourne, Eliza Wildes, previously widowed, mothered her own three children, his six, and in time their six—fifteen altogether. The couple also took in orphaned Joseph Alley, provided meals for John's shipyard workers, and depended on the help of various live-in kitchen maids. In 1828, the household of widowed

10-3. In 1837 the artist James Osborn (active 1820–37) captured the Thompson family of Oak Hill, Scarborough, with loving attention to detail. Captain William Thompson was a modestly successful master mariner who wed Rhoda Libby in 1819. In many ways the Thompsons were a representative middle-class family. Collections of the Maine Historical Society, Portland.

thirty-five-year-old Tobias Walker of Kennebunk included his two sons, ages seven and eight; his two widowed sisters; his unmarried brother; a hired hand; and a shoemaking apprentice, as well as assorted other workers who came in for varying periods of time to sew, dig potatoes, curry leather, hay, and perform other chores. In later years, after a second marriage, his household embraced, besides his new wife, four stepdaughters. Community responsibilities could extend this household cluster further. Schoolteachers were "boarded around" to various homes, which provided shelter and food for a certain period of time; and some families contracted with the town to board the indigent, who, as Parsonsfield's historian noted, were "set up at auction and provided for by the lowest bidder."

Social Welfare

As in other areas of social development, Maine's larger seaports provided the lead in matters of charity. In 1796, Portland founded a Marine Society dedicated to helping the widows and orphans of dead sailors. In 1805, the town built its second almshouse and inaugurated a "Portland Benevolent Society" to assist those needing forms of aid "different from that which is provided by law," and in 1805 the women of Wiscasset founded a Female Charitable Society. Economic crisis during the Jefferson embargo and the War of 1812 caused Portland's leaders to establish soup lines. By 1828, Portland had thirty different charitable organizations and was hailed as equal to any other town "of the same size on earth in its public spirit."

Methods of providing for those in need changed over time. In 1834, Parsonsfield opened a "poor farm" to house thirty paupers, for by the 1830s it was generally recognized in Maine that the "Poor House system, both as regards economy and comfort and the prevention of pauperism" was superior to bidding out the poor. Private alms-giving remained an important community tradition, however. The letters and diaries of Mary Knight of Otisfield, Florence Dole Brown of North Haven, and Barbara Wentworth of Cushing all mention the food, shelter, and "garments for the drunkard's child" that their families provided in the 1830s. "Pound parties," affairs to which everyone brought a pound of something for a struggling widow or indigent family, were still common at the turn of the twentieth century.

Traditionally, families or town governments cared for the insane locally. In 1803, the town of Temple was supporting the "partially insane" Jeriah Blake. Henry McCausland, a murderer who because of his religious delusions was judged insane in 1793, was kept in the Augusta jail for the rest of his life—thirty-six years.

Building a jail or lock-up was also a local responsibility. Here thieves, arsonists, debtors (by far the majority), murderers, and all other criminals could be held until their punishment was decided, or (until 1820) they could be dealt with at Massachusetts facilities. Methods of dealing with crime, as with poverty, followed a pattern of gradual change and improvement. Until about 1808, minor crimes were punished in a variety of ways: by placing the offenders in the stocks or on the gallows with ropes around their necks; by public whipping or branding on the face; by fines, servitude, or incarceration in the local jail. Gradually, as the judicial system was codified, the diversity in forms of punishment was reduced to jail sentences, monetary fines, or probation. In 1824, Maine completed the state prison at Thomaston. Here men, women, and children were kept in solitary confinement in "stone jug" vaults—five-by-nine-foot cells topped with grated trap doors into which the hapless prisoners descended by way of a ladder.

Many frontier towns participated in the larger New England thirst for self-improvement and a general intellectual curiosity by publishing a local newspaper. Frontier Maine established thirty-one newspapers between 1785 and 1820, a remarkable record not equaled by sister states. Most were printed in coastal or river towns, but from such centers the papers found their way into more remote communities. Reading material was considered precious and was shared or simply saved. Newspapers of the period carried little local news, but followed national and international developments closely, depending for their copy on larger metropolitan newspapers. As a result, even Maine's inland inhabitants shared a knowledge of the wider world. As with Maine's participation in the maritime trades, circulation of newspapers gave even the smaller villages a broad, even international outlook.

Rhythms of Work and Leisure

From advertisements and a scattering of local items in the newspapers themselves, it is possible to gain some insight into the work routines and life patterns of common Mainers. The length of the working day on the frontier was circumscribed by the severe limitations of a burning pitch-pine knot or tallow candle: people worked from sunrise to sundown. The Kennebunk family of Eliza Wildes Bourne, whose home weaving grew into a counterpane-making business, breakfasted by candlelight in order that no part of daylight would be lost to work at the loom in her "household manufactory," as the 1810 census-taker called it. Eliza Bourne's home-based work routines were typical. The household spinning of flax, wool, and imported cotton (sold by local traders) was universal. In 1810, in fact, there were sixteen thousand hand looms in Maine. Susanne Cook of Township Five (St. Albans) did not own a loom, but spun her yarn at home and carried it on horseback through the woods to a neighbor's house to weave it. Men who penned memoirs of their youth in the nineteenth century often recalled the comforting "whirr of the flax and spinning wheel; the pounding of the loom and the rush of the shuttle." Girls who worked with their mothers at the wheel and loom carried different memories into adulthood.

During the early decades of the century every town with water power had one or more mills. Home weavers could take yarn to a carding mill to be combed, or lengths of homespun cloth to a fulling mill to be cleaned, shrunk, and thickened. Woolen homespun for men's everyday clothing, usually light blue in color, was not fulled, but cloth for better wear was taken to the mill to be dressed. Tailor Betsey Segar of Bean's Corner (in Bethel) "made many a young man happy with his first fulled cloth suit, including a frock coat with gilt buttons." Finer weaves were for "nice wear." Women and girls wore linen, cotton, or wool dresses of blue, green, or brown homespun "pressed at the mill," with two cotton and wool underskirts, no underclothes, and "small blankets" on their heads. The clothing of the more affluent was made of imported silk trimmed with satin appliqué or metallic thread embroidery. Yarn was home-spun until the 1820s, when small woolen spinning and weaving mills began appearing in upland locations. Clothing, in turn, was handmade until the 1830s, when urban shops began mass-producing men's "ready-made." Cowhide boots and calfskin shoes were made by itinerant cobblers who traveled from house to house with their benches and kits of tools.

As men bartered their products and skills to secure family needs, so did the ability to make thread and cloth give women the wherewithal to help provide for their families. Fryeburg's Mary Stirling was paid in flax for caring for a new mother. She combed and dressed the flax, spun it on a linen wheel, and wove a web of cloth which her father took to Kennebunk and exchanged for "neces-saries" imported by a port merchant. In the 1820s Rebecker Copeland of Warren took in "webs" to weave for others, delivering them on horseback with a child riding pillion. Setting the web (or structure) of a piece of cloth was monoto-nous work frequently hired out to poorer women.

Able housewives scoured their unpainted tables, swept their sanded floors "into herring-bone," and worked at all phases of food and clothing preparation. They also made bedding, corn-husk or feather mattresses, homespun sheets, piece-work quilts, and the woven counterpanes that covered them. They sewed carpets, dipped candles, and made soap. They assisted their husbands in their businesses, whether farming or shopkeeping. They also provided medical care to whoever needed it. Babies were delivered by midwives, and neighboring women were called in whether the emergency was disease, broken bones, or death. Because basic medical knowledge was so widespread, most early doctors could not earn a living at their profession, and they supplemented their prac-tice with other work.

Much home and farm work called for mutual aid, and it provided fellowship and entertainment in the doing. Neighbors gathered for apple parings, corn-husking bees, barn raisings, and other annual chores best done en masse. In 1835 James Hunniwell organized his neighbors for a "hauling bee," assembling thirty-eight yoke of oxen and their owners to move to the water a fourteen-ton fish-ing vessel called the *Sarah Ann*, which he had built on his farm. Entertainment was by no means confined to work-related gatherings. Even the most remote country towns enjoyed a remarkable array of community activities—a flowering of local folk culture that expressed the close bonds between family, kin, neighbor, and fellow-worshiper in these closely knit frontier communities. Brunswick, for instance, offered a dancing school as early as 1799; Belfast youths simply gathered at a local tavern for dancing. In 1837 Otisfield's Mary Knight reported that she went to a ball and "stayed all night." Inland towns as well as seaports were treated to traveling entertainments, such as Punch and Judy shows. Psalmody was an important aspect of worship services, and singing schools were universally popular. Fortunate was the town with a blacksmith, miller, or minister who was musically talented and who held regular meetings in someone's home to teach his neighbors to sing in parts. Benjamin Messer, a cabinetmaker who came to New Sharon about 1830, was a typical singing master. He had a rich baritone and played the violin. From age eighteen he taught singing, traveling from town to town during the winter months. When spring brought warm weather and an increase in work for farm families, he returned home and took up his regular vocation.

School-related activities also provided entertainment, as did special occasions like weddings, ship launchings, and militia training days, while Court Week and Town Meeting Day provided entertainment of a sort for men and boys. The students of the one-room schoolhouses or the academies held "exhibitions" at which they spelled and recited for those who came to see what they had learned. The launching of a new vessel, with flags flying, bells ringing, and a pig roasting, was apt to bring out the town and close the schools. When a new church was dedicated in Saco in 1806, a mammoth tent was erected and a whole ox roasted. Training days on the first Tuesday in May and again in the autumn were annual festival days. From 1783 until 1841, every able-bodied man and boy between the ages of eighteen and forty-five was required by law to meet for company drill. While a gaggle of farmers and shopkeepers went through their unpolished maneuvers in someone's field at the edge of town, vendors hawked sheets of gingerbread to excited children, and their mothers talked under the trees.

The Fourth of July provided similar pleasures: orations, cannon firings, parades, picnics, and, primarily for the men, sit-down dinners at which numerous political and patriotic toasts were made. In later years, the Fourth became an artisans' holiday in the larger towns; working men in a variety of crafts marched in groups displaying their wares. If the anniversary of America's independence called for a community celebration, Thanksgiving was the great family holiday, observed in church attendance, parlor games, and the family feast: chicken pie and roast turkey with the usual accompaniments of apple and barberry sauce, mince and apple pies, and a plum pudding made with crackers, nutmeg, grated orange peel, raisins, sugar, milk, and eggs.

10-4. *Muster Day*, about 1845 by Saco's Charles Henry Granger (1812–93) is a window on his community's annual militia muster. In the distance, local units parade in good order, while a tipsy straggler sprawls in the foreground. A traveling Bible salesman holds forth from his wagon while Thomas Brannon offers "Bear O! Pi, Aiggs." Such gatherings offered a rare chance to drink, wager, dance, fight, and otherwise let loose in public. *Muster Day*, gift of Edgar William and Bernice Chrysler Garbisch, © 1992 National Gallery of Art, Washington, D.C.

Christmas did not become a universal holiday until mid-century. In 1836 the wife of the preceptor at the boarding school in Bucksport did not know that she was supposed to hang her stocking "at the door on Christmas Eve [so] Santa Claus (or something that sounds like it) will fill it." Student Elizabeth Freeman and her classmates hung one for her and filled it with homemade "nicnocs." They were rewarded with apples and raisins in the evening.

Just as holidays recognized events important to the nation's heritage, each town remained acutely aware of its own past and took note of events that recaptured or enriched the common sense of pioneer beginnings. In Brunswick, Dean Swift never forgot the day (around 1800) when the legendary Indian Chief Sabattis came to town, stopping at John Perry's store. Many years earlier, in 1757, Sabattis and other Indians had captured a local boy, Daniel Eaton, carried him to Canada, and sold him for four dollars. A year later Eaton returned home, and as an old man he still lived in Brunswick. Swift was sent to bring Eaton from his work, and the two old men, who remembered each other well, recalled the history they had shared in "wartime." A gathering of townspeople stood quietly by, and later each went home with a story to tell at the evening meal. They had seen history come alive.

Ethnic and Religious Diversity

By the early nineteenth century, Maine's Indians were already the stuff of legend in the settled portions of the state. A few, like Bethel's Molly Ockett, could be seen in town. Others followed in the old ways. Coffin, for instance, noted several Indians at Northport in 1796 felling trees, catching eels, and making baskets. Of these, some lived in scattered family bands and others in small communities: the Penobscot tribe at Indian Island near Old Town, and the Passamaquoddies at Pleasant Point on Passamaquoddy Bay. These two groups retained small fractions of their former tribal lands and pursued trades such as guiding, river driving, woods work, basket making, subsistence hunting, and trapping.

Maine Indians, along with a handful of blacks and scattered enclaves of Irish, Germans, and Swedes added a measure of diversity to Maine's largely English population. Early Maine censuses—1764, 1776, and the decennial censuses beginning in 1790—show a steady rise in the African-American population in Maine (although it always remained under one percent of the entire population of the state). Brunswick had an Irish community even before 1750 (in the records of the Pejepscot Proprietors they are referred to as the "wild Irish"). In 1845, Israel Shevenell, Biddeford's first permanent French-Canadian settler, arrived on foot from Canada, and many French Canadians worked in Maine mills

10-5. In spite of declining numbers and economic, social, and political pressures, Maine's native Americans clung to their identities and endured. This watercolor, painted by an unknown artist prior to 1860, shows Maliseet or Micmac salmon fishers dressed in a blend of traditional and manufactured attire. Collections of the Maine State Museum, Augusta.

long before they became a significant demographic influence in the state. But Maine's more pronounced cultural pluralism, based on an influx of Irish and French Canadians, came later, in the 1840s and 1860s respectively.

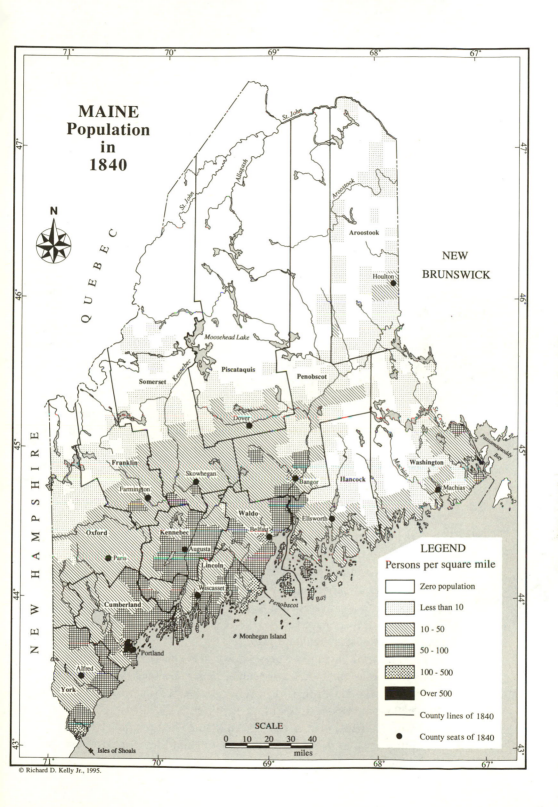

MAINE
Population
in
1840

N

Q U E B E C

NEW

BRUNSWICK

St. John

St. John

Allagash

Aroostook

Aroostook

Houlton

Moosehead Lake

Kennebec

Piscataquis

Penobscot

Somerset

Dover

St. Croix

N E W   H A M P S H I R E

Franklin

Skowhegan

Farmington

Bangor

Hancock

Washington

Passamaquoddy Bay

Machias

Machias

Oxford

Waldo

Ellsworth

Kennebec

Belfast

Paris

Augusta

Lincoln

Wiscasset

Cumberland

Penobscot   Bay

Monhegan Island

Portland

Alfred

York

Isles of Shoals

LEGEND

Persons per square mile

Zero population

Less than 10

10 - 50

50 - 100

100 - 500

Over 500

County lines of 1840

County seats of 1840

SCALE

0   10   20   30   40

miles

Before 1840 cultural diversity was most apparent in Maine in its religious denominations. No form of cultural influence was more pervasive in early nineteenth-century Maine than the church, and the early hegemony of Anglicanism and Congregationalism had been fragmented by this time. By the end of the Revolutionary War, all sects were tolerated; each family was free to choose its own denomination, and therein lay the root of the religious and social struggle that most communities experienced.

Following the Revolution, Congregationalists, traditionally the accepted denomination throughout New England, still controlled the tax money set aside by each town to support the "gospel." But during the early years of the century the Harvard-educated ministers who preached Calvinist doctrines from their two-story pulpits in galleried meeting houses were being challenged by Baptists, Methodists, and other religious groups who preached with "authority from Heaven," if not with tax dollars from the town.

As populations grew and families located away from the established centers, they found it increasingly difficult to journey into town to attend church. Their requests to the "orthodox" village minister for part-time pastoral services went unheeded, as did petitions for tax support of small neighborhood churches. Itinerant ministers from dissenting denominations—Baptists, for instance— were quick to fill the needs of these far-flung neighborhoods. Untrained preachers, often self-proclaimed (usually men, though a handful of women were active as well), conducted services in barns, orchards, schoolhouses, homes, or small buildings erected by their eager congregations. Some of these small churches were built as union churches, shared by members of quite different denominations.

The beginnings of the Baptist Church in Arundel (Kennebunkport) are typical. In 1798 inhabitants of the upper part of town built a small "meeting house" and invited the town's settled minister, Congregationalist Silas Moody, to preach in it "a third part of the time." Their request was ignored, and in 1802 they invited the itinerant, unordained Andrew Sherburne of Cornish to be their pastor. Sherburne augmented the meager stipend they could pay him by teaching school and serving as census taker. The village of Kennebunkport itself did not gain a Baptist church until 1820.

Aware of the growing number of new towns and villages, all denominations sent missionaries to the District of Maine. Newly ordained Baptist minister Isaac Case arrived in the Brunswick area in 1783; Methodism came to Maine in 1793, when Boston missionaries sent Jesse Lee through the district to form a circuit of town congregations. Lee established Maine's first Methodist Society at Monmouth in 1794. In 1828 there were sixty itinerant Methodist preachers in Maine. Although the Congregationalist missionary society in Boston sent ministers to Maine, the denomination also relied on its established town ministers to carry the gospel into the frontier. Like Buxton's Paul Coffin, the Reverend Daniel Little of Wells (Kennebunk) traveled and preached inland. Missionaries were so common, in fact, that when the people of an isolated town saw a man dressed in black ride into town, they assumed he was a minister and began to spread the word about an impending "meeting."

Methodists, Baptists in their various manifestations, and Congregationalists were Maine's most prolific denominations. At the turn of the century, Episcopalians, Universalists, Unitarians, Catholics, Quakers, and Shakers were all "new" or minor societies in Maine, but each added to the range of choices for church-going country people. Religious affiliation was not only diverse in Maine but also fluid. Benjamin Simpson of North Saco attended a different church every Sunday, or listened to the mid-week preaching of itinerants, until he finally became a tax-paying Cochranite in 1818. When that troubled sect was discredited, he became a Baptist, but many of his fellow Cochranites became Mormons when missionaries brought that faith to Maine in the 1830s. The "disorderly walk" of worshipers—the movement from church to church that grew out of this early period of religious upheaval—lasted well into the nineteenth century.

In addition to spiritual comfort, the churches provided the moral guidelines by which Maine people managed their daily lives, their families, and their towns. Religion structured social intercourse, culture, and educational goals. It was also a form of social entertainment. Poland's annual 1837 revivalist camp meeting offered worshipers seventeen tents and twelve ministers. New musical instruments, such as the bass viol, were introduced into many frontier towns at church services, and hard-working country people would have been slow to condone singing schools had they not had the unimpeachable purpose of furthering religious worship. Perhaps most important, it was through the influence of the churches that many of Maine's private schools and colleges were founded. Bowdoin College and Bangor Theological Seminary were Congregationalist; Westbrook Seminary (College) was a Universalist institution; and Waterville (Colby) and Bates colleges were started by the Baptists, as was an impressive roster of secondary institutions.

In fundamental ways the patterns of nineteenth-century rural life were established in the decades between 1789 and 1861. The coastal culture of Federalist refinement, the rhythms of work and play in the backcountry communities, the social and political institutions providing welfare, education, and government, and the diverse strains of religion took root in Maine during these heady years. Midcentury brought new economic and social developments: changes in agriculture and more dramatically a period of industrial development and political reform. Maine people, for whom the influence of frontier life was a recent memory, would meet these new challenges and make significant contributions to national affairs based on the legacy of the formative years of frontier expansion and town development.

For Further Reading:

Readers in search of bibliographic material on family and community life in Maine in the period under discussion will find that while primary and secondary sources are abundant, they are scattered and sometimes not easily accessible. The primary sources used for this study represent the kinds of documents that exist as well as the varied status of their ownership. The diaries of Eliza Wildes, Arundel (Kennebunkport), 1789–93; Abigail May, Portland, 1796; the Tobias Walker family, 1828–93, Kennebunk; Elizabeth D. Freeman, Bucksport, 1836; and Mary Knight, Otisfield, 1836–92, are in the collections of the Maine Historical Society. The Walker diaries are also on microfilm at the Brick Store Museum, Kennebunk. The Wadsworth-Longfellow family papers, ca. 1741–1900, are at the Maine Historical Society and at Craigie House, Cambridge, Massachusetts. Florence Dole Brown's memoir of her family's early history is owned by the North Haven Historical Society. Edward E. Bourne's history of his family is housed at the Brick Store Museum.

Some primary sources have been published. Eliza Southgate Bowne, *A Girl's Life Eighty Years Ago* (New York, 1888) contains the letters of a Scarborough woman, 1797–1809; the *Diary of Sarah Connell Ayer* (Portland, 1910) depicts life in Portland and Eastport from 1811 to 1833. The *Journals of Hezekiah Prince, Jr., 1822–1828* of Thomaston (New York, 1965) and the *Life of Elder Mark Fernald* of York (Newburyport, Mass., 1852) are also excellent sources.

The "Memoir and Journals of Rev. Paul Coffin, D.D." of Buxton, ca. 1796, appear in the *Collections of the Maine Historical Society* 4 (1856) and in Alice C. Cousens and Olive W. Hannaford, *Recollections of Old Buxton, Maine* (Farmington, 1972). *No Boughs on My Bonnet*, edited by Ruth M. J. Aiken (Augusta, 1983) is based on the privately owned journal of Barbara Copeland Wentworth, 1811–90, of Cushing. Laurel Thatcher Ulrich's *A Midwife's Tale: The Life of Martha Ballard, Based on Her Diary, 1785–1812* (New York, 1990) provides an important analysis of medicine and one woman's life in Hallowell from 1785 to 1812. Of further interest is the full *Diary of Martha Ballard, 1785–1812*, published for the Maine Genealogical Society (Camden, 1992). Henry David Thoreau's *The Maine Woods*, an account of three journeys into northern Maine in the 1840s and 1850s (New York, 1987), presents aspects of Maine frontier life as it was throughout the period under consideration. See also Mary Ellen Chase, *Jonathan Fisher: Maine Parson, 1768–1847* (New York, 1948), and Thomas Smith, *Journals of the Rev. Thomas Smith and the Rev. Samuel Deane* (Portland, 1849) for commentary based on first-hand observations in early nineteenth-century Maine.

Maine's nineteenth-century published town histories are rich with social history. Good examples are John Stuart Barrows, *Fryeburg, Maine* (Fryeburg, 1938); Edward E.

Bourne, *The History of Wells and Kennebunk* (Portland, 1875); Fannie S. Chase, *Wiscasset in Pownalborough* (Portland, 1941); Cousens and Hannaford, *Recollections of Old Buxton*; Ancient Landmarks Society of Parsonsfield, *History of Parsonsfield, Maine, 1771–1888* (Portsmouth, n.d.); William B. Lapham, *History of Bethel, 1768–1890* (Augusta, 1891); J. W. North, *History of Augusta* (Somersworth, N.H., 1981, 1870); Thomas Parker, *A History of Farmington, Maine* (Farmington, 1846); George A. Wheeler and Henry W. Wheeler, *History of Brunswick, Topsham, and Harpswell, Maine* (Boston, 1878); William Willis, *The History of Portland* (Somersworth, N.H., 1972, 1865). While these sources must be read judiciously to avoid the pitfalls of nostalgia, the memories they include are as valid as the oral history that is so avidly collected today.

Useful general overviews of Maine history include *Maine: A History*, edited by Louis Clinton Hatch (New York, 1919); *Maine in the Early Republic: From Revolution to Statehood*, edited by Charles E. Clark, James S. Leamon, and Karen Bowden (Hanover, N.H., 1988); and *Agreeable Situations: Society, Commerce, and Art in Southern Maine, 1780–1830*, edited by Laura Fecych Sprague (Kennebunk, 1987). The latter is a good reminder of the value of artifacts in helping us to interpret everyday life.

Useful studies of specific aspects of social history include Sandra S. Armentrout, "Eliza Wildes Bourne of Kennebunk: Professional Fancy Weaver, 1800–1820" and Joyce Butler, "The 'Single Parent' Households of Portland's Wadsworth-Longfellow House," *House and Home: Dublin Seminar for New England Folklife, Annual Proceedings, 1988* (Boston, 1990); Joyce Butler, "The Wadsworths: A Portland Family," and "The Longfellows: Another Portland Family," *Maine Historical Society Quarterly* 27 (Spring 1988); Frederick Gardiner Fassett, Jr., *History of Maine's Newspapers* (Orono, 1932); Jean Lipman, *Rufus Porter: Yankee Pioneer* (New York, 1968); Edwin A. Churchill, *Simple Forms and Vivid Colors: An Exhibition of Maine Painted Furniture, 1800–1850 at the Maine State Museum July 8, 1983–February 28, 1984* (Augusta, 1983); Deborah Thompson, *Maine Forms of American Architecture* (Camden, 1976); and George Thornton Edwards, *Music and Musicians of Maine* (Portland, 1928). William David Barry's *The History of the Sweetser Children's Home* (Portland, 1988) includes an invaluable study of the development of Maine's social service organizations. Thomas C. Hubka examines farm life and architecture in *Big House, Little House, Back House, Barn: The Connected Farm Buildings of New England* (Hanover, N.H., 1984) and "Farm Family Mutuality: The Mid-Nineteenth Century Maine Farm Neighborhood" (*The Farm: Dublin Seminar for New England Folklife, Annual Proceedings, 1986* [Boston, 1988]). In the same Proceedings, see also Marcie Cohen's "The Journals of Joshua Whitman, Turner, Maine, 1809–1846." The Turner journals themselves are privately owned, but copies are available at the University of Maine's Fogler Library (Special Collections Department) and at the Norlands Living History Center in Livermore.

11

Maine Agriculture,

1783–1861

JAMES B. VICKERY,

RICHARD W. JUDD, & SHEILA MCDONALD

*The years between the Revolution and the Civil War brought expanding opportu-
nity in rural districts, as stronger regional markets developed for Maine's farm
products. This chapter explores both the flavor of village life and the more general
forces of agricultural development. In reconstructing rural Maine's past, the authors drew in part on Maine's vast collection of rural local histories, particularly
those of Unity, Union, Buckfield, China, Brooksville, and Waldoboro, which provide excellent case studies of farm life in central Maine. Northern Maine's St. John
Valley, a distinctive region culturally and historically, is treated in a separate section by material culture specialist Sheila McDonald.*

*The four themes developed in this chapter are applicable to much of Maine's
nineteenth-century economy. First, the years between 1783 and 1861 brought initial
disappointments, then rapid growth as Maine products entered regional markets
in larger amounts. This two-stage trend came to characterize the entire Maine
economy. Second, environmental conditions in Maine added special risks and uncertainties to this already hazardous occupation. Third, agriculture was shaped by
a subtle tension between localism and external forces. As Joyce Butler pointed out
in the previous chapter, Maine was both provincial and cosmopolitan. Farmers
sustained close family and neighborhood bonds, but turned increasingly to external markets for sustenance. This halting shift from a local to a regional orientation
applies to other aspects of Maine's nineteenth-century economy as well.*

*Finally, like Maine's original inhabitants, nineteenth-century farmers re-
sponded to a harsh environment by diversifying their sources of income and
subsistence. They survived economically by combining a varied crop and livestock
production with a number of nonfarm crafts, such as baskets, pewterware, and
shingles. These varied occupations left a strong imprint on rural Maine.*

The development of Maine agriculture between 1783 and 1861 proceeded in three overlapping stages. Before statehood, most Maine farmers were preoccupied with the task of carving homesteads out of the eastern forests. Restrained by the intractability of the wilderness on one hand and by debts, poor markets, and conflicts with absentee proprietors on the other, farmers typically produced only enough food for their own survival. Roughly between 1820 and 1860, this pioneering effort gave way to an era of relative prosperity and commercial development. During this second period, farmers produced crops for regional urban markets and shipped produce to ports as far away as the Caribbean. As the antebellum era drew to a close, Maine agriculture stood on the brink of another transformation, in which western competition, brought closer to home by a spreading railroad network, prompted experiments with new techniques and new products in Maine. This period of adjustment, which also saw discouraging levels of outmigration, is discussed in a subsequent chapter.

During most of the colonial period, the insecurities of intermittent Anglo-Indian warfare limited European settlement to the southern coast of Maine. By the 1740s, however, English, Scots-Irish, German, and French Huguenot families were cautiously resettling lands as far east as Georgetown. The years after 1763 brought a mass settlement northward and eastward, as the more densely populated portions of New England discharged waves of settlers into the "Eastern Parts" to take up lands left nearly vacant by decimation or subjugation of the Indians. During these decades Maine's frontier expanded rapidly in three directions: up the Kennebec River to present-day Waterville; inland from Falmouth (Portland) as far as Gorham; and eastward along the coast to the Narraguagus and Machias rivers. Peopling this vast "eastern frontier" would be the largest instance of west-to-east migration in United States history.

♠   ♠   ♠

The Madawaska Communities in the St. John Valley
SHEILA MCDONALD

Far to the north of the English settlements a second migration to the Maine frontier was taking place along the St. John River valley above Grand Falls, a section of the river known as the Madawaska territory. In 1785 a group of sixteen families, mostly Acadians, moved upriver from present-day southern New Brunswick, looking for a peace and stability that had eluded them during the battles between England and France over control of Acadia. The Acadians, in turn, were joined by larger numbers of French Canadians from the lower banks of the St. Lawrence River. Both were attracted by the valley's fertile

11-1. French-speaking Acadian settlers crossed the St. John River into Madawaska Territory just after the Revolutionary War. The Roy House (Maison Roy), built in what became Cyr Plantation, is the best surviving example of a pioneer home. It is now in Van Buren where it joined sixteen other structures in the Acadian Village. Photograph by Anne Roy.

intervale lands—the alluvial soils along the river—and by the opportunity, as one Acadian land petitioner described it, "to obtain such lands for their families . . . and to have the assistance of a priest in the performance of the rites and ceremonies of their religion and the superintendence of their children's education."

Although the St. John River was an important communication route between Quebec and the seaport of Saint John, the Madawaska communities were a distant 70 miles from Rivière du Loup on the St. Lawrence and an even longer 170 miles upriver from Saint John, New Brunswick—the nearest population centers. Already isolated by geography, the Madawaska settlements were distanced culturally by the residents' French language and Catholic religion. The Acadian and French-Canadian way of life remained distinct from the Anglo-American communities that began to develop after a small band of Kennebec loggers arrived in 1816–17. This cultural isolation prompted one traveler through the valley in 1837 to comment: "It is curious to observe how perfectly they have retained all their French peculiarities. The forms of their houses, the decorations of their apartments, dress, modes of cookery, etc. are exactly as they originally were in the land of their ancestors."

St. John families were unusually large and tended to settle near each other, forming extended kin networks. Virtually everyone farmed, yet because the valley was so remote from population centers, agricultural produce was marketed largely within local communities or kin networks. Production and population balanced each other, and although farms were not necessarily self-sufficient, the larger region, for all practical purposes, was.

The lack of diversification implicit in the St. John Valley subsistence economy dominates both written observations about the area and census records. In 1831, John G. Deane and Edward Kavanaugh visited the valley and reported: "There are few blacksmiths and carpenters in the colony—they get their tools from the English provinces. . . . They manufacture agricultural implements which are crudely, badly made." The 1850 census does not indicate much change. Covering the entire valley population on the American side of the river, that document lists 393 farmers or farm laborers and 17 other heads of households engaged in nonfarming occupations. This dearth of specialized artisans continued into the second half of the century, although upriver lumbering operations diversified the economy somewhat in the 1850s. Madawaska's economy would change, but only when the arrival of railroads from New Brunswick altered the agricultural potential of the entire region in the 1870s.

♣   ♣   ♣

The Rise of Agriculture in Southern and Central Maine

As in Madawaska, Maine's southern settlement frontier remained primitive and isolated for most of the antebellum period. Maine's settlers were poor and many were illiterate. Nevertheless, these sturdy and resolute people recognized opportunities for their endeavors. Exaggerating somewhat, Henry Adams wrote about the frontier farmer: "Every stroke of the axe and hoe made him a capitalist and made a gentleman of his children." They sought out virgin land for the sake of commercial self-improvement, and, at least along the coast, maritime trade with the Massachusetts Bay towns, southern ports, and the West Indies offered commercial outlets for farmers. These outlets were not always sufficient to overcome the constraints of isolation, poor soil, dense forest cover, or unpredictable weather. Pursuits like fishing, lumbering, and home manufacturing—not farming—served as the primary export trade well into the nineteenth century.

The Pioneer Period, 1783–1820

Maine's frontier families often settled as groups of neighbors. Families from Massachusetts or New Hampshire negotiated with agents representing proprietors and then sent a delegation eastward to inspect the site, establish claims, and build cabins. After one season this vanguard would return, gather up families, neighbors, and possessions, and begin anew in the wilderness.

Establishing a new farm was a laborious process for the entire family. In the late fall settlers felled trees, often using a method calling "driving." After notching several trees on one side, they selected and cut a tall upslope tree called a "driver," which toppled into the others. The settlers limbed them, pitched the logs into a pile, and, after the wood had dried, burned them. They gathered the ashes and sold them for potash to make soap. During the next summer they used oxen to clear stumps.

The settlers' first cabins were small and primitive, perhaps sixteen feet by twenty and built entirely with hand tools. Squared logs were laid one above the other, chinked with blue clay, and matched at the corners. The low-posted, story-and-a-half affairs were shingled with split cedar. They consisted of a single room below, serving as kitchen, dining room, and sleeping room, and a loft, where children slept amid dried herbs and produce. The floors were split and hewn basswood. The building's few small, shuttered windows were covered with oiled paper. At one end, a huge fireplace was topped with a chimney made either of stone or "catsticks" placed "cob-house"-fashion and plastered with clay on the inside. A young woman with a dowry or furniture inherited from her family might set up housekeeping with articles such as a four-poster bed, a chest or bureau, a gate-leg table, a spinning wheel and loom, an iron kettle and skillet, dutch-oven, pewter dishes, and earthenware or wooden bowls. Families might live in their original cabins as many as twenty years.

Settlers in the first year cleared five or six acres and planted corn and some vegetables, subsisting on accumulated income, corn meal, and fish and game— moose, deer, bear, or wild fowl. Later they planted potatoes or other root vegetables, still supplementing this harvest by foraging. Frontier farming was backbreaking labor for both men and women. Men scraped together cash or credit to pay debts, taxes, and store bills by making shingles, staves, clapboards, or timber; by hunting and trapping; or by hiring out as farm workers. Women raised garden crops, processed the returns from the fall harvest, hunted the cows in the woods and milked them, and otherwise labored to feed their families. Many families grew flax and kept a flock of sheep; women combined the products into linsey-woolsey, a common form of frontier homemade cloth.

Timothy Dwight, who traveled throughout New England during 1806–7, noted that agriculture was improving in Maine in two respects. First, migrants from southern New England arrived in Maine in large groups, with the result that the farm economy increased significantly. Second, Dwight observed the New England farmers migrating to Maine were "much more skillful than their predecessors" so that agriculture grew intensively as well. Observers like Dwight agreed, however, that Maine farm families lived a grubbing existence. Raising livestock was precarious, and farm tools were primitive and cumbersome, made of heavy iron or hewn wood for heavy work. Settlers looked to the signs of the zodiac or the *Maine Farmer's Almanac* in planning activities such as planting, harvesting, and killing domestic animals, and superstitiously adhered to old proverbial advice. In this period farms yielded poorly; twenty cultivated acres might return only thirty or forty bushels of Indian corn or wheat. Farmers were ignorant of stock-breeding; they overcrowded their barns with livestock; and they often fed no grain during the winter.

Families that prospered eventually raised frame houses, which elevated their social standing and accommodated growing families. Most frame houses erected after 1815 were either two-story Federal-style homes or story-and-a-half capes. Either style had a central doorway with a fan-light, a staircase, and paneled and wainscoted rooms. Both upper and lower floors had fireplaces. At the front entry, the room to the right was a parlor, used only for funerals, weddings, or family reunions. On the left was a dining area and off this, a kitchen with a buttery and cupboards.

Among the many frustrations of this pioneer era were disputes with land proprietors. Massachusetts continued its colonial-era policy of granting huge tracts of Maine lands for speculative purposes after the Revolution. Between 1785 and 1793, for instance, General Henry Knox acquired the huge Muscongus, or Waldo Patent, and toward the end of the century two great proprietors— Knox, and William Bingham of Philadelphia—held around 3.5 million acres of Maine lands between them. Bingham's heirs lorded over a property nearly half as large as Massachusetts. Speculative ventures like these encouraged initial settlement, but the practice of holding the better lands for a rise in prices also limited further development and created smoldering resentments between settlers and proprietors.

Many of Maine's settlers, on the other hand, were squatters, who neglected to obtain title to their lands either because the land office was too remote from their clearings or because they were too burdened with debts and taxes to pay for land. Some, inspired by the republican ideology of the American Revolution, simply refused to recognize the rights of the nonresident land barons. Thousands of newcomers across the American frontier faced a similar predicament: having cleared and improved wilderness lands, they were subject to ejection by a land agent. Agents sometimes demanded foreclosure, not only on settlers' lands and improvements, but on their livestock as well. In Maine, as we have seen, this situation helped lay the basis for the movement to separate from Massachusetts. It also kept the frontier settlements in a state of civil unrest, as historian Alan Taylor has recently pointed out, through the first decade of the nineteenth century.

Tensions became so acute that in 1789 the General Court passed a law giving title to one hundred acres to families who had settled on public land prior to 1784, if they had cleared and "improved" sixteen acres and built a house. The law did not resolve the problem. Viewing the proprietors as oppressive, settlers repeatedly banded together, disguised themselves as Indians, and drove land surveyors or proprietors' agents from the area. "White Indians" burned houses or barns belonging to land agents or their sympathizers and threatened the offending officials physically. Riots occurred throughout Waldo and Kennebec counties.

A long-standing conflict between squatters and the Kennebec Proprietors came to a head in 1809 at Malta (now Windsor). In September, during an uproar brought on by several attempts to eject squatters, two local youths, Paul Chadwick and James Pratt, were hired to survey contested land. Having almost completed the task, they were confronted by several men disguised as Indians. When they resisted, three guns were discharged, one of which wounded Chadwick and caused his death two days later. With the perpetrators jailed in Augusta, considerable sympathy developed in Malta, and rumors circulated that they would be rescued and the jail, along with the houses of the proprietors or their agents, burned.

To intimidate the insurrectionaries, members of the militia fired cannons, rang steeple bells, and surrounded the jail. The so-called liberators dispersed, bringing a quick end to the "Malta War." Yet despite a long harangue by one of the judges encouraging a guilty verdict, the jury declared the Malta men innocent. The widespread sympathy for squatters' rights at Malta and elsewhere prompted the Massachusetts General Court to intervene and enabled the Malta settlers to obtain title to their farms at reduced fees. This cycle—smoldering resentment, a sharp clash with proprietors or their agents, and belated recognition by the General Court—occurred elsewhere on the eastern frontier. Arbitration and a growing conviction that resistance was in vain eventually settled most of the claims. The 1808 Betterment Act, which recognized settlers' claims to their improvements without admitting their claims to the land itself, encouraged negotiations, albeit heavily biased in favor of the proprietors.

Such incidents were part of a broader tension between frontier communities and more prosperous commercial towns throughout the young republic. The issues in this class and regional conflict ranged from taxes, debts, and paper money to land speculation, and they split the nation into two groups: propertied merchants, money-lenders, and land speculators on one hand, and indebted or cash-poor frontier farmers on the other. In Massachusetts these bitter frontier resentments fueled Shays's Rebellion in 1786; in Maine they formed the basis of the "squatters' wars" and shaped the movement toward statehood.

Debts and conflicts were only part of the problem. Maine farms were often remote from good markets, and, aside from the sea lanes, transportation was abysmal. In addition, soils were not as productive as they were in the states further south. Wheat, a primary export crop in colonial Maine, grew thick and yielded heavily on newly cleared lands, but after a few years yields declined. By 1800, troubles with a blight almost drove wheat from cultivation. Wheat growing rebounded briefly in the Penobscot Valley between 1807 and 1814, when Maine farmers circumvented federal trade embargoes against France and Great Britain by smuggling farm crops to the Canadian provinces. But these advantages disappeared after the War of 1812. Wheat from New York and Pennsylvania, grown under more propitious conditions, replaced native flour even in Maine's own farmhouses.

In addition to poor markets and sparse soils, Maine's climate was fickle. In 1816, the year known as "Eighteen-hundred-and-froze-to-death," there was a frost each of the twelve months. Crops were not harvested until October, and settlers were forced to rely on fish and game for survival. These hardships discouraged thousands and prompted a mass migration to the Ohio Valley, the beginnings of a long New England exodus that reached epidemic proportions after midcentury.

Primitive medical conditions added to the uncertainties of frontier life. Couples married young and had large families—ten or twelve children were not uncommon, and some families were as large as twenty. However, infant mortality was high and average life expectancy only twenty-five years. Consumption and epidemic diseases like measles, whooping cough, scarlet fever, smallpox, and diphtheria frequently swept through rural Maine. As in the colonial period, when tragedy struck a surviving spouse needed to remarry quickly because of the rigid division of tasks between husband and wife on the farm. Rural Maine's earliest doctors and midwives learned the medical arts as apprentices studying with older practitioners for a year or two. In 1820, the Maine Medical School in

11-2. *Corn Husking* (1860) by Lovell-born Jonathan Eastman Johnson (1824–1906) gives insight into the richness of Oxford County farm life on the eve of the Civil War. The writing on the Fryeburg barn door says "Lincoln & Hamlon" [sic], referring to the Republican ticket with Maine's Hannibal Hamlin as Vice President. Photograph by Courtney Frisse. Collections of the Everson Museum of Art, Syracuse, New York.

Brunswick began training doctors, and by mid-century formal medical practice had gone far to replace folk healing arts. By this time, even small towns had one or two doctors who would make house calls at any hour of the day or night, sometimes performing operations at patients' homes.

Expansion and Diversified Farming, 1820–61

In 1820, 55,031 farmers tilled some 78,964 acres of land. A "thrifty" farm of the time typically consisted of one or more barns, twenty to fifty acres of crops, more land devoted to pasturage, and a large woodlot. Livestock amounted to at least one yoke of oxen, a dozen cows, and a band of sheep. The old English Devon cattle had been replaced by purebred stock, an improvement that began in the 1790s, when the Vaughans of Hallowell imported from England the well-known Bakewell breed. In Hancock County, David Sears, owner of the "Great Farm" in Jackson, Maine, introduced from Massachusetts high-grade cattle and merino sheep, noted for their fine fleece. Oxen remained the principal draft animal for several more decades. Not only were these ponderous beasts able to pull heavier loads than horses, but they also supplied beef and leather. During the 1840s, horses became more prevalent for farm work, since they could also be ridden or used to pull a carriage, sleigh, or pung.

Confronted with poor markets, poor transportation, and a growing season filled with uncertainty, Maine farmers adopted a typically New England strategy of growing a broad range of subsistence crops to hedge against market or crop failure. Small farmers especially found it more prudent to mix market crops with a generous blend of subsistence items. "Mixed husbandry," a system whereby farmers raised the greatest possible variety of products for home use and export, persisted as a strategy through most of the nineteenth century. Hay and pasturage required the greatest amount of land, but farms also yielded pork, poultry, wheat, corn, barley, oats, apples, pears, plums, and vegetables. Under almost any circumstances, at least part of this harvest could be salvaged, and some of it bartered or sold. According to the state's Board of Agriculture, mixed cropping was "less subject to ups and downs by reason of fluctuating markets, as often occurs when the sale of one product has to be depended upon as a source of income."

In addition to raising diversified crops, farmers increased their incomes by processing hides into leather, shaving shingles, harvesting ice, or producing small hand-crafted items like boots, barrels, or ax handles, to be sold to a local merchant, who would in turn ship these products to city wholesale houses. Many of these products were made in small sheds or shops attached to farm outbuildings. Farm women made brooms or straw hats, sold eggs, caned chairs, wove cloth, or took in cut fabric or shoe parts to sew on consignment. Farms in this sense were "miniature factories," producing some form of saleable item almost every month of the year. Like mixed husbandry, this strategy assured the family a diversified source of income and fostered a sense of independence, ingenuity, and self-reliance that became proverbial when applied to the northern New England farmer.

These diversified activities gave a cluttered appearance to the Maine farm; barnyards and dooryards were strewn with various implements, tools, and materials. The State Board of Agriculture complained in 1883 of farm landscapes marred by unsightly objects: boards, fence posts, rails, wagon and cart parts, broken wheels, dilapidated hay racks, tinware, leather scraps, stovepipes, and limbs from orchards, all hidden among the thistles and burdock, which, the Board editorialized, "under the circumstances, become ornamental."

Yet these farms were not "self-sufficient" in a strict sense. They were involved in a very complex economy that included neighborhood trade and barter, several "market trips" yearly to neighboring communities, and exchanges with a local merchant or itinerant peddler. The nature of neighborhood exchanges varied widely. For each cash-based transaction, for example, two more might involve less formal exchanges, perhaps an item traded for the use of a neighbor's field or a promise to help bring in a harvest. These exchanges were part of a web of neighborhood cooperation, involving sharing, bartering, or borrowing, along with exchanges of labor, animals, tools, machinery, health care, or artisan skills. They blended almost imperceptibly with other forms of neighborhood cooperation—road work, schools, celebrations, barn-raisings, quilting bees, and the like—into a close-knit sense of mutual responsibility. Individual farms were far less "self-sufficient" than were these cooperating farm neighborhoods. As in Maine culture, the farm economy enforced a sense of localism that became characteristic of northern New England farm communities.

But even farms neighborhoods were not completely isolated from the broader commercial economy. A good part of farm income in the early 1800s came from transactions made on occasional trips to neighboring towns, where home-industry products, furs, hides, venison, pickled fish, maple sugar, dried apples, pork, wool, and an enormous range of other country products were traded or bartered. An important element in this broader exchange system was the village merchant, who took "country pay"—products from the woods or fields—for credit that often extended over the course of years. Merchants were the intermediaries between the metropolitan market and the barter economy of the village and farm. They stored country products like grains, beans, or shingles in bins or sheds and during the winter hauled them to the nearest port. These products were then shipped "along the shore" to other New England towns, southern ports, or to the Caribbean.

This complicated farm economy, a mix of local and regional markets, fostered a unique blend of values, the nucleus of which was the family. Family concerns overrode values such as individual self-interest and unbridled profit-making. True, farmers were engaged in a full-blown commercial-marketing economy, but they marketed only "surplus" crops—commodities left over after family and neighborhood needs had been met. Dedicated first to family security, most Maine farmers were really only casually dependent on external market forces. This balance of capitalistic, cooperative, and family concerns—sometimes called a "security-first" farming system—gave rise to a characteristic mix of New England values: Yankee shrewdness and a spirit of free enterprise balanced by enduring traditions of cooperation and individual self-sacrifice.

Village Life

Small, insular villages formed the heart of this rural society. Because overland travel was so difficult, villages were widely distributed throughout Maine; each cluster of stores, shops, mills, and public buildings served the daily needs of a neighborhood unable to travel great distances on a regular basis. For the same reason, towns themselves were divided into small, evenly distributed neighborhood school districts, and small stores and shops sprang up along the back roads wherever a merchant or dealer found suitable clientele to create a demand for these services.

The country store occupied a pivotal place in village life. It sold almost everything from molasses, sugar, salt, and pork to thread and cloth, and it had a distinctive aura of its own: a heady smell of kerosene, leather, spices, and coffee. It appeared crowded and cluttered, with glass cases displaying candy, tobacco, and sundries, and floor-to-ceiling shelves filled with dry goods—pants, "thick" boots, shoes, overshoes, farm frocks, harnesses, hardware of all sorts, patent medicines, tools, and crockery. By the counter stood a keg of molasses, a coffee grinder, and an open firkin of cheese inviting customers to help themselves. Stores were also social gathering places, frequented more often by men than women. Within, villagers gravitated to a pot-belled stove or hovered over a checkers match to discuss politics, farm conditions, or town problems.

Rum was a central item of exchange in these early country stores. A product of the West Indies, rum and its raw materials—sugar and molasses—were crucial as a return cargo for the loads of lumber and produce Maine shipped to the Caribbean. Maine historian William D. Williamson described the important place this truly ardent spirit occupied in Maine frontier society: "In its primitive state, [sugar or molasses] was an article of great use; and when distilled, it was supposed to be a needful drink for those engaged in the fisheries, in the lumbering business, in the military service, and in navigation—as better enabling them to endure hardships."

Another important ingredient of village life was the annual town meeting, the most democratic of any electoral system. These affairs often disintegrated into heated arguments over road-building or maintenance, schools, support for the town poor, unrestrained domestic animals, or use of the town's commons. Town government typically consisted of three selectmen or assessors, a town clerk, treasurer, and several constables, tax collectors, justices of the peace, and overseers of the poor. Minor officials might include fence-viewers (who arbitrated boundary disputes between adjacent landowners), surveyors of

11-3. The Congregational church and courthouse in the village of Norridgewock when
the town was the seat of Somerset County. The town's representative to the Massachusetts General Court, John Ware, led the effort to establish the new county and to make
Norridgewock the shire town by contributing land and funds to build a jail and do-
nating the use of a house as a court. The courthouse in the illustration was constructed
in 1820 and remodeled in 1847. The county seat was later moved to Skowhegan, which
had surpassed Norridgewock in population. Reprinted from *The History of Norridgewock*
by William Allen (Norridgewock: E.J. Peet, 1849).

highways, surveyors of wood and bark, sealers of leather, sealers of weights and
measures, and tithing-men. Since early cedar-rail fences were inadequate to
restrain stray animals, each town chose a hog reeve, who assumed custody of
livestock that strayed into cultivated fields. The animals would be confined to a
pound, where their owners could retrieve them after paying a small fine. The
office of hog reeve usually went to young, newly married males, because it was
an irksome chore.

Early in the century, these little communities manifested the social leveling
characteristic of frontier America. Distinctions of wealth existed, but they were
not translated into political power, simply because government was too limited
and informal and thinking too ardently republican in post-Revolution Maine.
Generally, a small group of men dominated town affairs, rotating town offices
among them, but the offices were largely functionary and the most elemental

decisions were made at the annual town meeting. Abuse of economic power by local merchants or landowners was likewise mitigated by the largely personal nature of exchanges, frequently involving neighbors or extended family members. Also, the close interface of religious, moral, family, and business values constrained mercenary impulses to some degree.

This "log-cabin" democracy, insular and innocent of high culture, contrasted sharply with the more stratified and cultured coastal society, where the new merchant aristocracy fed upon trade coming out of the developing interior. Gradually, however, even in the upland regions, some families gave up pewter and homespun for china and Boston fashion; the village "squires," with their more refined manners and paternalist instincts, assumed a dominating role in town politics. Moreover, as towns extended back from the rivers or main roads into the thin, rocky soils of the "backlots," neighborhoods or clans of poorer farmers coalesced. Men in these families worked mainly as wage laborers in the local grist or saw mills, in the fields of the more prosperous farmers, or on the decks of the coasting vessels plying the trade between Maine and the Bay towns.

These farm villages were changing economically as well as socially, with the appearance of larger saw or grist mills, foundries, tanneries, and leatherworking or woodworking shops. The first mills were primitive affairs, with slow, ponderous mechanisms; largely, they served the local farmers. In the 1840s these streamside mills were gradually replaced by complexes of steam-powered shingle, saw, fulling, or grist mills, tanneries, and woolen mills. The flowering of rural manufacturing was amazing: Maine's upland villages turned out chairs, cabinets, barrels, wagons, carriages, foundry products, shoes, saddles and harnesses, caskets, brick, hats, and—a Maine invention—toothpicks. Despite increasing involvement with outside markets for these products, village manufacturing was still invariably integrated into local agriculture. Like farm work, rural manufacturing was seasonal, slacking off when summer brought low water across the water wheels and alternative jobs in farming. Village trades experienced frequent interruptions for haying, planting, harvesting, or hunting. Labor routines remained flexible and casual to accommodate the seasonality and diversity of work in upland Maine towns.

In addition, many of these shops and mills supplied the surrounding farms. Most important was the blacksmith, who shod the oxen and horses, made iron plow points and axe heads, and repaired machines. In 1856, there were 974 blacksmith shops in Maine—about two for every town and village. Other complements to the farm economy were coopers, tanners, curriers, and millers. Shoemakers frequently traveled from farm to farm, staying with a household until they had made shoes for everyone in the family. Farm women took wool cloth to the local fulling mill, where it was colored and "pressed" and the better cloth sheared to give it a finished appearance.

Challenges at Midcentury

Humorist Seba Smith, who created the fictional Maine rustic Major Jack Downing, helped to stereotype the Maine farmer and fix a regional character for northern New England. Downing, as Smith's representative downeast Yankee, combined sharp wit and droll observation with a naive provincialism and a distinctive native dialect. Smith's work indeed reflected much of the real Maine character: provincial but shrewd, humble yet honorable. A more somber chronicler from eastern Maine alluded to the sometimes drab and severe aspect of the northern New England farm: Maine rural folk "worked, and that wasn't all; they calculated. . . . they didn't go into luxuries, and were frugal and saving. Their dress and living was plain." In 1868, Samuel Wasson complained to the State Board of Agriculture about rural Maine's proverbial conservatism. "Example begets example in full fruition," he wrote. "The practice of the father is the ideal of the son. He plows around the same rock heap, and up to the same headland; one furrow beyond would be sacrilege." Too often, Wasson complained, farming involved "muscle without mind."

This technological and financial conservatism was rooted in intergenerational farming. On New England farms, the elder sons usually received land as they reached maturity, and the youngest supported the parents and received the remaining estate. Along with the farm, the children inherited an obligation to care for their parents in their old age and to provide them, as one title transfer read, "with suitable meat, drink, lodging, and a horse and a carriage to ride when they think proper . . . and . . . medicine . . . and . . . a decent burial." Fathers and mothers passed down to the younger generation not only the farm itself, but also the techniques, habits, and philosophies of the older generation. Farms remained family institutions through as many as four or five generations, and the overlap of fathers and sons and mothers and daughters working together daily through most of their lives established patterns of thinking that were difficult to dispel.

Pressures eroding this rural conservatism, however, were at work. Commercial development itself brought more modern thinking. The years between 1820 and 1860 marked an era of increasing prosperity, accentuated by innovations that made home life more pleasant. Domestic improvement alleviated some of the drudgery of women's work. Kitchens were modernized with water pumps and butter churns made with revolving paddles instead of the awkward up-and-down plunger. Whale oil and then kerosene lamps replaced candles, and iron stoves, invented in the 1820s, saved wood and proved warmer and more efficient for cooking than fireplaces. Farm women used tinware instead of heavy cast-iron pots and kettles. Pottery ware—jugs, crocks, and later glass mason jars—made canning and preserving easier.

This outpouring of factory-made commodities lured farmers further into the market economy. Mixed-crop farms, Samuel L. Boardman noted as late as 1870, still formed "no inconsiderable portion of the agricultural community," but farming in general tilted toward specialized commercial production between 1820 and 1860. There were several reasons for this, in addition to the desire for "store-bought" goods.

First, as farm technology improved, farmers purchased more expensive equipment. Transition from the hand-held scythe, flail, and windlass to the horse-powered reapers, mowing machines, threshing machines, and hay rakes required capital or credit and drew farmers into the commercial system. Second, expanding manufacturing cities like Lowell, Lynn, Waltham, and Boston, and Maine's own Saco, Biddeford, Lewiston, Portland, and Gardiner provided attractive markets for farm produce, as did the state's vigorous maritime and lumbering activities. As industrialization proceeded on New England's lower river valleys, towns drew upon Maine farmers for sustenance. Third, Maine's railroad networks were edging into the upland farming districts by the early 1850s. Although the first lines were less than successful, they steadily gained more solid footing. Rail links to growing cities like Boston, Portland, and Lewiston provided better urban markets. Fourth, farmers recognized the advantages that regional specialization and factory production offered over home manufacturing and subsistence crops. They quickly gave up wheat growing when "Genesee flour" arrived via the Erie Canal in the 1820s, for example, and women were equally quick to abandon the laborious task of growing flax and preparing linen when other factory-made fabrics were available. Finally, commercial development was encouraged by a growing spirit of agricultural reform at midcentury. Farm reformers worked at dispelling prejudices of all sorts, and over the course of a decade or so, doubtful experiments in "scientific farming" became the new accepted wisdom. Reformer Samuel Boardman admonished Maine's prudent husbandmen to scrutinize their farms' potential more systematically for commercial potential, to specialize in clover, timothy, or other grasses, in apples, grains, beef, milk, or hoed crops, and to experiment with various implements for better production under given conditions.

Several important agricultural institutions helped pry farmers out of their old habits. Beginning in 1820 with the Kennebec Agricultural Society, farmers in local communities organized their own fairs for the exhibition of agricultural products. Farmers and their wives displayed poultry, pigs, cows, sheep, horses,

11-4. Threshing grain with a steam-powered engine (date unknown). Mechanized threshing was much more efficient than hand operations, but because the machinery was expensive it was often owned and used cooperatively. In this photograph the cut stalks are being brought by wagon to the threshing machine in the center, which separated grain from the hulls and stalks and then bagged it. Courtesy of the Maine Historic Preservation Commission, Augusta.

and household products and received premiums for exemplary displays. Partly to stimulate interest in better farming methods, Ezekiel Holmes founded the *Maine Farmer* in 1833. Published in Winthrop with Holmes as editor, the *Maine Farmer* was New England's second-oldest agricultural paper and the seventh in the United States. Holmes, Maine's premier agricultural publisher and reformer, fathered the commercial development of Maine farming; his paper reported on new breeds, seed, and stock, new markets, and new devices for threshing, mowing, raking, planting—even sewing machines. Holmes promoted state and local agricultural societies, served as the first secretary of the State Board of Agriculture, and helped organize cooperative seed stores and farmers' warehouses. He remained editor of the *Maine Farmer* for thirty-three years until 1865, when Nathan True became senior editor.

The Maine Board of Agriculture, founded in 1857 and active to the end of the century, also encouraged farmers to modernize, upgrade breeds of livestock, and improve depleted soil. The Board published annual reports providing valuable information about new developments and promoted rural uplift by organizing farmers' clubs in nearly every town in the state. County fairs sponsored by the clubs helped to demonstrate and reward scientific advances. Partly for the same reasons—to promote commercial agriculture and a rural way of life—the Maine State College was founded in 1868 and the Grange (Patrons of Husbandry) appeared in Maine in 1874.

Under the auspices of the *Maine Farmer*, the Board of Agriculture, and farmers' clubs across the state, methods of farming changed gradually. Farmers began to experiment with "artificial fertilizers" such as guano shipped from the Peruvian islands, phosphate of lime, bone meal, or gypsum. They adopted plans for better barns and cellars appearing in farm publications, improved breeds of swine and cattle, and searched for the crops best adapted to a given location or market.

This reform spirit would continue into the second half of the century, but increasingly agricultural development was overshadowed by new concerns: rural outmigration, competition from western farming districts, and in some areas soil depletion, loss of forest cover, and erosion. Rural commentary in the second half of the century swung between the poles of dogged optimism and discouragement. But between 1783 and 1861, farm men and women accomplished an epic transformation in the landscape that was mirrored in their unalterable faith in a more prosperous future. The optimism and sense of opportunity that pushed back the barriers of environment and geography were evident in Maine's other resource-based industries as well.

For Further Reading:

Students interested in the history of Maine agriculture will find an extensive literature and a wealth of primary resources available for further reading. Clarence A. Day's *A History of Maine Agriculture, 1604–1860* (Orono, 1954) and *Farming in Maine, 1860–1940* (Orono, 1963) survey not only Maine agriculture but also Maine rural life generally. Harold F. Wilson's *The Hill Country of Northern New England* (New York, 1936); Howard S. Russell's *A Long, Deep Furrow* (Hanover, N.H., 1982); and the Dublin Seminar for New England Folklife's annual Proceedings for 1986, titled *The Farm* (Boston, 1988), provide information on Maine agriculture in the context of New England history. The bibliography contained in the latter volume is extremely valuable. Hal S. Barron's *Those Who Stayed Behind* (Cambridge, 1984), a study of the upland Vermont town of Chelsea, suggests themes applicable to village society in western Maine. Alan Taylor's scholarly *Liberty Men and Great Proprietors* (Chapel Hill, 1990) offers insight into political and social life in rural central Maine, while Laurel Thatcher Ulrich's *A Midwife's Tale* (New York, 1991), Nancy F. Cott's *The Bonds of Womanhood* (New Haven, 1977), and Carolyn Merchant's *Ecological Revolutions* (Chapel Hill, 1989) provide feminist perspectives on early nineteenth-century rural society and agriculture in Maine and northern New England. Early local histories, used critically and interpretively, can also yield a wealth of detail about rural life.

Primary sources on Maine agriculture include farm diaries, account books, and journals, which may be found in such repositories as the University of Maine's Special Collections Department of the Fogler Library, the Maine Historical Society, and the Bethel Historical Society. The Dublin Seminar's *The Farm* offers a sampling of northeastern diaries and journals arranged geographically. The *Maine Farmer* (1833–1924), one of New England's most important agricultural newspapers, contains information on farm methods, technologies, rural attitudes and opinions, crops, and politics. The annual reports of the Secretary of the Maine Board of Agriculture, particularly the *Fifth* (1860), *Twelfth* (1867), and *Eighteenth* (1873), contain information on a variety of topics related to farming and rural life. Travel literature, autobiographies, and youth literature, particularly the stories of Elijah Kellogg and C. A. Stephens, also provide insight into everyday life on the Maine farm in the nineteenth century, as do the oral histories collected at the Northeast Archives of Folklore at the University of Maine.

ADDITIONAL SECONDARY SOURCES:

Agricultural Survey Commission, *Report of the Agricultural Survey Commission of the Maine Development Commission on Progress in Maine Agriculture, 1850 to 1920* (Augusta, 1929).

Baron, William R., "Eighteenth-Century New England Climate Variation and Its Suggested Impact on Society," *Maine Historical Society Quarterly* 21 (Spring 1982).

Baron, William R., and Anne E. Bridges. "Making Hay in Northern New England: Maine as a Case Study, 1800–1850," *Agricultural History* 57 (1983).

Beam, Lura, *A Maine Hamlet* (New York, 1957).

Cole, Alfred, and Charles F. Whitman, *A History of Buckfield* (Lewiston, 1915).

Churchill, Edwin A., and Sheila McDonald, "Reflections of Their World: The Furniture of the Upper St. John Valley, 1830–1930," in *Perspectives on American Furniture*, ed. Gerald Ward (New York, 1988).

Condon, Richard H., "Living in Two Worlds: Rural Maine in 1930," *Maine Historical Society Quarterly* 25 (Fall 1985).

Craig, Beatrice, "Early French Migrations to Northern Maine, 1785–1850," *Maine Historical Society Quarterly* 25 (Spring 1986).

Eves, Jamie, "'The Poor People had Suddenly Become Rich': A Boom in Maine Wheat, 1793–1815," *Maine Historical Society Quarterly* 27 (Winter 1987).

Grow, Mary M., "History," in Marion T. Van Strien, *China, Maine* (Weeks Mills, 1975).

Hubka, Thomas C., *Big House, Little House, Back House, Barn* (Hanover, N.H., 1984).

Johnson, Clifton, *Hudson Maxim* (Garden City, N.Y., 1924).

Konrad, Victor A., "Against the Tide: French Canadian Barn Building Traditions in the St. John Valley of Maine," *American Review of Canadian Studies* 12 (1982).

Mitchell, Robert J., "Tradition and Change in Rural New England: A Case Study of Brooksville, Maine, 1850–1870," *Maine Historical Society Quarterly* 18 (1978).

Sibley, John Langdon, *History of the Town of Union* (Boston, 1851).

Smith, David C., "Maine's Changing Landscape to 1820," in Charles E. Clark, James S. Leamon, and Karen Bowden, *Maine in the Early Republic* (Hanover, N.H., 1988).

Smith, David C., and Anne E. Bridges, "Salt Marsh Dikes as a Factor in Eastern Maine Agriculture," *Maine Historical Society Quarterly* 21 (1982).

Smith, David C., et al., "Climate Fluctuation and Agricultural Change in Southern and Central Maine, 1776–1880," *Maine Historical Society Quarterly* 21 (Spring 1982).

Stahl, Jasper Jacob, *History of Old Broad Bay and Waldoboro* vol. 2, *The Nineteenth and Twentieth Centuries* (Portland, 1956).

Taylor, Alan, "The Disciples of Samuel Ely: Settler Resistance against Henry Knox on the Waldo Patent, 1785–1901," *Maine Historical Society Quarterly* 26 (Fall 1986).

Vickery, James B., *A History of the Town of Unity, Maine* (Falmouth, 1954).

Wiggin, Edward, *History of Aroostook County* (Presque Isle, 1922).

12

Creating Maine's Resource Economy,
1783–1861

LAWRENCE C. ALLIN & RICHARD W. JUDD

Like agriculture, Maine's key export industries—lumber, granite, lime, and ice—grew spectacularly as regional markets developed. Also like agriculture, they were heavily dependent on the state's environment and natural resources. This chapter focuses on the natural and structural reasons for this period of economic ascendancy and the limitations of Maine's resource-based economy.

The story of Maine's largest staples industries highlights several points about the state's economy. First, it illustrates the richness and diversity of resources at Maine's disposal. That Maine at one time outproduced almost every other state in the nation in each of these industries tells us much about the state's self-confidence, its political vigor, and its impressive contribution to the development of the nation.

On the other hand, this chapter points out the economic limitations imposed by Maine's concentration on resource-based industries. Although these industries yielded spectacular profits and abundant opportunity, they produced few lasting capital investments. They offered difficult and dangerous working conditions and seasonal or unpredictable employment. These limitations would become all too apparent in the second half of the nineteenth century, which brought outside competition, technological obsolescence, and monopoly control. Such developments are the focus of another chapter, but Maine's economic vulnerability was apparent even in the age of economic ascendancy.

The story of Maine's resource-based economy demonstrates familiar themes: the commanding influence of climate, weather, topography, and natural resources; expansion of wealth and opportunity in the first half of the century; and increasing vulnerability to outside forces in the second.

The Nature of Resource Industries

LAWRENCE C. ALLIN & RICHARD W. JUDD

On a beautiful day late in May of 1884, the new three-masted schooner *William C. French* dropped down Penobscot Bay outward bound on a journey that illustrates much about the changes then sweeping through Maine's economy. Itself a product of the state's forest resources, the schooner carried on board 135,000 bricks—clay dug from the Brewer hillsides and fired with wood from local forests. On her manifest were three hundred casks of lime, quarried on the midcoast and burned with local spruce cordwood, in kilns built of native granite. Seventy-five thousand board feet of Penobscot lumber and 25,000 clapboards rode in the *French*'s hold. Sixty-three tons of hay, harvested from the coastal farmlands of Penobscot Bay, rode under canvas on her deck.

The schooner carried this harvest of Maine's natural resources to the French-owned islands of St. Pierre and Miquelon, off the south coast of Newfoundland. Leaving this cargo, the *French* took on a load of coal at Sydney, on Cape Breton Island, for the return trip to Maine. The return manifest reflected a newer source of economic growth, less dependent on natural resources locally available in the state of Maine.

Maine's economy, as the *French*'s manifest suggests, was heavily dependent on local natural resources. Lumber, clay, lime, and agricultural produce, along with granite and ice, were the backbone of the state's economy. These natural endowments brought tremendous wealth in the first half of the nineteenth century. But the national economy had changed profoundly by 1884. Coal-fired steam engines, for example, transformed the mills that once relied on natural water power as their source of energy, and they ran the locomotives and steamships that surpassed horses, oxen, and wind as means of transportation. Coal symbolized a new industrial order and a vast change in markets for Maine's traditional resource-based products. But as the *French*'s outgoing cargo made abundantly clear, the older economy, based on local natural materials, continued to exert a powerful influence over the state.

The products of Maine's resource-based economy shared several common features. Each experienced a period of rapid economic growth during the first half of the century, when Maine became the nation's leading producer of many of these natural commodities. Production peaked in most of these industries in the second half of the century, and shortly thereafter each was eclipsed by outside competition or technological obsolescence. Some adapted; others simply disappeared. While newer industries filled some of the gaps, the second half of the century was a period of difficult adjustment in Maine's economy.

In addition to their common patterns of growth, decline, and adaptation, these resource industries shared certain structural weaknesses. Low capital requirements, for instance, shaped each in two distinct ways. First, limited investments meant that they brought relatively little secondary industry to Maine. The rural trades required few roads, city services, or ancillary products; they were not generally springboards for further industrial development. Second, low capital investments meant that resource industries remained relatively unmechanized. Agriculture, lumbering, fishing, lime burning, and brick making were labor-intensive occupations; they involved direct human or animal manipulation of bulky raw materials. Even granite quarrying, perhaps the most capital-intensive of Maine's resource industries, remained technologically primitive. "Machinery has been tried in all forms," an official of the Maine Bureau of Industrial and Labor Statistics observed at the end of the century, "but, as yet, nothing has been found that will perform the labor that is now done by human power." Technology never replaced the backbreaking toil typical of the rural trades.

A third characteristic involves the outdoor setting for this work. Weather, climate, geology, topography, and other natural factors shaped these industries in profound ways. For one thing, exposure to the elements brought chronic uncertainty for working and business people. Lack of rain, too much rain, winters that were either too warm or too cold, abbreviated growing seasons, early frosts, November gales—any form of unexpected weather could mean disaster. Work in these industries was seasonal, giving rise to New England's widespread occupational pluralism, where farmers and other workers became accustomed to move from job to job according to the season. Exposure to unpredictable weather coupled with primitive technology and heavy, unresponsive materials also made these occupations unusually difficult and dangerous.

Fourth, Maine's resource industries were themselves unpredictable, vacillating between periods of boom and bust. Volatility was caused either by changes in markets or by cycles of abundance and depletion. In some cases, such as lumber and fish, the resource itself was depleted, requiring sudden shifts to different wood or fish products. In other cases, technology altered markets for the natural resource. Artificial refrigeration, for instance, undercut Maine's ice trade.

A final characteristic became apparent at the end of this period of ascendancy. Each of these industries, like other facets of America's economy, was transformed by monopoly capitalism after the Civil War. Forest lands, granite quarries, ice-cutting "privileges," and lime kilns were consolidated under giant firms, mostly using absentee financing. Maine people viewed this shift in economic control with profound ambivalence. On one hand, Maine needed capital to industrialize its economy; on the other, big-city financing threatened the rural state's independence and its republican values. This ambivalence was an important component of Maine's ongoing "love-hate" relationship with Boston, which symbolized the state's dependent status.

Resource-based industries had a mixed effect on Maine's economy. Limited development potential, labor intensity, seasonality, poor working conditions, resource depletion, wide market swings, and monopoly control left Maine vulnerable as national markets changed in the second half of the century. But during the period between 1783 and 1861, these limitations were outweighed by the spectacular growth and widening opportunities inherent in the development of Maine's resources. These themes— vigorous growth in industries with inherent underlying weaknesses—mark the period under discussion in this chapter.

Maine's Lumber Industry

RICHARD W. JUDD

The most valuable of Maine's resource-based products was lumber. An early leader in lumber production, Maine contributed heavily to the formation of American logging techniques and folklore, and Maine woods workers pioneered the industry as it moved westward across the United States. The annals of this colorful occupation were recorded by literary journalists like Timothy Dwight and Henry David Thoreau, novelists like Holman Day, and folklorists like Fannie Hardy Eckstorm, and they became part of the nation's frontier heritage. On a more prosaic level, lumbering shared the basic characteristics of resource industries noted above. It was, for instance, profoundly shaped by the natural environment, particularly by forest type, topography, river systems, and climate.

Maine was once nearly all forested. By 1860, this cover had been reduced to about 65 percent of the state's land area. With the decline of agriculture, trees reoccupied as much as 78 percent of the land by 1930 and nearly 90 percent by 1990, making Maine today the most heavily forested state in the nation. A line running from Gorham, New Hampshire, northeast to Bangor would mark a natural boundary between predominantly spruce and fir softwoods to the north, and pine and hemlock to the south, although there is considerable mixing in both regions depending on altitude, local topography, stand history, and soils. White pine, a soft, light, and durable wood, was the state's greatest natural asset through the antebellum period.

The forest economy enjoyed an important advantage in the even distribution of Maine's five thousand or so rivers and streams. Because timber is so bulky, transportation costs were an extremely important factor in its exploitation. Rivers offered a cheap means of moving logs to tidewater and also served as arteries for carrying supplies north into the remote logging camps. Their

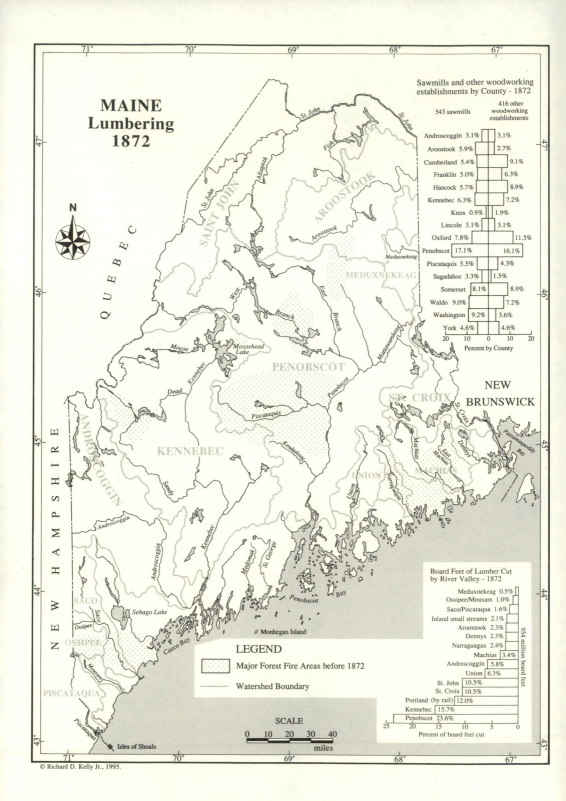

MAINE
Lumbering
1872

N

QUEBEC

SAINT JOHN

AROOSTOOK

MEDUXNEKEAG

PENOBSCOT

ST. CROIX

NEW BRUNSWICK

KENNEBEC

UNION

MACHIAS

NEW HAMPSHIRE

ANDROSCOGGIN

SACO

OSSIPEE

PISCATAQUA

Sebago Lake

Moosehead Lake

Casco Bay

Penobscot Bay

Monhegan Island

Isles of Shoals

Passamaquoddy Bay

Sawmills and other woodworking establishments by County - 1872

543 sawmills | | 416 other woodworking establishments

County			
Androscoggin 3.1%			3.1%
Aroostook 5.9%			2.7%
Cumberland 5.4%			9.1%
Franklin 5.0%			6.3%
Hancock 5.7%			8.9%
Kennebec 6.3%			7.2%
Knox 0.9%			1.9%
Lincoln 3.1%			3.1%
Oxford 7.8%			11.5%
Penobscot 17.1%			16.1%
Piscataquis 5.5%			4.3%
Sagadahoc 3.3%			1.5%
Somerset 8.1%			8.9%
Waldo 9.0%			7.2%
Washington 9.2%			3.6%
York 4.6%			4.6%

20   10   0   10   20
Percent by County

Board Feet of Lumber Cut by River Valley - 1872

River Valley	Percent
Meduxnekeag	0.5%
Ossipee/Mousam	1.0%
Saco/Piscataqua	1.6%
Inland small streams	2.1%
Aroostook	2.3%
Dennys	2.3%
Narraguagus	2.4%
Machias	3.4%
Androscoggin	5.8%
Union	6.3%
St. John	10.5%
St. Croix	10.5%
Portland (by rail)	12.0%
Kennebec	15.7%
Penobscot	23.6%

954 million board feet

25   20   15   10   5   0
Percent of board feet cut

LEGEND

Major Forest Fire Areas before 1872

Watershed Boundary

SCALE

0   10   20   30   40
miles

© Richard D. Kelly Jr., 1995.

abundance in Maine permitted tremendous economic activity in veritable wilderness areas, supported by only a few roads, trails, equipment depots, or farms. The use woods operators made of Maine's wide and even-flowing rivers drove down the cost of lumber and gave Maine a competitive edge in eastern wholesale markets. As the industry matured, operators harnessed the waterways even more intensively with dams, booms, and other alterations. Like other resource industries, lumber production developed with only minimal investments in transportation and other forms of overhead.

Cheap transportation and river distribution were also important because logging operations shifted frequently from place to place as timber was depleted. Also, rivers and streams were important because they provided power to process the timber. Lakes and ponds, many of them elevated well above sea level, provided stored energy to drive logs to market and to power the sawmills once they arrived. As a natural resource, water was at least as important as timber in determining the extent and growth of the lumber industry.

Topography was also critical to the movement of timber. Maine's largest rivers—the Saco, Androscoggin, Kennebec, Penobscot, and the St. John with its tributaries, the Allagash and Aroostook—all originate on the Appalachian plateau in the western part of the state. From the flanks of this mountain system, these swift-moving rivers carried timber from the westernmost corners of the state to the sea. Their headwaters interlink on this broad, relatively level tableland, facilitating movement across watersheds. This feature gave rise to several conflicts between loggers over the diversion of flowage and timber from one river system to another.

The most notable battle over flowage involved the "Telos Cut," named for a small pond located between the Allagash and Penobscot headwaters. In 1841, Penobscot lumber workers constructed a dam blocking the outflow from Chamberlain Lake, which drained into the Allagash River. The lake waters rose and spilled through a ravine into the East Branch of the Penobscot. The following season, water from Chamberlain Lake carried about nine million board feet of "Allagash" timber south to Old Town's mills. Disputes over tolls pitted river drivers against hired toughs protecting the cut in 1842. This "Telos War" ended without violence, but in the following decades Aroostook County mill owners, who needed Chamberlain Lake's water to drive timber down the Allagash, blew up the dam repeatedly.

Of four natural conditions—forest type, river distribution, topography, and weather—the latter dictated the timing of seasonal logging operations. Weather could mean the difference between a profitable season and disaster. Having constructed a transportation system based on natural elements, lumber operators were at the mercy of temperature and precipitation. They depended on the timely arrival of snow to cover the roads for the hauling sleds. Yet too much snow hindered the fellers and meant stumps would be cut high. Dry weather in the spring increased the cost and risk of river driving; too much rain destroyed the booms and scattered the logs. Like other nineteenth-century resource users, woods operators responded directly to Maine's mix of natural features and limited their overhead investments by utilizing in creative fashion the varied features of Maine's natural landscape.

Some sources place the first sawmill in North America in York, Maine, built in 1623 at the direction of Sir Ferdinando Gorges, although a more commonly accepted date is 1631, when proprietors built a mill on the Salmon Falls River in present-day South Berwick. At any rate, these installations multiplied rapidly. A visitor to Maine in 1682 counted twenty-four sawmills in operation, six of them at Kittery alone, each producing between 500 and 1,000 one-inch-thick pine planks per day. In addition, settlers produced hand-split clapboards, shingles, and oak pipe staves, largely for the West Indies trade. Over the next century, southern Maine also profited from a growing trade in oak, larch (tamarack), and cedar framing timbers and spruce and white pine spars and masts. Boston's cooperage (barrel-making) trade, a complement to the shipping industry, also prospered on Maine's raw materials.

Because loggers concentrated on a few valuable species, principally old-growth white pine, it is possible to trace in rough outlines a rapidly moving lumbering "frontier" extending eastward along the coast and northward up the major rivers. The fringe of this frontier reached Casco Bay in 1713 and edged north and east to the Kennebec, where by the 1750s a large mill at Gardiner was sending lumber to the West Indies. The lumbering frontier leapt eastward after extensive tracts of southern Maine forest were devoured by flames in 1761 and 1762. In the autumn of 1762, settlers from Scarborough, their crops and forests destroyed, sailed east to the marshlands beyond the Penobscot for hay for the coming winter. Encouraged by the recent building of Fort Pownall on the Penobscot and the approaching end of the Indian wars, they returned the following May to the Machias River to build a sawmill. Over the next few years several more were built on the Machias, and others appeared on Vinalhaven and Mount Desert islands and at Buckstown (Bucksport), Blue Hill, Gouldsborough, and Kenduskeag Plantation (Bangor). By 1800, there were about fifty-five mills between the Penobscot and St. Croix rivers.

While the edge of the lumbering frontier thrust eastward between 1760 and 1800, the central focus of the industry followed behind at a more even pace. The town of Saco, with seventeen mills clustered about its magnificent water power, was the heart of the industry at 1800; by 1820, the Presumpscot was the center of activity. After that came the Androscoggin, disgorging its drives of timber at

12-1. A logging crew in front of a temporary camp. Logging was done in the winter to allow the heavy logs to be moved easily over the rough terrain on sleds like those in the foreground. However, hard work in subzero temperatures required the loggers to consume large amounts of high-calorie food. The three women cooks in the center of the photo spent long hours preparing four meals a day for the workers. Courtesy of the Maine Historic Preservation Commission, Augusta.

Brunswick, and the Kennebec, with mills at Fairfield and Augusta. By 1832, the Penobscot cut reached 37 million board feet, leading all other river systems in Maine. By this time large pines on the Saco and Presumpscot were nearly gone.

Bangor, settled in 1769, thrived on the lumber trade. From this busy port, pine planks, house frames, and box boards were shipped to the West Indies in exchange for Spanish gold, molasses, and rum. Bangor also shipped "deals," or thick, semiprocessed planks, to England. Small, two-masted coastwise schooners carried lumber to ports along the East Coast, where rapid urban expansion created almost insatiable markets. Here in the magnificent pine of the lower Penobscot, the lumbering frontier paused only briefly. By 1860, the river basin was thinned of pine north as far as Medway; the following year, and increasingly thereafter, Bangor exported more spruce than pine. On the Kennebec and Androscoggin, woods workers had cut through the pine back to the spruce-clad Appalachian plateau two decades earlier, and in the late 1860s drives on the St. John similarly contained more spruce than pine. While some mills turned to spruce deals, others sent two- and three-inch planks to New York wholesalers. The "New York stuff" sustained the big mills on the Kennebec and Penobscot through the end of the century.

Bangor's brief reign as the world's most productive lumber port rested on several factors. The town served as the primary shipping point for the largest and most productive river system wholly within the state. Lumber surveyed at Bangor ranged from 145 to 211 million board feet yearly between 1850 and 1861, amounting to about 30 percent of the entire Maine cut. About six thousand workers labored to bring this harvest to the mills. In addition to this vast forest hinterland, Bangor enjoyed excellent harbor facilities. The breadth and depth of the "Bangor River" permitted direct passage for vessels ranging from small bay coasters to full-rigged ships. In busy seasons, up to a hundred vessels lay in the deep water between Bangor and Brewer.

Furthermore, the river towns directly above Bangor offered excellent water powers. From the mills at Old Town, Veazie, Great Works, Stillwater, and Basin Mills, lumber was rafted down to Bangor and loaded on the docks to await passage. Another impetus to Bangor's lumber economy was the construction of the Bangor and Veazie Railroad in 1836. Among the earliest in the United States, "Veazie's railroad" carried small lumber items like shingles and laths from the upriver towns to Bangor.

Finally, Bangor served as a labor recruiting center for the industry. About three thousand woods workers and river drivers received their season's pay in Bangor, after which they felt compelled, as one account politely put it, to "have a good time." After months of enforced sobriety and continence, the returning crews mixed with sailors in a general revelry that has occasioned colorful descriptions of Bangor ever since. "While their money lasts, they make Exchange Street lively enough in any year, and it is the harvest time for the saloon keepers, the boarding house keepers and the dealers in [cheap] ready-made clothing," an observer for the *American Lumberman* wrote.

That lumbering was the core of Bangor's economy was unmistakable to travelers. The huge brick warehouses near the river, the saloons and bawdy houses along Exchange and Harlow streets, the scream of the mills below the town, the smell of pine in the air, and the rows of elegant Federal-style mansions testified to the fortunes made in owning, cutting, driving, milling, or speculating in timber. Slab wood, edgings, and sawdust choked the river, sometimes leaving only a narrow channel through the thick bars of waste wood. According to some accounts, scavengers in small boats could pick enough lumber out of the river drift to complete a good-sized cottage in one summer. Bangor, more than any other town, represented Maine during the heyday of logging.

In addition to the advance of the lumbering frontier, three other changes were in process. First, sawmills were becoming more efficient, driving the logging frontier at an ever more rapid pace. Maine's earliest mills had been powered either by the ebb and flow of tides or by small tributary or coastal streams; their mechanisms simply converted the circular movement of the water wheel to oscillating motion that drove a heavy steel blade up and down in a timber frame. These "up-and-down" mills mostly served local customers on demand. Because local markets were limited, technology changed little between 1640 and 1840. As Maine's lumber economy matured, however, larger export or "merchant" mills appeared on the main rivers. Tied to expanding outside markets, these aggressive new mills adopted the latest technology: steam power in the 1820s, "gang" saws (entire rows of up-and-down saws) in the 1850s, and rotary or circular saws in the 1860s.

A second change was the rapid transfer of Maine's public lands into private hands. After statehood, Maine and Massachusetts (which still owned half of Maine's unsettled territory) each designated a land agent and systematically surveyed the public lands. Classified as either "settling land" or "wild land," the surveyed townships were auctioned to settlers or lumber operators. Maine used the proceeds from land auctions for various public projects. The state house, for instance, was built with the proceeds from twelve wild-land townships. As a result of these sales and auctions, about a third of the state eventually became the property of wealthy lumber barons and land speculators.

Many commentators later denounced the quick disposal of Maine's public domain as short-sighted or, at worst, an example of political chicanery. The state, they maintained, could have managed the land for long-term revenues, or at least used the sales as an inducement to agricultural development. In the context of the times, however, such a policy was unrealistic for several reasons. Maine did, in fact, encourage sales to small farmers, on terms that were far more liberal than those for federal lands prior to the 1862 Homestead Act. However, in competition with farmlands beyond the Appalachians, sales of Maine settling land languished. Much of it was eventually reclassified as wild land and sold in large blocks to woods operators or speculators. Second, most people expected that operators would remove the trees and then sell the cleared land to farmers. Few anticipated that they could profitably retain ownership after the old-growth trees had been cut. Third, timber theft and fire made forestland ownership extremely risky, and the state elected to pass this risk on to private speculators. Finally, Maine, like other states and the federal government, felt compelled to encourage private endeavors wherever possible. Public monopolies over timber rights had been, after all, one reason why America sought independence from Britain.

Disputes between Maine and Massachusetts over managing the alternating townships belonging to each state prompted Maine to buy the lands owned by Massachusetts in 1853. By 1873, the state had sold all but 213,000 acres, and much of this was sold in the last large state land auctions in 1874 and 1875. After this, the state retained only unmarketable lands and the "school lots" in each township, held in trust by the state to endow schools and churches when the township was settled.

Logging operations and river driving changed also, in response to expanding markets and the depletion of more accessible timber stocks. These changes, however, were marginal; overhead investments remained low, and operators continued their heavy reliance on resources and labor in lieu of capital. Even large-scale logging activities required only a few "winter roads" and basic river improvements, along with a set of buildings made from forest materials, a network of forest trails, and perhaps a central supply depot or woods farm. Woods operators became specialists in deriving maximum benefit from resources at hand in the woods itself. In part, however, this was accomplished at the expense of the woods workers: living and working conditions remained primitive throughout the nineteenth century.

Typically, a logging operation began with a survey of the site by a timber cruiser, an expert surveyor skilled at judging sound timber and suitable terrain. Disappearing into the woods for perhaps a month during the summer, the cruiser marked the "clumps" of pine on a rough map, counted the trees in a sample to judge the volume, noted where streams could be improved for driving, and evaluated good locations for camps and hauling roads.

Following the appraisal, the lumber operator bought timberland or stumpage rights. If the township was remote from farms, crews were sent in to cut and store wild hay. Later in the fall, laborers built a log camp from spruce cut on the spot, along with a shelter for the oxen or horses. They might also fabricate some of the logging equipment, using axes, augers, and a few pieces of forged steel hardware. The resulting camp accommodated from ten to fifty workers.

Food in these camps was rigorously simple, cooked in pots on swinging cranes over an open fireplace. Preparing the monotonous diet of biscuits, pork, and peas or beans was often a task shared among the crew, unless the camp was large enough to warrant a full-time cook. The bean pot was buried in the ashes of the fireplace. By midcentury, lumber operators were hauling cast-iron stoves into the woods camps, which permitted a more varied diet. Beans remained the woods workers' staple, but with the fireplace gone, they were cooked among live coals buried in holes in the ground. The technique, used earlier by New England Indians, yielded up the much-maligned or revered "bean-hole beans."

Seasonal logging operations, beginning in the late fall, lasted six months or longer, depending on the weather. Early on, trees were cut and hauled directly from the stump to a "landing" located on a nearby lake or stream, where they were piled, scaled (measured), and marked to await the spring drive. By mid-century, as woods operators worked farther back from the landings, the season was divided into two activities. During the light snows after November, workers concentrated on felling trees and "twitching" them to nearby yards, located along main hauling roads. When the deeper snows came, cutting operations were suspended and the crews began hauling logs to the landings.

By the 1850s, there were other changes. Earlier logging crews used oxen, because they were steadier than horses on rough roads and better at foraging. As improved roads made camps more accessible for hauling oats and hay, they switched to horses, which could traverse the lengthening hauling roads more rapidly.

The river drive began when snowmelt and spring rains created a "freshet" sufficient to flush the logs out of the streams to safe water in the lower rivers. The huge masses of timber were tumbled into the frigid water, and for one to three months, drivers rolled logs off the banks and ledges and herded them downstream. The work was, to say the least, dangerous. The uncounted victims of rushing water, grinding timber, or swamped boats were usually buried on the spot. One stretch on the West Branch of the Penobscot River, known as "the boneyard," was marked by a small graveyard containing forty wooden crosses.

Driving was made easier by four widely used innovations. Best known was an improved cant dog, a short pole to which a semicircular hook or "dog" was attached by an eyebolt. The levering or "canting" device was used for rolling or lifting logs. In 1858, Joseph Peavey of Stillwater improved the design dramatically by attaching the dog with a steel clasp that allowed it to swing on the pole in only one direction—in line with the pole—and by adding a sharp steel point to the end of the pole. The "peavey" offered a much more certain bite into the log, an extremely important consideration in the confused push and haul of waterborne timber.

River drivers also relied on a small boat called a "bateau." Of uncertain origin, the bateau was probably adapted for river driving from the ocean-going "whaleboat" of colonial times, itself a version of a French fishing dory. The bateau was double-ended, which increased its maneuverability, and it flared widely at the gunwales, which gave it stability in rough waters. On the drive, bateaux were used primarily for carrying equipment, clearing "center jams"— tangles of logs in the middle of a river—or bringing down a crew behind the main drive to clear the last of the logs from the river banks.

A third improvement to river driving was a system of dams used to control water or direct logs around obstructions. Dams were used in some cases to raise the water level along a rocky section of stream behind the dam and in other cases to conserve water until it could be used to "splash" logs farther downstream. This became increasingly important as lumber operations worked back into smaller tributary streams and branches near the headwaters. Booms, or strings of stationary logs held together by chains, were also important for herding waterborne logs or to keep them from washing up on the banks.

River driving was complicated by the fact that several different companies drove timber on each river during the spring freshet. The confusion was partially resolved by the use of log marks—individualized combinations of letters, numerals, and other symbols chopped into each log and serving, like cattle brands, to identify logs at the end of the drive. Maine lumber operators also developed specialized legal agreements designed to facilitate common use of a single river by various lumber companies.

More complicated was the fact that any company making alterations on a watercourse necessarily gave competing firms a "free ride" on these improvements. To distribute the costs of river improvements fairly, loggers used the public laws of Maine to form mutual-benefit companies, in which all users of the river held stock. These nonprofit corporations charged tolls for using the rivers and used the proceeds to build and repair dams, booms, and other facilities. The industry also innovated specialized log-driving associations to handle the entire drive on each river. Each employed a master driver, controlled the dams, and assessed logging companies according to the number of logs in the drive. Other corporations, also privately owned, were formed to sort the logs by marks at the end of the drive.

These inventions—the peavey, bateau, driving dams and booms, and mutual-benefit corporations—were perfected in Maine and diffused through the industry as the logging frontier moved westward. Indeed, Maine's lumber industry was a major force in the national economy in the first half of the nineteenth century. Maine's mills, along with those of Pennsylvania and New York, supplied the primary material for building the young nation's cities, its ships, and its industries. In the second half of the century Maine's lumber production was overshadowed by the lumber districts farther west—in the states around the Great Lakes and in the Pacific Northwest—but Maine's legacy endured, and indeed the state's output would increase steadily until lumbering fell behind wood pulp as the dominant use of Maine's vast forest resource.

Maine's Granite Industry

LAWRENCE C. ALLIN

As with other Maine resources, granite was used for local purposes before it became an export product. In all likelihood demand for granite foundations developed as settlers replaced log cabins with frame and brick dwellings in the colonial period. However, as early as 1812, Blue Hill's quarries began exporting granite as shipping ballast, and in 1820 Hallowell quarries supplied the cornices for Boston's Quincy Market. Vinalhaven began exporting granite perhaps in 1829, when a cargo of stone for a Massachusetts prison was shipped to Boston in a schooner appropriately named *Plymouth Rock*. The granite trade reached its zenith in the decades after the Civil War, an era of rapid urban expansion along the Eastern Seaboard.

Granite was used for foundations, façades, and, particularly in government buildings, for supporting walls, but the stone had a variety of other important uses, such as monuments, breakwaters, drydocks, curbs, street paving, and bridge abutments. Cemeteries up and down the Atlantic coast are memorial gardens of Maine granite, and, in a day when there were no parking meters, hitching posts carved from Maine granite were found in front of business establishments and private homes. To appreciate the enduring beauty Maine granite provided, one has only to see the figures carved for the New York Hall of Records, or, in the White House, the balustrades shaped from Franklin's hard, dark green stone.

As with lumber, Maine's granite industry was shaped by the configurations of the resource itself. New England granite comes from the cores of old mountain ranges worn down to their bases, largely by glacial action. The major granite-quarrying sites in Maine—the Hancock County coast, Vinalhaven, Deer Isle, and Hallowell—were determined by the structure of the stone and its feldspar and mica content, which determined the color, durability, and readiness to receive a polish. Quarries in Sullivan and Franklin produced gray and

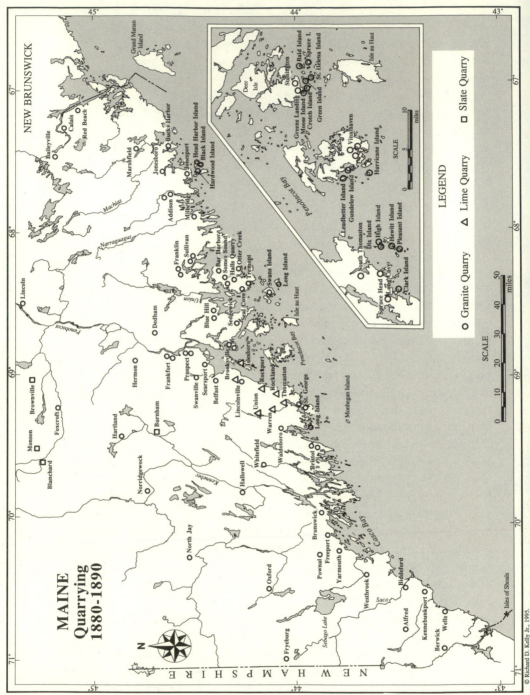

MAINE
Quarrying
1880-1890

N

NEW HAMPSHIRE

NEW BRUNSWICK

Penobscot

Machias

Narraguagus

Kennebec

Sebago Lake

Saco

Casco Bay

Penobscot Bay

Union

Isle au Haut

Monhegan Island

Isles of Shoals

Grand Manan Island

Baileyville
Calais
Red Beach
Marshfield
Jonesboro
Bucks Harbor
Head Harbor Island
Jonesport
Black Island
Hardwood Island
Addison
Milbridge
Franklin
Sullivan
Bar Harbor
Somes Sound
Halls Quarry
Otter Creek
Tremont
Swans Island
Long Island
Blue Hill
Sedgwick
Seal Cove
Isle au Haut
Brooksville
Islesboro
Rockport
Rockland
Thomaston
St. George
Long Island
Brooklin
Lincoln
Dedham
Hermon
Frankfort
Prospect
Searsport
Swanville
Belfast
Lincolnville
Union
Warren
Waldoboro
Whitefield
Bristol
Hartland
Burnham
Hallowell
Norridgewock
North Jay
Oxford
Fryeburg
Pownal
Freeport
Yarmouth
Brunswick
Westbrook
Biddeford
Alfred
Kennebunkport
Berwick
Wells
Lincoln
Monson
Brownville
Blanchard
Foxcroft

Deer Isle
Stonington
Greens Landing
Moose Island
Crotch Island
Green Island
Bald Island
Spruce I.
St. Helena Island
Vinalhaven
Hurricane Island
Leadbetter Island
Gundelow Island
High Island
Hewitt Island
Pleasant Island
South Thomaston
Spruce Head
Long Cove
Clark Island
Dix Island
Isle au Haut

SCALE
0   5   10
miles

LEGEND

○ Granite Quarry

△ Lime Quarry

□ Slate Quarry

SCALE
0   10   20   30   40   50
miles

© Richard D. Kelly Jr., 1995.

green granite, for instance, and Deer Isle and Mount Desert, pink-gray. The best sites contained fine-textured stone, lying in well-defined, even sheets ranging from one to thirty feet thick. The size of the blocks depended upon both the thickness of the sheets and their planes of fracture.

The largest and most stable market for Maine granite was for paving blocks, cut from relatively thin sheets of durable stone. For this, West Sullivan's granite was ideal, and the town's growth was directly connected to mushrooming demand in Massachusetts after the Civil War. For construction purposes and facing, large blocks with few faults, weaknesses, impurities, or veins were required. Stonington quarries excelled in this trade: their stone contained few blemishes; the fractures yielded large-sized blocks, and the big slabs could be cut at the water's edge and loaded on schooners with a minimum of hauling.

Along with the quality of the stone, other important advantages for Maine's granite quarries were their location, their minimal overburden, and their ease of drainage. Most were located on islands or along the shore. After a short haul to a pier, the granite could be put aboard a vessel ready to sail to markets on the fast, free winds and tides. In most locations decayed surface granite had to be blasted or scraped away in order to quarry the more durable stone beneath. Maine's good-quality granites, however, lay near the surface, minimizing the pick-and-shovel work necessary to open the quarries and the amount of lift required to bring the granite out of the ground. Once quarries were opened, ground water had to be pumped out and deposited far enough away that it would not seep back into the pit. Usually in Maine, the water was simply dumped into the sea.

As in the lumber industry, much of the quarry work was done by hand in the first half of the nineteenth century. At first, the rough stone was cut with hand-held drills or split free with steel wedges and sledge hammers. Pinches, or long iron bars, were used to carry the blocks about the quarry, and workers shaped the stones with hammers. Eventually, quarry operations employed blasting powder and later dynamite to dislodge the stone; steam engines to run the water pumps, cranes, pneumatic drills, and jackhammers; cable cars to move granite to the cutting and polishing sheds; and locomotives to carry the finished stone from the sheds to the wharves.

Quarry workers ranged from skilled construction stone cutters, among the finest artisans in Maine, to day laborers who handled the rough blocks. The construction cutters were paid by the day and worked in crews of six to twelve, each with a sharpener and blacksmith to keep the tools in shape. Paving cutters worked in separate areas, hammering out blocks and curbstones from the broken and waste stone in the quarries. This work required a quick eye to see the cleavage in the stone and cut the block to fit. The laborers came from

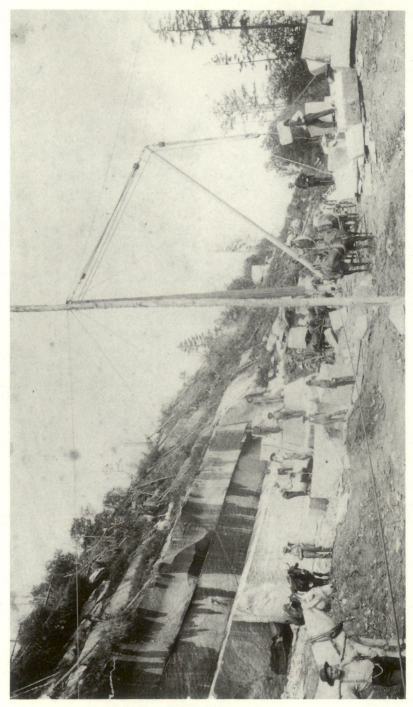

12-2. In 1870, Rockland's General Davis Tillson (1830–95) bought empty Hurricane Island, that "great pillar of granite," and opened quarries which he worked with laborers from Italy, Finland, Sweden, Scotland, and Ireland. The town of Hurricane flourished between 1878 and 1922, disappearing with the end of the granite trade. Courtesy of Hurricane Island Outward Bound School.

Scotland, Canada, England, Ireland, Italy, and Finland, as well as from Maine. Often granite workers lived in boarding houses and traded at the ever-present company store. At Vinalhaven Joseph Bodwell employed between twelve and fifteen hundred workers and literally ran a company town.

Like other resource-related trades, granite work was dangerous. Workers were surrounded by huge, moving blocks of granite, highly stressed steel cables, and frequent blasting. Those who understood English imperfectly suffered particularly high accident rates. Moreover, work in the polishing sheds was accompanied by a fine granite dust that resulted in a debilitating condition called "white lung disease." The introduction of machine tools stirred up dust in the quarries as well.

Stone cutters also complained about wages, which fluctuated with the dips in the construction industry. At times, their pay was withheld for weeks or months—in one notorious case for nine months—until a contract was completed. As in the lumber industry, work in the quarries was seasonal, and in isolated towns like Stonington it was difficult to find alternative employment. Unemployed workers fell into debt and became increasingly dependent on the company store, which, they complained, charged inflated prices for goods brought on credit.

Although vessels of all sorts were used to carry the granite to market, one type of craft was particularly suited for the trade. The "stone sloops" of Chebeague Island had a broad beam, a single mast, a clear, free deck, and a boom and gaff and derrick, worked at first by a hand windlass and then, after 1868, by steam winch. With this hoisting gear, the Chebeague sloops could easily load and offload large blocks. The last and most famous of these was the *M.M. Hamilton*, which plied the Maine coast from 1858 to 1929, carrying, among other things, stone for the building housing the State, War, and Navy departments in Washington, the Chicago Auditorium, the Chicago Board of Trade building, and the Washington Monument.

Listing even the outstanding works of architecture and engineering built of Maine granite would be difficult. A few examples, however, suggest the importance of Maine's stone to various aspects of the nation's heritage. The Yorktown (Virginia) Monument, cut by the Hallowell Granite Company, uses granite to preserve our national heritage; the Blue Hill granite in the US House of Representatives extension symbolizes the stability and strength of the national government. Maine participated in the westward movement by providing granite for the Union Pacific Building in downtown Omaha and the Hibernia Bank Building in San Francisco.

Maine granite undergirds many of the nation's engineering achievements: the Memorial Bridge across the Potomac River; the George Washington Bridge over the Hudson River; the Brooklyn Bridge over the East River; and the St. Louis Bridge across the Mississippi. The Portsmouth, New Hampshire, naval drydock, built of Stonington granite, marked the beginning of America's new navy. Maine granite also expressed the nation's cultural coming of age. Stone for the Ellis Island immigration building, symbol of America's cultural diversity, was cut at Blue Hill. The Boston Museum of Fine Arts was built of Deer Isle's granite, as were the eight columns of the Cathedral of St. John the Divine in New York City. The latter, cut between 1899 and 1904, were by some measures the largest granite blocks ever carved. Measuring fifty-four feet in length and six feet in diameter, they were turned on a special lathe and shipped in a specially constructed vessel.

Like other resource industries, granite production faced a difficult future in the face of monopoly capitalism and new building techniques and architectural styles. The industry declined steadily after 1900. But during its ascendancy Maine's granite industry contributed mightily to the state's vigorous economy. Symbolizing rugged durability and imperial power, it also contributed to the architectural expression of the American expansionist ideal as the nation extended its reach across the continent and into the Pacific rim.

Maine's Lime Industry
LAWRENCE C. ALLIN

Like the lumber and granite industries, lime production involved an interplay between natural conditions and human activity. In the millennia during which Maine's coastal area was submerged, the siliceous skeletons of diatoms, tiny single-celled plankton or algae, sank to the muddy sea floor. Their skeletons accumulated, mixed with silt from glacial streams, solidified under pressure, and became limestone. Under the weight of water, mud, and glacial ice, the bottom became Isleboro slate, into which intruded enormous fingers of granite-making lava, giving the coast its contours. This process ultimately provided an ideal resource for Maine: limestone close to the surface, easy to mine, and less than three miles from the sea.

Along with this, the Maine coast offered a long fringe of thick spruce forests, ideal for providing the fuel to transform the stone into powder and for making casks for its packaging. Coastal rivers and streams served as avenues for carrying wood to the kilns. Limestone, burned to a white powder, was used to bind bricks, lime interior walls, and later to restore soil fertility. By 1900, at least three-quarters of all the lime sold in greater New York was produced from Maine rock.

Among the first to tap the resources of the "lime coast"—the region between Thomaston and Lincolnville in western Penobscot Bay—was Samuel Waldo, a wealthy proprietor who in 1732 underwrote lime-burning experiments near the St. Georges River. Waldo's overseer, Robert McIntyre, shipped the product to Boston until 1750. When the Waldo patent fell to Henry Knox in the 1790s, the new proprietor launched an ambitious geological survey, constructed a series of kilns, wharves, and schooners, and entered the business on a larger scale.

These early efforts attracted others into the business. John and George Ulmer, son and grandson of a German immigrant, burned the first lime in what is now Rockland. Others shipped lime to New York City, which eventually became the lime coast's primary customer. By 1794, there were thirty-five kilns in the area. Each fired three to five times a year and yielded two hundred fifty-gallon casks of lime with each burning. Each firing consumed twenty-five cords of spruce.

As in Maine's other resource-extractive industries, lime burning required no large investments. The raw material was close at hand; the trade remained largely unmechanized, and lime-burning necessitated no large urban support facilities. The industry fed upon an almost unlimited natural resource, utilizing a transportation system that placed its product virtually on the doorstep of major metropolitan consumers.

The earliest kilns, "field" or "flare" kilns, were simply piles of limestone laid over wood, usually set in a field by a farmer or other part-time lime-burner. Indeed, lime was a byproduct of farm clearing, which necessitated cutting spruce and digging limestone out of the fields. By 1800, these field kilns were being replaced by rectangular "primitive" kilns, usually built against the side of a hill. Alternating layers of wood and rock were dumped into the kilns from above. The slow-burning fires were tended for a week or ten days, and then the lime powder was drawn off. By the 1830s, fifteen-foot high "pot" kilns, constructed of rock or cut granite and lined with clay, could produce three hundred casks at each burning. During this period, the kilns were relocated along the waterfront and the quarried rock was brought down from the interior, in order to expedite handling cargoes of kiln wood.

By 1845, Rockland alone employed 100 quarry workers, 150 kiln tenders, 204 ox wagons and rock carts, and 226 yoke of oxen. Hundreds of farmers in the surrounding towns cut hoop poles and made casks and barrels. As the trade flourished, the spruce forest receded from the coast and the nearby islands, and eventually lime-burners reached as far away as Eastport and the maritime provinces for fuel. Canadian woodboats entered the trade in the 1870s. These clumsy, carvel-planked, bluff-bowed vessels would poke into small creeks and inlets on the long stretch of coast between the Bay of Fundy and the kilns, paying a dollar and a half a cord at the creek and sometimes unloading the wood in Rockland for five dollars a cord. They frequently came into port so burdened their decks were awash.

As in the other resource-related industries, working conditions were difficult, dangerous, and seasonal. Stored lime in contact with water—either from high tides or rain—could heat, swell, burst its keg, and set the wooden sheds ablaze. Minor fires occurred almost weekly. In the quarries, great black powder charges called "giants" were used to pry the rock free; these sometimes exploded prematurely, blinding or maiming workers. So close together were the quarries that blasts in one might dislodge rocks in another, crushing unsuspecting workers. Toward the end of the century, however, workers benefited from new technologies, such as dynamite, wire rope, pneumatic drills, and stronger cranes, which made the work safer and physically less demanding.

Superior vessels were needed to carry lime, since the cargo could swell and even burn if it became wet. Ships sometimes carried extra lime kegs on deck, so that when the below-deck lime became wet and hot, the crew could open the on-deck casks, make plaster, and seal cabin doors, ports, and deck seams with fresh mortar. The hope was that this would starve the lime of oxygen and curtail its reaction. The vessel would be sailed to the nearest harbor and beached or moored until the results of these efforts were deemed successful.

Shipbuilding and lime-burning were complementary businesses. When Rockland split off from Thomaston in 1848, the former, boasting the largest lime quarries in the world, handled the lime burning, while Thomaston concentrated on building ships—among them the "limers," "kilnwooders," and "lumber coasters" necessary for the lime trade. Camden and Rockport likewise specialized, Camden being better suited for shipbuilding.

In the 1870s, competition from kilns at Glens Falls, New York, coupled with a surge in urban building and growing scarcity of wood, stimulated the development of "patent" kilns, which saved time and fuel in burning. In the 1880s and 1890s, businesses also experimented with coal, gas, and finally electricity to fire the kilns. These alterations, which followed a general transition from wood to fossil fuels in American society, left a gap in the coastal rural economy. The small woodboats and kilnwooders disappeared, and with them a casual way of seafaring characterized by random stops along the coast.

Maine's Ice Industry

RICHARD W. JUDD

Like lumber, granite, and lime, the ice industry embodied the strengths and as well as the pitfalls of Maine's nineteenth-century resource economy. Maine's renown in the ice industry came from the purity of its rivers and lakes coupled with the state's bracing climate. The Kennebec, in particular, possessed navigational advantages, an extensive surface area, and above all, a beautiful and

12-3. The lime industry flourished in the late nineteenth century. Lime deposits were located near the coast in Rockland and Thomaston, providing easy access to ocean transportation to East Coast urban markets for lime mortar and plaster. Moreover, abundant spruce trees were available to be harvested for use as fuel in the lime kilns and lumber for lime casks. Courtesy of the Maine Historical Society, Portland.

clear, crystal-blue ice that gave it a nationwide reputation. Kennebec ice set the standards for the industry. The ice industry also epitomized the resource economy's capacity for growth without large-scale investments—its "windfall" nature. Finally, it illustrates the impact of monopoly control and technological change on Maine's economy.

Local lore has it that the first large export of Maine ice was carried aboard the brig *Orion*, which arrived on the Kennebec in late fall 1824 and was frozen into the river in Pittston. In the spring, the vessel's captain took on a load of river ice, sailed to Baltimore, and sold the cargo for seven hundred dollars. True or not, the *Orion* story illustrates the windfall nature of the industry: the enterprising captain, with little effort and no investment, turned a mundane product of Maine's climate into a valuable commodity merely by transporting where scarcity gave it great value. This bountiful harvest, as one historian observed, required "neither seeds nor fertilizer." Nearby were large populations of farmers, carpenters, and others left idle by winter weather and willing to accept low pay for incidental work on the ice fields.

Maine's ice industry, like numerous others, began with Boston capital. To Frederic Tudor of Boston goes much of the credit for establishing world-wide markets for ice. Tudor began contemplating the possibilities of ice shipments in 1805 and sent his first cargo to the West Indies the following year. Prior to this, English and Boston shipmasters had carried "ice creams" to the West Indies in specially insulated packages; but without local storage facilities, the business languished. Tudor improved the trade by formulating better insulating material, perfecting the idea of above-ground icehouses, and inventing and distributing a household ice-box, or "refrigerator," to increase the usefulness of the ice.

In 1814, Tudor began securing ice monopolies in various West Indian and southern US ports. To doctors he demonstrated the healing virtues of ice packs and to barkeepers, the savory qualities of cold drinks rather than tepid ones. By the mid-1820s, Tudor and other Boston merchants were annually shipping south three thousand tons. Ice was altering the way people lived, what they ate, and how they served their drinks.

In 1826, Rufus Page built the first large ice house on the Kennebec near Gardiner and began selling ice to the Tudors. Page's business faltered, and to ensure a better supply, the Tudor Ice Company acquired its own houses near Richmond and Gardiner in 1831. The following years were relatively cold south of Boston, so no ice was shipped from Maine, but between 1841 and 1860, Maine's harvest increased, and new houses sprang up at Pittston, South Gardiner, and Farmingdale. Maine's primary markets at mid-century were port cities like New Bedford, New York, Wilmington, Philadelphia, Baltimore, Washington, Norfolk, Richmond, Charleston, and Savannah. The value of this trade depended on

No. 1084.

12-4. The lower Kennebec River produced some of the finest natural ice in the United States. In this photograph workers guide horse-drawn groovers to mark out a field of ice for cutting. On the shore are the huge, insulated warehouses where the ice was stored until it was shipped out on schooners to major East Coast cities. Courtesy of the Maine Historic Preservation Commission, Augusta.

weather along the eastern seaboard. If the Hudson River ice companies—Maine's largest competitors—suffered a warm winter, Maine's trade was brisk, bringing several weeks of welcome employment for every available worker along the lower river.

As with the lumber industry, ice harvesting utilized limited capital investments. Buildings were constructed of refuse spruce and pine and insulated with sawdust. Cutting the ice from the rivers was largely done by hand. The cutting areas were cleared of snow and surface ice by horse-drawn scrapers, and when the river ice thickened to about twelve or fourteen inches, the cutting began. The surface was scored into grid patterns, and a canal was opened to an ice house situated on the bank. Large sheets were sawn free and floated along the canal to an elevator. There they were sawn into smaller blocks and hoisted up an inclined conveyor into the house. The structure was filled, tier by tier, by increasing the incline of the endless chain. In the spring, the ice was loaded onto ships and surrounded by layers of sawdust. Ice shipped early in the season lost only about five percent of its volume.

Maine's ice industry epitomized the strengths and weaknesses of a resource-based economy. Like other industries, it provided spectacular profits with little capital investment and offered seasonal employment to farmers, carpenters, and other workers idled by winter weather. More dramatically than most, it illustrates the seasonal nature of employment in many rural Maine industries. Farmers and others developed multiple occupational strategies to deal with the risky and seasonal nature of work in the state. The resource-based industries that provided alternative employment in rural areas reinforced this pattern of seasonal part-time work. Occupational pluralism was especially pronounced among farm families. Farmers who chose not to specialize in commercial crops could find temporary supplemental work in industries like lumbering, fishing, quarry work, or ice-cutting. This prospect, not necessarily available in farming areas in other parts of the country, slowed the transition to full-blown commercial agriculture. But it also helped preserve a unique rural way of life in Maine and northern New England.

The ice industry, like other rural occupations, succumbed because the resource base proved too inflexible to meet the challenge of a changing national economy. Not all resource industries were so fated, but this drawback was a prominent feature of Maine's economy in the late nineteenth century. While it lasted, however, the ice industry contributed to a vibrant and buoyant state economy and a colorful, if demanding rural way of life.

For Further Reading:

Resources available for further reading in the history of Maine lumbering are extensive, beginning with John S. Springer's contemporary journalistic account titled *Forest Life and Forest Trees* (New York, 1851). Overviews of Maine lumbering may be found in Richard G. Wood, *A History of Lumbering in Maine, 1820–1861* (Orono, 1935); David C. Smith, *History of Lumbering in Maine, 1861–1960* (Orono, 1961); Philip T. Coolidge, *History of the Maine Woods* (Bangor, 1963); Smith's "The Logging Frontier," *Journal of Forest History* 18 (1974); and Richard W. Judd, *Aroostook: A Century of Logging in Northern Maine* (Orono, 1989). Chapters on early Maine lumbering can be found in Thomas R. Cox, et al., *This Well-Wooded Land* (Lincoln, Neb., 1985) and Michael Williams's *Americans and Their Forests* (New York, 1989). A more popularized account of Bangor in its lumbering heyday is in Stewart Holbrook's *Holy Old Mackinaw* (New York, 1938). The folklore of Maine lumbering is captured in the novels of Holman Day, particularly his classic *Rider of the King Log* (New York, 1919), and in two studies by Fannie Hardy Eckstorm: *David Libbey* (Boston, 1907) and *The Penobscot Man* (Orono, 1904). More recently this folklore has been detailed in Edward D. Ives's *Fleetwood Pride, 1864–1960: The Autobiography of a Maine Woodsman* (Orono, 1968) and his *Joe Scott, the Woodsman-Songmaker* (Urbana, Ill., 1978).

Secondary sources on the ice, lime, and granite trades are not as rich. They include Richard Osborn Cummings, *The American Ice Harvests* (Berkeley, 1949); Jennie G. Everson, *Tidewater Ice of the Kennebec River* (Freeport, 1970); and Florence E. Baker, "Maine's First Ice Business," *Sun Up* 10 (April 1932). Ernest Marriner's *Kennebec Yesterdays* (Waterville, 1954) and Robert P. Tristram Coffin's *Kennebec: Cradle of Americans* (New York, 1937) contain sections on ice. Local histories of the lower Kennebec River towns can be helpful. The granite and lime industries have been covered in Roger Grindle, *Quarry and Kiln* (Rockland, 1971); John Leavitt, "The Lime Droughers," in his *Wake of the Coasters* (Middleton, Conn., 1970); and in Cyrus Eaton, *History of Thomaston, Rockland, and South Thomaston* (Hallowell, 1867). A more recent study is Eleanor Richardson, *Hurricane Island: The Town that Disappeared* (Rockland, 1989).

Thousands of hours of taped and transcribed oral histories, the best source of primary documents on twentieth-century rural occupations in Maine, are available from the Maine Folklore Society at the University of Maine. A wealth of business records belonging to nineteenth-century Maine lumbering and timberland management firms can be found in the University of Maine's Special Collections at Fogler Library. Maine's premier trade paper, the Bangor *Industrial Journal* (1880–1918), and, to a lesser degree, the Portland *Board of Trade Journal* (1880–1918) follow logging, quarrying, and ice harvesting operations closely. On ice, for instance, see the March 10, 1898, edition of the latter journal. Material on Maine's resource-based industries can be found in the annual reports of the Maine secretary of state (1873), the Maine Department of Industrial

Statistics (1873–87), and the Maine Bureau of Industrial and Labor Statistics (1887–1911). These reports should not be overlooked by students of Maine economic history. The transcript copy of the International St. John River Commission hearings (1909–16), located in the Bangor Public Library, is an invaluable source of material on northern Maine river driving at the turn of the century.

ADDITIONAL SECONDARY SOURCES:

Averill, Albert E., "A Maine Boy at Sea in the Eighties [on the lime-coasting schooners]," *American Neptune* 10 (1950).

Chamberlain, Joshua L., *Maine: Her Place in History* (Augusta, 1877).

Elkins, L. Whitney, "Maine's Lime Industry," *Sun-Up* 2 (October 1925).

Grindle, Roger, "Bodwell Blue: The Story of Vinalhaven's Granite Industry," *Maine Historical Society Quarterly* 16 (Fall 1976).

Judd, Richard W., "Timber Down the St. John: A Study in Maine–New Brunswick Relations," *Maine Historical Society Quarterly* 24 (Summer 1984).

Lombard, Lucina H., "The Growth of Maine's Granite Industry," *Sun-Up* 9 (April 1931).

Lynch, Francis P., "Chapters in the Social and Economic History of Thomaston, Maine," M.A. thesis, University of Maine, 1941.

Smith, Joseph Coburn, "Maine and Her Trees," *Maine Naturalist* 7 (March 1927): 3–14.

13

Maine's Maritime Trades
in the Period of Ascendancy

WAYNE M. O'LEARY & LAWRENCE C. ALLIN

A combination of subsistence farming, fishing, and coastal commerce was a practical source of income for residents of rural areas on the Maine coast. This "occupational pluralism"—the seasonal movement between jobs—was part of a complex and interlinked system of mutually supporting economic activities along the coast of Maine. Environmental factors, such as thin soils, a rocky, indented coast, nearby fishing grounds, and a variety of locally available natural resources, established the parameters within which people could adjust this economy and survive in the face of changing national markets and new technologies.

In this chapter Wayne M. O'Leary and Lawrence C. Allin explore the period of rapid growth in Maine's maritime trades. Like the previous chapter, this story illustrates the richness of Maine's resource base, the interplay between environment and human agency, and the preeminence achieved by Maine in marketing its resources. Here again, though, the authors allude to the structural limitations in these traditional occupations. In the second half of the century, traditional fishing and shipbuilding succumbed to outside pressures. Since farming, fishing, shipbuilding, shipping, lumbering, and other resource-dependent activities were so intertwined, disruptions in any one trade altered the entire coastal economy. This period of crisis and adaptation in Maine's coastal economy will be the subject of subsequent chapters.

The Deep-Sea Fisheries in the Period of Ascendancy
WAYNE M. O'LEARY

Like Maine's other rural trades, the sea fisheries—that portion of the industry carried on beyond thirty miles from shore in vessels of the schooner class— were in large measure a product of the state's unique geography and environment. Their rise to national economic importance during the middle third of the nineteenth century was prompted in part by natural and economic circumstances that precluded most other forms of enterprise along the Maine coast. Coastal Maine's damp, cool climate and poor soil limited farming to a predominantly subsistence activity. Foreign trade and shipping, another economic alternative, required extensive capital assets, and the population of the Maine tidewater was relatively poor. Ownership and operation of large, square-rigged trading vessels was limited, therefore, to a few selected ports, Portland, Bath, and Waldoboro prominent among them.

In the early nineteenth century, most coastal inhabitants, particularly in the rural outports, found the complementary activities of small-scale or subsistence farming, fishing, and coasting in small vessels more practical and more congenial to their way of life than any other labor or capital investment. Hundreds of small operators were able to build small schooners to fish the offshore "banks" (or underwater shelves) in summer and carry their catch, along with some produce, to coastal markets in winter.

Fortuitously, the same geophysical forces that discouraged agriculture in tidewater Maine created the long, rock-bound coastline, with its innumerable protected harbors, that became the region's economic salvation. This coastal configuration, along with the state's vast interior woodlands, strongly encouraged maritime activity: shipping, shipbuilding, and fishing. Deep-sea fishing, in particular, was further stimulated by Maine's geographic location, which placed it enticingly close to the major offshore fishing banks of the North Atlantic, most of them underwater extensions of neighboring eastern Canada.

Excellent harbors, convenient stands of hardwood and evergreen forest, and geographic proximity to the best cod, mackerel, and herring grounds in the world did not, by themselves, produce a fishery: the missing ingredient was the human one. In the first decades of the nineteenth century, the pioneer coastal population migrated eastward, adapted to these harsh surroundings, and nurtured a generation of experienced and hardened seafarers, ready and able to fulfill coastal Maine's environmental imperative.

The specific character of the Maine sea fisheries was inevitably shaped by the economic circumstances of these hardy but relatively impoverished coastal inhabitants. The quintessential Maine fisherman of the early-to-mid-nineteenth century specialized in salted cod. Cod banking was, quite simply, the easiest and least costly form of offshore fishing. Because of the stolid nature of the quarry, salt-cod fishing required neither highly sophisticated equipment nor swift, expensive vessels. Fishermen simply sailed to the grounds, anchored, fished off the bottom by hand-line until the hold was full, and returned home. The salted catch was then sun-dried for preservation and carried to market in leisurely fashion. There was none of the frenetic and capital-intensive activity associated,

13-1. Many varieties of groundfish, such as cod, continued to be preserved in the traditional manner into the twentieth century. In this photograph taken on Vinalhaven, the fish have been dressed and placed on racks called flakes to dry in the sun. Workers turned the fish periodically and covered them at night and in inclement weather. Courtesy of the Maine Historic Preservation Commission, Augusta.

for example, with catching mackerel, a migratory fish pursued under sail in the most up-to-date and maneuverable vessels. That was typically left to the wealthier fishing merchants of Massachusetts. There was also no need to race home to market a catch that was liable to spoil, as was the case in the fresh fisheries of southern New England. Salt-cod fishing, more predictable and less economically and technically demanding, was perfectly suited to antebellum Maine's small-scale, locally financed enterprises. It stressed quantity, not quality or diversity, at a time when cod was a source of cheap protein in high demand.

That demand was both international and national in scope. Between 1830 and 1860, two outside historical influences impacted favorably upon the Maine sea fisheries. These were the rising tide of European immigration to North America and the growth of the slave population in the western hemisphere. The former brought to America a vast, impoverished, and largely Catholic population—a ready-made multitude of fish consumers motivated both by religious conviction and economic necessity. For a generation or more, fish served as the protein staple for the struggling immigrant working classes of the nation's cities, particularly those of the Northeast. The slave populations of the American South and the West Indies formed a second growing market for Maine seafood. Islands like Cuba and Puerto Rico, whose enslaved work forces grew with constant in-migration, vied for fish cargoes with cities like New Orleans and Charleston, whose agricultural hinterlands, despite the ban on importing slaves after 1808, still teemed with bonded labor. In both cases, the appeal to slave owners was the same: dried cod was an inexpensive, high-protein food that could withstand the debilitating effects of warm or tropical climates.

Driven by these two external markets, Maine's sea-fishing industry became a cornerstone of the national economy in the years prior to the Civil War. By the 1850s, the state had emerged as the leader in the American cod fishery, ranking near the top in most other fisheries as well. On the eve of the Civil War, Maine owned 51 percent of the nation's total sea-fishing tonnage, 57 percent of all cod-fishing tonnage, 44 percent of the total mackerel-fishing tonnage, and 51 percent of the tonnage in fishing vessels of twenty tons or more, including the important banker class. Maine dominated the United States cod fishery from 1849 to 1865, and its record of 68,680 tons of large cod-fishing schooners, attained in 1861, was never surpassed.

Geography, environment, and markets created an industry that transformed the Maine coast and absorbed a large portion of its population. The state was home to over ten thousand vessel fishermen during the late 1850s, and in some coastal towns, fishing was almost the sole occupation. At the end of the antebellum period, over half of the male inhabitants in the villages of Vinalhaven,

13-2. The typical Maine fisherman specialized in salted cod from the early to mid-nineteenth century because it was the easiest and least costly form of offshore fishing. Fishermen sailed to the cod grounds, anchored, and fished off the bottom with hand-lines. This scene depicts inshore groundfishing in Casco Bay. The catch was cleaned, salted, sun-dried, and marketed to meet a widespread demand for inexpensive protein. W. H. Bishop, *Fish and Men in the Maine Islands* (New York: Harper & Brothers, 1885).

North Haven, Deer Isle, Boothbay, Southport, and Westport, to name but a few, fished for their living.

The phenomenal growth of the Maine sea fisheries during the first two-thirds of the nineteenth century was nurtured by another force: government policy. Beginning in 1792, the United States Treasury instituted annual subsidies to cod fishermen based on the tonnage of their vessels. Payments were divided between owners and crews, with the fishermen's portion distributed according to each man's share of the catch. In 1819, the original "bounty law" was revised to the greater benefit of small-vessel owners, and it was this more democratic version of the law, enacted a year before Maine achieved statehood, that most influenced the industry down east. For individual fishermen, the subsidy provided up to 25 percent of their annual income in the years prior to the Civil War.

The law, enacted as an expression of eighteenth-century American mercantilism and kept on the books until 1866 as the crucial underpinning for a "naval nursery" essential to national defense, had several practical effects. In addition to encouraging the industry generally, the bounty tended to retard monopoly and centralization by subsidizing small entrepreneurs. In effect, it permitted the continued existence of a uniquely democratic, small-scale and broad-based industry long after the natural workings of the economy would have consolidated operations in a few hands. For the fishermen themselves, the bounty prevented the rise of a debilitating wage system by mandating profit-sharing between owners and crews. Simultaneously, it protected credit-dependent crew members from long-term indebtedness. In sum, the law safeguarded the fishing industry from the worst effects of nineteenth-century monopoly capitalism.

Under the protective umbrella of the cod bounty law and the stimulus provided by a growing national economy, the Maine sea fisheries reached their peak development. In the quarter-century from 1840 to 1865, they experienced a golden age of sorts, as a delicate balance was struck between national need, government action, geography, environment, population, technology and the nature of the state's economy. Conditions were right for the maturation of Maine's sea fisheries.

Several fisheries were pursued during this period. The most important to Mainers was, of course, the cod fishery, found to a limited extent in home waters but primarily in the waters off Atlantic Canada. Well before statehood, Maine fishermen were tapping the rich cod grounds in the Bay of Fundy, along the coast of Labrador, and in the Gulf of St. Lawrence. All three had the virtue of being relatively protected fishing areas compatible with the small craft Maine fishermen used. Even the northern Labrador fishery, which entailed a long sea voyage, was carried on in protected coves from small boats carried aboard the mother ship. As Maine fish merchants gradually accumulated capital and built larger schooners, the more exposed but potentially richer offshore banks became realistic options. Those off Nova Scotia and Newfoundland offered codfish that were substantially larger than the cod taken on the Labrador coast or in the Gulf of St. Lawrence. As the banks fisheries flourished in the 1850s, the Labrador coast enterprise fell into decline.

Of primary importance were the Grand Banks of Newfoundland, one to two weeks' sail from the Maine coast. This immensely rich area of several thousand square miles was visited by schooners from Portland, Castine, and Bucksport early in the century, but it played its leading role in the Maine cod fisheries in the decade after 1850. In the years immediately preceding the Civil War, dozens of large schooners, averaging a hundred tons or more, left Maine ports each spring for the Newfoundland grounds. They spent three to five months at sea and returned with cargoes that often exceeded thirty thousand fish. These were the "fisherman-coasters," a class of vessels developed in eastern Maine specifically to combine the functions of banks fishing in summer and long-distance coasting to the West Indies in winter. For a decade or more, beginning in 1850, they monopolized the Grand Banks fishery of North America. Eastern Maine ports—particularly those bordering on Penobscot Bay—dominated this branch of the industry, as they did most of Maine's cod fisheries.

Second only to the Newfoundland grounds as a source of large cod were the Western Banks, which comprised two distinct but contiguous fishing grounds: Western Bank proper (or Sable Island Bank) and Quereau Bank (or Banquereau), situated end-to-end about one hundred miles off the Nova Scotia coast. The Western Banks possessed the important advantage of closer proximity to Maine, allowing for quicker trips of about two months' duration. This appealed to the more diversified fishing ports west of Rockland, which limited their cod banking to the spring season. While Grand Banks ports like Castine, Bucksport, and Orland fished almost exclusively for cod, those in the vicinity of Portland and Boothbay sought both cod and mackerel.

Maine fishermen pursued mackerel, a migratory fish, in three different locations: the Gulf of St. Lawrence, or "the Bay," as it was called; the Gulf of Maine from Cape Cod to Fundy Bay, known as the "northern" or New England shore fishery; and the coastline from the Virginia capes to Cape Cod—the so-called "southern" fishery. These geographic demarcations essentially monitored the progress of the northward-schooling mackerel from the southern coast to Canadian waters.

The mackerel industry, unlike cod fishing, was characterized by numerous short voyages ranging from a few days in the New England shore fishery to a few weeks in the Bay. Once found, the elusive mackerel were caught quickly and, since they were perishable even when salted, transported to market with dispatch. Fast trips and multiple voyages in a season were commonplace. In the Bay, mackerel were "transshipped" when feasible. A practice unique to this branch of Maine's industry, transshipment meant landing the season's first catch at a Canadian Gulf port for shipment home by steamer or freighter, thus freeing the schooner to return immediately to the fishing grounds. Under the Reciprocity Treaty of 1854 (effective 1855–65), Canadian ports were opened to American fishermen for this purpose, and Maine vessels took full advantage of it.

The third major fish species pursued by Maine's deep-sea fishermen during these prosperous antebellum years was herring. Later the species would be captured exclusively in inshore waters using weirs, nets, and small boats, but prior to the Civil War herring played a key role in the state's offshore activities. The largest and most desirable herring for pickling and smoking were found in the northern Gulf of St. Lawrence near a chain of islands known collectively as the Magdalens, where they could be conveniently netted in harbors and coves.

Starting around 1820, the schooner fleets of eastern Maine sailed briefly each year to those waters before undertaking cod fishing voyages to the Labrador coast or the Bay. The Magdalen Islands herring fishery formed the basis for a smoked herring industry that eventually occupied most of the coastal towns east of Penobscot Bay.

At its height, Maine's cod, mackerel, and herring catch not only fed much of the United States and the West Indies, but served as an essential medium of exchange for the state's coastal economy. From Portland, for example, dried fish, along with lumber, went south to Havana and other Cuban ports in exchange for the raw brown sugar crucial to Portland's confectionery industry and the molasses that produced its rum. From Eastport, smoked herring was shipped to New York, Philadelphia, and other Middle Atlantic ports in exchange for basic foodstuffs like flour and corn, needed by a maritime region lacking in agricultural resources. From Castine and Bucksport, cargoes of cod and fish oil found their way to Boston in exchange for hardware, dry goods, and shipbuilding materials, as well as food items not available locally.

Of all the trades premised on fish exports, however, one stood out above the others. Salt figured in the preparation of every antebellum fish product, whether sun-dried, brine-pickled, or smoked. Until 1860, Maine's sources for this essential ingredient were primarily English and Spanish, and it arrived from Liverpool or Cádiz by way of the various transatlantic shipping trades, including the state's own southern-based commercial triangle. Typically, native cargoes of cod and mackerel left Penobscot Bay ports like Castine aboard square-riggers destined for a Deep-South market such as New Orleans. At New Orleans, the vessels exchanged their fish for cotton and sailed for Europe, eventually returning home with the saline preservative necessary to sustain the next season's fishing. This triangular fish-cotton-salt trade, inaugurated shortly after 1820, provided a crucial supply conduit that supported the regional fisheries until the outbreak of North-South hostilities.

The Civil War disrupted this trade, and the decades following the war brought further hardships for the Maine offshore fishing industry. During the antebellum years, however, cod, mackerel, and herring were mainstays of the coastal economy. Deep-sea fishing, combined in some form with other activities like coasting, shipbuilding, salt-water farming, lumbering, and lime-burning, provided a livelihood and, indeed, a way of life for coastal inhabitants. A second aspect of this maritime culture, equally as important as fishing, and equally as intermeshed into the diverse economy of the coastal region, was shipbuilding.

Shipbuilding and Shipping in the Period of Ascendancy

LAWRENCE C. ALLIN

In addition to fishing, the coastal Maine economy depended on two closely re-lated maritime trades: shipping and shipbuilding. During colonial times, shipyards of one sort or another lined the banks of virtually every harbor, salt-water creek, or tiny bay in New England. During this period, Boston, Essex, Salem, and the lower Merrimac River towns dominated the small-vessel indus-try, but gradually Maine ports usurped this position. By 1880, some fifty towns between Kittery and Machias were engaged in building vessels, employing in one way or another more than two-hundred thousand people. Although Maine's small ports continued the tradition of small-boat building, the con-struction of large vessels gravitated to a few of Maine's larger ports. In the second half of the century Maine's preeminent shipbuilding families not only pioneered the development of new vessel types, but also carried the craft of wooden shipbuilding to its apogee. This grand maritime tradition, still very much alive today, was founded on some of the same geographic, natural, and economic conditions that fostered Maine's preeminence in fishing.

By sea, Maine was not only close to magnificent fishing grounds, but also to a variety of excellent markets for fish and other products: the burgeoning urban-industrial complexes of the Eastern Seaboard, the fertile tidewater re-gions of the southern states, the sugar ports of the West Indies, and the cotton textile districts of England. Countless harbors and inlets offered cheap land for shipyards. Down the gently sloping banks of these tidal stretches slid thousands of vessels into deep, sheltered water, to be outfitted by the same skilled laborers who built them.

Maine's forests of pine, spruce, oak, and tamarack provided the diverse woods necessary to build sailing ships, and this inexpensive supply of timber was easily transported to coastal shipyards by a vast river system. White oak, which grew in abundance along the coast of Maine, provided dense, tough wood for the ship's ribbing, which was encased in lighter planking of pine or spruce. Larch (tamarack), an iron-hard, water-resistant wood, provided "ship's knees," the bracing that joined ribs to the deck timbers. Cut during the winter when the sap was dormant, trees for the hull were rough-hewn and hauled to the building yards. There the wood dried for several seasons before it was shaped into frame, planking, knees, and deck house. Before the vessel "swam"—before it was launched—caulkers forced oakum, or loosely braided rope, into the tight seams between the ship's planking. As the planks absorbed water, they swelled against one another, making a dry seal. The salt that preserved

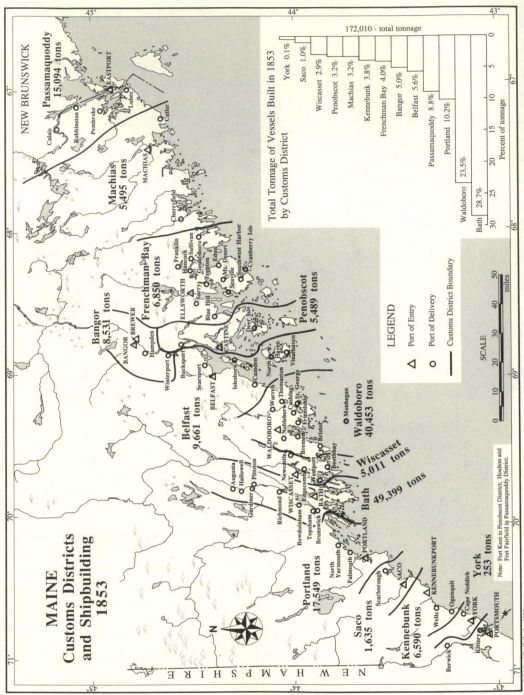

MAINE
Customs Districts
and Shipbuilding
1853

NEW BRUNSWICK

N E W   H A M P S H I R E

Passamaquoddy
15,094 tons

EASTPORT
Lubec
Cutler
Calais
Robbinston
Pembroke

Machias
5,495 tons
MACHIAS
Cherryfield

Frenchman Bay
6,850 tons
Franklin
Hancock
Sullivan
Gouldsboro
ELLSWORTH
Surry
Trenton
Mt. Desert
Blue Hill
Sedgwick
Southwest Harbor
Cranberry Isle

Bangor
8,531 tons
BREWER
BANGOR
Hampden
Winterport
Bucksport
Searsport
Winterport

Penobscot
5,489 tons
CASTINE
Deer Isle
North
Eagen
Vinalhaven

Belfast
9,661 tons
BELFAST
Islesboro
Camden

Waldoboro
40,453 tons
WALDOBORO
Warren
Nobleboro Thomaston
Bremen Cushing
Bristol St. George
Friendship
Boothbay
Monhegan

Wiscasset
5,011 tons
WISCASSET
Richmond
Newcastle
Edgecomb
Bowdoinham
Topsham Westport
Brunswick
BATH

Bath
49,399 tons

Augusta
Hallowell
Pittston
Gardiner

Portland
17,549 tons
PORTLAND
North
Yarmouth
Falmouth

Saco
1,635 tons
SACO
Scarborough

Kennebunk
6,590 tons
KENNEBUNKPORT
Wells
Ogunquit

York
253 tons
Cape Neddick
YORK
Berwick
Kittery
PORTSMOUTH

LEGEND
△ Port of Entry
○ Port of Delivery
— Customs District Boundary

SCALE
0   10   20   30   40   50
miles

172,010 - total tonnage

Total Tonnage of Vessels Built in 1853
by Customs District

York 0.1%
Saco 1.0%
Wiscasset 2.9%
Penobscot 3.2%
Machias 3.2%
Kennebunk 3.8%
Frenchman Bay 4.0%
Bangor 5.0%
Belfast 5.6%
Passamaquoddy 8.8%
Portland 10.2%
Waldoboro 23.5%
Bath 28.7%

Percent of tonnage

© Richard D. Kelly Jr., 1995.

13-3. Shipbuilding in Maine traces its origin to the Popham Colony in 1607. After the Revolution, Maine vessels and mariners were known throughout the world. Small and large ports launched everything from sloops and brigs to clipper ships. After the Civil War the square-rigged "Down-Easter" (three-quarters of which were built in Maine) dominated until the arrival of steel-hulled competition. Here a vessel is being launched from a small yard in Orrington in 1880. Courtesy of James B. Vickery.

the enormous quantities of fish New Englanders exported also helped keep this cargo dry: before launching, the majority of Maine's sailing craft had the substance poured between their outer skins and their inner ceilings. When the salt melted, it permeated the wood, acting as a preservative. In tropical waters, it also protected the wood from teredo worms, which bored into wooden hulls and weakened them.

Because Maine's white pines were so plentiful, easily worked, and comparatively long lasting, they yielded masts not only for local vessels but also for those of the British and American navies. As with other shipbuilding woods, pine masts were cut in winter, hauled to the building yards, and trimmed and rounded. Once shaped, the masts were ready to step, or place, on the ship's keel. Unlike the seasoned woods used in a vessel's hull, the masts had to be "wet"; the sap remaining in the wood made the masts more supple, so that they might withstand the enormous energy forces brought against them by wind and sail.

In addition to these natural resources and geographical advantages, coastal Maine supplied thousands of carpenters and sailors whose skills were honed by generations of dependence on the sea for sustenance and travel. Since Maine resisted industrialization until quite late, there were no booming inland cities to draw off these mariners, fishermen, and artisans, as in Massachusetts and other New England states. As wooden ships evolved, not only did ship's carpenters, mastwrights, and caulkers lend their labor to the construction, but so, too, did cordwainers, block makers, pump makers, and a host of other skilled craftsmen. The cordwainers operated the ropewalks in which they spun cotton or manila hemp into lines, hawsers, and anchor cables. Block makers made huge wooden contrivances through which two, three, or four lines ran to the masts, spars, and sails. The blocks provided leverage, guidance, and smooth passage for the lines that worked the sails. Pumps, each made of dozens of pieces of wood, were necessary because the enormous force of heavy seas and strong winds against a vessel's hull inevitably caused some leaks.

Excellent shipbuilding sites, good river and coastal transportation, a diverse supply of local timber, and a tradition of maritime skills were the circumstances that fostered the state's seaborne commerce. As important as the experience in building and sailing were Maine's skills in managing the vessels financially. To wrest a living from the sea, Maine people had to think as well as act; they deployed these vessels, large and small, as economic tools to generate profits and livelihoods. Without astute business management, they would have been nothing more than expensive floating cargo spaces.

Maine's shipbuilding skills were continually tested against the ever-changing demands of the maritime trades. The sea offered a variety of opportunities to make a living, each requiring a distinctive class of vessel. During colonial times, for instance, small, locally built shallops were used for fishing, while sloops, measuring around sixty tons, carried dried fish, lumber products, and foodstuffs to the West Indies. Cargo vessels fell into two broad classes: coasting vessels and deep-water sailers. The coasting trade ran from Maine ports down the coast to the West Indies. Later, it extended from Maine all the way around Cape Horn to ports located on the West Coast of the United States. The deep-water trades extended across the Atlantic, Pacific, and Indian oceans to foreign ports.

As we have already noted, codfish, sugar, rum, and salt were the elements of Maine's earliest seaborne commerce. This trade diversified quickly. Coasting

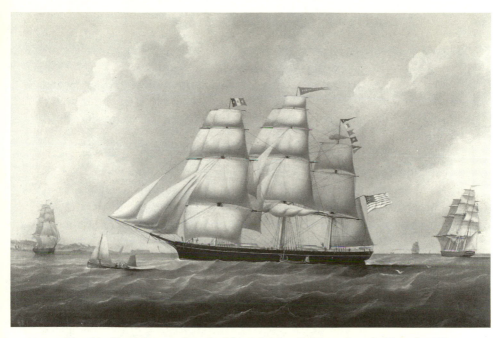

13-4. The ship *Samaritan* was launched from the Sewall shipyard on the Kennebec River in Bath in 1854. Boldly flying her house flag along with the Stars and Stripes, she took her place among the vessels making Maine famous throughout the world. Shipbuilding was the state's leading industry in the last century, and Bath remains its last important bastion. Collection of the Maine Maritime Museum, Bath.

vessels supplemented their cargoes of fish destined for the American South and the Caribbean with all kinds of Yankee-made wooden products, along with groceries from the Middle-Atlantic states. Once in a West Indies port, the ship-masters loaded boxes of crystallized sugar, great hogsheads of molasses, or distilled rum. Since the islands also grew indigo, cotton, cloves, and cocoa, other opportunities for profit existed. To reward their ship's officers and men, some captains allowed them to use cargo space to store a few pounds of "light pay," as these goods were called, to sell in their home ports at handsome markups.

At about the time of American Independence, schooners (fore-and-aft rigged vessels, some measuring a hundred tons) and brigs (two-masted, square-rigged vessels) moved into the "sugar" trade. While Maine shipping re-mained heavily oriented to the coasting trade, some of these larger deep-water sailers carried Caribbean goods, especially the rum, to Europe and returned to American ports with manufactured items. This deep-water trade received a tremendous boost during the Napoleonic Wars (1793–1809), when most European merchant ships were driven from the sea by France or England. Maine ships (the specific vessel type with three masts and square sails), some measuring 150 tons, moved into this lucrative "North Atlantic ferry route" as neutral shipping, carrying goods from the Caribbean colonies to US ports, and then "reexporting" them to the mother countries. Federal bounties, which heavily encouraged shipbuilding, fishing, and sailing, added further incentives for growth after 1819.

Much of the cargo carried in Maine vessels was, like salt cod, a home product. Building materials were the most important of these. Such materials included lime from the Rockland area, granite from the mid-coast headlands and islands, bricks (especially from Brewer), and the most spectacular of Maine construction products, lumber. Almost all Maine ports exported some lumber. Some, such as Pembroke, in Washington County; Franklin, in Hancock County; and Wiscasset, in Franklin County, had small hinterlands, or areas from which they took their exports and to which they brought in goods. Nevertheless, even these ports sustained booming lumber and shipbuilding trades until after the Civil War, when their hinterlands were cut over.

Larger rivers, such as the Androscoggin, Kennebec, and Penobscot, tapped deep hinterlands covered with seemingly inexhaustible stands of timber. Bangor's rise to national preeminence as a lumber-shipping port stimulated a prosperous shipbuilding industry on the Penobscot. During the nineteenth century, over five hundred vessels were launched in Bangor and its neighboring towns of Brewer, Orrington, and Hampden. Almost all these vessels left the Penobscot carrying some form of rough or semifinished timber. Among the most unusual were wooden "bricks" for paving factory floors or even public streets.

Because the "lumber-droughers" (vessels used to transport lumber) were constructed as general merchandise freighters and built to carry heavy commodities, they were difficult to handle when loaded with a light cargo like lumber. A conjunction of native Maine products and Yankee "know-how" helped solve this problem. Since the state abounds in good marine clays, ship masters consigned bricks as a complement to their relatively lighter loads of lumber or hay. Thus, while Bangor shipped lumber, its cross-river neighbor, Brewer, became a brick-making center of national reputation. Each winter, Brewer brick makers collected scrap wood from the sawmills, and when spring came they dug clay (the city is built around its old clay pits) and prepared it for firing. Since lumbering was primarily a winter occupation, brick makers had a ready supply of labor in the spring after the log drives reached safe water. Clay was shaped, dried, and stacked in and around wood to make the kilns. After brick makers fired and tore down their kilns, they furnished cheap bricks to sea captains who wanted to load their lower holds with balancing weight to make their vessels perform well at sea. Often the captains loaded casks of lime from the lower Penobscot Bay, making a complete "construction cargo" of bricks, lime, and lumber.

The mid-coast lime industry also created a demand for vessels to carry wood. These were usually two-masted schooners built in just about any port on the Maine coast, or "Johnny woodboats," small sloops or schooners built principally on the St. John River in New Brunswick. Larger, tighter and newer schooners, some four-masted, were used to carry the lime to its major distribution point, New York City. The lime trade helped make Camden, Rockland, and Thomaston major shipbuilding centers. Granite quarries created another cargo which also required specialized sloops to carry the stone.

The cargoes of construction materials were profitable partly because eastern cities were growing at such a phenomenal rate, and partly because sea captains found a steady return cargo in coal. Beginning in the 1820s, steam-powered engines gradually but steadily replaced the waterwheel as a source of mechanical energy. First wood, then coal fired these voracious steam boilers. Eventually, coal also fueled locomotives, tugboats, and steamships and supplied heat in cast-iron stoves and furnaces in large urban homes. But it was as much the need for light as it was for steam power that gave the coal trade its first boost.

It is little remembered that the Clapp brothers, William and Asa, were the first Portland entrepreneurs to use coal for light. In 1849, they set up a small coal gasification plant in Portland and piped the flammable vapors made by their little retort to twelve gas lamps in the yards of the Atlantic and St. Lawrence Railway. The lamps provided light so that the laborers from their shipping business could handle merchandise day and night.

In the years after 1849, similar coal gasification plants were built in other Maine cities. Scuttles to handle coal appeared on the waterfronts and, by the time of the Civil War, the trade in coal for gasification was booming. Streets were torn up and gas lines laid, supplying light, heat, and cooking fuel for homes, factories, and offices. Coal imports increased markedly in the gaslight era—the 1850s—then boomed with industrial expansion based on steam power after the Civil War.

Maine's deep-water carrying trade received another boost from the cotton textile industry in England and New England. In 1802, the brig *Androscoggin*, owned by Maine's first governor, William King, returned from New Orleans loaded with southern cotton. The voyage was successful, and for the next eighty years Maine dominated the carrying trade in raw cotton. Maine-built brigs and then ships dropped down the coast to the south's great cotton ports—Charleston, Savannah, Mobile, and New Orleans—carrying lumber, bricks, hay, or whatever cargoes they could find in northern ports. After taking on a cargo of baled cotton, they sailed for Liverpool, Le Havre, Bremen, or back up the Atlantic Coast to the mill cities of New England. European-bound vessels returned to the East Coast with manufactured goods or cargoes of immigrants; the human freight paid approximately the same rates for passage as inert cargoes.

This carrying trade also required a special design. Broad-beamed and bluff bowed, the cotton freighter had a high deckhouse and a deep hold, rounding out under water like a kettle. Two circumstances affected the way Maine built these vessels. One was taxes. In 1789 the new federal government passed a law taxing vessels according to a simplistic formula that did not account for how a vessel's hull was formed. The resulting "rule-cheaters," with their relatively narrow decks and wide waterline widths were less safe than conventional vessels, but they gained advantages in federal taxes. The second circumstance affecting the design—something of a countervailing influence—was the length of the voyage from Maine to New Orleans. The cotton droughers had to be well built to withstand the considerable punishment that often came on that difficult passage.

Perhaps the most famous of the early cotton freighters was the *Rappahannock*, built by Freeman Clark and William D. Sewall of Bath. Launched in 1841, she ran 179 feet in length and 37 feet at the beam and measured 1,133 tons. At this time, the *Rappahannock* was the largest vessel in the world—actually, one of the largest merchantmen built in the Western world since the Romans launched their great grain carriers at the time of Christ. In addition to the cotton trade, the ice industry created a demand for specially built Maine vessels. Again, local industries proved complementary: Maine's busy sawmills supplied cheap wood to build the ice houses, the mountains of sawdust with which to insulate them, and the vessels that carried the ice. One of the largest vessels in the trade used over two hundred cords of sawdust as insulation for its perishable cargo. Earlier cargoes went to market in brigs and two-masted schooners, but as demand grew, larger vessels, mostly schooners with three, four, and then five masts, were built to carry it. On board were finely crafted pumps to discharge water from the melting ice, along with any seawater that found its way through the seams. The schooners were built of the best materials, because their cargoes were heavy and the melting water subjected them to rot. Because their cargoes were perishable, they were also built for speed. In late summer or early fall, schooners sometimes carried bushels of Maine apples in their upper holds. Cooled by the ice below, the apples arrived in southern ports well preserved. The versatile schooners usually returned from the South laden with coal.

A fair way to describe the spirit and ingenuity of Maine shipbuilders is to examine the fabled but short-lived clipper-ship era. The bold creativity of American ship designers had been brought to the fore during the Napoleonic Wars, when a premium on speed as means of escape from privateers and war vessels dictated some daring departures in ship design. During the War of 1812 similar conditions produced the "Baltimore clipper," a schooner-rigged brig associated with the Chesapeake yards. After 1815, New York's East River shipbuilders produced a series of transatlantic packet ships that continued the quest for speed under sail.

But the true clippers emerged in the 1840s, combining in some fashion three square-rigged masts, a long hull tapering from the bow to a deeply concave stern, and a narrow beam, located farther aft than in earlier designs. Their long, thin, shallow-draft hulls were made for speed, and their sails were legion, catching whole rivers of wind to drive the clippers at startling speeds. Authorities bestow the title "clipper" only on vessels which made the passage from New York to San Francisco in 110 days or less, or equaled this feat on other voyages. Names bestowed on these vessels expressed the romance of this brief era: *Sovereign of the Seas, Flying Cloud, Hyperion, Romance of the Seas.* Their captains made handsome salaries, but drove their vessels relentlessly, running at times under full sail in conditions that defied caution.

The master artist of clipper-ship design was Nova Scotia–born Donald McKay, who worked in the yards in New York's East River, in Newburyport, and in East Boston. McKay's famous *Flying Cloud* was the epitome of the clipper. The 1,782-ton ship made the voyage between New York and San Francisco in eighty-nine days, carrying up to fifty-two sails and a crew of almost three score to work them. The *Flying Cloud* could make eighteen knots on a long passage, but like other clippers she sacrificed a third of her cargo space for speed, an economically unsound proposition in the long run.

Like other vessels built in Maine and elsewhere, the clippers were designed to meet specific needs—in this case, rapid deep-water passage and minimal cargo space. The California Gold Rush, which brought booming markets in San Francisco and Sacramento and a mass movement of gold-hungry easterners, stimulated competition after 1849, as did a later gold rush in Australia and a lucrative trade in low bulk, high value products from China—jades, brocades, china, tea, and spices. Six Maine-built vessels hold clipper records, and probably the best of the lot—the *Red Jacket*—was built in Rockland. The fabulous returns on transoceanic voyages, however, were not to last, and by the mid-1850s, the rush to build these exquisite "racehounds of the sea" had largely dissipated.

In addition to producing their share of clippers, Maine shipbuilders created what were probably the finest commercial sailing vessels ever built, the great

"Down-Easters." An exclusive New England design, the Down-Easters combined speed, handiness, cargo capacity, and low operating costs to a degree never before obtained in square riggers. According to Howard Chappelle, the best informed authority on American sailing ships, the Down-Easters were the "highest development of the sailing ship."

The Down-Easters were designed specifically to capture the Pacific grain trade, which began at midcentury when rudimentary improvements in health care caused a population explosion in Europe. Cheap wheat, grown in Argentina, Australia, Russia, and the American West, fed the burgeoning cities of Europe, and the cost of its transportation on these great transoceanic voyages played a large part in its final price. California was an important focus of this trade. After loading wheat in San Francisco, the Down-Easters often sailed westward across the Pacific and Indian Oceans, around the Cape of Good Hope, to Liverpool. On these long voyages, they became moving, floating warehouses; recent developments in the undersea telegraph meant that the wheat could be bought and sold several times en route.

Just as it is difficult to define a clipper precisely, it is difficult to define a Down-Easter. For our purposes, they were square-rigged sailing vessels which measured over a thousand tons and had slab sides, capacious mid-bodies that encompassed great cargo holds, and large but simple sail plans. Unlike the clippers, they featured steam winches to work their sails. The epitome of the Down-Easter was the *Henry B. Hyde*, a vessel built by Chapman and Flint at Bath in 1884. The *Hyde* measured 2,463 tons and ran 286 feet with a beam of 45 feet and a draught of 29 feet. On ten consecutive voyages, she averaged 116 days running from New York to San Francisco. Searsport, which bred around 10 percent of America's deep-water ship masters at midcentury, contributed a Pendleton or a Colcord to command the Hyde on many of these passages. Three times she made a clipper's passage of less than 110 days and twice more recorded a run of 113 days. Like most Down-Easters, the *Hyde* carried wheat from San Francisco Bay to help feed Europe's millions.

To win the carrying trade for Pacific grain, Maine shipbuilders built capacious, fast ships. They designed heavily timbered keels and frames, and thick, strong planking to withstand both the brutal weather of the lower latitudes and the strains produced by a shifting cargo of wheat. Maine shipbuilders were able to drive down production costs partly by using low-wage labor and partly by building ships of huge size. They used masts of "Oregon pine" (Douglas-fir), since Maine's great white pines were gone. Maine shipwrights used considerable amounts of metal for bracing in these great square-riggers.

The Down-Easters, the last of the large square-rigged vessels built in Maine, were eventually pushed out of the grain trade by steam vessels, and many ended their lives in a unique manner: plying the Alaska salmon trade. Beginning in 1893, the California-based Alaska Packers Association bought many of the great vessels, loaded them with box shooks, oil, tin plate for cans, fishermen, and laborers, and sent them north in the spring. Once in Alaskan waters, the Down-Easter tied up at a cannery wharf where fishing boats brought the salmon. The laborers processed the fish, made the cans, and packed the fish. At the end of the season, the Down-Easters sailed for San Francisco with a full cargo of fish and a crew of tired cannery workers.

The Down-Easters had another interesting facet in their careers: many ended their useful days in the "Hollywood Navy." Producer Cecil B. DeMille and the Metro-Goldwyn-Mayer studio, among others, bought the aging vessels for a song and took them to sea to make movies. Later, presumably, they were hauled up on deserted beaches and burned, so that the metal in them could be sold for scrap.

Wooden sailing ships remained a vital component of Maine's coastal economy through World War I and even experienced a brief revival during World War II. But increasingly in the second half of the nineteenth century the industry was on the defensive. Steam ships, made (usually in England) of iron, then steel, proved more efficient and dependable, and eventually they drove Maine's wooden sailing ships from the waters. But for a half a century after the Civil War, Maine shipbuilders met this challenge by producing wooden sailing ships to meet specialized markets. Just as Maine coast fishermen responded to the crisis in deepwater fishing by adapting to new markets, Maine shipbuilders continued to use their traditional skills and resources to meet new demands. The coastal economy survived the crisis of fishing and shipbuilding in the second half of the century, demonstrating again the versatility of Maine's resources and the adaptability of those who used them.

For Further Reading:

Essential to any consideration of the North Atlantic fisheries of the nineteenth century are a quartet of seminal works dealing with the broader aspects of the industry. Harold A. Innis's *The Cod Fisheries* (Toronto, 1940) is an unsurpassed model of research and synthesis covering both Canada and the United States. Also important is Raymond McFarland, *A History of the New England Fisheries* (New York, 1911), dated but still the best general study of that region's industry. A basic source on nineteenth-century fisheries history, technology, geography, biology, sociology, and economics is the monumental US Commission of Fish and Fisheries, *The Fisheries and Fishery Industries of the United States*, edited by George Brown Goode, 5 secs., 7 vols. (Washington, 1884–87). Emory R. Johnson et al., *History of Domestic and Foreign Commerce of the United States*, 2 vols.

(Washington, 1915) has several chapters by T. W. Van Metre that provide an overview of the various American fisheries from 1789 to 1910 and emphasize political, economic, and diplomatic developments.

A number of state and local studies bear directly on the Maine fishing industry. Foremost of these is Wayne M. O'Leary, "The Maine Sea Fisheries, 1830–1890: The Rise and Fall of a Native Industry" (Ph.D. dissertation, University of Maine, 1981), the only comprehensive treatment of the subject to date. A more superficial examination may be found in William H. Rowe, *The Maritime History of Maine* (New York, 1948), which devotes two chapters to the state's fisheries.

These works may be supplemented by several more narrowly focused studies. Charles W. Eliot's *John Gilley: Maine Farmer and Fisherman* (Boston, 1904) provides a unique biographical account of the life of a Maine inshore fisherman from the Mount Desert Island region. Francis B. Greene, *History of Boothbay, Southport and Boothbay Harbor, Maine* (Portland, 1906) is the best of the multitude of Maine coastal town histories from the standpoint of the fishing industry. Also worth mentioning is H. W. Small, *A History of Swan's Island, Maine* (Ellsworth, 1898), which presents a detailed look at a leading mackerel-fishing community. George L. Wasson and Lincoln Colcord, *Sailing Days on the Penobscot* (Salem, Mass., 1932) contains useful information on the fisheries of mid-coast Maine. Wesley G. Pierce's *Goin' Fishin'* (Salem, Mass., 1932) offers insights into the fisheries of the Portland and Boothbay areas, as well as an extensive examination of nineteenth-century fishing technology. In addition, two federal government publications of the late nineteenth century, the *Annual Report* and *Annual Bulletin* of the United States Commission of Fish and Fisheries, contain numerous monographs and statistical reports relating to various economic and technical aspects of Maine's fishing industry.

A considerable number of first-hand narratives illuminate the sea fisheries. Two of the best pertaining to Maine are Joseph W. Smith, *Gleanings from the Sea* (Andover, Mass., 1887), the memoir of a Biddeford Pool fisherman, and William H. Bishop, "Fish and Men in the Maine Islands," *Harper's New Monthly Magazine* 61 (August–September 1880), a journalist's account of the remote Maine outports.

Finally, no student of the North Atlantic sea fisheries should ignore the numerous fine works of fiction that lend flavor, drama, and an understanding of the fisherman's world. One that relates specifically to Maine is Elijah Kellogg, *The Fisher Boys of Pleasant Cove* (Boston, 1874). Superior as literature, and the recognized classic of the genre, is Rudyard Kipling's evocative *Captains Courageous* (New York, 1905).

Sources for researching Maine's shipping and shipbuilding trades include the commercial and shipping sections of newspapers from Maine's more important ports: the *Bangor Whig and Courier; Bath Times; Belfast Republican Journal; Eastern Argus* (Portland); *Eastport Sentinel; Hallowell Gazette;* and the *Rockland Courier-Gazette.* One should also consult the extensive archives of the Maine Maritime Museum in Bath and the Penobscot Marine Museum in Searsport. Maine's custom house records are located in the National Archives. A more extensive bibliography may be found in William A. Baker's *Maine Shipbuilding: A Bibliographical Guide* (Portland, 1974).

Rowe's *Maritime History of Maine,* along with his *Shipbuilding Days in Casco Bay, 1727–1890* (Yarmouth, 1929) and his *Shipbuilding Days in Old North Yarmouth* (Portland, 1924), provide a good starting point for secondary literature on shipping and shipbuilding. Other works of general interest are Robert G. Albion, William A. Baker, and Benjamin W. Labaree, *New England and the Sea* (Mystic, Conn., 1972); William S. Newell, *Shipbuilding in Maine: A Brief History* (Princeton, N.J., 1938); and Robert G. Albion's monumental *Forests and Sea Power* (Cambridge, Mass., 1926). Fine maritime graphics may be found in *The Age of Steam and Sail: Selections from the Allie Ryan Maritime Collection at the Maine State Museum* (Augusta, 1986).

For shipping and shipbuilding in specific locales, see William A. Baker, *A Maritime History of Bath, Maine* (Bath, 1973); Wasson and Colcord, *Sailing Days on the Penobscot;* George W. Rice, *The Shipping Days of Old Boothbay* (Boothbay Harbor, 1938); William T. Alexander, *Harpswell on Casco Bay* (Portland, 1973); Thomas W. Murphy, Jr., *The Landing* (Kennebunk, 1977); Cyrus Eaton, *History of Thomaston* (Hallowell, 1865); and Erminie S. Reynolds, *The Skolfields and their Ships* (Bath, 1987).

Some of the better works on specific topics include Basil Lubbock, *The Downeasters* (Boston, 1929); William A. Baker, "The Boston Boats from Sail to Steam," *Maine Historical Society Newsletter* 9 (August 1969); and Robert F. Duncan, *Friendship Sloops* (Camden, 1985). On women in the maritime trades, see Joanna C. Colcord's "Domestic Life on American Sailing Ships," *American Neptune* (July 1942); John F. Battick, "The Searsport 'Thirty-Six': Seafaring Wives of a Maine Community in 1880," *American Neptune* 44 (no. 3, 1984); and Julianna FreeHand, *A Seafaring Legacy: The Photographs, Diaries, Letters and Memorabilia of a Maine Sea Captain and his Wife, 1859–1908* (New York, 1981). Issues of the *American Neptune* carry many articles on Maine ships and shipbuilding.

14

Transportation & Manufacturing

JOEL W. EASTMAN & PAUL E. RIVARD

This chapter demonstrates the links between transportation, commerce, and manufacturing. Unlike Maine's resource-based industries, manufacturing did not always rely on locally available materials. Commerce—the influx of raw materials and the export of finished products—was thus vital to this sector of the economy. Joel W. Eastman, a business and economic historian, describes the development of transportation systems and the economic strategies upon which they were based. Paul E. Rivard, a material culture specialist, explains the "dual nature" of Maine's manufacturing—the huge textile mills operating in tandem with dispersed shop, home, and foundry activities.

A study of transportation, commerce, and manufacturing illustrates several important points about Maine's economy. First, the process of industrialization is much more complex than we might suppose. Manufacturing flourished at every level of Maine society, from the thriving mill towns to the dooryards and sewing rooms of upland Maine farmhouses. Although giant mills and factories may appear more symbolic of industrial development, small-shop and home manufacturing enterprises were just as important to Maine's productive capacity.

Second, the spread of manufacturing through the countryside dispels the myth that interior sections of Maine were isolated and self-sufficient. That rural Maine absorbed a vast and vigorous small-scale manufacturing economy without substantial demographic change helps explain the persistence of a rural way of life in the face of declining agricultural prospects. Third, this chapter emphasizes the important role women played in industry. Rural homes were tremendously productive in the aggregate, and much of this activity was traditionally the responsibility of women. Perhaps more surprising is the fact that women were the backbone of the state's first factory labor force. Finally, here again we find the essential connection between local activity—manufacturing in this case—and external developments. Maine was linked, early and intensively, with markets throughout the Eastern Sea-

board and across the Atlantic. This widespread commercial exchange is vital for understanding the evolution of Maine's economy and society.

Transportation Systems in Maine, 1820–80

JOEL W. EASTMAN

Manufacturing, like agriculture, fishing, and resource industries, benefited from certain geographical influences in Maine: proximity to metropolitan markets, river systems, and excellent prospects for seaborne navigation. Other geographical influences were less beneficial. Maine's location on the extreme northeastern edge of the nation left it somewhat isolated, particularly as east-west rail transportation replaced north-south seaborne traffic as the focus of American commerce.

Transportation systems were means by which Maine enhanced its geographical advantages and compensated for its disadvantages. Manufacturing activity depended heavily on these transportation developments, because it was woven into a much broader commercial network that involved outside supplies of raw materials, flows of semifinished products from place to place, and shipment of finished goods to metropolitan markets all across the nation. Commerce and the transportation infrastructure that supported it were the genesis of Maine manufacturing. Thus, the ways Maine people responded to the advantages and disadvantages of geography shaped the state's vigorous industrial life.

Overland transportation was not a major concern for the first Maine settlements, since they were located on the coast or on major river arteries. But as the frontier moved inland, the citizens of these interior communities recognized the necessity for improved transportation; products from landlocked areas could not be marketed competitively until they could be hauled in bulk. Roads and bridges were the first priority. Most towns levied a highway tax, which citizens paid off by working on the roads—cutting trees, removing stumps and rocks, filling holes, draining and leveling surfaces, and rolling snow for sleigh traffic in the winter. Bridges were more expensive than road maintenance, and usually required a direct appropriation of tax money.

With the population boom that followed the American Revolution, more ambitious projects were proposed. During the first decade of the nineteenth century, there was a flurry of enthusiasm for privately built toll roads or "turnpikes," so-called because of the barriers erected at the toll houses. Two toll roads were begun in 1802. The Camden Turnpike, running from that town to Lincolnville, was constructed over a six-year period at a cost of approximately

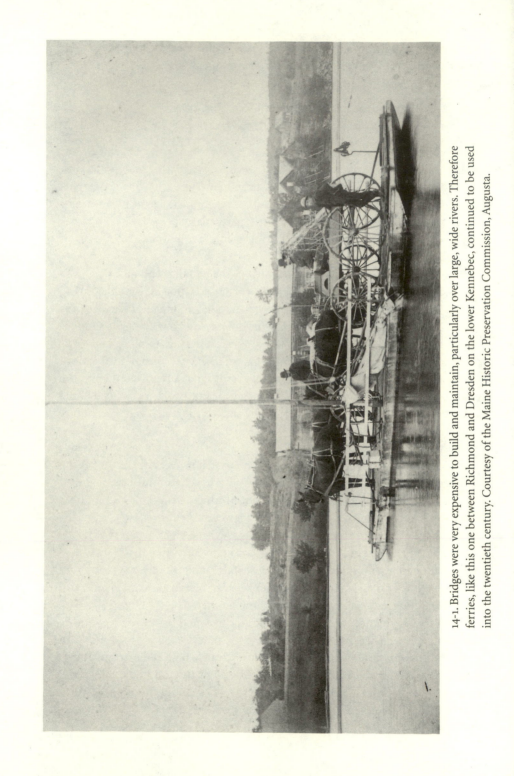

14-1. Bridges were very expensive to build and maintain, particularly over large, wide rivers. Therefore ferries, like this one between Richmond and Dresden on the lower Kennebec, continued to be used into the twentieth century. Courtesy of the Maine Historic Preservation Commission, Augusta.

six thousand dollars. The Cumberland Turnpike followed a portion of the current US Route 1 between the villages of Dunstan and Oak Hill in Scarborough. The latter operated until the 1850s with state-regulated tolls of eight cents for wagons and twenty-five cents for stage coaches. In 1803, the Wiscasset and Woolwich Turnpike was begun, and four years later, the Wiscasset and Augusta pike. In 1805, Bath entrepreneur and politician William King invested over sixteen thousand dollars in the construction of the eight-mile-long Bath Turnpike, which ran to Brunswick. The most ambitious and far-sighted proposal was put forward in 1804 by the Maine Turnpike Association, which advocated a toll road from New Hampshire through Portland to Augusta. The project was abandoned two years later, only to be revived 124 years later on the eve of World War II.

Despite the interest in turnpikes, the most modern form of transportation was the artificial waterway, or canal. Canal systems had been developed earlier in Europe and the British Isles, and Americans were building canals by the late eighteenth century. The earliest in Maine was the New Meadows Canal, a two-mile waterway from the Kennebec River to Casco Bay, chartered in 1792 by the Massachusetts legislature as a way to float logs to tide-powered sawmills on the New Meadows River and along Casco Bay. Plagued with high construction and maintenance costs, inadequate financing, and low traffic, it was abandoned in 1796. In 1793, the Georges River Canal was created to improve transportation into the interior of Knox County from the seaport of Thomaston. The first effort failed, but Henry Knox, who acquired much of the land in the county after the Revolution, operated the canal from 1803 to 1806. The canal again fell into disuse but was rebuilt in 1846 and then abandoned for good in 1854.

The most successful Maine canal was the Cumberland and Oxford, which ran from Portland to Sebago and Long lakes, about fifty miles inland. The canal was proposed as early as 1791, and a canal company was chartered. It failed, however, to raise sufficient capital, and the project languished until 1821, when a second corporation was chartered. Its prospectus reflects the high hopes this enterprise raised in the Portland area:

> Works of this stupendous character are not merely designed for the convenience and comfort of the passing age, but to endure beyond the ravages of time and revolution, and are of infinite value to posterity. If the present generation of men can be made sensible of their true interests, and awakened to a just sense of social duties, they will not only secure a plentiful harvest for their exertions . . . but will establish a chain of gratitude on the coming age, that shall ensure them an imperishable fame.

Despite this appeal, sale of the stock again proved inadequate. The directors returned to the legislature and obtained permission to operate a lottery, and when this device raised even less capital, they lobbied for a charter for a bank, agreeing to invest $75,000 of its capital in the canal in return for an exemption from state taxes. Even this was not enough to complete the construction of the waterway, which ultimately cost $206,000. The corporation was granted another $75,000 in loans by the Canal Bank to complete and open the canal in the spring of 1830.

The C&O prospered for over twenty years, with 150 boats traveling its waters. Tolls on cargoes of lumber and agricultural products paid the interest on the bank loans, but railroad competition eventually forced the canal into bankruptcy in 1858. The C&O was taken over and sold by the bank, and the new owners operated it until 1870. Although the canal was not able to repay its loans or pay dividends to its stockholders, the economic impact of its operation was positive. The canal brought efficient, inexpensive transportation to the interior of Cumberland and Oxford counties. This in turn boosted land values, stimulated agriculture, lumbering, and manufacturing, and helped to develop the city of Portland.

Other efforts were focused on improving navigation on rivers. A dam and lock built at Augusta in 1838 allowed steamboats to navigate the Kennebec River beyond Augusta Falls, until the lock was finally abandoned in 1895. A similar lock on the Penobscot River built in 1847 permitted steamboats to travel between Old Town and Lincoln until 1867. A small canal at Stillwater, which operated between 1840 and 1879, passed lumber around the falls at Orono. The "Telos Cut" between the Allagash and Penobscot watersheds was, despite the friction described earlier, among the longest lasting and most profitable of Maine's lumber canals, operating from 1846 until 1921. Although most canals were not as permanent as the Telos Cut, they did play a pioneering role in bringing improved transportation to the interior.

Canal development gave way to railroads as the benefits of this new system became apparent in the 1840s. In fact, the Maine legislature created a Board of Internal Improvements in 1834, which immediately focused on creating a railroad policy for the state. The board's underlying strategy was a system of railroads that would serve the entire state and be independent of outside control. It also commissioned the survey of a route between Maine and Canada, with the idea of promoting the state as a route to the Atlantic when the St. Lawrence River was blocked with ice. Competing Maine regions and industries made it impossible for the legislature to agree on a railroad policy, but a private citizen, John A. Poor, took on the task and achieved notable success.

14-2 The pioneering steam engines Lion (right) and Tiger in a railroad machine shop. Lion was built in 1846 for the Palmer & Machiasport Railroad. It was East Andover businessman-visionary John A. Poor (1818–71) who built the Atlantic & St. Lawrence (Grand Trunk) in 1853 and made Portland into Canada's ice-free winter port. Collections of the Maine State Museum, Augusta.

Poor was a Bangor lawyer who saw his first locomotive in Massachusetts in 1834. He immediately recognized the potential for opening up the interior of Maine and connecting the state with the rest of the world. Poor described the event: "As I reflected in after years, the locomotive engine grew into a greatness in my mind that left all other created things far behind it as marvels and wonders." After the tragic deaths of his wife and daughter, Poor moved to Portland and devoted the rest of his life to the task the state government had been unable to accomplish: promoting and building an independent railroad system for Maine.

The key to financing such a system, Poor felt, was linking Maine's railroads with other parts of the country and the world. As the entrepôt for other people's cargoes, Maine would receive jobs, taxes, and revenues. Railroads built to serve other areas would also be the core of a railroad system for Maine, which would allow Maine farmers and manufacturers to get their goods to market. This in turn would stimulate the economy, halt outmigration, and encourage immigration. In describing his dream, Poor wrote: "It was a vision, in which I saw the whole line pass before me like a grand panorama, and in continuation a vast system of railroads permeating the whole country, from the Bay of Chaleur to the Gulf of Mexico, . . . and the coast of Maine lined with cities rivaling the cities of the coast of the Baltic."

The first branch of the system was to be a railroad to serve Canada, which the Board of Internal Improvements had suggested in 1834. Canada needed an ice-free winter port, and in fact Boston had already attempted to convince business leaders in Montreal that it was the logical outlet. During a fierce blizzard in 1845, Poor dashed through western Maine to Montreal and argued persuasively that the route he had just traveled was the most expeditious winter passage to the Atlantic. Portland was indeed closer to Europe than Boston, and the route would bring rail service to more of eastern Canada. Convinced, Canadians organized the St. Lawrence and Atlantic Railway, while Portland business leaders created the Atlantic and St. Lawrence, with a $1.5 million loan from the city. Both companies built to meet at the international boundary. Poor then organized a company in Portland to manufacture locomotives and rail cars and convinced the Canadians to construct the rail line as a broad gauge, which he argued was more stable than the narrower standard gauge used by most American railroads. Not incidentally, it would also physically prevent rail traffic from being diverted to Boston.

As with the Cumberland and Oxford Canal, the Atlantic and St. Lawrence cost more to build than anticipated, and so when the Grand Trunk Railway of Canada offered to lease the line after it was completed in 1853, the owners consented, even though it meant loss of control over the route. Poor and Portland next constructed branch lines eastward to Bangor. As a result of the Atlantic and St. Lawrence, Portland did become Canada's winter port and benefited greatly from its commerce for seventy-five years. The importance of the railroad is reflected in a poem published in 1858 in Poor's newspaper, *State of Maine:*

> Portland is looking up and all her spunk
> Is centered in those noble words— "Grand Trunk":
> That iron arm that links Atlantic "Maine"
> With Huron's waters in a single chain;
> On whose smooth rail the swift, careening steed
> Shall cross Victoria Bridge, and onward speed,

Defying time and space—its journey o'er,
Shall slake its thirst in the Pacific shore:
While o'er our waters busy steamers ply
With flags of every hue, in peaceful harmony;
A neutral port with every flag unfurled
That floats on merchant ships throughout the world.

In the late 1850s, Poor unveiled his greatest dream: the European and North American Railroad, which he hoped would channel through Maine much of the passenger and freight traffic between Europe and the United States and Canada.

The key to Poor's scheme was the relative speed of railroads and ship traffic. Traveling by rail to Nova Scotia, which was closer to Europe by sea, would cut several days from a trip between New York and London. Poor held a railroad convention in Portland in 1850 which was attended by representatives of most of the cities and provinces to be served by the line. The delegates were enthusiastic, but raising capital for the project was another matter. Poor and the city of Bangor, which stood to benefit from the line, worked for years to sell stock and to obtain government aid; maritime Canadians likewise had great difficulties.

In 1864, Bangor loaned the company $500,000, and in 1869, the state legislature approved a land grant. Two years later the line from Bangor to Saint John, New Brunswick, was completed and appropriately dedicated by President Ulysses S. Grant and Canadian Governor General Lord Lisgor, along with the governors of Maine and New Brunswick and several other dignitaries. Ironically, the event took place just six weeks after Poor's death.

The railroad was untimely in another sense. As the speed of the Atlantic packet steamboats increased, the relative distance between Nova Scotia and Europe became less significant. By 1871, the concept behind the European and North American was no longer viable. Moreover, the railroad was inaugurated on the brink of one of the worst depressions in the nineteenth century. Still, the road brought transportation service to eastern Maine and provided a link between central Canada and the maritime provinces, via the Grand Trunk. The link was made more direct in 1885 with the construction of the Canadian Pacific Railroad across northern Maine.

Perhaps Poor's greatest legacy was the railroad that grew out of his branch lines to Lewiston and Bangor. These merged in 1862 to form the Maine Central Railroad. The Maine Central gradually leased or purchased other lines until it completely dominated the railroad system in the populated southern third of the state. The Maine Central abandoned the broad gauge for the widely used standard gauge in 1871, as it tied its system into that of the rest of the nation.

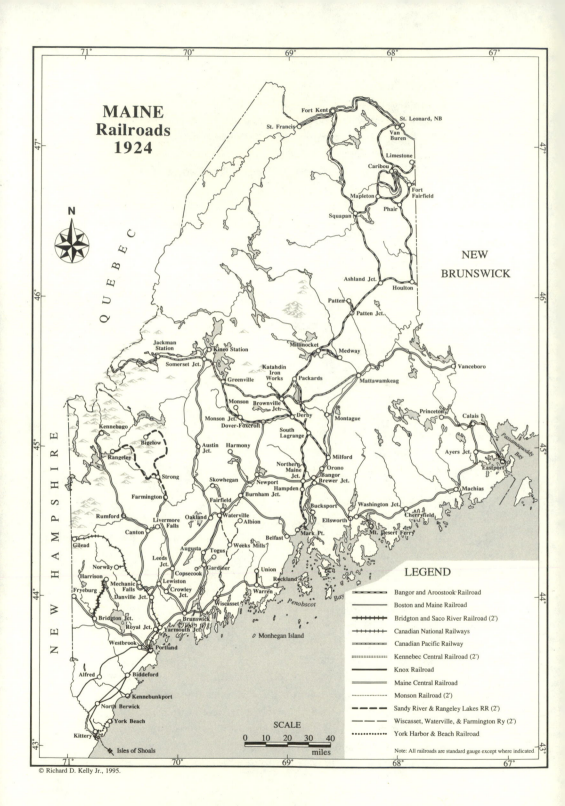

MAINE
Railroads
1924

N

QUEBEC

NEW BRUNSWICK

NEW HAMPSHIRE

Locations:
Fort Kent, St. Francis, St. Leonard, NB, Van Buren, Limestone, Caribou, Fort Fairfield, Mapleton, Phair, Squapan, Ashland Jct., Houlton, Patten, Patten Jct., Vanceboro, Millinocket, Medway, Mattawamkeag, Jackman Station, Kineo Station, Somerset Jct., Katahdin Iron Works, Greenville, Packards, Princeton, Calais, Monson, Brownville Jct., Derby, Montague, Ayers Jct., Eastport, Monson Jct., Dover-Foxcroft, South Lagrange, Machias, Kennebago, Bigelow, Austin Jct., Harmony, Milford, Rangeley, Strong, Northern Maine Jct., Orono, Bangor, Brewer Jct., Skowhegan, Newport, Hampden, Washington Jct., Cherryfield, Farmington, Fairfield, Burnham Jct., Bucksport, Rumford, Oakland, Waterville, Ellsworth, Mt. Desert Ferry, Livermore Falls, Albion, Belfast, Mark Pt., Canton, Gilead, Augusta, Togus, Weeks Mills, Union, Rockland, Leeds Jct., Gardiner, Norway, Copsecook, Lewiston, Mechanic Falls, Crowley Jct., Warren, Harrison, Danville Jct., Wiscasset, Fryeburg, Bridgton Jct., Royal Jct., Brunswick, Monhegan Island, Westbrook, Yarmouth Jct., Portland, Alfred, Biddeford, Kennebunkport, North Berwick, York Beach, Kittery, Isles of Shoals

Penobscot Bay, Passamaquoddy Bay

LEGEND

- Bangor and Aroostook Railroad
- Boston and Maine Railroad
- Bridgton and Saco River Railroad (2')
- Canadian National Railways
- Canadian Pacific Railway
- Kennebec Central Railroad (2')
- Knox Railroad
- Maine Central Railroad
- Monson Railroad (2')
- Sandy River & Rangeley Lakes RR (2')
- Wiscasset, Waterville, & Farmington Ry (2')
- York Harbor & Beach Railroad

Note: All railroads are standard gauge except where indicated.

SCALE

0   10   20   30   40
miles

© Richard D. Kelly Jr., 1995.

By the 1880s, the one major area of the state not served by rail transportation was Aroostook County. This situation was redressed when a group of entrepreneurs led by Albert Burleigh and Franklin W. Cram created the Bangor and Aroostook Railroad in 1891 and built a system to serve the county, stimulating both agriculture and lumbering. In other areas bypassed by the standard-gauge lines, a number of less expensive two-foot gauge railroads appeared in the 1880s, most of them operating successfully into the 1930s.

Maine people adopted the railroad system enthusiastically between 1840 and 1880, largely because it offered a new means of reintegrating Maine into the national economy, while it also served to link Maine to Canada's economy. Faced with the shift away from ocean shipping, where Maine had held a geographic advantage, to continental east-west rail travel, which left the state geographically isolated, Maine turned to the rail system to address the problem. Inland towns particularly benefited from the new form of transportation. The importance of railroads is evident in this poem written to commemorate the opening of the Bridgton and Saco River Railroad in 1883:

> And hark! Through the valley o'er hillside and plain
> The thunder is heard of the narrow gauge train.
> And cheers and huzzas from the spirited throng
> Greet the advent of progress now booming along.
> Eureka! The shriek of the engine declares
> And Bridgton Redeemed is the motto it bears.

Maine Manufactures, 1820–80

PAUL E. RIVARD

As we have noted, Maine's resource-based industries were shaped primarily by environmental factors. On the other hand, manufacturing—that is, the creation of finished products—was conditioned mostly by Maine's geography and its transportation systems. The relative ease of transportation along Maine's coast and river systems, coupled with the transportation networks developed in the middle of the nineteenth century, meant that Maine communities were seldom truly isolated, seldom remote from the centers of world or regional trade.

Initially, the accessibility of Maine's abundant natural resources stimulated commercial activity rather than manufacturing. From earliest times, Moses Greenleaf noted in 1829, Maine residents were a "commercial people." This, in turn, diminished the incentive to manufacture goods. Moreover, coastal and transatlantic shipping brought Maine communities a substantial supply of manufactured commodities, lessening the need to produce these goods at home. Compared with New England states to the south, manufacturing activity came to Maine slowly and somewhat late.

Eventually, however, this same waterborne trade network encouraged manufacturing activity. Rivers and harbors used to transport natural resources from the state could also be used to carry raw materials to Maine and finished consumer products to markets elsewhere. Furthermore, Maine's rivers and streams provided abundant water-power sites for the establishment of manufacturing centers. The rapid development of power machinery during the early decades of the nineteenth century made Maine's rushing water attractive to outside investment.

A romantic picture persists of preindustrial artisans working in small, self-sufficient communities to fashion handicrafts for their neighbors, an image that has little to do with the real story of manufacturing in Maine. Linked to metropolitan centers by Maine's excellent transportation situation, manufacturers worked within a much broader commercial network. In 1850, for example, the cotton factories of Saco produced over thirty million yards of cloth. At the same time, an establishment less than twenty miles away was manufacturing five thousand spinning wheels—for manufacturing yarn in the home! This apparent anachronism is easily explained: neither the cloth nor the spinning wheels was particularly intended for local sale. Likewise, shoes produced in Winthrop were destined for sale in California and the American South; bricks burned in Brewer were used in Boston and New York; and tinware fashioned in Westbrook was sold throughout Quebec and the Canadian maritime provinces.

Nor were the raw materials for Maine manufacturers always produced locally. Tinsmiths working in Stevens Plains (then a part of Westbrook, now Portland) imported tinplate from England; Maine blacksmiths commonly used imported Swedish and Russian iron; Maine stoneware pottery was produced from New Jersey clays; and brooms manufactured in Skowhegan utilized broom corn from Illinois. Maine's abundant routes of commerce opened the state's doors to the world, and through these doors passed every sort of raw material and commodity.

This link to a broader commercial network did not involve simply the large industries. The unprecedented productivity of factory cities has obscured the importance of smaller manufactures, not only of the easily identified products of artisan workshops—candlesticks, spoons, chairs, and pianos, for instance—but also the more generic goods, such as shoes, blankets, shirts, and carpets. These items demonstrate the dual nature of Maine's industrialization: the growth of prominent factories and mills, proceeding in tandem with an expansion of the dispersed, small-scale foundry, shop, and home activity that actually made the bulk of Maine's manufactured goods in the first half of the century. To appreciate the full spectrum of early nineteenth-century Maine manufactures, therefore, it is necessary to examine activities that were centered not just in the largest factories, but also in smaller mills, furnaces, artisan workshops, and in the home itself. These were essential units of the rural economy and an important part of Maine's manufacturing economy as well. Detailing the history of these small-scale and home manufactures demonstrates the degree to which the industrial "revolution" took place, not in great cities, but in rural and small-town America, without any significant disruptions in traditional culture, work patterns, or demographic structure.

The home is an important though overlooked context for nineteenth-century manufactures. Aside from sawmills, homes were the earliest workplaces in Maine. A great many commodities were produced as off-season activities by farm families and farm laborers. This winter work fostered a network of "farmer-craftsmen" engaged in the production of agricultural items. In Skowhegan, for instance, Eli Weston made plows, Albion Nay made ox yokes, Ebenezer Wentworth made spinning wheels and sap buckets, and John White made brooms. These men were farmers, but they were also small-scale manufacturers and, to some extent, merchants.

Off-season products included, among many other things, soap, candles, shoes, nails, barrel parts, straw bonnets, brooms, shingles, shoe pegs and shoes, furniture, and bedding. Enterprising merchants and shopkeepers recognized this vast productive potential and accepted home-manufacured items in trade for store merchandise. They stored the products, then sent them off to urban wholesale dealers in carload lots. The role of country merchants as intermediaries illustrates the commercial encouragements to activity in the home. Nowhere was this arrangement more significant than in the manufacture of textiles and clothing.

The weaving of cloth dominated home industry during the eighteenth and early nineteenth centuries. The importance of this activity can be measured, in part, by the extent to which cloth production exceeded the needs of Maine's own population. According to the somewhat incomplete census of 1810, over 2.5 million yards of cloth were woven "in families." This represents approximately 900,000 yards more than Maine families consumed themselves. In terms of the dollar value of finished products, cloth produced in homes was the largest manufacture in the Province of Maine. Moreover, the industry was widespread: approximately half of all Maine homes contained looms for weaving cloth in 1810.

Certainly, a large portion of the cloth produced in this way was intended for family or local use. The production of wool and flax on Maine farms encouraged weaving as a form of partial self-sufficiency. However, more than a third of the cloth woven during the period was not wool or flax, but cotton. By producing cotton cloth, Maine households necessarily participated in a larger regional trade which connected homes and local stores to the yarn spinning mills of New England.

Machines to spin cotton yarn were first employed in America in 1790, and by 1810 there were nearly ninety spinning mills in the country, most of them in the Northeast. However, power looms, which were used to weave the yarn into cloth, were not widespread until the late 1820s. During this 1790–1820 period, a glut of spun cotton yarns accumulated, creating a bottleneck as families struggled to turn them into finished cloth. This thirty-year period was the heyday of hand-loom weaving in American homes. During this generation, home weavers turned factory-made yarn into cloth for their own use and on contract with area merchants and mills.

In the case of cotton cloth, Maine households were necessarily part of a larger commercial network. Between 1819 and 1823, for instance, Henry H. Booty advertised a stock of seven to eight thousand pounds of cotton yarn available at his Portland store. A substantial part of his inventory was resold to upland shopkeepers, who distributed the product throughout the state. In addition, Booty itemized over eleven thousand yards of cotton cloth, with new shipments arriving every week. Even though many such cloths were woven by power looms in the 1820s, the "put-out" system of domestic weaving was still vigorous. Often the same merchants who sold finished cloth employed home weavers to manufacture the cloth on a per-yard basis. Thus in 1822 merchant Elias Kelsey advertised that he was seeking "immediately 150 good weavers to whom constant employ and fair prices will be given." Nathanial Crockett, John B. Cross, and Henry Booty advertised similarly the following year.

Ironically, even while cotton textile mills were spreading to Maine, the importance of home textile production was increasing. Initially, the two forms of industrial development—centralized mill production and home manufacturing—were by no means incompatible. Between 1820 and 1830, Maine produced more than $1.5 million in cloth, most of it in homes. This, in fact, represented nearly 40 percent of the total value of products manufactured in the state.

It was here that women made their most noticeable contribution to the economy of early nineteenth-century Maine. Moses Greenleaf alluded to this in 1829, when he wrote that the manufacture of cloth was "conducted chiefly in private families; and . . . confined almost wholly to the female part of the families, to whom other modes of profitable employment are generally not open." This largely hidden domestic production made an enormous contribution to the state's economy.

Textile factories eventually eclipsed home cloth production. The price of machine-made cloth, particularly cottons, declined markedly during the first half of the nineteenth century. This in turn fostered a "democratization" of clothing styles and enlarged most people's concept of wardrobe size. The "bottleneck" in textile production shifted to the sewing of cloth into garments. In the same way that machine-made yarns preceded machine-made cloth, thereby promoting a era of home weaving, power looms now preceded the perfection of sewing machines by thirty years. This fostered a new phase of the "put-out" system: merchants distributed garment parts to families to be hand sewn at home. Transforming millions of yards of power-woven cloth into clothing required an army of tailors and seamstresses, and in part, this army was found in Maine households. In the manufacture of "ready-made clothing," the Maine home was to see its greatest level of commercial activity.

The enterprise began in Maine in the 1830s and grew rapidly during the 1850s and 1860s. During these years Maine hosted nearly six hundred tailors; a fair number of these produced clothing wholesale by putting out men's apparel for sewing at home. After 1850, these merchant-tailors usually functioned as middlemen, engaged in a regional "put-out" system operating from garment centers in Boston and Providence. Because of its commercial orientation, this sewing work became widely known as "Boston work," and it engaged the labor of many tens of thousands of Maine women.

In the Augusta-Gardiner area, clothing manufacture was particularly intense, and the search for labor was often highly competitive. In July 1852, W. A. Luce of Gardiner advertised that "50 Coat Makers Can Find Employment of Boston Work," and the following March he increased his call to a hundred. In 1859, Luce advertised for "3 to 500 Coat Makers, to whom the best prices will be paid, and constant employment given." Luce was able to report in the 1860 census that he employed four men and eight hundred women producing clothing "for other [wholesale] houses."

Such advertisements reveal a tremendously productive, though dispersed, manufacturing economy in Maine. In Buxton, coat manufacturing was considered the most important industry in the town and a principal source of that community's wealth. Merchant Samuel Hanson produced some thirty thousand coats per year at mid-century—all of them sewn from parts supplied from Boston. At one point, the company's bookkeeper had apparently over twelve hundred names on the "woman's ledger." The largest single employer in the state was Josiah Buchnam of Minot, who claimed over fifteen hundred women at work, each in her own home. Although sewing machines hastened the centralization of garment making in factory settings in the 1870s, the put-out

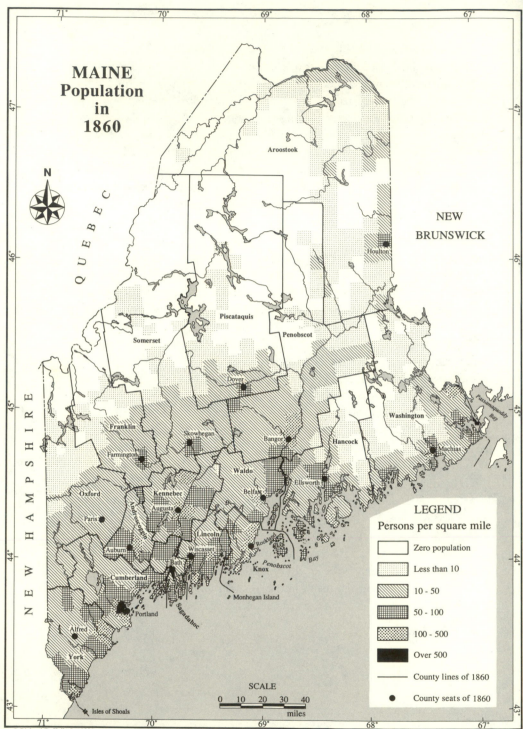

MAINE
Population
in
1860

N

Q U E B E C

Aroostook

NEW

BRUNSWICK

Houlton

Piscataquis

Penobscot

Somerset

N E W   H A M P S H I R E

Dover

Washington

Passamaquoddy Bay

Franklin

Skowhegan

Bangor

Hancock

Machias

Farmington

Waldo

Oxford

Kennebec

Belfast

Ellsworth

Androscoggin

Augusta

Paris

Lincoln

Rockland

Auburn

Wiscasset

Penobscot   Bay

Bath

Knox

Cumberland

Monhegan Island

Portland

Sagadahoc

Alfred

York

Isles of Shoals

LEGEND
Persons per square mile

Zero population

Less than 10

10 - 50

50 - 100

100 - 500

Over 500

County lines of 1860

● County seats of 1860

SCALE

0   10   20   30   40
miles

© Richard D. Kelly Jr., 1995.

tradition continued through most of the second half of the nineteenth century. In the 1880s, the number of Maine women engaged in this industry was so striking that the federal census appointed a special commissioner simply to count them and record the productivity of their work.

Craft manufactures like tinware, pewter candlesticks, painted furniture, and brass andirons were delayed in Maine, relative to domestic production, because Maine's heavy engagement in regional commerce filled most local needs, and the opportunities for livelihood in the Maine woods or at sea eclipsed those in the workshop. At statehood, in fact, a smaller portion of Maine's population was engaged in artisan manufactures than in any state north of Virginia. This was destined to change markedly in the decades from 1820 to 1850.

Despite Maine's relative backwardness in manufacturing, there were over seventeen hundred artisan workshops listed in the 1820 census. To be sure, many of these were not true manufacturing establishments. Blacksmith shops, for example, usually served local agricultural needs without producing any real "goods" for resale. Some, however, grew to serve a broader market for small agricultural tools, implements, and plows. In 1850, for example, Timothy Shaw of Exeter, working with one helper, assembled 190 plows, and Hiram Doe of Vassalboro, with four men, produced 250 plows and 30 cultivators. By 1850, there were nearly fifty manufacturers of agricultural machinery in the state, most of them operating on a small scale.

Other artisan workshops produced a seemingly infinite variety of items: fine furniture, bobbin spools, scythes, threshing machines, candlesticks, tin pails, carriages, barrels, clocks, and teapots. These, too, were part of a broader commercial network that supplied raw materials and accepted the finished products. A couple of examples illustrate the greater whole. The manufacture of tinware, floor coverings, and shoes share in common the fact that each was part of a regional network of trade and commerce, and none were fostered to any great extent by the availability of local raw materials.

Even within the simplest of artisan workshops, repetition in producing a small range of objects often increased productivity beyond the needs of a strictly local community. The benefits of specializing and mass producing objects for wider distribution are illustrated by the making of tinware at Stevens Plains. Utilizing a few specialized tools, Stevens Plains tin workers at mid-century could average thirteen finished articles per day—some four thousand items each year per person. These items were distributed widely throughout Maine by itinerant tin peddlers. Stevens Plains was Maine's principal emporium, not only for tinware, but for pewterware, brooms, combs, brushes, and other small commodities carried by peddlers.

Maine's premier tinsmith, Zachariah Stevens, opened his first workshop in Stevens Plains in 1789. Stevens not only formed and soldered a wide variety of tin containers and dishes, but he also painted decorations on these items. Later, the craft of painting tinware was put out to local homes. Stevens was joined in 1803 by a second tinsmith, Thomas Briscoe, who is credited with starting the first tin peddler's route from Stevens Plains. Straddling the major highway route from Portland to Montreal, the peddlers of Stevens Plains were able to distribute tinware to rural communities in New Hampshire, Vermont, and the province of Quebec. Later, similar routes took tinware from "the Plains" to northern Maine, New Brunswick, and Nova Scotia.

As these routes became established, they helped attract even more tinsmiths to Stevens Plains. By 1832, there were no less than eleven tin shops in the village, and by 1850, these workers were completing upwards of sixty thousand tin articles each year, including painted and decorated boxes, pots, pans, pails, and funnels. In fact, most Maine tinsmiths worked locally assembling stoves and making stove pipe, but the concentration of tinwork in Stevens Plains illustrates the influence of commerce in promoting and sustaining the mass production of goods. Specialization required access to a larger number of consumers, and in this case the need was met by itinerant peddlers. This pattern can be seen again in woven carpeting and oil-cloth floor coverings.

The abundance of yarn and lighter-weight cotton cloths fostered the weaving of coverlets and carpets. The center of this industry in Maine was Gorham, where professional weaver Hugh Gilroy began a carpet "manufactory" in 1827, largely to weave homespun yarns supplied by his customers. Gilroy's pioneer workshop was replaced in the late 1830s by two manufactories: the Gorham Carpet Factory and the Maine Carpet Manufactory. By 1850, Gilroy's successors were producing some 53,000 yards of carpeting each year and selling it throughout Maine and the region. Gorham's shops produced simple woven carpets known as ingrain (or Kidderminster). Although the power weaving of ingrains was perfected by Erastus Bigelow in Lowell in 1840, as late as 1850 thirty-two men and twenty-three women were still weaving carpeting by hand in Gorham.

Although hand-loom carpet manufacture was eventually superseded by machine improvements, the manufacture of oilcloth floor coverings was not. This industry began in Maine in the 1820s and 1830s and grew dramatically around 1840, when a number of shops were opened in central Maine. Winthrop manufacturers Charles and Moses Bailey produced three hundred thousand yards of floor coverings yearly, using both hand and horse power. Under the Bailey family enterprise, Winthrop became the largest oilcloth manufactory in New England and in the early twentieth century one of the premier manufactories in the nation.

The workshop examples selected—tinware, ingrain carpet, and oilcloth—reflect the impact of commercial enterprise on manufactures of all sizes in Maine during the 1820–80 period. Few of these workshops employed large numbers of people, but their cumulative impact was substantial. Two more industries—barrel and shoe making—illustrate the extent and the dispersed nature of workshop manufacturing in Maine.

Barrels were the preferred containers for shipping a wide variety of commodities in the nineteenth century. Whether apples or glassware, molasses or fish, beer or hardtack, the containers needed were barrels. Barrels were needed to ship Maine's own raw materials, but the containers themselves were also an item of export. Because there was little suitable wood for cooperage in the West Indies, barrels were commonly shipped as outbound cargo from Maine. They were shipped disassembled, or "shook"; coopers sometimes assembled these parts aboard ships. In 1826, Saco alone shipped some 1,616 "shooks" and headings, 4,000 barrel hoops, and over 65,000 barrel staves. They returned to New England as containers filled with sugar, molasses, and rum.

Some thirteen hundred Maine men called themselves "coopers" in the 1850 census. When the related work of loggers and sawyers is added, together with the largely hidden winter work of farmers preparing barrel parts and "poles" (hoops), the production of barrels emerges as an occupation of considerable importance to nineteenth-century Maine. At no location in Maine was the manufacture of barrels more widespread than on the central coast between Lincolnville and Rockland. Here lime production provided the most compelling and sustained need for barrels in the state. By 1835, lime exports required an estimated 750,000 barrels per year, and by midcentury production exceeded a million barrels per year. Around five hundred men worked in nearby communities assembling the needed casks.

Comparatively, though, this was not as significant or widespread as the production of shoes and boots. In the second half of the nineteenth century, the city of Auburn became one of the most important shoe-making centers in New England. Auburn hosted as many as twenty-one factories, employing between three and four thousand workers and producing nearly four million pairs of shoes per year. The industry had reached Maine communities a generation earlier, however, under the impact of a commercial system that was breaking down the custom production of shoes throughout New England.

The production of shoes and boots developed in a manner similar to the production of cloth. At the end of the eighteenth century shoes were largely custom made on demand, or "bespoke." As Maine's commercial networks broadened and merchants interjected themselves into the trade, this became less common. Even as early as 1819, for example, a Portland merchant advertised a

14-3. Shoemaking was the most widespread manufacturing industry in the first half of the nineteenth century. National demand made it an attractive investment for business-men, and one-third of the workforce was female. After the Civil War, shoemaking was mechanized, large factories were built, and Auburn became the center of the industry, producing 4 million pairs annually. The factory in this photograph is located in Norway. Courtesy of the Maine Historic Preservation Commission, Augusta.

stock of four thousand pairs of ready-made "Morocco and leather shoes." Under the aegis of urban merchants like this, shoes, like textiles and clothing, became standardized, generic products destined for distant markets.

During these transitional years, Maine homes and shops contributed to a commercial trade in ready-to-wear shoes. Controlled largely by merchant-man-ufacturers, a "put-out" system emerged similar to that in textile and clothing production. Skilled artisans, working in central workshops run by merchants or master shoemakers, cut shoe patterns out of leather; the merchant-manu-facturers sent these "uppers" out to small shops and households to be hand-sewn, then collected the uppers and redistributed them to shoeshops and households for lasting and soling at the cobbler's bench. This system remained a feature of Maine's household economy even into the last decades of the nineteenth century, a period dominated by large, centralized shoe factories.

Clearly, the manufacture of shoes was the most widespread workshop activity in Maine during the first half of the nineteenth century. The 1850 census identified 3,500 Maine men as shoe makers, but the actual number was much higher. Women, who may have made up nearly a third of the work force in shoe shops, were not counted by census takers prior to 1870, nor were women, children, and men working in their own homes on a part-time basis. The bulk of this work force was organized in and around relatively small, local shoe-making shops well distributed throughout the state—another example of the dual nature of Maine's manufacturing system.

Shoe making in Winthrop illustrates the range of shoe products produced on a workshop basis and the commercial orientation of this industry. Winthrop's trade in boots and shoes grew rapidly in the 1830s and 1840s. At mid-century there were no fewer than eight boot and shoe manufacturers in the town, employing 53 of the state's 3,500 male shoe makers, and 13 women. Together these shoe makers produced nearly 22,000 pairs of boots and shoes. Some had shops at their houses, each with several employees. The smallest in town was that of Elias Clark, who employed just three men and one woman to make 1,400 "thick Boots." One of the largest, Horace Parlin, employed ten men and four women in making 2,460 pairs of men's boots, 1,900 boys' boots, and 3,030 boots for youths.

Initially, most of the shoes were wholesaled in New England, then perhaps distributed nationally and internationally. However, Winthrop shoe maker Isaac Nelson shipped boxes of shoes directly to New Orleans and, after 1849, the Wing brothers, B. F. and Charles, sold a large part of their product, along with that of neighboring shops, in California. These and other small-town Maine shoe makers were part of a national trade network; here again, the impetus to manufactures was national commerce, not local self-sufficiency.

Shoe making proved to be an attractive investment for Maine merchants in the 1850s and the industry grew rapidly. In the town of Norway, J. and E. W. Howe rented a space in 1853 and hired thirty men and women to sew shoes. Soon after, Ezra Beal noted in his diary that shoe making was the "order of the day in the village." By 1856 employment in Norway's four shoe shops reached 250 persons, and early in 1857 Beal again noted that "Shoe making is flourishing, about 70 cases of shoes and boots are made pr. week."

Ezra Beal found Norway's shoe manufacture notable in part because it contrasted with his own previous investments in a more ancient Maine tradition: harnessing water power to run mills. Until late in the century shoe manufacturers operated largely without using an industrial power source. By comparison, the use of water power to drive sawmills stretched back in Maine history to the 1630s. Although sawing timber into boards was not a true manufacture—boards are raw materials, not finished products—the importance of sawmills to Maine industrial development involved considerable commercial enterprise. In terms of sheer numbers of mills, the role of this industry can hardly be overstated. In 1790, there were already 150 sawmills in the Province, and by the time of statehood, this number had jumped to 750; by 1840, the number reached nearly 1,400.

In a broad way, the proliferation of sawmills arose from a number of easily identifiable factors. First, there was the abundance of raw materials; secondly, there was an equal abundance of water-power sites; third, there was ample river and coastal traffic to provide for the easy export of the cut lumber. Maine had an ideal climate for lumbering and a relatively small farming population relative to the commercially owned forest. These added up to a favorable environment for the expansion of lumber industries.

Sawmills spawned a number of related sawing industries that included the making of shingles, clapboards, laths, and other "short lumber" products. In areas with hardwood forests, such as in Oxford County, mills sometimes manufactured dowels, bobbins, spools, and "novelty" products. Elsewhere, mills produced ready-made doors, sashes, and shutters. Until the arrival of textile factories on the state's larger rivers, these wood-product industries, particularly lumber mills, dominated the use of the state's water power, even though they used only a very small portion of it.

Other mills processed wool or home-made woolen textiles. Until the 1840s, the production of woolens remained largely a domestic activity. Mechanization in this enterprise took the form of small mill processes which assisted in home production of woolen cloth. The process of carding woolen fibers (brushing to prepare them for spinning) was laborious, and to mitigate this bottleneck, carding mills were built throughout the state beginning in 1790. The first of these was established in Gray by Samuel Mayall, perhaps the earliest of woolen manufacturers in the state. By 1820, there were over two hundred carding machines standing on Maine streams in the service of household woolen manufacture.

Unlike cotton cloth, good-quality woolens demanded considerable attention after the cloth had been woven. Commonly, the finished cloth was shrunken and thickened, brushed, sheared to a uniform nap, and dyed. These were jobs for trained clothiers equipped with mill equipment to "full" or felt the cloth after it was woven in the home. The 149 fulling mills in Maine in 1820 attest to the importance of domestic manufactures in this period; the skilled clothiers, carders, and laborers were engaged, albeit in an ancillary way, in the domestic manufactures of the state.

These milling industries—lumber, carding, and fulling mills—were alike in producing new forms of raw material rather than finished consumer products. Tanneries and furnace industries had similar functions. Tanneries were spread throughout the state in nineteenth-century Maine, but many located near a primary raw material for the tanning process, hemlock bark. In Maine, a region of particularly thick hemlock growth extends some two hundred miles from lower Aroostook County to Sebago Lake. Within this area, and particularly in the corridor from Waterville to Newport along the eastern side of the Sebasticook River, stood impressive stands of hemlock. The leather produced in those tanneries contributed to the robust development of shoe making in Maine.

Unlike the tanneries, Maine's four hundred brickyards were typically located near the state's urban centers. Brick makers in Saco and Biddeford, for instance, produced virtually all of the bricks needed in the considerable industrial expansion of those two cities. There were no fewer than seven brickyards in Saco in 1850, and five more in Biddeford. Together, these yards burned between six and ten million bricks a year. In addition to serving local needs, however, Maine exported large quantities of brick to Boston, New York, and other urban centers.

As we have already seen, the undisputed center of brick exports in Maine was Brewer. At the height of its business in the 1850s, Brewer boasted no fewer than twenty brickyards, producing over fifteen million bricks per year. The vast majority of these were shipped down the Penobscot, along with loads of lumber, to be sold at auction in the Boston market. Brewer brick was famous and became, for a time, a standard of manufacture cited in some government contracts: bricks everywhere were to be "constructed of Brewer brick or equal."

A second form of furnace work involved iron. Most ironwork manufacturers in Maine, aside from blacksmiths, remelted imported pig iron in casting furnaces for use in other manufactures, such as agricultural implements, tools, stoves, and other hardware. Aside from these casting furnaces, there were a few furnaces that actually produced iron from local bog ore. The most substantial of these was the Katahdin Iron Works, located north of Brownville. There were, in addition, two rolling and slitting mills which produced iron plates, bars of iron stock, and nail rods. The first of these was the Saco Nail Factory, founded in 1811. The Saco location permitted easy importation of raw materials—the iron used was either Swedish or Russian—and quick transportation to market. The company's nail-making machines turned out as many as 100 large nails and 150 shingle nails per minute.

In 1849, long after the Saco furnace had closed, a second rolling mill was started in Pembroke. This enterprise, more than any other, illustrates the importance of transportation and hence the commercial nature of most nine-teenth-century Maine manufactures. Like Saco, the Pembroke site was favored by the proximity of water power to sea routes. Beyond this, there were no com-pelling reasons for the iron mill to be located there. The pig iron used at Pembroke generally came from the Hudson River area; the iron ore from Lake Champlain; the wood from scattered points along the coast of Maine and the maritime provinces; and the labor to operate the mill and furnace from Ireland and England. The finished products of the mill were, not surprisingly, shipped to Boston and to axe-making centers in Taunton and Douglas, Massachusetts, and New Haven, Connecticut. By 1850, the Pembroke Iron Company was op-erating a fleet of ships to bring in supplies and take the bar iron and nails to other ports.

The Katahdin Iron Works, the Saco Nail Factory, and the Pembroke Iron Company stand virtually alone in the history of Maine industry; none of these enterprises triggered any significant development within the state; each was an anomaly to the state's manufacturing history. On the other hand, iron foundry work was an essential component of Maine manufactures, particularly where production depended on cast iron. Maine's fifty or so foundries produced cast-ings for plows, agricultural machines, stoves, ranges, fireplace doors, dampers, and, in some of the larger foundries and machine shops, water turbines and steam engines, textile machines, and fire engines. The largest of these manu-facturers was John A. Poor's Portland Company, founded in 1846 to build locomotive engines for the entrepreneur's Atlantic and St. Lawrence Railway. Ultimately, this company built over six hundred locomotives for companies throughout the United States and Canada, along with marine engines, boilers, pulp digesters, snow plows, fire engines and, in the early twentieth century, au-tomobiles.

Maine's domestic, workshop, mill, and furnace industries contributed sub-stantially to the economy of the state, but they did not generally lead to wholesale relocations of the population or to the creation of large manufac-turing centers. In fact, this industrial "revolution" changed the demographic structure of rural Maine very little, complementing rather than replacing a tra-ditional agricultural way of life. By and large, each establishment employed only a few people, although their aggregate contribution in some cases was large.

This was not the case with factory development, however. Factories cen-tralized work in huge complexes and sometimes required work forces ranging in the thousands. This irrepressible development changed not only the eco-nomic underpinning of the state, but its physical and demographic appearance as well.

In terms of the mid-nineteenth-century economy, three major factory industries belong in a distinct category by themselves: the manufacture of shoes, cotton textiles, and woolen textiles. These three hoarded the vast majority of capital invested in industry at midcentury, and they produced many of the demographic centers of population common to Maine today. The characteristics of these factory industries are substantially different. Shoe-making factories were established in Maine to exploit a relatively inexpensive labor market; cotton factories were built to exploit the water power of the major rivers; and woolen factories emerged from a grass-roots proliferation of small carding and fulling mills serving the needs of local households. Of these, the most significant in the 1820–65 period was the cotton industry.

The American cotton industry began in Rhode Island in 1790 with the first yarn spinning mills. Not until the development of the cotton factories in Waltham and Lowell, Massachusetts, however, were power looms actually used to weave cloth. The successful deployment of these looms provided at last an opportunity for merchants to control all aspects of the manufacturing process under one roof. Power weaving meant the eventual end of home weaving; the only limitations on factory size seemed to have been the availability of water power and labor. Merchant investors realized this quickly and rushed to exploit New England's largest rivers. This provided the major impetus behind Maine's cotton factory development.

Lowell's spectacular success set off a virtual stampede of land speculation aimed at the most attractive sites for large-scale manufacturing. The establishment of these planned "factory seats" depended on certain requirements: sufficient land at reasonable prices; ample water power; a pool of mechanics and laborers; and adequate transportation for both raw materials and finished products. There were many such sites in Maine. Most of the state's largest rivers were underutilized, if used at all; local mechanics and millwrights had avoided the substantial costs of damming the larger rivers because the scale of small, individual mills and shops had not required such power. Following the examples set by pioneer mill towns in Massachusetts, systematic development of these main river stems commenced in the 1820s and 1830s. Compared to the first thirty years of cotton production in Maine, the next thirty years brought unprecedented change. This era saw the development of a manufacturing economy that challenged the state's commercial underpinnings and created new cities, new jobs, and permanent changes in the state's demography.

The Saco River was the most noticeable of Maine's water-power opportunities. With its headwaters in the White Mountains, the river had an ample, reliable supply of water. The waterpower locations near the village of Saco were, in addition, adjacent to sea traffic; ships could approach the wharves abutting the potential mill sites themselves. The most favorable locations, on Indian Island (later called Cutts Island), were superior to most sites already employed in Massachusetts and Rhode Island.

The organizers of the Saco Manufacturing Company were mostly Boston merchants, who apparently held the opinion that the success of the Lowell factories depended on their size. In Saco, they set out to build a factory of truly massive proportions for its time. The building, completed in 1826, was a 210-by-47-foot, seven-story structure. This was by far the largest cotton factory yet built in America. Unfortunately, manufacturing had barely commenced in Saco when in 1830 the entire building burned to the ground. This brought to an end the immediate fortunes of the Saco Manufacturing Company, along with any plans for building more such structures of wood.

Under the continued influence of Boston developers, new projects began quickly. Between 1831 and 1850, the construction of factory buildings, tenements, offices, and boarding houses continued unabated, an activity that spawned twelve brickyards in the Saco area. Factory and construction work brought thousands of workers to Saco and Biddeford and transformed the twin cities into Maine's premier manufacturing center. By 1850, a village based on lumbering, farming, and fishing had been remade into a city of brick, machines, and cotton cloth.

The York Mill's 750 power looms produced over six million yards of cloth per year at mid-century, employing some 250 men and 1,000 women. Following the opening of the Pepperell Manufacturing Company in Biddeford between 1850 and 1855, that city boasted some eleven separate factories, along with numerous related buildings, shops, dye houses, bleacheries, and tenements. Where sawmills had stood twenty-five years before, a hundred thousand spindles were now turning, under the guidance of three thousand men and women.

The productivity of the Saco-Biddeford factories was astounding, amounting to some ten thousand yards of cloth produced for each employee per year. This statistic helps to explain the decline of domestic cotton weaving, as well as the impetus that followed for sewing ready-made clothing at home. Textile manufacture led the way in the industrialization of New England, bringing profound changes in the relative importance of home manufacture.

To find labor for these gigantic factories, the Saco proprietors utilized a pattern previously developed in Lowell. Men were commonly employed as machinists, loom fixers, laborers, and operators of some machinery, but the bulk of the work fell to farm girls and young women mostly between the ages of fifteen and twenty-five. The population of Saco became skewed by 1850,

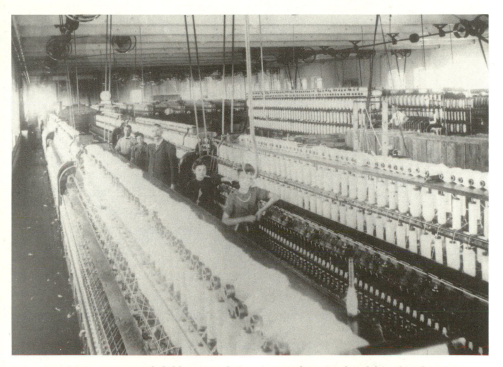

14-4. Men, women, and children, mostly immigrants from Quebec, labored in the great textile mills of Biddeford-Saco and Lewiston. In this photograph from around 1900, workers and their foreman are shown on station in the cotton-spinning room at Lewiston's Hill Mill. Courtesy Franco-American Collection, Lewiston-Auburn College, University of Southern Maine.

with some 2,553 females living in the city compared to only 1,855 males. Those working on Factory Island lived at home, with local families, or more generally, in housing units adjacent to the factories themselves. By 1840, there were some twenty-six "housemothers" in various houses providing guidance and supervision for a large complement of women living away from home. If women were an important, although overlooked, component of Maine's domestic economy, they were certainly a significant part of Maine's early factory development as well.

The emergence of Maine as a major cotton manufacturing state can be traced directly to the opportunities provided by water power sites. Needless to say, the raw materials did not come from Maine, nor were the products meant for resale in the state. Here the potential offered by Maine's rivers for both transportation and water power became the primary locational advantage for a major export industry.

Lewiston, Maine's second major cotton textile center, was located at considerable distance from shipping lanes. For this reason alone the town's development awaited a new solution to the problem of inland transportation. Rail lines, as we have noted, began to appear in the 1840s, signaling the beginning of industrialization along the Androscoggin Valley. In 1845, the Lewiston Falls Cotton Mill Company was incorporated. Quickly reorganized as the Lewiston Water Power Company, then the Franklin Water Power Company, it assumed a broad development role, building dams, canals, and factory buildings, fabricating machinery, and acquiring real estate. Between 1850 and 1870, the Franklin Company managed the most aggressive cotton factory development in Maine and built some of the largest cotton mills then standing in New England.

Under the leadership of Boston capitalists, particularly Thomas Hill and Benjamin Bates, the Franklin Company provided the basic overhead investments for Lewiston's new industries. In 1852, Bates Manufacturing Company commenced operation. More mills were completed the following year, and in 1854, the Hill Manufacturing Company opened. In the span of years between 1852 and 1866, the small rural town of Lewiston saw the construction of eight huge cotton mills, employing thirty-three water wheels and 220,000 spindles. In the years just after the Civil War, the production of cotton cloth approached thirty million yards yearly and employed over 3,500 women and 1,500 men.

At the onset of Lewiston's industrial development, the American cotton industry was in a mature stage of development, both economically and technologically. Lewiston was not an experiment, but rather a well-calculated business endeavor that took as its precedents the numerous similar, if often smaller, cotton mill developments elsewhere in New England. Lewiston's development was relatively late, but its mills were among the largest and the most modern in America.

For labor, Lewiston's industrialists again followed the Lowell pattern that has been used in Saco and Biddeford: the machines were operated largely by young women attracted by cash wages to live in local homes or company boarding houses. Through the Civil War period, this labor force came overwhelmingly from rural farms in Maine and northern New England. The influx of Irish families to these factory towns began in the 1840s, and the enormous immigration of French-Canadian families commenced in the last third of the century. During this period, mill operators turned away from young women and relied increasingly on children.

14-5. Workers in their street clothing pose for a photograph in front of the office of the Madison woolen mill. The brick factory is in the background. Most woolen mills were small operations, allowing them to operate on smaller rivers and in smaller communities than many of the huge cotton textile mills. Courtesy of the Maine Historic Preservation Commission, Augusta.

Woolen mills developed at a steady but much less spectacular rate. Early on, the industry was tied to local wool growers and family weavers, and this attachment was not easily transcended. Because of this tradition of local supply, woolen mills usually began as small enterprises. Large-scale factory developments were neither common nor particularly successful for wool production, and the development of woolen mills exhibits a pattern somewhat different from cotton textiles. Woolen mills did not create new industrial cities; nor were these mills complemented by the construction of boarding houses or the immigration of non-local labor. Like Maine's small-scale and home manufactories, the woolen mills thrived in the context of Maine's predominantly small-town demography.

The emergence of woolen factories in Maine began in the mid-1830s in small communities like South Paris, Lewiston, Sanford, South Berwick, Windham, and Dixfield. By midcentury, there were no fewer than thirty-eight woolen factories in Maine, spread across a wide geographic region. By the 1870s the industry ranked third in value in the Maine economy, behind cotton goods and lumber products.

While woolen textile production remained relatively stable, shoe manufacturing was transformed from a domestic trade into a factory industry as a new body of industrial manufacturers began mechanizing the industry after the Civil War. Auburn became the shoe manufacturing capital for Maine, with an annual production approaching four million pairs per year. In numerous Maine communities, however, smaller "shoe shops" were built. While these shops, like the woolen mills, existed within the framework of local labor pools, they nonetheless provided a growing network of factory jobs for Maine people.

The period from 1820 to 1865 witnessed a truly profound change in Maine's commercial economy. However, as massive and oppressive as the developments in Saco and Lewiston might first appear, they existed side-by-side with numerous smaller manufactures in rural Maine. The era that saw production of ten thousand yards of cotton cloth for every mill worker in Saco was also a period that provided employment for tin manufacturers in Stevens Plains, barrel makers in Bridgton, and spinning wheel builders in Alfred. Despite the enormity of industrial change, the commercial aspects of Maine's geography and history continued to provide opportunities for rug weavers, oilcloth printers, pewter turners, and seamstresses.

The dual nature of Maine's manufacturing—the huge textile mills in tandem with dispersed shop, home, and foundry activities—illustrate three important features of the state's economy. First, Maine's predominantly small-town demography was sustained, despite heavy agricultural outmigration, by a vigorous and rapidly evolving small-scale manufacturing economy. Although these manufactures felt the impact of broader economic changes, they helped to preserve the essentially rural nature of the Maine landscape. Second, the connection between manufacturing and commercial activity in Maine remained strong through this period; commercial forces, more often than not, were behind the changes in Maine's early nineteenth-century manufacturing economy. Finally, no single description of "industrialization" can embrace the totality of Maine's manufactures in the 1820–65 period. The spirit of enterprise—and commerce—flourished on all organizational and financial levels. These points considered, the nineteenth-century manufacturing economy had much to do with the making of modern Maine.

For Further Reading:

The *Acts and Resolves* and *Laws* of the Massachusetts General Court and the Maine legislature contain the charters of the early turnpikes, canals, railroads, and industrial corporations and the laws regulating them. Reports of the various departments and agencies of state government, many of which regulated transportation and industry, are contained in the *Maine Public Documents*. The Maine State Archives hold the unpublished records of state agencies, such as the Board of Internal Improvements. The annual reports of the Maine Railroad Commissioners offer yearly descriptions of operating lines. The corporate records of the Cumberland and Oxford Canal are available at the Maine Historical Society. Most railroad records are still held by the original companies, such as the Bangor and Aroostook Railroad, or by the corporations which currently control predecessors' lines, like Guilford Transportation, which operates the Maine Central and Boston and Maine.

On manufacturing, primary sources include old deed records, which provide information on mill construction and ownership. County and local histories also contain a wealth of largely factual information on early manufacturers and manufacturing, but these must be used cautiously. Newspaper advertisements are a little recognized source of valuable information on manufacturing in the first half of the nineteenth century. Statistical information can be found in Moses Greenleaf, *A Statistical View of the District of Maine* (Boston, 1816) and his *A Survey of the State of Maine* (Portland, 1829). In 1850 the US Census Bureau began compiling an *Industrial Census*, which provides a relatively complete account of manufacturing in each community, including the quantity and value of raw materials used, the products produced, the labor employed, and the principal machinery and power sources used. Maine's industrial census records are available on microfilm at major libraries in the state. Old photographs, buildings, and artifacts themselves are valuable sources of information. Good photograph selections may be found in the Maine State Museum, the office of the Maine Historic Preservation Commission, and the Special Collections Department of the University of Maine. Finally, the best source of tangible information on manufacturing remains the "Made in Maine" exhibition at the Maine State Museum in Augusta.

ADDITIONAL SECONDARY SOURCES ON TRANSPORTATION:

Anderson, Hayden L. V., *Canals and Inland Waterways of Maine* (Portland, 1982).

Baker, George P., *The Formation of the New England Railroad Systems* (New York, 1968).

Carter, Harland Hall, "A History of the Cumberland and Oxford Canal" (M.A. thesis, University of Maine, 1950).

Chase, Edward E., *Maine Railroads* (Portland, 1926).

Harlow, Alvin F., *Steelways of New England* (New York, 1946).

Holt, Jeff, *The Grand Trunk in New England* (West Hill, Ontario, 1986).

Kirkland, Edward C., *Men, Cities, and Transportation; A Study in New England History, 1820–1900*, 2 vols. (New York, 1968).

Leavitt, H. Walter, *Some Interesting Phases of the Development of Transportation in Maine* (Orono, 1940).

Moody, Linwood W., *The Maine Two-Footers: The Story of the Two-Foot Gauge Railroads of Maine* (Berkeley, Calif., 1959).

Potter, Edward W., "Public Policy and Economic Growth in Maine, 1820–1857" (Ph.D dissertation, University of Maine, 1974).

White, John William, "The Bangor and Aroostook Railroad" (M.A. thesis, University of Maine, 1952).

Wood, Frederic J., *The Turnpikes of New England and the Evolution of the Same through England, Virginia and Maryland* (Boston, 1919).

SECONDARY SOURCES ON MANUFACTURING:

Bishop, J. Leander, *A History of American Manufactures from 1608–1860* (Philadelphia, 1868).

Branin, M. Lelyn, *The Early Potters and Potteries of Maine* (Augusta, 1978).

Davis, William T., *New England States: Their Constitutional, Judical, Educational, Commercial, Professional, and Industrial History*, 4 vols. (Boston, 1897).

Eastman, Joel W., "A History of the Katahdin Iron Works" (M.A. thesis, University of Maine, 1965).

Everson, Jennie G., *Tidewater Ice of the Kennebec River* (Freeport, 1970).

Glover, John G., *The Development of American Industries* (New York, 1959).

Hart, Albert B., editor, *Commonwealth History of Massachusetts*, 5 vols. (New York, 1896).

Hatch, Louis, *Maine*, 5 vols. (New York, 1919).

Hussey, Philip W., *The Hussey Manufacturers, 1835–1960* (North Berwick, 1960).

Knowlton, Evelyn H. P., *Pepperell's Progress: History of a Cotton Textile Company, 1844–1945* (Cambridge, Mass., 1948).

Maine State Museum, *Cabinet-Makers of the 19th Century Who Practiced Their Trade in Maine* (Augusta, 1970).

Maine State Museum, *Maine Furniture Makers* (Augusta, 1976).

Ostroff, Susan, *A Woman's Place . . . : The Maine Point of View* (Augusta, 1977).

Rivard, Paul E., *Lion: The History of an 1846 Locomotive in Maine* (Augusta, 1987).

Rivard, Paul E., *Made in Maine* (Augusta, 1985).
Rivard, Paul E., *Maine Sawmills* (Augusta, 1990).
Williamson, William D., *History of the State of Maine*, 2 vols. (Hallowell, 1832).
Yorke, Dane, *The Men and Times of Pepperell* (Boston, 1945).

15

Defending Maine & the Nation

JERRY R. DESMOND, JR.,

JOEL W. EASTMAN, STANLEY R. HOWE, RICHARD W. JUDD,

& EDWARD O. SCHRIVER

During the nineteenth century Mainers participated in four significant military conflicts or near-conflicts: the War of 1812, the Aroostook War, the Civil War, and the Spanish-American War. In two of these, the War of 1812 and the Aroostook War, Mainers were engaged in defending their native soil. The former war has been discussed briefly in chapter 8, and the latter is discussed below. The Civil War and the Spanish-American War were largely external to the state; Mainers participated as part of the American experience, but these conflicts were only indirectly part of Maine history. Yet the Civil War had an impact on Maine even more lasting than that of the Aroostook War.

Maine sent a sizable portion of its population—73,000 youths—off to preserve the Union. Some lost their lives; others came back fundamentally changed; still others, having seen the world beyond the farmstead or town line, abandoned their native state for good. During the Civil War decade, Maine was one of only two states in the nation—New Hampshire being the other—that experienced absolute declines in population. Just as important, the wartime crisis brought Maine distinction in national history. Powerful political figures from Maine dictated national policy during these years, and in several instances Maine leaders and troops stood at crucial turning points in the course of the war itself.

The Civil War was also a watershed in Maine politics. The national crisis helped to crystallize Maine's modern party system and strengthen the Republican grip on offices across the state. The war also contributed to the eclipse of the Democratic party, still wracked by internal dispute and now suffering the onus of being the "party of rebellion." Finally, the war was an economic watershed, partly because the momentous events of the war changed Maine industries, and partly because the postwar period brought profound alterations in American capitalism generally. Thus, two wars, the Aroostook War directly and the Civil War indirectly, figure prominently in Maine history.

Maine's Defenses in the Early Nineteenth Century

JOEL W. EASTMAN

Between 1839 and 1865, Maine fought two wars. The first, the Aroostook War, was largely confined to Maine, with related skirmishes in New York, and it involved no real combat. Nevertheless, the "bloodless Aroostook War" settled a long-festering boundary dispute with New Brunswick, drew attention to some of the best potential farmlands in the state, and established the basis for a lasting international lumbering economy along the St. John River. The Civil War, although it did not directly involve Maine territory, was nevertheless significant to the state's history, in part because Maine contributed so conspicuously to national events during the crisis, and in part because the war had a tremendous indirect effect on Maine's politics and economy.

By the time of the Aroostook War, Maine had weathered a long string of military crises, including military occupation by enemy troops twice in the generation between 1779 and 1814. The state's geography—its long, exposed coast and its boundary location—presented formidable prospects, and nineteenth-century Maine citizens took the matter of defense seriously. Thus, the Aroostook War and the Civil War, although neither threatened the state directly, fit into a broader context of historic concern about the military defense of Maine.

Maine's earliest European colonies, Popham, St. Sauveur, and Pemaquid, had begun as fortified settlements, and with the coming of the French and Indian wars, defensive fortifications became a continuing concern of residents, proprietors, and the colonial government. The Massachusetts General Court responded to the needs of its colonial frontier by building several fortifications at strategic spots on rivers and the coast.

Ironically, most of Maine's colonial forts failed when put to the test of a formidable assault by a determined enemy. In 1690, Fort Loyal was surrounded by a large force of Indians and French, and the inhabitants were massacred after they surrendered. Fort William Henry at Pemaquid, called by the governor of Massachusetts the strongest fort in North America, proved to be structurally unsound, and it was surrendered to another force of Indians and French in 1696. Fort Pownal, at the mouth of the Penobscot River, was destroyed to keep it out of British hands after the outbreak of the Revolution. In general, however, these and other early forts provided a presence of troops and served as nuclei for small communities on the frontier.

15-1. The United States relied on state militias as its principal means of land defense into the first decades of the nineteenth century. Every town had its own company of militia and a secure powder house, like this one in Wiscasset, in which to store gunpowder for use in emergencies. Courtesy of the Maine Historic Preservation Commission, Augusta.

Like the colonial wars, the American Revolution demonstrated the vulnerability of seacoast towns to seaborne attack, particularly after the burning of Falmouth in 1775. This act prompted the construction of numerous small coastal fortifications aimed at preventing further attacks during the early phase of the Revolution. After the Revolution, defense became the responsibility of the federal government, although the states still continued to build and operate local fortifications in time of war. In 1794, shortly after the outbreak of conflict in Europe, the first federal fort was constructed in Maine. Fort Sumner guarded the entrance to Portland, the state's most important port. As the international situation deteriorated again, a second generation of defenses was authorized in 1807. Portland received two new fortifications—forts Preble and Scammel. Kittery was given Fort McClary, and other smaller forts were built at ports along the Maine coast. The War of 1812 again demonstrated the inadequacy of these defenses, and a new generation of forts—huge, multistory masonry fortifications—was designed by the US Army Corps of Engineers. However, the cost of constructing these new works was so great that Maine initially was not included in the new defense program.

Maine approached the Aroostook War with an ambiguous military legacy. During the French and Indian wars, the Revolutionary War, and the War of 1812, the region had proved difficult, if not impossible, to defend. The coastline was impossibly long, and navigable rivers cut deep into the heart of the territory. While a string of coastal fortifications added some security, Maine's best defense, as Falmouth's leaders had commented in 1775, was its military insignificance.

The Aroostook War, 1828–42

RICHARD W. JUDD

It was both ironic and fortuitous that Maine's next military encounter occurred far inland, on the northeast boundary of the state. The so-called Aroostook War culminated a half-century dispute between Maine and New Brunswick over the entire eastern and northern frontier of the state of Maine. Following its admission to the union as a separate state in 1820, Maine was anxious to define a boundary that had been in question since the end of the Revolutionary War. New Brunswick, with an economy dependent upon the expanding mast and timber trade, was equally interested in the heavily timbered region on the Aroostook and St. John rivers. Each felt that history justified its claims to the disputed territory.

The conflict grew out of ambiguities in the 1783 Treaty of Paris that ended the American Revolution. Little was known about the geography of the north-

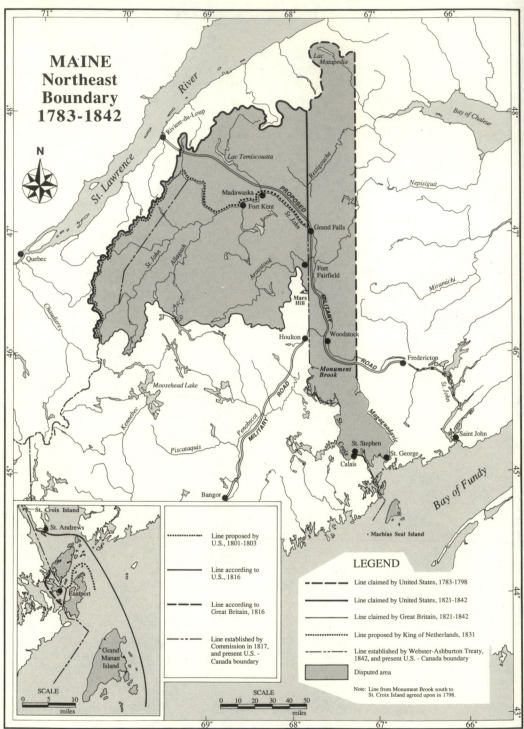

MAINE
Northeast
Boundary
1783-1842

N

St. Lawrence River
Rivière-du-Loup
Lac Temiscouata
Quebec
Chaudière
St. John
Madawaska
Fort Kent
Allagash
Aroostook
St. John
PROPOSED
Restigouche
Grand Falls
Fort Fairfield
Mars Hill
MILITARY
Lac Matapedia
Bay of Chaleur
Nepisiguit
Miramichi
Houlton
Woodstock
Monument Brook
ROAD
Fredericton
St. John
Saint John
Moosehead Lake
Kennebec
Penobscot
MILITARY ROAD
Piscataquis
St. Croix
Magaguadavic
St. Stephen
St. George
Calais
Bangor
Bay of Fundy
Machias Seal Island

St. Croix Island
St. Andrews
Eastport
Grand Manan Island

SCALE
0   5   10
miles

.... Line proposed by
          U.S., 1801-1803

——— Line according to
          U.S., 1816

— — Line according to
          Great Britain, 1816

—··— Line established by
          Commission in 1817,
          and present U.S.-
          Canada boundary

LEGEND

— — — Line claimed by United States, 1783-1798

——— Line claimed by United States, 1821-1842

——— Line claimed by Great Britain, 1821-1842

••••••• Line proposed by King of Netherlands, 1831

—··— Line established by Webster-Ashburton Treaty,
          1842, and present U.S.-Canada boundary

          Disputed area

Note: Line from Monument Brook south to
St. Croix Island agreed upon in 1798.

SCALE
0   10   20   30   40   50
miles

© Richard D. Kelly Jr., 1995.

eastern boundary area at the end of the Revolution, and no precise boundaries had been established. Two issues remained unsettled. First was the true location of the St. Croix River, the ancient boundary between New Brunswick and Maine. The eastern boundary of the state was to run from the mouth of this river to its headwaters, and then due north to the second problematic geographical feature of the Treaty of Paris: the watershed or "highlands" dividing the rivers that empty into the St. Lawrence River from those that drain into the Atlantic ocean. In addition, the boundaries of northern New York and Vermont and the area to the west of the Great Lakes were in question.

Three rivers actually conformed to the treaty's description of the St. Croix River, and predictably New Brunswick claimed the Schoodic, the westernmost, while Maine claimed the easternmost Magaguadavic as the "true" St. Croix. Between them lay seven or eight thousand square miles of disputed territory. A number of Loyalists living in Maine at the end of the Revolution had relocated in the coastal area between the two rivers, assuming they were securely inside British territory. These residents were understandably anxious to see that their new homeland remained British soil.

A joint commission of surveyors began searching for clues to the eastern boundary in 1796. After a series of disagreements, they settled on the middle river as the St. Croix and ran a "monument line" due north from the headwaters to the as yet unlocated "highlands." This second geographical ambiguity proved more difficult. Topographically, no continuous highlands actually transect the disputed territory. British surveyors pointed out that the St. John River drains into the Bay of Fundy; the Penobscot, strictly speaking, is the northernmost river draining "into the Atlantic." The height of land thus lay above the Penobscot. However, American surveyors insisted the line ran north of the St. John.

At the federal level, American politicians would have welcomed any reasonable settlement in the remote and inaccessible land. Few outside the state were willing to risk a third war with Great Britain for these vague claims to wilderness territory. On the other hand, Maine and Massachusetts (which still owned alternate townships in Maine's unsettled territories) were important constituencies, and, especially in this era of states' rights, successive administrations drew back from any settlement unfavorable to them. Britain's position was similar; the boundary agitated the province more than it did the mother country.

Following the War of 1812, Britain and the United States, without consulting either Maine or New Brunswick, agreed to submit the boundary question to arbitration. King William I of the Netherlands deliberated, and divided the disputed land into roughly equal shares. His decision, however, was turned down handily by Maine in 1831, and this firm rejection left both the Jackson and Van Buren administrations without further strategy; no settlement could pacify

Great Britain and at the same time retain Maine within the Democratic fold. Thus, procrastination seemed the better part of valor.

Maine's forbearance in the boundary matter was tested in the 1830s by three developments. First, the issue assumed a crucial role in the ongoing partisan tug-of-war between Maine's Whigs and Democrats. The latter, resolved to support the vacillating federal policy, hoped to downplay the issue without appearing to compromise Maine's position. Whigs, on the other hand, highlighted the value of the territory and accused the Democrats of undermining Maine's prosperity by ignoring the boundary issue. As long as they remained in power, Democrats kept the matter in hand; when the Whigs took office, the situation became incendiary.

A second issue for Maine was the chronic problem of timber theft, or "trespass" on the public lands in the area. Most galling was the fact that timber cut in the territory, either by Mainers or New Brunswickers, was by geographical necessity floated out of Maine on the St. John River to the New Brunswick port of Saint John, on the Bay of Fundy. In 1824, the provincial government, given temporary jurisdiction over the territory, responded to Maine's protests by issuing a ban on all lumbering operations in the area. Trespass continued nonetheless. Most of the local inhabitants hailed from New Brunswick and were accustomed to lumbering on Crown timberlands that were practically lying open to all comers. Even those who moved north from Bangor harbored a limited regard for their own state's timber rights. In 1825, Maine and Massachusetts land agents estimated that trespassers had carried off more than a fourth of the merchantable white pine on the public lands. Their estimates were exaggerated, but the report suggests the desperation with which the State Land Office viewed the situation.

A third development that exacerbated the crisis on the St. John was the arrival of Yankee settlers in the region. In the winter of 1816–17, a small group of Kennebec farmers settled on the north bank of the St. John above the Acadian community. By 1825, a small American settlement had grown up around John Baker's saw and grist mill and store. By the late 1820s, New Brunswick agents, at Maine's urging, were strengthening their surveillance of the upper watershed, and in 1827 when Baker floated a raft of lumber to Fredericton, he was placed under arrest and his timber was confiscated. Baker was released, then arrested again following an incident at his store. This time the event brought strong protests from Augusta. Tempers flared again in 1831 when legislators insisted on incorporating Madawaska as a Maine town, and once more in 1837, when a Maine census-taker, presuming that Madawaska's residents were Maine citizens, was arrested. Such incidents caused tremendous agitation throughout the state, highlighting the boundary dispute and forcing partisan issues into high relief.

In June 1828, federal troops were sent to Houlton, just south of the disputed territory, to reassure (and perhaps restrain) local citizens. The garrison was only lightly fortified and the troops employed mainly in clearing a road from the Penobscot at Mattawamkeag to the frontier outpost at Houlton. The so-called Military Road, built to move soldiers and supplies through the forest and to provide a line of retreat for the far-flung garrison, was completed in 1832, providing the first overland transportation route between Bangor and northern Maine.

Despite the unsettled circumstances, the boundary controversy was in some ways laying the groundwork for future settlement and development. A series of survey expeditions carried out in connection with the boundary dispute heaped attention on the resources of the area. In a series of letters to the *Bangor Whig and Courier*, agriculturalist Ezekiel Holmes, who had explored the disputed territory in 1831, urged Bangorians to extend roads and canals into the north country in order to ensure their own "eternal prosperity." On the assumption that development would substantiate the state's claim to the territory, in 1831, Maine began constructing the Aroostook Road, which would connect the Penobscot, the Aroostook, and eventually the Fish rivers. As early as 1832, farms and sawmills were appearing along the rough trail.

In 1838, Whigs gained control of the state house, after having aimed a barrage of criticism at Democratic policy on the border. Governor Edward Kent, compelled by his party's political brinkmanship to take action, resolved that Maine would run its own boundary survey through the territory. Noting this, Halifax papers observed that New Brunswickers could "anticipate a fracas on the roads and some amusement cut out for the 43d Light Infantry as well as our own militia." Bangor editors responded with a demand for more federal troops. President Martin Van Buren cautioned restraint and hoped privately that the federal garrison at Houlton could quell the incipient crisis.

In August 1838, the Land Office secured reports of alarming depredations on timber and sent a state surveyor, George W. Buckmore, to the Aroostook to gain a better account of the situation. Buckmore reported that the territory was alive with trespassers from Maine and New Brunswick operating with absolute disregard for the state's claims. These "violent and lawless men," he insisted, were undeterred by the feeble contingent of deputies who patrolled the area. The surveyor estimated that $100,000 worth of timber would float illegally to Saint John that spring.

Democratic Governor John Fairfield, who replaced Kent in 1839, brought the situation before the state legislature in late January. He sent State Land Agent Rufus McIntire, Penobscot County Sheriff Hastings Strickland, and a band of two hundred Bangor woods workers to Masardis, on the upper Aroostook

River. The "posse" descended the Aroostook, seizing lumbering teams and equipment, breaking up lumber camps, and arresting or scaring off lumbering crews. Near the confluence of the Aroostook and the St. John, McIntire and two others were taken captive by a small band of armed men. Stationed further upriver, Sheriff Strickland succumbed to rumors that an army of New Brunswickers was advancing up the Aroostook. He and the posse retreated with unbecoming haste to Masardis.

Governor Fairfield dispatched a letter to New Brunswick Lieutenant Governor John Harvey demanding an explanation for McIntire's arrest, and Maine prepared for war. Towns mustered and drilled their militia, and the legislature authorized $10,000 to defend the border. In mid-February, the second and third divisions of the state militia, nearly two thousand strong, began an armed occupation of the territory. Fortifications were constructed near the mouth of the Aroostook. Maine, the *Bangor Whig and Courier* announced, had "had enough of diplomacy." New Brunswick's lieutenant governor ordered two companies of provincial infantry to the Madawaska area, and British regulars were moved into position at Tobique, Madawaska, and Temiscouata Lake. With the Maine militia on the Aroostook and Fish rivers and the British troops across the St. John, peace in the region seemed precarious indeed.

In March 1839, President Van Buren sent General Winfield Scott to Augusta with full authority to restore peace or defend the nation's honor. Defusing the crisis was surprisingly simple once amicable communications were established. General Scott, an outsider, viewed the situation dispassionately and quickly renewed an old acquaintance with Governor Harvey. Scott and Harvey simply sanctioned the existing occupation of the territory; Maine remained in control east of the monument line and south of the St. John. Harvey promised not to interfere in the area, and Maine agreed to muster out the militia, leaving only a civil force to control trespassing. By late March the "war" was over, and in mid-April the last of Maine's volunteers returned home to heroes' welcomes.

To protect the timber, the posse constructed log booms and fortifications at the mouths of the Aroostook and Fish rivers. Forts Fairfield and Kent were threatened several times by bands of provincial lumber crews, and in late April 1839, the blockhouse on the Aroostook was burned, presumably by a disgruntled New Brunswick lumberer. Despite this and several other acts of sabotage, neither garrison saw any real military encounter. Indeed, discipline and desertion proved to be the main problem; a disorderly house across the British line did "great nuisance" to the routine at Fort Fairfield, and a near-mutiny on May 5 brought work on roads and fortifications to a halt. Nevertheless, the booms and sorting gaps functioned reasonably well during the few years that the posse occupied the territory. Timber theft on the waters of the Aroostook and Fish rivers was curbed, and a major source of frustration to Maine was brought to a halt.

15-2. Friction between American settlers and New Brunswick timber harvesters nearly led to war in the 1830s and sparked several important surveys of the largely unexplored Northeast Boundary region. The Federal Talcott Survey was completed in 1842 and produced sixteen camera-lucida views, including this view of surveyors at the southern end of Co-cum-go-muc Lake. Collection of the National Archives, Washington, D. C.

To negotiate the final boundary settlement, Great Britain selected Alexander Baring, an immensely powerful British banker. Baring—Lord Ashburton— although English, had an abiding interest in Maine's welfare. Earlier he had purchased more than two million acres of Maine timberland (although not in the disputed territory) from William Bingham and Henry Knox. Later he married Bingham's daughter. Britain gave Ashburton loose instructions, which amounted to retaining a crucial land route to Quebec north of the St. John River, protecting the "just rights" of the Madawaska Acadians, and beyond that making the best settlement possible. Daniel Webster, his American counterpart, took with him to the bargaining table an understanding that Maine would concede the territory north of the St. John in return for rights of navigation on the lower portion of the river.

Negotiations were complicated by the fortuitous appearance of several maps, each purported to have been used by American or British negotiators at the 1783 Treaty negotiations and incised with red lines authenticating American or British claims according to the Treaty of Paris. Neither Ashburton nor Webster pressed these claims publicly, however. Once Ashburton had conceded the Madawaska communities on the south bank of the river, and Webster the territory north of the St. John, the settlement had essentially been reached. In addition to the Aroostook territory, Maine received the land south of the lower St. Francis River and a cash settlement from the federal government to compensate the state's military expenses.

The Treaty of Washington, or Webster-Ashburton Treaty, was signed August 9, 1842. It established the boundary in Maine and along the New York and Minnesota-Wisconsin frontier as well. Maine received 7,015 square miles of the disputed territory, and the provinces 7,098. Maine's portion was slightly less than the settlement suggested by the king of the Netherlands in 1831, but the land ceded, as Daniel Webster pointed out, was considered of slight value for timber or farm. The state retained the fertile Aroostook River valley and the valuable pines of the Allagash, upper St. John, and St. Francis rivers. The treaty's most significant feature was a clause dictating that the navigation of the St. John River and its tributaries would be "free and open to both parties and . . . in no way . . . obstructed by either." This provision gave Aroostook lumber operators rights to float timber to sea at Saint John, and acknowledged an economic interdependence between Maine and New Brunswick that had been developing since the earliest days of logging on this international watershed.

The 1839 war and its resolution in 1842 had a tremendous effect upon the development of the northern section of Maine. The new boundary, sadly, split the Acadian community on the upper St. John River in two, leaving half the Madawaska settlement on the New Brunswick bank of the St. John and half on the American shore. Individual land claims in the Madawaska region would remain in dispute throughout the century. But aside from this, the treaty opened the door to settlement in northern Maine. It secured peace and laid to rest many of the uncertainties that plagued farmers and lumber operators in the region. The war and its settlement also highlighted the area's resources and changed attitudes about the vast northern territory, permitting Maine to market its best remaining public lands and to proceed with developing its northern frontier. In response to provincial incursions into the area, Maine built roads and sent out surveyors, receiving back reports of surprisingly fertile soil and a vast wealth of trees. The resulting exposure and the increased accessibility spurred settlement once the dispute had been resolved.

In addition, Maine won the right of free navigation on the lower St. John River through New Brunswick. This international river, a trade route of incalculable importance to both Maine and New Brunswick, allowed lumber operators from either nation access to Aroostook County's timber resources and New Brunswick's port facilities. The right of free navigation on the St. John established the legal basis for a unique transnational lumbering economy along the St. John River. It encouraged the development of several American-owned sawmills on the lower river in New Brunswick and gave Aroostook County lumber operators the right to enter, duty-free, all ports in the vast British empire. Without the treaty, the timber resources of the north would have remained landlocked, and virtually valueless until railroads entered the territory in the 1870s.

Maine Political Leaders in the Civil War Era

JERRY DESMOND, EDWARD O. SCHRIVER, & STANLEY R. HOWE

The impact of the Civil War on Maine history was more subtle and indirect; the long-term political bearing of the war and its effect on the Maine economy will be discussed in subsequent chapters. On the other hand, Maine people had a significant impact on national wartime politics and on the war itself. During the era of the Civil War, Maine made some of its most important contributions to national leadership. In fact, the war launched a forty-year period during which "Maine ruled Washington." Mainers served with distinction on the Supreme Court, in the presidential cabinet, in diplomatic and territorial posts, and in important positions of power in the United States Congress.

In good part, Maine's national preeminence reflected the Republicans' success in forming a solid state organization out of the chaos of new party alignments in the 1850s. In Maine, the Republican party began with a charter partially written by William Pitt Fessenden. Indeed, it may have been Fessenden who suggested the name for the new party. The party's power increased dramatically in the state elections of 1858, and in 1860, Maine Republicans won an overwhelming endorsement for the national ticket. With over 57,000 votes, Abraham Lincoln far outdistanced his closest rival, Northern Democrat Stephen Douglas, who finished with slightly over 27,000 votes.

The Democratic party, on the other hand, remained in disarray. Following the secession of the southern states and the firing on Fort Sumter in 1861, the party split into two factions, the Peace Democrats and the War Democrats. Marcellus Emery, owner and editor of the weekly *Bangor Democrat*, was perhaps the most ardent supporter of the states' rights position in all of the North. Following the news of the disastrous Union defeat at the battle of Bull Run, Emery called for a peace convention in Bangor, which triggered rumors of impending violence against his press.

The owner of the city block in which the *Democrat* was housed, J. G. Clark, realized that an attack on the office was inevitable and warned Emery to vacate. Emery refused, and Clark began eviction proceedings, hoping to avoid damage to other offices in the block. It was too late. Around noon on August 12, 1861, the leaders of the plot against Emery rang the fire alarm from the First

Congregational and Episcopal churches in order to divert attention. A mob apparently led by a blacksmith forced its way into the *Democrat* office, broke up the press, and dumped the contents of the office into the street, where they were burned. Emery appeared briefly on the scene but was convinced by friends to withdraw. A barber friend of Emery's picked a fight with one of the mob, which resulted in his shop being demolished as well. Then the violence subsided.

The editors of Bangor's *Republican Whig and Courier* denounced the riot and explained that they had "carefully abstained from any comments which might instigate violence against the establishment." But not coincidentally, the *Whig and Courier* had published an editorial on the morning before the attack explaining why Democrats who favored compromise with the rebels were not much more than traitors. This was directly followed by a news article on the recent destruction of the *Democratic Standard* offices in Concord by some members of the First New Hampshire Regiment, recently returned from Bull Run, who were upset with the paper's pro-rebel stance. Emery filed civil suits against several of the leaders of the mob, as no criminal charges were ever made. Eventually, a jury awarded him $916.60 in damages, far below even the value of the printing press. The *Bangor Democrat* resumed publication in January 1863, as unrepentant as ever.

Democratic journals in Maine, like the party itself, were split over the issue of disunion. In the gubernatorial election of 1861, the *Bangor Democrat*, the *Saco Democrat*, the *Machias Union*, the *North Anson Advocate*, and the *Franklin Patriot* supported the Peace Democrats and their candidate, John Winchester Dana. The *Bath Times*, the *Augusta Age*, the *Belfast Journal*, the *Lewiston Advocate*, and the *Rockland Democrat* supported the pro-war Democrats and their candidate, Charles D. Jameson. The results of the election demonstrated the strength of the Union position in the state, as the Republican incumbent, Governor Israel Washburn, was reelected with 58,689 votes. Jameson finished second with 21,935 votes and Dana last, with 19,801 votes. Although the Democrats were able to unite later in the war, they never came closer than eleven thousand votes to winning the governorship, and even this narrowing of the margin was due to the fact that many Republican supporters were off fighting in the war.

Unlike the Democrats, the Republican party presented a surprisingly solid front, given the chaos of the times. Overwhelming support for the Republican ticket demonstrated that Mainers were not in the mood to give in to the demands of the South. Indeed, the Republican party in Maine was controlled by its more radical fringe. Interestingly, four sets of brothers dominated the radical element: Abner and Stephen Coburn of Skowhegan; Anson and Lot Morrill of Augusta; Frederick and James Pike of Calais; and the seven Washburn brothers of Livermore Falls and Orono, of whom the most prominent were Israel, Cadwallader Colder, Elihu Benjamin, and William Drew. (At one time during the war, three Washburn brothers sat in the US House of Representatives at the same time, representing Maine, Wisconsin, and Illinois.) For a time during the Civil War, these four sets of siblings played a variation of political chair-swapping as they rotated in and out of the governorship, the Senate, and the House of Representatives.

When not involved in Maine politics, these men often contributed their talents to the war effort in other ways. For example, Cadwallader Colder Washburn served as a Union general during the war. His brother, Elihu Benjamin Washburne (he added the extra *e* himself to make the name appear more English), became the chief sponsor of a young general from his adopted home town, Galena, Illinois, helping Ulysses S. Grant rise to prominence during the war. James Shepard Pike worked as the Washington correspondent for Horace Greeley's *New York Tribune* and was appointed by Lincoln as US ambassador to the Netherlands.

The party's strength in Maine, and consequently in national politics, was in good part a result of remarkably effective leadership during the war years. The Republican leader emerging from the shadows during the Civil War was James G. Blaine of Augusta. Originally from Pennsylvania, Blaine became the editor of the *Kennebec Journal,* speaker of the Maine House of Representatives, and head of the Republican party in Maine during the early war years. Blaine even found the time to win a seat in the US House of Representatives in 1863, beginning his rise to national prominence.

The two most prominent Maine politicians on the national scene during the Civil War were Vice-President Hannibal Hamlin and Senator William Pitt Fessenden. Hamlin was born in 1809, and as a youth in Paris, Maine, he pursued a rather aimless existence. Among other things, he worked as a cook, a wood-cutter, and even a water carrier. Having failed at these occupations, he resigned himself to become a lawyer. With Horatio King, he assumed managing editorship of the *Oxford Jefferson,* then sold his interest in the paper and went into farming.

Hamlin's next major change in direction took him to Hampden, Maine, where he finally put down roots. He joined the town council, the school committee, and the Hampden Rifles. The people of Hampden elected this pillar of society to the state legislature, where he distinguished himself as an ardent Jacksonian Democrat. Elected to Congress in 1843, Hamlin fought the infamous "gag rule" that prevented discussion of antislavery proposals and petitions. He moved from the House to the Senate in 1847. There he was known for his strong stand against slavery and the Kansas-Nebraska Bill. In 1856, he once again changed course—this time with dramatic results: he abandoned the Democrats to join the Republican party. Whatever his motives—conscience or expediency—he turned to the new party at an opportune time, just as it was gaining control of Maine politics. At the expiration of his Senate term in 1857, he ran for governor. Easily elected, Hamlin soon resigned to return to the Senate.

In 1860, Hamlin was picked by the Republican National Convention as its vice presidential candidate to run with Abraham Lincoln of Illinois. As an easterner, former Democrat, and perceived supporter of Lincoln's rival, William Seward, Hamlin provided balance on the ticket. A man of swarthy complexion, Hamlin provided southern editorialists with endless opportunities to comment about "that Black Republican Lincoln and his mulatto running mate."

Actually, becoming vice-president was a bad break of sorts of Hamlin; it took him out of any real position of power. After the first year in office, he was rarely invited to Lincoln's council meetings, and his only official function was the rather boring one of presiding over the Senate. His biographer, H. Draper Hunt, noted that he felt like a "fifth wheel on the Presidential carriage." During his years in the Senate, he almost never missed a session of that body, but as vice-president, Hamlin often passed the duties of moderator over to the president pro-tempore. Indeed, he took off most of the summer of 1864 to serve as a cook with the Maine Coast Guards at Fort McClary in Kittery.

Still, Hamlin expected to run again with Lincoln in 1864. Instead he was dropped at the Baltimore convention in favor of Tennessean Andrew Johnson, an overture to the Confederate border states. Johnson, of course, became the seventeenth president of the United States after the assassination of Abraham Lincoln in April 1865. It is interesting to speculate on how history might have been changed had Hannibal Hamlin been in Johnson's place. A radical himself, he probably would not have resisted the Radical Republican reconstruction program. Hamlin returned to the Senate, where he became chair of the Foreign Relations Committee. Later, he spent a term as Envoy Extraordinary and Minister Plenipotentiary to Spain. He retired to his Hampden home, where he died July 4, 1891.

With Hannibal Hamlin in vice-presidential purgatory during the war, the most influential man from Maine was US Senator William Pitt Fessenden of Portland. Fessenden was born October 16, 1806. Although there was some question whether Daniel Webster or Samuel Fessenden was his father, the latter accepted Pitt as his son and raised him as his own. The young man grew up in New Gloucester, attended North Yarmouth Academy, and entered Bowdoin College. After a rocky college career, Fessenden graduated in 1823 and spent a few agonizing months as an apprentice in his father's law office in Portland. Although he disagreed often with his father, he accepted many of the older

Fessenden's social and political views, including abhorrence of slavery and alcohol and allegiance to the Whig party's program of high tariffs and internal improvements.

Fessenden spent two years in Bridgton, then returned to Portland as a law partner of William Willis. He briefly entered the Maine legislature, then in 1837 traveled "out west" to Pittsburgh with Daniel Webster. By 1840, Fessenden was back in the state legislature, and in the next year he was elected to Congress from the second district. The young Whig occupied his time attempting to implement Henry Clay's programs, but overall, Fessenden gave the Whig party low marks for accomplishment.

Elected to the Senate in 1854 by an antislavery majority of the legislature, Fessenden rose to become one of the most important members of that body. Temperance and antislavery convictions energized his performance. In fact, his first great speech in that chamber came only a week after his swearing in, as he rose in opposition to the Kansas-Nebraska Act sponsored by Stephen Douglas. The next year, he left the Whig party to become a Republican.

During the war, three of Fessenden's four sons enlisted in the Union Army, while his two brothers joined him in Congress. Fessenden served on the Senate Finance Committee, the Committee on the Conduct of the War, and finally as Lincoln's secretary of the treasury—all powerful positions during a period of national crisis. As chair of the Senate Finance Committee, he virtually controlled the vast outlays of money necessary to conduct the war and the revenue bills necessary to raise that money. He supported, for the most part, the policies of the Lincoln administration under Treasury Secretary Salmon P. Chase's direction, although he opposed the issuance of paper money ("greenbacks") to support the war effort. His 1862 speech on the dangerous inflationary problems associated with paper money is still considered a classic on that subject. Perhaps his greatest achievement as chair was guiding the politically dangerous but much needed first income tax legislation through Congress in 1863. Upon Chase's resignation as secretary of the treasury in 1864, President Lincoln nominated Fessenden to that post, a position that Fessenden accepted with reluctance but in which he served with distinction.

After the war, Fessenden returned to the Senate, serving as chair of the Joint Committee on Reconstruction. Fessenden sided, to a certain degree, with the Radical Republicans who demanded severe punishment for the South. While he considered southerners a "conquered people" and favored harsh terms for readmittance into the Union, his views were generally less strident than those of more radical Republicans, such as Charles Sumner and Thaddeus Stevens. In 1868, when Radicals became engaged in a bitter struggle with President Andrew Johnson over this and other issues, the House voted a bill of impeachment against the president. Radicals assumed that Fessenden would side with them on the Senate vote. In perhaps the bravest political act of his career, he voted against conviction. The final Senate vote was thirty-five to nineteen—one vote short of the required two-thirds needed for impeachment. The vote might have ended his career, had Fessenden not died after a lingering illness in 1869, before the Maine State Legislature had the opportunity to unseat him. Fessenden was buried on September 11, 1869, in Evergreen Cemetery in Portland.

Maine in the Civil War

JERRY DESMOND

Maine's record of contributions to the war effort was no less impressive than its role in the political arena. Following the firing of the first shots of the war at Fort Sumter, Governor Washburn issued a call for ten regiments of volunteer infantry to be formed within the state, along with three regiments of militia, both groups to be armed, equipped, and drilled at the expense of the state. Although the initial call to arms fell short because of poor organization, eventually the state had no trouble meeting the various yearly quotas set by the federal government. Indeed, Maine continued to send volunteer regiments long after other states had resorted to paying bounties.

Approximately seventy-three thousand Mainers served in the Union Army and Navy during the Civil War, the highest figure in proportion to its population of any northern state. Maine's more than eighteen thousand casualties rank second only to Vermont (again, in proportion to its population). Maine furnished thirty-one regiments of infantry, three of cavalry, one of heavy artillery, seven batteries of field artillery, seven companies of sharpshooters, thirty companies of unassigned infantry, seven companies of coast artillery, and six companies for coast fortifications. In addition, over six thousand Mainers served in the Union Navy during the war, a number three times larger than any other state in the Union. Thirty-one Union generals came from Maine, together with several prominent naval officers. Maine leaders and regiments fought in almost every battle of the eastern front.

Three Maine generals, Adelbert Ames, Joshua L. Chamberlain, and Oliver O. Howard, exemplify the important contribution Maine made to the Union effort. Ames was born in Rockland in 1835. After graduating fifth in a class of forty-five from West Point in 1861, he almost immediately saw action as a second lieutenant of artillery in the first land battle of the war at Bull Run. Although seriously wounded in the thigh, Ames continued to direct the fire of his battery until loss of blood made him too weak to sit upright. For this action, he was promoted to brevet (temporary) major and later awarded the

15-3. The Seventh Company, unassigned Maine Infantry, commanded by Captain A. Thompson, poses in front of the Maine State House during the Civil War. Early in the war Maine's quotas were easily filled, but as the war dragged on, towns and cities resorted to paying bounties to encourage men to volunteer so that a compulsory draft would not be needed. Courtesy of the Maine Historic Preservation Commission, Augusta.

Congressional Medal of Honor. Breveted three additional times during the war for bravery, Ames saw action in almost every campaign of the Army of the Potomac, including Antietam, Fredericksburg, Gettysburg, and the final campaigns before Petersburg. The "Ames" division of the 24th Corps was instrumental in the capture of Fort Fisher at Wilmington, North Carolina in January 1865, thus closing the last open port of the Confederacy. By the end of the war, Ames had achieved the rank of brevet major general of volunteers at the tender age of twenty-nine.

There is no question that Maine's best-regarded military leader was Joshua L. Chamberlain of Brewer. Seven years older than Ames, Chamberlain graduated from Bowdoin College and completed a course at the Bangor

Theological Seminary, returning to Bowdoin to teach religion, rhetoric, and modern languages. In 1862, he was granted a leave of absence from Bowdoin for study abroad but instead enlisted as a lieutenant colonel of the Twentieth Maine Regiment.

Taking part in twenty-four major battles, Chamberlain was wounded six times. During a desperate charge at Petersburg in 1864, which brought him promotion on the spot to brigadier general, Chamberlain received a severe wound that shattered his hips. Doctors declared that he would die of the wounds, and he did—of lingering complications some fifty years later in 1914. Chamberlain is most remembered for his role in the valiant stand taken by his regiment at Little Round Top during the battle of Gettysburg, for which he was awarded the Congressional Medal of Honor. Of all of Grant's generals, he was chosen to receive the surrender of the Confederate Army at Appomattox in April 1865, an event dramatically portrayed in his posthumously published book, *The Passing of the Armies* (1915). Following the war, Chamberlain served as governor of Maine, president of Bowdoin College, and surveyor of the port of Portland.

Oliver Otis Howard was born at Leeds, Maine, in 1830. A graduate of both Bowdoin College and West Point, Howard led the Third Maine Regiment at the first battle of Bull Run and rapidly gained promotion to brigadier general. At Fair Oaks, during the Peninsula Campaign, he sustained two serious wounds and lost his right arm; he was later awarded the Congressional Medal of Honor for his actions. Promoted to major general, he commanded the Second Corps and, later, the Eleventh Corps during the Chancellorsville and Gettysburg campaigns. Unfortunately, his reputation has suffered serious damage; military critics have held him responsible for Union reversals on the first days of these battles, especially at Chancellorsville, where his troops were surprised and routed by "Stonewall" Jackson's flanking attack. He did, however, receive the thanks of Congress for choosing Cemetery Hill as a defensive position at the battle of Gettysburg. Transferred to the western theater of the war, he took command of Sherman's right wing and joined his famous march to the sea.

After the war, Howard was appointed commissioner of the Freedman's Bureau, in charge of newly freed African Americans. He founded and served as the first president of Howard University, a noted historically black institution in Washington, DC. Later he was appointed peace commissioner to the Apache Indians by President Grant and commanded an expedition against the Nez Percé Indians in 1877.

While there can be no doubt that the Twentieth Maine Regiment is the most famous and celebrated of the thirty-one infantry regiments to come from the state, several other regiments made impressive contributions during the war. The Second Maine Infantry Regiment, recruited from the Bangor-Orono area,

15-4. Combat artist Winslow Homer (1836–1910) sketches two six-foot-seven privates from Company F of the First Maine Regiment, believed to be John J. Handly of Wilton and Edwin Farrar of Bethel. The illustration appeared in *Harper's Weekly,* May 17, 1862. After the war Homer moved to a studio at Prouts Neck, where he painted some of his greatest landscape and marine canvasses. Private collection.

was one of the first to leave the state and saw important action in the early years of the war. However, the regiment was severely disciplined following the first battle of Bull Run. The regiment had signed up for a two-year enlistment period, and when several ninety-day regiments bivouacked nearby began to go home, the Second Maine decided not to turn out for duty. General George McClellan cracked down swiftly and had sixty-three of the toughest cases sentenced to Fort Jefferson, a disciplinary barracks in the Dry Tortugas off Key West, Florida, for the rest of their two-year enlistment period. The sentence was later commuted, and most of the offenders were assigned to the Second New York Regiment, then returned to the Second Maine.

At the battle of Antietam, the Seventh Maine Infantry performed bravely in a desperate situation. The regiment had been ordered to clear out some Confederate sharpshooters positioned near the Piper farm. In his book, *Following the Greek Cross: or, Memories of the Sixth Army Corps* (1894), Major Thomas W. Hyde describes how he led 240 of the regiment up to the Piper farm buildings. They soon found themselves surrounded on three sides by four Confederate regiments. Only sixty-eight soldiers were able to fight their way back to their lines, to the cheers of the other Union regiments looking on. Hyde received the Congressional Medal of Honor for this action and remarked after the battle that with a little more support the Rebel line could have been broken and the battle, perhaps even the war, could have been won. Company A of the regiment was made up of Aroostook County recruits, mostly from Presque Isle and Houlton.

The Seventeenth Maine Infantry Regiment took part in most of the battles along the eastern front. Recruited in 1862 from York, Cumberland, Oxford, and Androscoggin counties, the regiment ranks twenty-second in percentage killed in action among all federal regiments in the war. It eventually became so decimated that it was united with the Third Maine. At Sayler's Creek, Virginia, during the final week of the war, the regiment captured over two hundred prisoners and a stand of colors.

The First Maine Heavy Artillery has the dubious distinction of suffering more battle losses than any other federal regiment, in part because the regiment had twelve companies rather than the usual ten, with a total enlistment of over 2,200. The primary reason, however, was its role in the Petersburg campaign. Recruited mostly from the Penobscot Valley, the regiment was originally trained to operate the large guns in forts protecting Washington, DC. General Grant, having suffered incredible casualties during the summer of 1864, decided to strip the defenses of Washington and convert the "heavies" to infantry regiments. In a desperate and hopeless attack on the Petersburg defenses on June 18, the First Maine suffered 632 casualties (out of 900 engaged) in about ten minutes.

With over 350 Congressional Medals of Honor, the Twenty-seventh Maine Infantry Regiment was certainly the most decorated of the war—an honor bestowed in large measure because criteria for awarding the medal were lower at the beginning of the war and because of confusion over what medal should be given to the regiment. The Twenty-fifth and Twenty-seventh Maine regiments were nearing the end of their enlistment period in the middle of the Gettysburg campaign. The regiments, assigned to protect Washington, DC, were asked to re-enlist. The Twenty-fifth refused, but 350 members of the Twenty-seventh decided to stay on. The medals were awarded for this dedication to duty.

While it is often easy to recall the heroic regiments and their gallant leaders, it is important to remember that war is fought by individuals. There are countless stories of personal acts of bravery, but only a few must suffice. Many city mayors and town leaders, for example, enlisted and served during the war. Hiram Berry, former mayor of Rockland and colonel of the Fourth Maine Infantry Regiment, was killed leading a bayonet charge at the battle of Chancellorsville on May 3, 1863. Aroostook County, although sparsely populated, sent several companies and hundreds of soldiers to war. Captain Black Hawk Putnam of Houlton, the dashing leader of Company E of the First Maine Cavalry, was wounded and captured at the battle of Middleton. Escaping across the mountains of Virginia, Putnam made it back to Union lines to become, in his later years, a leader of veteran organizations. His boot, complete with bullet hole, can be found at the Aroostook County Historical and Art Museum in Houlton.

Several Maine women served as nurses during the Civil War. Dorothea Dix of Hampden, already famous as an advocate for reform in prisons and insane asylums, served as superintendent of women nurses during the war. Amy Bradley began her war experience as the nurse for the Third Maine regiment. She eventually took charge of the *Knickerbocker,* a hospital ship, and the Soldier's Home in Washington, DC. However, the experience of Isabella Fogg was probably more typical. She followed her son after his enlistment and served in field hospitals during the Peninsula Campaign, Antietam, Fredericksburg, Chancellorsville, Gettysburg, and Cedar Run. At Cedar Run her son was seriously wounded and she nursed him back to health, eventually collapsing from overwork herself.

While due consideration must be given to Grant's capture of Vicksburg, there is little doubt that the biggest and most important battle of the Civil War was fought at Gettysburg, Pennsylvania, on the first three days of July 1863. General Lee's plan was to drive into Union territory, capture supplies to feed his hungry army, and swoop down on Philadelphia, Baltimore, or even Washington, DC, from the northwest. He hoped a victory would convince Great Britain and France to recognize the Confederacy. Over 150,000 soldiers fought at Gettysburg with over 50,000 casualties during the three-day battle, making it the largest land battle ever fought in North America. Maine had ten regiments of infantry, three artillery batteries, and one cavalry regiment at Gettysburg. Their presence and performance in this battle were crucial elements in the Union's victory.

The first day of the battle saw Confederate troops marching on Gettysburg from the northwest as outnumbered lead units of the Army of the Potomac tried to slow their advance. Both the Second Maine Artillery Regiment and the Sixteenth Maine Infantry Regiment were instrumental in this delaying action. The Second Maine battery, under the able leadership of Captain James Hall, coolly held off several charges of Confederate infantry while holding down the left flank of the makeshift Union line on Seminary Ridge. Forced from their advanced position, Hall's troops eventually retreated to a more tenable line on Culp's Hill.

Meanwhile, on the extreme right of the Union line near Oak Ridge, the Sixteenth Maine Infantry Regiment was in a desperate fix. With only two hundred troops, the regiment had been ordered to hold that position at any cost. Eventually cut off from the rest of the army, each soldier tore off a piece of the regimental flag and attempted individually to return to the new Union position on Cemetery Hill just south of the town. Only thirty-five of the regiment reached their destination that evening. By the end of the first day, the Army of the Potomac was able to secure important defensive positions, thanks in large part to the holding efforts of units like the Second Maine Artillery and the Sixteenth Maine Infantry.

The second day of the battle saw some of the most desperate fighting of the entire war. General Lee ordered General Longstreet to take his entire corps and make a flanking maneuver around the Union left. The objective was to capture two important positions, Little Round Top and Big Round Top, from which the Confederate army could force a collapse of the Union lines on Cemetery Hill. Several Maine regiments were in position to meet this advance, including the Seventeenth Maine Regiment, which eventually lost 199 soldiers near the Devil's Den, and the Third Maine regiment, which lost 122 in the famous peach orchard.

It was the Twentieth Maine Infantry Regiment that played the greatest part in stopping the Confederate advance on that day. Rushed to the crest of Little Round Top, the Twentieth Maine, under the command of Colonel Joshua Chamberlain, was barely able to reach its position at the extreme left of the Union line before being hit by a charge of Confederate infantry, mostly regiments from Alabama. Somehow maneuvering his troops under fire, Chamberlain was able to extend his line to the left, bent back in the middle. Sending one of his companies off to the left to find additional positions, Chamberlain and his regiment withstood several charges of attacking Rebels. Desperately low on ammunition, Chamberlain finally took the only course of action left to him.

Unsure whether his missing company was dead or alive, realizing that retreat was impossible, he ordered his troops to fix bayonets on their empty rifles and charge down the hill. For some reason, it worked. Suddenly, his missing company appeared from behind some rocks on the Confederate flank, raking it with gunfire. The Confederate line wavered and then broke as Chamberlain's troops pursued them, taking over four hundred prisoners. Chamberlain himself

15-5. Fort Scammel on House Island in Portland Harbor. Built in 1808, the fort was manned in wartime and continually expanded and modernized into the 1890s. This photograph shows the large Rodman guns in place at the time of the Spanish-American War. Photo courtesy of the Maine Historical Society, Portland.

recalled that one Confederate officer fired at him with a pistol in one hand while offering his sword in surrender with the other. The Twentieth Maine was so jubilant in their advance, some shouting "On to Richmond," that Chamberlain had some trouble getting his troops to halt at that position. The left flank of the Union Army had been saved by a gritty and determined combination of loggers, fishermen, and farmers from central Maine, under the leadership of a college professor. One hundred and twenty-five of their comrades were lost in the engagement.

The third day of the battle saw General Lee take the desperate gamble of attacking the Union center on Cemetery Hill. The Nineteenth Maine Regiment was near the center of the line during Pickett's charge, and participated in repelling the Confederate attack. The charge brought disastrous losses to Pickett's forces, which demoralized the Confederate army. By some accounts, the charge was the watershed of the Civil War, the point beyond which Confederate chances of victory grew steadily dimmer.

Maine Fortifications: The Civil War and Beyond

JOEL W. EASTMAN

Geographically, Maine was remote from scenes of battle such as Gettysburg, but limited congressional funding for Maine seacoast defenses left the state vulnerable by sea. In 1842, the Maine congressional delegation had been able to convince Congress to fund the construction of a fort to defend the entrance to the Penobscot River, which the British had invaded during the Revolution and again during the War of 1812. Fort Knox, in Prospect, was Maine's first new fortification since 1807. Several years later, in 1857, Congress authorized a new fort for Portland, Fort Gorges, and one to guard the mouth of the Kennebec River, named Fort Popham.

With the outbreak of the Civil War, construction of these new forts and modernization of old ones were given high priority. The presence of these impressive structures, however, did not discourage Confederate activity in the Gulf of Maine. Confederate commerce raiders operated off the Maine coast, seizing fishing boats and one passenger steamer, which was taken to Canada. In 1863, Confederates raiders sailed into Portland on a captured fishing boat with plans to set fire to shipping and seize another passenger boat. Although their plans to destroy shipping were frustrated, the rebels seized the federal revenue cutter *Caleb Cushing* and sailed it out the north end of the harbor, away from the forts. A citizen spotted the boat leaving and notified the mayor of the city, who gathered a group of civilians and a few soldiers, commandeered a steamboat, and gave chase. The Confederates set fire to the *Cushing* as the steamboat approached. The vessel exploded, and the raiders were captured. Although the Confederate effort failed, news of it caused a panic up and down the Atlantic coast, forcing the federal government to build temporary installations to defend even small ports, including several in Maine.

With the outbreak of the war with Spain in 1898, cities all along the Atlantic coast feared an attack by the Spanish navy, and so forts were occupied and temporary defenses erected. Maine's congressional delegation was able to use its influence to have two obsolete cruisers assigned to the coast, and obsolete Civil War surplus cannon were emplaced temporarily to defend small harbors such as Rockland and Bar Harbor.

Coincidentally, work was underway around the country and in Maine on the most extensive system of coast defenses in American history. In the late 1880s, Congress had approved a modernization program, and construction began in the 1890s at the most important ports in the country. Fort Preble in Portland was upgraded and four new forts were built to protect the harbor. Fort Baldwin was built at the mouth of the Kennebec, and Fort Foster in Kittery was con-structed as part of the defenses of the Piscataqua River.

Although the North Atlantic coast never again became a theater of war, as it had been during the French and Indian wars, the American Revolution, and the War of 1812, these coastal defenses provided a measure of security for Maine citizens. Indeed, in World War I and World War II enemy warships appeared off the Maine coast, as they had during the Civil War. Still, in the twentieth century, Maine's best defense as a region proved to be, as it had been after 1775, its mili-tary insignificance.

Insignificant or not as a military objective, Maine played an exemplary mili-tary and political role during the Civil War years. The state provided troops, political leadership, and generalship to conduct the war effort elsewhere. The impact of the Civil War on Maine's own history, particularly on the state's poli-tics and economy, will be detailed in the following chapters.

For Further Reading:

A wealth of original sources exists on Maine's military history. The records of the Union and Confederate armies and navies have been published and are available in most li-braries. The annual reports of the Secretary of War cover federal fortifications in Maine, while the reports of the Maine Adjutant General provide details on the Maine militia and volunteers. Civil War veterans' organizations published first-hand accounts, and there are numerous published diaries available. Many excellent biographies and histories cover the role of Maine and her people in the Civil War.

Additional bound primary documents include *The Maine Bugle* (Rockland, 1894–98); *Annual Report of the Adjutant General of the State of Maine* (Augusta, 1862–67, 1898–1902); us Navy Department, *Official Records of the Union and Confederate Navies in the War of the Rebellion*, 30 vols. (Washington, DC, 1894–1922); us War Department, *The War of the Rebellion: A Compilation of the Official Records of the Union and Confed-erate Armies*, 70 vols. (Washington, DC, 1880–1901); *Civil War Unit Histories, Part 2: The Union, New England: Regimental Histories and Personal Narratives* (Bethesda, Md., 1991). See also Bryan L. Dilts, 1890 *Maine Census Index of Civil War Veterans or Their Widows* (Salt Lake City, Utah, 1984).

Useful first-hand accounts by Maine people in the Civil War include George H. Coffin, *Three Years in the Army* (Lincoln, Mass., 1976); Abial H. Edwards, *"Dear Friend Anna": The Civil War Letters of a Common Soldier from Maine* (Orono, 1992); and H. Draper Hunt, editor, *Dearest Father: The Civil War Letters of Lt. Frank Dickerson, A Son of Belfast, Maine* (Unity, 1992).

The Aroostook War has been covered in a number of volumes, perhaps most exten-sively in Henry Burrage's *Maine in the Northeast Boundary Controversy* (Portland, 1919), and more recently in Howard Jones's *To the Webster-Ashburton Treaty: A Study in Anglo-American Relations, 1783–1843* (Chapel Hill, N.C., 1977), and Geraldine Tidd Scott's *"Ties of Common Blood": A History of Maine's Northeast Boundary Dispute with Great Britain,* 1783–1842 (Bowie, Md., 1992). Jones treats the Aroostook War in the context of a series of boundary disputes and negotiations between Great Britain and the United States culminating in the 1842 Webster-Ashburton Treaty.

Primary documents on the Aroostook War abound, particularly in the form of diplomatic correspondence and boundary survey reports. Most are collected in several volumes published by the state, the federal government, and the British government, available in the larger libraries in the state under various ponderous titles refering to the "Northeast Boundary." Newspaper accounts are also voluminous, since the issue was at the heart of Maine politics and political campaigns between 1839 and 1842. See especially the *Bangor Whig and Courier* (Whig) and the *Eastern Argus* (Democrat). The journals, letterbooks, and annual reports of the Maine land agents, located in the Maine State Archives, are also revealing.

SECONDARY SOURCES ON MAINE FORTIFICATIONS AND THE CIVIL WAR:

Bowden, Murray, "The Problem of Conscription in Maine during the Civil War" (M.A. thesis, University of Maine, 1948).

Bradley, Robert L., *The Forts of Maine, 1607–1945* (Augusta, 1981).

Carpenter, John A., *Sword and Olive Branch: Oliver Otis Howard* (Pittsburgh, 1964).

Chapin, John E., "Impact of the Civil War on Maine Shipping and Shipbuilding" (M.A. thesis, University of Maine, 1970).

Dunnack, Henry E., *Maine Forts* (Augusta, 1924).

Eastman, Joel W., *The Modern Defenses of the Coast of Maine, 1891–1945* (Augusta, 1988).

Grindle, Roger L., "Into the Breech: The Life Story of Major General Hiram G. Berry" (M.A. thesis, University of Maine, 1962).

Hunt, H. Draper, *Hannibal Hamlin of Maine: Lincoln's First Vice President* (Syracuse, N.Y., 1969).

Hutchinson, Vernal, *A Maine Town in the Civil War* (Freeport, 1967).

Jellison, Charles A., *Fessenden of Maine* (Syracuse, N.Y., 1962).

Lewis, E. Raymond, *Seacoast Fortifications of the United States* (San Francisco, Calif., 1979).

Maine Gettysburg Commission, *Maine at Gettysburg* (Portland, 1898).

McCormick, Donald M., "A Cross-Section of Maine History during the Civil War Period" (M.A. thesis, University of Maine, 1934).

Mundy, James H., *Second to None: The Story of the 2d Maine Volunteer Infantry: "The Bangor Regiment"* (Scarborough, 1992).

Olson, Sandra G., "The Archaeology of Fort Pownal: A Military Outpost on the Maine Coast, 1759–1775" (M.A. thesis, University of Maine, 1984).

Parkman, Aubrey, *Army Engineers in New England* (Waltham, Mass., 1978).

Pullen, John J., *A Shower of Stars: The Medal of Honor and the 27th Maine* (Philadelphia, 1966).

Pullen, John J., *The Twentieth Maine* (Philadelphia, 1957).

Smith, Mason P., *Confederates Downeast: Confederate Operations in and around Maine* (Portland, 1985).

Trulock, Alice R., *In the Hands of Providence: Joshua L. Chamberlain and the American Civil War* (Chapel Hill, N.C., 1992).

Wallace, Willard M., *Soul of the Lion: A Biography of General Joshua L. Chamberlain* (New York, 1960).

Whitman, William E. S., *Maine in the War for the Union* (Lewiston, 1865).

Zimmerman, David, *Coastal Fort: A History of Fort Sullivan, Eastport, Maine* (Eastport, 1984).

ADDITIONAL SECONDARY READING ON THE AROOSTOOK WAR:

Day, Clarence A., *Aroostook: The First Sixty Years* (Presque Isle, 1981, ca. 1952).

Jones, Wilbur D., "Lord Ashburton and the Maine Boundary Negotiations," *Mississippi Valley Historical Review* 40 (December 1953).

Le Duc, Thomas, "The Maine Frontier and the Northeastern Boundary Controversy," *American Historical Review* 53 (October 1947).

Lowenthal, David, "The Maine Press and the Aroostook War," *Canadian Historical Review* 32 (December 1951).

McDonald, Sheila, "The War after the War: Fort Kent Blockhouse, 1839–1892," *Maine Historical Society Quarterly* 29 (Winter–Spring 1990).

Melvin, Charlotte L., *Madawaska: A Chapter in Maine–New Brunswick Relations* (Madawaska, 1975).

Scott, Geraldine Tidd, "Fortifications on Maine's Northeast Boundary, 1828–1845," *Maine Historical Society Quarterly* 29 (Winter–Spring 1990).

Sprague, John F., *The North Eastern Boundary Controversy and the Aroostook War* (Dover, 1910).

Steinhauer, Dale R., "A Class of Men: United States Army Recruits in Maine, 1822–1860," *Maine Historical Society Quarterly* 30 (Fall 1990).

16

The Republican Ascendancy: Politics & Reform

EDWARD O. SCHRIVER & STANLEY R. HOWE

The sectional crisis and the Civil War ushered in a period of Republican domination of state politics that lasted well into the twentieth century. This chapter explores the almost-century-long era after 1854, during which Maine has been characterized—not entirely accurately—as a one-party state. The basis for Republican control in the second half of the century remained much the same as it was in the Civil War years. Strong leadership, appealing issues, the appearance of unity, ties with business, and the legacy of the Civil War kept the party in power.

Republicans continued to send astute politicians to Washington. Leaders like James G. Blaine and Thomas B. Reed were seasoned veterans whose leadership influenced the nation's destiny. Republican power was not monolithic, however. The party's long tenure naturally led to complacency, a trend underscored by Democrat William R. Pattangall's incisive commentary on late-nineteenth-century Maine politics. Democrats, fragmented though they were, were quick to seize the opportunity when discontent split the Republican constituency.

In part, dissatisfaction arose because Maine people, despite their reputation for conservatism, were still sensitive to the spirit of reform, whether marshaled on behalf of old crusades like temperance or new issues like currency, abolition of capital punishment, and women's suffrage. Usually Republicans were able to contain these reform sentiments within their organization; when they did not, they found themselves, at least temporarily, out of office.

The Republican party emerged from the chaos of the Civil War years with a strong and unified organization. The young party attracted an impressive phalanx of astute leaders and quickly established control over state politics, at a time when the Democratic party was disintegrating under the intense pressures of slavery, states' rights, Southern secession, and war. Building on these considerable advantages, the Republican party went on to dominate Maine political life almost without interruption until the election of Edmund S. Muskie in 1954.

16-1. William Pitt Fessenden (1806–69), a Portland lawyer, served in the Maine legislature and U.S. Congress. In 1854, he was elected to the U.S. Senate, chaired the important Senate Finance Committee during the Civil War, and was appointed Secretary of the Treasury by Abraham Lincoln. Fessenden returned to the Senate after the war and was one of a few courageous Republicans to vote against the impeachment of President Andrew Johnson. Courtesy of the Maine Historical Society, Portland.

Although the party's grip was far from complete, this one-hundred-year ascendancy was nonetheless impressive. Between 1858 and 1901, for instance, Republicans elected fourteen of the sixteen governors, twenty-eight of the twenty-nine speakers of the Maine House, and all thirty-four presidents of the Maine Senate.

What accounts for this long hold on Maine voters? Certainly lingering memories of Maine's participation in the Civil War helped the party that denounced slavery and preserved the Union, as did continuing links to the Grand Army of the Republic, a politically powerful Civil War veterans organization. Strong intergenerational ties in this predominantly rural state perpetuated such allegiances well beyond the Civil War generation. Other answers to this question lie in the nineteenth-century fixation on issues such as temperance, currency, and tariffs. The party's stand on these matters gained wide appeal, and its superficial unity, in contrast to vacillating and divided Democratic positions, held voter loyalty.

Some credit also goes to the party's extraordinary political leaders. Nationally powerful Maine figures like Vice-President Hannibal Hamlin and Secretary of the Treasury William Pitt Fessenden enhanced the image of the party in their home state. For over twenty years (1859–81), the charismatic James G. Blaine ran the party as his own personal fiefdom from his position as head of the Republican State Committee. A natural leader and astute political boss, Blaine used his enormous influence to make certain the party nominated effective candidates for governor and Congress. Blaine's leadership helped Republicans survive internecine party warfare and weather the broader conflicts between radical temperance advocates and those less enthusiastic with the course of this reform.

Nineteenth-century political habits also played a part in establishing Republican rule. Voters during these decades formed their political loyalties early, and it took catastrophic events to move most party regulars from their moorings. After years of Republican triumphs, some Mainers no doubt felt duty-bound to stand by Republican candidates. Success paved the way for further victories in more practical ways as well. Republicans controlled important appointive offices and, as the dominant party, they gathered in the most able and ambitious of the rising politicians in the state.

Moreover, as the nineteenth century wore on, big business became an increasingly important factor in political decision making. While the Democrats were not without their adherents in the commercial world, Republicans elected several business leaders to the governorship, helping to fuse a strong link between the party and Maine's business elites. A final factor was the party's sensitivity to tensions between eastern and western Maine—to the Bangor and the Portland-Lewiston bases of the party. Geographically balanced tickets paid dividends in election after election.

A long span of Republican successes between 1857 and 1879 set the stage for the party's dominant role in Maine politics. Lot M. Morrill, brother of former governor Anson P. Morrill, became Maine's chief executive in 1857, and except for the tensions caused by the approaching break-up of the Union, little threatened the security of his tenure. Maine's wartime governors, Israel Washburn, Jr., Abner Coburn, and Samuel Cony, were all Republicans. Joshua L. Chamberlain, hero of the Battle of Gettysburg, was governor from 1867 until 1871, and he was followed by two Republican temperance leaders: Sidney Perham (1871–74) and Nelson Dingley, Jr. (1874–76). Selden Connor, another Civil War veteran, was governor between 1876 and 1879. Collectively, these figures represent the party's postwar strengths: symbolic connection to the cause of the Union and a strong stand on temperance and high tariffs. The party's remarkable unity on these issues, particularly in contrast to the divisions plaguing the Democratic party, explains much about their control over nineteenth-century Maine politics.

It was during Selden Connor's term that the first serious challenge to the Republican ascendancy emerged. The campaign of 1878 hinged on the question of currency, a reform issue the Republican party was not able to absorb within its well-orchestrated consensus. In 1862, the federal government had been forced to issue paper currency to finance the Civil War effort. Eventually some $4 million was circulated, supplementing the prevailing system of gold and silver. After the war, the government set out to redeem the "greenbacks" in hard currency, but hard-pressed farmers and debtors opposed the move. Increasingly restive during the mid-1870s, many farmers and workers pressed for another greenback issue to boost employment and farm prices and ease the crushing burdens of debt and foreclosure. Congress nevertheless passed the Resumption Act of 1875, which continued the hard-money policy. This, coupled with the rise of the state Grange, brought new militancy to farmers in Maine and elsewhere.

The Greenback party made its appearance in Maine in 1875, running candidates who advocated paper money and other reforms to benefit farmers and working people. The movement's most colorful adherent was "Uncle" Solon Chase, who stumped the state in an ox cart denouncing monopolies and the money power. This insurgent party drew farmers away from the Republicans and, in the election of 1878, pushed the Democrats into third place. Because none of the parties' gubernatorial candidates received a majority of the popular vote, the matter, as specified in the state constitution, went to the legislature for resolution. In the House, Greenbackers and Democrats outvoted the Republicans to eliminate Selden Connor from consideration. This presented

PLAISTED—"When can I reach the State House, neighbor?"
HONEST FARMER—"Never, my friend, with that load."

16-2. Lisbon Falls native D. D. Coombs (1850–1938) captured the ragtag Republican opposition in this splendid cartoon. The rise of the agrarian Greenback party, led by Solon
Chase of Turner (carrying the banner), led to a deadlock in the gubernatorial election of
1878. The state Senate chose Democrat Alonzo Garcelon (center), and a deadlock the
following year led to a Republican chief executive, after near insurrection. In the next
election the Fusion Party (Democrats and Greenbackers) elected Harris W. Plaisted
(pointing to the State House with his sword). Courtesy of William and Debra Barry.

the Senate's majority Republicans with an unhappy choice: Democrat Alonzo
Garcelon, or Greenbacker Joseph L. Smith. Historian Louis C. Hatch concluded
that they preferred Garcelon, even though he ran a poor third in the election,
because he was "weaker" than Smith. Garcelon became the first Democrat to
hold the position since 1857.

Currency reform continued to churn the waters of Maine politics in 1879,
disrupting the consensus Republicans had maintained for a quarter century.
The 1879 elections gave Republican candidate Daniel F. Davis a plurality, but

again, the election was transferred to the legislature, since there was no clear majority. This time Governor Garcelon and his council took it upon themselves to certify the election returns for state legislative seats, and there was some confusion over who had won various races. By the governor's count, Republicans maintained sixty-one seats, but the Fusionists (Greenbackers and Democrats) held seventy-eight. Twelve seats were left vacant. The Republicans appealed to the State Supreme Court, but the issue remained unresolved.

Tempers flared and nerves grew raw. Worried about violence and possible damage to state property, Governor Garcelon implored ex-governor Joshua L. Chamberlain to act as military custodian of the peace until the matter was settled. Reluctantly, Chamberlain agreed to serve, but by this time the controversy had turned Augusta into an armed camp. Slowly, however, anger cooled, tensions relaxed, and the legislature was seated. When cooler heads prevailed, the legislature selected Republican Daniel F. Davis to succeed Garcelon.

The election of 1880 demonstrated that Republicans had not yet regained control of the situation. Democrats and Greenbackers joined forces, giving Fusion candidate Harris M. Plaisted 73,713 votes to Republican Daniel F. Davis's 73,544. Despite the close vote, Republicans chose to avoid a second challenge, and Plaisted became governor. By this time, however, the United States was back on the gold standard, Maine farmers were enjoying relative prosperity, and Greenbackism was in remission. The movement had cost the Republicans two terms in office, but the 1882 election (held biennially after 1880) returned them to power.

Governor Frederick Robie again demonstrated the Republicans' recipe for success. "Colonel" Robie had been an officer during the Civil War; he was managing director of a railroad and business manager of a Portland newspaper, signaling the party's growing alliance with Maine businessmen. Although Robie was not a farmer (his Gorham estate, Democratic critics pointed out, was "cultivated by his tenants"), he had risen to prominence as master of the increasingly powerful state Grange, a position that boosted several later politicians into the governor's seat as well. The party's link to the Grange demonstrated its success in absorbing the agrarian discontent that had fed the Greenback movement earlier.

A popular governor, Robie was easily reelected, and his administration marked the beginning of a thirty-year Republican hold on the executive branch. His successors were also powerful entrepreneurs: Joseph R. Bodwell was an immensely wealthy business leader with holdings in granite quarries, timberlands, sawmills, ice cutting operations, water supply companies, and farms; Edwin C. Burleigh was an Augusta business executive and timberland speculator.

During these years, Democrats could do little but offer criticism of their effectively unified Republican counterparts. William R. Pattangall, a leading

Maine Democrat, later wrote a series of short political vignettes satirizing political figures for the *Machias Union*. In these "Meddybemps Letters," Pattangall summarized his impressions of Republican governors and noted the party's growing complacency in the last years of the century. His characterization of Governor Burleigh was typical:

> A good man is Mr. Burleigh. . . . He has had great opportunities to serve the public, great chances to do something for the good of his state, and for the people who have loyally supported his ambitions for 40 years. That he has done nothing for them in return for their loyalty goes without saying. Politics to him has been a business, a means of making money, of advancing personal fortunes, of helping his personal friends and relatives. Perhaps this is not his fault; men bred in the narrow school of modern Maine Republican politics do not take a very broad view of their public duties. Any why should he worry about the people? They vote for him right along. What more does he want?

Although this commentary could have been applied to a number of Gilded Age politicians, Republican and Democrat, it does suggest that Burleigh was beginning to take his party's preeminence for granted.

Pattangall, in a sarcastic humor, labeled John F. Hill of Augusta (1901–5) a "magnificent" governor, who avoided all the mistakes of his predecessors by doing absolutely nothing at all. "He just sat still and let the boys run things as easily and quietly as possible." Hill's successor in 1905, lime-quarry owner William T. Cobb of Rockland, won Pattangall's grudging admiration for honesty. Cobb's major political shortcoming, Pattangall felt, was his belief that the party meant what it said in its platform. Cobb's strict approach to liquor law enforcement alienated many voters and narrowed his margin of victory in the 1906 election.

In fact, Republican majorities in state elections after 1900 were growing slimmer, for several reasons. First, Republican administrations were increasingly vulnerable to Democratic charges of extravagance. Second, prohibition proved to be a thorny issue. Temperance leaders had long complained that Republican administrations failed to enforce the laws Republican legislators so conspicuously endorsed. In response, the 1905 legislature passed the so-called Sturgis Law, which empowered a special commission to enforce the law. The commission's deputies so irritated the public, however, that Republicans lost favor. Finally, the presidential administration of William Howard Taft alienated many Maine Republicans who hoped for more progressive measures nationally. Others, particularly in eastern Maine, resented Taft's policy of trade reciprocity with Canada, which included lumber, fish, and potatoes on the tariff-free list. In sum, the organizational unity that kept the Republican party in office was disintegrating under the pressures of turn-of-the-century reform. By 1908, the Republican majority had fallen to six thousand votes.

Cobb's successor in 1909, cannery operator Bert M. Fernald, brought to an end a string of Republican successes dating back to 1883. A moderate reformer, Fernald brought the national progressive movement to Maine; his stand on reducing the state bureaucracy, creating a state road system, and conserving forest, water, and wildlife resources shook the now somewhat rigid state party machine. Fernald, like Cobb, mishandled the prohibition question, this time alienating radical prohibitionists by vetoing a bill designed to stiffen liquor-law penalties.

Fernald was also too closely associated with the politically powerful Ricker family of his native town of Poland. The Rickers, proprietors of the massive Poland Spring House and the equally impressive Samoset Hotel in Rockland, were tireless advocates of state measures to promote tourism through better conservation laws and better highways. Edward P. Ricker, in Pattangall's opinion, was determined "to control the politics of the State of Maine," and Fernald's nomination in 1908 was largely a result of Ricker financing and organizing skills. As an ally of the reform-minded Ricker family, Fernald was caught in the middle of a feud between progressive and conservative wings of the Republican party. Progressive reform, sweeping the nation between 1901 and World War I, disrupted Republican unity and provided an opportunity for Democrats.

The 1910 election brought national attention to Maine; since state elections were held in September, two months before the November national elections, it was widely heralded as a measure of the Republican party's prospects for weathering the pressures of reform. And indeed, as Maine went in 1910, so went the nation in 1912, electing Democrat Woodrow Wilson as President. Fernald's genial but less than shrewd nature, his connection with Ricker money and Ricker ambitions, and his inability to hold together factions within the party spelled disaster for Republicans. In 1910, voters selected, along with Democrat Frederick W. Plaisted, son of Harris M. Plaisted, their first Democrats in Congress since 1880 and their first Democratic legislature since the 1850s. This legislature in turn chose the first Democrat—Grange Master Obadiah Gardiner—to represent Maine in the US Senate since 1857. Maine's other Senator, William P. Frye, died in the summer of 1911, and to complete the Republican rout, Governor Plaisted choose as his successor Democrat Charles F. Johnson of Waterville.

The hiatus in Republican rule proved short-lived. Even though the Republican party was wrenched apart nationally in 1912 by the formation of Theodore Roosevelt's Bull Moose party, in Maine Republican progressives and conservatives agreed to join forces in the state elections and then take sides during the national campaign. Democrats, in their brief tenure in office, managed to implement several progressive reform measures: a Corrupt Practices Act; an amendment to the Direct Primary Law; and resolutions favoring the direct election of US Senators and the federal income tax. But standard Republican issues ruled the day. Republicans labeled their opponents the "party of free rum and free trade," and in 1912, Governor Plaisted was replaced by another Republican, William T. Haines.

Thanks to disruptions in the dominant party caused by progressive insurgency, Democrats elected one more governor, Oakley C. Curtis, in 1915, but after the 1916 elections Republicans were back in full force. They continued their grip on the governorship until Louis Brann brought the Democrats back to power during the tumultuous Depression decade. In the waning years of the Depression, Republicans elected Lewis O. Barrows, and Maine voters did not again deviate from the party until Edmund S. Muskie shattered the Republican hegemony in 1954.

Despite these continuing successes, the long Republican ascendancy was brought to an end by the 1910 rout. Republicans continued to win elections, but victory was no longer assured by a wide margin of success. In good part, the party's weakening grip was a result of internal disturbances—wrangles between progressives and regulars—rather than growing Democratic party strength. Internal squabbling was a deadly game in the battle for public favor. Temperance, too, had become a divisive issue. Republicans traditionally managed to straddle divisions in the party and the electorate by taking a firm rhetorical stand on the liquor question coupled with lax enforcement. But when two governors, Cobb and Fernald, mishandled the issue, it helped bring an end to the era.

But sheer complacency was a problem as well. In presenting Fernald for the gubernatorial nomination in 1908, Mayor I. L. Merrill of Auburn had sounded a warning to Republicans:

> It is not wise or prudent for us to ignore the fact that within the past few years there has been a growing feeling of discontent and dissatisfaction among the rank and file of the Republican party. It appeared to a great many thinking people that a few gentlemen who were enjoying the offices of the State and the emoluments thereof were selecting the candidates and shaping the policies of the administration rather than the great mass of the intelligent and conscientious Republican voters.

Merrill's sage admonition went unheeded. Perhaps it is fair to say that the Republicans became too complacent and too divisive in the new century; nothing erodes a party's effectiveness faster than internal dissension or overconfidence. The Republicans learned important lessons from their 1910 defeat, but the era of the party's ascendancy was over.

Maine Republicans in National Politics

As it had during the Civil War, the Republican party's seemingly invincible grip on the state house provided a solid foundation for national leadership. Nothing illustrates Maine's influence on the course of national events better than historian Samuel Eliot Morison's account of an 1889 conversation between New York financier John Sargent Wise and Thomas B. Reed of Maine, then speaker of the US House of Representatives. Visiting Reed in his office, the business executive asked: "Who's running this government anyway?" The speaker is said to have replied: "The great and the good, of course, be calm." Next Wise observed that all the "great and good" appeared to come from Maine. Not only was his host from the Pine Tree State, but everyone he dealt with seemed to have a Maine connection: the secretary of state, James G. Blaine; the acting vice-president, William P. Frye; the leader of the US Senate, Eugene Hale; the chair of the House Ways and Means Committee, Nelson Dingley; and the Naval Committee chair, Charles A. Boutelle. As Wise and the speaker left for lunch with US Supreme Court Chief Justice Melville Weston Fuller—from Maine—the speaker, according to the story, turned to Wise and said, "Yes, John, the great and good—and the Wise. The country is safe." Such were the considerable fruits of party success over many years; all, except for Fuller, were Republicans.

Of Maine's political leaders in Washington in the post–Civil War era, perhaps the most notable were James G. Blaine and Thomas Brackett Reed. Blaine was born in Pennsylvania in 1830. His connection with the state of Maine came through his Augusta-born wife, Harriet Stanwood, whom he met at the Millersburg Seminary in Pennsylvania. They were married in June 1850, and three years later they moved to Maine. In 1854, Blaine became editor of the *Kennebec Journal*, and he later acquired part ownership of the larger *Portland Advertiser*. Journalism provided an excellent base for a political career, and Blaine quickly moved from a position as head of the Republican State Committee to the legislature, where he became speaker. In 1863, he was elected to the US House of Representatives. Between 1869 and 1875, Blaine served as speaker of the House, exerting his power to push the Republican program through Congress. Blaine demonstrated a remarkable aptitude for making friends and enemies alike; colleagues either loved or hated him. Representative Roscoe Conkling of New York, once asked to support Blaine's bid for the presidency, replied that as an attorney he did not engage in criminal practice.

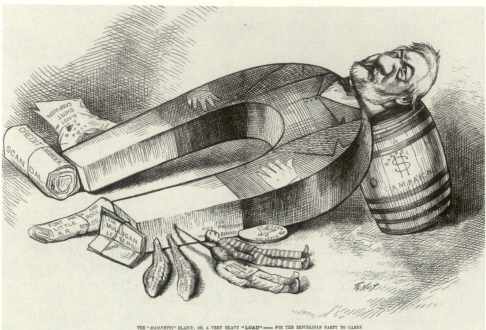

THE "*MAGNETIC*" BLAINE, OR, A VERY HEAVY "**LOAD**"—even FOR THE REPUBLICAN PARTY TO CARRY.

16-3. James G. Blaine (1830–93) was Maine's most controversial politician of the post–Civil War era, as this cartoon from *Harper's Weekly* (May 8, 1880) by Thomas Nast suggests. "The plumed knight" served as Speaker of the U.S. House of Representatives, as a U.S. Senator, twice as Secretary of State, and he was the G.O.P. presidential candidate in 1884. Private collection.

"The Plumed Knight," as Colonel Robert Ingersoll once called Blaine, was appointed to the United States Senate in 1876. A leader of the Republican "Half-Breed" faction, he worked on the Appropriations and Naval committees, battled back the tide of Greenbackism, and campaigned to stop the immigration of foreign workers into America. Blaine was appointed Secretary of State in 1881, but President James A. Garfield's assassination later that year cut short that appointment. In 1884 Blaine received the Republican nomination for president, and although heavily favored to win, he was defeated by Grover Cleveland. Now unemployed, he used his time to reflect upon his years in Washington and write a classic political memoir, *Twenty Years in Congress*.

Blaine's respite from office was short-lived. The election of Republican Benjamin Harrison as president in 1888 enabled Blaine to serve as Secretary of State again. In this last meaningful political accomplishment of his illustrious career, he helped to initiate what became America's Good Neighbor Policy toward the countries of Central and South America. He resigned his post as Secretary of State to return to private life in 1892; not long after, ill health overtook him.

A quintessential party man, James G. Blaine mirrored the values, or lack of values, of his party and his nation at a critical time in history. Reflecting the general disregard for conflict of interest in Gilded Age politics, Blaine carried with him the odium of a questionable stock manipulation deal involving the Little Rock and Fort Smith Railroad. Blaine repeatedly professed his innocence, but the insinuations dogged him through his unsuccessful bids for the presidency. For good or for ill, he left his mark on American politics, as speaker of the House from 1869 to 1875 and as a major contender for the presidency in 1876, 1880, and 1884. When he died on January 27, 1893, Maine lost an influential voice in Washington.

Thomas Brackett Reed stands as the preeminent exemplar of Maine's role in national politics during the Republican ascendancy. As speaker of the US House of Representatives, the Portlander amassed so much power he was often referred to as "Czar Reed." He ran for president in 1896 but was no match for the wily Mark Hanna, whose effort on behalf of William McKinley prevailed. A man of principle favoring female suffrage, civil service reform, and open immigration, Reed resigned his seat in Congress to protest the American drift toward empire as a result of the Spanish-American War.

Thomas Brackett Reed was born in Portland on October 18, 1839; he was educated there and at Bowdoin College. With the aid of a loan from William Pitt Fessenden during his senior year, Reed graduated in 1860 and served in the Navy during the Civil War. He returned to Portland after the war to prepare for the Bar, and in 1868, he was elected to the legislature. After a stint as state attorney general, Reed was elected to the US House of Representatives in 1877.

During his lengthy career in Congress, Reed fought diligently for orthodox Republican principles, but on occasion he did deviate. Like Blaine before him, he vigorously opposed the Greenback philosophy, but he also pressed harder and longer for women's rights than most members of his party. On the matter of suffrage, Reed wrote in a congressional report that, "No reason on earth can be given by those who claim suffrage as a right of manhood which does not make it a right of womanhood also." Reed also fought against the Chinese Exclusion Bill and supported Civil Service reform.

As speaker of the House between 1889 and 1891, Reed became one of the most powerful political figures in America. After the election of 1888, the Republicans controlled both houses of Congress, and as speaker Reed used his position to his party's advantage. For instance, Democrats sometimes attempted to block legislation by refusing to answer the roll call, thereby denying the

16-4. Thomas Bracket Reed (1839–1902), a Portland lawyer, served in the Maine legislature and was elected to Congress as a Republican in 1876. In 1889 Reed became Speaker of the House, one of the most powerful positions in the federal government; he served in Congress until his resignation in 1899. In this photo, taken about 1901, Reed is welcoming Theodore Roosevelt to his home in Portland. Collections of the Maine Historical Society, Portland.

House a quorum. Reed met this ploy head on; he leaned over the podium, identified the offender, and pronounced him present. For this, the speaker gained the nickname "Czar Reed."

When Democrat Grover Cleveland was reelected in 1892, Reed served briefly as minority leader, but he assumed the speakership again in 1896. At the conclusion of his second speakership, Reed retired to practice law in New York City. He returned to Maine to visit and, on occasion, to speak at Bowdoin College. In November 1902, it became evident that his huge body was wearing out after many years of abuse. Severe chest pains, kidney failure, and appendicitis finally struck him down on December 6, 1902. His remains were brought home to Portland to be buried in the same cemetery that held the body of William Pitt Fessenden.

The era of Republican ascendancy brought some of Maine's political leaders to the highest levels of national policymaking, and, at the state level, it offered up a band of seasoned politicians who in most cases rendered competent if not distinguished service. More important, perhaps, it provided stability to a state wracked by political turbulence in the years between statehood and the Civil War.

Reform Movements in the Era of Republican Ascendancy

Although a conservative state dominated by a conservative party, Maine was periodically swept by currents of reform. Such issues as economic development, tariff reform, currency adjustment, Civil War veteran benefits, and, of course, temperance attracted attention at various times during this era. The course of three of these reform movements—the abolition of capital punishment, temperance, and women's suffrage—reveals this reform aspect of the Republican ascendancy. Each, except possibly temperance, was handled by the Republicans in a manner apparently satisfactory to a majority of Maine people.

The movement to abolish capital punishment began in Philadelphia in the Revolutionary War era as an attempt to limit the number of capital crimes. Thomas Eddy's *Reflections Occasioned by a Public Execution at Boston* touched off the debate in Maine. Maine's Code of Statues for 1821 mandated the death penalty for the crimes of treason, murder, arson, rape, burglary, and robbery. In 1829, rape, burglary, and robbery were deleted from the list, and in 1837 the state provided that condemned prisoners were to be confined for a year and a day before execution, and that a warrant from the governor would be necessary to carry out the hanging.

From the very beginning there were those who found state-ordered executions repulsive and misguided. What galvanized their opinion to a great degree was the case of Joseph Sager, whose wife died suddenly in 1834 under suspicious circumstances. After an investigation, Sager was arrested, tried, convicted of murder, and sentenced to hang. He went to his death protesting his innocence on a bitter January day in 1835, before a crowd estimated at eight to twelve thousand persons. In a bizarre series of events, his body was then whisked away to Hallowell, where attempts were made to bring him to life "by means of galvanism and other fruitless experiments."

Adverse reaction to the Sager hanging influenced subsequent deliberations in the legislature. A small but growing minority argued largely along Biblical lines that capital punishment was not demanded by Scripture, and that government had no moral right to take life unless public safety required it. According to an 1836 legislative report, the Sager hanging neither reformed the guilty nor restored the injured party.

Although the abolitionists failed to achieve their goal in the 1830s, two sensational murder trials in the 1840s revived the question and drew it to a conclusion. The first involved Thomas Thorn, charged with murdering Elisha Wilson at Harpswell in a rivalry over Wilson's wife. The second involved Dr. Valorus P. Coolidge of Waterville for the poisoning of Edward Matthews, apparently over a debt owed to Matthews. Coolidge violently protested his innocence and was supported by several opponents of capital punishment, including the Reverend Sylvester Judd of Augusta, who had for years lobbied to abolish capital punishment. Both Coolidge and Thorn were sentenced to hang, but, as it turned out, neither sentence was completed. Coolidge died at his own hand, and Thorn remained at the state prison because no governor was willing to issue his death warrant. He was pardoned in 1872. The only other capital sentence carried out in Maine before the Civil War was by federal decree, and it involved two sailors convicted of mutiny and hanged in the Auburn jail yard in 1858. Thus, by the Civil War, the state of Maine had executed no one since 1837, even though the law requiring hanging had not been abolished.

It took a brutal and senseless murder to force a Maine governor to sign the warrant necessary to allow an execution. The victim was Richard Tinker, warden of the Maine State Prison at Thomaston, stabbed without apparent provocation by an inmate. The *Bangor Whig and Courier* reflected opinion around the state when it editorialized, "Our prisons are filled with knaves. Ordinary punishments have no effect on them." Governor Samuel Cony agreed: if imprisonment itself was the harshest penalty for murder, then prison officers like the hapless Richard Tinker had no protection in the law.

Between 1869 and 1875, three more official hangings took place. In the case of John True Gordon, who apparently hacked to death his brother, sister-in-law, and one of their children, the condemned was found lying motionless in his cell on the day of the execution; he had stabbed himself and was semi-conscious. Nevertheless, Gordon was taken to the gallows and hanged. A second incident, on Smutty Nose Island in the Isles of Shoals, involved Louis F. H. Wagner, a Prussian immigrant who was caught in the act of robbing a home. Wagner murdered two of the women who discovered him; the third escaped to tell the story. Wagner, executed alongside Gordon, went to the gallows claiming that he was innocent.

The hangings of Gordon and Wagner helped open the abolition debate once more. Quakers repeated longstanding arguments for abolition, and when the legislature assembled in 1876, a bill was introduced to abolish capital punishment, substituting hard labor for life. It passed both houses by comfortable margins. Farmers and manufacturers generally voted to abolish capital punishment; merchants and lawyers, to retain it. Of those who reported religious preferences in their biographies, Universalists and Liberals voted to abolish, and Congregationalists and Baptists voted to retain the death sentence.

For the next seven years Maine law prohibited the death penalty. During the seven years before 1876, there had been eighty-six homicides, and in the seven years following, forty-eight. Nonetheless, in 1882, a state prison warden complained that since abolition "life sentences are increasing yearly," while many legislators remained convinced that capital punishment should not have been abolished. In January 1883, "An Act to Restore the Death Penalty" was presented to the legislature and voted into law.

Murder with malice aforethought was once again punishable by hanging. Certain provisions suggest that legislators were more circumspect, however. Among other things, the delay between sentencing and execution was increased to as much as fifteen months; the governor was given power to pardon, reprieve, or commute the sentence; the indicted person was allowed an increased number of juror challenges; and the defendant was guaranteed a competent counsel. Still, the debate over capital punishment did not end with this restoration. Among others, ex-governor Anson P. Morrill and the Reverend George W. Quinby of the *Gospel Banner* continued to argue for abolition. Judge William Penn Whitehouse asserted that during the period in which there was no death penalty, there had not been a single acquittal in a murder indictment, while in a similar period under the death penalty, there had been eight. He insisted that the efficacy of punishment depended upon its certainty and celerity, not its severity.

Events in 1884 further eroded support for the death penalty. Daniel Wilkinson, who murdered a police officer while robbing a store in Bath, and two Italian laborers, Raffaele Capone and Carmen Santore, who murdered a fellow laborer, were sentenced to death. All three were hanged in 1885. Once again, the horrors of execution by hanging stirred feelings. As the 1887 legislative session opened, some members moved to postpone the matter to the next session. By a wide margin the House rejected postponement, and the Senate followed suit. "An Act to Abolish the Death Penalty" passed, 87–27, and once more hard labor replaced hanging for first-degree murder.

From the beginning of statehood, Maine people were reluctant to apply the death penalty. On codifying their reluctance into law, Maine became one of two states in New England and six across the country to abolish capital punishment in the nineteenth century. Given that most states had, and still have, capital punishment laws, Maine stands as a significant exception. And judging from the unsuccessful attempts to revive the death penalty in the 1970s, it appears that Maine will remain an abolition state.

The struggle for woman suffrage was another national issue Maine addressed during the Republican ascendancy. Despite the reality of widespread female wage labor, women in the nineteenth century were idealized as homemakers who looked after the needs of the family and provided moral training for the children. As guardians of society's more refined virtues, they were supposed to exhibit piety, purity, submission, and domesticity. Although many Maine women worked outside the home and some became notable political figures, these sanctions generally barred them from active participation in important arenas of political and economic life.

There were a few organized attempts to break the "bonds of true womanhood." John Neal, Portland writer and editor, spoke and wrote for women's rights, and as an old man in 1873, he and a small group of women and men organized the Maine Woman Suffrage Association (MWSA) in Augusta. For the first few years, ironically, the MWSA was led by men. Joshua Nye, Augusta lawyer and temperance advocate, was elected to the presidency of the organization, but under his direction the MWSA languished.

That the leaders of the MWSA were males reflected prevailing negative attitudes toward females in public life; wresting control from them required someone with considerable determination. Hannah J. Bailey was born on July 5, 1839, in Cornwall, New York. A Quaker, she married Moses Bailey, a Winthrop, Maine, oilcloth manufacturer. When her husband died in 1883, she dedicated herself and her financial resources to promoting peace, temperance, and woman suffrage. In 1891, she was elected president of the MWSA, a position she held until 1896.

Bailey's final address to the members of the MWSA very clearly illustrates what she wanted for American women. She opened her talk by observing that the time had come for women to lead a women's organization. She called for the right to vote, a demand that rested on basic human considerations. "It is humiliating to be disenfranchised or unenfranchised. When the government wished to punish Jefferson Davis, it considered that the worst punishment it could inflict upon him was to deprive him of his right to vote." She ended her remarks with these words:

> May the time come apace when women shall be no more weak politically, but when she will be elevated to the highest sphere of her own possibilities. Then she will elevate the unborn generations, both men and women, her own posterity to a place beside herself in the sphere of human heights.

Appeals to the legislature were unsuccessful. The MWSA requested the right to vote in school board elections, in town elections, in state elections, and in national elections—all to no avail. By the late 1890s, the MWSA was discouraged, its membership declining, and its future dim. Susan B. Anthony, who had come to Maine in 1857 to promote woman suffrage, returned in 1898 to Hampden to speak before a MWSA meeting on the same goal. She delivered her thoughts to just fifty-six members who had gathered for the MWSA annual convention.

The women persisted in persuading their male friends to introduce suffrage bills in the legislature. Most bills, however, did not progress beyond referral to committee. On occasion, committees added insult to the repeated recommendation, "ought not to pass," by indicating that the sponsors of the bill "had leave to withdraw" their request for passage.

However, through the years the Republican party had generally, although not wholeheartedly, supported the franchise for women, and by 1917, the MWSA goal appeared to be in sight. The legislature passed an act submitting the issue to a referendum, and Republican Governor Carl E. Milliken, a staunch temperance and women's suffrage supporter, gladly signed the enabling legislation. As the September 1917 referendum approached, MWSA members and their friends blanketed the state appealing for male support. Speakers came from around the nation to participate.

Unfortunately, their efforts were hampered by internal fighting. The most damaging dispute involved the followers of Katherine Reed Balentine, daughter of Thomas B. Reed and head of the MWSA, and Florence Brooks Whitehouse, leader of the more militant Congressional Union, which had picketed the White House and, many thought, harassed President Wilson unwisely in a time of national wartime crisis. Another divisive aspect of the Maine campaign was the ongoing rivalry between Katherine Reed Balentine's Portland organizers and the Bangor movement, headed by Deborah Knox Livingston. Tensions between the two fronts resulted in a lack of coordination.

The referendum arrived on September 10, and the results dashed the hopes of the suffragists. The vote stood 40,000 to 20,000 against them. Anti-suffrage leader Margaret Rollins Hale, pleased with the outcome, declared that the vote settled the question of female suffrage for good. Portland had turned the women down 4,581 to 1,792; Lewiston, 1,315 to 654, and Bangor, 1,875 to 502.

Events in 1919 belied Hale's pronouncement, however. Republican Senator Guy Gannett of Augusta introduced a bill in the legislature giving Maine women the right to vote in presidential elections. It passed and was signed by Governor Milliken. In Congress, the Susan B. Anthony Amendment giving women the right to vote by constitutional mandate was sent out to the states for ratification. When the amendment reached the Maine legislature in

November 1919, the miracle the women of Maine had been praying for occurred. The House ratified by a margin of 72–68, and the Senate was unanimous in support. By August 1920, enough states had ratified for passage, and American women had the vote.

In Maine the drama had one more act to play, according to a rather odd set of circumstances. Gannett's bill, passed and signed by the governor, was called into referendum by the anti-suffragists prior to passage of the Anthony amendment. When the amendment became binding, legislators suggested that the referendum be canceled. The Maine Court ruled that it had to take place, however, and in September 1920, men and women voted in a meaningless exercise to decide whether women should vote. Mainers gave the Nineteenth Amendment an 88,080 to 30,642 vote of confidence.

Allied with woman suffrage was the prohibition question. Republicans who supported prohibition also supported woman suffrage, on the assumption that women opposed alcohol to protect their families and, if given a chance to vote, would continue to support prohibition. Maine Democrats, who as a party opposed prohibition, saw this connection all too clearly, and joined with "wet" Republicans to exclude women from voting.

Neal Dow continued to fight for the Maine Law and in 1880 was nominated by the Prohibition party for president. Of more importance to Maine, however, was Dow's work in making prohibition a part of the state constitution. The legislature approved this action in February 1884, and the law took effect in January 1885. The Twenty-Sixth Amendment to the Maine Constitution declared that the manufacture and sale of intoxicating liquors, excluding cider, "are and shall be forever prohibited." The law made exemptions for liquors used for "medical and mechanical purposes and the arts." The legislature was to determine appropriate penalties.

After 1885, prohibitionists fought a long, hard battle to protect their victory. Neal Dow was growing too old to fight, and when he died in October 1897, his place was taken by the Maine Christian Civic League. For the next forty-nine years, the Democrats and their "wet" Republican allies struggled to remove the Twenty-Sixth Amendment from the Constitution. Lillian M. N. Stevens, leader of the Maine and later the national Woman's Christian Temperance Union, fought "resubmission" of the amendment to the voters. It took until December 16, 1933, to obtain approval from the legislature for another constitutional amendment—the Fifty-Fourth—to repeal the prohibition. This amendment read simply that "the Twenth-Sixth Amendment to the constitution is hereby repealed." The victory was proclaimed by Democratic Governor Louis J. Brann on October 1, 1934.

Repeal of the prohibition amendment, following on the defeat of national prohibition under the Roosevelt administration, brought an end to one of the most comprehensive pieces of moral reform legislation in Maine history. In the twentieth century, other forms of restrictive legislation were removed from the law books. In 1909, Maine became the first eastern state to pass the direct initiative and referendum. Maine extended the suffrage to Indians in 1954 and to paupers in 1965. The state passed basic civil rights legislation in 1963, and in 1988, voters approved an amendment to remove all sexist language from the constitution.

Since 1900, there have been several attempts to reinstate the death penalty, but none has succeeded. The first was in 1925, an initiative by Representative Ellsworth Piper of Jackman. In 1973 a bill to reestablish the death penalty was introduced at the request of students at Biddeford High School, who were studying the issue. Both attempts failed in committee. The most concerted attempt was made by Stanley Laffin, representative from Westbrook. In 1975, 1977, and 1979, Laffin introduced bills to reestablish the death penalty for various crimes. The Laffin bills coincided with two landmark Supreme Court decisions, *Furman v. Georgia* (1972) and *Gregg v. Georgia* (1976); the first found the measure unconstitutional; and the second allowed capital punishment to stand. Nevertheless, the Laffin bills went down to defeat in Maine. The battles for civil rights, temperance, and abolition of capital punishment have been long ones in Maine; the struggles are not yet over.

For Further Reading:

Sources about the Republican party in Maine from the 1850s to the 1930s are diverse, and little of a scholarly nature has been written about the entire period. There remains a rich lode for researchers working in newspapers and in the personal and political papers of various political leaders.

For the national party perspective, which has implications for Maine, see Leonard D. White, *The Republican Era* (New York, 1958). William E. Gienapp's *The Origins of the Republican Party, 1852–1856* (New York, 1987) offers the fullest and most comprehensive treatment of that subject in one volume. Also useful is Eric Foner, *Free Soil, Free Labor, Free Men* (New York, 1970) and George H. Meyer, *The Republican Party, 1854–1864* (New York, 1964). *Leslie's History of the Republican Party,* vol. 2 (New York, n.d.) is an indispensable reference work on nineteenth-century Republicans.

The best general discussion of Maine's Republican party in the nineteenth and early twentieth centuries is still found in *Maine: A History,* edited by Louis C. Hatch (New York, 1919). Useful for the origins of the party in Maine is Richard R. Wescott, *New Men, New Issues* (Portland, 1986). Also essential is H. Draper Hunt, *Hannibal Hamlin of Maine*

(Syracuse, N.Y., 1969) for this leading figure of the Maine Republican party. The best biography of Blaine is David S. Muzzey, *James G. Blaine* (New York, 1934). A new biography is badly needed for this central figure of Maine Republicanism. Also useful is *James Gillespie Blaine: A Documentary Study and Source Book*, edited by Norman E. Tutorow (New York, 1989), with its insights into the "Plumed Knight's" political career in the introductory essay. Gail Hamilton's *Biography of James G. Blaine* (Norwich, Conn., 1895) is useful because of her close family ties. (Hamilton wrote under a pseudonym. She was Mrs. Blaine's first cousin, known to her family as Mary Abigail Dodge.) Of less utility are other Blaine biographies, including Theron C. Crawford, *James G. Blaine* (New York, 1893) and Charles Edward Russell, *Blaine of Maine* (New York, 1931). In the same category for Hamlin is the biography by his son, Charles E. Hamlin, *The Life and Times of Hannibal Hamlin* (Cambridge, Mass., 1899) and for Fessenden, the biography by *his* son, Francis E. Fessenden, *The Life and Public Service of William Pitt Fessenden* (Boston, 1907). Democratic party leader William R. Pattangall's often hostile commentary regarding Republicans of this era is contained in his *Great Men of Maine* (reprint; Brewer, 1985). The best biography of Fessenden is Charles A. Jellison, *Fessenden of Maine* (Syracuse, N.Y., 1962).

Brian C. Lister's Ph.D. dissertation, "Alonzo Garcelon, 1813–1906: The Man and his Times" (University of Maine, 1975) provides significant insights into the political career of a prominent Maine Democrat who upset the Republican hold on the governorship in 1879. Charles Scontras has presented details of the issues, particularly those facing labor in Maine politics, in his "Decade of Organized Labor and Labor Politics in Maine, 1880–1890" (M.A. thesis, University of Maine, 1965) and his "Two Decades of Organized Labor and Labor Politics in Maine, 1880–1900" (Ph.D. dissertation, University of Maine, 1968). The post–Civil War career of Blaine has been examined in Hiram Otis Noyes's M.A. thesis, "James G. Blaine: Reconstruction Congressman" (University of Maine, 1970). Also important for the postwar period is George Thomas Barton's M.A. thesis, "Joshua L. Chamberlain: Governor of Maine, 1866–1871" (University of Maine, 1975). Thomas L. Gaffney's M.A. thesis, "A Study of Maine Elections, 1930–1936" (University of Maine, 1968) contains essential background on the history of the Republican party. His doctoral dissertation, "Maine's Mr. Smith: A Study of the Career of Francis O. J. Smith, Politician and Entrepreneur" (University of Maine, 1979) is significant for the perspective of a leading Democrat of the mid-nineteenth century. Other M.A. theses which contain useful information are: Elizabeth Ring, "A Study of the Progressive Movement of 1912 and the Third Party Movement of 1924 in the State of Maine" (University of Maine, 1926); Richard Pitt Erwin, "Maine and the Election of 1896" (University of Maine, 1949); Everett L. Meader, "The Greenback Party in Maine, 1876–1885" (University of Maine, 1950).

Edward Schriver has provided an extensive discussion of one of the leading issues of the late nineteenth century in "Reluctant Hangman: The State of Maine and Capital Punishment, 1820–1887," *New England Quarterly* 63 (June 1990). Finally, Robert M. York's observations on the Republican party in "The Maine Election of 1912," *Maine Political Yearbook, 1962*, explain some of the problems facing the party in the early years of the twentieth century.

17

Traditional Industries in the Age of Monopoly, 1865–1930

WAYNE M. O'LEARY,

LAWRENCE C. ALLIN, JAMES B. VICKERY, & RICHARD W. JUDD

The Civil War was a watershed in Maine's economy, just as it had been in Maine politics, at first simply because of the effects of wartime disruptions. But the changes in Maine also paralleled a fundamental transformation of the national economy after midcentury. Monopoly capitalism profoundly altered industries in Maine, as it did regional economies everywhere. These two fundamental turning points— war and economic consolidation—set the stage for our discussion of the crises in Maine's traditional industries: fishing, shipbuilding, agriculture, lumbering, granite, lime, and ice.

The second half of the century brought additional challenges from outside Maine: rising costs, new technologies, changing government policies, competition, and new consumer tastes. Again, Maine responded creatively to these external forces, finding new ways to market traditional skills and resources. Industries that succumbed to the pressures were replaced by new forms of enterprise, a topic to be discussed in the next chapter. Another familiar theme characterizes the history of these traditional industries: the presence of social antagonisms, this time between owners and workers. This subject, too, will be explored in greater detail in a subsequent chapter.

Crisis and Decline in the Deep-Sea-Fishing Industry
WAYNE M. O'LEARY

In the decades after the Civil War, Maine's traditional industries underwent fundamental changes, most of them triggered by larger economic trends in the American economy. Fishing, shipbuilding, lumbering, agriculture, granite quarrying, lime production, and ice harvesting each faced a grave crisis in the second half of the century. As far as possible, Maine producers adapted to the new realities of nationwide competition, corporate financial structures, new consumer tastes, and new technologies. Characteristic of these challenges from outside the state was the rise of monopoly in the resource industries, usually under the aegis of large outside corporations. In some cases, monopoly control meant that Maine's traditional industries gained access to the capital-intensive technology that kept them competitive in broader, nationalized markets. In other cases, it meant that these industries became increasingly rigid at a time when the state's economy needed maximum flexibility to adjust to new markets. Some industries faltered, and this narrowing economic base helps explain Maine's dramatic rural outmigration in the second half of the century. Most, however, survived in some form, perhaps finding smaller, more specialized niches in older markets. In either case, the Maine economy was vastly changed in the years following the Civil War.

Maine's traditional sea fisheries exemplify the dual effects of wartime disruptions and broader changes in the American economy. In 1861, Maine was the most important sea-fishing state in the Union. Five years later, its fisheries were in decline, and within a generation, they had become insignificant in national terms, accounting for just a fraction of American tonnage by 1890. The reasons for this sudden turn of events were many and complex, but the initial factor was the Civil War.

The war was a mixed influence. Under its stimulus, the demand for seafood products and the prices they commanded reached all-time highs. Unfortunately, the wartime costs imposed on the industry also rose, and eventually costs outpaced the returns realized by merchants and fishermen. The price of salt, cordage, sail canvas, anchors and chains, and almost every other item used in preparing vessels for the banks increased geometrically during the war, as did the foodstuffs stocked for fishing voyages. These inflated outfitting costs were matched by dramatic increases in marine insurance. Under the threat of Confederate commerce raiders, insurers more than doubled their rates during the war years.

Augmenting the negative impact of wartime inflation were new government policies. Between 1861 and 1864, tariffs on imported necessities used in the industry were increased by the protection-minded Republican party that took power at the onset of the war. Particularly damaging were the new salt duties imposed at the behest of domestic producers in 1861 and 1862. Rates on imported salt, relatively low under earlier tariffs, rose eightfold within a few months. Almost as harmful were tariff increases on a host of other imported items: hemp, iron, manila cordage, copper, and foodstuffs like coffee and molasses. As a result of this government-imposed inflation, the cost of building and equipping a cod-fishing schooner in eastern Maine doubled before the end of the war. Tariffs remained high for almost a generation, as did insurance rates, imposing onerous burdens on the fragile industry.

Most damaging of all, the federal fishing bounty, which might have eased the postwar situation, was repealed at the close of the war in 1866. The repeal was a product of three developments. First, the newly dominant Republican party espoused a philosophy of laissez-faire economics that rejected direct government subsidies. Second, wartime naval actions demonstrated the superiority of iron and steam over wood and sail and undermined the longstanding argument that the fisheries were an essential nursery for the training of naval seamen. Finally, Congress, absorbed in debates over transcontinental railroads and westward expansion, lost interest in preserving legislation that enhanced Atlantic maritime activities.

The repeal of the bounty was especially devastating to Maine's sea fisheries, based as they were on great numbers of marginal operators. Large fishing firms, like those dominating the Massachusetts industry, were less dependent on the subsidy, and as time passed they chaffed under its rules and regulations. To the small outport merchant or independent fisherman, however, the bounty was the key to survival. Its loss meant a restructuring of the industry in Maine, as vessel ownership and fishing operations were concentrated in fewer hands and at fewer places.

The war years thus completed the first stage in the decline of Maine's deep-sea fisheries. Overall, tonnage fell by about 50 percent, and the state's share nationwide dropped from close to half to about one-quarter, roughly the same proportion as in 1830. Ownership of that remaining tonnage also changed, as operations shifted from the eastern outports to larger mercantile centers in the western part of the state, and large fish dealers replaced individual boat operators as the controlling force in the industry. This diminished and consolidated fishery maintained its viability for another twenty years, but its character was fundamentally altered.

The postwar change from eastern to western dominance, from independent to mercantile ownership, and from decentralized to centralized operations was accelerated by two developments, one economic and one technological. The first was the nationwide financial panic of 1873 and the depression that followed. The onset of hard times drove many of the surviving small merchants and owner-fishermen out of business. Large merchant firms at places like Portland and Boothbay withstood the crisis and eventually profited from it by picking up the assets and trade lost by the faltering outports. Western Maine, home to just one-third of the state's fishing tonnage in 1865, accounted for two-thirds of the total by 1880, and Portland, acquiring 25 percent of Maine's fleet, became firmly established as the center of the state's fishing industry, with

Boothbay emerging as a secondary satellite. By the early 1880s, Portland's supply merchants monopolized Maine's outfitting business, and its fish buyers controlled the wholesale packing and shipping trade. The city's fishing fleet of approximately a hundred large vessels, owned by eleven large firms capitalized at an average of $100,000 each, dominated statewide fishing operations.

Portland's hegemony, purchased at the expense of smaller ports elsewhere in Maine, was only partly an outgrowth of the economic dislocations of the postwar years. It was also a result of the technological revolution that swept the fishing industry in the Civil War era. Until midcentury, both groundfish and mackerel were caught by the time-honored and straightforward hand-line method. Fishing was done from the decks of vessels, and no major expenses for gear were necessary. Beginning in the late 1850s and early 1860s, however, several costly innovations were introduced. In the cod fishery, dory hand-lining and trawl fishing with multi-hooked set lines began to replace traditional deck hand-lining. In the mackerel fishery, the purse-seine, essentially a huge net with a drawstring, began to supplant old-fashioned hooking or "jigging" by hand. By the 1870s, the new techniques had become nearly universal.

These novel methods enhanced efficiency, speeded the fishing process, and greatly increased catches, but they also brought adversity to the traditional coastal economy. The new technology required significant outlays of capital. Trawling and seining gear, as well as dories and seine boats, added hundreds, even thousands, of dollars to outfitting costs. It was an expense easily met by the heavily capitalized merchant firms, but not by Maine's smaller independent operators, who were gradually forced from the scene. Any who managed to remain were faced with a wholesale fish market dominated by large buyers able and willing to use price-fixing arrangements to limit competition and maximize profits. For most, it was an untenable situation.

Maine's small, independent fisheries entrepreneurs were not the only ones who suffered from the changed postwar realities. Crews working on the state's fishing vessels were victimized as well, first by the new technology adopted by the industry after 1860. Fishing was always a dangerous occupation. Throughout the first half of the nineteenth century, the loss of vessels in the fisheries was commonplace. The chance of being swept ashore or wrecked in a gale, being run down by a merchant ship in the busy sea lanes, striking an unmarked rock or shoal along a strange coast, or simply springing a leak and foundering at sea were among the risks facing vessels and their crews. Until the introduction of dory fishing, however, fishermen at least worked in comparative safety aboard their schooners. Dory fishing separated the men from their mother ships and left them susceptible to capsizing in their small boats during sudden storms or to being lost in the thick fogs that periodically enveloped the offshore banks.

17-1. Baiting hooks on a trawl line on a fishing sloop at Port Clyde in 1916. The line, with hundreds of hooks attached to it, was set out with anchors at each end; later it would be hauled in and the fish removed. Photograph by Sidney M. Chase, courtesy of the Maine Maritime Museum, Bath.

Isolated deaths from drowning, starvation, dehydration, and exposure rose markedly among vessel crews in the 1870s and 1880s, as dory fishing became commonplace in the offshore fleets.

Increased danger was accompanied by harder work. Trawling schooners did not rest on Sundays, as had been the tradition in the deck-fishing era. The greater labor necessitated by setting and tending trawls, which involved miles of rowing and hours of hauling heavy lines, increased the hardship. Crews worked around the clock to use up a supply of fresh bait before it spoiled and to process the larger catch now realized. In the mackerel fisheries, too, rigorous exertion and long hours became the new hallmarks of a formerly sportive activity. Seining crews went for days without sleep in order to exhaust the schools of fish they located, and handling cumbersome pursing gear entailed backbreaking labor unknown in the early years of the industry. New technology, as employed by the large merchant-operators, meant an increasingly hard life for fishermen, with more hazards, harsher work conditions, and reduced leisure.

The postwar era brought economic as well as physical hardship to the ordinary crew members in Maine's deep-water fleet. Repeal of the bounty law removed a source of money they desperately needed to pay off the outfitting debts they incurred each spring. The repeal also legalized, for the first time in the cod fisheries, monthly or seasonal wage payments. This development changed the entire nature of relations between owners and workers.

Historically, the cod fisheries had proceeded on the "share" or "lay" system. Owners and crews shared in the expense of outfitting the vessel and likewise shared the proceeds from the voyage. In the early years of the industry, vessels typically fished "at the quarters" or "at the fifths," meaning that the owner provided one-quarter or one-fifth of the outfit and took a similar portion of the returns; the crew provided the rest of the outfit and divided the balance of the returns according to each member's share of the catch. In later years, many ports favored the half-lay system, essentially an equal split of responsibilities and rewards between owners and crews. Whatever the precise nature of the arrangement, mutual investment and profit-sharing was the essential characteristic of the business, and that concept, mandated by federal law under the bounty, guaranteed at least a modicum of economic democracy in the industry. No vessel that paid its crew in wages could legally collect a government subsidy.

Repeal of the bounty, however, relieved owners of the necessity of treating their crews as co-investors in a cooperative venture. Crew members ceased being "sharesmen" and became wage earners, and low wages quickly became the rule throughout the cod fisheries. New technological developments provided the rationale for the change. Individual crew members could not easily provide their own fishing gear according to the traditional share-fishing compact when that gear included trawls and dories. The essential motivation, however, was that owners could greatly increase their percentage of the profits from any given voyage under the wage system. The crew's share remained set, while the owner's increased with the success of the enterprise.

For ordinary fishermen, elimination of the protections furnished by the bounty law brought home the stark reality of poverty and indebtedness. Real income for working crewmen, never great under the best of circumstances, declined considerably after 1865, even as mercantile profits grew. Perpetual debt to a company store owned by the fish or supply merchant became a way of life for many, and the debilitating credit system created a new, downtrodden class of fishermen. By 1880, a definite social division, not readily apparent a generation earlier, had emerged between those who fished and those who owned and serviced the vessels.

Hundreds of native fishermen abandoned the industry for more certain livelihoods elsewhere. For some, this meant safer work and slightly better pay in southern New England factories; others succumbed to the lure of the West. Still others migrated to Gloucester, Massachusetts, New England's premier fishing port, which provided a number of advantages not available in Maine. These included remunerative winter fishing and the chance for year-round employment, as well as better credit terms and immediate cash payments upon returning from sea, which freed crews from the infamous company store. For captains, Gloucester also offered the possibility of part ownership in a vessel, and for ordinary fishermen, it offered an elaborate system of social security that included survivors' benefits for families of those lost at sea.

As coastal Mainers deserted the sea fisheries, their places were taken by fishermen from the Maritime provinces, who were allowed to serve on American vessels without restriction following repeal of the bounty law. Canadians were drawn south for a variety of reasons: geographic proximity; lack of economic opportunity at home; the superior qualities of the American schooners; and the better food aboard Yankee vessels. After 1865 the number of Nova Scotians and other Maritimers serving in the Maine fishing fleet increased sharply. By 1880, when Canadian seasonal or permanent immigration reached its peak, close to one-fifth of Maine's vessel crew members were from the Maritime provinces. The availability of this imported workforce kept Maine's diminished deep-sea industry alive during the immediate postwar decades.

Until about 1885, the state's deep-sea fisheries, although altered considerably, remained a viable force in the US fishing industry as a whole. A second stage of economic decline, however, reduced them within a few years to statistical insignificance. This new development was precipitated by fundamental changes in markets and marketing, including the arrival of new competitors in the domestic and international marketplace and a revolutionary alteration in the nature of food products and food consumption patterns.

New domestic competition for the Maine sea fisheries, and the New England industry as a whole, came in the form of the rapidly expanding fisheries of the Gulf of Mexico, the South Atlantic Coast, the Great Lakes, and the Pacific Northwest. The first two of these largely eliminated Maine's traditional southern markets, already disrupted by the Civil War. Undeveloped in 1865, the South's Gulf and native inshore fisheries achieved local market dominance by 1880. Simultaneously, Great Lakes landings increased fivefold, edging New England products out of their traditional western and midwestern markets during the 1870s. A third fish-producing region, the Pacific Northwest, also entered the competition against New England in the 1870s and challenged eastern fish merchants in their own backyard. By 1885, Pacific salmon, both canned and whole, had become a common sight in the fish markets of New York, Boston, and even Maine.

More critical than interregional competition or the growth of the inshore fishery was a change in American eating habits that culminated in the period after 1880. Prosperity before the war was based on supplying consumers with salt fish, and until midcentury the state's industry was in tune with consumer preferences. But eating habits began to change under the influence of diet reformers, European cuisine, and growing urban affluence. Salted fish was increasingly stigmatized as a food of the poor, and a preference for beef and poultry spread gradually throughout American society. This revolution in American taste was reflected in the growth and development of the western meat-packing industry in the years following the Civil War. Facilitated by the building of the transcontinental railroads, the invention of the railroad refrigerator car, the consolidation of the midwestern stockyards, and the creation of national distribution warehouses, shipments of fresh processed beef from Chicago and other meat-packing centers flooded into eastern cities after 1880. During the last two decades of the century, such shipments increased by 500 percent. The competing New England fishing industry had nothing to compare with the beef packers' vast, highly organized processing and marketing juggernaut.

In addition to the shift from fish to beef, the late nineteenth century witnessed a growing preference for fresh over salted fish, encouraged in part by improvements in home refrigeration. Among the many reasons for the final decline of Maine's sea fisheries, the rise of fresh fish marketing stands out; it struck at the very core of the state's deep-sea industry.

It was clear by the 1880s that Maine could retain its share of the domestic market only by shifting to fresh products, but this was an adaptation that, by and large, coastal merchants were unable to make. One word—*geography*—explains that failure. Fresh fish was a highly perishable product, and proximity to large urban markets was critical. Isolated in a distant corner of the Northeast, Maine lacked that essential advantage. Refrigerated railroad cars permitted swift transport of iced products over long distances, but coastal Maine's rocky and irregular shoreline discouraged rail development. No tracks were built into the important fishing regions of eastern Maine until the end of the century, and those laid along the western coast largely bypassed the fishing ports, most of which were situated on long and inaccessible peninsulas.

Among Maine ports, only Portland, the state's rail center, developed a viable fresh fishery. Even Portland, however, was restricted by the direction of its railroads, most of them trending north and east, away from the major urban markets of the United States. Its limited fresh fishery, therefore, was based primarily on shipments to northern New England, upstate New York, and central Canada, all of them relatively stagnant markets. After 1890, the city slowly declined as a fresh fishing center.

It was Massachusetts, with its great marketing and rail center at Boston, that emerged as the leader in the American fresh-fishing industry. Boston's celebrated "T" Wharf, a massive commercial facility, was able to accommodate hundreds of vessels at one centralized location, and the city's numerous rail lines fanned out in a southerly and westerly direction toward the nation's population centers. Boston's own substantial fish landings were augmented by those from other nearby ports, each connected by a rail feeder line. By 1880, Massachusetts ports accounted for close to three-quarters of New England's total fresh fish landings, and Boston alone processed and shipped more than half of the region's production.

Isolated from the fresh-fish markets, Maine was forced to rely on its historic salt-fish trade with the West Indies, the one marketing region untouched by changes in consumer tastes and diet. Yet even there, the state faced new and formidable competition. Beginning in the 1850s, Nova Scotia merchants, who had traditionally sold their salt cod in the British-owned islands of the region, turned increasingly to markets in the Spanish West Indies, including Cuba and Puerto Rico, which New England fish exporters had long considered their own.

Atlantic Canada enjoyed several advantages in its competition with Maine. Its salt cod was cheaper than the American variety, and it was dried harder, proving less perishable in the tropical marketplace. Moreover, Nova Scotia ports were nearer to the major cod banks, permitting additional fishing voyages at reduced expense. In addition, building and outfitting Canadian vessels cost less, due to local softwood resources and lower Empire tariffs. By the 1870s and 1880s, Nova Scotians were entering the deep-sea fisheries with at least one-third less overhead than their American rivals. The savings thus realized went into the purchase of trawls and other highly competitive technology. Furthermore, Canadian fishermen benefited after 1882 from a federal fishing bounty law of their own that was roughly similar to the American legislation repealed over a decade earlier. Under its stimulus, the provincial cod-fishing fleets of the 1880s, particularly those of Nova Scotia, increased dramatically in size and quality, becoming an overwhelming numerical presence on the Grand and Western banks. They were operated, ironically, by many of the same crewmen who had formerly shipped aboard New England schooners.

By cutting off Maine's pool of imported labor and encouraging the growth of its chief rival, the Canadian bounty law critically undermined Maine's salt-cod fisheries and guaranteed their eventual collapse. The rise of the Canadian fisheries placed the state in a competitive vice, between two powerful and resourceful competitors—Massachusetts and the Maritime provinces, each possessing natural advantages grounded in geography and economics. Mainers could not compete with Massachusetts in the burgeoning fresh fisheries; nor could they prevail against Nova Scotia in the traditional dried and salt fisheries. It was an impossible situation, and one that portended the gradual disintegration of the state's deep-sea-fishing industry. By the end of the nineteenth century, that process was largely complete.

While Maine's position as a premier deep-sea-fishing state was being undermined by regional competitors, the state's shore fisheries—those carried on in coastal waters using small boats—experienced unprecedented growth in the postwar years. The statewide menhaden ("porgy"), lobster, and inshore herring fisheries drew many former vessel fishermen away from the cod and mackerel fleets, especially after 1880. Of these localized fisheries, lobstering was the most important and far-reaching in its impact, occupying over three thousand workers by the turn of the century. Stimulated by the growing tourist trade, it held out the promise of high monetary returns on minimal capital expenditures, and it permitted independent fishing operations to be carried on close to home in comparative safety. The appeal of the herring-weir fishery that supplied the growing sardine canning industry was much the same: low capital requirements; adequate returns; economic independence; and proximity to home and family. By the end of the century, these and other shore fisheries occupied 80 percent of Maine's total fishing population. While the coastal fishing economy experienced painful adjustments in the post–Civil War period, it survived in reduced and altered form, and, perhaps more important, continued to offer opportunities of a sort to the small, isolated farming-fishing villages that lined the ragged rock-bound coast.

Shipping and Shipbuilding in the Age of Steam and Steel
LAWRENCE C. ALLIN

Another aspect of Maine's traditional maritime industries was under pressure during these years. Maine's wooden sailing vessels, the core of the nation's merchant fleet in the pre–Civil War years, faced a challenge posed by the development of steam-powered iron and steel ships. Like the deep-sea fisheries, the shipbuilding industry succumbed to external competition and changing technologies, but it, too, left its legacy on the Maine coast.

Although their hallmark was the wooden sailing vessel, Maine shipbuilders were no strangers to steam. In 1814, less than a decade after Robert Fulton's successful experiment with steam navigation on the Hudson River, Jonathan Morgan built a wooden-hulled, steam-powered vessel at Alna, Maine. By mid-century little steamers were common on Maine's rivers and coastal waters. Beginning in 1875, for instance, Captain Samuel Henry Barbour of Brewer built a fleet of twenty-six small, wooden-hulled, steam-powered coal burners to carry freight and passengers—including tourists—between Brewer and Bar Harbor. Small steam vessels provided similar packet service for Maine islands elsewhere.

Although Americans assumed an early lead in ocean-going steam-powered vessels, it was Great Britain's iron and steel vessels that drove wooden sailing ships from the seas. British shipbuilders were experimenting with screw-propeller steam vessels by the 1840s, about the same time they began substituting iron for wood. The high tensile strength and malleability of iron, and later steel, made larger, safer, and dryer vessels possible. By 1854, Lloyd's Register was charging a higher rate on American wooden vessels than on British iron ships.

Maine's Down-Easters were in some senses a response to the competition from steam and steel. Maine shipbuilders designed the Down-Easter specifically for the Pacific grain trade, where long deep-water voyages in regions without developed coal deposits or depots made sailing ships more profitable. Indeed, as knowledge of ocean currents and prevailing winds in the southern Pacific improved, sailing vessels actually bettered their competitive position over steam in the 1860s.

Better steamship technology and refueling facilities in the Pacific, however, fated the Maine industry. The last hurrah for Maine's Down-Easters, from a business standpoint, was Arthur Sewall's "Big Four": the second *Rappahannock*, the *Shenandoah*, the *Susquehannah*, and the *Roanoke*. Launched in the early 1890s, these massive vessels were Sewall's attempt to prove that America's wooden sailing vessels could compete with Britain's iron, steel, and steam. Sewell's great square-rigged ships proved uncompetitive, but the effort was a grand one: Maine's Down-Easters generally—their size, efficiency, and low cost—had extended the age of the square-rigger in the face of steam and steel impressively. The last Down-Easter, and the last wooden square-rigger built in the United States, went into the Kennebec from the shipyard of Charles Minot in Phippsburg on July 13, 1893. This was the *Aryan*, built not far from where the first Maine sailing vessel, the "pretty pinnace" *Virginia*, was launched in 1607.

A second area where Maine's wooden ships remained competitive was the coasting trade, since federal laws passed in 1817 banned foreign vessels from the trade between American ports. Here, of course, sailing vessels faced pressures from a growing rail network after the Civil War, but they still remained competitive in hauling coal from the Chesapeake to New England and other coastal regions.

The coal trade challenged the ingenuity of downeast shipbuilders. A high bulk–low value cargo, coal had to be transported in the most economical fashion: first, by small, two- or three-masted schooners, and then, as the coal trade expanded, in schooners of four, five, and even six masts. The demand for these larger schooners had two effects on shipbuilding in the state. First, because of their size, they needed steeper, longer ways for launching and deeper water to receive them on launching. This requirement put many yards out of business. Second, their size affected the way the vessels were built. Many had centerboard trunks and centerboards built into them. The centerboard served as a keel, which could be lowered from the trunk to give a vessel more purchase and stability in deep water. Retracting the centerboard gave the schooners access to shoal waters or upriver ports, an important advantage in the coasting trade. The first four-masted schooner built for the coal trade, the *William L. White*, came out of the Goss, Sawyer, and Packard yard in Bath in 1880. She was a centerboard schooner measuring 996 tons.

Although Bath was the center of production for the big schooners, other yards built some notable examples. Leverett Storer of Waldoboro launched the first five-masted schooner, the *Governor Ames*, in 1888. In Camden, Holly Bean built the first six-masted schooner, the *George W. Wells*. When launched in 1900, Bean's schooner rivaled the largest square-rigged ships in size. Eleven six-masted schooners were built in the United States, nine in Maine and seven of them in Bath by the Percy and Small yard.

The 3,730-ton *Wyoming*, built in 1909, was 328 feet in length—the largest wooden American sailing craft operated in commercial service. This record-setting vessel typified Maine shipbuilding ingenuity. For added strength, Percy and Small used several hundred tons of metal in her standing rigging and for bolts and strapping. However, like so many of her antecedents, the *Wyoming* met a tragic end. The details of her loss are unknown, but it is believed she foundered and broke up on the south shore of Cape Cod during a severe storm in 1924.

Although the era of the wooden ship ended at the turn of the century, Arthur Sewall was determined that American commercial sailing vessels could prevail. After preliminary experimentation, he ordered steel punching, bending, edging, and other machinery to convert his family shipyard for building steel ships. The Sewall firm built nine steel square-riggers, a steel five-masted schooner, and a steel tank barge. Ultimately, however, the steel sailing ships proved unprofitable and the Sewalls quit building vessels.

Maine's shipbuilding industry survived the eclipse of wood and sail, but it was altered fundamentally and became concentrated in fewer locations, most notably in Bath. Thomas Worcester Hyde, one of Arthur Sewall's Bath neighbors, had acquired metalworking experience building steam-powered windlasses for sailing vessels. Hyde convinced Sewall and others to join him in the establishment of the Bath Iron Works (BIW) in 1884. Ironically, the firm's first project, a steam-powered vessel, had a wooden hull. Like Sewell's steel sailing ships, Hyde's wooden steamship was unsuccessful. In 1890, however, BIW received a contract to built two gunboats for the United States Navy. The USS *Castine* and the USS *Machias* were the first all-steel vessels of any type to be built in the state. As BIW gained experience and the American steel navy grew, Hyde received other warship contracts, many of them for torpedo boats. In 1901, his firm constructed the only battleship ever built in Maine, the USS *Georgia*.

During World War I, BIW constructed destroyers for the Navy while the Sewalls leased their shipyard to the Texaco Company to construct tankers. Elsewhere, Maine carpenters were asked to build more four-masted schooners to help carry war supplies through submarine-infested waters. Boothbay and Camden led in this effort, and Stockton Springs helped, as did other towns along the Penobscot. The *Horace E. Monroe*, built under wartime conditions, was the largest and last wooden vessel constructed on the Penobscot. This flurry of activity proved to be a brief epilogue to the story of Maine's wooden sailing ships, however. After the war, these smaller yards quickly passed into oblivion. The big schooners continued to ply the waters of the New England coast into the 1930s, but one by one they were towed into back bays and abandoned or burned for their metal, each a victim of sharpening competition from steamships, rising maintenance costs, and a dwindling supply of youths willing to dedicate their lives to the backbreaking toil of a voyage before the mast.

The tradition of building with wood was continued, however, in numerous small yards up and down the coast that produced small vessels for the shore fisheries. Builders in Friendship, Maine, for instance, created the versatile Friendship sloop for local use. It became a mainstay of the growing lobster trade, much admired for its fine sailing qualities. The internal combustion marine engine, developed around the turn of the century, nicely complemented this tradition of small-craft building, and it helped stabilize Maine shipbuilding in a variety of ways. For instance, scallop draggers had resisted using steam engines because they were too heavy to carry, pounded their wooden hulls unmercifully, and wore out the bracing. For the same reason they resisted steam-powered winches to raise and lower their drags. When the draggers were

forced into deeper water to locate scallops, they turned to gasoline engines, realizing two advantages: the powerful engines pulled their drags in deeper water
and helped lift the bulging nets aboard their vessels. Lobstermen and other
fishermen also saw the advantages of gasoline or diesel, and thousands of powered fishing boats were constructed in Maine. "Rum runners," attracted by
Maine's proximity to Canada and its innumerable hidden coves and inlets, also
used the new engines to great advantage during Prohibition. While the great
sailing ships were a thing of the past by the 1920s, Maine wooden vessels, and
the steel ships built in the yards of Bath, continued to serve useful purposes in
America's maritime trades.

Agricultural Crisis and Adaptation, 1861–1900
JAMES B. VICKERY & RICHARD W. JUDD

Although changes in Maine agriculture were less dramatic than those in deep-
sea fishing and shipbuilding, this industry, too, experienced a period of crisis
and adaptation. Between 1860 and 1880, Maine's farms grew in number from
55,698 to 64,309, a greater increase than in any previous period. After 1880, however, both the number of farms and the amount of acreage under cultivation
declined. Farmers responded by experimenting with crops better suited to postwar market conditions, and they achieved some notable successes. Nevertheless,
the nature of the industry changed considerably during these years.

Maine agriculture faced a number of difficulties in the final decades of the
century. On one hand, many of the rural industries that provided farmers with
supplemental incomes or markets—small tanneries and lumber mills, shipyards, fisheries, and foundries—fell on hard times. More important, farmers
began to feel the impact of interregional competition as railroads created national produce markets. Even though Maine was closer to eastern metropolitan
markets, western producers enjoyed several decisive advantages: their soils were
richer, the growing season longer, the lands flatter, and the farms larger. Federal
grants and subsidies, such as the 1862 Homestead Act, the transcontinental railroad land grants and subsidies, and later the federal irrigation projects, also
helped to reduce the relative costs of farming in the West.

Many Maine farms were poorly suited to meet this competition. "Salt-water"
farms, for instance, provided a good mix of supplemental incomes for farmers,
like coasting, fishing, and lumbering, but soils along the coast were sandy, and
the damp climate limited yields. Although coastal farms produced good hay
and pasture, they were in no position to compete against western produce in
eastern markets, especially after coastwise commerce gave way to interior rail
service. Upland farms faced similar constraints: hill-top or ridgetop locations

were suitable for Maine's first farmers, because higher ground provided dryer and sunnier locations and the predominant hardwood forest was easier to clear. Commercial cropping, however, quickly eroded these thin soils, and in the hilly upland terrain, transportation to market was difficult and costly—a factor not terribly important until farmers became more dependent on commercial crops. "Hill country" and "salt water" farms, however suitable during frontier days, were less than ideal in the commercial age, especially those located in eastern-most Washington County.

As Maine farmers elsewhere turned to specialized crop production, they too hastened the exhaustion of already thin soils. Hay, the state's most valuable export, is illustrative. Hay became important in Maine as southern New England's more expensive farmland was adapted to higher-yield crops. Coastal Maine farms, in particular, shipped thousands of tons of hay south yearly. Some farms paid for themselves several times over by this brisk trade, but specialization meant fewer livestock and consequently less manure. Young families bought farms on credit and met their annual payments, interest, and taxes by entering into year-long contracts with merchants to deliver specified amounts of hay, potatoes, barley, oats, or straw each year until the debts were paid. Locked into commercial production by rising debts, they continued to skim the soil, while declining yields merely drove them deeper into debt. In Waldo County, according to an 1873 report, the "once teeming fields that bore bounteous harvests, now show a deplorable state of deterioration."

For these reasons and others, many rural young people left Maine and moved west after the Civil War. Others, weary of farm drudgery, found better opportunities in the shoe or textile factories of Waterville, Lewiston, Auburn, or Biddeford. Opportunities declined and entrenched farmers intermarried, crystalizing local elite structures that had been forming since the beginning of the century. Wealthier citizens often acquired the abandoned farms.

The loss of prospective farmers exacerbated the situation. Mixed-crop farming was an ideal strategy for family-based enterprises where unpaid labor was available from family members. With large families, farmers could afford to produce a full range of marginally profitable crops. But family size declined in the second half of the century, and when family members left the farm and the rural population thinned, labor costs rose appreciably. To survive, some farmers narrowed their cultivation to the single most profitable crop they could produce. Increasingly dependent upon fluctuating markets, high-priced machinery, costly fertilizers, and hired labor, farmers confronted a world in which success and failure were no longer matters one family or one community could control.

Thus, the steady increase in the number of farms and the acreage under cultivation came to a halt in Maine in the 1880s. As farms were abandoned, forests edged back over the cleared fields and pastures, first in the "hill country" and along the eastern coast and then in the more productive valleys. In part, the reduction in acreage and farms simply reflected a change in the structure of farming in Maine: the remaining farms were consolidated into larger units, and production and value of farm produce, as opposed to farm acreage or number of farms, continued to rise throughout the first two decades of the twentieth century. The total value of Maine farm products in 1919, corrected for inflation, stood three times as high as the 1879 value, and except for oats and corn, acreage in Maine's major crops actually increased. Nevertheless, the steady decline in population in rural villages and the conspicuous increase in abandoned farms, houses, and fields was a matter of great concern throughout the agricultural community.

The rise in value of farm goods indicated that Maine farmers were adapting as well as possible to the new realities of nationwide agricultural competition. In part, this was possible because farmers developed new institutions to aid their search for new markets. Among the most important was the Maine State College of Agriculture and the Mechanical Arts, founded in 1868 and located in Orono. The college was funded primarily through the federal Morrill Land Grant College Act of 1862, which gave grants of land from the national domain to states and territories to found colleges for the benefit of agriculture and the mechanical arts. Prompted by Ezekiel Holmes and other agricultural reformers, the legislature created the college in 1865, and after considerable debate over the location, the trustees settled on a 370-acre farm on the banks of the Stillwater River near Orono village. On September 21, 1868, the college opened its doors to its first class of twelve students. Dedicated to disseminating information about new farming techniques, the college gradually broke down rural prejudice against "book farming," and the institution assumed a leading role in promoting progressive farming in the state.

One of the college's most ardent supporters was the Maine State Grange, or Patrons of Husbandry. As a national movement, the Grange began in the late 1860s; Maine's first "subordinate Grange" was formed in Hampden in 1873. Like the local and county farmers' clubs formed earlier in the century, the Grange was dedicated to disseminating modern methods for farm improvement through lectures, discussions, and publications. It also served a social function; Grange halls, built in almost every agricultural community, were gathering places and community centers that brought a surprising variety of local and outside talent, entertainment, and culture to the isolated towns.

With the help of institutions like the Grange and the Maine State College, farmers learned to adapt to the new realities of interregional competition. With the Western Plains producing quantities of meat that were shipped east from

17-2. The development of canning was pioneered in Maine in the mid-nineteenth century. One of the most popular vegetables canned was sweet corn. Local canneries, like this one in Bridgton, packed corn grown in the immediate area, providing a market for farmers and seasonal employment for residents of all ages. Courtesy of the Maine Historic Preservation Commission, Augusta.

the Chicago stockyards, local farmers reduced beef and increased dairy herds. Maine remained competitive in producing fresh products like milk, cheese, or butter, which could not be hauled great distances. The 1870s brought a proliferation of cheese factories, some of them manufacturing up to sixty tons of cheese a year. Two decades later farmers discovered a market for cream and milk in summer resorts and, with refrigerated railroad transportation, found ready buyers in Massachusetts. The Turner Center Dairying Association, founded in 1882 and relocated in Auburn in 1898, was by 1900 one of the three largest dairy manufacturers in the United States. Although regional competition eventually restricted local dairy production, the industry remained an important staple for Maine agriculture.

Market gardening was another instance where the emphasis on fresh delivery insulated Maine farmers from western competition. Large cities in Maine and Massachusetts offered a booming market for a diversified array of garden crops. After 1870, agricultural reformers heartily endorsed the appearance of huge textile and paper mills, recognizing the potential for agricultural markets.

Maine farmers also responded to western competition by planting crops especially suited to Maine's soil or climate, reaching markets in which Maine held natural advantages. Orchard production—apples and pears principally— became profitable, partly because Maine's cool climate produced popular varieties. As early as 1850, even small towns in Kennebec, Franklin, and Waldo counties were producing up to ten thousand bushels yearly for eating, drying, and cider. In the 1870s, encouraged by the Maine Pomological Society, farmers experimented with new varieties of apples and shipped huge quantities to England, where Maine apples were highly regarded. Wild blueberries, another Maine "specialty," became an important export crop in the late 1860s, when canneries were established in the eastern towns of Cherryfield, Harrington, and Columbia Falls. The great "barrens" in Washington County, regions of acidic, thin soils where few trees grew, produced bounteous crops of blueberries.

Sweet corn was another adaptation especially suited to Maine's even and abundant summer rainfall. In 1862, the Portland Packing Company diversified from seafood into corn-canning and began building plants throughout southwestern Maine. In the 1870s, other large canning companies appeared, including Fernald and Keene, and Burnham and Morrill, bringing Maine a nationwide reputation for the quality of its sweet corn. For several decades these "corn factories" were economic mainstays for rural towns. In the fall, farmers carried the corn in wagons to the factory to be husked, typically by local women and children. Later, packers extended the busy season by canning apples, string beans, peas, beans, and pumpkins, then shifting operations to the coast for seafood.

The greatest gains for commercial farming in Maine came with the opening of the eastern sections of Aroostook County to agriculture. As early as the 1780s, the St. John River valley—the Madawaska region—had been settled by French-speaking farmers from the Maritime provinces and Quebec, but commercial production in this remote and landlocked section of Maine depended on improvements in transportation. In 1832, in response to the northeastern boundary controversy, Maine opened the "Military Road" between the Penobscot River and Houlton, the first such road linking central Maine and the Aroostook frontier. At the conclusion of the controversy in 1842, Yankee farmers moved north in large numbers, settling to the south of the Acadian community. Although Houlton and points south thrived on trade

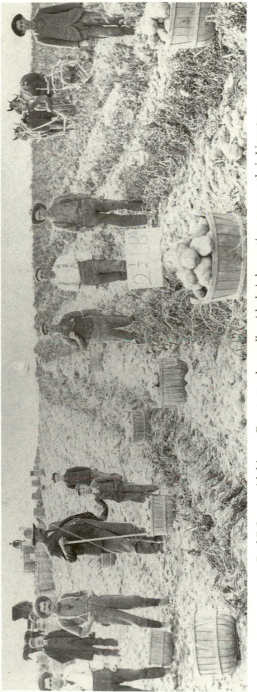

17-3. Fred F. Spear, with his son Forest, stand proudly with their harvesting crew on their Limestone farm, around 1900. When the opening of Aroostook County late in the nineteenth century, potatoes became an important part of Maine's agricultural economy. Courtesy of Jane Russell Stanford.

with Bangor, northern Aroostook County developed more slowly. Presque Isle in 1860 contained only 732 inhabitants.

While the eastern Aroostook townships were cleared for farming, western Aroostook saw massive lumbering operations managed from Houlton, Caribou, Fort Kent, and the more isolated mill towns of Eagle Lake, Portage, and Ashland. Lumber camps offered an essential market for pioneer farmers' crops, since regional isolation left these settlers few marketing alternatives. The remarkably fertile "Caribou loam" lying between Mars Hill and the Aroostook River valley, coupled with the energies of the region's Acadian, Irish, Canadian, and Yankee farmers, soon outproduced these limited lumber-camp markets, however. When railroads reached over the New Brunswick border to tap the farming districts of the eastern county in the 1870s, agriculture expanded at a spectacular rate. By 1880, there were seventeen starch factories located at Presque Isle or adjacent towns, taking the cull from Aroostook's table-grade potatoes.

It soon became apparent that "the County" offered the best farming facilities in the Northeast for potato production. This vast acreage became known as the "Garden of Maine," specializing in the commercial production of potatoes. With the completion of the Bangor and Aroostook Railroad in 1894, the county attained national importance for its potato crop. During the next five decades Aroostook reigned as a veritable potato empire, with some 42,000 acres under cultivation in 1900.

Maine farming, like fishing and shipbuilding, faced a crisis in the post–Civil War years, as western competition, new technology, and outmigration challenged this traditional mainstay of the state's economy. Farmers developed new institutions to meet the challenge and experimented with new crops to find permanent niches in the altered markets for agricultural produce. Like fishing and shipbuilding, the industry survived and in places thrived, but it too was an industry structured much differently than it had been before the war.

The Lumber Industry in an Age of Change
RICHARD W. JUDD

Maine's lumber industry also faced a number of challenges in the second half of the century, the most serious being interregional competition and rising stumpage prices and operating costs. These pressures drove Maine producers to seek new markets. The industry survived largely by diversifying into a broad array of alternate wood products, as traditional markets for dimension lumber (lumber used for construction) were captured by western producers.

Maine loggers responded to growing competition from the Great Lakes states and the South by increasing the size and efficiency of their mills and woods operations, particularly after the depression of 1873. While the number of mills in Maine declined after 1873, their average capitalization and work force increased significantly. The F. W. Ayer mill, built in the late 1870s, occupied a mile of waterfront along the south Brewer shore of the Penobscot. Farther north, the St. John Lumber Company mill, completed in 1903 near Van Buren, gathered up nearly half the entire production of logs from the Allagash and St. John rivers, producing 250,000 board feet of lumber daily along with 350,000 shingles. The Ashland Manufacturing Company at Sheridan undertook a similar grand-scale reorganization of the Aroostook River drainage. These mills, some of the largest in the nation at the time, were fully automated and equipped with multiple high-speed band saws. No longer an aggregation of independent machines, the mills blended the various stages of lumber manufacturing into a single, continuous-flow process.

At the same time the industry continued to migrate northward. Between 1884 and 1904, lumber shipments from Bangor averaged around 154 million board feet annually; this dropped to less than 114 million between 1904 and 1910, and to 80 million between 1910 and 1915. In the same period, lumber production in Aroostook County grew spectacularly. The St. John, Allagash, and Aroostook rivers, first logged in the late 1840s, still contained tracts of old-growth pine and spruce when the Bangor and Aroostook Railroad opened the territory to large-scale operations in 1893. In the two decades between 1903 and 1923, new mills at Van Buren, Portage, Eagle Lake, and Sheridan rapidly transformed Maine's last stands of old-growth timber into dimension lumber.

This northward shift in the focus of the industry reflected the difficulties of procuring stocks of old-growth spruce suitable for dimension lumber south of the St. John. Indeed, as pulpwood cutting increased, stumpage and timberland prices were driven further upward. As timber near the drivable streams thinned under more intensive cutting, logging operations moved deeper into the woods. Expenses soared when hauling roads extended several miles back from the streams, especially when logs could no longer be hauled directly downslope to a landing.

Another indication of the rising price of old-growth timber was the appearance of logging operations in upper watersheds once considered inaccessible to river driving. Gulf Hagas, a precipitous gorge on the upper West Branch of the Pleasant River, was tamed for river driving in 1879 with an expensive series of dams and channel clearings. Similar efforts permitted logging on Wassataquoik Stream north of Mt. Katahdin in 1881–84 and on the upper St. John River after the turn of the century. Log jams of epic proportions on these twisting channels brought financial disaster for smaller operators.

Conflicts over river use added to the expense and precariousness of logging operations at the turn of the century. Disputes arose partly because of the changing nature of lumber transportation. Earlier sawmills had crowded close to tidewater, where sawn lumber could be conveniently loaded onto ships. Once rails replaced ships as the forest industry's primary transportation system, new sawmills and paper mills were built upriver near the timber supplies, thereby shortening the costly river drives. Delays caused by sorting logs for the upriver mills sparked legal, and sometimes physical, battles between operatives for the older tidewater mills and those in the new upriver facilities.

The most spectacular altercation involved upriver mills on the St. John River in Maine and those at tidewater in the New Brunswick city of Saint John. In this case, the situation was complicated by the industry's international complexion and by the 1842 Webster-Ashburton Treaty, which stipulated that the St. John was to remain free and open for navigation between Maine and New Brunswick. Sorting logs for the new upriver mills at Van Buren delayed the spring drive in 1904 and in every subsequent year through 1909. During years when the freshet subsided before the drive was passed through Van Buren's sorting gaps, the logs remained upriver. In 1905, this situation resulted in a near-war between river drivers and Van Buren mill workers.

To sort out this international confrontation, the two federal governments inaugurated an International St. John River Commission, which met sporadically between 1909 and 1916. After recording some four thousand pages of testimony, the commission concluded that mill development and log driving were, indeed, compatible on the St. John, if coupled with an ambitious program of water conservation and a framework for international arbitration.

Other conflicts involved pulp and paper producers, particularly their requirements for hydroelectric power storage. In the 1890s, for example, dams built to furnish power for paper mills brought an end to log driving on the lower Androscoggin, Kennebec, and Presumpscot rivers. On the Penobscot River, difficulties between the Great Northern Paper Company and Bangor-area sawmill owners over flowage on the West Branch yielded a spectacular legal battle that reached the halls of the state legislature in 1901. The huge Millinocket mill delayed the West Branch drive by drawing off water for hydropower generation while the drive was in the upper lakes, then shutting down the water after the drive had passed Millinocket. Seeking firmer control of the West Branch, the paper company placed a bill before the 1901 legislature to replace the old Penobscot Log Driving Company with a new organization more responsive to its own needs. The legislative fight resulted in a draw. Despite favorable rulings in the courts, the downriver loggers gradually yielded control of the West Branch; the last long-log drive came down the Penobscot in 1928, and thereafter the river was used for pulpwood driving until 1958.

17-4. In the spring of 1900 and 1901 George Hawley Hallowell (1871–1926) joined Luther R. Rogers of Patten in his logging operations in the Katahdin region. His wonderful *Wissataquoik River Drive* shows loggers at work on what was probably the most difficult stream for long log driving in Maine. George Hawley Hallowell, *Wissataquoik River Drive*, oil on canvas, ca. 1920. In the collection of the Corcoran Gallery of Art, Washington, D. C. Museum purchase, William A. Clark Fund.

Skyrocketing river-driving costs, increasingly unpredictable flowage on cut-over watersheds, and the economic advantages of producing lumber or pulp on the upper rivers fated the outcome of each of these controversies. Generally, the balance of forces in the disputes was dictated by trends well beyond the courts and legislative halls of Maine.

In addition to their difficulties on the rivers, lumber operators faced a growing labor shortage during the second half of the century. At a time when pulp and paper mills were increasing the demand for labor, many woods workers were leaving Maine for better wages in the western lumber districts.

Populations in farm towns, a traditional source of labor, were stabilizing or declining. Labor recruiters advertised for workers throughout the region, bringing loggers from New Brunswick, Nova Scotia, Prince Edward Island, Quebec, and even northern and central Europe. Migrant work crews, especially those from the Maritimes and Quebec, excited bitter rivalries in the camps at times; locals complained that Canadians worked for less money and tolerated more primitive conditions. In general, though, labor scarcity boosted wages. This, along with rising costs for provisions, forced many marginal operators out of business.

New substitutes for wood products added further stresses on the industry. Items such as kraft paper, barbed-wire fencing, compounds based on petroleum or other chemicals, clay-based materials, metal, concrete, and brick drove per-capita lumber consumption in the United States down from 516 board feet in 1906 to 375 feet in 1915. In the East, with its older, more established cities, this figure dropped even lower. Maine's lumber production peaked in 1909 and again in 1915 at around 1.1 billion board feet, and thereafter declined steadily to 200 million board feet in 1932.

As markets for lumber declined and stocks of high-grade pine and spruce grew more scarce, the big mills, with high capital costs and equipment geared to dimension-lumber production, were increasingly at a disadvantage. The high-capacity mills on the Penobscot closed shortly after the turn of the century, and the northern Maine mills at Van Buren, Portage, Sheridan, and Eagle Lake shut down during the sharp construction slump after World War I.

By the late 1920s, smaller mills, principally in Aroostook, Cumberland, Oxford, Penobscot, and York counties, once again dominated the lumbering scene. These flexible, low-overhead operations served local markets, found small niches in the construction lumber business, or turned out "short-lumber" products like box boards, tool handles, sashes and frames, or novelties. New hardwood mills manufactured flooring, veneer, bobbins and spools, spokes and hubs, shoe pegs, clothespins, tool handles, or toothpicks. These smaller mills, better adapted to shifting markets and changing tree species, persisted. After World War II, trucks and better highways encouraged larger, centrally located mills once again, but these, by western standards, were still relatively modest in scale.

The more fundamental change in the forest industries in Maine came with the growth of the pulp and paper mills in the 1880–1920 period. Drawing huge reserves of capital from outside Maine, paper manufacturers built mills, then integrated backward—that is, bought up pulp mills, water rights, and timberlands. By the 1920s, huge companies like Great Northern Paper Company and International Paper Company dominated Maine's lumber districts. Their presence reinvigorated the state's forest industries at a critical point in time, but the industry was vastly different from the operations of the pre–Civil War years.

Granite, Lime, and Ice in the Age of Monopoly
LAWRENCE C. ALLIN & RICHARD W. JUDD

Most of the trends identified in the lumber industry apply to Maine's other resource-based industries as well. While lumbering operations in Maine were influenced by the development of giant pulp and paper corporations, similar changes in business organization affected the granite, lime, and ice industries.

Maine's granite quarries were first opened by local companies using local capital. These were usually small firms with fewer than twenty-five employees. The business was fiercely competitive, as was the construction industry generally, and wages and profits fluctuated widely. In the second half of the century, the industry was stabilized through two developments. During the 1870s, the federal government issued lucrative contracts for public buildings, known as "fifteen percent contracts" because they guaranteed that amount of profit to the builders and, by extension, to the suppliers. Several large quarry owners gained a monopoly over these contracts and profited heavily.

The second development was the rise of a new breed of quarry owners. Spurred by the rising expense of quarry machinery, these aggressive business leaders began consolidating ownerships in the 1860s. Joseph R. Bodwell, Maine's most prominent example, began his empire on Vinalhaven in 1852, extended it to Spruce Head, St. George, Hallowell, and Jonesborough in the next decade, and created the Bodwell Granite Company in 1871. In 1887, he became governor of Maine. He died in office that year, but as late as 1891, the Bodwell Granite Company was still reputed to be the largest granite company in the United States.

As the industry was monopolized, relations between workers and managers deteriorated. Many complained that wages were too low to provide a decent living, and in hard times companies refused credit at their stores. Granite cutters on Vinalhaven charged in 1887 that they were being "crushed down" by Bodwell's "soul-destroying corporation."

As more companies were swallowed up by the granite "ring," workers sought alternatives to the terms it offered. In 1877, they began organizing affiliates of the Granite Cutters' Union and vowed to establish uniform wage rates and better working conditions. Quarry owners, represented by the powerful Granite Manufacturers' Association of New England, blacklisted those who showed interest in the union, and in 1878, about two hundred Vinalhaven workers struck. Their protest was only partially successful, but by 1887, Maine's ten branches of the union reported a total of five hundred union members. In 1892, some twelve thousand striking cutters idled quarries throughout New England, and in the following January the strike was settled on terms favorable to the workers.

Between 1890 and 1914, the older generation of Maine's granite-industry leadership was replaced by out-of-state capital and control. In some cases, general contracting companies or granite dealers from the larger cities leased entire quarries and set up their own operations in order to increase profits, efficiency, and dependability. Monopolizing the supply of granite, part of a larger process of consolidation in the metropolitan building and construction industries, shifted control over this portion of Maine's economy to outside financial centers. Still, these new sources of capital kept the quarries competitive. Maine was the nation's second largest granite producer in 1890, when over two million tons of granite were wrenched from the coastal ledges and sent to build American cities.

By 1890, the structure of the lime industry had changed too. Once again, the trend toward consolidation began locally. As early as 1869, Francis Cobb and twenty-four other lime manufacturers had experimented with a syndicate to control prices. Although their Lime Exchange functioned poorly, in 1871 Cobb stabilized the venture by merging his family firm with seven other businesses. But this attempt at price fixing also failed, and in 1900, Cobb's son, William, merged the new company with several others, producing the Rockland-Rockport Lime Company. This "lime syndicate," which owned quarries, sheds, kilns, railroads, and the shipping subsidiaries, then controlled much of the Atlantic coast lime trade.

The ice industry also inspired several attempts to introduce stability through local consolidations. In 1861, James L. Cheesman, a New York retailer and Hudson River ice dealer, built several ice houses near Farmingdale and within five years developed a controlling interest in the Kennebec ice trade. Cheesman lost his hold on the trade in 1868 and sold out to the Knickerbocker Ice Company of Philadelphia.

Other large-scale, outside firms followed: the Great Falls and Independent ice companies of Washington, DC, located in Pittston; the Cochran and Oler Ice Company of Baltimore at Dresden; the Consolidated Ice Company, controlling the wholesale and retail business of New York City; and Charles Russell and Company of Boston. Most of these large companies shipped ice in their own vessels and handled retail business in the metropolitan centers.

The most important consolidation came under the direction of Charles W. Morse of Bath, founder of the Consolidated Ice Company. In the 1890s, this gigantic firm owned sixty ice houses and shipped nearly one million tons of ice in as many as a thousand vessels. In 1899, Morse's "ice trust" swallowed up several more competitors and became the American Ice Company. Gaining a virtual monopoly on ice sold in Boston, New York, Philadelphia, Baltimore, and Washington, the "Ice King" doubled prices overnight. Strong popular indignation forced the company into litigation, and Morse was compelled to reorganize.

As in granite and lime production, the rise of ice empires like Morse's provided the capital and drive to expand the industry. The larger companies introduced steam-powered elevators, bigger ice houses, and more efficient scrapers. Between 1880 and 1900, Maine seldom shipped less than a million tons yearly. But here, too, monopoly control had negative effects as well. By 1900, absentee owners controlled about 85 percent of production in Maine, and on the Hudson River as well. In command of both the markets and raw materials, the syndicates cut ice in Maine only when the Hudson River remained open or mushy. Maine shipped an extraordinary three million tons of ice south in 1890, since the Hudson remained open through the winter, but in 1901 and 1902, almost no ice was cut in Maine. "Harvesters are idle," a concerned journalist noted, "the houses are neglected, and the machinery rusting, and the big schooners that will bring coal to Maine next summer will have to go away empty, instead of having cargoes of ice to take back as in former years."

Granite, lime, and ice succumbed to monopoly control at the turn of the century, which brought welcome infusions of capital, but also left the companies somewhat inflexible in the face of changing circumstances. During these decades, Maine's resource-based industries also faced grave challenges as new technologies brought competition from other directions.

In the 1880s, architects began using structural steel frames to support large buildings. Previously, granite had provided the strength to bear a building's weight, but now granite facing could be "hung" on a steel skeleton. Granite began to serve ornamental and artistic, rather than structural, purposes, but even in this regard it faced growing competition from other materials, particularly concrete.

Buildings of steel and concrete, increasingly common in the 1890s, could reach higher and enclose more floor space than granite buildings. Also, American architectural tastes changed dramatically after the turn of the century, as did American attitudes toward corporate power, as it was reflected in office buildings. The imposing and sometimes garish symbolism of granite gave way to something new: an architecture in which form followed function. America's new "faceless" corporations demanded efficient space, efficient form, efficient construction. The tendency to see buildings as memorials to America's corporate titans faded. With that pharaonic tendency went the market for granite.

Granite faced other challenges, apart from the new construction materials. Asphalt and concrete replaced paving blocks in the nation's streets. Changing fashion in monument materials and in the regulations of cemetery associations cut into another sector of the trade. Less obvious was competition from marble as a facing material for buildings. These changes forced the consolidation or abandonment of the smaller quarries, and only those well situated with good granite and transportation facilities survived.

Quarries began closing at an accelerating rate during the First World War. Between 1900 and 1919, seventy-two quarries closed. The Great Depression brought a further dwindling of demand, and the shock of World War II was the final blow to granite quarrying as an important industry in Maine. In the otherwise bright year of 1946, thirty-four Maine quarries closed.

Like granite, the lime industry experienced the vicissitudes of technological changes. In 1903, the New England Lime and Cement Company began production of cement in Thomaston, using the area's limestone deposits. Substitutes for lime plaster and lime fertilizers appeared in the 1920s, and after this point lime production declined. In 1949, lime was burned in Thomaston for the last time.

During these years, the ice industry suffered a similar fate. Ice cutters were vexed by the tons of shavings and sawdust dumped into the rivers by upstream mills. Sewage, too, blighted Maine's reputation for pristine ice. More important, the production of manufactured ice was progressing steadily. "Chemical ice" had been available since 1866 but was not competitive with Maine's naturally produced product in price or quality until the end of the century. As manufactured ice subsumed the natural ice industry, the "ice empires" disintegrated, or in some instances metamorphosed into artificial ice or ice-cream manufacturers and distributors, operating on a much reduced scale. Although pollution killed the industry on the big rivers, ice harvesting continued on smaller lakes and ponds into the 1940s, serving very restricted markets.

Maine's traditional industries—fishing, shipbuilding, agriculture, lumbering, granite quarrying, lime burning, and ice harvesting—underwent tremendous changes in the years after the Civil War. Outside pressures, such as new competitors, new capital structures and business organizations, changing technologies and transportation systems, and new consumer tastes, were responsible for most of these new developments. Creative response to these shifting conditions brought new life to some traditional industries, but others succumbed to modern forces. At the same time, however, several new industries were on the rise, taking up slack in the economy. Maine's industrial landscape was much changed at the end of the century, but the economy on the whole remained prosperous. And remarkably, a way of life that had existed in rural and coastal Maine since the pre–Civil War years remained largely intact.

For Further Reading:

For bibliographical information on agriculture, shipbuilding, and the lumber, granite, ice, lime, and fishing industries in the post–Civil War era, please see the suggested reading lists following chapters 11, 12, and 13.

18

New Industries in an Age of Adjustment,
1865–1930

NATHAN R. LIPFERT,

RICHARD W. JUDD, & RICHARD R. WESCOTT

*In the decades after the Civil War, Maine's natural resource industries were eroded
by trends in the national economy. Producers responded creatively by moving into
markets where Maine's resources, labor, and location still offered competitive advantages. As they altered the traditional industries, they generated economic
growth in a variety of new sectors, principally shore fishing, paper production,
tourism, and hydroelectric power.*

*These new enterprises, ranging from small owner-operated fishing boats to mas-
sive mill complexes, shared one common feature. Like antebellum manufactures,
each expressed the dual nature of Maine's economy, which has generated small-
scale traditional enterprise as well as large-scale corporate capitalism. Maine
continued to exhibit an extreme local orientation while at the same time maintaining powerful links to out-of-state agents of finance and control.*

*The new shore fisheries, for example, were locally oriented, while paper produc-
tion epitomized the "colonial" nature of Maine's economy, that is, its links to
outside metropolitan finance. Tourism, a mixture of magnificent resort hotels and
locally generated services, spanned the two economies. And finally, hydroelectric
power development brought these two ways of life into direct confrontation.*

*Once again, Maine's resources—fish, forests, landscape, wildlife, water power—
offered vast potential for economic growth. Here, however, we begin to see a new
variation on this old theme: early awareness of the need to conserve these resources.*

The Shore Fisheries, 1865–1930
NATHAN R. LIPFERT

In the years between statehood and the Civil War, Maine experienced an
industrial "golden age" of sorts, when the state's mix of natural resources corre-

sponded closely to the needs of the young nation. In an age of wood, Maine offered a bounty of white pine within easy sailing distance of expanding Atlantic coast cities. Maine's fishing industry provided inexpensive protein for a hungry nation of immigrants, while granite, ice, lime, and other resources enjoyed similarly booming markets.

In the second half of the century these industrial foundations were eroded by changes in the national economy. As long as commerce followed a north-south axis along the Atlantic sealanes, Maine's economy moved with the pulse of national development. But when railroads, running west from seaboard cities, shifted trade flows to an east-west axis, Maine was left isolated. The nation's center of gravity shifted westward, and with it went the processing centers, markets, and transportation networks vital to a prosperous regional economy.

In 1865–1930, as before, Maine felt the impact of irrepressible outside events. But this was not an era of decline. Certainly some traditional industries succumbed to national forces, but others changed form, entered new markets, and molded themselves to new circumstances. This is best illustrated by four new industries that arose after the Civil War: shore fisheries, paper production, tourism, and hydroelectric power development.

Between 1865 and 1930, Maine's shore fisheries grew to dominate the state's maritime activities as a result of declining profits in the traditional banks fishery and improved markets for inshore species. In the 1880s, the banks fisheries withered under the multiple discouragements of adverse government policy, interregional competition, rising operating costs, expensive new technology, and consolidated markets. Livelihoods in the small downeast coastal villages were threatened, but this same discouraging decade brought new opportunities in the shore fisheries, particularly with expanding markets for herring and lobster.

The extent of direct occupational transfer from the offshore to inshore fisheries is difficult to judge, but traditionally there had been considerable overlap between the two. The shore fisheries provided informal apprenticeships for those destined to a life aboard the offshore fishing schooners, and older workers who lacked the strength to go offshore often returned to the shore fishery. Some catchers alternated between shore fishing in winter and offshore fishing in summer. Thus the skills honed on the far-off banks and bays of Newfoundland and Nova Scotia served well to exploit the inshore trade when markets presented themselves, and the shift in energies to the shore fisheries was probably considerable.

Traditionally, the shore fisheries carried far less prestige than the banks fishery, and some claimed—probably without much justification—that only smaller workers, unable to take the physical abuse of the offshore life, were forced to make a living in this trade. Shore catchers generally made less money and tended to live more humbly, but they enjoyed certain other advantages: they could choose the weather they went out in, since they started from home each morning; and they could live more normal, uninterrupted family lives. This, combined with the lure of independent boat ownership and self-mastery, attracted many to the shore fisheries when fortunes in the offshore industry had begun to decline. One way that shore fish catchers could sometimes equal the income of their offshore compatriots was to become "campers," leaving home for the spring and summer to live in a hut, tent, or boat nearer the inshore fishing grounds, thereby saving a great deal of travel time. If the fish failed or a fishing ground was affected by a closed season, moving to another location was easy. Deserted coastal islands often sprouted these seasonal fishing camps. The practice is still occasionally seen today.

Shore catchers routinely accomplished difficult and courageous feats at sea, but they also succumbed to the temptations of sociability common to close-knit fishing communities, violating the general late-nineteenth-century work ethic. Said one writer in 1887: "When at home, the fisherman of this class passes most of his time lounging about with his companions, relating personal adventures and talking superficially over the outlook."

This characterization misses an important point about the coastal livelihoods: although flexible in their work habits, fish catchers were far from indolent. Overlapping patterns of season and weather, fish migrations, crop yields, and market changes conditioned a way of life that blended subsistence farming and commercial fishing into a broad mix of incomes. Shore fishers moved quickly and easily from one fishery to another according to the availability of species and fishing regulations. They worked some combination of lobster traps, otter trawls, line trawls, or weirs, and in slack times supplied bait to the banks vessels, "smacked" (transported) fish, wood, or produce to other ports, and farmed. The sheer complexity and variety of their economic exchanges left them relatively independent of any single source of income, thus leading them to appear at loose ends to outsiders. But this occupational pluralism, characteristic of the entire North Atlantic rim, was a rational response to geographic isolation, acute capital shortages, and the seasonality of resource-based work which precluded year-round professions for all but a few.

In this multifaceted trade, boys destined to fish for their livings often left school at an early age; girls in fishing communities were likely to be better educated. One nineteenth-century observer remarked that fishermen were often less capable of business than their wives, observing that the women acted as agents for their absent spouses. Dealers frequently considered a wife's word better than that of her husband, and, in fact, women were not infrequently the decision makers in the family enterprise.

Maine's shore fish catchers were preoccupied in the 1865–1930 period with the worry that the industry was in decline. Fish and lobsters were smaller and fewer, and the future seemed to hold little hope, beyond the possibility of opening new markets and exploiting new species. (This concern continues in most fisheries today but was uncommon before the 1860s.) Many attributed the diminished catches to overfishing and thought protective measures were called for, but most catchers regarded conservation laws as just another obstacle to keep them from earning a good living. That conviction has altered in the years since 1930, but to an earlier generation the late-nineteenth-century development of a state fisheries bureaucracy and a scientific approach to the study of fish biology and behavior seemed more antagonistic than helpful.

Several post–Civil War innovations increased the productivity and market reach of the inshore fishery. Trawl lines, with their many hooks, increased the landings of cod, pollack, herring, and mackerel, the species that dominated the inshore fisheries until the turn of the century. In 1842, the state's first seafood cannery was established in Eastport, using techniques borrowed from France and Scotland. Canneries proliferated after the Civil War, and the wide public acceptance of hermetically sealed or canned food helped diversify coastal fishing during the years when salt cod was losing ground in the American diet. Finally, the extension of rail networks along the coast in the late 1800s and the increased use of motorized trucks a few decades later carried fresh fish and live lobsters to previously inaccessible markets.

The greatest advances came in the lobster fishery. Commercial lobster fishing began in the 1820s on the western coast of Maine and extended eastward, reaching Eastport about 1855. By 1887, around two thousand Mainers considered lobstering their primary occupation. Lobsters were trapped with gear much like that used today, and then collected from isolated locations by lobster smacks, small coasting vessels equipped with seawater wells. The skippers followed a somewhat regular schedule, moving from cove to cove, cultivating individual suppliers with special prices, small commissions of household goods, and credit to purchase equipment and supplies. The smacks transported live lobsters to Boston, New York, and other northeastern coastal cities, where they were sold to restaurateurs.

The early development of this fishery, however, owed much to the growth of seafood canneries, since lobsters could not be shipped to inland markets in any other form. But as canneries increased, the size and number of lobsters seemed to diminish, and in the 1870s and 1880s, the state legislature began experimenting with size limits, closed seasons, and pricing by weight instead of number. No solution satisfied all factions of catchers and dealers, however; nor was the understaffed Fisheries Commission equipped to enforce these legislative decrees.

Another marketing innovation came in 1875, when Boston fish dealers Johnson and Young experimented with holding live lobsters in a fenced-in cove near Vinalhaven to await the most advantageous prices. Pounds, as they were called, soon came into common use and improved the distribution of fresh lobsters. With markets for live lobster increasing, fresh-fish dealers began to view canneries as a problem. Since canners purchased only the smallest lobsters, which were cheaper than those sold fresh to restaurants, they rapidly depleted the breeding stock. Sometimes twenty or thirty tiny "snappers" were used to fill a one-pound can. In 1883, the legislature established a minimum ten-and-a-half-inch size limit, which eventually drove the lobster canneries from the coast, often to neighboring Canada. In 1895, the last Maine cannery stopped putting up lobsters.

The gap left by the canneries was more than filled, however, by the burgeoning coastal tourist industry. Promoters estimated that around three hundred thousand tourists summered on the Maine coast at the turn of the century. This trade sustained the industry, as did a growing restaurant market along the eastern seaboard and new techniques for packing fresh lobster in barrels for long-distance rail shipment to inland cities.

In 1880, Maine landed around fourteen million pounds of lobster. The catch remained stable until after the turn of the century, when it rose to a peak of twenty million pounds in 1910, then dropped to eight million pounds in 1930. The Great Depression hit the industry with devastating force. As a luxury item, lobster was an easy consumer sacrifice during hard times. During these years Maine also faced growing competition from Nova Scotia lobster fisheries, as dealers began experimenting with refrigerated rail shipments and fresh-frozen Canadian lobster meat. Lobster landings fell off dramatically in the 1930s, largely because fewer traps were being fished. The coming of the Second World War would see this trend reversed. Lobster landings rebounded quickly and in the 1950s exceeded pre-Depression figures by substantial amounts.

Digging soft-shell clams was a second important shellfish industry. In the early nineteenth century, clams were considered of no particular commercial value, but after 1850, pickled clams were used as bait for the banks fishery. Diggers began stocking clams in October, and they sold the catch in the early spring to fishers leaving for the banks. Aware of this new bounty, shore owners attempted to charge for the right to dig on their flats, but in view of the long-standing custom of public access, the courts declared the flats open to all. By 1880, around three million pounds of clams were being harvested; about 60 percent were shucked and salted for bait. The industry faltered momentarily as the banks fishery declined and fishers shifted to fresh bait, but within a few years orders for clams in the shell began arriving from Boston hotels. About the same time local canneries began putting up clams.

Clams provided a valuable winter income for coastal inhabitants, especially in eastern Maine. In 1901, Maine furnished about three-fourths of all clams used in chowder in the nation, and demand was increasing steadily. By 1914, the annual harvest had grown to twenty-six million pounds. However, flats in the vicinity of canneries and summer hotels were being depleted. The situation caused friction between locals and diggers from "away," and the legislature debated several conservation measures, including a ban on exporting live clams from the state, establishment of clam "preserves," and size or seasonal limits. Adding to other difficulties during the 1930s, out-of-state dealers began questioning the hazards caused by pollution on the Maine flats. Important areas along the southern Maine coast were declared off-limits to clam diggers. Resolution of this problem awaited effective pollution-control legislation in the 1970s.

Another important branch of this industry was weir fishing. Weirs are aquatic fences built near shore by driving tall stakes into the mud and weaving them with brush or, in later years, nets. The weirs intercepted schools of fish swimming close to shore and led them to an inner enclosure or pound, from which they were unlikely to make their escape. Fish catchers then collected them with a purse seine or a dip net. Adopted from Indian cultures, weirs came into use in Maine about 1820; about 1865 fishers began building weirs in deeper water, so that they stood twelve to fourteen feet deep at low tide.

Although practical for a variety of migratory fish, weirs were most profitable in the herring fishery. On the eastern coast of Maine, smoked herring was an important industry throughout this period. However, it was small compared to the sardine industry, which was also supplied by weir fishers. In 1875, an experiment was made to substitute juvenile herring for "Russian sardines"; the original European version of this delicacy had become rare. The attempt was successful, and canning became an important eastern Maine industry. The tiny herring were cleaned, salted, fried, and canned in oil or vinegar and spices. As canneries increased, particularly at Eastport and Lubec, "sardines" were transformed from a luxury item into a staple seafood. By 1880, Maine was canning over six million pounds of sardines valued at $772,176; by 1910, state canneries were producing sardines worth $5,078,587—an impressive value for a species used mostly for bait forty years before.

There were a number of other options for shore fish catchers. In this period they also fished for cod and hake with hand lines and trawl lines and they dragged for scallops. From the rivers they harvested salmon, shad, alewives, smelt, striped bass, eels, tomcod, and sturgeon, using drift nets, gill nets, weirs, fyke nets (bag nets), hand lines (often through holes in the ice), traps, seines, dip nets, spears, set nets, and stop nets.

A wide variety of small boats were used by nineteenth-century shore fishers, many of them distinctive to a particular region. On the western coast, for instance, Maine fish catchers used Hampton boats or an associated type, the Crotch Island pinky, both derived from a New Hampshire model known as the Hampton whaler or New England boat. The eastern coast produced the Eastport pinkies, or Quoddy boats, and the Reach boats. The midcoast region had its own distinctive types, including the double-ended peapod, the Cape Rosier wherry, the Matinicus boat, and the Maine sloop boat (now known as the Friendship sloop), with its predecessor, the Muscongus Bay sloop. Most were used in a variety of ways, but some, like the Lincolnville salmon wherry, were associated with particular fisheries. Dories were ubiquitous, although hardly unique to Maine. Larger vessels—small schooners—were occasionally used on the inshore fishing grounds.

Marine gasoline engines suitable for installation in small boats became available about 1895. Fishers were quick to see the advantages of marine motors, even the early two-cycle make- and-break engines that weighed roughly a hundred pounds for every horsepower they produced. By 1910, most shore fishers had motors in their boats, and in the 1920s, the lighter and more powerful four-cycle marine engines transformed the fisheries. Such an engine could not only propel the boat, but it could run a trap-hauler, pump out bilge water, force sea water through a live well, and even heat the fisherman's steering shelter. Not all the Maine sailing and rowing craft were easily adaptable to power. Many fell out of use or, like the Friendship sloop, were adopted by yachtsmen. The Hampton boat and the Reach boat were best suited to motorization and, together with the peapod, evolved into a shape that present-day observers would recognize as a "modern" Maine lobster boat.

The Pulp and Paper Industry, 1865–1930

RICHARD W. JUDD

Although Maine was less competitive in nationwide lumber markets after 1880, the region provided unrivaled opportunities for a new forest industry: pulp and paper production. In contrast to the shore fisheries, which continued the legacy of small-scale, independently owned fishing enterprise, the emerging pulp and paper industry represented capitalization on a grand scale. Creation of entire new cities in the wilderness to serve the needs of this industry symbolized the power of metropolitan capital to alter the Maine woods. Wrestling with the consequences of this massive transformation in the forest industries, Maine people pioneered some of the earliest forest conservation measures in the nation.

Natural resources destined Maine to become an important producer of pulp and paper. The state's abundant supply of water provided cheap log transportation and hydroelectric power, and huge tracts of spruce, an ideal source of pulp, stood nearby. The paper industry began its expansion in 1827, when a European machine called the Fourdrinier was brought to New England. It produced paper in a continuous-flow process, rather than in batches or in individual sheets. Rising demand for paper and limited sources of rags for pulp inspired a search for new sources of fiber, and shortly after the Civil War paper makers began experimenting with wood. After trying a variety of species, by the 1880s most producers settled on poplar or spruce; both could be ground up easily, and they yielded strong, lengthy fibers.

Paper making is a relatively simple process, although producing several hundred tons per day required huge outlays of capital. The wood was barked, trimmed, and cooked to extract the glutinous matter and resin. The remaining fine fuzz was mixed with rag pulp and paste and processed into long sheets. Soda, and later sulphite, solutions aided in breaking down the wood. Sulphite worked best on spruce, a boon for Maine, which contained the largest stock of this species in the nation.

Using capital from the lumber trade and from Boston and New York, paper makers built mills on the lower Penobscot, Kennebec, and Androscoggin rivers in the 1880s. This decade brought one of the most active periods of industrial expansion in Maine's history. Since the 1850s, Maine lumber barons had been investing in midwestern timberlands and sawmills; paper making reversed this capital drain by drawing new investments into the state. As the mills expanded, newsprint makers diversified into boxes, baskets, and packing cases. New uses for wood pulp, appearing almost daily, prompted a Bangor trade journal to speculate that barrels, pails, cornices, picture frames, eating utensils, plates, cups—even fishing rods, steamships, and passenger balloons—might be rendered from pulp. The world, it announced, had entered the "Paper Age." In 1885, Maine boasted 12 pulp mills and 9 paper mills, most built with outside capital. By 1906, the industry, now with 109 mills, ranked first in the state in value added to product.

Changes in business organization in the industry followed national trends in the development of monopoly capitalism. The 1893 depression brought a decade of destructive price wars in the overextended industry, prompting experiments with various means of keeping prices stable. When "pools," or agreements to maintain prices, proved ineffective, industry leaders began consolidating ownerships. In late 1897, Portland's Hugh J. Chisholm and several other backers managed to bring more than a score of paper companies in New York and New England together under one firm: International Paper Company. The new giant controlled two-thirds of the industry's productive capacity.

18-1. Few examples illustrate the importance of the pulp and paper industry in Maine better than the community of Millinocket, shown here in 1939. In 1900, eight individuals lived in the township, but within a few months an entire city went up around the Great Northern plant. Collections of the Maine Historical Society, Portland.

The International Paper Company consolidation panicked the newspaper industry and touched off a series of congressional investigations of the "paper trust" between 1908 and 1916. Partly in reaction to International Paper, in 1899 a number of Boston and New York capitalists underwrote a massive new investment in woodlands and mill property on the upper Penobscot River. Two years earlier, home-grown speculators from Bangor had chartered the Northern Development Company, in order to develop a water-power site near the confluence of the east and west branches of the Penobscot. Having secured the Millinocket Stream location, the Bangor group began buying up large tracts of forestland. By 1899, the company controlled eleven townships and around three hundred million feet of standing timber on the West Branch.

In the spring of 1898, the company announced plans to build the world's largest pulp and paper mill on this tract of northern Maine wilderness. The proposal, however, had grown too ambitious for local lumbermen, and the firm, now Great Northern Paper Company, was acquired by the Boston and New York financiers. Newspaper publisher Joseph Pulitzer, wary of International Paper's growing power over newsprint prices, figured in the background.

Millinocket would become the crowning achievement of this powerful new industry. In a remote wilderness region the company built an entire industrial city wholesale, complete with an enormous hydroelectric plant, city water utilities, a library, hotels, several business blocks, and homes for thousands of workers. The mill, centerpiece of this colossal undertaking, was capitalized at $4 million and had a capacity of 250 tons of paper a day. The company's timberland holdings would eventually amount to a tenth of the state's total land area.

As the Maine paper industry expanded, the story of "Magic Millinocket" was repeated on a lesser scale in several other locations, including Woodland in eastern Maine and Rumford Falls in west central Maine. The transformation of watersheds with dams and reservoirs, the construction of new cities, roads, and railroads, and the acquisition of vast timberland estates all demonstrated the power of these big firms and the tremendous capital resources at their disposal. Maine's rivers became transport systems for their pulpwood, sources of hydroelectric energy for their mills, and conveyers of their mill wastes. Great Northern Paper Company launched an ambitious program to harness the West Branch; a decade and a half of dam, canal, and reservoir development was capped by construction of the huge Ripogenous Dam at the outlet of Chesuncook Lake in 1917. By 1920, the paper industry, and secondarily the textile industry, enjoyed a virtual monopoly over Maine's larger river systems.

The industry was likewise gaining dominance over Maine's forests. By 1900, the pulp and paper industry was consuming nearly half the annual cut of timber in the state. In an article reproduced in several Maine papers in 1901, publicist Francis Wiggin recognized this unsettling increase in timber production: "Whether our forests can continue to stand this constant annual drain or not, is one of the most serious questions confronting the people of Maine today."

Maine forestland owners responded to the increased demand for timber with several pioneering forest protection measures. As one of the earliest states to market second-growth timber as a recognizably limited, though renewable resource, Maine developed some of the earliest state conservation practices on the continent. In 1895 Allagash timberland owners began posting signs along the river to caution outdoors enthusiasts and river drivers against wildfires. They also joined together to hire "forest rangers" to watch for fires. After 1903, this system spread to other areas of Maine. Working through their timber scalers (those who measured and recorded the cut timber), landowners also imposed more stringent cutting regulations upon lumber operators. Rising prices for timber, imposed by growing pulpwood cutting, prompted a new appreciation for the value of the Maine woods. The work these scalers did shaded into practical woods engineering and forestry in the 1920s.

Interest in forest conservation stemmed from broader concerns as well. Farmers speculated (incorrectly, as it turns out) that forest denudation altered Maine's climate, drying the soil and hence decreasing rainfall. Concerned that denuded lands would not effectively retain rainfall, southern Maine legislators called for protection of forests on the Sebago Lake watershed, which supplied water for Portland. Similar concerns were expressed for the Androscoggin, source of power for Lewiston's textile mills. Governor William T. Haines pointed out in 1913 that rivers deforested at their headwaters would become "practically useless as sources of water power." Tourist promoters, concerned about Maine's reputation for fishing and hunting, similarly called for better forestry to protect wildlife habitat.

Successful lobbying by the Maine State Grange, the Maine Board of Agriculture, the Maine Forestry Association, and interested individuals resulted in creation of the Maine State Forest Commission in 1891. This agency took on greater importance after a series of devastating fires in 1903–5 highlighted the problem of underfunding. In the latter year a cooperatively funded state and private fire patrol system was inaugurated, and Maine built three fire lookout stations on the upper Kennebec watershed, reportedly the first such structures in the nation.

Between 1901 and 1907, an acrimonious debate over timberlands taxation animated the conservation debate. Loggers and landowners responded to pressures for more equitable taxation by pointing out that timber was a low-yield, high-risk investment and arguing that since the public enjoyed unrestricted use

of private forestland for recreational purposes, landowners should not be subjected to higher taxes. The land, they argued, was a public, as well as a private
trust. Assessments were raised over the next few years, but landowners effectively fended off moves toward comprehensive tax reform. Nevertheless, the
long debate fostered conservation thinking in several ways. First, it brought
landowners and lumber operators together in a defensive association which, in
the process of lobbying for favorable taxes, proposed several conservation measures. Second, the debate articulated a compromise on private and public
responsibilities for the forest, based on a multiple-use approach: private lands
would be open to the public for recreational purposes in return for generally
low tax assessments and some public responsibility for forest protection. This
compromise, coupled with a new round of forest fires in 1908–9, set the stage
for a new approach to fire-fighting administration.

The Maine Forestry District, created in 1909, resolved two dilemmas. Maine's
forest commission, because of underfunding, had been unable to implement
needed fire prevention programs. At the same time, landowners, although well
prepared to fund fire-suppression programs, lacked the comprehensive authority to involve all land-owning parties in their programs. The Forestry
District was funded mostly by a special assessment levied by the state on forest
landowners in Maine's unincorporated wilderness. With ample funding and
comprehensive oversight by the state, the Forestry District achieved impressive
successes in reducing the yearly loss of timber to wildfire.

Following national trends, Maine's pulp and paper companies also demonstrated some concern for proper forestry practices. Guided by pioneering
surveys made by Maine-born Austin Cary, charting the growth and distribution
of spruce and fir forests in western Maine, companies conducted forest inventories, encouraged fire prevention, and designed cutting plans to reduce waste
and encourage new growth. By 1930, some maintained staffs of private foresters, supplied, in good part, by the University of Maine, where the College of
Agriculture began offering a course in forestry in the fall of 1900. Although
these state and private developments left much to be done, they provided a
basis for future fire prevention and scientific forestry programs.

Tourism in Maine
RICHARD R. WESCOTT

Although tourists visited Maine in limited numbers before the Civil War, it was
during the last three decades of the nineteenth century that the industry
became an important part of the state's economy. Like shore fishing and paper
production, tourism helped to fill the void left by older declining industries.

This emerging industry typically comprised small-scale guiding, boat-building, camping, and other locally financed enterprises. Yet tourism attracted larger players as well, exemplified by the impressive promotional efforts of Maine's steamship and railroad companies, well-financed land syndicates, and massive resort hotels.

The "second discovery of the Maine Coast," as one commentator put it, began with wealthy easterners seeking relaxing settings where they could escape the cities' summer dirt and heat and enjoy social pursuits with their peers. In the 1870s, Maine's reputation for scenic coastal vistas, cooling breezes, and abundant fish and game also drew increasing numbers of middle-class tourists from southern New England, the middle Atlantic states, and the Midwest. The *Bangor Industrial Journal* characterized the new summer migrants as "professional and other over-worked and brain-wearied men from the large cities."

Ironically, it was Maine's lack of development—its relatively rural landscape—that provided the conditions for this economic transformation. Improved rail and steamship travel aided the industry by placing Maine at the very doorstep of the urban Northeast. A national mania for the "outdoor life," the quickening pace of professional and managerial occupations, changed social values that encouraged conspicuous display among the wealthy, deteriorating sanitary conditions in East Coast cities, and certainly the extensive promotional efforts of Maine's railroad and steamship companies and boards of trade all contributed to the spectacular growth of tourism in the last years of the century. As in so many other industries, Maine's resources—its landscape, wildlife, culture and folkways, and its healthy climate—presented a vast potential for economic growth.

At first, tourists settled into hotels and boarding houses that catered to the "summer trade." By the late 1860s, a few resorters began building their own cottages, and in the next decade, this growing interest in summer home construction led to a frantic speculative boom in coastal lands. Syndicates, formed by home-grown speculators or those from Massachusetts and New York, bought up large stretches of shoreline and carved them into lots that sold for thousands of dollars per acre. The Cushing Island Company, formed by a group of New York investors, was typical. It bought Cushing Island in Casco Bay, built a large hotel, and divided the rest of the island into house and cottage lots. The company provided a network of roads, scenic parks, and a wharf and launched a lavish promotional campaign to sell the attractions of the location. Frederick Law Olmsted, the famed designer of Central Park in New York City, testified in a brochure that Cushing Island was "the finest and most picturesque locality east of New York." Land speculation on this scale continued through the 1880s and slowed only with the panic of 1893. Regardless of whether such

18-2. Summer visitors began arriving in Maine before the Civil War to enjoy the cool climate and beautiful scenery. In the affluent postwar period, scores of huge summer hotels, like the Poland Spring House in Poland, were built to cater to wealthy persons who came for long visits. Courtesy of the Maine Historic Preservation Commission, Augusta.

enterprises returned a profit to their investors, their promotional campaigns and boom-time hoopla showed Maine to be a desirable vacation destination.

To house the growing flood of visitors, both native and nonresident speculators built new hotels and opened boarding houses by the dozens along the seacoast. Tourist accommodations also sprang up in almost every Maine town that was near a lake, river, mountain, or mineral spring. By the early 1890s, the boom had pushed the total room capacity in Maine to over 33,000, nearly two-thirds of it in York, Cumberland, Penobscot, and Hancock counties. The Maine Hotel Proprietors Association was organized to promote the industry.

The prominent Poland Spring House in South Poland is a prime example of the large-scale investment in facilities that tourism inspired in Maine. The establishment was founded in 1797 by Jabez Ricker, and under Jabez's son it became the Wentworth Ricker Inn. In 1844, the Ricker family discovered a nearby mineral spring, and in 1856 they began selling barrels of mineral water.

Capitalizing on the "curative powers and remarkable purity" of the water, the family built the Poland Spring House in 1876 and promoted the resort as a spa. The hotel complex was enlarged over succeeding years. A lavish blend of Italianate and French Provincial architecture with generous rooms and layers of verandahs, the hotel purveyed to its guests each week during the summer season nearly three thousand pounds of beef, two thousand pounds of lamb, and ten thousand eggs. The Rickers published their own roadmaps and their own monthly magazine, the *Hill-Top*. At the turn of the century they added the Samoset Hotel at Rockland and the Kineo House on Moosehead Lake to their business holdings.

Like the Poland Spring House, the Kineo House illustrates the distinctive blend of opulence and rusticity that was a hallmark of Maine tourism. Built in 1844 and enlarged for the tourist traffic several times thereafter, the Kineo House was a splash of elegance in a remote wilderness setting. Despite its remote location, the hotel had its own steam and gas plants, its own farm and dairy, and acres of landscaped woods, lawns, and golf links. The establishment epitomized the features that attracted well-off resorters to inland Maine: rustic charm, modern opulence, a remote wilderness or pastoral landscape, and plenty of hunting or fishing opportunities nearby. The Rangeley Lake House, for instance, offered steam heat, solid brass beds, mahogany furniture, tennis courts, golf links, billiards, pool, a casino, a "Boston orchestra," and moonlight skiff rides—all in a remote western Maine setting. A night's run from Boston by rail, these hotels combined country charm with the amenities expected by a pampered class of urban travelers. The resulting influx of summer visitors was a seasonal economic boon to nearby communities, boosting demand for goods and services ranging from groceries to fishing tackle and from carpentry to boat rentals.

Intensified promotion of the state's attractions was an important factor in the growth of tourism. During the summer months, Maine newspapers were liberally sprinkled with advertisements by hotels, railroads, and steamboat lines. Little use was made of out-of-state newspapers, although Maine resort hotels occasionally advertised in New York City. Tourist promoters preferred to rely on guidebooks and pamphlets. The Maine Central Railroad, which devised the slogan "Maine, the Nation's Playground" in 1884, was the leader in publishing and distributing such material, with its own monthly travel magazine and more than two dozen guidebooks and brochures on various regions of the state. The state government promoted tourism by arranging a display of photographs of Maine's natural scenery as part of its pavilion at the New Orleans Exhibition of 1884. It made an even stronger effort at the Chicago World's Fair in 1891, and, with funding from the Maine Central Railroad, Maine sponsored a booth at the

18-3. Cornelia T. "Fly Rod" Crosby (1854–1946), the noted Maine guide and outdoors writer, fishes in the shadow of Mt. Kineo. Born in Phillips, she attended finishing school before taking to the woods to improve her health. A great promoter of hunting and fishing in Maine, Crosby was the state's licensed guide number one. Collections of the Maine Historical Society, Portland.

annual Madison Square Garden Sportsmen's Exhibition featuring a live moose, a log cabin, and lectures on fly tying and casting by famed Maine guide Cornelia T. ("Fly Rod") Crosby.

Despite the promotional extravaganza, many local citizens entertained doubts about this new sector in the state's economy. Some felt that the sale of land along the coast threatened to cut off access to the shore. Others worried that the creation of exclusive fish and game preserves for out-of-state sports would close off hundreds of square miles of forests, lakes, and streams to native fishers and hunters. But the chief fear was that a way of life was being permanently altered; some residents felt that they were being crowded out of their

18-4. The Progressive period at the turn of the century placed great emphasis on providing a healthy environment for young people. Hot, dirty, congested cities were obviously undesirable places for children to spend their summers, and so hundreds of private summer camps, like Camp Maranocook in Readfield, were created to cater to the children of wealthy urban families. Courtesy of the Maine Historic Preservation Commission, Augusta.

own towns. As one wrote, "With strangers navigating our waters, occupying our houses, enjoying our scenery, and sympathizing with our history, what is there left to us for our exclusive possession?"

As tourism developed, the state government gradually and somewhat begrudgingly became more involved in nurturing the industry. The state Fisheries Commission, created by the legislature in 1867, recognized early that the decline in salmon, trout, and togue threatened an important food supply for rural Mainers. By the time the boom in tourism began in the 1870s, the state had already taken some steps to protect its inland fisheries from decimation by dams, sawmill waste, and overfishing during spawning runs. It was not until the late 1870s, however, that the commissioners admitted that sport fishing and tourism were important enough to justify an extensive fish propagation program. Impressed by the commissioners' success in saving inland sport fishing, the legislature in 1880 made them responsible for protecting Maine's moose, deer, caribou, and other game. To assist the commissioners in dealing with the problem, it enacted a new, stringent set of game laws in 1883. Gradually, in the face of stiff and sometimes violent opposition, the game wardens were able to curb illegal hunting.

Tourism continued to grow rapidly in the twentieth century, but new national developments changed its character. "Summer people," who owned their own cottages or settled into hotels and boarding houses for the season, still came to Maine, but they were gradually superseded by more transient visitors who traveled by automobile. The number of sporting camps for hunters and fishers declined, but summer camps, bringing thousands of children to Maine on special trains from Boston and New York, more than made up for the slack.

Tourism experienced a temporary setback during the national emergency of World War I, but the industry revived and flourished in the 1920s, with the help of vigorous advertising programs such as that mounted by the Maine Central Railroad in midwestern and southern newspapers and national magazines. The Bangor and Aroostook Railroad helped to bring the Allagash and St. John region to national attention through its widely distributed annual magazine, *In the Maine Woods.* Printed on heavy slick paper, the profusely illustrated publication contained articles on hunting, fishing, canoe trips, mountain climbing, and other activities of interest to prospective visitors, as well as extensive advertising for tourist facilities. Before the war, the Maine Hotel Proprietors Association had helped fund the Maine Bureau of Information to disseminate facts about Maine industries and resorts; in 1922, the agency was replaced by the Maine Publicity Bureau, which began receiving limited state funding a few years later.

Automobiles provided a new aspect to tourism beginning in the 1920s. The state highway commission had worked since 1905 to improve major roads, and since 1912 the Maine Automobile Association had issued road guidebooks and maps. But it was not until after World War I that substantial numbers of tourists began to wend their way through the state by motorcar. With a sharp drop in the cost of buying and operating motor cars in the 1920s, "the automobile week-ender or extreme transients," as a disgruntled cottage owner called them, became common on Maine's highways. While auto tourists continued to stop at hotels, a new type of accommodation—overnight tourist cabins—sprang up like mushrooms along the roadsides. These modest motor courts gradually replaced the huge summer hotels, and gave Maine tourism, with its highway-oriented façade, the look we associate with the industry today.

Over the years between 1865 and 1930, tourism grew in importance. For better or worse, the changes wrought by the industry were permanent and profound. Yet at a time when several of the state's major manufacturing industries were in decline, resort and recreational accommodations generated tens of millions of dollars in income each year. While the direct economic benefits of tourism were substantial, the indirect effects were not insignificant. Resort developments drove up property values and added substantially to the tax rolls in Maine communities, even though assessors commonly set low valuations on such properties in order to encourage their construction. In some towns, more than half the total taxable real estate was owned by nonresidents, who ended up paying over half the towns' taxes, even though they received few services.

Tourism also encouraged small rural service enterprises like farmhouse boarding, liveries, craft shops, diners, boat works, and the like. Offsetting the unsettling changes brought by a flood of "outsiders," the industry in this respect complemented Maine's tradition of small-scale rural occupations. Also, by contributing to the movement to protect the fish, wildlife, and forests upon which the industry depended, tourism helped spur Maine's conservation thinking. Thus, despite the changes tourism brought, it helped preserve, in both economic and natural terms, a landscape that was closely identified with the Maine character.

The onset of the Depression in 1929 hit the industry hard, for vacationing involved discretionary spending. Transient visitors, who had become the mainstay of the tourist industry, stayed away from Maine in droves, and the industry did not fully revive until after World War II. The very wealthy who owned palatial Bar Harbor cottages were not as affected by the hard times, but while the nation wrestled with the problems of poverty and destitution, elites discreetly abandoned the vogue for conspicuous displays of wealth. This helped to end an older form of genteel tourism already in decay in the coastal "colonies" and giant hotels.

Hydroelectric Power Development

RICHARD W. JUDD

Maine's inland lakes and rivers, a drawing card for thousands of tourists, had another role to play in the economic life of the state. The water system offered two important features that favored hydroelectric power development: an impressive change in altitude between the source of Maine's rivers and the sea; and abundant water storage in headwaters lakes. Maine's new hydroelectric industry promised many things to many people: better lighting for city streets; new interurban trolley systems; more industry; and surcease from the backbreaking toil that drove young men and women from Maine's farms. These possibilities were not always compatible; in fact, the question of how Maine's vast water power resources were to be allocated became one of the most divisive political issues of the day. Maine's emerging industries offered support for a small-scale traditional economy and at the same time helped move Maine into the age of monopoly capital. In this case, these two developments came into direct conflict.

Thomas Edison invented the incandescent lamp in 1879–80, and within a decade Americans were beginning to light their streets, run their trolleys, and power their industries with electricity. Although Maine switched on its first electric light as early as January 1880, at a spool mill belonging to the Willimantic Thread Company, the state was slow to realize the possibilities of this new energy source. In the mid-1890s, for instance, the *Lewiston Journal* still worried that trees next to electric street lights would not be able to "sleep at night." However, as the state's traditional industries entered a period of crisis, business leaders began to see hydroelectric power as a means to restore economic competitiveness.

Maine's traditional water-powered industries had been limited by the energy available from local streams. Maine ranked third in the nation at the turn of the century in terms of developed power sites, but most of these were small, scattered sources generating a few horsepower each, and they were poorly suited to support competitive industries in the age of giant enterprise. Transmission of power via electric wires, on the other hand, offered the prospect of consolidating the output from these small facilities and laying the foundation for large-scale industry. Hydroelectric power development, in short, promised to reintegrate Maine into the world of monopoly capitalism.

Farmers as well as business investors were enthusiastic about hydroelectric power, but they harbored a different vision of Maine's future. While industrialists viewed transmission lines as a means of consolidating Maine industry, farmers saw in them the potential for diffusing energy throughout the countryside, bringing industrial advantages to remote areas and reinvigorating the small inland processing centers that were so vital to Maine's rural economy. Moreover, electric power could be used to light country homes, cut wood, grind corn, milk cows, and pump water, thus mitigating much of the drudgery that was driving youth from the Maine farms.

The tension between these two visions placed hydroelectric power at the heart of Maine politics. Whether water power was to be developed in the "interests of all the people, or . . . monopolized and exploited by the 'big business interests,'" as the State Grange stated the issue, was the "great, vital, and all-absorbing question" of the day, and it launched a political battle that lasted from the first decade of the century through the 1930s.

By 1899, Maine towns were served by numerous hydroelectric plants, and new ones were constantly coming into operation. Most were small, isolated, and locally controlled plants serving one or two communities each. Typically marginal business propositions, they offered little potential for revolutionizing Maine industry.

Much of their income came from operating street railroads or trolleys, which the electric companies themselves often underwrote. Built down the middle or along the sides of streets and highways, these "electrics" provided inexpensive, frequent public transportation to small and large communities alike, and they eventually spread throughout the populated areas of the state, carrying fifty-four million passengers in 1914. Trolley lines ran in a continuously inter-linked network stretching from the Kennebec Valley and Portland all the way to Boston, where lines connected with New York.

At the turn of the century most electric utilities were still owned and operated locally, but as the systems expanded and developed greater capital needs, they were absorbed into larger companies, such as Central Maine Power, Cumberland County Power and Light, Gould Electric Company (later Maine Public Service Company), and Bangor Hydro-Electric Power Company. The most prominent figure in this period of consolidation was Walter S. Wyman. Born in West Waterville (Oakland) in 1874, Wyman entered Tufts College in 1893 and specialized in electrical engineering. Before his senior year he left college and went to work for the Waterville and Fairfield Railway and Electric Company, and in 1899 he purchased the plant.

The Oakland plant, typical of Maine's small hydroelectric facilities, consisted of a thirty-horsepower generator located under an old mill on the Messalonskee River. The plant served several score of customers and lit the village streets until ten PM—except on moonlit nights. Appreciating the potential of the site, Wyman and partner Harvey D. Eaton of Waterville incorporated the Oakland Electric Company and embarked on an expansion program in 1905. The company built dams on the Messalonskee and Sebasticook rivers, established a steam plant in Farmingdale, and contracted for street lighting in several Kennebec river towns and for a street railroad between Lewiston and Waterville. In 1910, the firm became Central Maine Power Company (CMP), and by 1924, it had acquired thirty-seven separate electric companies and served about sixty-two thousand customers. The ambitious nature of this program reflected Wyman's vision of hydroelectricity as a solution to the localism inherent in Maine's industrial economy. CMP's interconnected power system would provide energy to launch Maine into the age of giant enterprise.

Others, of course, shared this vision. A key figure in the emerging politics of Maine hydroelectricy was Governor Bert M. Fernald. Born to modest wealth in West Poland, Maine, Fernald married Annie Keene, the daughter of a resort proprietor in the area. In the 1880s, Fernald and his in-laws went into the corn-canning business, and in 1899, Fernald became a state senator, largely under the tutelage of the Ricker family, owners of the massive Poland Spring House and tireless promoters of Maine tourism. In 1908, Fernald became governor, having utilized to good advantage, as an unkindly commentator put it, the "shrewd business ability of the men who have made a fortune from a boiling spring in a state containing half a million just like theirs."

Acting on a platform heavily influenced by the needs of the tourist industry, Fernald signed into law several forest, water, and wildlife protection measures, including provisions for the pathbreaking Maine Forestry District. Along with this, he founded a commission to study the state's water systems and to "devise plans for the development of our water power under ultimate state ownership and control, so far as possible." More important was a controversial piece of legislation passed in 1909 and known as the Fernald Law, which prohibited the export of hydroelectric power from the state.

The Fernald Law was championed by Representative Percival P. Baxter of Portland, heir to a Maine seafood canning fortune and a man of considerable wealth and prestige. Prohibiting power exports, Baxter argued, would ensure Maine the full benefits of local waterpower development. It would draw outside industry to the state and guarantee that Maine would not become a power colony of the industrial centers to the south, particularly those in the Boston area. Baxter noted that for years Maine had "given [away] franchises, flowage rights, dam rights, eminent domain rights, rights to flow and . . . [to] public lands and everything else that belonged to the people of this State." The Fernald Law acknowledged the people's right to contol resource development in their own interests.

Between 1917 and 1919, Baxter, now a state senator, fought for a constitutional referendum to give the state the right to buy up and develop Maine's remaining water storage potential. In late January 1921, Governor Frederick H. Parkhurst died in Augusta, and Baxter, then speaker of the senate, succeeded him and remained in office until 1925. The cornerstone of Baxter's administrative policy was waterpower conservation, an idea that had gained broad popular appeal. The Fernald Law had become a political given among the electorate, and the next step in securing Maine's water powers seemed to be a system of state-controlled reservoirs.

At the center of the water storage controversy was CMP's plan to develop the Dead River, on the upper Kennebec watershed, for water storage. In 1923, Governor Baxter vetoed legislation granting the company a franchise to the river, claiming that public lots located there gave the state rights to the flowage. Walter Wyman subsequently shifted CMP's plans to the Moose River, northwest of Moosehead Lake, but the legislature refused to give Baxter permission to develop sites like the Dead River under state ownership. Although Baxter's attempts to place storage reservoirs under state authority were frustrated, he was able to attach to some forty new hydropower charters provisions that specifically prohibited power exports—a hedge against repeal of the Fernald Law.

The anti-export provisions of the Fernald Law also impacted on CMP's plans for expansion. In 1925, Wyman launched a vigorous development program calling for $20 million in new funding for dams on the Androscoggin, Kennebec, and Moose rivers. The Bingham (Wyman) Dam on the Kennebec, CMP's president predicted, would produce the "cheapest power available in the United States east of the Mississippi River, with the exception of Niagara Falls." For capital, Wyman turned to Chicago utilities magnate Samuel Insull, architect of a massive holding company called Middle West Utilities. Wyman permitted an Insull subsidiary, New England Public Service Company (NEPSCO), to absorb CMP in 1925. This done, CMP began laying plans for the new dams. This new capacity, however, would outpace Maine's limited markets for electricity. Where Wyman had voiced mild objections to Fernald's export ban when it was passed in 1909, he become outspoken on the subject in 1925.

Confined by the Fernald Law to markets inside the state, CMP became directly concerned with the welfare of Maine's big industrial consumers. By 1925, Lewiston's textile mills, the most important industry in the territory served by the company, were almost seventy years old. Disadvantaged by obsolete equipment and complacent management, the mills competed poorly with the rapidly growing southern textile industry. The Lewiston mills continued to rely on water turbines, belts, gears, and shafts, while their newer competitors in the South absorbed the benefits of more efficient electrical power, cheaper labor, better transportation, newer machinery, and factories designed to accommodate unit-drive electrical motors. In the grip of a deepening recession in the late 1920s, Lewiston mill owners realized that they faced a massive renovation program.

In the midst of Wyman's $20 million expansion program in 1928–29, the owners of the Androscoggin, Bates, and Hill mills decided to liquidate. After a brief consultation between Walter Wyman and J. Martin Insull, Samuel's brother, Middle West Utilities bought the mills to preserve CMP's key power consumers. These, and later the Edwards Mill in Augusta and the York Mill in Saco, were turned over to NEPSCO, along with control of several key water storage systems owned by the mills. With money supplied by Middle West Utilities, the Androscoggin Mill was reconditioned to become one of the largest producers of rayon in the world. The Bates Mill began specializing in tablecloths and bedspreads.

By this time, conditions seemed favorable for an industry assault on the Fernald Law. With construction of the huge Bingham Dam under way, CMP's credibility, a well as that of the Insull money, seemed to rise. Wyman pointed to the "great waste of power" running to the sea for lack of markets and announced that even larger dam projects were in the offing if the Fernald Law were repealed. Wyman argued that modern industry obtained much of its efficiency through size and economies of scale. Competing in the modern world, he continued, required huge investments, broad markets, a worldwide outlook, and a scientific eye to resource use. A regional power grid could help link the state's smaller water powers to greater industrial complexes and promote large-scale industrial development, Maine's only recourse in the age of monopoly.

Others saw the question of size differently, however. Critics were left uneasy by what they perceived as a growing monopoly over Maine's water power and its basic industry. NEPSCO had acquired interest in several Portland banks, and close connections existed between Walter Wyman and Maine's largest newspaper chain, the Guy Gannett Press. To rural people in particular, the Fernald Law represented a safeguard against monopoly control over Maine's natural resources. Farmers saw hydroelectric development as a key to reinvigorating traditional small-scale rural industries and were loath to see Maine water power exported to fuel big business in Massachusetts. Throughout most of this period, the State Grange clung to the Fernald Law, fearing that power exports would delay rural electrification.

The late 1920s saw the rise of another important Fernald Law supporter in Ralph Owen Brewster, governor of Maine between 1925 and 1929. Brewster's xenophobic stand against Catholic and immigrant influences won him the support of the politically powerful Ku Klux Klan in Maine in the late 1920s, and it also predisposed him against "foreign" capital in the development of Maine's water powers. Although initially amenable to certain changes in the Fernald Law, Brewster gradually became one of its strongest proponents.

In 1927, the legislature passed a bill drawn up by a CMP lawyer to allow export of "surplus" hydroelectric power from the state. The "Smith bill" passed both houses of the legislature but was vetoed by Brewster, who was concerned that abolishing the Fernald Law would place Maine hydropower under the control of the Interstate Commerce Commission, as specified by the recently passed Federal Waterpowers Act. The 1929 legislature voted to put the issue before the people in a special referendum in September.

As the debate quickened in the weeks before the referendum, Percival Baxter, at odds with Brewster over the latter's reputed KKK connections, actually endorsed a modified export bill, as did Edward P. Ricker, an early Fernald Law supporter. CMP President Walter Wyman offered to invest up to $150 million in Maine industries and hydropower development if the Fernald Law was modified. The Gannett Press splashed Wyman's offer across the front pages of the daily news and, after some hesitation, Republican Governor William Tudor Gardiner endorsed the limited export measure. Democrats, as usual, remained split on the issue.

Despite the endorsement of Baxter, Ricker, and Gardiner and lavish campaign funding from Wyman, the referendum lost and the Fernald Law remained intact. The vote to sustain the law was heaviest in the rural areas, where uneasiness over the prospects of monopoly power and Wyman-Insull-Gannett influence was strongest. If economic development meant draining Maine's resources to feed big metropolitan industries, rural folk were not interested; better to keep Maine's power at home, servicing a traditional, diversified rural economy.

When the September referendum denied CMP the authority to export surplus energy, NEPSCO launched plans for a new paper mill at Bucksport to consume the excess power from the Bingham project. In addition to Bucksport's new Maine Seaboard Paper Company, NEPSCO also lent money to the Crosset Shoe Company in Auburn, to Keyes Fibre Company in Waterville, and to the Bath Iron Works, warding off bankruptcy in these important industries during the difficult early Depression years. Middle West Utilities, often cited as the foremost practitioner of the type of stock manipulations that led to the 1929 stock market crash, collapsed in 1932. Walter Wyman, however, organized a stock purchase at greatly depreciated prices and regained control of CMP and the other operating utilities and industries in Maine. Back in safe hands, the textile mills operated at relatively high capacity through the dark days of the 1930s. The Public Utility Holding Company Act of 1935 prohibited power companies from owning manufacturing interests, and in 1945 CMP divested its control over the industrials. Although the Fernald Law had not lived up to its early expectations, it did affect Wyman-Insull operations, and it helped to propel Walter Wyman into his remarkable role as the major support for Maine's tottering industries in the Depression crisis.

Between 1865 and 1930, Maine gravitated between two worlds: an older order of rural landscapes arranged around small-demand, resource-extractive industries, and a new system based on monopolies, national competition, and capital-intensive development. The debate over the Fernald Law reflected this ambiguity. In the years after World War II, Maine continued to wrestle with the problem of reconciling a tradition of small-scale industry with an expanding corporate-capitalist system. The choices made in this postwar era echoed those made in the past.

For Further Reading:

Secondary sources on Maine's pulp and paper industry include David C. Smith, *History of Papermaking in the United States* (New York, 1970), and Richard W. Judd, "The Emergent Pulp and Paper Industry, 1900–1929," in his *Aroostook: A Century of Logging in Northern Maine* (Orono, 1989). Dorothy Laverty's history of Millinocket and John J. Leane's history of Rumford provide local perspectives on the larger paper mill towns. For a recent assessment of the Androscoggin River paper mills, see Page Helm Jones, *Evolution of a Valley* (Canaan, N.H., 1975). More critical views can be found in William C. Osborn, *The Paper Plantation* (New York, 1974), which is the published report of Ralph Nader's Study Group on the Pulp and Paper Industry in Maine; in Jonathan Falk, "The Organization of Pulpwood Harvesting in Maine" (New Haven, 1977); and his "Regional Inequality and Rural Development: The Maine Paper Industry" (Cambridge, 1973). Typescripts of both are located in the University of Maine's Special Collections Department of Fogler Library.

Primary sources for a study of the pulp and paper industry are similar to those for the lumber industry; see listings for chapter 12. In addition, the extensive collection of the papers of the Great Northern Paper Company are available at the University of Maine's Special Collections Department. These papers are the basis for a multivolume unpublished history of the company by John E. McLeod, also available in the Special Collections Department. The annual reports of the Maine Bureau of Industrial and Labor Statistics, especially for 1899 and 1911–12, and the Maine Forest Commission after 1891, contain information on the paper industry. See also Great Northern Paper Company's magazine, *The Northern*, published during the 1920s.

The history of hydroelectric power development in Maine can be pieced together from Richard W. Judd, "Reshaping Maine's Landscape: Rural Culture, Tourism, and Conservation, 1890–1929," *Journal of Forest History* 32 (October 1988); James S. Leamon, *Historic Lewiston: A Textile City in Transition* (Auburn, 1976); John A. Rand, *The Peoples History of Lewiston-Auburn Maine, 1875–1975* (Freeport, 1975); Lincoln Smith, *The Power Policy of Maine* (Berkeley, Calif., 1951); and, for a less dispassionate account, Jerome G. Daviau, *Maine's Life Blood* (Portland, 1958).

Primary sources on Maine hydroelectric power include the writings and speeches of Percival P. Baxter, found in the Baxter Collection at the Maine State Library. Various pamphlets by Baxter are scattered throughout the major state libraries. The annual reports of the Maine State Water Storage Commission, the Maine Water Power Commission, the Maine Public Utilities Commission, and the Maine Development Commission, especially the latter's *Report on Water Power Resources of the State of Maine* (Augusta, 1929) are useful. Company papers from more than a score of small hydroelectric power plants around the turn of the century can be found in the University of Maine's Special Collections Department.

ADDITIONAL SECONDARY SOURCES (SEE ALSO READINGS FOR CHAPTER 12):

Ayres, Philip W., "Is New England's Wealth in Danger?" *New England Magazine* 38 (April 1908).

Baxter, Sylvester, "The Redevelopment of an Old State," *American Monthly Review of Reviews* 33 (1906).

Cary, Austin, "Forest Management in Maine," *Journal of the Association of Engineering Societies* 23 (August 1899).

Dow, Edward F., "Public Utility Regulation in Maine" (Ph.D. dissertation, Harvard University, 1932).

Smith, David C., "Wood Pulp Paper Comes to the Northeast, 1865–1900," *Forest History* 10 (April 1966).

Staples, Arthur G., "Conservation Problems of Central Maine," *Sprague's Journal of Maine History* 12 (1924).

Wilkins, Austin H., *The Forests of Maine*, Maine Forest Service Bulletin no. 8 (Augusta, 1932).

Wilkins, Austin H., *Ten Million Acres of Timber* (Woolwich, 1978).

By far the most useful analysis and history of Maine's shore fisheries is Goode, listed below. Created as part of the industrial census of 1880, this work is encyclopedic in its coverage of the fisheries. Unfortunately, there is nothing comparable on the fisheries for the twentieth century. Primary material relating to commercial fishing is scarce; fishers and fisheries industries tend either not to create records or not to preserve them. There are, however, important collections of oral-history interviews relating to the shore fisheries at the Northeast Archives of Folklore and Oral History, University of Maine, Orono, and at the Maine Maritime Museum, Bath.

SECONDARY SOURCES:

Ackerman, Edward A., *New England's Fishing Industry* (Chicago, 1941).

Bishop, W. H., *Fish and Men in the Maine Islands* (New York, 1885).

Chapelle, Howard I., *American Small Sailing Craft: Their Design, Development, and Construction* (New York, 1951).

Clifford, Harold B., *Charlie York, Maine Coast Fisherman* (Camden, 1974).

Cobb, John N., "The Lobster Fishery of Maine," *Bulletin of the United States Fish Commission* 19 (1901).

Dow, Robert L., and Theodore Trott, "A Study of Major Factors of Maine Lobster Production Fluctuations," unpublished manuscript, Bigelow Laboratory for Ocean Sciences, West Boothbay Harbor, 1956.

Goode, George Brown, et al., *The Fisheries and Fishery Industries of the United States* (Washington, DC, 1887).

Lunt, C. Richard K., "Lobsterboat Building on the Eastern Coast of Maine: A Comparative Study" (Ph.D. dissertation, Indiana University, 1975).

Maine Bureau of Industrial and Labor Statistics, *Ninth Annual Report. . . , 1895* (Augusta, 1896).

Maine Bureau of Industrial and Labor Statistics, *Twenty-fourth Annual Report. . .* (Augusta, 1910).

Martin, Kenneth R., and Nathan R. Lipfert, *Lobstering and the Maine Coast* (Bath, 1985).

May, Earl Chapin, *The Canning Clan* (New York, 1938).

Thompson, Winfield M., "The Passing of the New England Fisherman," *New England Magazine* 13, no. 6 (February 1896).

The history of Maine tourism has received little scholarly attention, but the archival sources are voluminous. Among the most important are the Portland *Board of Trade Journal* (1886–1918) and Bangor's Industrial Journal (1880–1918). In addition, the University of Maine's Special Collections Department holds an extensive collection of materials relating to camping in Maine, including the excellent Bert Call photographs of the north woods and the Fannie Hardy Eckstorm Papers, which contain the writings of her father, Manly Hardy, a celebrated Maine guide and forester. The Maine Historic Preservation Commission has collected numerous pamphlets, maps, and other items relating to Maine's summer homes and hotels. Publications of the Maine Publicity Bureau and the Maine Inland Fish and Game Commission and their successor agencies are helpful. Periodicals published by Maine's two largest rail lines, titled *The Maine Central*, and *In the Maine Woods* (Bangor and Aroostook Railroad) are rich sources of information, as are two papers devoted to outdoor life in Maine: *The Maine Sportsman* (Bangor) and *Maine Woods* (Phillips). All of these were in publication in the decades around the turn of the century.

SECONDARY SOURCES:

Carleton, Leroy T., *Maine as a Vacation State* (Portland, 1902).

Dulles, Foster Rhea, *America Learns to Play* (New York, 1940).

Lowrey, Nathan S., "A Historical Perspective on the Northern Maine Guide," *Maine Historical Society Quarterly* 26 (Summer 1986).

The New Northeast 1 (July 1894).

Wasson, George, "The Rusticators at the Cove," in *Capt'n Simeon's Store* (Boston, 1903).

Wescott, Richard R., "Economic, Social, and Governmental Aspects of the Development of Maine's Vacation Industry, 1850–1920" (M.A. thesis, University of Maine, 1959).

Wescott, Richard R., "Early Conservation Programs and the Development of the Vacation Industry in Maine," *Maine Historical Society Quarterly* 27 (Summer 1987).

19

Work & Workers in the Industrial Age, 1865–1930

ROBERT H. BABCOCK,

YVES FRENETTE, CHARLES A. SCONTRAS, & EILEEN EAGAN

In this chapter, labor historians Robert Babcock, Yves Frenette, Charles Scontras, and Eileen Eagan describe the age of industrial adjustment from the perspective of Maine's working class. Focusing on families, communities, and work in three representative industrial cities—Portland, Lewiston, and Auburn—they demonstrate the ways working people experienced and responded to the rise of industrial capitalism.

Mirroring the growth in Maine's economy, the state's wage-earning labor force more than doubled between 1865 and 1930. And like Maine's expanding industrial landscape, its working class was diverse. Some, like Roscoe Fillmore and Adelard Coté, were recent immigrants; others could boast an American heritage of several generations. Distinctions of occupation, sex, age, ethnicity, and skill complicate the matter of describing the "typical worker" in this changing economy. As Eileen Eagan points out, considering women's roles in Maine industry requires the historian and student to redefine the word "work." In Maine, as in the nation at large, women's work was shaped by the ideology of "separate spheres"—occupational roles defined by gender.

Most working people, however, shared the experience of Roscoe Fillmore and Adelard Coté in that they were on the move. Immigrants and Yankees, women and men, traveled from job to job according to the shifting locus of industrial opportunity. This was part of the incessant quest for a better life that animated nineteenth-century American workers generally, and it reflected the uncertainty and instability of industrial work in Maine's changing economy.

For some working people, mobility was a means of controlling the conditions under which they toiled. Others responded to economic uncertainty by transforming kinship or friendship networks or immigrant communities to meet new conditions. Some turned to unions and others to politics. Collectively, through these institutions, laborers, foundry and streetcar workers, textile operatives, and those who worked in the home were agents of history, helping to forge Maine's new industrial order.

Industrial Growth and Worker Uncertainty

ROBERT BABCOCK

Among the thousands of ordinary people who lived and worked in Maine at the turn of the century, few recorded their experiences. Among those who did was Roscoe Fillmore. Writing in the late 1950s, he recalled leaving behind his rural New Brunswick home at age sixteen to go to work in Portland, Maine. His grandmother and several uncles had preceded him, and young Fillmore boarded with these kin. "I moved from job to job, [accepting] casual work with no particular future," he wrote. He tried to stay in touch with his sweetheart, "but at that distance and with a pen in hand I wasn't so shy and, foolishly, I suppose, [I] declared my love for her. That ended the correspondence as her parents thought her too young to receive such declarations."

Why did young Fillmore come to Maine? "Portland was not a large city then," he recalled, "but it was huge to my country-bred eyes and it was full of wondrous things." Like other working-class city-dwellers, he patronized a growing number of commercial amusements: Portland's Bijou Theatre, perhaps, or vaudeville shows at nearby Riverton Park and Old Orchard Beach. "I never tired of watching the wonderful stunts, the chorus girls, the tumblers, acrobats, hypnotists and sundry other acts that made up the recreation of that day," Fillmore recalled. For him as for so many others, the city spelled opportunities and excitement. And besides, some of his relatives had already paved his way.

During this period of industrial capitalist revolution, rural migrations to Maine's factories, mills, or quarries were considerable. Between 1865 and 1930, the number of wage earners more than doubled, while the value of the goods they produced increased nearly ten-fold. A close examination of the figures in Table 19.1 reveals a period of erratic but general expansion between 1860 and 1925. Industries prospered and declined, while others rose to take their place; in the aggregate, the remarkable fluctuations in this economy represented a shifting and confusing pattern of opportunity and hardship. In all, these decades were disruptive ones for Maine's working people.

Table 19.1

THE RISE OF INDUSTRY IN MAINE, 1860–1925

Year	Workers	Value/Product (in dollars)
1860	34,619	38,193,254
1870	49,180	79,497,521
1880	52,954	79,829,795
1890	70,374	95,689,500
1900	74,816	127,361,485
1910	85,501	176,029,393
1920	88,651	456,821,783
1925	73,849	371,849,000

In 1860, cotton textiles employed the largest number of Maine wage-earners, followed by lumber products, men's clothing, boots and shoes, woolens, and shipbuilding. Over the next seventy years, these industries expanded at uneven rates, offering different employment outlooks to workers in each sector. The number of textile workers, for instance, doubled between 1860 and 1910, peaking at 14,500. After that, southern competition provoked a decline. The woolen industry followed a similar, if somewhat steadier path, reaching a high of 12,000 employees by 1925. Lumber production experienced erratic growth between 1870 and 1910, reaching a high of 15,000 employees before declining dramatically in the 1920s. With the put-out system still in flower, the boot and shoe industry employed just 6,500 people in factories in 1890, but when capitalists began bringing shoe workers together under one roof, the wage-earning work force mushroomed; by 1925, shoemaking was the second greatest employer in the state, with 12,000 workers.

The pulp and paper industry experienced phenomenal growth between 1890 and 1920, but at the same time job prospects in other industries were worsening. Men's clothing employed 4,500 hands in 1870, but out-of-state competition virtually eliminated this sector after the turn of the century. Wooden ship-building peaked at 2,000 wage earners in 1850, declined briefly, then leveled off for the remainder of the century. Tanning suffered from the exhaustion of hemlock bark supplies and the introduction of new tanning extracts. Canning,

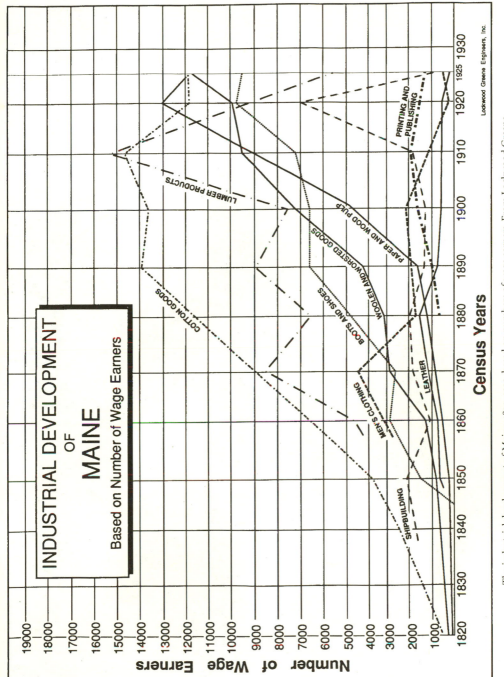

INDUSTRIAL DEVELOPMENT
OF
MAINE
Based on Number of Wage Earners

Number of Wage Earners

19000
18000
17000
16000
15000
14000
13000
12000
11000
10000
9000
8000
7000
6000
5000
4000
3000
2000
1000

1820 1830 1840 1850 1860 1870 1880 1890 1900 1910 1920 1925 1930

Census Years

COTTON GOODS

LUMBER PRODUCTS

WOOLEN AND WORSTED GOODS

BOOTS AND SHOES

PAPER AND WOOD PULP

MEN'S CLOTHING

LEATHER

SHIPBUILDING

PRINTING AND PUBLISHING

Lockwood Greene Engineers, Inc.

The industrial development of Maine, 1820–1930, based on numbers of wage earners. From Lockwood Greene Engineers, *Report on the Industrial Resources of the Part of Maine Served by Companies Affiliated with the New England Public Service Company* (New York, 1929).

which earlier employed thousands of men, women, and children part-time, stagnated because of outside competition.

As the graph on page 451 shows, the wage-earning labor force grew most rapidly during the apex of competitive capitalism in Maine from 1880 to 1910. Together, production of cotton goods, lumber, boots and shoes, pulp and paper, and woolens added 28,000 new jobs to the work force and accounted for two-thirds of all Maine workers hiring out their labor. Women, as Table 19.2 shows, made up a surprisingly high proportion of Maine wage earners. In all, the data on Maine workers bear out historian David Montgomery's observation that the rising productivity of American industry at the turn of the century owes more to increased labor inputs than to the application of new technologies.

Table 19.2

PERCENTAGE OF WOMEN AMONG WORKERS
IN MAINE INDUSTRIAL SECTORS, 1920

Cotton goods	48%
Printing	42%
Boots/shoes	38%
Woolens	35%

Increasing job opportunities and shifting patterns of industrial growth brought new people to Maine and kept them on the move, as thousands like Roscoe Fillmore left their rural homes for better fortunes in Maine's industrial centers. In 1890, 26 percent of all Mainers lived in urban areas; forty years later the urban population stood at 40 percent. Most of this growth, with the exception of Aroostook County, took place where industrialization was most rapid.

Table 19.3

AGGREGATE POPULATION BY COUNTY, 1870–1930

	1870	1890	% change	1910	% change	1930	% change	% change 1870–1930
Androscoggin	35,866	48,968	36.5	59,822	22.2	71,191	19.0	98.5
Aroostook	29,609	49,589	67.5	74,664	50.6	87,764	17.5	196.4
Cumberland	82,021	90,949	10.9	112,014	23.2	134,232	19.8	63.7
Franklin	18,807	17,053	-9.3	19,119	12.1	19,921	4.2	5.9
Hancock	36,495	37,312	2.2	35,575	-4.6	30,506	-14.2	-16.4
Kennebec	53,203	57,012	7.1	62,863	10.3	70,571	12.3	32.6
Knox	30,823	31,473	2.1	28,981	-7.9	27,519	-5.0	-10.7
Lincoln	25,597	21,996	-14.1	15,976	-27.4	15,437	-3.4	-39.7
Oxford	33,488	30,586	-8.7	37,700	23.3	41,446	9.9	23.8
Penobscot	75,150	72,865	-3.0	87,684	20.3	92,157	5.1	22.6
Piscataquis	14,403	16,134	12.0	20,554	27.4	18,216	-11.4	26.4
Sagadahoc	18,803	19,452	3.4	23,021	18.3	16,874	-26.7	-10.3
Somerset	34,611	32,672	-5.6	37,171	13.8	39,108	5.2	13.0
Waldo	34,522	27,759	-19.6	21,328	-23.2	20,275	-4.9	-41.3
Washington	43,343	44,482	2.6	41,709	-6.2	37,724	-9.5	-13.0
York	60,174	62,829	4.4	70,696	12.5	72,832	3.0	21.0

Like Roscoe Fillmore, many of these rural migrants came from foreign countries—first from the British Isles and Germany, then from Scandinavia and Canada, and finally from eastern and southern Europe. The most important of these migrations came from French Canada. At the turn of the century, Franco-Americans represented 12 percent of Maine's population, largely concentrated in northern Aroostook County and in the textile centers of central and southern Maine.

The percentage of women and young girls in Maine's work force rose from 14 percent in 1880 to 22 percent in 1930. The largest number of wage-earning women—30 percent—were employed in domestic and personal service. Employed females, more than their male counterparts, were concentrated in the ten- to twenty-nine-year-old age group. Women tended to leave the wage-earning work force when they married and bore children, a reflection of sex role divisions, the patriarchal ideology of the time, and the absence of household technology designed to lighten daily home chores.

19-1. With the coming of the Industrial Revolution, many newly created jobs came to be segregated by sex. These women in a Portland hat factory worked long hours in poor surroundings for wages that were much less than those for comparable work performed by men. Collections of the Maine Historical Society, Portland.

An Old Mercantile Center in Transition

ROBERT BABCOCK

Economic change was evident in Maine's largest cities, too, where the volatility of urban industries meant uncertainty for working people. Certainly one of the greatest concentrations of urban workers was in the city of Portland. Until the mid-nineteenth century, Portland's economy was dominated by commerce. The entrepreneurs who built the port city's impressive merchant fleet lived in sumptuous mansions on High Street. From their second-story windows, these great merchants could look out across the waterfront districts, where hundreds of mechanics, laborers, and longshore workers toiled and lived hand-to-mouth existences. Artisans, who occupied a station in life substantially above those in the waterfront trades, supplied the city's wholesalers and retail merchants with craft products. These middling merchants, in turn, controlled local and regional markets in woolens, hardware, dry goods, and groceries. Portland's hierarchical society reflected these class distinctions in a variety of ways.

Although Portland's independent artisans acknowledged the leadership of the merchant elites, they considered themselves the backbone of the community. They still responded to the ideals—if not the reality—of an older tradition, in which young aspirants worked years as apprentices and journeymen to learn the skills of a trade, then spent their mature lives as master artisans. Most embraced a "producer ideology," which celebrated the material contributions made by mechanics and workers. By the 1840s, however, depression conditions had widened the gap between master artisans and journeymen or apprentices. When many of the former established factories to produce goods more cheaply, an increasing number of the latter found their living standards lowered; some were even imprisoned for debt. As the gap between the rich and poor widened, sporadic street violence broke out.

In the midst of this turmoil, Portland's elites adopted a new strategy to stimulate the city's economy. Guided by the mercantile vision of railroad promoter John A. Poor, they began planning the construction of a railway from Portland to Montreal, hoping to transform the Maine entrepôt into a flourishing commercial and industrial metropolis. The industrial component of this venture was the Portland Company, built in 1846 on the site of old Fort Burrows at the eastern end of the harbor. Funded with capital raised by public subscription, the foundry attracted machinists, blacksmiths, boilermakers, patternmakers, and laborers, who fashioned pig iron into locomotives and rolling stock. By the 1850s, the Portland Company was the largest employer in the city, with customers as far away as Chicago and Galveston.

The Civil War era proved to be a watershed in Portland's industrial development; the Portland Company produced cannon, machinery, and gunboat engines for the Union forces, and shortly after the war a new rolling mill was built near the Fore River to produce hardware for ships and railroads. Other metals firms turned out sawmill equipment. By 1880, there were no less than 302 manufacturing establishments in the city providing jobs for 7,129 wage earners.

During the 1880s and 1890s, Portland labor force weathered difficult times. Intensified regional competition weakened markets in lumbering, metalworking, and shipping, while consolidations within the sugar industry, combined with the introduction of cheap cloth bags, wiped out the city's cooperage, shook, and sugar refining activities. In the early 1880s, the Portland Company's 525 employees had produced over one hundred large, eight-wheel locomotives for James J. Hill's transcontinental railway, but competition from locomotive works in New York and Ohio placed the Portland firm in difficulty; by 1889, employment had fallen to 175 and the company was on the ropes. The Portland Rolling Mill faced similar problems; a fire destroyed the shuttered mill in 1899. It appeared that the larger East Coast port cities would siphon off Portland's economic sustenance and leave little more than the shell of a viable community.

As monopoly capital reintegrated northeastern financial and marketing structures, Maine received an infusion of large-scale outside investments in pulp and paper, granite and slate, lumber, and other industries (see graph, page 451). These exploding hinterland sectors generated demands that breathed new life into Maine's urban areas. The Portland Company, for instance, abandoned the highly competitive locomotive industry to build pulp digesters and soon offered steady employment to five hundred workers—among them, Roscoe Fillmore. The city's leading clay pipe firm hired several hundred unskilled workers to manufacture special brick for the paper industry and sewer tiles for the East Coast's expanding suburbs. Portland's consumer-goods industries— clothing, shoes, processed foods—served the burgeoning single-industry mill and quarry towns of northern New England. French consumers savored lobster canned in Portland, while western cowboys and miners chewed Curtis spruce gum. By 1900, the city's industrial output had surpassed Lewiston's, signifying the maturation of Maine's largest city as a diverse commercial and manufacturing center.

After World War I the manufacturing sector of Portland's economy again yielded to labor-intensive mercantile and service activities, this time led in good part by the phenomenal growth of the tourist industry in the Casco Bay region. As Table 19.4 reveals, the manufacturing sector continued to decline throughout the 1920s, as did the number of wage earners in Maine generally (see Table 19.5). Between 1899 and 1919, they had increased by nearly 27 percent; they dropped by one fifth by the end of the 1920s. As we shall see, not all Portland elites saw this as an unwelcome trend.

Table 19.4

MANUFACTURING ESTABLISHMENTS, WAGE EARNERS,
& VALUE OF PRODUCTS IN PORTLAND, 1910–29

	1910–11	*1919*	*1929*
Firms	217	308	213
Workers	5,891	6,710	4,518
Value of product	$11,950,000	$29,168,000	$28,291,351

Source: United States Census, 1910, 1920, 1930.

Table 19.5

MANUFACTURING WAGE EARNERS IN MAINE, 1899–1929

1899	69,914
1909	79,955
1919	88,651
1929	70,159

Source: United States Census, 1930.

Factory Work in Lewiston and Auburn

YVES FRENETTE

While Maine's largest city was changing from merchant port to industrial hub, other communities were growing from farm towns to multi-ethnic factory districts. Again, urban growth brought new jobs and uncertain prospects for Maine's new industrial workers. Lewiston is perhaps the best example of these new industrial towns. Lewiston's mills, built in the 1840s, grew rapidly after the Civil War. In 1871, the city's seventeen large companies included nine cotton mills producing a total of more than thirty-two million yards of cloth yearly. In the early 1890s, immigrants from Quebec accounted for 80 percent of the labor force in these mills, having rapidly replaced Yankee and Irish operatives

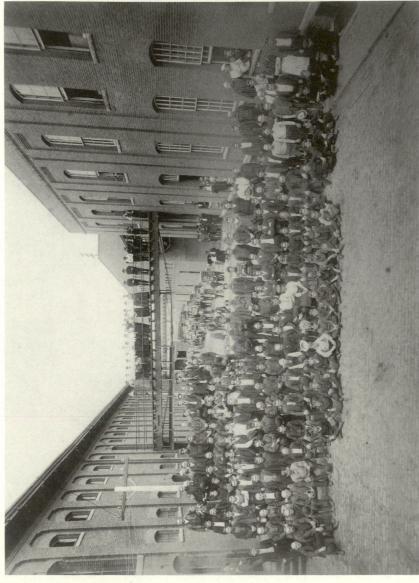

19-2. Millworkers pose outside a cotton textile mill in Lewiston. The huge waterfalls on the Androscoggin River at Lewiston provided the power for a complex of canals which powered scores of large factories. The mills attracted large numbers of immigrants, particularly Québécois, and family members of all ages and sexes took jobs in the factories. Courtesy of the Maine Historic Preservation Commission, Augusta.

as a source of cheap labor. At the turn of the century, French Canadians were followed by eastern and southern Europeans, including many Jews, but the character of the community increasingly became French-Canadian. On the eve of the Great Depression, Lewiston was the second largest city in the state with a population of nearly thirty-five thousand.

The textile industry, which by 1900 employed 70 percent of the city's labor force, led the industrial transformation of Lewiston. Small shops were built to supply items to the larger mills; department stores, hospitals, and other facilities, including a few brothels, served the growing working population, and municipal authorities struggled to keep up with the fast-paced growth. The problems of growth were endless. In the 1860s, no year passed without someone suing the city for injuries sustained on the poorly maintained streets or sidewalks. School facilities were unable to absorb the growing number of children, and teachers were ill-equipped to deal with the students' diverse ethnic backgrounds.

Auburn, across the river from Lewiston, also underwent rapid industrialization, propelled largely by the demand for shoes caused by the Civil War. Although the put-out system remained a feature of industry until late in the century, increasingly shoes were produced in Auburn's new central factories. In 1863, Ara Cushman moved his shoe business from West Minot to Auburn, and in subsequent years he built the largest shoe factory in the world. In 1871, banker and manufacturer Jacob Roak and other investors erected a factory and store complex that would become the "cradle" of the Auburn shoe industry. Smaller shoe firms rented space, then moved on to larger quarters as they expanded. Auburn's industry was gradually consolidated; its ten largest factories in 1890 provided work for 1,800 people, who produced 220,000 cases of shoes. Central to Auburn's success was its growing labor force, composed of outworkers in neighboring towns, semiskilled factory workers—mostly Irish and French Canadian (American-born and immigrants)—and a cluster of highly skilled artisans. This force was welded together by a bold, ferociously anti-union community of entrepreneurs.

Although Auburn's population doubled between 1870 and 1890, the shoe industry did not foster the massive changes that characterized Lewiston. Auburn retained an atmosphere more typical of a quiet, church-going New England town. On the nearby hills, business leaders and professionals built cozy, sometimes sumptuous residences and summer cottages, giving the community a resort-like atmosphere. In 1883, the Lewiston Horse Railroad set up an amusement park on the shore of Lake Grove that would remain a favorite attraction for many decades. In 1923, the city government made recreation more accessible by opening Pettingill Park near the downtown area. These developments contributed to a sense of superiority over rival Lewiston—the "immigrant city."

Women and Work in the Industrial Age, 1865–1930
EILEEN EAGAN

Women's wage work in the canneries, textile mills, and shoe factories was only a small part of their overall contribution to the Maine economy. Much of their work was unpaid. "Unemployed" women, in addition to maintaining households, worked in a variety of other ways: bearing and raising children, keeping boarders, cultivating farms and gardens, making home products, providing a broad range of services to extended family members and neighbors, and emerging from that particular sphere of work from time to time to engage in the civic, cultural, and social activity that built Maine's communities. But because this work was not measured in income, it has been undervalued by historians and others.

Middle-class and upper-class women in Maine, like those nationally, participated in the women's-club movement of the late nineteenth century and in some of the reform movements of the early twentieth. Members of the Women's Literary Union in Portland and the Woman's Club of Castine found ways around the limitations on women's education and on women's formal role in politics. The Bangor Federation of Women's Clubs was actively involved in city-planning efforts in 1911 after a major fire destroyed much of the downtown area. Like other women's groups, the Bangor women supported the idea of planned development rather than laissez-faire growth, but in Bangor and elsewhere in Maine, the Women's Club endorsement of planning and the city-beautiful movement largely lost out to the free-wheeling capitalism of Maine businessmen. In other ways, such as in their support for parks and playgrounds, women's groups were more successful. The familiar Civil War memorial statues found in town greens across Maine owe much to the work of women's groups, especially the Women's Relief Corps.

Women were also active in developing social services to alleviate some of the problems associated with rural or urban poverty. In this area, religious orders played an especially important role. The Grey Nuns (Sisters of Charity) from Montreal founded a major hospital in Lewiston and played a key role in that city's health-care system. Like the Catholic sisters, Jewish and Protestant women engaged in social service work. In Portland, the Fraternity House, which coordinated and dispensed social services in a poor neighborhood, preceded Chicago's famous Hull House as a kind of settlement institution.

Women played a major role in Maine's cultural life as well. For married women, supporting or contributing to the arts was a respectable occupation. Writers like Sarah Orne Jewett and photographers like Emma Sewell and Chan-

sonetta Stanley Emmons expanded the sphere of women's options while remaining largely within the bounds of acceptable behavior. For middle-class
women, the arts offered professions and careers, but their range of choices was
usually confined by rigid Victorian strictures. Emmons's photography, for instance, produced from the late 1890s to the late 1930s, reflects both a celebration
of new trends and ideas and a nostalgia for a comfortably idealized rural past.
Her bold career undertaking after her husband's death and her relationship
with women's clubs and colleagues illustrate the opportunities and the limits
inherent in the "bonds of womanhood." Similarly, the opening of the state
system of normal schools in Maine provided women with an education and a
way to make a living, but did so within a rigidly paternalistic administrative
structure.

Workers and Community Control
ROBERT BABCOCK & YVES FRENETTE

Beyond the diversity of settings typified by Portland, Lewiston, and Auburn,
working people shared common experiences. Among the most important was
a political structure that left working people essentially powerless in the industrial communities. In Portland, by the turn of the century, city elites were
having second thoughts about the effects of smokestack industries on their city.
Fearing that new industry would attract an unsavory labor force, they promoted a "City Beautiful," with tree-lined avenues and small shops patronized
by tourists. Portland renewed itself as the gateway to Maine's vacationland. Even
without new industrial investments, local business elites controlled the city's
destiny, dominating both the Board of Trade and the City Council.

While Portland business leadership was generally local, Lewiston's pace for
growth was set early on by Boston-area industrialists, who built the mills,
canals, boarding houses, and other features of the town's new economy in the
1840s and 1850s. This tight-knit group of financiers owned controlling shares in
each of the town's most important enterprises. They hired the mill workers, determined the ethnic mix in the city, paid most of the city's property taxes, and
contributed heavily to local cultural institutions they deemed appropriate for
Lewiston. City politics, controlled by industrialists and merchants and their
representatives in the Republican party, reflected this economic power. Lewiston's first five mayors were all Republican, and three were intimately associated
with the mills.

After 1870, however, control over Lewiston politics fell to a rising group of
professionals, small-business owners, and shopkeepers. This shift was symbolized by the election of Alonzo Garcelon as Lewiston's first Democratic mayor

in 1871. Although Garcelon was from an old patrician family, he was best known as a devoted doctor and a friend of immigrants. Lewiston's Democratic party recruited principally among Irish Catholics. But as elsewhere in the state, the Irish were unable to challenge the Republicans successfully without support from other ethnic groups. Lewiston's French-language newspaper, *Le Messager*, founded in 1880, helped to cement a Franco-Irish Democratic alliance. With Franco-American backing, Lewiston elected its first Irish mayor, Daniel J. McGillicuddy, in 1887. After 1914, Franco-Americans dominated city politics, with Irish support. Although the ethnic political machines in Lewiston and other mill towns were controlled by middle-class Irish or Franco-Americans, they were more responsive to their largely working-class constituents. By the First World War, Republicans, too, backed Franco-American candidates and were able to win office in both Biddeford and Lewiston.

Despite claiming some voice in mill-town politics, working people were largely powerless to improve neighborhood conditions. Workers' housing varied according to the precariousness of their condition. In Lewiston, only a third of the city's families possessed their own homes. Single working people often lived in company boarding houses; some families rented company housing, but most lived in private tenements. The Cabot Company's one-hundred tenements in Brunswick were likewise overcrowded; too often, humans shared the premises with rats. Outside, piles of garbage, open pools of filth, and other sanitation problems encouraged epidemic diseases. Lewiston's Board of Health in 1888 declared "Little Canada," a swampy piece of land located between the Androscoggin River and the canal, the "worst and most dangerous place in the city." Epidemics ravaged Brunswick and "French Island" in Old Town. Harsh living conditions explain the high mill-town mortality rates, especially for working-class infants.

Unlike Portland, in Lewiston working people achieved some voice in local politics. Still, the structure of politics, the ideology of limited government, and restrictive municipal budgets placed these neighborhood problems beyond their control.

Control at the Workplace
CHARLES SCONTRAS & YVES FRENETTE

Workers had even less control at the workplace. Wages were generally low, and varied greatly—from $609 a year in the large pulp and paper mills to $415 in the woods and $390 in cotton mills in 1910. Women were paid less than men, the worst wages being offered for domestics, waitresses, and saleswomen. Moreover, workdays ranged between nine and fifteen hours, usually for a six-day week. Although working hours decreased between 1865 and 1930, the work often became more intense. Textile mill owners, for instance, met southern competition by adopting sophisticated machinery that increased the pace of work.

Unemployment was a constant threat. Each decade after 1850 saw a slump that resulted in shortened hours, lower wages, and ultimately work stoppages and layoffs that wiped out a family's savings. Even the excellent markets for cotton textiles in 1879–80 left 31 percent of the French-Canadian work force in Lewiston unemployed for periods ranging from a few days to several months. In some industries such as shoes, mechanization resulted in a decrease in the number of employees. Elsewhere, work remained seasonal or dependent on variable markets. Declines in cotton textiles and granite production in the 1920s brought permanent unemployment.

Those most affected by irregular income were the day laborers. Digging ditches, grading streets, and other such tasks were not only physically taxing, but also erratic. Bad weather brought work to a halt, as did the onset of winter. Some workers had to leave their families in order to find a job. Indeed, the line between day labor and destitution was thin. In Maine, as elsewhere, the ethnic groups most associated with day labor were the Irish and Italians.

In a variety of ways, some still discernible today in court cases, state agency reports, and union documents, workers gave voice to the perils and problems they encountered at work. Many complaints stemmed from the fact that industrial buildings and internal working arrangements were not designed with worker comfort or health in mind. In summer, the oppressive heat of the mills taxed workers' endurance; in the winter, they were forced to wrap themselves in shawls and jackets. Workers labored in multistoried factories that lacked fire escapes, with machines that lacked safeguards, or in rooms where ventilation was so poor that the cry for fresh air could be heard with monotonous regularity. Cotton factories were known for their deafening noise, inadequate lighting, and high summer temperatures. Heat prostration was common. The high humidity necessary to keep the threads pliable often caused bronchitis, and cotton dust choked the lungs. Accidents were common. A homesick operative wrote in 1872 that moving from Bethel to Lewiston was "like going from the heavens to earth."

Facilities for washing or changing clothing were a luxury. Female textile operatives, who customarily exchanged street clothes for lighter garments in the mills, often had to disrobe behind the looms and spinning frames. They were given a storage box near their place of work, but this left their street clothes damp and cold when they donned them again. If workers were fortunate enough to have access to a toilet, it was often uncovered and uncared for.

Sometimes toilets were located in the boiler room; women found this particularly disquieting, since they had to pass male work crews to reach the facility.

Some complaints stemmed even more directly from the lack of control workers exercised over their jobs. Factory doors were sometimes locked after the workers entered to prevent them from leaving. As a condition of employment, workers often signed "iron-clad" contracts, in which they agreed not to join a union. Other contracts left workers liable for all injuries they sustained in the increasingly dangerous workplaces. Sometimes workers were required to trade at the company store as a condition of employment; others found work only by paying a supervisor a substantial fee for the privilege. Employers sometimes dictated how workers should vote. It was not until 1891 that the legislature, petitioned by thousands of Maine working men and women, stipulated that citizens could vote in secrecy. Workers were sometimes fired for expressing political views, joining a union, or testifying publicly.

As in community politics, workers had little recourse against such conditions in the state legislature or in the courts. The prevailing view was that government should remain aloof from the economic playing field. For instance, three state supreme court judges in 1871 informed the legislature that "the less the State interferes with industry, the less it directs and selects the channels of enterprise, the better." Other judges spoke of the "inexorable" law of supply and demand or "the sagacity shown in the acquisition of capital" as the best regulator of working conditions.

Another limitation on workers' rights was the widely held view that in America an individual's position on the social pyramid was dictated solely by personal effort. Those who possessed the appropriate character traits—capacity for hard work, perseverance, frugality, foresight, temperance—would surely rise above the work place and its miseries. According to this view, the social order was not to be tampered with; disparities in wealth, power, and status were inevitable manifestations of individual character.

Religious doctrine reinforced the view that Providence rewarded hard work and punished lassitude, but it also fostered at least a limited sense of social responsibility on the part of owners of capital. Some employers aided their workers in cases of injury, illness, or death of a family member, provided them with periodic excursions and entertainment, or overlooked certain minor offenses against property. In order to prevent labor problems, the Ara Cushman Shoe Company instituted a profit-sharing plan in 1886; five years later, the S. D. Warren Company did likewise, soon to be followed by other paper companies. Company welfare programs, although essentially paternalistic in outlook, provided some surcease from the problems of the workplace.

Coping with Uncertainty
YVES FRENETTE

Company welfare was limited and random, however. Most workers, faced with difficult conditions in the workplace and neighborhoods, found strength in institutions of their own making. These sources of support provided a measure of stability and control that the established structures of power in the mills and communities denied. Surviving letters from female textile-mill operatives reveal a regionwide network of relatives and friends that worked both as an employment agency and a psychological support system. Neighbors from towns miles from Lewiston often worked in the same factory, even in the same room. "If you could only be here," confided a young Lewiston woman to a Bethel cousin. "There are so many friends [from back home]." French-Canadian immigrants also relied on their families for support; indeed, whole families of French Canadians moved to mill towns. In fact, it was often specifically to preserve the integrity of their family that people left Quebec for Maine, where there would be work for all members of the family. Many households comprised, in addition to parents and children, relatives and friends who boarded with the family.

In order to accumulate savings or just to make ends meet, members of a household combined incomes. Between 1850 and 1880, over 70 percent of French-Canadian children in Biddeford and Lewiston aged ten to fourteen worked in the mills. Citywide figures for child labor, at least by official count, dropped to 0.7 percent for girls and 1.6 percent for boys in 1930, the result of changing economics, new attitudes toward education, and child labor legislation. True figures were higher, however; in 1908, for instance, a year after state legislation forbade employment before fourteen years of age, at least 270 youngsters could be found in Lewiston mills. "When the truant officer was about to come," reminisced a Franco-American, "they'd send us home for the day." Wives and mothers, as opposed to single women and young girls, rarely worked outside the home. In 1880, only 12 percent of the city's French-Canadian married women were gainfully employed. On the other hand, those who stayed home often took in boarders, in addition to taking care of a husband and numerous children.

Working people reacted to economic instability by moving, which again provided some measure of control over their lives. Laborers—loggers or construction workers—were sometimes recruited by employers and relocated to a work site, but most working people moved on their own, often responding to the call of a relative or friend. Many went back and forth between their place of origin and one or two locations where they found work, following the caprices of the economy. A number of young women worked in Lewiston ten months out of the year but returned to Bethel for the summer. French-Canadian families did likewise, leaving in June and returning in September. Some alternated between mill work and farm labor, fishing, or woods work.

Geographic mobility was thus an important part of working-class life. Adelard Coté was born in St. Sophie, Quebec, in 1889. When he was a child, his family moved to neighboring St. Pierre Baptiste. After four years at school, Adelard entered the world of work on the family farm and as apprentice at the local blacksmith shop. From St. Pierre Baptiste, the young man traveled to Biddeford, where he was welcomed by an aunt and a sister who had migrated before him. Easing into this urban world with the help of his relatives, the young immigrant plied his blacksmith's skills at the Pepperell Manufacturing Company. Moving on quickly with a brother to New York, he worked in a light-bulb factory. He returned to Biddeford, then departed almost immediately for Manitoba and Saskatchewan, where he lived four years. In early 1920, he again returned to Biddeford, then bought a blacksmith shop in Westbrook. Three years later, he married in Biddeford, where he spent the rest of his life. By the beginning of the twentieth century, thousands of French Canadians had followed the same winding path; some had been on the move for two or three generations.

In Old Town, only 13 to 36 percent of the Franco-Americans remained locally for as long as ten years; the population was in flux between Canada, the St. John Valley, and industrial centers throughout New England. In Biddeford, between 1870 and 1890, the turnover of French Canadians was 50 percent every three years, making the city one of the most transient in New England. Lewiston's turnover approached 66 percent in the decade of the 1870s. Since they did not sink deep roots, French Canadians were largely insensitive to the rhetoric of union organizers. When a strike or a lockout occurred, they simply looked for another job. Failing this, they returned to Canada or went elsewhere in Maine or New England.

In contrast to geographical mobility, social mobility was sharply limited. In Lewiston, thirty years after their arrival in the 1850s, 60 percent of foreign-born Irish were still unskilled laborers. Of the rest, most were semiskilled factory operatives. A lucky few took advantage of the numerous opportunities created by a booming community to become merchants. For children of immigrants and people who arrived young in the United States, the situation was not so bleak. Only 20 percent of second-generation Irish were confined to unskilled employment. The majority entered the textile and shoe factories, and a fairly large number became skilled construction workers. Second-generation Irish were less likely to send their children into the mills, and with the benefit of an education, this third generation could achieve middle-class status in the first decades of the twentieth century.

Ethnic Enclaves

YVES FRENETTE

Ethnic identity formed another source of collective support and control. In politics, ethnic groups allied and fought, but social contacts between people of different origins were usually kept to a minimum. To go onto Old Town's French Island, one had to cross a bridge, a symbol of the separateness of the residents. Among Lewiston's several European minorities, only the Italians did not show residential concentration. Other groups held firmly to their territory.

To this neighborhood exclusiveness was coupled a social distancing. Maine's three leading liberal arts colleges, located near the downtown sections of Brunswick, Lewiston, and Waterville, either ignored or condescended toward the sizable working-class communities in each town. Cultural and linguistic barriers reinforced these exclusive identities. Eva Aubé, who immigrated to Lewiston in 1919, never learned English. "Why should I?" she explained. "My doctor speaks French. . . , my hairdresser speaks French. . . , my grocer speaks French. . . , my landlord speaks French." Like her, thousands of Franco-Americans could live with a minimum of contact with Yankees and other ethnic groups. They worshiped in French-language churches, sent their children to parochial schools, joined their own clubs, read their own French-language newspapers—twenty-eight statewide in 1935—played music in their own bands, celebrated their patron saint each year, and shaped a culture of their own. Like the more recent immigrant groups, Portland's older African-American community developed a range of institutions and services that helped insulate its members from oppression and racism.

Even though reduced to a minimum, contacts nevertheless occurred, and acculturation of immigrants took place. Ethnic groups concentrated in certain neighborhoods, but they very rarely monopolized them. On the street, on the streetcar, at the factory, at the vaudeville or silent movies, cultures mixed. Acculturation was especially rapid for the second generation and in settings where an ethnic group was in the minority. Born in Old Town in 1873, Mike Pelletier learned to play the accordion as a child; his repertoire consisted of American, rather than French songs. He loved stories about the Wild West, and as a grown man, he belonged to the Catholic Foresters and the Grange, two non-Franco associations. His real given name was Magloire but he preferred the Americanized "Mike." In Lewiston and Biddeford, mixed marriages were rare, and the people who took this less-traveled road were likely to be suspected or ostracized; but in Old Town, they accounted for nearly one-third of Franco-American unions between 1925 and 1929.

19-3. While the majority of immigrants to Maine at the turn of the century clustered together in larger communities, a few moved to smaller towns in search of opportunity. Italian-American Amedeo Christopher and his family established a produce store in Madison. Courtesy of the Maine Historic Preservation Commission, Augusta.

By 1930, smaller Franco-American parochial schools had evolved into general Catholic schools with French language studies occupying a minor position in the curriculum. Larger schools still emphasized the language, but no longer were the teachers preaching love of Canada and its history. In fact, schools and other ethnic institutions had always helped immigrants adapt to American life as much as they helped keep alive their national traditions. Ethnic professionals and business leaders too helped validate acculturation in the eyes of their compatriots by forming cross-cultural friendships and borrowing middle-class traits from American culture—even when they preached a strong attachment to ethnic traditions. Acculturation, of course, was not a one-way street. At the cotton mill, many supervisors learned French to communicate with their Francophone employees, and the entire mill might close when a popular Franco-American personality died. In some cases, acculturation took place twice: several of Lewiston's Italian and Polish immigrants joined the Franco-American community before being absorbed into the larger American culture.

Despite this accommodation, ethnic conflict was part of the social and cultural landscape of Maine. The Franco-Irish political alliance was not a marriage of love but of convenience. Fights between youths of the two groups were part of everyday life. French-Canadian immigrants grew unsatisfied with the Irish-dominated Catholic churches and asked for their own parishes, which they generally obtained, or the opposite happened: Irish Catholics, when their churches were taken over by French Canadians, reformed into separate congregations. Franco-Irish tension culminated in open political war in the first three decades of the twentieth century. Militant members of the Franco-American petty bourgeoisie challenged the Irish-American Catholic hierarchy of Portland, led by Bishop Louis S. Walsh, over financial control of the parishes, nomination of Franco-American priests and bishop, and the overall question of Francophone assimilation. Casualties in the crisis, called the Corporation Sole Controversy after the system of parish administration in Maine, included six Franco-American lay leaders who were interdicted from the Catholic Church in 1911.

Initially, middle-class Yankees accepted French Canadians as a necessary evil in industrial towns. Hostility increased, however, when immigrants from the North increased in numbers and claimed a share of political power. Symbolic of this friction was the verbal duel between *Le Messager* and the *Lewiston Evening Journal*, whose view of Franco-Americans was quite unflattering. In Biddeford, the English-language newspaper offered a positive view of Franco-Americans, but letters to the editor left no doubt about the xenophobic sentiment of many Yankees. Wrote one in 1907: "We are not French, neither Irish. We are true born Americans and we don't want to read anymore about the exploits of the French in Biddeford, nor of the Irish neither, for one is no better than the other." The municipal government in Saco prevented Francos from living there by refusing to permit construction of big tenements. After the first World War, "Americanization" became state policy when the Legislature specified that all school instruction, public and parochial, was to be in English, and that American history and civics were to be taught.

Anti-Catholicism was an element of Yankee xenophobia. In 1871, the second pastor of Saint Peter's parish in Lewiston, Pierre Hevey, was unable to find convenient lodging when he arrived in town: no one would rent to a disciple of the pope. The most dramatic manifestation of anti-Catholicism in Maine after the Civil War was the popularity of the Ku Klux Klan in the 1920s. In Catholic cities such as Biddeford and Lewiston, the Franco-American population reacted virulently, sometimes violently, against the Klan, but in Saco, a largely Protestant community, Franco-American reaction was more restrained, for fear of physical abuse.

Within the working class, economic competition contributed to ethnic conflict. Immigrant workers who faced a hostile reception in the textile and pulp and paper industries refused to join Yankee workers in unions or collective action. At the beginning of the twentieth century, when many Franco-Americans did join unions, the tables were turned. Victims, now, of strikebreakers and scabs from southern and eastern Europe, some Francos advocated restrictions on European immigration. Jews were also subject to Franco-American intolerance, and during World War I the French and English newspapers of Biddeford united in a propaganda campaign against the Turks and pro-German Greeks, contributing to a climate of fear and narrow-mindedness. Ethnic identification brought mixed blessings: on one hand, ethnic communities provided support for individuals who faced uncertainty and powerlessness in the workplace; on the other hand, ethnic tensions divided groups of workers who shared a common interest in better wages and working conditions. In Maine, as in America generally, ethnic tension was a fundamental weakness of the trade union movement.

Protest and Organization
CHARLES SCONTRAS

Workers found a source of control and stability in family networks, geographic mobility, or ethnic enclaves. Others expressed their discontent by organizing unions. In a state with a very complex occupational, ethnic, and class structure, workers' grievances were varied, and so were their attitudes toward unions. In some cases they responded with pledges of solidarity and union organization; in others, they bore their grievance with smoldering resentment, unable to overcome the cultural, economic, or personal sanctions against organizing and confronting the bosses directly.

Nevertheless, a growing number of workers joined the chorus of dissenters who refused to accept the cluster of values that celebrated the free market, unrestrained competition, and individualism. The editor of the *Bangor Whig and Courier* noted in 1869 that it was "the Day of Isms," as he cataloged a variety of alternative beliefs, values, and attitudes that had emerged to challenge the established patterns of thought. Dissidents became increasingly convinced that equality of opportunity and freedom of contract had given way to gross inequalities in power between capital and labor. Collectively, workers struggled to regain some measure of dignity and control in an world where they were increasingly viewed as an impersonal factor of production.

While sporadic labor organization and protest reach back in Maine as far as the 1830s, it was not until the 1860s that a sustained drive to organize Maine workers was discernible. Labor unions were organized in major cities of the state during and immediately after the Civil War, and the number of strikes, official and unofficial, so increased that Portland's *Eastern Argus* complained in 1867 that they were "the order of the day." A proliferation of labor unions like the Knights of St. Crispin, the Sovereigns of Industry, and the Granite Cutters' National Union, along with workers' cooperative enterprises, labor parties, and eight-hour leagues, all symbolized the rise of class consciousness in Maine.

In 1882, the Knights of Labor, the nation's first major labor movement, reached Maine, and by 1887, it reported 27,900 members distributed over 127 locals. The Maine state organization became District Assembly 86. Originally a craft society, the Knights adopted a policy of inclusive unionism, designed to bring into one big union all those engaged in "honorable toil"—men and women, skilled and unskilled, black and white, merchants, farmers, and employers. This did not include, however, bankers, stockbrokers, lawyers, professional gamblers, liquor manufacturers and sellers, and, at least initially, doctors. The organization sought to uplift all of humanity; in place of a society based on class antagonism and competition, the Knights envisioned a world governed by the principles of brotherhood and cooperation.

The rapid growth of the Knights belied the view held by many that Maine was a ideological fortress impenetrable to unionism. Knights' literature, "sown broadcast," reached throughout Maine. Organizers used songs, poems, plays, picnics, and dances to reach Maine working people, while labor mugs, pins, stationery, newspapers, broadsides, official proclamations, and documents seemed to be everywhere. School children in one case, caught up in the craze for organization, struck for shorter hours. Most adherents were attracted to the Knights' immediate demands: an eight-hour day, abolition of contract, convict, and child labor; equal pay for both sexes; health and safety legislation; and a legal labor holiday—which became a reality in 1881. Although the Knights lost momentum in the late 1880s, others implemented many of their reforms in the twentieth century.

Leadership of the labor movement passed to the American Federation of Labor. Nationally organized in 1886, the new labor movement accepted the outlines of the capitalist economic order. Unlike the much more inclusive Knights, the AFL was a federation of craft unions—independent organizations of skilled workers addressing matters particular to their own interests. Along with this exclusive craft structure, advocates of the new "business unionism" narrowed their focus to immediate "bread and butter" issues, unlike the Knights of Labor, which worked to uplift all of humanity.

In May 1891, delegates from the various craft unions formed a state branch of the American Federation of Labor. The dislocations and hardships brought about by depression conditions destroyed the young organization in 1897 and left the labor movement ill-defined and fragmented. General union membership in Maine plummeted from an estimated fifteen to twenty thousand in 1891 to between three and six thousand. In the early years of the new century, organized labor again entered a period of explosive growth, bringing membership to 13,609. By 1914, the state branch claimed nearly 18,000 members.

Activities symbolic of this revival were everywhere: reports of organizational drives, strikes, jurisdictional quarrels between unions, ideological disputes over ends and means, educational and public relations campaigns, and an endless list of speakers and dignitaries from the world of labor filled the press. The state branch sponsored social events—union picnics, concerts, dances, "smoke" talks, and other forms of entertainment. Once again labor unions spawned countless petitions and resolutions; members trekked to the legislative halls in Augusta, flirted with independent labor politics, and forced the major political parties to carry labor planks in their platforms.

Some differed with the AFL's economic philosophy of organizing workers into separate crafts and trades and its political philosophy of nonpartisan alignment. Syndicalism, socialism, and anarchism gained adherents as organizations such as the International Laborers' Union (1903), the Socialist Trades and Labor Alliance (1903), and the Industrial Workers of the World (1906) brought their brand of solidarity, class war, and revolution to Maine workers. While never significant in terms of numbers, the radicals' insistence on the abolition of capitalism as a condition for the emancipation from "wage slavery" widened the boundaries of debate on labor questions. Even though the AFL remained the dominant labor movement in the state, its affiliated branches counted for only 107 unions out of Maine's 390 in 1920. Like Maine's working class itself, philosophies of working-class emancipation were diverse.

During the 1920s, the labor movement entered a period of decline as statewide and national anti-union campaigns took their toll. Membership dropped to around ten thousand late in the decade. The Depression exacerbated matters; in 1933, for the first time since its founding in 1904, the state federation failed to hold a convention. The favorable labor legislation of the New Deal era, coupled with the emergence of the aggressive Congress of Industrial Organizations, sparked a revival late in the decade and ushered in a new chapter in the history of organized labor in Maine.

On Strike!

ROBERT BABCOCK

The most dramatic means by which working people sought control over their lives and work was a strike. For a number of reasons, union organizing and strike activity were more intense in some industries than in others. Because sawmill workers labored seasonally, they remained for the most part unorganized, and relatively few of them ever walked out. Among shoe workers, only the most skilled lasters and cutters generally found themselves in a position to declare strikes. On the other hand, granite cutters, well-organized into an association by 1890, waged massive struggles over the next decade throughout New England. Young women, braving enormous cultural sanctions against female militancy, spontaneously walked off the job at several Maine cotton and woolen mills, risking their livelihoods long before unions had appeared in their line of work. Pulp and paper workers unionized during the first World War but then lost a titanic three-year struggle with International Paper Company during the early 1920s. After 1900, many service employees, such as laundry workers, trolley conductors, and telephone operators, declared strikes in order to win union recognition.

Most Maine wage-earners walked out for a combination of reasons: shorter hours, higher pay, improved working conditions, or the preservation of a measure of control over their workplace. Unskilled workers, easily replaced from the regional pool of unemployed, usually chose boom times to express grievances, since employers then found it more difficult to replace them. Thus, mill workers along the Penobscot River won a shorter workday in 1889, and in 1917, three hundred hands at a pulp and paper mill in Howland achieved a three-shift, eight-hour day after a brief walkout. During the inflationary years around World War I, strikes for higher wages were increasingly common, but after the war employer resistance stiffened. When 125 molders at the Saco-Lowell shops in Biddeford walked out to demand higher wages, the owners hired replacements, feeding and housing them in the mill. The strike was ultimately defeated.

Arbitrary action by a supervisor or a sudden wage cut sometimes provoked spontaneous strikes. In 1896, weavers at the York Mill in Saco, for example, shut down the entire plant to protest a wage cut. During the same year textile workers in Biddeford, Lewiston, and Waterville, facing a depression-induced 10 percent wage cut, persuaded management to give them the reduction in hours instead. Weavers at a woolen mill in Gardiner walked out in 1900 when their supervisor was "unfairly" discharged. Most such disputes were resolved within a few days or weeks.

Strikes called by trade unions increasingly replaced those occurring spontaneously, and more of these struggles centered upon issues involving control over conditions at the workplace, rather than simple improvements in wages or hours. Even without strikes, the trade unions helped workers to gain new respect: "Before we formed the union the bosses wouldn't speak to us on the

19-4. After the Civil War street railways were built to meet the public transportation needs of every city and large town in Maine. By the turn of the century, urban lines had expanded into surrounding communities to provide inexpensive regional transportation. Labor problems with the Portland Railroad Company led to a successful general strike in 1916. Collections of the Maine Historical Society, Portland.

street," one Portland worker observed in 1916, "and now they invite us into their autos when they meet us." But not always: the resistance to union recognition was often bitter and dogged. In 1890, for example, the powerful Granite Cutters' Protective Union demanded higher wages, a nine-hour day, and enforcement of the union shop against imported Italian cutters. When the owners declined, about eight thousand went out on strike, some for nearly two years. Dissatisfied with their settlements, in 1900, the cutters at West Sullivan, North Jay, and Stonington joined quarry workers all over New England in a massive strike.

Ethnic tensions were a part of union politics. When cutters at the Mt. Waldo Granite Company in Frankfort first walked out in 1889–90, for example, the firm's owner hired 150 Italian workers to replace them. After assaulting a native laborer, one immigrant was discharged; thereupon, all the Italian cutters quit, demanding that the Americans be fired. At the height of the conflict union and non-union workers waged pitched battles on Saturday nights at the local tavern in Frankfort.

Occasionally, the inevitable tensions between labor and capital escalated into battles that paralyzed whole communities. A struggle considered by some the greatest strike known in Maine up to that time occurred in Portland during the summer of 1916. Streetcar workers had been bitter over poor wages for some time. When the company, owned by Philadelphia interests, discharged eight men who had been trying to form a union among the three hundred employees, the men joined the Amalgamated Association of Street and Electric Railway Employees and walked out in a body. Trolley service quickly ground to a halt.

Refusing to negotiate, management imported strikebreakers from Boston. The company ran a few trolleys at infrequent intervals and housed the replacement workers under police protection in the car barns. The inexperienced operators occasionally drove their trolleys off the tracks and into automobiles. Striking workers marched through the city, drawing widespread support because of their peaceful conduct, their good standing among riders, and growing dissatisfaction with the company. A group of strikers, emerging en masse from a theatre, passed a shop full of women. Lifting their caps in unison they shouted: "Will you walk?" Back came the cry: "We'll walk." Others joined in refusing to ride trolleys run by scabs, and those who owned autos went out of their way to provide lifts.

By the end of the week, public pressure on the company officials was mounting. Portland's mayor criticized them for importing strikebreakers; the city attorney threatened to prosecute them for reckless operation of the trolleys; the board of health complained about unsanitary conditions at the car barns; and newspaper editorials commended the strikers for their good order and called upon management to negotiate. "It is bad enough to fight the employees," the trolley's manager lamented, "but what can you do when you have the public on your back as well?" Local merchants appointed a blue-ribbon committee to bring both sides together, and after a marathon bargaining session the company conceded all the strikers' demands.

The crucial role of public support for Portland's striking trolley workers was well illustrated a month later when Bangor's conductors walked out for similar reasons. The outcome could not have been more different. First of all, about a third of the workers remained on the job or returned within a short time. More importantly, as a result of the strikers' disunity, the public was little inconvenienced and did not take much interest in the struggle. The company quickly hired non-union workers, and the union was forced to call off the battle.

The outcome of the 1916 Portland trolley strike suggests that workers by the first decade of the twentieth century had come some distance in their struggle for control over their lives. The Amalgamated Association demonstrated the power of collective action; what is more, the union articulated their cause in a way that won support from Portland's citizens. Workers in Portland had, by this time, learned to use their power as voters, too. Workers had transferred their political allegiance from the Republican to the Democratic party, which proved more receptive to their demands. Some even began to offer themselves for local office, and by 1920 nearly a third of the officials in Portland had been elected from blue-collar ranks. As in Lewiston, politics in Portland had become another means of accommodating to an inherently unequal society.

Despite the prevailing ideology of economic individualism, even the Maine state government gradually became involved in workplace issues. In the 1870s, the legislature established a Bureau of Industrial and Labor Statistics to collect data on working conditions. Early in the twentieth century the state set up a board of arbitration to mediate strikes, and by the first World War state agencies were intervening frequently to get talks started. The creation of a state workers' compensation board also provided a mechanism to redress grievances.

It should be apparent that labor-management struggles in Maine, as elsewhere, emerged from the contradictions inherent in the rapidly changing capitalist economy. Wage-earners invariably faced a mix of difficulties compounded of long hours, low wages, death or injury from industrial accidents, seasonal and cyclical joblessness, and sometimes physical or mental abuse from workplace supervisors. Just as regularly, workers' responses alternated between protests and accommodation. Angry wage-earners relied not only upon strikes, but also upon other strategies at their disposal, including quitting one job in favor of another, surreptitiously restricting their output, engaging in occasional acts of sabotage, or, on a few occasions, trying to short-circuit the profit-driven economy by organizing cooperative factories and stores.

A few shared experiences similar to Roscoe Fillmore's. One workday evening in 1904, he strolled along Congress Street in Portland, stopping occasionally to browse in the booksellers' stalls. At Monument Square, Fillmore joined a small crowd listening to a soapbox orator who was talking in animated terms about the virtues of a socialist economy. A half-century later Fillmore still believed that his exposure to socialism on that memorable evening had "changed the whole course" of his life. Doubtless his eighteen months of hard toil in Portland's foundries and machine shops had helped to prepare him for the orator's message. At any rate, upon his return to Canada, Fillmore devoted all his spare time to the propagation of a socialist cure for the ills of the modern industrial society. The cause he espoused was one more facet of the workers' search for stability and control in Maine's industry.

For Further Reading:

There is no single collection of primary sources dealing with Maine's working class and its ethnic groups. The State Archives in Augusta remain a rich but untapped source. Records of departments and agencies, such as the Superintendent of Public Schools, the State Board of Health, the Registrar of Vital Statistics, and the Bureau of Industrial and Labor Statistics all deal with aspects of working-class life. At the county level, Registries of Deeds maintain land records that allow researchers to study land and home ownership and the formation of ethnic neighborhoods and working-class suburbs. Municipal archives are a gold mine for historians: street records, vital statistics records, assessors' rolls, city council minutes, and municipal court records provide information on an array of topics. The manuscript schedules of the decennial federal census, available through 1920, are essential tools for the social historian, and business records stored in damp basements should not be overlooked. Relations between ethnic groups and the Irish-dominated Catholic hierarchy of Portland are documented in diocesan and parish archives. In addition, the latter contain information on ethnic life in general. Data on Maine population distribution and the economy in this chapter is from the compiled US Census reports, 1860–1930.

Major collections and publications of national labor federations and unions are indispensable for labor research in Maine. These contain reports from local organizers, secretaries, labor leaders, and state labor organizations touching upon a wide range of topics. Particularly valuable are the proceedings and publications of the Knights of Labor (major depository, Catholic University, Washington, DC) and the American Federation of Labor (located in the George Meany Memorial Archives in Silver Spring, Maryland). The University of Maine's Special Collections Department in Fogler Library contains the twentieth-century records, correspondence, and papers of the Maine State Federated Labor Council Collection (AFL).

The annual reports of the Maine Bureau of Industrial and Labor Statistics, which begin in 1887 (with titles that vary over time), are useful for information concerning particular local unions in various towns and cities. Also of great value for researchers of the contemporary period are the files of the Bureau of Labor Education, University of Maine, and the Maine AFL-CIO located in Bangor.

Some records of the Portland Company can be found in the collections of the Maine Historical Society, Portland; others are located at the Harvard School of Business Administration, Cambridge, Massachusetts. On elite strategies for promotion of Portland and vicinity, see the *Portland Board of Trade Journal*, 1886–1918. On the industrialization of Maine, see the *Industrial Journal*, a weekly (later monthly) newspaper published in Bangor, 1880–1918. The papers of Roscoe Fillmore are found in the Dalhousie University archives, Halifax; see also Nicholas Fillmore, *The Life and Times of Roscoe Fillmore* (Toronto, 1991).

Primary sources on women and work include the Maine Women Writers Collection, Westbrook College; the Oral History Archives, New England Studies Program, University of Southern Maine; interviews for Portland's West End Working Class Women's History Project; and *Maine Revised Statutes, Annotated*, title 19, sections 162, 163. See also Judy Litoff and Hal Litoff, "Working Women in Maine: A Note on Sources," *Labor History* 17 (1976).

Life stories, either put down on paper by workers themselves or recorded by interviewers, are rare. The few that exist fill large gaps in our knowledge of the Maine working-class. In this respect Franco-Americans are especially blessed with interviews made in Old Town during the Great Depression published in C. Stewart Doty, *The First Franco-Americans* (Orono, 1985) and with life stories of two ordinary French Canadians who migrated to Maine in the 1920s. They are Normand R. Beaupré and Stephen O. Muskie, *L'enclume et le couteau: The Life and Work of Adelard Coté, Folk Artist* (Manchester, N.H., 1982); and Mary Elizabeth Aubé, "Mes entretiens avec Mémère," (Ph.D. dissertation, Brown University, 1985).

The Pine Tree State's working class still awaits a comprehensive history. For specific groups of workers, see Roger L. Grindle, "Bodwell Blue: The Story of Vinalhaven's Granite Industry," *Maine Historical Society Quarterly* 16 (1976); David C. Smith, *A History of Lumbering in Maine 1861–1960* (Orono, 1961); and Richard W. Judd, *Aroostook: A Century of Logging in Northern Maine* (Orono, 1989), pp. 109–28, 190–96. The urban setting of the Maine working class remains for the most part *terra incognita*. Exceptions are Robert Babcock's articles on Portland listed below and the fine popular history by Jacques Downs, *Cities on the Saco* (Norfolk/Virginia Beach, Va., 1985).

In the late nineteenth and early twentieth centuries, a good portion of Maine's workers were first- and second-generation immigrants. By far the most studied group has been the Franco-Americans. One should start with the annotated bibliography by Alice R. Stewart, "The Franco-Americans of Maine: A Historiographical Essay," *Maine Historical Society Quarterly* 26 (1987). Two useful overviews are: Gerard J. Brault, "The Franco-Americans of Maine," *Maine Historical Society Newsletter* 12 (1972); and James P. Allen, "Franco-Americans in Maine: A Geographical Perspective," *Acadiensis* 4 (1974). Many pages and tables in Ralph Vicero's unpublished dissertation deal with the Pine Tree State: "Immigration of French Canadians to New England, 1840–1900" (Ph.D. dissertation, University of Wisconsin, 1968). On migration patterns, see also James P. Allen, "Migration Fields of French Canadian Immigrants to Southern Maine," *Geographical Review* 42 (1972). The difficult relations between Franco-Americans and the Irish Catholic hierarchy are chronicled in Kenneth G. Woodbury, Jr., "An Incident between the French Canadians and the Irish in the Diocese of Maine in 1906," *New England Quarterly* 40 (1967); and Michael Guignard, "Maine's Corporation Sole Controversy," *Maine Historical Society Newsletter* 12 (1973). For a fresh look at this controversial matter the reader should consult Yves Roby, *Les Franco-Américains de la Nouvelle-Angleterre (1776–1930)* (Quebec City, 1990), pp. 253–67.

Several Franco-American communities have been researched. For Old Town, see Marcella Sorg, "Genetics of Deme Formation in a Franco-American Population, 1830–1903" (Ph.D. dissertation, Ohio State University, 1979); for Augusta, Maurice Violette, *The Franco-Americans* (New York, 1976); for Brunswick, William Locke, "The French Colony at Brunswick, Maine," *Les archives de folklore* 1 (1946); for Biddeford, Michael Guignard, *La foi–La langue–La culture* (n.p., 1982); for Lewiston, Yves Frenette's "*Understanding the*

French Canadians of Lewiston, 1860–1900: An Alternate Framework," Maine Historical Society Quarterly 25 (1986); his "Lewiston's Ethnic Majority: The Francos," *Bates: The Alumni Magazine,* 86th Series (1988); and his "La genèse d'une communauté canadienne-française en Nouvelle-Angleterre: Lewiston, Maine 1800–1880," *Historical Papers/ Communications historiques* (1989).

On Maine's Irish, see James Mundy, *Hard Men, Hard Times: Maine and the Irish, 1830–1860* (Scarborough, 1990). The post–Civil War Irish badly need a historian. The only work in the field is Margaret J. Buker, "The Irish in Lewiston, Maine: A Search for Security on the Urban Frontier, 1850–1880," *Maine Historical Society Quarterly* 13 (1973). Randolph Stakeman has begun to uncover the history of Maine's African-American population. See his "The Black Population of Maine 1764–1900," *New England Journal of Black Studies* 8 (1989).

For a broader view of this period from the perspective of American workers, see David Montgomery, *The Fall of the House of Labor* (New York, 1987). On the labor movement in Maine, see Charles A. Scontras, *Organized Labor and Labor Politics in Maine, 1880–1890* (Orono, 1966); his *Two Decades of Organized Labor and Labor Politics in Maine, 1880–1900* (Orono, 1969), his *Organized Labor in Maine: Twentieth Century Origins* (Orono, 1985); and his *The Origins of Labor Day in Maine and Historical Glimpses of Labor in Parade in Early Nineteenth Century Maine* (Orono, 1989). On left-wing politics in Maine at the turn of the century, see Scontras, *The Socialist Alternative* (Orono, 1985). Studies of the Ku Klux Klan in Maine include Rita M. Breton, "Red Scare: A Study of Maine Nativism, 1919–1925" (M.A. thesis, University of Maine, 1972) and Lawrence W. Moores, Jr., "The History of the Ku Klux Klan in Maine, 1922–1931," (M.A. thesis, University of Maine, 1950). On the harbor at Portland, see Robert H. Babcock, "The Rise and Fall of Portland's Waterfront, 1850–1920," *Maine Historical Society Quarterly* 12 (Fall 1982). On the merchant/artisan community in Portland, see Babcock, "The Decline of Artisan Republicanism in Portland, Maine, 1825–1850," *New England Quarterly* 63 (March 1990). On the Portland trolley strike of 1916, see Babcock, "'Will You Walk? Yes, We'll Walk!': Popular Support for a Street Railway Strike in Portland, Maine," forthcoming in *Labor History.*

On women, see Karen Blair, *The Clubwoman as Feminist: True Womanhood Redefined, 1868–1914* (New York, 1980); Miriam Anne Bourne, *The Ladies of Castine* (New York, 1986); Eleanor George Down, "Working Women in Bangor" (M.A. thesis, University of Maine, 1988); Judith S. Goldstein, *Crossing Lines: Histories of Jews and Gentiles in Three Communities* (New York, 1992); Theodora Penny Martin, *The Sound of Their Own Voices: Women's Study Clubs, 1860–1910* (Boston, 1987); and Marius B. Peladeau, *Chansonetta: The Life and Photographs of Chansonetta Stanley Emmons, 1858–1937* (Waldoboro, 1977).

20

Maine & the Arts

WILLIAM DAVID BARRY

In this chapter William David Barry describes the many facets of Maine arts and culture, focusing on the characteristic expression of Maine art forms in the nineteenth and early twentieth centuries. He shows us how Mainers perceived themselves—how they expressed a distinctive self-image—and created a literary and artistic tradition that is uniquely Maine's.

Not surprisingly, Maine's cultural traditions correspond with other aspects of the state's history. Maine artists, musicians, and literary figures, for instance, were part of the mid-nineteenth-century fluorescence that distinguished Maine nationally. And Maine expressed through its cultural forms the remarkable diversity we have seen in other aspects of its history. The development of Maine culture might be perceived, as with Maine politics and economic growth, as a search for autonomy—for an identity freed from the powerful influences of Europe, Boston, or New York. "Why . . . should [we] not aim at independence, with respect to our mental enjoyments, as well as for our more substantial enjoyments," asked early novelist Madam Wood. In the nineteenth century, Maine residents, and those who came to Maine to express their art, provided another basis for that independence.

Another parallel between Maine arts and culture and other historical trends is the characteristic blend of frontier or natural influences and cultivated expression. Maine art thrived on a fusion of refinement and raw nature. Finally, nineteenth-century Maine art forms express the creative tensions between national and local influences we have seen in other aspects of the state's history. Maine art was thoroughly grounded in local identity but also benefited from national innovations and especially from a constant influx of artists from "away." In this, as in other aspects of state history, Maine people transformed national themes and impulses into expressions of their own compelling sense of place. The result was a dynamic and uniquely Maine cultural outpouring that continues to the present day.

"I've traveled the world over—talk about your chalk cliffs . . . —talk about the 'wonderful scenery' anywhere in Europe—Maine has it all over them," opined the celebrated American painter George Luks in the *Maine Library Bulletin* of July–October 1927. The artist rounded out his vision of Maine by concluding: "And your characters—there are real American types; types that you will find nowhere else." Like so many creative individuals before and after him, Luks responded to what he perceived as Maine's uniqueness of place, people, and spirit. Indeed, through the years the relatively small state has attracted and inspired the likes of Thomas Cole, Henry David Thoreau, Frederic Edwin Church, Winslow Homer, E. B. White, Marguerite Yourcenar, Andrew Wyeth, and Berenice Abbott, to select a few names from a remarkable constellation of stars. Maine has also given birth to such giants as Henry Wadsworth Longfellow, Sarah Orne Jewett, Edwin Arlington Robinson, Marsden Hartley, Edna St. Vincent Millay, John Ford, Kenneth Roberts, Walter Piston, and Stephen King. Thus, in the sweep of our nation's recorded cultural history, Maine has played a substantive and outsize role.

Though Maine's impact on American art and literature became most apparent at the outset of the nineteenth century, its roots extend back to the first recorded visits of Europeans, and beyond them to the vibrant native cultures that ebbed and flowed across the landscape over time. Although a study of the cultures of the pre-contact centuries is not in the scope of this chapter, one must never lose sight of the tremendous contributions of Indian civilizations. Many of the extant artifacts from these cultures were utilitarian, but they were also decorated in manners that combined religious, social, and political ideas into a vital whole.

Early European visitors found the native inhabitants of what became Maine to be well adapted to their coastal, river, and forest surroundings. They had developed beautifully designed canoes and snowshoes, which for swift movement were not improved upon for centuries. As one seventeenth-century observer noted, Indians were "always celebrating feasts and having songs, dances, and speeches." In addition, they developed a powerful, sustaining cosmology in which all aspects of daily life were combined. In particular, they shared tales of the hero Gluskap, perhaps the most enduring figure in Maine native American cosmology.

Maps may be considered the first of the European visual arts focused on Maine. The explorer Giovanni da Verrazano, who visited in 1524, provided the first literature about Maine and a name, "Oranbega," which altered to "Norumbega" remained till the seventeenth century. So too, "Arcadia" or "Acadia," his name for the Carolinas, gradually migrated north to become the French colony in Maine and the Maritimes. Starved for information about the unknown shore, decorative mapmakers illustrated "Norumbega" with fanciful images. Decades of maps bearing the name inspired new rounds of European visits.

Samuel de Champlain's drawings of the St. Croix settlement, the large Indian town at the mouth of the Saco, and other places mark him as the first European visual artist to live here. Probably the earliest painting of an inhabitant of Maine is the extraordinary full-length oil portrait entitled "Mme. Penobscot." Thought to have been painted shortly after 1605, it hangs in a great house called "The Vyne" in Basingstoke, England. The artist is not identified, and all that is known of the sitter is that she is said to have been an Indian woman brought back from the banks of the Penobscot. She became a ward of the Crown and her stylish clothing suggests that she was an early target of acculturation. For now, "Mme. Penobscot" remains a tantalizing enigma.

A more illuminating, although less lovely, light was cast on the region by the famous Capt. John Smith, whose work marks the divide between the literature of exploration and that of settlement. Smith's popular and influential illustrated map, "New England Observed," appeared in his *Generall Historie of Virginia, New England, and the Summer Isles* (London, 1624). Therein, the name New England replaced Norumbega for the region.

John Josselyn's two volumes, *New England Rareties Discovered* (1672) and *An Account of Two Voyages to New England* (1674), have the first real claim on local literature and describe his visits to Black Point (Scarborough) in 1638–39 and 1663–71. He offers scenes of life among Indians and whites, discussions of a hundred or more plants, and considerations of native medicine. Recorded also are stories of mermen and sea serpents, giving him the title of "Maine's first folklorist." The New England historian Paul J. Lindholdt has also pointed out that Josselyn's writing would later attract and delight the likes of Longfellow and Thoreau.

Maine had no settled portrait painters prior to the Revolutionary War, but likenesses could be had by the well-to-do, providing they could travel to Boston or Europe. Having a portrait made was a tangible sign of status and taste in a poverty-stricken land. Robert Feke's opulent full-length oil of Brigadier-General Samuel Waldo graces the Bowdoin College Museum of Art, while John Smibert's portrait of Sir William Pepperrell hangs at the Essex Institute in Salem, Massachusetts. Around 1767, the beautiful Elizabeth Ross voyaged to Boston to sit for John Singleton Copley. The result of that visit is in the Museum of Fine Arts, Boston. The first itinerant painter to visit Maine was an unknown portrait painter who worked in the Piscataqua River area around 1710. But aside from practical craftworkers such as potters or blacksmiths, there were no specialized artisans in Maine. Only the most successful inhabitants could afford luxuries, and they had to travel to find them.

By 1760, Maine boasted some twenty thousand inhabitants in fifteen towns, the largest of which was Falmouth (now Portland, Falmouth, Cape Elizabeth, South Portland, and Westbrook). The line of settlement ran from the New Hampshire border to the Kennebec but extended only some twenty miles inland. Roads were poor and most transportation was by water. Some of our best insight into the everyday culture of this period comes from the journals and letters of future-President John Adams, then a young attorney obliged to travel the backcountry on court business. In 1767, he recalled: "From Falmouth . . . to Pownalborough There was an entire Wilderness, except North Yarmouth, New Brunswick [*sic*] and Long Reach, at each place were a few houses. . . . The Roads where a wheel had never rolled from the Creation, were miry and founderous, incumbered with long Sloughs of Water. The Stumps of the Trees which had been Cutt to make the road all remaining fresh and Roots crossing the path some above ground and some beneath so that my Horse's feet would frequently get between the Roots and he would flounce and blunder, in danger of breaking his own Limbs as well as mine."

On the other hand, many frontier elements were giving way to more cosmopolitan tastes. By the 1760s, Cumberland and Lincoln counties joined York, erecting elegant new courthouses in the shire towns of Falmouth and Pownalborough (now Dresden). In Falmouth, America's largest masting port, the inhabitants built a workhouse (1761), organized a Masonic lodge (1762), and opened a library (1766) to paying members. Impressive two-and-one-half-story homes dotted the landscape, although most homes remained more modest. On one visit to Falmouth, Adams wrote: "I thought I had got into the house of a nobleman."

The English Proclamation of 1763, which ruled out settlement west of the Appalachians, directed New England settlers to the terra incognita of Maine, northern New Hampshire, and what later became the Republic of Vermont. The Maine frontier assumed greater visual focus in 1760 and 1761, when British Lieutenant John Montresor led expeditions from Quebec to the headwaters of the Kennebec and Penobscot rivers. A number of coastal surveys were prepared by the Royal Navy prior to the Revolution and published following 1777 as part of J. F. W. Des Barres's *Atlantic Neptune*. Often called the most splendid collection of charts, plans, and views ever published, they gave visual shape, in the eyes of the world, to Kittery and Machias, among other places.

By the time of the Revolutionary War, a fifth of New England's population lived on the Eastern frontier. These people ranged from poor, uneducated squatters to such luminaries as the Reverend James Lyon, who had graduated from Princeton and become one of the first published musicians in America (*Urania*, 1761) before settling at Machias. The most honored profession remained the ministry, although attorneys and physicians had begun to appear. These latter professionals did not have a "public education," but their training gradually improved. A few artisans, notably part-time silversmiths, appeared, but furniture, gravestones, and portraits still had to be imported.

During the Revolutionary War a number of young go-getters took over political, economic, military, and religious niches once held by the colonial elite. However, scant literature was produced, aside from journals, tracts, and letters. One exception was Hugh Henry Brackenridge's *The Death of General Montgomery* (Providence, 1777), which includes lines about Arnold's march and is perhaps the first mention of Maine in a play. Visual images are equally rare. John Norman's engraving, "The Town of Falmouth, Burnt by Captain Moet, October 18, 1775," appeared as an illustration in James Murray's *An Impartial History of the War in America* (Boston, 1782). It is an innocent, if largely accurate, view of the attack. A sketch of the Piscataqua, including the Kittery shore, was made by a French officer named Ozanne and is now at the Musée de la Marine in Paris. The finest painting of Maine during the Revolution is Dominic Serres's great marine oil, *The Battle of the Penobscot in 1779*, which resides in the National Maritime Museum, Greenwich, England.

At war's end Maine had some political identity as one of Massachusetts's three electoral districts, but the primary political loyalty of the citizens was to town. Though one of the first New England places to be settled, its people rarely thought of themselves as "Mainers." They were Machiasfolk, Gorhamites, or Kennebunkers. But in the years between 1783 and 1820, the population grew from 56,000 to 300,000. Transportation improved, as did commerce, with Portland becoming the nation's sixth largest port by the 1790s.

Leisure now became affordable to a growing middle class, and by the second decade of the nineteenth century, sailing and island picnicking became popular. Portland, in particular, evinced a growing demand for public entertainment. The Columbian Hall displayed a leopard in 1809 and an elephant in 1816 and hosted Bradley's Museum in 1817 and "The Travelling Hindoos" in 1819. The elephant, "Old Bet," the first to tour America, was shot in Alfred by an unknown person. In an age that gave little newspaper coverage to human murder, great indignation was expressed. Today, a roadside plaque marks the animal's grave.

In 1794, Maine's first theater opened at Assembly Hall in Portland with a comedy called *The Lyar*; a song, "The Learned Pig"; and a farce, *The Merry Mourners. Macbeth* was staged in 1805, but the favorite was *The Sultan, or the Captive*, set in Tripoli and featuring the popular Maine hero Commodore Edward Preble. In 1806, a new Puritanism reared up, and Portland passed a law banning plays. This prohibition lasted until 1820.

There were also a number of visual artists at work. Artisans, including silversmiths, furniture makers, ornamental painters, and carvers of ships' figureheads, found employment in the larger communities, especially Portland. In 1815, skilled workers there banded together to become the Maine Charitable Mechanic Association, which encouraged and promoted the mechanic arts, maintained a library, and offered practical instruction for poor boys. In 1801, Rufus Porter came to Maine, entered Fryeburg Academy, and commenced a career as a decorative painter. In later years he achieved note as an artist, an inventor, and founder of *The Scientific American*. By the 1790s Bartlett Adams became Maine's first settled stonecutter or sculptor, and gravestones no longer had to be imported from Boston.

After 1783, a roadshow of traveling artists plied the East Coast from Halifax to the West Indies. Included were miniature painters, portrait painters, silhouette cutters, and panorama painters. Among the early visitors were painters Dr. Josiah Flagg, Jr., John Brewster, Jr., Moses Cole, Nathaniel Hancock, Henry Williams, and John Roberts. Michele Felice Corné brought his grand panorama, the *Bombardment of Tripoli*, to Portland in 1807. The hero of that event, Commodore Preble, was a resident of Portland. Viewing this sixty-by-ten-foot painting cost a substantial fifty cents and was as much an entertainment as contemporary art event. Visiting artists usually exhibited in store windows and were inevitably given notice in the growing number of local newspapers.

In 1818, painter Moses Pierce opened a gallery in Portland after spending a year studying the art collection at Bowdoin College. Maine's first college had been founded in 1794, and in 1811, the institution was bequeathed 142 drawings and 70 paintings by Governor James Bowdoin III of Massachusetts. This was the first institutional art collection in the state and one of the nation's earliest as well. Moses Pierce's Portland gallery failed, and for some time there were no settled professional artists. However, the town of Blue Hill could boast the Reverend Jonathan Fisher, whose avocational skills included those of surveyor, writer, teacher, architect, musician, and painter of portraits, landscapes, and genre works.

Music had been frowned on by the early religious establishment, and the Congregationalists remained indifferent to it in the pre-Revolutionary world. This changed during the 1780s, as the number of denominations grew. By then, even among Congregationalists, hymns were sung, and organ and instrumental music came into vogue. In 1785, the composer Supply Belcher settled in Hallowell for a few years and later pushed west to Farmington. His collection, *The Harmony of Maine* (1794), included compositions named for communities—Hallowell, Farmington, York, Friendship, Readfield, Bath, and New

Sharon among them. Hallowell and Portland became regional centers for musical events and publications. In 1789, the musician John Merrick came to the former town and in 1815 led the statewide Handel Society of Maine. In 1817, the *Hallowell Collection of Sacred Music* was issued by E. Goodale. In the following year the Reverend Jonathan Fisher formed the Hancock Music Association, and in 1819, the Beethoven Musical Society was begun at Portland. Music became not only an enjoyment but a necessary part of upper- and middle-class family life. A very special and enduring music emerged from the state's Shaker communities. Music was one of the first endeavors to link citizens across the District of Maine.

Some achievements were registered in the field of writing. One of the most outstanding figures was Stephen Sewall of York, professor of Hebrew and Oriental languages at Harvard between 1765 and 1785. Among the first in a long line of Down-East dons, Sewall produced a Hebrew grammar, orations, language translations, and some verse. Diarists, including the Reverend Thomas Smith, the Reverend Samuel Deane, and midwife Martha Ballard, helped illuminate their times, although their efforts did not reach print until years later. The Reverend Deane also wrote Maine's first newspaper poem and the more durable study, *The New England Farmer*, a practical guide that ran through three editions between 1790 and 1822. Blue Hill's Parson Fisher also produced insightful journals as well as published work that included *The Youth's Primer* (1817), which was illustrated with twenty-nine of his animal woodcuts.

Maine always attracted visitors who published travel accounts, including those of Talleyrand, the Duc de la Rochefoucault, Dr. Timothy Dwight of Yale, the Reverend Paul Coffin, and Edward Augustus Kendall. Satisfying the thirst for knowledge about the place was future Massachusetts Governor James Sullivan, a native of Berwick, who wrote the classic study *The History of the District of Maine* (1795). In 1785, publishers Thomas B. Wait and Benjamin Titcomb, Jr., commenced the first newspaper, *The Falmouth Gazette*, and by the middle of the next century most towns had a paper. They served as a unique forum for dissent, rebuttal, and occasional flights of poetry.

In the sphere of fiction writing, Sally Sayward Barrell Keating Wood stands virtually alone. Born in York in 1759, "Madam Wood" produced Maine's first novels, including *Julia and the Illuminated Baron* (1800), *Dorval; or The Speculator* (1801), *Amelia; or The Influence of Virtue* (1802), *Ferdinand and Elmira; A Russian Story* (1804), and *Tales of the Night* (1827). In *Dorval,* Wood urged her neighbors into literary activity: "Hitherto we have been indebted to France, Germany, and Great Britain, for the majority of our Literary pleasures. Why we should not aim at independence, with respect to our mental enjoyments, as well as for our more substantial enjoyments, I know not. Why, must the amusements of our leisure hours cross the Atlantic and introduce foreign fashions and foreign manner, to a people, certainly capable of fabricating their own? Surely we ought to make a return in some way." The younger set took Wood as a model, and she lived to see a more-than-favorable return in literary production.

Self-confidence was also expressed in the building of three-story homes and new commercial buildings by the growing merchant class. Important works include Alexander Parris's Portland Bank Building, the Matthew Cobb House, and the Joseph Holt Ingraham House in Portland; Nicholas Codd's James Kavanaugh House and St. Patrick's Church in Damariscotta Mills; and buildings by the Melchers at Bowdoin College and in Brunswick. While great merchant homes were lofted along the coast, back-country settlements continued to produced more humble, yet enduring habitations. The Roy House at the Acadian Village in Van Buren is a fine example of structures built by French-speaking inhabitants of the St. John Valley from the 1780s into the next century.

At statehood in 1820, Maine chose the vaunting motto *"Dirigo"* (Latin for "I Lead" or "I Direct"). Ranking twelfth out of twenty-four states in population, Maine was growing rapidly and saw itself taking a prominent place in the Union. Portland, the largest town and commercial hub, became the first state capital and built a two-story statehouse. However, a number of towns continued to compete for the honor, and in 1827, Augusta won out. In 1832, Charles Bulfinch's bold Greek Revival State House was completed, and all functions of government moved to Augusta. Up through 1910, numerous attempts were made to move the capital back to Portland, but Augusta remained triumphant. In 1822, the Maine Historical Society was founded. The fourth oldest society of its type, the society attracted a unique collection of documents and artifacts. Benedict Arnold's correspondence concerning his march across Maine to Quebec during the Revolution was presented to the society by former Vice President Aaron Burr.

In this era Maine was remarkably productive in political, social, and business activities, but it was in the arts that her citizens dazzled. Portland often rivaled Boston as an art center; artists of all types loomed large and, occasionally, prosperous. A generation of children emerged who had been educated and steeped in music, drawing, and literature. Although parents had usually intended that such exposure would enhance rather than sustain their careers, some young men and women traveled new paths.

Henry Wadsworth Longfellow, born in 1807, the year of the Jefferson embargo, became America's most widely read Victorian poet. A Portland native, he attended Bowdoin during a time that included such fellow students as Nathaniel Hawthorne, Franklin Pierce, John Brown Russwurm, John S. C. Abbott, and Frederic Mellen. In an age that loved verse, Longfellow popularized

20-1. Henry Wadsworth Longfellow (1807–82) of Portland attended Bowdoin College; later he taught there and at Harvard College. His popular poetry made him one of the most famous poets of the nineteenth century and the first American to be honored by having his bust placed in England's Westminster Abbey. Collections of the Maine Historical Society, Portland.

American Indian myth, humanized the dour Pilgrims in *The Courtship of Miles Standish,* and in *Evangeline* wrote eloquently of the Acadians dispersed at the hands of the English. In popularizing local and regional history, Longfellow performed a tremendous service, and his poetry was translated into many languages.

20-2. Charles Codman (ca. 1800–1842) painted this view of Augusta, Maine's new capital, in 1836. The Kennebec River town replaced Portland as the political center of the state, a role it has retained. At the center of this scene is the original Greek Revival State House designed by Charles Bulfinch (1763–1844). Collections of the Maine State Museum, Augusta.

Historian Francis Parkman might speak disparagingly of downeasters in his 1843 notebook, written during a visit by coach to Maine. But citizens of the new state continued to influence colleges, including Harvard. Longfellow himself became Harvard's professor of modern languages and belles lettres in 1835; Simon Greenleaf, who grew up in New Gloucester, was given the Royall Professorship of Law in 1833, and John Langdon Sibley of Union was Harvard's librarian and author of the first three volumes of *Biographical Sketches of Graduates of Harvard University*.

Maine attracted talents from afar as well. There were visitors like the journalist Anne Royall; itinerant visual artists, including J. G. Cole, Master Hanks, A. G. Hoit, Anthony Meucci, Susanna Paine, and Caroline Hill Wardwell; and engravers, the first among them Abel and Sidney Bowen, Danforth Newcomb, and the brothers O. H. and D. S. Throop. Harriet Beecher Stowe is perhaps the best-known example of a writer from away who was active in Maine in this period. While her husband taught at Bowdoin, she labored on her influential novel, *Uncle Tom's Cabin* (1852). Another non-native, Charles Codman, became Maine's first settled professional landscape painter when he came to Portland in 1822. It was Codman who co-founded Maine's vibrant local visual arts tradition, the first generation of which included William Matthew Prior, Charles O. Cole. J. T. Harris, Charles E. Beckett, and Frederic Mellen. They were quickly followed by notable landscape painters J. R. Tilton and Harrison Bird Brown.

The spirit of this productive period in local culture was embodied in John Neal. Born in Portland in 1793, he became an itinerant artist, read for the law in Baltimore, and learned to box and fence. He then pushed off to England and lived in the household of philosopher Jeremy Bentham. While there, he wrote novels and the first criticism of American art for British magazines. Returning home in 1827, Neal was met by a mob whose members took issue with finding themselves in the pages of his fiction. Neal forged an alliance with writers and artists and published a literary magazine, *The Yankee*, through which he helped discover or promote Poe, Whittier, Rembrandt Peale, and others, including the next generation of Maine artists and sculptors. For his part, Neal wrote novels, such as *Seventy-Six* and *The Down-Easters*, but aside from insightful reviews and a delightful autobiography, produced no masterwork. As America's first art critic, talent scout, and an active proponent of total equality for women, John Neal loomed large on the national scene.

A number of popular artists won national or international fame. Ann S. Stephens, a Neal protégé, published and edited the *Portland Magazine* and *Portland Sketchbook* in the 1830s. These volumes drew the talents of Longfellow, Codman, Neal, and many others. Stephens went on to New York, where she edited and published monthly magazines and wrote successful dime novels.

20-3. Wreathed in laurels in this portrait by Jared B. Flagg (1820–99) is the author, lecturer, and reformer Elizabeth Oakes Price Smith (1806–93). Born in North Yarmouth, she is the first woman known to have climbed Mount Katahdin. Beginning in the 1840s she wrote popular fiction for national magazines and seven novels, including the bestselling *Bald Eagle*. A feminist, she married humor writer Seba Smith; their children were surnamed Oaksmith. Collections of the Maine Historical Society, Portland.

Portland-born Samuel Colman, son of a bookseller, became a noted painter, also working from New York. Portland produced N. P. Willis, journalist, travel writer, and member of the Knickerbocker group. His sister, Sara Payson Willis Parton, wrote bestsellers under the pen-name "Fanny Fern" and in 1855 was making the then-remarkable wage of a hundred dollars a week writing for the *New York Ledger*. Elizabeth Oakes Smith of North Yarmouth was a nationally popular author and feminist. Two brothers from Maine, Jacob and John S. C. Abbott also turned to writing. Jacob produced some two hundred works, notably the "Little Rollo" series for children. John's most noted work was a much-read biography of Napoleon. Isaac McLellan, Jr., a favorite of the small but growing contingent of outdoors enthusiasts, won the title "Poet of Rod and Gun."

The wilderness beckoned many, and Bangor became the principal gateway to Mount Katahdin, Maine's highest peak and one of the first recreational goals of what is now known as Vacationland. The first recorded climb was completed by seven hikers from Bangor in 1804. In 1849 Elizabeth Oakes Smith became the first white woman to reach the summit. Parts of this wilderness were still largely terra incognita when Moses Greenleaf brought out his *Survey of the State of Maine* (1829). The eminent Dr. Charles Thomas Jackson became state geologist in 1837 and began a survey that included important visual images of Maine. In 1842 the federal government's Talcott survey was completed along the northeast boundary. With this careful mapping came sixteen camera-lucida watercolor views that now rest in the National Archives. In 1832 naturalist John James Audubon explored Washington County and, according to contemporary historian Herbert Adams, completed some fourteen bird portraits in-state.

As Maine's wilderness was explored and better understood, it also served as inspiration for artists and essayists. The celebrated landscape painter Frederic E. Church trekked to Katahdin and the surrounding woods between 1852 and 1879, and the trips inspired a number of his works, including the masterpiece *Twilight in the Wilderness* (1860). Henry David Thoreau journeyed to Katahdin, Moosehead Lake, the West Branch of the Penobscot, and the Allagash between 1846 and 1857, producing extraordinary journals later published as *The Maine Woods*. Complementing his account is John S. Springer's *Forest Life and Forest Trees* (1851), a fascinating account of logging in the north woods.

The coast was even more popular among artists and rusticators. In 1844, landscape painter Thomas Cole visited Bar Harbor and the dramatic headlands nearby. He was followed by the painters Thomas Doughty, Alvan Fisher, and the incomparable marine visionary Fitz Hugh Lane. By the 1830s newly built hotels and cottages were catering to the growing demand of summer visitors. In 1848 Appledore House appeared on the Isles of Shoals and, under the aegis of author Celia Thaxter, that place soon blossomed into the state's first summer art colony.

Nearly every town produced a visual artist or two. Sculptor Edward Augustus Brackett, whose *Drowned Mother and Child* was a Victorian favorite, hailed from Vassalboro. His brother Walter, a noted painter of game fish, was born in

Unity. Saco was home to genre artist Charles Henry Granger, and Rumford could boast the Wardwell family of painters and their cousin, Jonathan A. Bartlett. Eastman Johnson was born in Lovell, and although he moved out of state, he came back to produce some of his best paintings. Bangor, the great cultural rival of Portland, boasted portrait painter Jeremiah P. Hardy and his sister Mary Ann, together with a second and third generation of family talents. The first daguerreotypist visited in 1840, and by 1869 there were eighty-nine professional photographers. In Kingfield, F. O. and F. E. Stanley began as painters, turned to portrait photography, and later developed the dry-plate photographic process.

Through the 1860s, no one city dominated the American art scene. Instead there were a number of small markets scattered across the land, with Portland and Bangor contributing particularly important practitioners and patrons and attracting major artists, actors, and traveling exhibitions. William Dunlap's large oil, *The Christ Rejected*, failed to attract interest in Boston, so in 1822 the disappointed artist shipped his picture "further east, to Portland where the tide of fortune turned." Thomas Sully's famous *Passage of the Delaware* followed in 1823, and Hiram Powers's marble *The Greek Slave* visited in 1851. In 1826, 1838, 1854, and 1859 the Maine Charitable Mechanic Association held craft fairs. Beginning in 1838, art catalogues accompanied the efforts. These were large, well-covered shows spotlighting contemporary artists and local collectors. C. O. Cole organized similar large showings in 1845 and 1849. In 1829 a theater appeared in Portland, and soon first-class actors like Edwin Forrest were drawn to town. The strange Prof. F. Nicholls Crouch, composer of *Kathleen Mavourneen*, headed the Portland Sacred Music Society, causing little but disharmony. Hermann Kotzschmar left Germany after 1848 and became the veritable music czar of Maine for the next forty-seven years. Under his firm hand, Portland became a "must stop" for musicians.

Perhaps the most famous Mainer was a fictional character escaped from the pen of Buckfield journalist Seba Smith, husband of Elizabeth Oakes. Major Jack Downing first appeared in the *Portland Courier* in 1830. The rural Down-Easter blundered into Portland and then on to Washington, where, through a series of happy accidents, "Major Jack" became an advisor to President Andrew Jackson. People from other regions recognized elements of themselves in the attitude and dialect of this citizen from "jest about the middle of down east." Smith produced two books: *The Life and Writings of Major Jack Downing of Downingville* (1833) and *My Thirty Years out of the Senate* (1859). The "Major Jack" character was pirated by others and appeared at the elbow of Jackson in the best political cartoons of the day. Smith made little money from his writing, but he initiated a Maine tradition of humor that persists, for better or worse, into the present.

His work, along with the verse of Longfellow, the paintings of Eastman Johnson, the political prominence of Hannibal Hamlin and William Pitt Fessenden, and the observations of writer Fanny Fern combined to give Maine and Mainers a commanding presence within the nation.

Maine Arts during and after the Civil War

In 1860, as the nation moved closer to civil war, Eastman Johnson returned to the haunts of his boyhood and produced *Corn Husking*, one of his most enduring images (see page 250). The painting used as background a barn in Fryeburg; it shows a sturdy laborer carrying a basket of corn, and behind him, a young couple and an elderly man with a toddler. A gun, a brace of ducks, and the words "Lincoln & Hamlon" scratched into the door complete this scene of self-sufficiency. Few works better depict life at the brink of the Civil War, and it was reproduced widely as a Currier and Ives print.

The challenge to the Union was met on the cultural front as well as in the field of arms. Abraham Lincoln was fond of Longfellow's poetry and claimed that most of his "historical knowledge" derived from the histories of Brunswick's John S. C. Abbott. Lincoln was much impressed by Harriet Beecher Stowe's *Uncle Tom's Cabin*, which was followed in 1862 by Stowe's best Maine work, *The Pearl of Orr's Island*.

Following in the comic tradition of Seba Smith, Charles Farrar Browne of Waterford and his creation, "Artemus Ward, the genial Yankee showman," took center stage. Beginning in the pages of the *Cleveland Plain Dealer*, the character caught on, leading to national articles, a tour of the US and Europe, and several books. *Artemus Ward, His Book* (1862), complete with "ingrammaticisms," was a favorite of Lincoln's and immediately sold forty thousand copies. During the war, Ward was a great supporter of the Union.

Historian Herbert Adams has pointed out that at the time of Fort Sumter's bombardment, John Wilkes Booth was appearing at Portland in *Rafaelle, the Reprobate* and *The Corsican Brothers*. A few weeks later, the great actress Charlotte Cushman was performing in town. Throughout the Civil War, headliners continued to appear in well-attended productions.

Miss Cushman was a friend of critic John Neal and sculptor Benjamin Paul Akers, who had recently completed his neoclassic masterpiece, *The Dead Pearl Diver*. When Akers died in 1861, his place as Maine's leading sculptor was taken by Franklin Simmons, who became one of the chief artistic beneficiaries of the war. Simmons began with a life-sized equestrian statue of Rockland's slain Gen. Hiram C. Berry and produced portrait-busts of Lincoln's cabinet members. From this point until the turn of the century, the sculptor met the

20-4. Benjamin Paul Akers (1825–61) of Westbrook began his career in Portland under art critic John Neal and became very successful after moving his studio to Italy and specializing in neoclassical sculpture. His *The Dead Pearl Diver* is among the best of its type of Victorian sculpture, and it was a model for Nathanial Hawthorne's *The Marble Faun.* Courtesy of the Portland Museum of Art, Portland, Maine, gift of Elizabeth Akers Allen et al.

demand for images of fallen heroes and rising politicians. Even during the conflict, painters came to Maine to work, and in 1864–65 Sanford R. Gifford produced his masterwork, *The Artist Sketching at Mount Desert, Maine.* However, the market for both landscape views of the region and portrait painting began to fail as photography and prints became more available, affordable, and desirable.

With nine thousand dead in the war and eleven thousand wounded or disabled, and with a war debt of $18 million, Maine entered troubled times in the second half of the century. "The fact of the matter is, that in our way of doing business Maine has become an old and exhausted State, before her true wealth has begun to develop," warned Joshua L. Chamberlain in 1876. Both the economy and the cultural scene changed, as old ways of making a living faltered or failed. Many ambitious young people had to leave the state to seek their fortune, including those involved in the arts. They were, to some degree, replaced by immigrants from Quebec and Europe and by an infusion of summer people and established artists seeking an inexpensive, pressure-free environment. Although Portland's cultural rivalry with Boston faded quickly, Maine still managed to boast such impressive figures as Sara Orne Jewett in literature, Winslow Homer in painting, and Madame Lillian Nordica in music.

The seashore had beckoned to earlier generations of artists, but in the postwar era improved transportation, including steamships and railroads, drew more talented people to sundry down-east watering places. By 1872 Bar Harbor had fifteen luxury hotels, and through the 1920s leading American architects concocted lavish summer cottages for the country's wealthiest citizens, including the Rockefellers and Joseph Pulitzer. Islesboro provided an ideal summer setting for notables such as illustrator and painter Charles Dana Gibson. In 1901 a Belfast newspaper gushed: "Imagine an island, barren save a few scattered houses and settlements three years ago, to have grown to be a beautiful villa-dotted paradise."

This beauty was captured in Winslow Homer's enduring images of the Maine coast, which caught the public imagination. Beginning in 1883, he worked from a studio in Prout's Neck, Scarborough, and generations have been introduced to the state through his much reproduced and imitated marine images. His arrival signaled the influx of artists from away who found Maine a perfect work environment. Often arriving as full-blown successes, with gallery connections in New York or Boston, the new artists had little to do with "native" artists. As late as the 1870s John Neal had welcomed the English watercolor painter Elizabeth Heaphey Murray as one of "the Portland painters." By contrast, John T. Hull's *Handbook of Portland* (1889) refers slightingly to "that New York painter Winslow Homer."

By 1880 the once-rich Portland art scene was failing. The young Franklin Stanwood produced some of our finest marine paintings but lived hand to mouth, while the fine landscape painter Charles F. Kimball was reduced to being a weekend artist. Painter Charles L. Fox ran schools in Portland and Bridgton. Younger artists like the Auburn sports-painter Scott Leighton, Brewer sculptor Charles E. Tefft, Portland impressionist Walter Griffin, and Kennebunkport's Hannah Skeele, the most technically complex Maine artist of her time, made their careers out of state. When they achieved success, many returned to summer or to live permanently.

In Brunswick, Kate Furbish achieved fame as a painter of exquisite and scientifically accurate botanical specimens and the discoverer of two new plants, including the Furbish lousewort (a rare species which prevented construction of the proposed Dickey-Lincoln dam in 1980s). Artist Annie Eliza Hardy survived in Bangor, and jack-of-all-arts Harry H. Cochrane did so at Monmouth. In smaller towns, photography became the supporting visual art form. Still, it is only recently that the photographs of Kingfield's Chansonetta Stanley Emmons, Amity's Isaac Simpson, Bath's Emma D. Sewall, Dexter's Bert Call, and Norway's Minnie Libby have gained special recognition.

Most outsiders thus saw Maine through the paintings of newcomers like Homer at Prout's or Childe Hassam, who produced an extraordinary group of impressionist views at the Isles of Shoals. In the 1880s, Charles Woodbury, who turned Ogunquit into an art colony, began holding his renowned beachside landscape classes. Soon summer art colonies sprang up in Bridgton, Poland Spring, Boothbay, Monhegan, and Eastport, and the likes of painters Maurice Prendergast, Rockwell Kent, Robert Henri, George Bellows and illustrators N. C. Wyeth and W. H. Foster began to discover the Pine Tree State.

By the late nineteenth century, architecture had become an honored profession which, in the wake of Greek Revival, Gothic Revival, Italianate, Mansard, and other styles, now favored the Queen Anne and Colonial Revival forms. Maine's foremost architect from the 1880s on was John Calvin Stevens, a pioneer of the Shingle style, perhaps the most successful domestic form ever to grace the coast. It was also an age of impressive public structures built from Maine granite. One of the great concentrations is arranged near Portland's Lincoln Park and includes the Cumberland County Courthouse (1910), the Federal Courthouse (1911) and City Hall (1912). These buildings bespeak order, tradition, and civic duty. Parks, fountains, and war memorials were also popular public art forms during these years.

Musical societies prospered under such indomitable personalities as Hermann Kotzschmar and George W. Marston. When Paderewski gave a recital in Portland in 1892, he was stunned by the size and warmth of his audience. Kotzschmar had seen to it that musicians from all over Maine were in attendance. The Bangor Opera House opened in 1882 and drew the best performers. In 1896 the Bangor Symphony, the nation's second-oldest continuously operating symphony, began. In the next year, the Maine Music Festival under William R. Chapman began a fruitful life. John Knowles Paine of Portland became the nation's most noted composer of the time and in the 1860s was appointed director of music at Harvard, holding one of the country's first chairs of music.

Maine women contributed to the success of opera. Annie Louise Cary of Wayne was the first to win international acclaim and tour widely. Madame

Nordica, formerly Lillian Norton of Farmington, made her debut in Milan and achieved world fame as a prima donna, with twenty-one roles at the Metropolitan Opera House. Her childhood home is now a museum. Emma Eames, born in Shanghai, grew up in Bath. Attending her debut in Paris, one critic called hers the "finest soprano voice I ever heard." The fourth figure, Madame Scalar, formerly Minnie Plummer, had a successful career in European opera before retiring to Maine.

Portland and Bangor continued to host the best dramatic and vaudeville performers, and by the turn of the century many summer theaters were in operation in such diverse places as Cape Elizabeth and Skowhegan. Films were shown in the 1880s, and the first movie house was operating by 1907.

Sara Orne Jewett was the stand-out writer of the era in her clarity of style and skilled observations of Mainers. Her short stories, particularly those included in *The Country of the Pointed Firs* (1896), remain classics. Longfellow died in 1882, and in 1888 Portlanders erected a public statue to him in Longfellow Square. In 1907 his boyhood home was opened to the public. Novelist William Dean Howells, "the father of American realism," drew the likes of Mark Twain, Henry James, and Thomas Bailey Aldrich to his summer cottage at Kittery Point. At Appledore, Celia Thaxter penned *Among the Isles of Shoals* (1873) and *My Island Garden* (1894). Laura E. Richards of Gardiner authored *Captain January* (1890), light poems, and good biographies, sharing the first Pulitzer Prize for biography in 1917. Calais's Charles Townsend Copeland was a distinguished professor of writing at Harvard, while Harriet Prescott Spofford, of the same town, was a frequent contributor to the *Atlantic Monthly*. Bill Nye of Shirley and William Robinson Pattangall of Pembroke continued to work the vein of Maine humor. Laboring in the wings was poet Edwin Arlington Robinson of Head Tide, while in nonfiction scholars such as Fannie Hardy Eckstorm, Henry Burrage, and James Phinney Baxter enriched our understanding of folklore and local history.

This was a golden age of children's authors. Kate Douglas Wiggin worked in Hollis to produce *Rebecca of Sunnybrook Farm* (1903), James Otis Kaler of Winterport and South Portland wrote the circus classic *Toby Tyler* (1880), and for decades Clarence E. Mulford lived at Fryeburg, where he wrote of "Hopalong Cassidy." Rebecca Sophia Clarke, "The Dickens of the Nursery," created the "Dotty Dimple" and "Flaxie Frizzle" stories. The Reverend Elijah Kellogg, Jr., entertained generations of boys with his tales of the sea, Dr. Charles A. Stephens followed with six decades of boy's adventure in the *Youth's Companion* magazine, and Gilbert Patten of Corinna created the sports hero "Frank Merriwell." Vassalboro's Holman Day also wrote juvenile fiction before turning to novels of lumbering and liquor smuggling.

Other Mainers founded magazines. Cyrus H. K. Curtis left the region to start the *Saturday Evening Post, Ladies Home Journal,* and other familiar periodicals. In 1869 E. C. Allen founded the *People's Literary Companion* and turned Augusta into the mail-order capital of the world. W. H. Gannett of the same city started *Comfort Magazine,* the first magazine to circulate to a million readers. In 1891, Thomas Bird Mosher pioneered modern fine printing and made Portland his headquarters. In Maine's mill towns, newly arrived Franco-Americans were able to preserve their culture and language through journals, including *Le Messager* (1880–1910) and *La Justice* (1896–1950).

At the turn of the century, Maine's Yankee elite began a period of retrospection and codification. In 1892–94 Bowdoin College gained its new Walker Art Building, designed by the prominent New York architectural firm McKim, Mead and White. Although the Portland Society of Art was founded 1882, it was not until 1911, through the generosity of author Margaret Jane Mussey Sweat, that the collecting institution found a permanent home. In 1893, the booklet, "Leaflets of the Artists," was organized to preserve what was best about the nineteenth-century flowering of art in Bangor. In 1910, architect G. Henry Desmond's new designs for the State House were carried out, with Gardiner sculptor W. Clark Noble's figure of "Wisdom" placed atop the dome. In spite of this activity, the attitude of most Mainers was perhaps summed up best in an 1889 *Sunday Telegram* observation: "We know that it is a too frequent characteristic of Portland people to deem everything which emanates from our city inferior." Such an outlook would have shocked John Neal.

Maine Arts in the Early Twentieth Century

In the period that followed World War I, local artists were eclipsed by a surge of well-known figures migrating to Maine. However, in-state markets were limited, and artists still needed visibility beyond Maine. Mary Neal Richardson of Mt. Vernon worked in Boston and summered in Canton. Lewiston's master painter, Marsden Hartley, made frequent trips to Maine but spent much of his brilliant career in New York and Europe, although his last years were spent in his home state. Biddeford's John G. Lyman became a key figure in Canada's art scene. W. Herbert Dunton of Augusta became an illustrator of the American West. The best-known native-born artist to flourish critically while living in-state during the early twentieth century was Waldo Pierce of Bangor, but he was perennially out-of-pocket.

This was the heyday of the Ogunquit art colony. Some artists, like Georgia O'Keeffe, stayed for only short periods. Yasuo Kuniyoshi, Henry Strater, Robert Laurent, Bernard Karfiol, Rudolf Dirks, Isabella Howland, and the nearby Walt

20-5. *Old Pine* by Charles Hovey Pepper (1864–1950), a native of Waterville, Maine. Following art studies in New York and Paris, where he had his first one-man show, Pepper visited Japan in 1903 and then settled in Massachusetts. Beginning in 1912 he summered each year at Maine's Attean Lake, near the Canadian border, where *Old Pine* was painted. Japanese influence is evident in the painting. Collection of the Colby College Museum of Art.

Kuhn had a more lasting local impact. Edward Hopper painted in Portland and Cape Elizabeth; Marguerite and William Zorach settled in Robinhood. John Marin put down roots at Cape Split, and Ivan Albright worked at Corea. Sculptor Gaston Lachaise made Georgetown his home, and Kennebunk was enlivened by the dual personalities of Mildred Burrage and Edith C. Barry, founder of the Brick Store Museum in 1936.

In the field of music, lyric soprano Evelyn J. Shah-Nazaroff left Rockland to pursue a career that took her to the Metropolitan Opera. By the 1920s, Maine's best-known composer, Walter Piston of Rockland, began his teaching career at Harvard. In 1923–24 Portland followed Bangor in founding a symphony. The Maine Music Festival continued until 1926. On a more popular level, the pier at Old Orchard Beach attracted the big bands, including Rudy Vallee and his Connecticut Yankees. Vallee grew up in Westbrook, attended the University of Maine, and became a radio sensation. In 1930 he made the University's "Stein Song," written by his friend Lincoln Colcord, the number-one hit in the nation.

In literature, Edna St. Vincent Millay captured the essence of her defiant generation with the line, "My candle burns at both ends." Born in Rockland, Millay grew up in Camden and graduated from Vassar in 1917, the same year she published *Renascence and Other Poems*. In 1923 she won the Pulitzer Prize for poetry. Summers she spent on Ragged Island in Casco Bay. During this period Maine artists had an almost magnetic hold on Pulitzers. Laura E. Richards shared the prize in 1917 for a biography of Julia Ward Howe. Booth Tarkington, who summered in Kennebunkport, won for *The Magnificent Ambersons* (1919) and *Alice Adams* (1922), and at the time was probably America's highest paid novelist. After years of struggle, Edwin Arlington Robinson came into his own with *The Man Against the Sky* (1916). Robinson won Pulitzers for poetry in 1922, 1928, and 1936. His narrative poems and wonderful psychological portraits were often set in or influenced by Maine, and his closeness to the place is as palpable as any poet before or since. Rounding out the Pulitzer winners of the era is Robert Peter Tristram Coffin, who won for poetry in 1936. Though often overlooked today, Coffin's best verse has tremendous power.

Owen Davis, born in Portland and raised in Bangor, stands as Maine's major playwright. Davis wrote hundreds of melodramas and was the most successful Broadway writer of his era. In 1923, he won a Pulitzer Prize for *Icebound*, a remarkable study of a dysfunctional family set in the town of Veazie. In later years, the writer lived in and produced plays at Lakewood Theater near Skowhegan.

Livermore Falls was the home town of Louise Bogan, one of America's finest poets and long a reviewer-editor and essayist for the *New Yorker*. In 1932 Elizabeth Coatsworth and Henry Beston settled in Nobleboro to pursue long careers in writing. Blue Hill's Mary Ellen Chase distinguished herself as an author and professor at Smith College from 1926 to 1955. In 1933, E. B. and Katherine White bought a farmhouse in Brooklin. The influx of literary personalities also included Erskine Caldwell who, having lost his job as a book-reviewer, took his stacks of free review copies to Portland and opened a used bookstore. Caldwell's first fiction was written in Maine and included *The Bastard* (1929), which was censored by local authorities. Gladys Hasty Carroll grew up in South Berwick, graduated from Bates College, and produced her best known novel, *As the Earth Turns*, in 1933. The expansive list of worthy writers would also include Virginia Chase, Lincoln Colcord, Wilbert Snow, and Marsden Hartley.

Interest in folk literature came to include Roland Gray's collection, *Songs and Ballads of the Maine Lumberjacks* (1925) and Fannie Hardy Eckstorm and Mary Winslow Smyth's excellent *Minstrelsy of Maine: Folk Songs and Ballads of the Woods and Coast* (1927). The University of Maine made important contributions to history and literature while the *New England Quarterly* was published on campus. Under Milton Ellis and George Davis Chase, the crucial "Maine Studies–Second Series" began. The series included Richard G. Wood's history of lumbering and Ava Chadbourne's history of education, along with biographies and monographs that greatly extended our knowledge of Maine culture. In 1938 and 1941 Elizabeth Ring's landmark *Reference List of Manuscripts Relating to the State of Maine* took its place as a standard. The distinguished South Portland historian Robert G. Albion's classic *Forests and Sea Power* appeared in 1926. Albion served as Gardiner Professor of Oceanic History and Affairs at Harvard. Samuel Eliot Morison, noted maritime historian, summered at Northeast Harbor, and literary historian F. O. Matthiessen also wrote in Maine; his first project focused on Maine writer Sarah Orne Jewett.

During the late 1920s changes in cultural styles and mass media further wove Maine into the national fabric. Maine cultural expression, however, retained a strongly regional flavor. Maine became a frequent setting for the emerging film industry. *Way Down East* (1920), although actually filmed in New Hampshire, created a vision of Maine for a mass audience. Maine's Holman Day produced such successful films as *The Rider of the King Log* (1921) before going to Hollywood. Portland's Hiram Abrams became president of Paramount in 1914 and later headed United Artists. Actors William and Dustin Farnum of Bucksport became film stars, as did Indian Island's Molly Spotted Elk and Portland's Francis Feeney, who changed his name to Ford in Hollywood. Ford's brother John followed suit and directed 112 movies, including *Stagecoach* (1939) and *The Grapes of Wrath* (1940). John Ford won six Academy Awards.

Maine's cultural scene was further transformed by world events, including the Great Depression and World War II. The Works Progress Administration (WPA) and other Depression-inspired programs provided new outlets for Maine cultural expression. Prior to the 1930s, except for municipal organists, the arts had been a private affair; now came inventories of town records and local histories funded by the WPA, the most notable result being *Maine: A Guide Down-East* (1937). Post offices were adorned with murals, although at Kennebunk, Booth Tarkington and Kenneth Roberts led the fight to remove Elizabeth Tracy's *Bathers*, which they termed "bumpy" and "very ugly." The Federal Art Project, headed by Dorothy Hay Jensen, lasted from 1935 to 1942 and sustained numerous local artists who produced scenery for theaters, school murals, signs for fish hatcheries, and entries for the *Index of American Design.*

The archetypal Maine author of the 1930s and 1940s was Kennebunk native Kenneth Roberts. Though often dismissed as a regionalist, Roberts has a just claim to be the "inventor of the modern historical novel." His sweeping vision and attention to historical detail led to such popular and underrated books as *Arundel* (1930), *Rabble in Arms* (1933), and the peerless *Oliver Wiswell* (1940). Roberts's unabashed views brought outrage on both the left and right, but his exploration of the nature of individuals and their relation to great events is unsurpassed. Roberts's hatred of the "Vacationland" promotionals and their byproducts led to his call in 1930 for Mainers to "go forth with rope and grappling irons and tear the offending billboards down." It would be decades before his wish was granted, but once again a "Maine original" was holding forth.

As war approached, the literary scene again played a productive role. East Orland's Walter van Tilburg Clark wrote *The Ox-Bow Incident* (1940), a notable western seen in its time as a warning against the Nazis, but in fact a study in human nature that rises above genre. Leon Tebbetts's *O Big Earth* (1938) was a satire directed against Hitler and totalitarianism. During these years Ben Ames Williams, a transplanted Mississippian, produced two of our finest historical novels, *Come Spring* (1940) and the uncompromisingly dark study, *The Strange Woman* (1941). Louise Dickinson Rich brought out *We Took to the Woods* (1942), an unadorned account of life in the Maine wilderness.

In Hollywood, *The Ox-Bow Incident* became a popular film, with Portland's Francis Ford as a cast member. Few in Hollywood took the war more seriously than director John Ford, who filmed the *Battle of Midway*, a documentary that won him a Purple Heart as well as an Oscar. Ford also co-directed the Academy Award–winning documentary, *December 7th*. Historians Samuel Eliot Morison and Robert G. Albion were placed in charge of operational and administrative histories of the United States Navy during the conflict. Mildred Burrage produced notable images of the South Portland shipyards, and William Muir created a splendid series of paintings focused on life at the Brunswick Naval Air Station.

At the close of World War II, Maine entered a new era of cultural and artistic expression, broadened in many ways by the state's immersion into national trends in politics, economics, and arts and letters. Maine artists and writers operated in the national scene, incorporating new creative concepts and using media inspired by national developments. At the same time, national media— radio, film, syndicated newspapers, popular magazines, and television— penetrated even the remotest sections of the state. The challenge of preserving a regional identity and at the same time meeting new and changing national standards would be greater than ever. That Maine artists, musicians, and writers continued their stellar production in the face of these new trends is the subject of another chapter.

For Further Reading:

The most readily available primary sources on Maine artists are the works they produced, whether paintings, books, or buildings. In addition to the museums mentioned below, students of Maine arts might consult the Maine State Museum's exhibition, "12,000 Years in Maine," which contains some 2,400 objects crafted by Maine's native peoples. The University of Southern Maine has recently received two important map collections that can aid scholars interested in early European images of Maine. Historical societies, libraries, and museums have grown in towns and cities throughout the region, and the authors of this book have availed themselves of many of them. Special mention should be made of the excellent Canadian Studies program at the University of Maine, the Maine Women Writers Collection at Westbrook College, the New England Studies Program at the University of Southern Maine, and the unexcelled special collections at Bowdoin College. One can experience the past directly through living history programs in such operations as the Acadian Village in Van Buren or Norlands, the nineteenth-century farm school in Livermore.

Locating information on individual artists themselves can be difficult. The best sources are contemporary newspapers and business directories. I have spent twenty years searching the sources with my colleague Philip N. Grime, and I have exchanged information with a variety of historians including William B. Jordan, Jr., F. M. O'Brien, Earle G. Shettleworth, Jr., Miriam Barndt-Webb, Harry Walker, Gael May McKibben, Richard Durnin, and the late Arthur Gerrier, to name a few.

A full bibliography of Maine and the arts has yet to be published, and for now I would suggest that the reader turn to the many catalogue publications of the Bowdoin College Museum of Art, Colby College Art Museum, Portland Museum of Art, Olin Art Center, or the William A. Farnsworth Library and Art Museum. There are also fine biographies, such as Philip C. Beam's *Winslow Homer at Prout's Neck* (Boston, 1966). Similarly, books like *The County, Land of Promise: A Pictorial History of Aroostook County, Maine,* edited by Anna Fields McGrath (Norfolk, Va., 1989) reveal many lesser known artists. Future study will benefit from the Maine Historic Preservation Commission's series, "A Biographical Directory of Architects in Maine." A short, sampler bibliography could include the following publications.

Beem, Edgar Allen, *Maine Art Now* (Gardiner, 1990).

Churchill, Edwin A., *Simple Forms and Vivid Colors: Maine Painted Furniture, 1800–1850* (Augusta, 1983).

Curry, David Park, *Childe Hassam* (New York, 1990).

Edwards, George Thornton, *Music and Musicians of Maine* (Portland, 1928).

Joan Whitney Payson Gallery of Art, *Women Pioneers in Maine Art* (Portland, 1981).

Joan Whitney Payson Gallery of Art, *Women Pioneers in Maine Art, 1900–1945* (Portland, 1985).

Maine Literature Project, *Maine Speaks: An Anthology of Maine Literature* (Brunswick, 1989).

Mellon, Gertrude A., and Elizabeth F. Wilder, editors, *Maine and Its Role in American Art, 1740–1963* (New York, 1963).

Miller, William B., editor, *Maine Artists, 1850–1899: Maine State Museum Checklist Series* (Augusta, 1976).

Sadik, Marvin S., *Colonial and Federal Portraits at Bowdoin College* (Brunswick, 1966).

Scott, Geraldine Tidd, *Isaac Simpson's World: The Collected Works of an Itinerant Photographer* (Falmouth, 1990).

Simpson, Mrs. C. C. W., *Leaflets of Artists* (Bangor, 1893).

Skolnick, Arnold, editor, *Paintings of Maine* (New York, 1991).

Thompson, Deborah, editor, *Maine Forms of American Architecture* (Camden, 1976).

Tragard, Louise, et al., *Ogunquit, Maine's Art Colony* (Ogunquit, 1987).

Woodman, Katherine, and Grace L. Barney, *A Century of Portland Painters, 1820–1920* (Portland, 1970).

21

Maine in Depression & War, 1929–1945

RICHARD H. CONDON,

JOEL W. EASTMAN, & LAWRENCE C. ALLIN

Seldom have Americans witnessed such profound changes as those that came between 1929 and 1945. In this chapter, historian Richard Condon (with help from Joel W. Eastman and Lawrence C. Allin on World War II) discusses the two cataclysmic events that shaped this period: the Great Depression and World War II. Here a recurrent theme, the impact of national or world events on Maine history, becomes pervasive; indeed, national events seem to eclipse state history in the mid-twentieth century.

But Maine experienced these outside events in the context of its own past. Maine citizens, for instance, voted against the immensely popular Roosevelt administration in all four presidential elections during these years. In part, this can be explained by Maine's specific disappointments with the New Deal. Although the multitude of federal programs did benefit many, Maine farmers received less aid than in most states, the Passamaquoddy Tidal Power Project was canceled, Maine suffered under the administration's Reciprocal Trade Agreement, and union organizing under the National Labor Relations Board failed. But more significantly, Maine's voting behavior reflected characteristic attitudes toward federal welfare programs and deficits, a long-standing distrust of outside control, whether from Boston capitalists or Washington bureaucrats, and Maine's uneasy acceptance of the new economic order of the 1930s. All of these attitudes were rooted deep in the state's own past.

The fifteen years between 1929 and 1945 brought some of the most dramatic changes in the history of the state and the nation. Economic disaster, a new role for the federal government, and the agony of world war changed the face of Maine in a variety of ways, bringing the "outside" world into the daily lives of Mainers to an unprecedented degree. Indeed, this was an age of transition, but

Maine's response to these cataclysmic events showed the marks of its own past. Maine continued its distinctive dialogue with the world around it.

Rural and Urban Maine in Transition: 1929

On the eve of the Great Depression, the rural landscape that had proved so resistant in the late nineteenth century was already in the throes of change. Three-fifths of Maine's eight hundred thousand people still lived in rural areas, but this proportion was falling. During the 1920s, for instance, more than forty thousand Mainers forsook rural life, some moving to nearby cities and others leaving the state. In fact, about a quarter of Maine's native sons and daughters lived in other states in 1930, while only 9 percent of the American-born population of Maine came from "away." This was the second-lowest ratio of in-migration to out-migration in the country. Since so many left and so few came, the rural population remained relatively homogeneous. More than three-quarters of the rural farm population in 1930 were native-born of native parentage, the highest proportion in New England.

Vestiges of subsistence farming lingered among Maine's fifty thousand farmers and farm workers, with families in central and southern Maine using 15 to 30 percent of their farm's product for domestic consumption. Still unable to make ends meet, 45 to 55 percent of the farmers outside Aroostook County worked at other jobs. Many in inland and northern sections of Maine cut pulpwood and sawtimber from the forests that still covered nearly 80 percent of the state's surface area. Along the coast, fishing, lobstering, clamming, cannery work, and caretaking for "summer people" helped made ends meet.

Between the hill country and the shore lay pockets of marginal or even submarginal land where abandoned farmhouses and barns could be seen caving in upon themselves and cleared fields giving way to brush. Elsewhere in this belt, however, many mixed farms operated. Though nearly half were still classified as part-time, self-sufficient, and general, their owners specialized much more than their grandparents had done in 1880. Adapting and modernizing shrewdly, some managed nicely with apples, poultry, eggs, sweet corn for canning factories, and above all, milk for local and Boston markets.

More than anywhere else in Maine, Aroostook County farmers were adopting modern business techniques. The deep soils on the long, broad ridges that are so distinctive of Aroostook County were still productive after a half-century of intensive commercial agriculture. Harvesting about one-eighth of the total U.S. potato crop, Aroostook farmers led the nation in both production and yield per acre. They used nearly one-half of the state's tractors and enjoyed, in the very good year of 1929, the highest farm income in the sixty-four counties

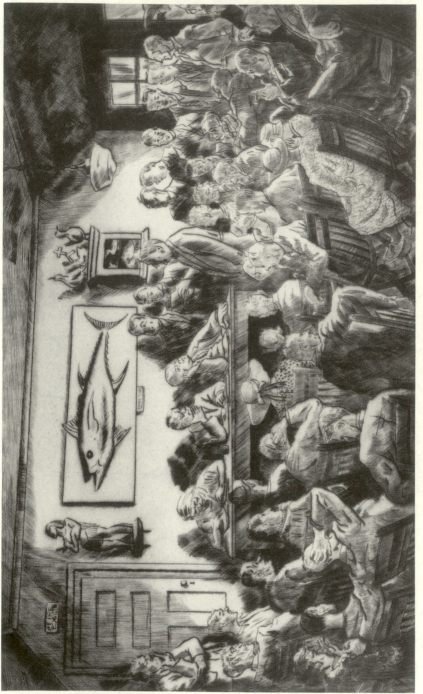

21-1. *Maine Problems* (1941), a drypoint by Peggy Bacon (1895–1987), pokes gentle fun at the town meeting, perhaps the purest form of democracy. Bacon, one of the few artists able to support herself during the Depression, settled in Ogunquit. Courtesy of the Portland Museum of Art. (Gift of Harold Shaw, 1984.)

of New England. But other years saw low prices or short crops. As the Aroostook ditty went, "When the price is high enough, we have a little cash; and when the market's on the bum, we eat a lot of hash."

In "the County," mortgage debt per farm exceeded the very low levels found in the rest of the state. Notorious gamblers on business deals, Aroostook farmers were also confirmed individualists. Eschewing cooperative marketing projects, each traded directly with dealers, who increasingly represented chain stores and other large, faraway customers. Moreover, potato farmers faced declining consumption patterns and increasing competition from Idaho and many other states. Obsessed with potatoes, Aroostook farmers generally neglected garden crops, livestock, and other diversified sources of income.

Social life in rural Maine was, as always, organized around the villages and small towns. Here, farmers traded, banked, visited their doctors, attended church, and went to the movies. A number of traditional town functions, however, were being performed in new ways. One-room rural schoolhouses, for instance, were giving way to consolidated district schools, as improved highways allowed more children to ride into the village centers. Although still "poorly lighted, poorly heated, poorly equipped, [and] poorly maintained" by comparison to urban schools, the consolidated schools offered advantages over their nineteenth-century predecessors.

As in earlier times, town budgets and other aspects of local administration were decided at town meetings held across the state in late winter. The assembled townspeople deliberated appropriations for roads, fire and police protection, street lighting in the village, libraries, and a growing number of other rural necessities. Towns still cared for their own poor, but they no longer auctioned "paupers" to the lowest bidder. Many still operated "town farms" or "poor farms," but these were more likely to be simply neglected refuse heaps for a few aged or mentally handicapped persons. Needy families, on the other hand, were normally provided with food and clothing orders and firewood. Before 1930, there were very few such unfortunates to relieve, at least in part because of a strong Yankee aversion to "taking charity."

Although towns were still responsible for local roads, by 1929, the State Highway Commission maintained a twenty-thousand-mile network of "trunk" highways that linked various regions of the state. Farmers and other rural folk had ceded authority over Maine's roads reluctantly at the turn of the century. Rather than trunk lines, farmers wanted "market roads" leading from the farm to the nearest village or railhead. Using limited funds derived from state bond issues and automobile license fees, state officials tried to placate the rural constituents in the face of strong pressure from the tourist industry and urban businesses for better intercity and coastal routes. Over declining rural

21-2. Although trains and coastal steamers had already made Maine a vacation destination for the well-to-do, it was the automobile, and a gradually improving road system,
that revolutionized things. As this 1928 view of Main Street in Farmington shows, cars
and trucks, along with gas stations and garages, had replaced horse-drawn vehicles and
livery stables. Courtesy of the Farmington Historical Society, Farmington, Maine.

opposition, the state road system expanded in the 1920s, bringing city and
country closer together and drawing more country traffic, trade, and people
into the cities each year.

The flexibility of auto travel appealed to all Americans, but it was particularly attractive to Maine people, so many of whom lived on farms or in small
villages. Maine residents purchased automobiles as soon as inexpensive, reliable
ones were available after 1910, and the impact on railroads, streetcars, and
steamboats was evident even in the early 1920s. Railroad passenger service
dropped from 4 million in 1920, to 1.9 million in 1927, and to 375,000 in 1933;
freight revenues declined from $14 million in 1920 to $8 million in 1933. Soon
the focus of transportation improvements was highways, a concern supported
by increasing state and federal funding.

Maine's urban 40 percent saw changes in the 1920s as well. Portland's seventy
thousand citizens were employed mainly in small, diversified manufacturing in-

dustries, services, trade, and tourism. The city's superb port facilities had been neglected in the late nineteenth century as maritime trade all across the nation declined. Like Portland, Bangor, with twenty-nine thousand people, turned away from its seaport functions to perform commercial services on a smaller scale for a huge, thinly populated central Maine region. Farther north, Presque Isle, Caribou, and Fort Fairfield shared the role of outpost for Bangor.

Other cities hosted mills, and their heavy manufacturing component gave a different texture to urban life. Biddeford, Lewiston, and Augusta produced mostly cotton textiles; Millinocket, Westbrook, Rumford, Jay, Woodland, and Bucksport produced paper products; and the twin cities of Auburn and Lewiston, especially the former, produced most of the state's shoes, although Gardiner, Wilton, Augusta, and Hallowell contributed as well. Paper, textiles, and shoes composed the "big three" of Maine manufacturing, but Maine communities produced many other items, ranging from canned fish, fruit, and vegetables to wood products like lumber, toothpicks, and furniture. Shipbuilding, once Maine's specialty, survived—but just barely—in Bath. Although these and other industries employed over twice as many men and women as Maine's farms, the state still ranked twenty-seventh in the value added by manufacturing. Maine produced only about six-tenths of one percent of the nation's total. Its firms were mostly small-scale: of more than fifteen hundred manufacturing establishments, only ten made products that earned them more than $5 million each, and only twenty-six had more than five hundred wage earners.

Although the paper mills thrived in the "Coolidge prosperity" of the 1920s, neither textiles nor shoes had done as well. Cotton textiles, hard hit by new synthetic fabrics and new fashions requiring less yardage, migrated to the southern states for more accessible raw materials, lower labor costs, and cheaper power. Refinancing of the Lewiston, Saco, and Augusta mills by Central Maine Power Company President Walter Wyman postponed the crisis in Maine textiles for about three decades, but the shakeout in the industry in 1928–29 was a clear foreshadowing of what was to come. Shoes, another low-wage industry employing many women, faced less out-of-state competition; in fact some companies moved to Maine to escape paying higher wages in Massachusetts.

Indeed, Maine wage-earners received less than their fellows in most northern states. Employing a string of euphemisms, a 1929 industrial survey suggested that the state's chief industrial asset was its cheap, docile labor force. Maine, the report contended, offered "excellent quality of labor"; a "large potential supply of labor"; "reasonable labor laws, including a 54-hour week for women"; and "reasonable wage rates." As the report summarized it, "a contented labor element results. Non-union or open-shop conditions prevail in most industries."

Ethnic tensions in Maine's cities in the 1920s marked the culmination of a half-century of changing demography. By 1930, more than a third of Maine's people were first- or second-generation Americans; about 12 percent were foreign-born, and another 22 percent had at least one foreign-born parent. The largest number came from French Canada. With a few exceptions, like the Finns who scattered throughout rural Maine and the Acadians and Franco-Americans in the St. John Valley, most immigrants chose to resettle in urban areas—Lewiston, Biddeford, Waterville, and Augusta, for example. Their foreign language, their Roman Catholic or Jewish faiths, their customs, even their factory jobs jarred the sensibilities of some rural Mainers, giving rise to a period of proscriptive "Americanism." In 1924, the Ku Klux Klan claimed more than fifty thousand members in the Pine Tree State. Although these figures may have been exaggerated, there were enough to maintain an impressive Portland headquarters, to march and burn crosses in many Maine towns, and exert considerable political pressure at the state level. The movement was moribund by 1930, but its prejudices lingered.

Politics in the Early Depression Years, 1929–33

Although rural and urban society showed the strains of new developments in the 1920s, Maine politics remained remarkably stable. As in the nineteenth century, mill towns like Lewiston, Biddeford, and Waterville generally voted Democratic, and nearly all rural areas voted in some degree Republican. Given the mix of population, this meant that, barring Republican splits or gross misconduct, Maine continued as a one-party state.

The 1928 elections brought a predictable GOP triumph, but in 1929 Republicans fell to squabbling, ostensibly over the referendum to abolish the twenty-year-old Fernald Law banning the export of hydroelectric power from Maine. Governor William Tudor Gardiner favored repeal, but other Republicans, led by Mayor John Wilson of Bangor, disagreed. Sectional jealousies over control of the party added fuel to the fire. Sensing a possible comeback, Maine Democrats prepared early and worked hard for the 1930 election. Fate would deal them some unexpected high cards.

Concentrating on the upcoming political campaigns, Maine newspapers showed only passing interest in stock prices in the fall of 1929. Immediately following the devastating October 24 stock market crash, the *Kennebec Journal* announced that speculators got what was coming to them. The editors joked that the stock market was "flashing its Halloween bogy and having better success in scaring folks than the average urchin," then cautioned against panic: "The crash directly affected not more than one percent of the population."

Clearly, Maine political commentators saw Prohibition as a more substantial political issue. Most politicians, especially Republicans, backed Maine's controversial 1851 temperance law and endorsed the 1919 National Prohibition Enforcement (Volsted) Act. Some tried to straddle the prohibition issue; but news stories, day after day, highlighting drunken driving convictions, seizures of homemade spirits, and arrests of bootleggers kept the issue before the public. One editorial attributed the supposed decline in alcoholism in Maine to strict enforcement of prohibition, but only four days earlier the same editorial column had carried the following instructive tale:

Recently in a given store not many miles from Lewiston a woman said she wanted a can of malt syrup to make beer. "Can't sell it for beer making," replied the manager. "It is against the law." "Oh well, give me a can for cooking," she concluded, and departed happily with her package.

The prohibition issue surfaced briefly at the 1930 Republican state convention. One delegate who charged angrily that the officially dry GOP had plenty of booze at their conclave was himself arrested for "drunken driving" on his way home. But the party took its time-honored stand against Demon Rum. Nevertheless, savage infighting continued to plague the party. Mayor John Wilson of Bangor challenged Governor William Tudor Gardiner for renomination and took about 40 percent of the vote. Another candidate from the northeast, Ralph Owen Brewster, ran even better against Senator Wallace White, the official choice of the "Kennebec Ring" (a bloc of leaders from central and southern Maine) but also lost.

With all this dissension in the enemy ranks, the Democrats, under Edward C. Moran of Rockland, saw their chance. They lashed the Republicans for their heavy spending, for a series of "scandals" in the State Highway Commission, and for the GOP's ties, through the Central Maine Power Company, to the huge, unpopular, and now financially undone utilities empire of Samuel Insull. Republicans defended themselves listlessly, and many probably stayed away on election day. In the general election of 1930, Republicans still garnered 55 percent of the vote and the Democrats 45 percent, with Governor Gardiner receiving 66,000 fewer votes than he had won in 1928.

Although the worsening depression probably had little to do with the close election, the next two years drove the economic crisis home in Maine. In rural Maine, the impact of the Depression was uneven. Some farm families, partly self-sufficient and isolated from national markets, had endured generations of hard times and hardly noticed the slump after 1929. Indeed, for many, rural life was an attractive refuge from the Depression; more people actually lived on farms in Maine at the end of the 1930s than at the beginning.

But for most of those in rural Maine, the Depression years offered a pinched existence. Maine's dairy and poultry industries rebounded somewhat after 1931, but apple producers lost export markets due to the collapse of the British pound, and potato farmers were in deep trouble. At the going price of 45 to 50 cents a barrel, the 1931 potato crop was worth about one third the 1930 harvest. The following year brought further declines. Purchasing power for potato farms dropped to less than half the 1910–14 levels. Part-time farmers who tradition-ally "got by" with cutting wood found it harder to make money that way, with both employment and wages in the woods industries off 22 percent between 1929 and 1931.

The 7,500 Mainers who tried to live wholly or partly by fishing and fish pro-cessing faced similar discouragements. Their industry had been declining for decades, and income fell off by more than 50 percent during the 1930s. Some coastal residents tended lawns, cooked, and kept house at the "cottages" where the wealthy vacationed or worked at the many large hotels along the coast. But the "summer people" left around Labor Day. Then, as one local put it, "You knew you had to work and you had to do whatever you could to earn a cent . . . whether it was clamming or cutting wood or whatever."

Some remained optimistic through the summer of 1932. Mayor Cony of Au-gusta told the Kiwanis Club that the Depression was a blessing in disguise, for "hard times make one realize the value of a place to sleep, a humble meal, a few friends, a daily laugh." But the news columns told a different story. Towns from Kittery to Fort Kent, from Bethel to Machiasport, shared in the growing crisis. Tourist travel was down 20 percent in 1932, and the state's largest railroad, the Maine Central, which had posted a profit of $1.1 million in 1931, sustained a loss of $63,000. Annual town reports showed similar signs: growing lists of tax delinquents, swelling payments for poor relief, and pay cuts for road laborers, teachers, and other town employees. Income tax collections in Maine were 36 percent lower in 1932 than in 1931. Fewer married and fewer registered cars than in the preceding year.

The state's mill towns were hardest hit. Although unemployment remained relatively low during the first years of the Depression, by 1933 about 20 percent of Maine's manufacturing workers were on the street. Even in the high-paying paper industry, production was down 50 percent and payrolls off almost as much, with nearly three thousand out of work altogether by 1933. In Lewiston, the hard-pressed city government experimented with a "work-for-aid" system in the summer of 1932. All physically fit males were to report daily at 8:00 AM and work eight hours for their relief allotment, the amount depending on family size, up to a maximum of eleven dollars per week. After weeks of grum-bling, some 150 men demonstrated peacefully at the mayor's place of business.

About five weeks later, the city dropped the idea. The problem of unemployment persisted, however, and in 1933 the city opened a commissary for those on relief to receive supplies in return for tickets.

Despite the hard times, in 1932 the state's Republicans seemed unworried. Rather than face the economic crisis, the Republican campaign emphasized the tired prohibition issue; even the staunchly Republican *Bangor Daily News* jabbed at the "frayed and frazzled traditionalism" in the platform. Meanwhile, the Gardiner administration refused to ask for federal Reconstruction Finance Corporation funds to help the unemployed and simply ignored the $1.6 million allocated to Maine for public works jobs on highway construction. The Democrats, ably led by Edward C. Moran, selected a dynamic nominee: Louis J. Brann, a Lewiston lawyer, judge, six-time mayor, and former member of the Maine legislature. Brann's call for outright repeal of prohibition helped the Democratic cause, as did the Republican feuds and political blunders. The voters endorsed Brann by a narrow margin and chose two Democratic congressional representatives. Although the three years of hard times undoubtedly helped the Democrats to victory, the issue was not decisive; two months after Brann's election, Republican President Herbert Hoover carried the state handily with 56 percent of the vote. Only five states joined Maine in Hoover's column, while forty-two went for the charismatic governor of New York, Franklin D. Roosevelt.

Maine and the New Deal, 1933–40

Mainers who had radios listened with the rest of the country to the new leader's inaugural address at noon on a rainy Saturday, March 4, 1933. They heard the ringing, confident tones give new life to reassurances like "the only thing we have to fear is fear itself," but they also listened to the promise to ask Congress for broad executive powers should that be necessary to deal with the crisis.

Banks were the immediate problem. Everywhere in the United States people were withdrawing deposits from banks to convert them to currency or gold, and many were sending the gold out of the country. Many banks failed under this pressure. To save those still left, a large number of states had declared "bank holidays." By executive order Roosevelt temporarily closed the rest, calling Congress into session three days later. The lawmakers rapidly confirmed his action and took others to rescue and reopen the viable banks. Nevertheless, some larger banks collapsed, like Maine's Casco Mercantile Trust and the Fidelity Trust Company, both of Portland. The latter, controlled by Guy P. Gannett of the *Portland Press Herald* and Walter Wyman of Central Maine Power Company, was the centerpiece of a fourteen-bank empire. Eventually, its depositors got ninety-four cents on the dollar of their deposits. Some banks never did reopen, but most eventually returned to business.

Relief was another Democratic priority. During the heady "First Hundred Days" of the new administration, Congress endorsed the scores of federal relief agencies that made up the core of the New Deal program. These agencies signaled a fundamental change in the relationship between the federal government on one hand and state and local governments and the economy. Maine people, of course, participated in these changes, but managed to express a longstanding rural, conservative bias against federal powers, state-run welfare programs, and economic regulation at the same time.

Lorena Hickok, a reporter and confidant of Eleanor Roosevelt, spent nine days in Maine in September 1933, as a field investigator for the Federal Emergency Relief Administration. In her acute and detailed eleven-page report, she told FERA head Harry Hopkins that thousands of families should be getting federally funded relief, but weren't. And why not? Partly because a "Maine-ite . . . would almost starve rather than ask for help." It was considered a "disgrace in Maine to be 'on the town.'" Given that attitude, those who did ask for help (especially Franco-Americans, she said) got little. To receive aid, people had to be "deserving cases"—that is, they had to be living up to "purely conventional moral standards."

Hickok's impressions provide some understanding of the limited endorsement Maine people gave Franklin Roosevelt's New Deal. Rather than ask for state or federal aid, town officials cut expenses to the bone, reducing everything from food orders for town "paupers" to teachers' pay. Everywhere she went, from the potato fields of the St. John Valley to bleak and empty canneries in Eastport, people needed help. In Rockland and St. George—the "gloomiest of all" Maine towns—the Depression had killed the demand for limestone, granite, ships, and fish. Hickok counted thirty vacant stores in Rockland. Officials were doing the best they could, but "their ideas simply do not fit in with ours, that's all."

Between 1930 and 1932, town governments provided most of the relief, inadequate as it was. As conditions worsened, resources husbanded by town governments, private charities, the Red Cross, and the Salvation Army were depleted. State government, at least until 1935, simply refused to do more than aid those who had no "settlement" in any particular town. Bangor's relief bill increased 50 percent from 1930 to 1933, and Portland saw a 500 percent rise over the same period. These enormous expenditures, roughly 10 to 15 percent of town expenditures throughout the decade, came at a time when tax collections were plummeting.

By 1933, some communities were unable to continue normal services, service bonded debt, or pay state taxes, much less to provide relief for the growing

numbers of unemployed. Maine turned to the federal government, albeit reluctantly, to answer the Depression decade's desperate needs. The first relief
program to pass Congress, and first in the hearts of many Maine people, was
the Civilian Conservation Corps, established in April 1933. The CCC recruited
young men, and later young women, and put them to work on various con-
servation-related projects in return for food, lodging, and thirty dollars a
month, twenty-five of which was sent home to their families. A company commander directed each camp, assisted by group leaders, a mess sergeant, a
surgeon, a chaplain, and an educational adviser.

About sixteen thousand Maine youths belonged to the CCC during its nine-
year life. The Maine Forest Service supervised the majority of the camps. The
CCC built four hundred miles of roads, planted trees, completed most of
Maine's section of the Appalachian Trail, worked at the eradication of the
gypsy moth and other insect pests, constructed the campgrounds at Acadia
National Park, and created Camden Hills State Park. CCC youths also fought
forest fires and cleaned up thousands of trees felled by the great hurricane
of 1938.

A more comprehensive relief program was the Federal Emergency Relief
Administration, also started in 1933. The agency granted funds to a state authority staffed by more than five hundred persons. This agency, in turn, made
grants to localities for direct relief. It also supervised a number of work-relief
projects, ranging from construction and sewing to preserving historical
records. In 1935 the Emergency Municipal Finance Board built thousands of
yards of new sewers. The Works Progress Administration (WPA), also established in 1935, constructed and improved airports from Portland to Houlton.

Women, 25 percent of Maine's unemployed, undertook a wide variety of
WPA projects. Some canned vegetables, fruits, and meats for school lunches,
using food supplied by the Federal Surplus Commodities Corporation. Others
sewed garments and articles of bedding, and still others acted as nurses, day-
care providers, and housekeepers for those unable to take care of themselves.
Unemployed men and women cataloged and preserved historical records, tu-
tored illiterates, and participated in cultural programs under the so-called
"Federal One." This branch of the WPA employed artists, writers, and musicians to bring theater, painting, sculpture, and music to citizens who had
seldom, if ever, experienced them before. In Maine one hundred musicians
played in a traveling orchestra, and forty actors participated in a theater project. About fifty persons worked on the famous WPA *Guide to the State of
Maine*, as well as on guides to U.S. Highway 1, to Maine's capital, and to Portland. Still, for all its accomplishments, the WPA could have done much more.
Its principal historian, Lawrence Lashbrook, concludes that "administrators

were concerned as much with operating a conservative, economical program as they were with employing the destitute." This was at least as true in Maine as it was elsewhere.

Under the WPA umbrella, the National Youth Administration (NYA) attempted to deal with the special needs of young people. NYA part-time jobs allowed, on an annual average, more than nine hundred high school students and about three hundred college men and women to stay in school. Many others worked for their towns on everything from drafting and painting to serving hot lunches. Some from outlying rural areas even stayed and worked at resident centers. At the largest of these, the Quoddy Regional Work Experience Project, hundreds of young men received vocational training and help in finding jobs.

In addition to immediate relief, the New Dealers also drew up plans for recovery. The most important of their programs for the country as a whole, although not for Maine, was the original Agricultural Adjustment Act of 1933. Its fundamental purpose was to raise farm prices until farmers had purchasing power equivalent to what they had enjoyed in the good years of 1909–14. This would be achieved by contracting with farmers to reduce production of "basic commodities." No crop grown commercially in Maine was on the "basic commodity" list, however, so Maine was one of only two states to retire no acres of any crop, and its farmers received the lowest sum paid to any state in rental and benefit payments.

During some early Depression years, Aroostook potato farmers sold their crops for prices far below the cost of producing them. The county's representative in Congress moved in vain to add potatoes to the list of AAA "basic commodities." In 1935, over the objections of the Secretary of Agriculture, the head of the AAA, and many others, Congress passed the Warren Potato Control Act. Acreage of spuds would now, it seemed, be under compulsory control, once the farmers signed their contracts. Growers supported it, but before it could take effect, the Supreme Court declared the first AAA unconstitutional, and Congress repealed the Warren legislation.

Cooperating far more than usual, potato growers, shippers, bankers, Granges, and the Farm Bureau formed the Aroostook County Council. The Maine Potato Growers Association, a marketing cooperative, flourished and farmers stabilized their acreage. In addition to this voluntary restriction, the disappearance of a thousand farms between 1935 and 1940 was a major factor in reducing farm surplus. Going beyond direct self-help, the beleaguered farmers pushed the state legislature in 1935 to mandate use of US standard grades in packing the spuds. Two years later, another act levied a small tax on each barrel of potatoes to finance advertising and agricultural research.

Aroostook farmers also benefited from New Deal agricultural programs. A temporary substitute for the AAA, the Soil Conservation and Domestic Allotment Act of 1936 continued to pay farmers who substituted grasses and clovers for wheat, corn, cotton, tobacco, and other "soil-depleting" crops. Maine farmers took a modest part in this program in 1936 and a larger one in 1937. As part of its nationwide bid to keep agricultural prices from falling further, the Federal Surplus Commodities Corporation bought up certain crop surpluses—among them, Maine potatoes.

The Farm Credit Administration served as an umbrella for various schemes, including those which refinanced mortgages so that farmers would not be driven off their land. By 1941, two of its branches held about one-third of the farm mortgage debt in the state. Another limb of the FCA provided loans at planting time for seed, fertilizer, and other materials. It was very active in Maine, especially in Aroostook County, with more than $5 million in outstanding loans at its peak in mid-1936. Still another unit, the Farm Security Administration—the only one directed specifically to the rural poor—was always underfunded and unpopular with conservatives. Nevertheless, about 4,600 Maine farm families (more than 10 percent) took out over $9 million in FSA loans between 1934 and 1942, when its enemies finally killed the program.

Federal help saved some farmers, but the 1935 Reciprocal Trade Agreement, which lowered tariffs on Canadian potatoes, soured many on the New Dealers. Indeed, a letter-writing campaign against the agreement had led to the formation of the Aroostook County Council. Moreover, the New Deal seemed to offer no permanent solution to the agricultural depression. Although no subsequent year was as bad as 1934, prices in the late 1930s usually hovered around the break-even level. Despite federal aid, people fell behind in mortgages, taxes, and store bills; more than 40 percent of the families in the town of Van Buren were fed and clothed by federal relief during the winters of 1936 and 1937. Some towns took farm products as payment for taxes and then doled them out to the destitute.

Maine Reacts to the New Deal, 1936–39

In Maine, the greatest disappointment with the New Deal centered on the Passamaquoddy Tidal Project. The idea of using the powerful tides of Passamaquoddy Bay to generate hydroelectric power began in the early 1920s with Dexter Cooper, an engineer who owned a summer home at Campobello Island—as did President Roosevelt. Impressed with the bay's extremely high tides, Cooper thought they could be harnessed with dams and holding basins to provide cheap, plentiful electricity. After Canada rejected his original international plan in 1929, Cooper designed a smaller but expandable all-American project. He believed the bay's tidal power would attract industry to perennially depressed Washington County. People in the area waxed enthusiastic: $65 million in federal money, six to seven thousand construction jobs, and new industries all promised a new era.

The project failed its first test when the Public Works Administration refused to fund it. Roosevelt, himself, revived the idea with a letter to a Maine congressman. Then Harold Ickes, head of PWA, visited Eastport with Governor Brann and Dexter Cooper. Ickes requested new studies, including one by the newly created Maine State Planning Board, which predictably urged immediate construction of the project. Congress appropriated $10 million for the project, and when the news reached Eastport, the street filled with cheering people. Bands paraded and church bells rang; at Lubec free beer was provided.

On July 4, 1935, the Army Corps of Engineers arrived and construction began. Erecting a "model village" to house more than a thousand clerks, draftsmen, engineers, technicians, and workers wiped out the relief rolls in Eastport. As the work proceeded on the village, the engineers drilled rock, tested currents, and carried out many other preliminary tasks. After three months of euphoria, the first warnings of trouble filtered into eastern Maine. The Bureau of the Budget halved the allocation to the hydro project, and partly as a result, about a thousand workers were laid off early in 1936. A nervous Brann scuttled off to Washington and returned with reassurances, but "Quoddy" was, in fact, in deep trouble. When the Senate's crucial vote on another survey of Quoddy and a Florida canal project came up, Maine's Senators voted against the latter, whereupon four southern Senators shifted their position on Quoddy. A narrow Senate vote on May 30, 1936, effectively killed Cooper's dream. By the end of the year, only 350 were still at work. Although $7 million had been spent, only two small dams and the Quoddy Village (soon taken over by the National Youth Administration for a trade school) remained.

In the balance, Maine people responded unenthusiastically to the New Deal. In the 1936 presidential elections, Roosevelt lost the state by about 57 to 43 percent, reflecting Maine attitudes toward federal welfare programs, deficits, and the local impact of the Reciprocal Trade Agreement. Only Vermont stood with Maine, causing FDR's campaign manager to reword the old political axiom to "As goes Maine, so goes Vermont." At the New Hampshire end of the Kittery-Portsmouth bridge, some wits erected a large sign: "You are now entering the United States"!

Worse yet for Maine Democrats, in 1936 Brann lost a bid for the Senate, and Republican Lewis O. Barrows beat the Democratic choice for governor. Brann had won easily in 1934, when Quoddy was steaming ahead, federal relief money was helping thousands, and Navy destroyer contracts were breathing new life into the Bath Iron Works. But over the long run the unpopularity of the New Deal with Maine voters hurt Brann, even though he tried to distance himself as much as possible from the federal help he received from Washington. Between 1934 and 1936, Republicans resolved their differences while Brann feuded with the Moran faction of the Democratic party, which was far more loyal to Roosevelt and the New Deal than Brann himself was. Brann's actions drove away some Democrats, and the governor's reputation fell further when his friend John MacDonough, director of the Maine Emergency Relief Administration, escaped serious corruption charges on a mere technicality. Brann's defeat in 1936 was one more indication of Maine's uneasy acceptance of the new economic order of the 1930s.

The later 1930s brought new federal strategies, among them an attempt to foster what one historian has called "countervailing forces" to balance the power of big business. During the so-called "Second New Deal," President Roosevelt attached increasing importance to a new American labor policy. That the government should support the right of workers to form unions and bargain collectively was unprecedented. When the leaders of the tiny Maine Federation of Labor realized that this was what the famous section 7(a) of the National Industrial Recovery Act (1933) said, they tried to take advantage of it. But in Maine unions were relatively weak, and the Bath Iron Works, textile and shoe factories, and many other industries remained unorganized. The unions knew that tradition and the weight of public opinion were against them.

Unsurprisingly, they had little to show for their first efforts. The International Brotherhood of Pulp, Sulphite, and Paper Mill Workers, stronger than most unions before 1933, improved its position. On the other hand, when Maine textile workers participated in the nationwide textile strike in September 1934, they got nowhere. In Augusta, Skowhegan, Pittsfield, and Waterville, workers did go out for a few days; in Lewiston heavy pressure from the mayor (who warned that strikers would receive no relief), from the Roman Catholic pastors, and from five companies of National Guard troops meant that only a few struck. The strike failed, but the new Congress of Industrial Organizations (CIO), set up to organize the mass-production industries across the country, later signed up the Maine textile mills.

Although in 1935 the Supreme Court killed the NRA, under which the union revival of 1933–34 had taken place, labor soon got something better. The National Labor Relations (Wagner) Act reaffirmed the commitment to collective bargaining, banned certain "unfair" practices used by industry to frustrate unionization, and set up the National Labor Relations Board to oversee workers' rights to choose or reject organization. If a majority voted for the union, management had to bargain collectively—or so the law appeared to say. Employers generally hated the Wagner Act and assumed for nearly two years that the Supreme Court would nullify it. To their surprise, the long-awaited decision upheld it.

That ruling came during the largest, longest, and most bitter strike in Maine during the 1930s. The walkout, which began in March 1937, closed or crippled nineteen shoe factories in Lewiston-Auburn; it ended three months later with a defeat for the United Shoe Workers of America–CIO. The strike was a stormy one from the start. Local workers, dissatisfied with low pay and poor workplace conditions, invited union organizers from Massachusetts to the Twin Cities. After several weeks in the community, the chief organizer asked a tumultuous meeting of several thousand workers to vote a strike up or down. They cheered it on, and walked out the next day, asking for a 15 percent pay hike, a forty-hour week, and union recognition. The last demand was probably the most controversial, because for decades the industry had operated on the "open-shop" principle. Only five years before, owners had crushed a brief attempt to set up a local union.

By Maine standards, the strike was violent, involving blacklists, strike-breakers, sabotage, and vandalism. The Auburn police, augmented by sheriffs' deputies and the state police, kept pickets away from the factories and arrested strike leaders for violating Maine's conspiracy statute. Those detained were able to obtain bail, but a local judge granted an injunction against the strike, bringing matters to a head. A band numbering around five hundred strikers marched to the Lewiston-Auburn bridge and was turned back; the following day, a crowd twice as big tried again, only to be dispersed by tear gas and clubs. Several strikers and police were injured in the melee. After this affair, dubbed "Red Wednesday" by the bitterly anti-CIO Lewiston papers, Governor Barrows sent in five hundred National Guardsmen. The strike leaders again found themselves under arrest, this time for contempt of the injunction. Denied bail, they remained under lock and key until the strike was over.

The NLRB held hearings in Auburn and decided to conduct elections in the factories. Most workers voted for the CIO but the factory owners simply ignored the results. The NLRB threatened court action, but to no avail. Elsewhere across the nation the CIO achieved spectacular successes in the textile, auto, and steel industries, but in Maine, inexperience, editorial condemnation of the "outside agitators" brought in to organize the strike, strong opposition from state, press, and church, the use of force, and—most important—the poverty of workers who simply could not afford to stay out of work, defeated the union and the Wagner Act as well.

Nationally, the later 1930s brought a sharp recession in 1937–38, followed by gradual improvement. In Maine, textiles continued to decline and the potato industry remained mired in debt. The 1937–38 recession was fatal to any chances Maine Democrats might have had to recover from their 1936 debacle. Brann ran a close race with the unpopular Barrows by avoiding the New Deal label, but the Republicans successfully identified his try for a third term as governor with Roosevelt's possible bid for a third presidential term. Both sides favored the resurrection of the Quoddy hydro project, but the Republicans hammered on the federal administration's unpopular trade agreement with Canada.

During 1939 and 1940, the economic picture slowly brightened in southern Maine. Tourism improved slightly, textile mills showed more profits, and shipyards at Bath and Kittery added workers as a slow naval build-up continued. On the other hand, some twenty-seven Aroostook County towns were said to be "practically bankrupt" by the field representative of the Federal Surplus Commodities Corporation. He added that 19,206 individuals out of 43,484 people in those towns were on relief.

In Maine, the Great Depression hurt most those who were already poor, especially those living in hard-pressed areas like the St. John Valley, the fishing and lumbering towns of Washington County, and the hills of Waldo and neighboring mid-coastal counties. Such distress spawned serious health problems. George W. Leadbetter, director of the Maine Department of Health and Welfare, claimed in early 1939 that five thousand people in Aroostook had scurvy, a disease caused by vitamin c deficiency, and George W. Coombs, director of the state Bureau of Health, warned of thousands of cases of malnutrition, adding that the prevalence of scurvy in northern Maine was "not over-emphasized." Local doctors took varying stands, and Governor Barrows—without visiting the area—denied the claim. While we are unlikely to extract the true figures from this thicket of political opinion, it is likely that malnutrition stalked Maine families in a number of economically marginal areas, a result of long-term unemployment coupled with a traditional reluctance to take "charity" and an equally firm resistance to giving it on the part of town and state officials.

To cope with this unprecedented drop in an already low standard of living, Mainers had first turned to self-help. But neither this, nor charity, nor the usual last resort, town relief, were adequate to meet the growing problem. State authorities were slow to move, with no broad-based taxes to tap, with a conservative Democrat in the Blaine House, and with the usual conservative Republican majority across the street in the legislature. The federal government did more, but states like Maine that squeaked the least got less oil. New England and the southern states rejected federal "interference" more than western and mountain states did, and consequently dropped to the bottom of the list of New

Deal expenditures, loans, and insurance. On a per capita basis, Maine came in thirty-second, although it received more than any other New England state except Vermont.

Politically, as we have seen, the New Deal changed few Mainers' minds about the Democratic party or about the wickedness of federal programs. If pushed hard enough, Mainers took Washington's help, grudgingly. But approving it with a vote was another matter. Perhaps this is a result of habit, but it also owes something to the fact that, however distressed some areas of the state might have been, Mainers generally weathered the Great Depression better than urban workers in the big cities of the East and Midwest.

Maine in World War II, 1939–45
RICHARD CONDON, WITH JOEL W. EASTMAN & LAWRENCE C. ALLIN

As their candidate for governor in 1940, the Republicans picked a wealthy newcomer, Sumner Sewall. The much-decorated World War hero won easily, probably aided by Maine people's concerns about the outbreak of war overseas. By November 1940, Hitler dominated Europe, his bombers pounding London every night. Living in the state nearest to England and bordering Canada on two sides, most Mainers rejected the isolationist thinking then common in the Middle West and other sections. This bias, and the dangerous world situation, probably explain why FDR, as America's commander-in-chief, came closer in 1940 to carrying Maine than he had in the previous two elections, losing by only seven thousand votes.

Slightly more than a year after the election of 1940, the US was at war with Japan, Germany, and Italy. During 1940 and 1941, naval construction picked up momentum. The Bath Iron Works, which had built several navy destroyers during the Depression, received a contract on July 1, 1940, for six vessels and later for twenty-five more, in addition to contracts for 10,000-ton cargo ships for Great Britain. BIW expanded its operations to East Brunswick and increased its work force, including sixteen hundred new women ship workers.

Early in 1941, BIW, in conjunction with Todd Shipbuilding Company, won a contract to build thirty cargo ships for Great Britain and began construction on a new yard in South Portland, featuring four huge basins. Only four months later, the Maritime Commission ordered a second shipyard with (eventually) six conventional ways for launching American "Liberty" ships. The two adjacent yards finally merged into the New England Shipbuilding Corporation, employing more than thirty thousand workers at their peak, including nearly four thousand women, and launching a total of 266 ships. At the third major

21-3. President Franklin D. Roosevelt (1882–1945) arrives in Rockland after his secret shipboard conference with British Prime Minister Churchill in August of 1941. Shown here with (l-r) Capt. John Beardall, Thomas Qualters, and Harry Hopkins, Roosevelt had just announced his "Atlantic Charter," which prolonged America's neutrality in World War II but moved it economically closer to the Allies. Courtesy of the Franklin D. Roosevelt Library, Hyde Park, New York.

war production site in Maine, the Portsmouth Naval Shipyard in Kittery, nearly nine thousand were working when the United States entered the war.

Maine's harbor defenses had been upgraded during and after World War I with the addition of anti-aircraft batteries and long-range heavy guns. In the fall of 1940, the coast artillery regiment of the National Guard, which had been responsible for Maine's harbor defenses in time of war, was called to active duty to operate the forts and train troops chosen by the country's first peacetime draft. After the United States entered the war, the defenses of Portland harbor were again modernized to defend the port, which had become a US naval station and the terminus of an oil pipeline from Montreal.

21-4. World War II brought the nation together as never before and stimulated industry, especially shipbuilding. In South Portland, the new Todd-Bath shipyards employed some 30,000 persons. Bath Iron Works itself turned out more destroyers (83) than any American yard. This print by Wiscasset artist Carroll Thayer Berry (1886–1978) shows a destroyer under construction at Bath in 1941. "Destroyer at Bath—Maine," a wood engraving by Carroll Thayer Berry from *The Down East Printmaker: Carroll Thayer Berry,* a catalogue raisonné by Elwyn Dearborn, published by Down East Press, Camden, Maine, 1983. Courtesy of Elwyn Dearborn.

Rearmament brought recovery, but even as late as March 1940, unemployment stood at 15.5 percent in Maine. During that last year of peace, the per capita income of Mainers stood at $523, higher than any year since 1930. In 1941, it finally topped the 1929 level. That same year, however, the cost of living rose sharply, as did taxes.

War was in the air during the autumn months of 1941. Gasoline had to be conserved, and there were war movies at the theaters, appeals for relief of the British in the editorials, and new government programs for selling defense bonds and stamps. Even more ominous, the draft boards began calling up men under the Selective Service Act of 1940. The state's other National Guard regiments were called into federal service in February as part of the 43rd Infantry Division, training in the South. The governor formed a state guard to take their place in Maine.

When war finally came, on Sunday afternoon, December 7, 1941, it was a shock to all, despite the warning signs. The papers commented on Maine's exposed position, with Nazi Germany's submarines operating off the coast. But other commentators assured that Maine people were so scattered that "it would take more bombs than the whole Nazi air force could tote over here in a year to kill a dozen people." Despite the brave humor, barbed wire barricades were thrown up—presumably to prevent sabotage—at the Carlton Bridge between Bath and Woolwich; coastal gun crews practiced at Fort Williams on Cape Elizabeth; and community Civil Defense Councils worked out plans for emergency defense. A December 10, 1941, *Kennebec Journal* headline really said it all: "U.S. Faces Long, Hard War."

During the war, firms like Goudy and Stevens, the Hodgdon Brothers, and Harvey F. Gamage of Boothbay Harbor built wooden torpedo boats and minesweepers for the Navy, and yards in Camden produced patrol craft and wooden auxiliary vessels. But Maine's greatest shipbuilding achievements of the war came out of BIW, which produced eighty-two destroyers for the Navy, arguably the finest afloat. Over the four years of the war, the South Portland yard produced 30 Ocean-class freighters and 236 Liberty ships to carry war supplies through submarine-infested waters.

Although Maine's harbor defenses were never put to the test, a number of vessels were sunk off the Maine coast by German submarines. In June 1942, a U-Boat was spotted in Casco Bay, and late in the war a submarine landed two spies on Hancock Point in Frenchmen's Bay; they were later arrested by the FBI. When Germany surrendered in May 1945, U-Boats surfaced and were escorted to the submarine base at the US Naval Shipyard in Kittery.

Preparing for the Postwar World

During this "long, hard war," unemployment finally melted away in Maine and elsewhere. Personal income rose to record levels. Aroostook farmers planted potatoes "fence post to fence post" and enjoyed record prices, with German prisoners of war assisting with the harvest to compensate for a shortage of pickers. At the other end of the state, the long-neglected port of Portland not only turned out the Liberty ships but also served as a major naval base, with as many as twenty-five hundred sailors on liberty in its streets at once.

On August 14, 1945, President Harry S. Truman, in office four months since the death of Franklin D. Roosevelt, announced the Japanese surrender. The Germans had given up in May, so the war was completely over, and Americans celebrated for days. Massive crowds jammed every downtown. One Portland paper ran a picture of sailors cavorting with women and bottles and a second photo of a car sporting a large banner reading, "To Hell with Hirohito!" The accompanying story, however, quoted a decorated Marine's comment that "they wouldn't be so wild if they'd seen the blood that paid for this." He spoke for the 80,000 Mainers who had served, and especially for the 1,634 who never returned.

Those who did come back found their state prosperous, although apprehensive, with the rest of America, about a postwar depression. It never came. Instead a new era emerged from fifteen years of economic catastrophe, unprecedented government activity, and total war. Good times did not erase the changes that had come since the 1920s. The New Deal "revolution," shorn of its emergency features, remained much in effect: the national security state kept its forces in Maine and exacted high taxes; big government came to stay; and in due course Mainers became accustomed to it.

For Further Reading:

Newspapers are an essential primary source for state and local history, and they provide coverage for even the smallest community. Some large public libraries maintain card indexes to local papers. In addition, most libraries maintain a local history file, and historical societies often maintain scrapbooks of clippings on matters of local interest. Government agencies like the Maine School Finance Commission and institutions like the Aroostook County Council often publish reports and recommendations on topics of contemporary concern. During the Great Depression and World War II, the federal government undertook numerous studies of economic, military, and social topics, some of which were published; others are available at the US National Archives. The New England regional branch of the National Archives in Waltham, Massachusetts, includes records of such agencies as the Farmers Home Administration and the Works Progress Administration, both of which are useful for researching Maine in the Great Depression. For World War II, records of the Office of Price Administration, the First Naval District, the Selective Service System, and the War Manpower Commission are available at Waltham. Finally, many persons who lived during these years are still alive and can be interviewed.

Secondary sources on the period are not abundant, but graduate students at the University of Maine have produced a number of excellent studies that are available on interlibrary loan. These and other important secondary works are included in the following list:

Allen, Mary Moore, *Origin of Names of Army and Air Corps Posts, Camps and Stations in World War II in Maine* (Goldsboro, N.C., 1952).
Aroostook County Council, *A Long-Term Agricultural Program for Aroostook County: A Panorama of Aroostook Farm Problems* (n.p., 1936).

Butler, Joyce, *Wildfire Loose: The Week Maine Burned* (Kennebunkport, 1979).

Coffin, Harold W., *Assignment in Military Intelligence* (Old Town, 1972).

Condon, R. H., "Bayonets at the North Bridge: The Lewiston-Auburn Shoe Strike, 1937," *Maine Historical Society Quarterly* 21 (Fall 1981).

Condon, R. H., "Living in Two Worlds: Rural Maine in 1930," *Maine Historical Society Quarterly* 25 (Fall 1985).

Devino, W. Stanley, *A Study of Textile Mill Closings in Selected New England Communities* (Orono, 1966).

Doty, C. Stewart, *Acadian Hard Times: The Farm Security Administration in Maine's St. John Valley, 1940–43* (Orono, 1991).

Dunnack, Henry, *Rural Life in Maine* (Augusta, 1928).

Earley, Sharon, *Walter Wyman and Five Maine Mills, 1925–1933* (Lewiston, 1973).

Eisenmenger, Robert W., *The Dynamics of Growth in the New England Economy, 1870–1964* (Middletown, Conn., 1967).

Gaffney, Thomas, "A Study of Maine Elections, 1930–1936" (M.A. thesis, University of Maine, 1962).

Holmes, Theodore C., "A History of the Passamaquoddy Tidal Project" (M.A. thesis, University of Maine, 1955).

Jones, Herbert G., *Portland Ships Are Good Ships* (Portland, 1945).

Lashbrook, Lawrence, "Work Relief in Maine: The Administration and Programs of the WPA" (Ph.D. dissertation, University of Maine, 1977).

Lowrie, Walter, "Roosevelt and the Passamaquoddy Bay Tidal Project" *History* 30 (1968–69).

Maine Civilian Defense Corps, *Official History of the Maine Civilian Defense Corps* (Hallowell, 1946).

Maine Development Commission, *It's Easy To Get to Maine by Train, Bus or Plane* (Augusta, 1942).

Maine School Finance Commission, *Financing the Public Schools of Maine* (n.p., 1934).

McGuire, Harvey P., "The Civilian Conservation Corps in Maine, 1933–1942" (M.A. thesis, University of Maine, 1966).

Merriam, Paul G., *Home Front on Penobscot Bay: Rockland during the War Years, 1940–1945* (Rockland, 1991).

Moffat, Alexander W., *A Navy Maverick Comes of Age, 1939–1945* (Middletown, Conn., 1977).

New England Homefront, WW II (Camden, 1991).

Tardiff, Shirley, "Maine Politics at the End of the Second New Deal" (M.A. thesis, University of Maine, 1975).

United States Navy, *War Diary, Eastern Sea Frontier, December 1941–August 1945* (Wilmington, Del., 1984).

Veazie, Carl E., "The Maine Economy, 1940–1975," *Thomas Business Review* 3 (Fall 1975).

Webber, Edwin W., *An Evaluation of the Political History of Maine (1930–1940)* (Orono, 1952).

Wright, John G., editor, *New England's Prospect, 1933* (New York, 1933).

York, R. M., "The Maine Economy, 1900–1940," *Thomas Business Review* 3 (Fall 1975).

22

Maine Out of the Mainstream,

1945–1965

RICHARD H. CONDON

The previous chapter explored the impact of national and world events on Maine's history; this chapter focuses on Maine's internal development between 1945 and 1965. During these years, Maine's resource-based industries grew more slowly than the national economy, presenting fewer opportunities for Maine people. Other signs that Maine remained "out of the mainstream" during these two decades can be found in statistics on population growth, wage levels, and funding for social services, including education.

In part, Maine spent less on social services because state government had fewer taxable resources. Underfunding also reflected complacency in Maine's ruling circles, however. The situation prompted a major debate over the pace of economic and social progress, leading to the rebirth of a two-party system and finally to greater emphasis on industrial development, education, and the environment.

This chapter raises four important points. First, from a pedagogical perspective, it demonstrates the way statistics can be used to illustrate social issues. It shows that statistics can be blended with social history to draw a precise, yet richly detailed picture of the past. Second, this chapter, although more subtly than the last, illustrates the tension between national trends and the development of Maine. In a period of national growth and prosperity, Maine appeared to be mired in the past, and at a time of changing partisan alignments, Maine clung to its old Republican standard, at least until 1954. This again raises the question: what makes Maine different?

Third, the postwar period again shows the precariousness of Maine's resource-based industries and demonstrates the profound impact this traditional economy had on all forms of opportunity in Maine. And finally, this chapter, too, shows Maine in a period of transition, a state in the process of realigning its economy and political structure with that of the rest of the nation. By the mid-1960s, it would appear, Maine was moving back into the mainstream.

In 1947 Arnold Toynbee published his massive interpretation of the rise and fall of civilizations, *A Study of History.* Although the work attracted much attention, even bringing its author to the cover of *Time* magazine, most of those who noticed it in Maine did so because of a few lines buried deep in one of its many volumes. They described the Pine Tree State as a backwater where a few miserable hunters and fishers eked out a barren existence among the Indians. Outraged, Maine editors lambasted the English academic, and the state's premier historical novelist, Kenneth Roberts, brought out a longer refutation called, "Don't Say That about the State of Maine!"

The tempest soon blew over, but more than a decade later Maine heard from other critics. Although they were less harsh than Toynbee, their well-founded analyses were more to the point. In the March 1963 issue of *Down East,* George H. Ellis, a native of Maine who had served as president of the Federal Reserve Bank of Boston, squarely faced the fact that the state was "less fortunate" than the other New England states and prescribed a shift to newer, research-based industries. These would require a better-educated work force, higher state expenditures for schools on all levels, and a state income tax to pay for them.

Three months after Mainers received these home truths, journalist William Ellis discussed "The Trouble with Maine" in *The Nation,* a liberal political weekly magazine. He saw "a state gasping for breath, bogged down in the muck of supreme depression—a state dedicated seemingly to the humiliation of its own people." The quaint façade of "Vacationland" hid substandard living conditions, low wages, closed factories, declining farms, high utility rates, polluted rivers, powerful interests, captive politicians, and bland newspapers. Leaving the detailed remedies to others, Ellis saw Maine's greatest need as a "thundering voice of dissent"—a Paul Revere to awaken a state in desperate trouble.

In more temperate terms, the Armour Research Foundation, hired in 1960 by the state's Department of Economic Development to plan for economic growth, had already sounded a call for change:

> Probably the most important improvement opportunity is the conversion of the general lethargy of many of the people of Maine to a dynamic outlook. . . . We found a surprisingly large number of Mainers who appeared to be convinced that the State was doomed toward economic failure. There was hope in many people, but it seemed to be overshadowed by a rationalization that the outlook was dim.

These observers leveled their criticisms of Maine during the decades when the United States enjoyed the longest era of economic growth and prosperity in its history: the quarter century that stretched from the end of World War II to the

Arab oil embargo of the mid-1970s. These good times owed much to the population explosion touched off by the 1947–63 "baby boom," which itself profoundly changed American society. New technologies also fueled economic growth. Children who grew up in these decades experienced the coming of television, computers, and other new electronic equipment, superhighways, shopping malls, jet travel, the conquest of polio, and many other rapid changes.

How correct were Maine's critics in placing the state on the sidelines as the good years of the "American century" rolled by? The answer to this question has two parts, both addressed in this chapter. First, the decades from the mid-1940s to the mid-1960s brought economic growth to Maine, but it was indeed slow. Second, the problems the critics identified prompted a major political debate between those who, out of apathy or complacency, were satisfied with the pace of change and those who were not. Out of this debate came a major political shift during the period, which in turn began closing the "opportunity gap" between Maine and the nation at large.

People and Economy

Why did Maine's economy lag behind that of the nation as a whole? To some degree, Maine's growth pattern was predicated on slowly rising population figures. Population growth slower than the national average was nothing new in Maine. The rapid peopling of the District in the years just before statehood eased markedly before the Civil War, and for decades after that conflict the pace slowed to a crawl. Once entitled by population to eight representatives in Congress, Maine had only three by the early decades of the twentieth century. Only in the 1930s did Maine's population increase of 6.2 percent almost reach the nation's anemic 7.3 percent. For those who wanted growth, much worse news lay ahead. In the 1940s, Maine grew at a rate slightly more than one-half the United States figure; in the 1950s, Maine could manage only about one-third the national average.

The reasons for this had little to do with Maine's birth or death rates; both were near the national average in the 1950s. A look at the age structure, however, turns up a clue. Although the median age of the people of Maine in 1960, 29.5 years, was exactly the same as that of the American people, there was a slightly smaller proportion of persons in the critical age groups between 20 and 44 years: 30.2 percent of the total, as against 32.1 percent across the nation. Why were there fewer men and women in the age groups that enter the work force and start new families? Evidently they were following the old Maine tradition of seeking greater opportunities elsewhere. In the 1940s, 21,000 more persons left the state than came in it; in the booming 1950s, the figure rose to 65,000; and in the 1960s, the net outmigration was 70,000.

The fact is that thousands of Mainers knew that they could do better economically elsewhere. In the two decades from 1945 to 1967, per capita personal income in Maine averaged only 84.1 percent of the nation's average. (Maine did worse, relatively, in these boom times than it had during the Great Depression.) Moreover, states with far better personal income figures were not far away: New Hampshire outdid Maine at 91.2 percent of the national level and Massachusetts at 110.1 percent. Connecticut stood at 128.9 percent of the national average; no wonder some in Lewiston referred to East Hartford as the "second capital of Maine."

In part, these per capita income figures reflected weaknesses in Maine's older resource-based enterprises. Mainers who farmed, fished, or lumbered, or who processed these resources, faced serious challenges in the postwar years. At the end of the war, Maine farmers, already adapting for decades to western competition by specializing, mechanizing, and expanding saw the pace of change increase rapidly. The "mechanical-biological-chemical revolution," as economist David Vail and historian Richard Wescott call it, increased crop yields, but required less labor and more ready capital. Large farmers were able to afford the high costs of the new era, and the smallest operators continued to farm but relied increasingly on other sources of income. But middle-sized producers left the business in large numbers. As farms closed down, many rural communities lost people and services, creating conditions that drove even more of Maine's young people off the farms. Some farm towns became suburbs to larger municipalities and changed their character substantially; others stagnated as populations declined and the social and institutional supports for rural neighborhoods withered away.

Where farms survived, they became more specialized. Potatoes, dairy products, broilers, and eggs accounted for more than 70 percent of farm production by the early 1950s. Potatoes, the only Maine crop of great national importance, lost ground steadily. Markets failed to grow, and western farmers took more of what was left. Even in Maine, it seemed, people demanded "Idaho potatoes," and Maine ceased to be the nation's primary spud producer. Statewide, Maine farms echoed national trends in increasing size and capitalization, but the value of farmland, buildings, and output grew at a slower pace than in the nation at large, while the numbers of farms and farm acreage dropped more rapidly.

Against this story of decline may be set the curious growth of the contract broiler industry. During the war, demand shot up for poultry, which was not subject to wartime rationing. New York processors began supplying Maine farmers with chicks, feed, litter, and medicine. Farmers housed and cared for

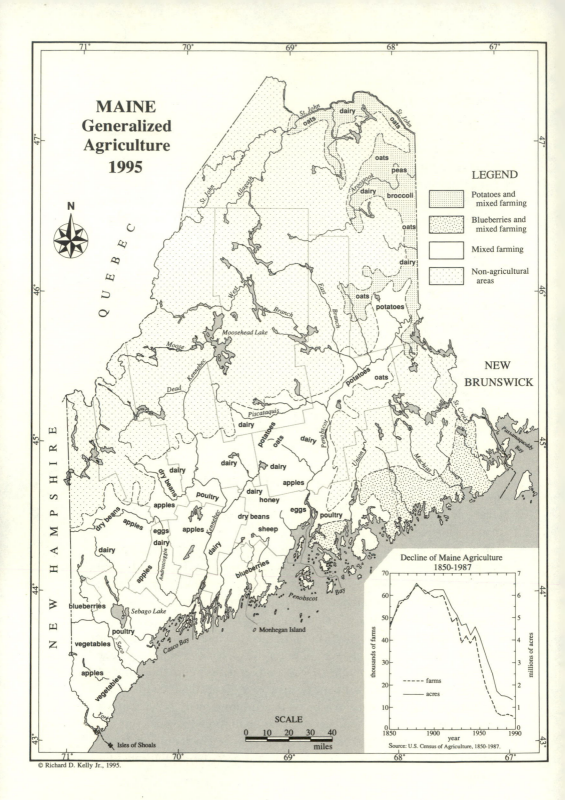

MAINE
Generalized
Agriculture
1995

N

Q U E B E C

N E W H A M P S H I R E

St. John

Allagash

St. John

West

Branch

Moosehead Lake

Moose

Kennebec

Dead

Piscataquis

East

Branch

Kennebec

Androscoggin

Saco

Sebago Lake

Penobscot

Casco Bay

Monhegan Island

Penobscot Bay

Union

Machias

St. Croix

Passamaquoddy Bay

NEW
BRUNSWICK

oats

dairy

oats

oats

peas

dairy

broccoli

oats

dairy

oats

potatoes

potatoes

oats

potatoes

oats

dairy

dairy

dairy

dairy

dairy

dairy

apples

dairy

honey

dry beans

poultry

apples

eggs

apples

dairy

dairy

eggs

poultry

sheep

dry beans

apples

dairy

dry beans

apples

dairy

apples

blueberries

blueberries

poultry

vegetables

apples

vegetables

York

Isles of Shoals

LEGEND

Potatoes and
mixed farming

Blueberries and
mixed farming

Mixed farming

Non-agricultural
areas

SCALE

0 10 20 30 40

miles

Decline of Maine Agriculture
1850-1987

thousands of farms

millions of acres

--- farms

— acres

year

Source: U.S. Census of Agriculture, 1850-1987.

their flocks under supervision from the large out-of-state combines. During the postwar years this became big business, and in the 1950s poultry—unlike nearly every other form of agriculture—continued to grow.

Maine's fisheries workers saw their catch, and income from it, swing broadly up and down in the postwar years. Again, this repeated national movements. The 1967 landings, 197.4 million pounds, were only slightly higher than the 1945 figure, but other years brought well over 300 million pounds. The value of the catch hovered around $20 to $25 million in the mid-1960s, about one-tenth of the value of Maine farm products sold at that time.

Maine's third traditional resource-based industry, lumber production, held relatively steady, following a precipitous decline in the 1920s and 1930s. As farm acreage fell, even more of Maine returned to forest; eventually about 90 percent of the state's land area was under forest cover, making Maine the most heavily wooded state in the nation. Millions of these forest acres belonged to a few great landholders, traditionally wielders of great power in Augusta and in areas of the state dependent on forest products for economic survival. In the postwar years, about 15 percent of Maine's manufacturing force worked in logging camps and sawmills. However, sawmills and small wood-turning operations produced only about 18 percent of the total value of Maine's forest products in 1959, and all other wood products, from shingles to railroad ties, from maple sugar to Christmas trees, made up only another 2 percent of the total dollar value.

Paper production, on the other hand, which accounted for the other 80 percent of the forest's bounty, experienced a sustained increase in the 1950s. While Maine's paper companies employed only a few thousand more people than the woods operations and sawmills, they turned out nearly three dollars of every ten generated in the state. The largest Maine producer was Great Northern Paper Company, which made newsprint paper at the "Magic City of the North," carved out of the woods by hundreds of immigrant laborers at the turn of the century. The Millinocket plant produced nearly a thousand tons of paper a day, and almost as much came out of a newer facility built at East Millinocket in 1954. Great Northern lived up to its name by owning well over two million acres of the state—about 11 percent of its total land area. Other giants included Oxford Paper Company in Rumford; Fraser in Madawaska; S. D. Warren in Westbrook; International in Jay; and Scott in Winslow. Together they made Maine the eighth ranking paper-making state in the nation.

From the end of World War II to the late 1950s, the industry spent more than $180 million adding new paper machines and upgrading older ones. By 1970, these six expanding paper companies owned nearly one-half of the state's commercial forestland, a proportion in private hands higher than that held in any other state. One-quarter of Maine's manufacturing work force was employed in the paper mills.

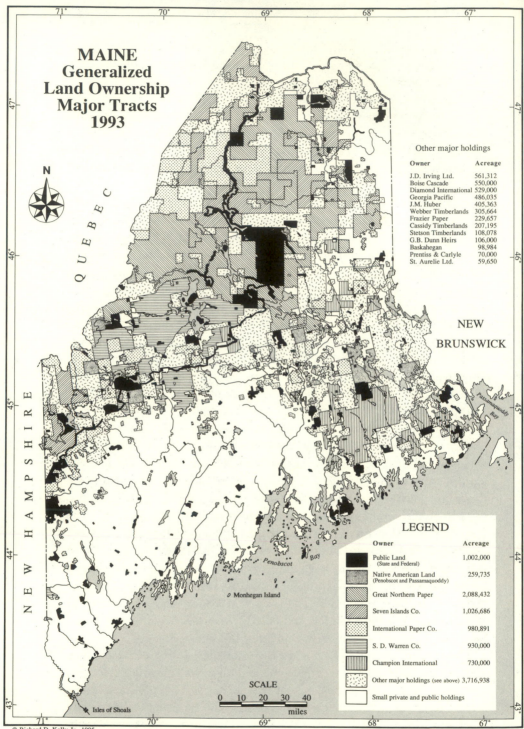

MAINE
Generalized Land Ownership Major Tracts 1993

N

QUEBEC

NEW BRUNSWICK

NEW HAMPSHIRE

Passamaquoddy Bay

Penobscot Bay

Monhegan Island

Isles of Shoals

Other major holdings

Owner	Acreage
J.D. Irving Ltd.	561,312
Boise Cascade	550,000
Diamond International	529,000
Georgia Pacific	486,035
J.M. Huber	405,363
Webber Timberlands	305,664
Frazier Paper	229,657
Cassidy Timberlands	207,195
Stetson Timberlands	108,078
G.B. Dunn Heirs	106,000
Baskahegan	98,984
Prentiss & Carlyle	70,000
St. Aurelie Ltd.	59,650

LEGEND

Owner	Acreage
Public Land (State and Federal)	1,002,000
Native American Land (Penobscot and Passamaquoddy)	259,735
Great Northern Paper	2,088,432
Seven Islands Co.	1,026,686
International Paper Co.	980,891
S. D. Warren Co.	930,000
Champion International	730,000
Other major holdings (see above)	3,716,938
Small private and public holdings	

SCALE

0 10 20 30 40
miles

© Richard D. Kelly Jr., 1995.

22-1. Frances Allen and other union picketers go out on strike at Factory Island, Saco, in 1945. Throughout World War II workers remained on the job, despite the fact that their pay stayed nearly flat and even though the mills were earning huge profits from war contracts. Courtesy of the York Institute Museum, Saco, Maine.

Growth in the paper industry was a bright exception to the economic malaise of the 1950s and 1960s. Here, too, however, clouds lay on the horizon. A 1970 US Forest Service report pointed out that some valuable species were being cut faster than they were regenerating. If this continued, total hardwood removals would exceed growth within a few years, and even softwoods—the basic requirement of the paper industry—would reach that point by the turn of the century.

Other important Maine industries faced much darker skies in the postwar years. The cotton textile business, concentrated in Lewiston, Biddeford, Waterville, and Augusta, had been beleaguered since the 1920s. Maine was too far from the raw material, and its workers' pay envelopes were fatter than those of the desperately poor rural populations of Virginia, the Carolinas, and Georgia. Finally, the southern mills were newer than many New England facilities and their owners far more aggressive competitors.

Five leading Maine mills—the Bates, Hill, and Androscoggin in Lewiston, the Edwards in Augusta, and the York in Saco—survived the Depression after a takeover by Walter Wyman's New England Public Service Company. Wyman, president of the state's largest utility, Central Maine Power Company, needed large electricity consumers to absorb power from the huge dam and reservoir projects CMP completed on the Kennebec and other rivers. Under these circumstances, textile profit or loss was secondary to the new owners, so the mills remained open and thousands continued to enjoy steady work. Although profits rose during the war years, they disappeared again afterward. Still, keeping the mills in Maine to buy power counted most.

All this changed abruptly in 1955, when Lester Martin, a New York financier who had hankered for the mills for years, announced that he now controlled 51 percent of the stock. The test now, of course, was whether the mills made money as textile producers, not as consumers of power. The new management soon closed two of the mills; two others closed in the early 1970s, and the Bates mill buildings were sold to the city of Lewiston in 1964.

Maine's other traditional, nondurable-goods industry, shoe manufacturing, suffered less than textiles from out-of-state competition. Auburn remained a major manufacturing center in the postwar years, but there were "shoe shops" in many Maine towns. Like textiles, the industry predominantly employed women and paid low wages. Textiles and shoes did most to keep the average weekly earnings of Maine employees at 77 to 78 percent of the national scale from the late 1950s to the late 1960s.

Mainers who worked in defense-related occupations were more prosperous than mill workers, but even during the height of the Vietnam buildup in the mid-1960s, Maine had fewer jobs relative to other states. In June 1968, 8,400

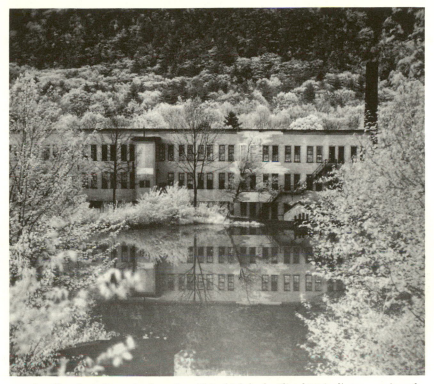

22-2. Small and medium-sized textile mills, which had utilized Maine's streams since the nineteenth century, began to vanish from the scene after World War II. The Hughes Woolen Mill was one of the five such operations clustered along Camden's Megunticook River. It ceased production in 1952, and the building was turned into the Penobscot Poultry Company's chicken hatchery. The structure burned in 1964 and is now the site of a trailer park. Courtesy of John J. McAuliffe.

Mainers were in defense-generated employment, only 2.1 percent of the total civilian work force. They worked in shipbuilding at Bath Iron Works, at the Portsmouth Naval Shipyard, and at bases at Limestone and Brunswick. Dow Air Force Base in Bangor and a missile site in Presque Isle closed during the early 1960s.

Maine continued to have a higher share of its work force in manufacturing than the national average at the end of the 1960s. The proportion fell slightly, however, and the trade and services segments grew slightly, although it remained below the U.S. figures. The state's center of trade and services had traditionally been its largest city. Portland enjoyed wartime prosperity, but at the end of the war the Navy sailed away and no one needed "Liberty ships." Historian William David Barry wrote of the "profound economic and attitudinal slump" during the 1950s and 1960s—the "dark ages of twentieth-century Portland." The old city's population dwindled as the suburbs grew, stores closed or moved, and tourism declined. In 1961, the decline of the city was symbolized by the tragic destruction of the beautiful Union Station, which in its heyday had seen sixty-five trains a day arrive and depart. But, as Barry points out, there were a few signs of life in the ruins: the airport grew modestly, an Airport Industrial Park opened, and Greater Portland Landmarks began to urge that many historic buildings should be preserved and adapted to new uses. Not until the 1970s, however, would the winds of change blow strongly through the Old Port.

Portland's stagnation during the first two postwar decades was a microcosm of the state's economic problems. Neither the older resource-based economy, excepting paper making, nor the newer nondurables like textiles and shoes expanded. At the same time, a nearly static population meant that residential construction remained sluggish, as did trade and services, the spearheads of change elsewhere.

Social and Educational Change

As a state with a lagging economy, a small population, and (for New England) a large territory, Maine found it difficult to maintain, much less improve, social services. When health, education, and welfare programs fell further behind those available elsewhere, outmigrants had another reason to leave. As they did, of course, progress was harder yet to achieve. Tables 1 and 2 make it clear where Maine's money for social programs came from, where it went, and how state income and expenditures compared with national levels. These figures suggest several conclusions. First, Maine leaders had less to spend than their counterparts elsewhere, on average. Second, leaning on federal funds helped more (as a portion of total revenue) in the 1960s. Third, Maine depended more than other states on the property tax. Fourth, Maine spent more on highways than the national average, and less on education, welfare, and health. Fifth, despite great increases in education spending between 1959 and 1967, the gap actually widened between what Mainers spent per capita on these functions and what the rest of the country saw fit to spend on them.

Table 22.1

REVENUE PER CAPITA BY SOURCE

		Total	From Fed. Govt.	From Taxes	From Prop. Tax
1959	ME	$237	43	171	86
1959	US	$257	36	184	85
1967	ME	$334	74	260	126
1967	US	$386	78	308	132

Table 22.2

FEDERAL, STATE, & LOCAL GOVERNMENT EXPENDITURES

PER CAPITA, BY FUNCTION

		Total	Education	Highways	Welfare	Health & Hosps.
1959	ME	$251	81	72	22	17
1959	US	$277	98	54	23	22
1967	ME	$400	157	88	35	20
1967	US	$472	192	70	42	34

Chronic underfunding, however it can be justified, left its mark on institutions and programs maintained by the state government. A series of newspaper headlines in 1950 suggests the scope of the problem: "Mental Hospital Budgets Sadly Low"; "Crowded Prisons Require Big Outlay"; "Five Plants Cite Rise in Costs"; "Welfare Expenses Poser for Maine"; "Costs of Old Age Program Pose Acute Problem to State." A story under the last of these banners pointed out that the state's old-age assistance program was outrunning its revenue sources. As of 1950, fourteen thousand persons were receiving aid; but there were nearly four times that many who were sixty-five or over and drew neither from the state program nor from Social Security. The state's commissioner of health and welfare worried, "One cannot tell when some of them might apply." He also noted that Maine had more older people and fewer recipients of aid proportionate to population than the rest of the nation. Although persons became eligible for assistance at age sixty-five, the average age of Mainers in the program was seventy-four, suggesting to the author that "people do not apply for assistance until the actual need hits them."

For those receiving institutional care, the picture in 1950 was at least as bleak. Mentally ill persons went to the state hospitals at Augusta or at Bangor. Augusta was seriously overcrowded, with 294 more female patients than could be accommodated. Both spent far less on food per patient than the national average; both were handicapped by high staff turnovers and high job vacancy rates, problems blamed on poor pay and working conditions. Augusta needed renovations to meet plumbing, electrical, and elevator code requirements, while Bangor's maintenance needs had not been met for ten years. At the state's facility for the mentally retarded, Pownal State School (Pineland), many of the same deficiencies existed for the rapidly growing population of thirteen hundred. It takes little imagination to picture conditions at the institution, where "279 must be dressed and undressed; 257 are untidy all the time."

Seventeen years later in 1967, reporter William Langley investigated "Poverty, Maine Style" (*Portland Sunday Telegram*, December 31, 1967). He concentrated on the rural poor, probably justified when one recalls that well over half of the state's people were rural and about two-thirds of rural families had annual incomes of less than $3,000—considered the poverty line in 1967. Langley described rural Maine existence at or below this line:

> One mother in northern Hancock County lives with her four children in a two-room dwelling covered on the outside with black tarpaper. The shack sits on the edge of the woods and the small yard is littered with piles of rags, tin cans, pails and tubs, assorted cardboard, and other refuse. . . . There is no indoor bathroom. There is no running water or electricity. The furniture consists of two tables, five wooden upright chairs, one semi-upholstered chair, one cupboard on the wall, a wood stove and three beds without sheets.

Maine's poorest counties—Hancock, Washington, Waldo, Aroostook, and Lincoln—had too much seasonal work, too little steady employment, too few doctors and dentists, too much illness, too many hungry children and elderly people, too few decent houses.

Education, generally regarded as a way out of such squalor, was as underfunded as other social services in postwar Maine. Educators, editors, and even a few politicians brandished reams of statistics to prove that Maine was near the bottom of every ranking—except that of rejection of draftees for mental and educational deficiencies!

Throughout the period, Maine teachers' salaries remained among the lowest in the nation, resulting in a serious shortage of qualified instructors. Superintendents had been hard put to find them during the war years, and peace brought little or no relief. During 1945 and 1946, about seven hundred teachers left Maine. This was not drastic enough to force schools to close, as happened in some other states, but it did mean that many poorly trained persons got jobs. Nor did the future look better. Most new teachers came from the state's five "normal" (teacher training) schools, which together produced fewer than two hundred graduates a year. (In the late 1920s, incredibly, they had sent out between four and six hundred annually.) With the average teacher's salary only $1,748 per year in 1946–47—several hundred dollars less than factory wages—it is clear why so few contemplated a teaching career.

By the early 1950s, when the first baby boomers were entering school, Maine had a shortage of elementary teachers. The teachers' colleges graduated 247 that year for 391 openings for beginning teachers. No wonder, then, that only 21 percent of Maine's elementary teachers held degrees. Since 1947, the average salary had risen to $2,300, but only a few states, mostly southern, still paid less. Although 1954 brought a state minimum pay schedule for teachers, their salaries slid to forty-fourth in the nation by 1956–57, about $1,200 below the national average.

Averages, although sometimes useful as blunt instruments of comparison, can conceal as well as reveal. For instance, it was long understood that Maine's many poor rural towns were struggling to support schools on a limited property tax base. Cities with thriving industries or other sources of wealth could afford to spend much more on their children's education. Although the state had made modest efforts at "equalization" since 1919, little could be done when the state itself bore only about 18 percent of the total cost of public education (1953–54). Four hundred and ninety cities, towns, and plantations supported schools; only a handful had formed community school districts to share the load. As a result, approximately 40 percent of the secondary schools in the state had a hundred pupils or less. Such small units seldom had enough teachers able to present knowledgeably a varied curriculum; libraries and laboratory equipment were antiquated.

In view of these problems, the 1955 legislature authorized a thorough investigation of Maine's schools. The resulting report, the Jacobs Study, laid the foundation for thoroughgoing educational reform in Maine. Behind the study lay a bipartisan agreement by Republican president of the state senate, Robert N. Haskell, and the new Democratic governor, Edmund S. Muskie, that increased school subsidies and district consolidation had to come. Out of their cooperation came the landmark Sinclair Act of 1957. Passed by large majorities, but only after bitter arguments from some towns defending local interests, the law made the state more responsible than ever before for public education.

Backed by a 1 percent raise in the state sales tax, the state began paying each local authority, according to its need, a per-pupil allowance intended to support a minimum foundation program. The act also provided that towns could join or create School Administrative Districts (SADS) by a simple majority vote at town meeting. Besides this carrot, there was a stick: the law withheld state funding from high schools with fewer than five hundred pupils. This was a major incentive for small towns to consolidate their resources.

Beginning with SAD 1 (Presque Isle and neighboring towns) in 1958, seventy-seven districts formed in the next two decades. Probably the most obvious immediate change was the gradual disappearance of most of the smaller high schools. The larger schools that replaced them could offer better programs, a process the State Department of Education tried to foster after the mid-1950s with an accreditation program for high schools.

As the baby boomers made their way upward through the grade levels, even structural reforms like the Sinclair Act fell short. Another positive step was the 1965 Uniform Effort principle, which obliged each town or district to levy a base property tax rate for schools. If the revenue from that rate was insufficient to provide a "foundation" program, as was the case in many smaller and poorer communities, the state would make up the difference. By the mid-1960s, the state was shouldering about 27 percent of the support for schools, and some of the worst conditions of the 1940s and 1950s had begun to disappear.

As the crisis in elementary and secondary schools cleared and the school-age population bulge moved upward, higher education became the focus for fundamental change. Reformers wanted an increase in the numbers of Maine high school graduates going on to higher education. In 1957, Maine ranked fifteenth among the states in the percentage of its young people completing secondary school, but only thirty-ninth in those finishing four or more years of college. Few states had such a gap between the two figures. The explanation seemed to be that Maine parents attached great importance to the high school diploma, but less to a college degree: only 4.8 percent of the state's residents had four years or more of college.

President Charles F. Phillips of Bates College, speaking at a 1957 conference called by Governor Muskie, attributed the wide gap between high-school and college graduates to lack of motivation, alleging that New Hampshire and Vermont, states comparable to Maine in wealth, sent nearly twice as many of their high-school graduates to college. Dennis Blais, a labor leader, argued for greater financial aid for students, as well as expansion of educational facilities, to be financed, if necessary, by tax dollars. If root causes were in doubt, they and the other participants agreed that the problem was serious and needed immediate attention.

If the numbers of Mainers attempting higher education were to keep rising (as they already had, dramatically, from the Depression years), what schools would they attend? If they stayed in Maine, a few would attend one of the select private liberal arts colleges—Bates, Bowdoin, or Colby. The majority, however, would choose a public institution. The most glaring weakness in the state's array of choices was vocational education; the state had only one post-secondary vocational-technical school. Located in South Portland, it was described by a 1960 report on school financing as "doing an excellent job of training young men and women in eight specialized areas, even though it has received meager support from the state and has had to depend on ingenuity and the availability of federal surplus property to provide, in large part, its equipment and facilities."

For a much longer time the state had taken responsibility for training elementary teachers. Secondary school teachers, except for home economics and industrial arts instructors, graduated from the University of Maine and the liberal arts colleges, or arrived from out of state. The five state teachers' colleges had made considerable progress since their low point in the immediate postwar years. Enrollment, at 730 in 1946–47, had risen to 1,700 by 1960–61. But an estimated 2,900 students would be necessary to provide the teachers the state needed, and the teachers' colleges were suffering from long years of neglect. Only one of the five—Farmington—was accredited. Each needed "higher faculty salaries, improved libraries and laboratories, more classroom and dormitory space, improved curriculums and additional scholarships" (*Report on School Financing by the Governor's Advisory Committee on Education*, October 1960).

The largest educational facility in the state was the University of Maine, established at Orono in 1865. The campus suffered the same deficiencies as the rest: the state spent less on it than other states spent on their land-grant institutions—$600 per student per annum less than the average. As a result, professors received lower salaries and had higher work loads than their counterparts elsewhere. Further, UM students paid almost twice the average tuition charged at public universities across the country. Even while the high costs of tuition kept some deserving young people from attending, officials predicted rising numbers in the college-age group and sharply higher enrollments in the 1960s.

As always, financing was the key. Ever since the coming of the automobile, Maine had opted to spend a far higher proportion of its limited resources on highways than on schools. In 1910, when Henry Ford had just begun to produce the Model T, Maine devoted one-third of its governmental revenues to public education. By 1940, this had fallen to 11 percent. By 1960, although education had crept back up to 14 percent, highways took nearly three times as much of the state's cash. To be sure, Maine is a large state with a scattered population that needed to be linked with roads sufficiently well built to withstand the climate. But construction interests had a loud voice in the legislative halls and enjoyed a bountiful cow to milk: revenue from the gasoline tax was dedicated to roads. The 1960 report on education pointed out, a bit sourly perhaps, that "Maine is probably making the strongest effort of the 50 states in improving and maintaining its highways and bridges."

It is tempting to say that Mainers could at least drive on good roads from tarpaper shacks to their substandard schools. Fairness obliges the further observation that relatively few Mainers were victims of violent crime, and nearly all could breathe clean air (though water pollution was a serious problem). Few endured urban slums and the kind of hopelessness that they increasingly meant, and many were even happy with what later times would call the "quality of life" here.

A Political Sea-Change

Post-World War II Maine shared little of the economic boom most of the country was enjoying, and the rapid changes accompanying the good times came more slowly here. Political development lagged similarly. Across the northern United States, the Great Depression had shifted voters from a predominantly Republican orientation to the Democratic column for five consecutive presidential elections and for the majority of congressional races as well.

Maine marched to the beat of a different drummer. Franklin Roosevelt never carried the state, and Harry Truman's upset win in 1948 got no help from the northeast corner. In fact, after a brief flirtation with Democrat Louis Brann between 1933 and 1937, Mainers returned to the old ways in gubernatorial elections. Republican candidates for governor averaged two-thirds of the popular vote in the seven elections between 1940 and 1952, with no Democratic hopeful getting more than 39 percent. The state legislature was equally uncompetitive. In the early 1950s, a little more than one-fifth of the state's registered voters called themselves Democrats, a slightly larger number were independents, and the other 55 percent were Republicans. The Democratic Party was active only in a handful of mill towns. Stigmatized by its ethnic base in Maine's mill towns and nearly broke, the organization needed a decent burial or a miraculous resurrection.

In a longer perspective, signs of hope for the party show more clearly than they did at the time. First, the ruling party creaked at the seams with overconfidence and factionalism. Leaders had little time for younger members; in

1948, many of the latter successfully backed Margaret Chase Smith for the Senate nomination over two of the party chieftains. In 1952, Neil Bishop, after losing in the Republican primary for governor, kicked over the traces, stayed in the race as an independent, and earned a respectable 35,000 votes. He lost both elections to Governor Burton Cross, an Augusta florist who two years later sought the virtually automatic second term. No governor had ever been denied it in the state's history.

Naturally, Cross was confident. But despite a good showing in the 1954 primary, he was unpopular in many parts of the state. One such area was staunchly Republican and desperately poor Washington County, where unemployment stood at 15 percent and per-capita income was less than $1,400 a year. Visiting the Sunrise County early in 1954, Cross proclaimed that he saw no depression and advised the people to "lift themselves up by their bootstraps." Some voters attributed this imperious attitude to Maine's traditional one-party rule. Others grew restive with the party's perceived domination by the paper companies and the public utilities; the former owned, directly or indirectly, half the state's land area, and the latter charged some of the highest rates in the country for their power.

In some ways, Governor Cross had been effective and progressive, cleaning up a scandal in the state liquor monopoly and installing more professional leadership for the highway program. But he had trod on many toes in the process. During his campaign he stood on "principle," refusing to bend to political winds on certain local issues. Two weeks before the election, he toured the state and declared that devastation from a recent disastrous hurricane "wasn't as great as I had anticipated," thereby downplaying the losses suffered by thousands of Mainers. Cross was beatable, but the old political adage runs, "You can't beat somebody with nobody!" Who did the Democrats have?

Until very late in the election process it looked as if they would have no one. But the Democrats had been changing internally as well. Although the old chiefs were tenacious, a handful of reformers challenged them for control. The upstarts included Frank Morey Coffin, an Anglo with deep roots in the Democratic and heavily Franco-American city of Lewiston. Although a brilliant scholar and graduate of Harvard Law School, Coffin lacked political experience and was less comfortable on the campaign trail than a Waterville lawyer and former state representative, Edmund S. Muskie.

Coffin and Muskie were by no means alone, but they dominated the reform group and worked well as a team. Both were on the Democratic National Committee, and in 1954, Muskie and others maneuvered Coffin into the post of state chairman. Coffin used the post to develop a grassroots platform, sending out questionnaires and holding open forums for citizens to make their ideas

22-3. Edmund S. Muskie, a Waterville lawyer, led the effort that brought about the rebirth of the Democratic party in Maine after a century of Republican dominance. Muskie was elected governor in 1955 and U.S. Senator in 1959. He was the Democratic vice-presidential nominee in 1968 and ran unsuccessfully for the presidential nomination in 1972. Muskie later served briefly as U.S. Secretary of State. Photograph by Nelin Studio, Lewiston, Maine. Courtesy of the Edmund S. Muskie Archives, Bates College, Lewiston.

known. This was so revolutionary that hundreds of Mainers, from all walks of life, took part. A platform, however, was of little value if no one could be found to stand on it.

Muskie called a long list of possible candidates as the filing deadline approached, but repeatedly he heard that he should run himself. Reluctantly, he became a candidate and faced the difficult task of assembling the rest of the ticket, raising campaign funds, and getting his message across before the September 13 elections. The Democrats managed to raise a sum paltry even by their standards: $18,000 to finance all the races. Every Democratic candidate ran that year on the proverbial shoestring and none more so than Muskie. He and a friend crisscrossed the state in Muskie's 1949 car until it gave out, and then switched to his friend's newer model. The campaign, and the candidate's personal finances, were often quite literally down to small change.

But the crowds, even in normally Republican towns, were larger and friendlier than anyone anticipated. Muskie spoke simply of things that mattered to Mainers. He emphasized the need to create jobs for young people, so that they could stay in their native state if they wished. Muskie also used television, then a new and inexpensive campaign tool in Maine. The Republicans used it heavily as well, but Muskie particularly benefited from the quick name recognition it could give. He was telegenic, and many independents and even Republicans agreed when he spoke of moving the state forward with new ideas, jobs, and a real two-party system.

On election day Muskie received about 54 percent of the vote. By cutting into Cross's totals in heavily Republican towns and swamping the governor in the normally Democratic cities (five to one in Lewiston, and six to one in Biddeford), he pulled off one of the great upsets in the state's history. All the other Democrats lost, however, and the Republicans continued their stranglehold on the state legislature. The new governor had a difficult job before him.

Edmund Muskie, forty years old when he took the oath of office, grew up in the paper-mill town of Rumford. His family, headed by his immigrant tailor father, was staunchly Roman Catholic. The young Muskie suffered his share of ethnic and religious prejudice, which peaked in Maine in the 1920s and simmered long afterward. With work and scholarship aid, Muskie graduated Phi Beta Kappa from Bates College in 1936, then borrowed cash to go to Cornell Law School and to buy a law practice in Waterville. During World War II the young attorney served in the Navy in both the Atlantic and Pacific theaters. Discharged as a lieutenant in 1945, Muskie ran for the legislature in 1946, won the election, and was reelected in 1948. In 1950, he married Jane Gray and settled down to a growing family. This background, combined with Muskie's quiet, reasonable campaign style, helped convince enough voters that this Democrat did not fit the "bogeyman" stereotype.

Muskie needed public support, political skill, and luck to survive a session with the overwhelmingly Republican legislature. In a last-minute lame-duck session, the old legislature saddled the incoming governor with commitments to raise state employee salaries and teachers' retirement allowances and to construct a new state office building. Muskie asked for thirty-seven pieces of legislation in his inaugural address and ended up with twenty-two of them. As a prelude to action on his major campaign theme, more and better jobs, he reorganized the Development Commission into a full-scale Department of Industry and Commerce. Lawmakers also agreed to increase appropriations for education and for state institutions, but they demurred on the governor's pleas to streamline state government, a battle that Governor Curtis would finally win in the early 1970s.

Muskie lost other fights as well. The state's power, timber, and manufacturing interests—called by political historian Duane Lockard the "Big Three" of Maine's legislative lobbies—showed their considerable muscle by helping defeat an increase in the minimum wage for intrastate employees to seventy-five cents an hour and a proposal to broaden sales tax exemptions and make up the difference with a state income tax and a corporate franchise tax. Another loss was most interesting, considering Muskie's future role as an environmental advocate. The governor's appeal to speed up the task of classifying Maine's waters and to increase "public" representation on the Water Improvement Commission ran into stiff resistance from the paper companies, whose longstanding practice of using nearly all of Maine's major rivers as their private sewers seemed by this time unassailable. Maine's industrial and municipal interests were unwilling to spend money on sewage-treatment plants, and legislators refused to consider any proposal that might cause the paper companies to relocate. Hydroelectric power interests, another strong lobbying force, supported the existing abuse of the rivers since paper companies were their largest industrial customers. Muskie himself was no radical on the pollution issue: he argued that it was "essential that our policy in this field be firm and progressive while avoiding damage to our industrial structure." The battle for cleaner waters lost this round.

Governor Muskie, however, proved that his upset in 1954 was no fluke by winning reelection easily in 1956. It should have been more difficult, with the beloved President Eisenhower topping the Republican list on the "big box" ballot Maine then used; it featured a single box at the top of each slate to simplify the check-off process for straight-ticket voters. But the governor won and this time faced a friendlier legislature. Democrats were far from close to con-

22-4. Margaret Chase Smith (b. 1897) on the lawn of her Skowhegan home just after her election to Congress in 1940. In 1948 she defeated two former Maine governors in a successful run for the Senate. In 1950, she delivered her courageous "Declaration of Conscience" denouncing the excesses of Joseph McCarthy. Senator Smith was nominated for President during the Republican convention in 1964. Collections of the Maine Historical Society, Portland.

trol, but at least they could generally sustain a Muskie veto. The popular governor no doubt helped pull Frank Coffin to victory in Maine's second congressional district, although the GOP held on to the other two districts.

Encouraged by the vote of confidence, Muskie took a bolder line in his second term. Again, economic development was a clear priority. The legislature agreed to set up the Maine Industrial Building Authority, using the state's credit to assist new plant construction, and approved (as did the voters) large bond issues for highways and improvements at hospitals, the University of Maine, and the teachers' colleges. A proposal to bring Maine into line with the rest of the country by moving state elections to November also passed, as did a four-year term for the next governor.

Muskie continued Maine's switch to a two-party system by winning election to the US Senate in 1958 as the first popularly elected Democratic Senator in the state's history. That year Coffin won a second term, James Oliver won in the first congressional district, and Clinton Clauson was elected governor. The Republicans' only major victory was in northern Maine's third district, though they still held both houses of the state legislature.

In the Senate, Muskie joined the able and popular Republican Margaret Chase Smith. Elected to succeed her deceased husband as representative from the second district in 1940, she had gone to the Senate eight years later and won reelection easily in 1954. In her first term as Senator, her conscientious, informed, and independent style was already apparent. Never missing a roll call, she also gained fame for her "Declaration of Conscience" speech of June 1, 1950, at the beginning of the national anti-Communist hysteria fomented by Wisconsin Senator Joseph McCarthy. Almost alone among Senators and Representatives of either party, she made it clear that character assassination and wild accusations of disloyalty were contrary to American's political traditions. Although Maine was not one of McCarthy's greatest strongholds, her stand brought criticism here.

Muskie, as Maine's junior Senator, also left no doubt that he would make up his own mind on the issues. When he went to Washington, Texan Lyndon B. Johnson was majority leader and "king of the Hill." Muskie's independence got under Johnson's skin, and the Maine man found himself left off all his preferred committees. But he made the most of what he had, especially on the Special Air and Water Pollution Subcommittee of the little-regarded Public Works Committee. He began to make a name for himself on an issue of growing importance, followed a moderately liberal path, and was easily reelected in the big Democratic year of 1964.

That year Lyndon Johnson not only won a landslide presidential victory in his own right, after finishing the term of John F. Kennedy, but even carried

Maine, a feat no Democrat had accomplished since 1912. None had done it in a two-way race since 1852. But Johnson won easily, even sweeping a Democratic legislature and representatives in with him. Fortunately for the Republican Governor John Reed, elected after the early death of Clauson in 1960 and reelected in a very close race in 1962, he was not required to run in 1964.

By the mid-1960s, the revived Democratic party had come of age, and Maine was a competitive two-party state after a century of nearly unbroken Republican government. Signs of other changes also began to appear. Education was becoming a higher public priority; the pace of industrial growth had accelerated; and awareness of environmental problems was increasing. But while many issues had been raised, few had been resolved. Here Maine echoed, if faintly, the questioning, striving, struggling tenor of the 1960s in America. Old ideas, old ways, old authorities, the older generation generally, were on the defensive everywhere. What about Maine?

For Further Reading:

Suggestions for additional reading about Maine in the 1945–65 period are included with the listing for the years 1967–88 that appears at the end of chapter 23.

23

The Tides of Change,
1967–1988

RICHARD H. CONDON *&* WILLIAM DAVID BARRY

Writing the history of the recent past is a perilous undertaking. Given our limited perspective on these years, it is difficult to isolate the underlying themes and pinpoint the most significant events—those that define the course of history—from the complex of personalities and events that make up an era. Historian Richard Condon takes on this formidable task by demonstrating continuities and contrasts between the most recent decades and those he has described in the previous two chapters.

Three themes bear close attention. First, during the 1970s and 1980s, Maine did indeed "enter the mainstream," increasing in population, per capita income, and state revenues. Developments in lumbering, electronics, the defense industries, and real estate shaped an economy more closely resembling national patterns. In politics, the revitalized Democratic party implemented major reforms in education, taxation, the environment, and the organization of government, narrowing if not eliminating the gap between Maine's social programs and those across the nation.

A second point, that growth and prosperity remained uneven in the Pine Tree State, is just as important. The glaring contrast between Maine's image as a "Vacationland" and the reality of persistent poverty received much comment in the 1980s. Despite the creation of a more professional and active government, Maine failed to root out the social problems that had marked the years between 1929 and 1967. Finally, the two most positive trends in recent history have been Maine's performance in the environmental field, where advances in water pollution control put Maine in the forefront of national trends, and in the field of arts and letters, where Maine succeeded in projecting its own vision of the world onto the national arts scene. Rounding out this chapter, William D. Barry details Maine's cultural achievements in the postwar era.

These themes—economic growth, limited opportunity, the environment, and cultural expression—all have roots in the past. And it is safe to say that they will persist as important issues into the new century.

One metaphor historians have used for the United States since 1945 is a "troubled feast." In the immediate postwar decades, as the previous chapter argued, Maine shared only marginally in the national good times. And its troubles were largely traditional ones, peculiar to the sort of place it had long been. After the mid-1960s, however, Maine's population and economy grew more rapidly than before, at times even more rapidly than the nation as a whole. With relative prosperity, Maine edged further into the mainstream of American life, for better or for worse. Economic and demographic growth brought a host of concerns and social strains, but the state was able to contend with its problems more effectively than it had in the 1950s. A competitive political system that produced generally honest and competent leaders helped, and the state combined the best in its heritage with new ways and ideas brought by the many migrants who wanted a share of Maine.

Migrants, Growth, and New Concerns

Maine's population growth, stagnant since the Civil War, remained sluggish in the first postwar decades. Optimists pointed to the attractions of a slow-paced, uncrowded rural life, but many others worried about a drain of educated young people, especially in an age that demanded more professional expertise with each passing year. In 1967, the newly inaugurated Governor Kenneth M. Curtis promised to deal with the flight of youth, while newspaper correspondents like Frank Sleeper of the state's dominant Gannett chain of newspapers pointed to gloomy statistics of out-migration since 1950 and followed them with even darker projections for future decades.

A half-decade later, these pessimistic predictions had dissipated. Although the 1970 census count fell seven thousand short of the magical one million mark, Maine's population expanded dramatically over the next ten years. The increase, 13.2 percent between 1970 and 1980, exceeded the national figure for the first time since the Civil War. This had nothing to do with more babies; the baby boom had become the baby bust here as elsewhere. Rather it resulted from in-migration, which exceeded out-migration by more than seventy-five thousand.

Who were these immigrants and where did they come from? Ironically, many of them were the same sort of people Maine had long been losing. Some *were* the same people—returning natives; the rest came mainly from other northeastern states. They tended to be relatively young, well-educated ex-urbanites with professional or managerial training or experience, much like the class of out-migrants that had been the focus of concern during the years of the "brain drain."

23-1. Kenneth M. Curtis, governor in the years 1967–75, presided over the modernization of Maine state government and the enactment of some of the most advanced environmental legislation in the country. He served as U.S. ambassador to Canada from 1979 to 1981. Courtesy of the Maine Historic Preservation Commission, Augusta.

Why did they come? Maine's "quality of life" was the usual answer, but that, of course, meant different things to different people. In the early days of the immigration, when the nation was divided over the war in Southeast Asia, relocation meant a break with a way of life many rejected. To these newcomers, Maine's historic failure to industrialize made it a sort of utopia-by-default. Some hoped to go "back to the land," homesteading on still-inexpensive acreage in some remote part of the state, painting, writing, perhaps earning money from pottery or weaving, perhaps raising sheep, growing organic vegetables, cutting wood, or holding some part-time job in a neighboring town. Native Mainers reacted to this group of newcomers in varied but interesting ways: some saw them as naive outsiders; others dismissed them as communists (synonymous for some Mainers with communes); still others viewed them as curious individuals with challenging ideas.

For most in-migrants, however, the decision to relocate reflected expanding opportunities in the state. The nationwide recession of 1974–5, in large part a result of the Arab oil embargo in 1973–74, hit Maine hard, but it also spurred conservation and a search for new energy supplies to reduce the state's heavy dependence on imported oil. The next recession, in 1981–83, mattered less, largely because Maine lacked the steel mills and other heavy industries that initially suffered most, while the sharp drop in oil prices, so burdensome to the "oil patch" states, was a benefit here. Maine's mix of tourism, services, paper, and light manufacturing withstood the times relatively well.

Statistics tell us little about how people experienced this new prosperity in their daily lives, but they do allow for comparisons over time and with other states. Two seem important in this regard. From the end of World War II to 1981, Maine's unemployment rate was greater, almost every year, than that of the United States as a whole. But, interestingly, between 1981 and 1988, the reverse was true. During 1982, with national unemployment peaking at nearly 11 percent, between 9 and 10 percent of Mainers were idled. After this, the rate dropped steadily to 3.5 percent in late 1988.

Second, although Maine's per-capita personal income remained at about 85–86 percent of the national figure, it increased at a rate consistently faster than the national average through the early 1980s. As a result, Maine rose from forty-first to thirty-first in per capita personal income between 1980 and 1987. In constant dollars—the only meaningful measure in an age of inflation—Mainers earned well over $2,000 more per person in 1985 than in 1970.

Maine's oldest industries, farming, fishing, and lumbering, turned in a mixed performance. Farming, long in decline, continued to slide. Only 3 percent of the state's area was cropland in 1982; one in thirty-five of the state's workers was regularly employed in agricultural production. The number of farms, declining for a century, bottomed out at about seven thousand in 1974, and even rose slightly in the early 1980s, although the new farms were generally small, part-time operations. The overall size of farm operations continued to grow, as rising operating costs squeezed those too small to benefit from economies of scale. During the early 1980s, expenses regularly exceeded gross farm income, producing a net loss. By 1986, nearly half of Maine's farmers relied on Farmers' Home Administration "last resort" loans, the highest percent of any state in the nation.

Eggs, milk, and potatoes, all about equal in receipts, generated nearly three-quarters of the state's agricultural returns. The broiler industry, important from the 1940s to the 1960s, died at the hands of well-financed, well-managed, and well-advertised competition centered in the Delmarva (Delaware-Maryland-Virginia) peninsula. While Maine ranked first in blueberry production, by the mid-1980s it had fallen to third or fourth in potatoes, producing not much more than one-half the 1950 crop (when it was still first in national production). In 1987, the state had fewer than half as many potato growers as in 1969. The survivors persisted by raising popular varieties and promoting them vigorously.

Such developments changed many rural communities. In Aroostook County, a sign of the times was the gradual abandonment of the traditional three-week school recess during the September potato harvest. Less immediately apparent but probably more important, a large number of farm communities in all sections suffered high unemployment. Continuing out-migration from these rural communities left behind an older population more dependent upon aid of one sort or another. Some farm towns became bedroom communities for nearby cities, as Maine shifted from about a 60 percent rural population in 1940 to about 52 percent in 1980.

Maine fisheries responded well to the passage of the two-hundred-mile limit in 1976, with the value of the catch nearly tripling between 1970 and 1980. But by the mid-1980s fishing was again in trouble, with landings for most species falling off. The value of the catch rose only because of inflation. On the other hand, income from lumber and other wood products rose during the 1970s, although employment changed little. Indeed, the number of jobs in the paper industry declined slightly. Heavy cutting and a spruce budworm epidemic increased earlier worries that Maine could run out of its greatest resource.

Labor relations, traditionally stable in the woods industries, changed sharply in the mid-1970s. Woods operations were the first to feel the impact of deteriorating industrial relations. Small pulpwood contractors were squeezed between sharply rising equipment costs and stagnant prices for pulpwood at the millgate. Company-paid pulpwood cutters, on the other hand, were threatened by competition from so-called bonded workers: Canadians brought over the border on contract, with exemptions from certain federal migrant-worker regulations. In 1975,two thousand Maine workers organized the Maine Woodsmen's Association and called a work stoppage to force the mills and the state government to recognize their complaints. The courts quickly enjoined the association to prevent picketing at the mills, and over the next year the organization disbanded. During the same time, however, the United Paper Workers' International Union organized the north woods and gained representation for nearly half the region's company-paid wage workers.

In the next decade, workers in the mills lost a series of strikes when the huge paper-producing conglomerates went on the offensive against unions across the nation. The first in Maine was a bitter three-month strike at Boise Cascade in Rumford in 1986. Paper companies cited rising costs and foreign competition as reasons for cutting benefits in contract proposals, but unionists pointed to high profits made by the companies. About three hundred strikers lost their jobs at Boise Cascade. In 1987–88, three or four times as many were replaced by new workers in the seventeen-month walkout at International Paper Company in Jay, the longest and certainly one of the ugliest strikes in the state's history.

The textile and shoe industries, like agriculture long in decline and like paper beset by heavy foreign competition, also lost incomes and jobs. Clothing bearing labels from Taiwan, Sri Lanka, Turkey, Yugoslavia, and the Philippines gave clear evidence that cheap labor, once an advantage for Maine manufacturing, had ceased to be so. Some displaced workers found jobs in new manufacturing plants, electronics among them, although these too offered mainly low-skill, low-wage positions.

Maine's largest private employer, Bath Iron Works, added to its work force during the defense buildup of the 1980s. Competition in the world shipbuilding industry slowly put BIW out of the commercial shipbuilding business, but the shipyard continued to receive important Navy contracts. Bath shipbuilders launched their first Aegis cruiser, the *Thomas S. Gates*, in 1986 and sent the first Aegis-class destroyer, the USS *Arleigh Burke*, into the Kennebec in 1990. In addition, the Portsmouth Naval Shipyard in Kittery, the oldest of the Navy's shipyards, employed thousands of Maine people building and repairing nuclear-powered submarines.

Opportunities in electronics and shipbuilding were only part of a changing economy as Maine moved through the 1980s. Parts of the state underwent rapid development for second homes, condominiums, marinas, ski areas, and other resort facilities. Starting on the southwest coast, a land boom inched toward the northeast after the late 1970s. By the late 1980s, the pace had definitely slowed in the original locations, where surging demand had steeply inflated land prices. A prime piece of shorefront property in the Mount Desert Island area, for example, went for about $10 a front foot in 1960, $100–200 in the mid-1970s, $500

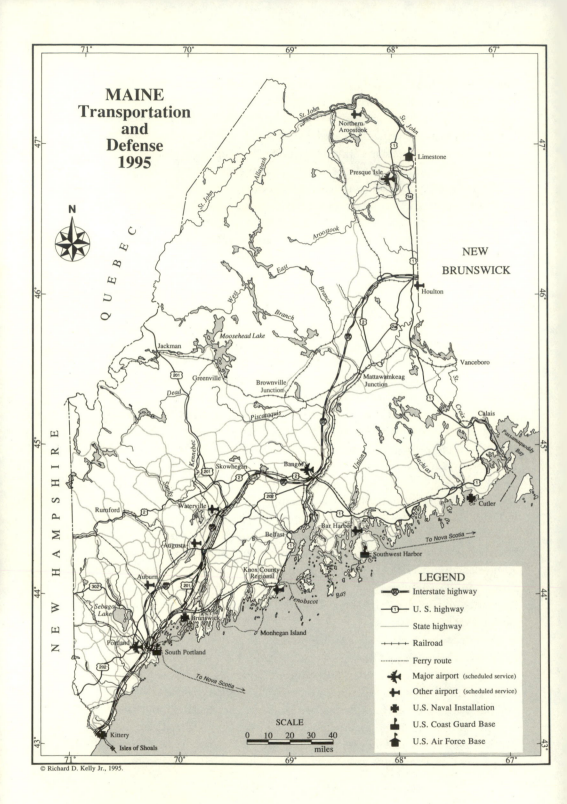

MAINE
Transportation
and
Defense
1995

QUEBEC

NEW BRUNSWICK

NEW HAMPSHIRE

St. John

Northern Aroostook

Limestone

Presque Isle

Allagash

St. John

Aroostook

East

West

Branch

Houlton

Vanceboro

Jackman

Moosehead Lake

Greenville

Brownville Junction

Mattawamkeag Junction

Dead

Piscataquis

St. Croix

Calais

Passamaquoddy Bay

Rumford

Skowhegan

Bangor

Kennebec

Waterville

Sandy

Belfast

Bar Harbor

Machias

Cutler

To Nova Scotia

Southwest Harbor

Augusta

Knox County Regional

Penobscot Bay

Monhegan Island

Auburn

Sebago Lake

Brunswick

Portland

South Portland

To Nova Scotia

Kittery

Isles of Shoals

LEGEND

Interstate highway
U. S. highway
State highway
Railroad
Ferry route
Major airport (scheduled service)
Other airport (scheduled service)
U.S. Naval Installation
U.S. Coast Guard Base
U.S. Air Force Base

SCALE

0 10 20 30 40
miles

in 1986, and $1,000 in 1987. The town of Carrabassett Valley, created around the Sugarloaf USA ski resort, had an assessed valuation of $3.6 million in 1971, $88 million in 1985.

The enclosed shopping mall came to Maine after 1970, first with the Maine Mall at South Portland, and later with regional malls at Bangor and Auburn. In downtown areas, nearly every city attempted some kind of a "revitalization" project. Most notable was Portland's Old Port Exchange, where run-down shops and warehouses were transformed into chic restaurants, boutiques, and specialty shops catering to Portland's expanding professional population.

Portland epitomized the changing styles of the 1970s and 1980s. The old city celebrated its 350th birthday in 1982 with a large, glossy booklet that predictably hymned its subject as "a miracle of prosperity in a period of economic and political chaos." That might have been a bit strong, but there was indeed a new, positive mood. The Maine Medical Center and the Jetport expanded, and the new Cumberland County Civic Center offered headline entertainers and an American Hockey League team. The city received an outstanding art museum building. Federal dollars and local efforts to raise matching funds all contributed to Portland's renaissance and helped win it national recognition as a livable city in a fine natural setting.

Portland's growth emphasized, as it had in the past, the service sector. Throughout Maine, service industries, especially trade, health services, and education, continued to grow rapidly, as they did elsewhere. Between 1970 and 1980, income from service industries rose 10 percent and employment 29 percent. This shift was partly responsible for Maine's relatively light brush with the 1981–83 recession. But Maine's new economy was vulnerable in other ways. As a form of "taking in each other's washing," service industries fail to attract money from outside the region, as do export-oriented industries. Moreover, Maine's good times owed much to a special demographic circumstance: the maturing of the "baby boom" generation, as that cohort in the American population moved into the twenty-five-to-forty-four age band, typically entering the work force, starting businesses, buying first homes and cars, and creating demand for services.

The 1980s economy produced other concerns. The persistence of poverty was a seeming anomaly in a state that had carefully groomed a national image characterized by a colorful yet homogeneous and middle-class rural population. However, Maine's poverty, like its prosperity, mirrored national trends. The 1980s saw upper-income groups increasing their share of national wealth, middle groups struggling to stay even in real-money terms, and the poorest Americans growing even poorer. An "underclass" grew, heavily composed of single mothers and children dependent on income maintenance (welfare) programs. Maine's poverty rate, which had remained nearly constant at 13 percent in the 1970s, rose to 16 percent in the early 1980s. Even in prosperous Cumberland County, the number of food-stamp recipients rose from 12,193 to 15,277 during the 1983–85 "recovery" years.

Contrary to popular belief, many of the poor had jobs. Even among Portland recipients of General Assistance, the "last source of aid for low income people," the numbers working full-time doubled, to 10 percent, between 1984 and 1986. Ironically, some were put into this predicament by one aspect of the boom: runaway real estate prices, which drove up rents. Some, especially elderly low-income persons, benefited from federally subsidized housing programs, which enabled them to pay a fixed proportion of their income for shelter. Others joined the growing ranks of the homeless on the streets, especially in Portland—a darker side of Portland's spectacular gentrification.

High utility costs hit poor Mainers especially hard. One study claimed that poverty-level residents in Maine paid 64 to 71 percent of their monthly incomes for utilities; in California, where heating costs were obviously lower, the equivalent income group paid 11 percent. As a result, California's poor had ninety-one dollars a week left for rent and food; Yankees, twenty-one. The latter also paid heavily for foodstuffs that had to be trucked for long distances.

Underemployment explains much of the gap between Maine's image as a "Vacationland" and the reality of persistent urban and rural poverty. Sixty percent of the jobs created in Cumberland County between 1979 and 1984 were in the low-paying retail trade and service sectors. Conventional statistical reporting hides a great deal of substandard income; for example, working ten hours a week at a fast-food outlet, at the minimum wage and with no fringe benefits, officially qualifies a person as "employed." In order to escape paying benefits, many employers favor hiring two part-time workers rather than one full-time. In federal statistics, this practice appears as two jobs, masking significant weaknesses in the local economy.

Persons working part-time, or even full-time at the bottom end of Maine's new service sector, especially those priced out of decent housing, were in some sense a "new poor." The boom sparkling around them made this more poignant. But what of the "old poor," especially those living in the traditionally low-income parts of the state?

Maine's cities had always had their slums, but most of Maine's poorest men and women had generally lived in or just outside isolated villages in areas lacking successful mills or commercial agriculture. Many such sections were in the interior parts of mid- and eastern coastal counties, in the foothill and central highlands regions, and in Aroostook County.

The two decades from the mid-1960s to the mid-1980s produced no major changes in this pattern. In 1985, 17 percent of rural Mainers were poor, 12 percent of those in towns and suburbs. In the south-coastal counties, York, Cumberland, and Sagadahoc, per-capita personal income in 1984 was at 95 percent of the U.S. mean; in eastern Maine, 78 percent; in northern Maine, 71 percent. In the north, the brutal shakeout of potato farming caused Aroostook County to lose population, the only county to do so between 1970 and 1980. But Waldo County, hard hit by the collapse of the broiler industry, generally ranked poorest of all. As poultry processing plants closed, the farms that supported them followed suit. Shoe factories in the county shut down as well. A guidance counselor at Belfast Area High School noted with some resignation that graduates could look forward to nothing but "almost make-work employment." By 1988, newcomers, mostly from out of state, began buying land in Waldo County, a few of them starting small businesses, such as silkscreening T-shirts, smoking meat, and cabinet-making.

During the late 1980s, growth slackened in York and Cumberland counties and increased to the north and east. L. L. Bean, the massive Freeport retailer, located its telemarketing operations in an abandoned department store in Lewiston, one symbol of the trend. Another was the development of manufacturing jobs, especially in durable goods, in places like Lewiston. Industries moving northward, up the Interstate 95 "corridor," softened the sharp contrast between the much-discussed "two Maines."

Maine and the Environmental Movement

Economic growth at times conflicted with another important development of the 1970s and 1980s: environmental protection. As early as the 1940s, pollution of Maine's river and coastal waters began to worry fishing enthusiasts, resort proprietors, coastal and riverside residents, and business leaders in afflicted towns. Pollution control made little progress until the late 1960s, but long before that, newspaper articles began to raise concerns about water quality. A 1966 four-part series in the Portland *Sunday Telegram* revealed that coastal towns poured raw sewage into the sea, relying on the ancient notion that the tide would "carry it away." Newspaper publicity and grassroots pressures spurred the Water Improvement Commission (WIC), formed in 1941, to speed classification of river basins and coastal waters, and this, in turn, encouraged some towns to build primary sewage treatment plants. Old Orchard Beach had done so as early as 1959, after a WIC report classified the waters off the famed "Coney Island of Quebec" as "heavily polluted, quite unfit for swimming." Federal and state matching funds for up to 50 percent of the cost of new municipal treatment plants encouraged other towns to begin construction.

Municipal sewage was not the biggest problem, however. Casco Bay, for instance, received thousands of tons of filth daily from industries in Portland and several smaller towns. The giant S. D. Warren paper mill at Westbrook used the Presumpscot River as its open sewer to the bay. In 1960 a firm of Boston civil engineers found that "the bed of the river was covered with a layer of slime and mud varying in depth from a few inches to five feet. No signs of aquatic plant growth or fish life were to be noted." A surface layer of foam and bubbles made the river's condition obvious to the most casual observer. In the next six years, S. D. Warren began primary treatment and cut waste discharges by about one-quarter, but even the mill's director of stream improvement admitted that the company "still [had] a long way to go."

In the late 1960s and 1970s, local and even national media stepped up the attack with statistics and impassioned pleas. The *Maine Times*, a statewide weekly paper first published in 1968, specialized in environmental issues. In 1967 the Portland *Sunday Telegram* traced the course of the Androscoggin from its source at Lake Umbagog in Maine, where it remained clean enough to drink as far as Berlin, New Hampshire. There, and over the remaining 160 miles to the sea, it absorbed municipal sewage and paper mill wastes. At Rumford, the Oxford Paper Company contributed 100,000 pounds of waste *a day*, about one-half the river's total load. The International Paper Company's mill at Jay threw in another 50,000 pounds. The author summarized this dismal story:

> Lovely little white houses will get yellower and yellower; the river beds of organic waste will, like cheese, become riper with age, and their fumes will make people physically sick; the clams, shrimp, scallops and lobster that mean so much to Maine will become inedible or die; fishing will further decline both as a sport and as a commercial venture; and who will want to swim among the suds and the other substances that will be increasingly present?

The next installment of the series, "Decline and Fall of the Kennebec," told of one Harland Iverson, an octogenarian of Cedar Grove, who awoke on a fine morning in the late 1950s to an incredibly foul odor on his property. Thousands of dead fish were rotting in the sun on the river bank, attended by millions of flies. The tide didn't help; nor did the state (it was an "act of God," according to the head of the Health and Welfare Department); and so Iverson had to take action himself. He plowed a large ditch and with a shovel and wheelbarrow dumped at least fifteen thousand fish into it. He commented, "I know I'll never see it get any better, but I wish something could be done so that some day other people will enjoy it the way we used to."

An exhibition of photographs taken by John McKee, "As Maine Goes," attracted attention at the Bowdoin College Museum of Art in 1966. It was later published in book form and excerpted by the *Maine Digest.* Chemical scum on the Androscoggin, pipes emptying raw sewage on a beach, billboards blocking fine views along US 1, roadside trash, and an abandoned car filled with garbage on Popham Beach were some of its striking images.

In 1973, J. A. Pollard published *Polluted Paradise: The Story of the Maine Rape.* This broad-scale, closely documented book touched on every form of environmental degradation, including herbicides, road salt, clearcuts, soil erosion, pesticides, and water and air pollution. The following year, Ralph Nader's Center for the Study of Responsive Law published *The Paper Plantation,* based on a two-and-one-half-year investigation of Maine. The author, William Osborn, claimed that Maine was "a land of seven giant paper and pulp companies imposing a one-crop economy with a one-crop politics, which exploits the water, air, soil, and people of a beautiful state." Each of the seven, all headquartered outside Maine, had gross revenues in 1970 exceeding Maine's total tax revenues. International Paper Company took in six times as much as the state did!

By the early 1970s, environmental politics had become a dominant issue in Maine. One of the precipitators of this modern movement, along with the question of water pollution, was the Dickey-Lincoln power project. A 1965 proposal to build a huge dam on the St. John River at Dickey and a smaller one a few miles away at Lincoln School started a fight that lasted well over a decade. Arguments that it would flood 140 square miles of wilderness, destroy wildlife habitat, and spoil fishing and canoeing on the almost-pristine St. John and Allagash rivers disposed many against the dam. But more effective politically was the heavy lobbying by private power companies. Congress, after once authorizing Dickey-Lincoln, denied funding to build it time after time. The power companies also (in their view) removed the need for it by putting on line the gigantic Maine Yankee nuclear station at Wiscasset in 1972, capable of more than three times the power Dickey-Lincoln promised. Maine Yankee, in time, became a hard-fought issue itself; three times in the 1980s voters rejected, in referendum elections after successful petition drives, proposals to close it.

Land use issues added to the complexity of Maine's environmental scene in the 1970s. In 1970, liberal Republican Harrison Richardson proposed to organize the vast unorganized townships of the state into eight "grand plantations." This would not only bring government and direct representation to the scattered inhabitants, it would also allow for greater resource management and equitable taxation and terminate the rights of the paper companies to cut timber on nearly four hundred thousand acres of "public lots." These scattered lots had never been *sold* to the companies; the right to cut on them was ceded until the territory was organized—which, of course, it never was. Another Republican, Attorney General Jon Lund, pointed out the issue: "Shall the resources of the people of the state that belong to all the people be deeded to corporate interests forever, or shall the people be entitled to share in the benefits accruing from those resources?" Stung to the quick, the paper companies mounted a full-scale offensive on Richardson's bill.

The lobbying, along with other political considerations, sent the "grand plantation" bill down to defeat in 1974, but the flap spurred the paper interests to begin negotiating with the state about the public lots. In 1981, the state Supreme Judicial Court ruled that the state owned the cutting rights, and the paper companies settled out of court with land exchanges. The state thus found itself the owner of a huge acreage, encompassing three outstanding mountain ranges and miles of frontage on remote lakes, rivers, and streams.

With the growing public awareness catalyzed by publicity and controversy, and symbolized in Maine as elsewhere by the celebration in April 1970 of the first Earth Day, laws slowly began to change. In the 1970s, the legislature addressed wetlands, air pollution, solid waste, land use, pesticides, shoreland zoning, siting of major facilities, and oil handling, among other issues.

The Department of Environmental Protection supervised the enforcement of these laws, a challenging mandate because the agency was chronically understaffed. There were, however, several victories. In addition to the public lots, the state acquired other "critical habitat" areas to protect them from development. Approved by referendum, the purchase of Bigelow Mountain forestalled a plan for a huge ski area there. Another environmental gain was the "bottle bill," providing for recycling of beer and soda bottles and cans. Spearheaded by state representative John McKernan, it was passed by referendum and retained after an overwhelming victory in a second popular vote.

There were also defeats. The environmentalists had hardly organized when one of the worst examples of pollution in the name of progress surfaced in the late 1960s. Fred Vahlsing, Jr., a New Jersey transplant, operated a potato processing plant at Easton in Aroostook County. Its wastes had already destroyed the once-pure water of Prestile Stream when Maine received a federal quota to raise sugar beets in 1964. Trumpeting the crop as an alternative for Aroostook potato growers, Vahlsing applied for a $6 million federal loan to build a beet refinery. To get it, he needed assurance that the Prestile would be reclassified at so low a grade that virtually any pollution load could be deemed legal. The Democratic legislature, prodded by Republican Governor John H. Reed and Senator Edmund Muskie, endorsed Vahlsing's request, and threw in

$8 million from the state's industrial building authority. The project turned into a costly fiasco; Aroostook farmers proved reluctant to plant beets, and poor management finished off the business.

This episode was a mere overture to the seemingly endless struggle by one group or another to site an oil refinery along the coast of Maine. The saga began in 1967 with plans for Machiasport by Jack Evans, an independent soon bought out by Armand Hammer's Occidental Petroleum Company. It presumably died with the abandonment of the Pittston Company's project for Eastport, which was under consideration from 1973 to 1982. Oil refinery projects attracted many supporters, including bankers, businessmen, unemployed and underemployed local residents, and politicians—among them, Governor Kenneth M. Curtis and Senator Muskie.

They also drew many opponents: most of the fishing, lobstering, and tourism industries, and others who feared the consequences of an oil spill in the narrow, fog-bound channels that 250-thousand-ton supertankers would have to negotiate on their way to the deep-water ports. Environmentalists, especially those writing for the *Maine Times*, stressed the danger of spills and other drawbacks of the oil schemes. As with Dickey-Lincoln, opponents had help from an unlikely source: big Louisiana-Texas oil producers, with friends in the Nixon administration, resented interference with their oil market in New England.

High oil prices, recession, lack of support from Washington, and budget cuts blunted the environmental movement in the later Reagan years, but continuing concern over acid rain, the nuclear disaster at Chernobyl, global warming, solid waste, ozone along the Atlantic corridor, and the horrendous Alaskan oil spill kept the environment in the news. A massive popular outcry turned back an ill-conceived plan to bury nuclear wastes generated in the eastern states near Sebago Lake, a source of drinking water for Portland and other towns. Maine's larger newspapers, twenty years after their first salvos, ran lengthy articles, in installments, in 1988 and 1989 on threats to Maine's lakes, its forests, and to the Gulf of Maine.

Environmental problems continued to command public attention in the late 1980s; seven cities and towns were found to be still discharging untreated sewage into coastal waters, a problem compounded by some three thousand private overboard discharges. At Boothbay Harbor, researchers discovered crabs with high concentrations of lead, possibly a result of auto exhausts in the crowded resort town. Overcrowding was, indeed, a problem along the coast, which was home to 58 percent of the state's people. More affluence meant more recreational boating and larger marinas. Lakes, too, showed signs that too many people loved them too much. Malfunctioning septic systems, phosphorus runoff from farm and lawn fertilizers, and clearcutting along lakeshores came under shoreline zoning regulations, but such laws were routinely violated. The underfunded Department of Environmental Protection, with twelve enforcement workers for the whole state, was hopelessly short-handed, while many local officials were, to put it charitably, unfamiliar with the laws.

A Competitive but Civil State

Environmental protection was but one of the many new demands on Maine's government. As Maine entered the mainstream in terms of competitive, two-party politics, it also modernized its government. As elsewhere, Maine's state bureaucracy became more professional and systematic, with research staffs, cost-benefit analyses, and greater emphasis on accountability. Federal programs and dollars, along with population growth, meant a more active state government. "A sleepy Augusta came alive with public and private entrepreneurs shepherding projects from conception to fruition," according to the 1983 study called, appropriately, *Maine: Fifty Years of Change.*

New demands for state services required new sources of revenue. The 2 percent sales tax of 1951, later raised in steps to 5 percent, began the process. In 1969, Maine adopted a personal and corporate income tax. Arguably the most important piece of legislation accomplished by Governor Kenneth M. Curtis (1967–75), it passed by only one vote in each house, despite the support of Republican house leader Harrison Richardson. Moreover, it almost cost Curtis the traditional second term; he squeaked through in 1970 by less than 900 votes. Yet in 1971, a referendum comfortably upheld the tax.

An attempt in 1974 to institute a uniform state property tax to equalize educational spending between richer and poorer communities was turned back after a hard-fought referendum campaign. A few wealthy towns led the fight against the tax, but the unfolding "Watergate" scandals in Washington convinced a majority of Maine people that government on any level was suspect. Nevertheless, growth of the broad-based income tax and the assumption of a greater share of school costs by state government made the property tax less important than it once was.

Modernization of state government was another Curtis priority. A state labyrinth of more than two hundred departments, bureaus, boards, and agencies, often with overlapping responsibilities, reduced executive efficiency. By 1973, the legislature agreed to group all state agencies and activities into fifteen restructured departments, each headed by an officer appointed by the governor for a period coterminous with the governor's own time in office. Another accomplishment of the Curtis administration was abolition of the Governor's Council. Only two other states still retained this relic, and in both cases the council was at least elected by the people. Maine's legislature chose the council, giving that Republican-dominated body one more tool to control a Democratic governor. A referendum in 1975 finally abolished it.

The state's higher education facilities underwent a complete restructuring as well. An act of the legislature in 1968 created a new university system for Maine. The "Super-U," as its critics dubbed it, included the University of Maine, with its main campus at Orono and its branches at Portland and Augusta; the associated law school in Portland; and the five state colleges. The system was guided by a single board of trustees and a chancellor. The new system embarked on a wide range of programs, including a two-year community college in Bangor, marine research and graduate programs at the Darling Center in Walpole, cooperative education (with business and industry) at all campuses, and an expanded Maine Public Broadcasting Network for both radio and television transmissions.

Cultural services expanded as well. A building completed in 1971 near the Capitol provided a modern home for the Maine State Library, Archives, and Museum. Over time, the museum's expanded professional staff created innovative exhibits highlighting Maine development from prehistoric times to the present. As early as 1974, the museum attracted nearly a hundred thousand visitors in the course of the year. Beginning in 1966, the Maine Arts and Humanities Commission aided a variety of endeavors, from the highly visible Portland Symphony Orchestra and the Theater at Monmouth to arts programs in various public schools.

State expenditures rose rapidly to pay for these expanded services. To help control them, Curtis in 1972 asked for a comprehensive survey of state government operations by a team of businessmen. The Maine Management and Cost Survey, chaired by Lewiston insurance executive James B. Longley, submitted a report in the fall of 1973, containing more than eight hundred recommendations. The majority of the ideas were implemented by Curtis or passed by the legislature during 1974, although some of the more sweeping concepts were rejected outright or slated for reconsideration.

Longley, disappointed over the limited endorsement of his report, entered gubernatorial politics himself as an independent. A number of circumstances, obvious only in hindsight, won him the seat as Maine's first independent governor. First, he ran in 1974, the year Richard Nixon's resignation of the presidency lowered the public's estimation of all "professional politicians." Second, the Republicans, after a bitter primary, turned down the liberal Harrison Richardson and nominated the much more conservative James Erwin, who had lost to Curtis in 1970. Third, Longley's Lewiston base was critical to any Democratic hopeful. Fourth, Longley was a most effective campaigner. He claimed, for instance, to have shaken four hundred thousand hands around Maine in five months. And finally, he had an unbeatable program: efficiency, adequate services, and lower taxes—all at once. Although neither Erwin nor the Democrats' choice, George Mitchell, took Longley very seriously, he attracted many nonvoters, as party loyalty continued to erode, and won a narrow minority victory, with 39 percent of the vote against Mitchell's 37 percent and Erwin's 24 percent.

The pace of change in Maine government slowed during the Longley years (1975–79). The new governor attempted to "hold the line" in taxes, cutting the state's work force by 5 percent. Gaining few friends in the state office building with this program, he also suffered testy relations with the Democratic legislature. Longley vetoed a record number of bills and was overridden a record number of times. He also jousted with the chancellor and trustees of the University of Maine, with lasting effects on the university's budget. Nevertheless, the governor retained considerable popularity to the end of his term.

In 1978, Longley announced that he would not seek a second term. His successor was Democrat Joseph Brennan, a former state legislator from Portland and attorney general. A quiet, cautious politician, perhaps more conservative than Curtis, Brennan nonetheless saw government as a positive force. Reelected in 1982 with the largest vote ever cast for a governor in Maine, Brennan called for higher standards at state institutions, "a comprehensive plan for the wise use of . . . our rivers," and higher appropriations for education in Maine. He also took pride in the creation of thousands of new jobs, reductions in the state's bonded debt, and curbs on rising hospital and workers' compensation costs.

In 1986, a complex election involving two independents as well as major party candidates made Republican John R. McKernan governor. In his inaugural address he painted a picture of Maine as a "caring place, a state that meets the needs of our elderly and our veterans," and as the "opportunity state." For McKernan, as for Edmund Muskie a generation before, economic development and educational improvement were priorities. Promising not to increase the sales or income taxes, he also claimed that his would not be a "status quo administration."

The Democratic victories of the 1950s had indeed ushered in an era of reinvigorated two-party politics. From 1967 to 1989, for example, four men served as governor: two Democrats, a Republican, and an independent. Control of the house and senate likewise fluctuated. Maine's most successful politicians on both sides, however, tended to be moderates. This was true of Maine's senators and representatives in Washington as well. In the late 1960s, veterans Margaret Chase Smith and Edmund Muskie balanced the parties for Maine in the Senate. Smith ran for a fifth term at the age of seventy-four in 1972 and was narrowly defeated by Representative William Hathaway. In 1978, Hathaway's seat fell to

Republican William Cohen, well known for his service on the House committee that heard the Watergate testimony. Muskie served until the spring of 1980, when he resigned to become secretary of state in the last year of the Carter administration. Muskie's term in the Senate was completed by appointee George Mitchell, a Democrat who won broad majorities in the 1982 and 1988 elections and went on to become majority leader of the United States Senate. He and Cohen won much acclaim for their performances on the committee investigating the Iran-Contra affair.

These leaders generally took positions near the center or somewhat to the left of it. Maine voters, dividing fairly evenly between Democrats, independents, and Republicans, almost always kept the incumbents and often split tickets. For instance, Republican Richard Nixon won big in 1972 at the same time Smith lost to a liberal Democrat; Muskie, a Democrat, won by his usual landslide in 1976, while Jimmy Carter was losing a very close race in Maine to Gerald Ford.

Like the political achievements of the two decades since 1967, the economic and environmental accomplishments were mixed. Maine citizens experienced new economic growth, but this took shape alongside persistent older problems. The state achieved a number of environmental victories, but faced new threats, often more complex and more difficult to control. State politics became more competitive and pluralistic, but at the same time political figures from both parties competed for votes with generally centrist programs.

Maine Arts

WILLIAM DAVID BARRY

During these years dizzying changes in mass media, along with new trends in artistic, musical, and literary expression, transformed the cultural scene nationally and in Maine. The state continued to produce significant cultural works and to foster creative expression by attracting important talent from outside. Despite dramatic changes in the arts, Maine sustained its national reputation as a setting for notable creative activity.

The immediate postwar years brought changes in mass media that fostered a truly nationalized popular culture. Maine participated in this trend, which included a growing readership for popular magazines, consolidation of newspaper publishing and national radio broadcasts, and the rise of television. By 1949, some homes in southern Maine could pick up fuzzy television images from Boston, and in January 1953, WABI in Bangor went on the air, ushering in the television era for Maine. Additional commercial stations in Portland, Bangor, Poland Spring, and Presque Isle appeared, and local programming flourished alongside national broadcasts.

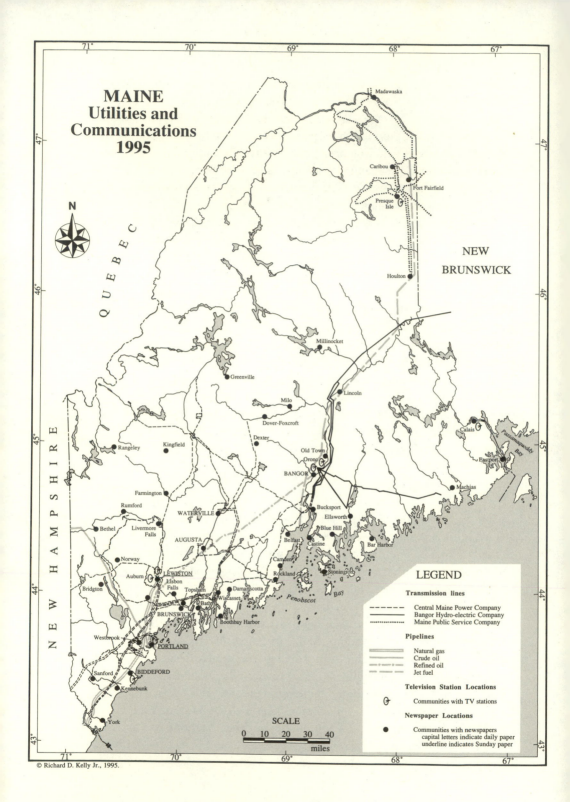

MAINE
Utilities and Communications
1995

N

QUEBEC

NEW BRUNSWICK

NEW HAMPSHIRE

Madawaska

Caribou
Fort Fairfield
Presque Isle

Houlton

Millinocket

Greenville

Milo
Lincoln

Dover-Foxcroft

Dexter

Rangeley   Kingfield

Old Town
Orono
BANGOR

Calais

Eastport

Passamaquoddy Bay

Farmington

Rumford

WATERVILLE

Bethel   Livermore
          Falls

AUGUSTA

Norway

LEWISTON
Auburn   Lisbon
          Falls
Bridgton   Topsham
                  Bath
          Damariscotta
          Wiscasset

BRUNSWICK
          Boothbay Harbor

Westbrook

PORTLAND

Sanford   BIDDEFORD

Kennebunk

York

Bucksport
Ellsworth
Blue Hill
Belfast   Castine   Bar Harbor
Camden
Rockland   Stonington

Machias

Penobscot Bay

LEGEND

Transmission lines

– – – Central Maine Power Company
— — — Bangor Hydro-electric Company
· · · · · Maine Public Service Company

Pipelines

═════ Natural gas
───── Crude oil
─ ─ ─ Refined oil
─ · ─ Jet fuel

Television Station Locations

⊖ Communities with TV stations

Newspaper Locations

● Communities with newspapers
   capital letters indicate daily paper
   underline indicates Sunday paper

SCALE

0 10 20 30 40
miles

© Richard D. Kelly Jr., 1995.

Small-town newspapers, a thriving industry in the nineteenth century, survived in fewer communities, and largely as weekly papers. Reflecting national trends, Portland's Guy Gannett publishing company consolidated the city's morning and evening papers, along with several other mid-Maine publications. Journalistic expression remained diverse, however; Maine readers supported several alternatives to the larger city papers. The most important of these was founded in 1968 when John Cole and Peter Cox began the statewide weekly *Maine Times* with a focus on the environment, arts, and quality of life.

Maine's regional identity was also enhanced by several state-based magazines. By far the most polished and influential was *Down East*, published at Camden-Rockport since 1954. Its popular visions of Maine life have been responsible for shaping Maine images throughout the United States. Down East Publications also produced books by Maine writers and introduced the popular "Bert and I" records of Marshall Dodge and Robert Bryan. These light, humorous yarns featuring local characters tap into the Seba Smith tradition but were spun by out-of-staters primarily for newcomers or outsiders. Mainer Tim Sample follows in the Jack Downing tradition as well, and the "Wicked Good Band" has combined music, wit, and a bold appraisal of social realities in Maine. Preserving Maine folklore in a more scholarly venue is a reason for the Maine Folklife Center, directed by Edward D. Ives at the University of Maine. Similarly, *Salt* magazine has since 1972 dealt with aspects of everyday life from truck driving to book selling to lobstering. Assuming similar missions, Northeast Historic Film created a tremendous archive of regional film footage in Bucksport, and the Maine Women Writers Collection was formed at Westbrook College.

Maine writers have continued to achieve national acclaim in a number of fields. Rachel Carson, who first visited Maine in 1946 and wrote from Southport, provided the first popular warnings about global pollution. She authored *The Edge of the Sea* in 1956 and the famous *Silent Spring* in 1961. In 1951, Helen and Scott Nearing pulled up stakes in Vermont and began a homestead in Harborside. Their experiments in alternative ways of living, publicized through volumes like *Living the Good Life* (1954) prefigured and helped generate the back-to-the-land movement of the 1960s and early 1970s.

The performing arts continued to hold a special place in community life. Acting companies like the Portland Players, Mad-Horse Theater, and Lyric Theater were joined each summer by operations ranging from the venerable Lakewood to the Shakespeare Theater at Monmouth, the Ogunquit Playhouse, and Hackmatack Playhouse in Berwick. Among the finest operations is the Maine State Music Theater at Brunswick, begun by Victoria Crandall and others in 1959. Nor was professional dance wanting, for the Ram Island Dance

Company has grown in stature since its founding by Millicent Monks in 1967. Sam Costa and Dancers and the Casco Bay Movers are other indications of this art's growth. Two ballet companies were established in the 1980s: Portland Ballet and Portland Ballet East.

Music continued as an active force in Maine life. In 1947 and 1961, Walter Piston won the Pulitzer Prize for Music. Piston's love for his native place included close working connections with the Portland Symphony Orchestra. The composer dedicated his last composition to the distinguished Portland String Quartet. Both the Bangor and Portland symphony orchestras have flourished as professional groups, and Maine boasts active classical, jazz, folk, and country and western artists and composers.

After the war, Maine continued to attract prize-winning authors. The Belgian-born writer Marguerite Yourcenar, whose remarkable skills won her election to the formerly all-male L'Académie Française, settled at Mount Desert in 1950. Among her works are the *Memoirs of Hadrian* (1951) and the haunting *Two Lives and a Dream* (1987). An inventory of writers living or working in Maine is far too long for this study but would have to claim E. B. White for his essay on Maine speech and his timeless *Charlotte's Web* (1952). That superb poet and writer of journals, May Sarton, has spent productive working years living on the coast in York. Robert Lowell, who won a Pulitzer for poetry in 1947 and 1974, and his wife, Jean Stafford, who was awarded the Pulitzer for fiction in 1970, resided for a time in Damariscotta Mills. Lowell later focused on Castine; his "Fourth of July in Maine" in *Near the Ocean* (1967) gave a different slant on small-town life. Poet Richard Eberhart, another recipient of the Pulitzer and a summer resident of Cape Rosier, produced a powerful volume titled *Maine Poems* (1989). Philip Booth, one of the most consistently fine poets working in the area, captured the car culture perfectly in "Maine" (1960). Both Kenneth Roberts and E. B. White won Special Pulitzers in 1957 and 1978 respectively.

No one has so neatly expressed the cadence of Bar Harbor life as B. J. Morison in her little murder mysteries, beginning with *Champagne and a Gardener* (1982). Martin Dibner, resident in Casco, authored such fast-paced novels as *Ransom Run* (1977) and the nonfiction beauty, *Seacoast Maine* (1973). Michael Kimball's *Firewater Pond* (1985) is a picaresque novel of the finest kind. John Preston earned a nationwide audience for his fiction and nonfiction focused on gay life. Certainly the artistry of Susan Kenney's *In Another Country* and *Sailing* is of the highest order.

Nativity is probably quite irrelevant when it is remembered that such ultra-regionalist writers as John Gould and Bill Clark were born beyond the Piscataqua. Still, not since the days of Longfellow and Neal have natives contributed so much to literature. Beginning with Gott Islander Ruth Moore, who joined the ranks of Roberts, Coffin, and Virginia and Mary Ellen Chase, the list

23-2. Writer Stephen King, a Portland native, attended the University of Maine, where he majored in English. His "horror" novels caught the public fancy and made him one of America's most successful contemporary writers. King resides in Bangor. Photograph by Tabitha King.

has grown. Consider the mix that includes Hemingway biographer Carlos Baker of Biddeford, short-story master Fred Bonnie of Bridgton, and the outstanding poet Leo Connellan, who grew up in Rockland. In terms of clear style, compassionate human insight, and story-telling ability, few authors can rival Margaret Dickson in *Maddy's Song* (1985) and other novels. Carolyn Chute's exploration of the bleak underside of rural life in *The Beans of Egypt, Maine* (1985) sparked high praise from critics and outcries from locals who did not appreciate her characterization of Maine poverty. Topography and atmosphere served the horror genre well, as seen in the popular novels of Rick Hautala, Tabitha King, Christopher Fahy, Cris Starks, and, most spectacularly, in the twenty or more thrillers by Stephen King. The author's ability to scare through artful tales led to one of the most spectacular successes in publishing history. Not since Longfellow has a native Maine writer been so widely acclaimed and read.

Maine nonfiction, especially in the field of history, has also been exemplary, ranging from first-rate town histories like William B. Jordan, Jr.'s *A History of Cape Elizabeth, Maine* (1965) to John J. Pullen's best-selling regimental history, *The Twentieth Maine* (1957). Recent Pulitzer Prize winners included Portland native James Phinney Baxter III, who gained the prize in 1947 for his *Scientists Against Time*, and Laurel Thatcher Ulrich of the University of New Hampshire, who was honored in 1990 for *A Midwife's Tale*, based on the diary of Augusta's Martha Moore Ballard.

In the years since the World War II, the state has provided inspiration for a bewildering number of visual artists. Year-round commercial galleries appeared in number, and the level of criticism and study of contemporary Maine artist improved. In 1948, Rockland's William A. Farnsworth Library and Art Museum opened and soon became famous for works by Andrew Wyeth, one of the few late twentieth-century painters to achieve the status of a household name. Wyeth's *Christina's World* (1948), owned by the Museum of Modern Art, made Cushing, Maine, and Christina Olson world-famous. Critics were often not so kind, but Wyeth's images of Maine were the most popular since those of Winslow Homer. Wyeth's son Jamie, working from Monhegan, made his own rich explorations of the figurative tradition.

In the first post-war years, summer art colonies remained the pulse of Maine's art scene. In 1946, painter Williard Cummings and others established the unique Skowhegan School of Painting and Sculpture. Governed by and for artists, it attracted the nation's most dynamic practitioners. Other important schools include Haystack on Deer Isle, the Center for Creative Imaging in Camden, and the Maine Printmaking Workshop. The first public collection dedicated to contemporary and modern art was Henry Strater's Museum of Art of Ogunquit, opened in 1951. In 1958, the Barn Gallery was founded to showcase living artists with area connections and the distinguished Hamilton Easter Field Collection, later placed at the Portland Museum of Art.

Nonobjective works were little appreciated and difficult to sell in Maine during the first postwar decades. The great sculptor Louise Nevelson, who grew up in Rockland, made her career in New York. Subtle changes began to reshape attitudes beginning in the 1960s with important contemporary shows at Portland's Temple Beth El. In 1966, painter Thomas Crotty opened Frost Gully, the state's first year-round commercial gallery. The appearance of Lewiston-born William Manning's pure, elegant, nonrepresentational canvases furthered the community's growing interest in serious paintings. In 1969, Manning and painter Polly Brown established the short-lived but influential Concept School in Portland, and the rather traditionally oriented Portland School of Art (now the Maine College of Art) shortly after underwent a revolution of its own. By the 1970s, an economic boom in Portland, centered around the Old Port with its craft shops, cinemas, and galleries, reestablished the city as an art center of note.

Coverage in the local press, especially Philip Isaacson's reviews in the *Maine Sunday Telegram*, elevated the level of discussion. However, it was the *Maine Times* that really made a mark by hiring Edgar Allen Beem as the state's first full-time art critic. Often controversial, Beem's weekly essays probed various aspects of local art in a way that has not been done since John Neal. In the 1990s, the *Casco Bay Weekly* followed by taking on Margot Brown McWilliams as its art critic. On occasion the two writers differed, exchanging barbs and creating something close to an exciting cultural dialogue.

New museum facilities appeared at the University of Southern Maine (1966), Colby (1973 and 1991), Bowdoin (1976), Westbrook College (1977), the Portland Museum of Art (1983), Bates (1986), and the University of Maine (1986). The Portland Museum's vast new wing, designed by Henry Nichols Cobb of I. M. Pei and Partners, has helped transform the previously drab Congress Square. An equally successful building, though on a smaller scale, is Winton Scott's new gallery for the Maine Maritime Museum in Bath. At Westbrook College, the Joan Whitney Payson Gallery of Art saw many of the region's finest contemporary exhibitions in the 1970s and 1980s, before closing its doors.

A census of artists connected with the state in recent years would certainly make a mighty throng. The choice is vast, ranging from the photography of Berenice Abbott and Eliot Porter to the sheer beauty of a Beverly Hallam still-life, the snap and tug of a John Laurent oil inspired by fishing, the witty political cartoons of Michael Ricci, and the tough urban realism of a Michael Waterman oil. It would include the exciting paintings and lithographs of John Muench, the commanding sculpture of Celeste Roberge, and the bold, naive oils of Eastport by Judith Colemann.

At the dawn of the 1990s, however, the seemingly robust economy began to twist apart, and a number of familiar old questions about making a living were posed. In 1991, the Joan Whitney Payson Gallery of Art closed, and its collection was transferred to the Portland Museum of Art. Important full-time commercial galleries in Brunswick and Portland went out of business or left for more lucrative areas of the nation. Indeed, the performing arts and collecting institutions, along with government programs, felt the pinch and began to face a future of uncertainty. Boom or bust, however, has always characterized Maine's cultural and economic life, and some of the best work has been done in times of adversity. Maine will continue to produce distinctive forms of art in good times and bad.

Maine's Minorities

Along with new politics, new economics, and new cultural expressions, the 1970s and 1980s brought Mainers a new sense of ethnic awareness. To be sure, especially since America's industrial transformation, at least small numbers of nearly every European people, as well as African Americans, Asians, and Hispanics have come here. In the 1970s and 1980s, refugees from many world conflicts joined them; a March 1989 newspaper article counted 1,616 arrivals in the preceding five years. These new Mainers came from such culturally distant points of origin as Vietnam, Cambodia, Poland, Afghanistan, and Iran, among others. A year later, the 1990 census revealed that 0.4 percent of Maine's people were African Americans, 0.5 percent American Indians, 0.5 percent Asians, and 0.6 percent Hispanics.

Centuries earlier, when parties of native Americans met French explorers on its shores, Maine began a long and contentious history of cultural interchange. Both Indians and French have been an integral part of this story ever since. Maine's Francophone peoples have been linked to the settlement of the upper St. John River valley since the 1780s, and to the rise of the textile mill towns in southern and central Maine since the 1870s. Despite the persistence of prejudice and their seemingly perpetual minority status, for Franco-Americans, the 1920s and 1930s were in some senses a golden age. World War II and the subsequent collapse of the textile industry precipitated a flight from the tidy world of parish, parochial school, and extended family, and in the next decade television and an increasingly secular society impinged upon the remaining "petits Canadas." By 1970, assimilation had gone so far that the total disappearance of any "separateness" seemed possible, even likely. Early in that decade, however, the first signs appeared of a reaction against total identification with the surrounding Anglo-Saxon world.

At the University of Maine at Orono, for instance, Yvon Labbé (who had once used the name "Ivan" in an effort to assimilate) founded the Franco-

American Resource Group (FAROG). Its acronym was deliberately chosen to appropriate and defuse a long-time ethnic slur. Its newspaper, the FAROG *Forum*, first published at the university in 1973, attracted more than seven thousand subscribers, giving it the largest circulation among French-language publications in the United States. FAROG's purpose, according to Labbé, was to open "doors that allow pride to come out." At about the same time in Lewiston, the Franco-American Heritage Center opened. A museum for artifacts, correspondence, and other documents, the center also presented films and other educational programs. By the later 1970s, such efforts were encouraged by a flowering of ethnic consciousness all through the United States, and in 1977, Franco-Americans got official federal recognition as a distinct ethnic group. This opened access to federal support of bilingual education programs.

In the 1980 census, 266,000 Mainers—just short of one-quarter of the state's total—listed themselves as wholly or partly of French descent. Most were located in Aroostook (41 percent), Androscoggin (38 percent), and York (29 percent) counties, while Knox County ranked lowest with nearly 9 percent. Among Maine towns of more than 5,000, Lewiston, Biddeford, and Portland had the greatest numbers of persons of French ancestry.

For Paul Paré of Action for Franco-Americans of the Northeast (ACTFANE), Maine's most substantial minority still suffered the legacy of the years of discrimination. Too few Franco-Americans had reached decision-making levels in business, banking, or education. Lingering prejudice was partly to blame; other factors included educational disadvantages, aspirations lowered by too many dead-end jobs, and a legacy of rural conservatism. In the mid-1980s, a lengthy series in the Lewiston-Auburn Sunday newspaper explored issues of image, language, and religion and the general outlook for the Maine's Franco-Americans. One woman told the reporter that the French majority in the area had been "treated as a minority, and that was because we allowed that to happen to ourselves." Kept ignorant of their past and made to feel ashamed of their Canadian French dialect, Franco-Americans were "divided by an ill-defined sense of self."

Yet the signals were decidedly mixed. In 1986, the Roman Catholic Diocese of Maine reported 280,057 practicing their faith—up over 12,000 since 1970. Lewiston's St. Domenic's Regional High School had fewer students in 1989 than in 1970, but it was growing again. On the other hand, five parish schools in Lewiston-Auburn had closed in recent years, and enrollment was still declining in the three surviving institutions. As for the other traditional pillar of Franco-American culture, the language, two points seemed clear: it was less often heard in homes, stores, or on the street; yet a growing number of children and young people were interested in learning it. Erosion of the French language in Maine posed the question: can ethnic identity survive without the language? Perhaps a stronger sense of ethnic or family history, coupled with the influence of six million French speakers in Quebec and New Brunswick, will keep it alive in altered form.

In these ways Maine's largest minority reflected some national concerns in the 1970s and 1980s. At the same time, one of its smallest but oldest minorities, the native Americans, played out their part in the great civil rights struggle of the 1960s and 1970s.

The affair eventually known as the Indian land claims suit began in 1964, when a white man decided to cut timber on land he had purchased from the town of Princeton. The land lay within Indian Township, a Passamaquoddy reservation in eastern Maine near the New Brunswick border. The township had been reserved to the Passamaquoddies by a Massachusetts treaty of 1794, but by 1965 some six thousand acres had been sold off, much of it by the state of Maine acting as trustee for the tribe, but without consulting the Passamaquoddies or obtaining their consent. At the same time, about 75 percent of the tribe was unemployed, the majority depended on welfare, and many suffered from alcoholism.

In the face of this degradation, and the most recent provocation, some dreamed of regaining their land—for a start, at least, the six thousand lost acres in Indian Township. Maine's Penobscot tribe had experienced a similar historic pattern. In 1796, they had signed over to Massachusetts more than two hundred thousand acres in return for an annual subsidy of trade goods. Treaties with Massachusetts in 1818 and with Maine in 1833 ceded the remainder of their ancestral lands, except for islands in the Penobscot River north of Old Town.

After the Indians' first lawyer left the state under threat of a prosecution for marijuana possession, a new Mainer, Thomas Tureen, took up the case in 1969. After extensive legal research and reading in historic documents, Tureen realized that the treaties violated the Indian Nonintercourse Act of 1790, which prohibited the sale of Indian lands without the express approval of Congress. Nevertheless, convincing authorities in Maine that the treaties were invalid would take exactly a decade. The dispute peaked in the late 1970s, and in 1976, the Indians won their case when a federal court agreed that the 1790 law applied to the Maine tribes. A negotiated settlement seemed in order, but Governor Longley refused to consider the matter seriously. Attorney-General Brennan would not commit himself, and the Great Northern Paper Company, which controlled most of the land claimed by the Indians, had nothing to say.

This widespread complacency was brought up short when bonds issued by towns within the claim area were deemed doubtful by out-of-state banks; indeed, legal experts warned that real estate transfers were probably void, and

23-3. On October 10, 1980, President Jimmy Carter signed the Maine Indian Claims Settlement Act, a ceremony witnessed by (from left to right) Gov. Joseph E. Brennan, U.S. Secretary of State Edmund S. Muskie, Sen. George Mitchell, and Indian representatives Terrance Polchies and Andy Akins. After a long legal battle, Maine's Penobscots, Passamaquoddies, and Micmacs gave up claims to millions of acres of land in exchange for a $54.4 million trust fund. Courtesy of Jimmy Carter Library.

mortgages might soon become unavailable. Twelve and one-half million acres were affected. The Maine congressional delegation proposed a bill to extinguish the Indians' land title in return for monetary damages. Tureen and the Indian leaders rejected the offer and sought help from Harvard Law School professor Archibald Cox. Cox was probably at that time the most famous lawyer in the country; he was the special prosecutor fired by President Nixon in 1973 at a climactic point in the Watergate scandal. Governor Longley, for his part, brought in the almost equally well-known Washington trial lawyer, Edward Bennett Williams, as a consultant.

At this point, President Carter assumed responsibility for a settlement and appointed a Georgia supreme court justice to work one out. His proposal, which became the basis for resolution, was ready by 1978, but two more years would pass before all obstacles had been cleared. Longley still strongly opposed any settlement, and the state's two Congressmen, David Emery and William Cohen, would go no further than a cash buy-out. However, the state's two Senators, Edmund Muskie and William Hathaway, were now urging the state's officials, including the new governor, Joseph Brennan, to consider the administration's offer.

Settlement was still not a popular solution in Maine; Hathaway's recommendation to settle was one reason for his drubbing at the hands of Cohen in the 1978 senatorial race. Still, final resolution came in 1980. In effect, the federal government bailed out Maine with $81.5 million, which would allow the Indians to purchase 300,000 acres of land; $27 million of the total were set aside in a trust fund. In return, the Penobscots and Passamaquoddies gave up all claims to the millions of acres at issue. Carter signed the bill in October 1980 and Congress, in the waning days of the Carter administration, approved the money to pay for it.

For Maine's Indians, the settlement brought a complicated mixture of progress and setbacks. The two tribes purchased land, a cement plant, blueberry farms, a radio station, and made other investments which, by the late 1980s were bringing about $300 annually for each of the more numerous Penobscots and $1,000 for each Passamaquoddy. The population of Indians doubled, as persons who were at least one-quarter Indian proved their ancestry and joined the tribe. The death rate from alcohol-related causes was sharply reduced from an incredible 60 percent to a still formidable 25 percent. Some of the credit for this belongs to a modern health center with twelve full- and part-time workers and an annual budget topping $1 million at the Passamaquoddies' Pleasant Point village.

Ironically, the Indians faced their successes with mixed feelings: tribal leaders agreed that economic development was the answer to poverty and alcoholism; but one stated that "when I was a child I was poor, but rich in culture and tradition. . . . Now it's the other way around."

Like the recent history of its oldest inhabitants, the history of Maine over the last few decades is a mixture of achievements and setbacks, new developments and old problems. Maine's experience between 1929 and 1967 placed it largely out of the "mainstream" of American economic and political development. In the three following decades, the state's political system was transformed, revitalized, and brought back into the compass of American competitive two-party politics. State government and state institutions were given an infusion of new expertise and new funds, and the state tackled some of its thorniest environmental problems.

Yet, like Maine's Franco-Americans and Indians, Maine people generally mixed their faith in progress with a sense of loss for the world as it was. Progress through development, while somehow preserving the best of the past, has been Maine's dilemma in the late twentieth century, which brought accelerating social change. All who have experienced that change will make their own judgments on the choices we made, the pace we set, and the outcome we desired.

For Further Reading:

Primary sources on recent Maine history are scattered and, like those for chapter 21, do not yield well to generalization. The best sources for a general overview of the recent period are Maine newspapers, journals, and magazines. Subject indexes for some, such as *Down East* Magazine and the *Maine Townsman*, are available in major libraries, especially the University of Maine's Special Collections Department in Fogler Library. The *Maine Times*, a valuable resource for the later period, began publication in 1968 and is indexed. Topics covered in chapter 23 are summarized in two *Maine Times* anniversary issues, October 1983 and October 1988.

Newspapers supply a wealth of information. See, for instance, a series of articles by Edward D. Talberth in the *Portland Press Herald*, October 27, 1950, and succeeding days, dealing with underfunded state institutions. Updates can be found in an unsigned article titled, "More Liberal Public Aid Program to Cost State Less" (October 18, 1957). A similar series on pollution and the environment can be found in: the *Portland Sunday Telegram* (July 3–August 7, 1966); articles by William Williamson in the *Portland Sunday Telegram* (December 31, 1967–January 14, 1968); by Tux Turkel and Joanne Lannin in the *Maine Sunday Telegram* (August 28–September 25, 1988); and in a *Maine Sunday Telegram* series (August 20–September 10, 1989). On education, see "Maine Teachers' Salaries," *Lewiston Daily Sun* (February 25, 1947); *Maine Teacher* (May 1952); Nick Panagakos, "Dr. Phillips Hits Attitude on Education in Maine," *Waterville Morning Sentinel* (October 30, 1957); and Lance Tapley, "Maine Higher Education," *Maine Sunday Telegram* (March 26–May 14, 1972). An unsigned article in the *Maine Sunday Telegram* (July 15, 1984) gives some insights into the state's changing population mix.

Organizations formed around special concerns like conservation, business, fish and game, commercial fishing, education, and wood-products industries also produce a variety of specialized periodicals that should be consulted. Recent issues can be perused in the reading room of the Maine State Library. Maine government reports also yield much information about the state's economy, environment, and political structure.

ADDITIONAL SECONDARY SOURCES:

Banks, Ronald F., editor, *A History of Maine* (Dubuque, Iowa, 1969); see articles by Arthur M. Johnson, Staff of Maine Business Indicators, Edgar Miller, Richard Barringer, Edmund S. Muskie, and John McDonald for recent Maine history.

Barry, William D., *A Vignetted History of Portland Business, 1632–1982* (Portland, 1982).

Brault, Gerald, *The Franco-American Heritage in New England* (Hanover, N.H., 1988).

Carrier, Paul, "The Franco Factor, Lewiston Journal *UNDAY* (September 21–October 19, 1986).

Coolidge, Philip T., *History of the Maine Woods* (Bangor, 1963).

Cummings, Bob, "The Public Lots," *Maine Sunday Telegram* (June 15, 1983).

Ellis, George, "Issues and Decisions," *Down East* (March 1963).

Ellis, William, "The Trouble with Maine," *Nation* (June 22, 1963).

Franklin, Lynn, "'The Indian Nation is Vanishing, That's a Fact,'" *Maine Sunday Telegram* (September 16, 1973).

Giguere, Madeleine, "The French Ancestry Population of Maine, 1980," Annual Meeting of the Maine Canadian Studies Association, University of Maine at Farmington, April 1983.

Hayward, Mark, "Maine Tribes: Beyond the Settlement," Lewiston Journal *Sunday* (October 2–9, 1988).

Hendrickson, Dyke, *Quiet Presence* (Portland, 1980).

Hoose, Shoshana, "Maine's Indians," *Maine Sunday Telegram* (September 25–October 2, 1988).

Hoose, Shoshana, "Religion in Maine," *Maine Sunday Telegram* (February 12–26, 1989).

Irland, Lloyd C., *Wildlands and Woodlots* (Hanover, N.H., 1982).

Judd, Richard W., "The Coming of the Clean Waters Acts in Maine, 1941–1961," *Environmental Review* 14 (Fall 1990).

Langley, William, "Poverty, Maine Style," *Portland Sunday Telegram* (December 31, 1967).

Leamon, James S., *Historic Lewiston* (Auburn, 1976).

Lippmann, Theo, Jr., and Donald C. Hanson, *Muskie* (New York, 1971).

Lockard, Duane, *New England State Politics* (Princeton, N.J., 1959).

Maine State Governor's Advisory Committee on Education, *Report* (Augusta, October 1960).

Maine Transportation Capital Improvement Planning Commission, *Transportation to the Year 2000: A Capital Improvement Plan for Maine* (Augusta, 1990).

Maine's Indians: Legacy of the Land Claims," *Bangor Daily News* (September 9–15, 1989).

"Maine's Infrastructure Crisis: A Report to the State," Maine Today (March 1983).

Nickerson, Kermit S., *One Hundred and Fifty Years of Education in Maine* (Augusta, 1970).

"Northern New England: Land of Myths and Contrasts," *Boston Sunday Globe* (October 2, 1983).

Pease, Allen, and Wilfred Richard, editors, *Maine: Fifty Years of Change, 1940–1990* (Orono, 1983).

Peirce, Neal, *The New England States: People, Politics and Power in the Six New England States* (New York, 1976).

Pollard, J. A., *Polluted Paradise: The Story of the Maine Rape* (Lewiston, 1973).

Treadwell, David, "Rural Areas' Economies Stagnant," *Maine Sunday Telegram* (December 23, 1990).

Treadwell, David, "Recession Wipes Out Gains on Poverty in New England in 1980s," *Maine Sunday Telegram* (October 29, 1991).

Veazie, Carl, "The Maine Economy, 1940–1975," *Thomas Business Review* 3 (Fall 1975).

Wescott, Richard, and David Vail, "The Transformation of Farming in Maine, 1940–1985," *Maine Historical Society Quarterly* 28 (Fall 1988).

24

Epilogue

RICHARD H. CONDON

As we acknowledged in the headnote to chapter 23, history does not necessarily become easier to write as it becomes more recent. Bias is an obvious danger to the contemporary observer, but perhaps even worse is the absence of perspective. All that said, there is reason for us to think that in the 1990s Maine started down a different road. The hardest times since the 1930s abruptly ended a prosperous era and precipitated bitter political struggles that culminated in a two-week shutdown of state government.

By the last decade of the twentieth century, over 1.2 million people resided in Maine. Their numbers increased about 9 percent during the 1980s boom, a lower rate than during the previous decade but close to the 10 percent national population growth rate for the decade. The southwestern counties, Cumberland and York, already Maine's largest, continued to grow most rapidly, while Aroostook continued to lose people.

As the census was taken in the spring of 1990, the Maine and New England regional economy had already begun to falter. The 1988 growth rate of 4.7 percent fell to a nearly static 0.7 percent in 1989. All the growth sectors of the 1980s economy—construction, real estate, and retail sales—turned downward. The free-fall continued in 1990, with real economic growth slipping 2.6 percent from September 1989 to September 1990. That month, the *Maine Sunday Telegram* reported that Mainers were cutting back their spending; during the same autumn, unemployment neared 7 percent of the work force. Year-end news summaries used headlines like "Layoffs, plant closings hit the [Lewiston-Auburn] area"; "Unemployment soars in Oxford Hills region"; "Hundreds face loss of jobs in Twin Cities."

Such conditions inevitably reduced more persons and families to poverty. With just over 12 percent of its population below the official poverty line in 1990, Maine remained slightly below the national figure, but it had by far the highest rate in New England. Aid to Families with Dependent Children (AFDC) caseloads shot up 30 percent between 1989 and 1991, as thousands of parents and children were caught in the "welfare trap" explained in a major series in the Lewiston Sunday paper. Few jobs were available in any case, many were low-wage, and transportation and child-care costs added to the AFDC recipients' difficulty in finding work that would justify giving up their benefits.

Maine was hardly alone in its misery, as the national economy began to move into recession by late 1990. That year, the rapid growth of the 1980s still showed up in per-capita income figures, with Maine ranking 28th among the states. Furthermore, experts thought that Maine now had a more diversified economic base. Perhaps, but paper and tourism continued to be first and second in the state's mix. Fortunately, neither took as severe a hit as real estate suffered. Maine's paper mills, which in 1988 turned out over 10 percent of the nation's product (second to Wisconsin), survived sharp profit declines without wholesale layoffs or plant closings. They did, of course, delay or cancel planned expansions and improvements.

Tourism, which contributed $2 billion to the Maine economy at the turn of the decade, generally held its own through the hard times. Yet observers had questions about its future. Maine's natural beauties, within easy reach of tens of millions of urbanites in the crowded Northeast, continued to attract. But with cheaper transportation, might not a reviving economy tempt holiday-makers to more distant "Vacationlands"? Would development gradually destroy the attractions that brought people here in the first place? Would Maine's government continue to slash funds for promotion of the industry (only two states spent less on it in the late 1980s)? Would Mainers ever make up their minds about the visitors? (Residents continued to welcome tourist dollars and the more than 45,000 jobs they provided; but some local cars sported bumper-sticker slogans such as "Welcome to Maine. Now Go Home," expressing Mainers' ambivalence about tourism.) For the moment, Canadians escaping high taxes and southern New Englanders unable to afford longer trips kept tourism healthy.

By the spring of 1992 there were signs that the free-fall had halted. No more banks seemed likely to fail. (In 1991 two of the state's largest, Maine Savings Bank and Maine National Bank, had gone under.) Moreover, job losses had stabilized. In February 1989, 525,300 Mainers were working. Two years later, the figure was 500,400; by February 1992 the total was almost identical. Observers cautioned that part of the leveling-off of unemployment came from people leaving the state. Still, those who remained were spending 8 percent more at the stores than in the first quarter of 1991.

Recovery, if it existed, was anemic. To stimulate the economy the voters agreed in June 1992 to borrow nearly $80 million for state highway, bridge, ferry, pier, and railroad projects; for grants to municipalities for infrastrucure improvements; and for business loans. A more innovative proposal called for nearly $10 million to provide tuition at Maine's technical colleges for up to three thousand jobless Mainers; it and most other bond issues went down to defeat in November 1992.

Recovery plans aside, attitudes toward growth remained ambiguous. A few months before, voters had rejected a costly proposal to widen the Maine Turnpike to six lanes between Wells and South Portland. It is impossible to say how much this decision owed to the hard times and how much to opposition to development and other environmental concerns, but previous large road projects, such as a planned Route 1 bypass at Wiscasset, had also run into fatal opposition. Environmental groups mobilized enough strength in 1986 to persuade the Great Northern Paper Company to give up its "Big A" dam proposal; a scheme for an ash dump in Washington County's remote Township 30 was abandoned after public outcry. Similar concerns surfaced in other communities chosen as possible sites for special wastes or for low-level nuclear waste. In the summer of 1992, a fourth referendum on closing the Maine Yankee atomic power station appeared likely. A newspaper commented that "Mainers are developing the will power and the legal and technical expertise to fight big business and big government." Those that do so, and the development interests they opposed, seemed at times to be speaking entirely different languages.

Generally, environmental concerns were not an obvious issue in state politics in the 1988–92 years. The political debates of those years were no less bitter, however, and the root of the problem seemed to be the boom-bust economy, compounded by divided government and strong personalities in conflict.

During the good years, state government seemed capable of meeting the new expectations and demands of Maine citizens. Governor Joseph Brennan's eight budgets had contained increases ranging from 7.3 percent to 12.9 percent over previous years' expenditures. His successor, John McKernan, proposed, and successive legislatures passed, even larger budget hikes, peaking at 19.7 percent in 1989. By then, the state's total outlay, which rose from $482 million to $961 million during the Brennan era, had jumped to $1.52 billion. The number of state employees, which decreased slightly during the Brennan years, climbed from 12,492 to 13,710 in McKernan's first term. The governor also raised their pay a total of 19 percent in those years. He pumped money into such programs as ASPIRE, designed to provide education, job-training, child care, and transportation for families receiving AFDC or food-stamp benefits.

In 1989 the administration proposed a $41 million property-tax-relief package, and the 1989–91 state budget carried a 25 percent spending increase, on the assumption that the economy would remain healthy. This had to be revised downward in July. In the spring of 1990, the governor and legislature, facing a shortfall of more than $200 million, were forced to agree on another round of budget cuts.

In the 1990 election year, the race for the governor's office pitted the Republican McKernan, seeking the traditional second term, against his predecessor. Democrat Joe Brennan had just spent two terms representing Maine's first congressional district in Washington. His place would be taken by another Democrat, Tom Andrews, who decisively defeated former Congress member David Emery. In the huge second district, six-term Republican Representative Olympia Snowe, never before seriously challenged, narrowly won reelection over challenger Pat McGowan. Another veteran, Senator Bill Cohen, won handily over a surprisingly strong Neil Rolde, who ran on one issue: health insurance. These races attracted much interest, as did a successful referendum drive allowing all stores to open on Sundays.

But the struggle for the governorship stood out. Brennan made the state's budget problems virtually his only issue, predicting large shortfalls and promising to end the crisis, although his platform was short on specifics. Governor McKernan insisted, however, that the 1990 budget revisions had resolved the problem. The race was complicated by third-party candidate Andrew Adam. A virtual unknown, he attracted 47,500 votes. McKernan won with 239,000 to Brennan's 226,000 votes.

Immediately after the election, the McKernan administration announced that state tax revenues would fall another $106 million below previous projections, forcing more budget cuts in March 1991. Among the casualties were the state's fledgling health-insurance plan, the ASPIRE program, and much of the property-tax relief. A new lottery game was introduced, payments to cities and towns for the state's share of school costs were slashed, and state pension reserves were raided.

By the summer of 1991, the seemingly unending budget mess, bitterness about the election (which left the legislature strongly Democratic), and personal ill feeling between the governor and the entrenched leadership of the House and Senate, Speaker John Martin and President Charles Pray, exploded in a government crisis unprecedented in the state of Maine.

The immediate trigger was the state Workers' Compensation law, a program providing income support to employees disabled on the job. Very expensive for employers, its high premiums were alleged to discourage new enterprises from locating in the state. On the other hand, many Maine industries—especially woods work—were very dangerous. Unions and their supporters tended to blame unsafe working conditions for high costs, while employers pointed to individuals receiving generous benefits for dubious problems. Governor McKernan, who

24-1. President George Herbert Walker Bush (b. 1924), a lifelong summer resident of Walker's Point, Kennebunkport, continued to make many visits to Maine during his term in office. Heads of state, including President François Mitterand of France (shown here) came to Maine as guests of the forty-first President. This visit occurred on May 20, 1989. Photograph Carol T. Powers, courtesy of the White House, Washington, D.C.

wanted more change than the Democratic legislature would allow, refused to sign the new 1991 budget until the lawmakers gave him what he asked for. Without a budget, state functions came to a stop on July 1, except for those of the state police. Unpaid state workers thronged the Capitol, staging noisy demonstrations, and tempers rose as legislative deliberations continued inside in the summer heat. After more than two weeks of grueling, late-night sessions, both sides backed down: reforms were made and a commission was established to recommend further Workers Comp changes. The budget, including higher taxes and more cuts, became law. State government began to function again, but the "civil" state described in chapter 23 had lost a large degree of civility in the process. By the summer of 1992, the emotions of the previous year had subsided, and the state budget ended the fiscal year in balance, as constitutionally required, but just barely.

In early 1993, the legislature worked on meeting yet another deficit before another fiscal year ended. Beyond that task there would be, they knew, some very hard choices to make for the next biennium's budget. The 1992 elections had returned another Democratic legislature, though the Republicans had gained a few seats. At the same time, Maine voters joined those of most other states in choosing Bill Clinton as president; but they also gave independent candidate H. Ross Perot, who edged out incumbent President Bush for second place, his highest percentage of votes (30 percent) of any state in the country. Unsurprisingly, considering the difficult times since 1989, about seven of ten Maine voters had voted for change.

As the twenty-first century loomed, Maine shared in most national trends and problems and faced others more peculiar to its own nature and history. Perhaps the most enduring and pressing problem was summarized by a popular line of the time: "Maine is a great place to live, but a poor place to make a living."

The Contributors

LAWRENCE C. ALLIN is a historian employed by the Oklahoma City Air Logistics Center Office of Public Affairs. His Ph.D. is from the University of Maine. Dr. Allin is the author of numerous scholarly articles on Maine's history as well as historical sketches for various state newspapers. He conceived and directed the Maine Historical Data Program.

ROBERT H. BABCOCK is Professor of History at the University of Maine and the author of *Gompers in Canada: A Study in American Continentalism before the First World War* (Toronto, 1974). His Ph.D. is from Duke University.

WILLIAM DAVID BARRY is a public historian whose articles and reviews appear regularly in the *Maine Sunday Telegram* and other publications. He is the author of *The Sweetser Children's Home: A Century and a Half of Service to Maine Children* (Portland, 1988) and several exhibit catalogs.

BRUCE J. BOURQUE is Chief Archaeologist for the Maine State Museum and a Lecturer in Anthropology at Bates College. He is the author of scholarly articles about archaeological investigations in Maine and the maritime region and the book *Prehistory of the Central Maine Coast* (1992). His Ph.D. is from Harvard University.

JOYCE BUTLER is Curator of Manuscripts for the Brick Store Museum in Kennebunk. She has written extensively about Maine history and is a contributor to *Agreeable Situations: Society, Commerce, and Arts in Southern Maine, 1780–1830* (1987), *Maine in the Early Republic: From Revolution to Statehood* (1988) and *Sketch of an Old River: Shipbuilding on the Kennebunk* (1993).

EDWIN A. CHURCHILL is Chief Curator for the Maine State Museum. He is the author of *Maine Communities and the War for Independence: A Guide for the Study of Local Maine History* (1976), *Simple Forms and Vivid Colors: Maine Decorated Furniture, 1800–1850* (1983), and *Hail Britannia: Maine Pewter and Silverplate, 1824–1941* (1992). His Ph.D. is from the University of Maine.

RICHARD H. CONDON is Professor of History at the University of Maine at Farmington. He has contributed scholarly articles to the Maine Historical Society *Quarterly*. He was awarded the 1993 James Phinney Baxter Prize for a recent contribution to the journal. His Ph.D. is from Brown University.

JERRY DESMOND is a Ph.D. candidate at the University of Tennessee at Knoxville. He has taught courses in Maine and U.S. history and is the author of "Maine and the Elections of 1860" (*New England Quarterly*, forthcoming).

EILEEN EAGAN is Assistant Professor of History, University of Southern Maine. She is the author of *Class, Culture and the Classroom: The Student Peace Movement of the 1930s* (Philadelphia, 1982). Her Ph.D. is from Temple University.

JOEL W. EASTMAN is Professor of History, University of Southern Maine. He has written extensively about Maine history for scholarly and popular publication and wrote, co-produced, and hosted "Never in Anger: The Forts of Portland" for USM Television in 1987. His Ph.D. is from the University of Florida.

ALARIC FAULKNER is Professor of Anthropology, University of Maine. He is the author, with Gretchen Fearon Faulkner, of *The French at Pentagoet, 1635–1674: An Archaeological Portrait of the Acadian Frontier* (Augusta, 1988). His Ph.D. is from Washington State University.

GRETCHEN FEARON FAULKNER is Development Coordinator, the Hudson Museum, University of Maine, where she is also a Ph.D. candidate. She is the author with Alaric Faulkner of *The French at Pentagoet, 1635–1674: An Archaeological Portrait of the Acadian Frontier* (Augusta, 1988).

YVES FRENETTE is Associate Professor, Glendon College of York University, Toronto. He has written extensively about the Franco-American population of Maine and New England. His Ph.D. is from the Université Laval.

DAVID L. GHERE is Assistant Professor of History, University of Minnesota. His Ph.D. is from the University of Maine. He writes and teaches about native American history and colonial American history.

STANLEY R. HOWE is director of the Bethel Historical Society. His Ph.D. is from the University of Maine. He is the author of *Dr. Moses Mason and His House* (Bethel, 1981) and serves as book review editor for the Maine Historical Society *Quarterly*.

RICHARD W. JUDD is Associate Professor of History, University of Maine. He is the author of *Aroostook: A Century of Logging in Northern Maine* (Orono, 1989) and the editor of the Maine Historical Society *Quarterly*. His Ph.D. is from the University of California at Irvine.

RICHARD DAMIAN KELLY, Jr., the cartographer who prepared the maps for this volume, has contributed maps to other publications, including the *Maine Bicentennial Atlas* (Portland, 1976), *The Maine Coastal Inventory: A Natural Resource Inventory* (Augusta, 1974–77); and *Maine Land in State and Federal Ownership: A Cartographic Inventory* (Augusta, 1989).

JAMES S. LEAMON is Professor of History, Bates College. He co-edited *Maine in the Early Republic: From Revolution to Statehood* (1988) and authored *Revolution Downeast: The War for American Independence in Maine* (1993). His Ph.D. is from Brown University.

NATHAN R. LIPFERT is Library Director, the Maine Maritime Museum. He has authored scholarly articles and with Kenneth R. Martin wrote *Lobstering and the Maine Coast* (1985).

SHEILA McDONALD is Resource Administrator with the Bureau of Parks and Recreation, Maine Department of Conservation. She has written about Maine history for scholarly publications as well as prepared interpretive materials for a number of state historic sites. She curated the exhibit "Chez-Nous: The St. John Valley" for the Maine State Museum.

WAYNE M. O'LEARY is an independent researcher and writer with a particular interest in Maine maritime history. He is the author of *The Tancook Schooners: An Island and Its Boats* (forthcoming, 1994). His Ph.D. is from the University of Maine.

HARALD E. L. PRINS is Assistant Professor, Kansas State University. He has written extensively about the history of the native Americans of Maine and the maritime provinces. He is co-editor of *American Beginnings: Exploration, Culture, and Cartography in the Land of Norumbega* (forthcoming). His Ph.D. is from the New School for Social Research.

PAUL E. RIVARD is Director, Museum of American Textile History, North Andover, Massachusetts. Formerly he was director of the Maine State Museum in Augusta. His extensive writings about a variety of topics in Maine history include numerous exhibit guides and catalogs.

EDWARD O. SCHRIVER (1931–94) retired as Associate Professor of History, University of Maine. He was the author of *Go Free: The Anti-Slavery Impulse in Maine, 1833–1855* (Orono, 1970), and he edited *The French in New England, Acadia and Quebec* (1973) and co-edited *Maine: A History through Selected Readings* (1985). His Ph.D. was from the University of Maine.

CHARLES A. SCONTRAS is Professor of Special Studies with the Department of History and Research Associate with the Bureau of Labor Education at the University of Maine. He is the author of *Organized Labor in Maine: Twentieth Century Origins (1985)* and *The*

Socialist Alternative: Utopian Experiments and the Socialist Party of Maine, 1895–1914 (1985). His Ph.D. is from the University of Maine.

JAMES B. VICKERY is the author of *History of the Town of Unity, Maine* (1954) and *A Bibliography of Local History: The Town Registers of Maine* (1965) and editor of *John E. Godfrey Journals* (1979) and *Pictorial History of Brewer, Maine* (1976). He was photograph editor for *An Illustrated History of Bangor, Maine* (1976) and *The City of Brewer, Maine: Centennial, 1889–1989* (1989).

RICHARD R. WESCOTT has retired as Professor of History, Monmouth College (New Jersey). He is the author of *"New Men, New Issues": The Formation of the Republican Party in Maine* (1986) as well as several articles about topics in Maine history. His Ph.D. is from the University of Maine.

Index

Note: Page numbers in italics refer to illustrations, captions, and maps.

K

L

MAINE

The Pine Tree State from Prehistory to the Present

was composed in 10/13 Minion
on a Macintosh system with LaserWriter output
by Books International;
printed by sheet-fed offset
on acid-free 50-pound Glatfelter Supple Opaque Recycled stock,
Smyth sewn and bound over 98-point binder's boards
in Roxite B cloth with Rainbow endpapers
and wrapped with dustjackets printed in four color process
on 100-pound enamel stock finished with film lamination,
also notch bound in signatures with paper covers
printed in four color process on 12-point C1S stock
finished with film lamination
by Thomson-Shore, Inc.;
designed by Will Underwood;
and published by

The University of Maine Press

ORONO, MAINE 04469-0150